Francis Patrick Kenrick

The Primacy of the Apostolic See

Francis Patrick Kenrick

The Primacy of the Apostolic See

ISBN/EAN: 9783744748582

Printed in Europe, USA, Canada, Australia, Japan

Cover: Foto ©ninafisch / pixelio.de

More available books at **www.hansebooks.com**

THE PRIMACY

OF

THE APOSTOLIC SEE

VINDICATED,

BY

FRANCIS PATRICK KENRICK,

ARCHBISHOP OF BALTIMORE.

"Ipsa est petra quam non vincunt superbæ inferorum portæ.
Augustinus, in Ps. contra partem Donati."

SEVENTH REVISED EDITION.

BALTIMORE:
PUBLISHED BY JOHN MURPHY & CO.
182 BALTIMORE STREET.
1875.

TO

His Holiness,

POPE PIUS IX.

THE FOLLOWING VINDICATION OF THE RIGHTS OF HIS SEE,

AND

THE ACTS OF HIS PREDECESSORS,

IS INSCRIBED,

AS A TOKEN OF FILIAL SUBMISSION AND DEVOTED ADMIRATION,

BY THE AUTHOR.

On the presentation of the last edition of this work to His Holiness Pius IX., the author was honored with a letter, of which the following is a translation :—

PIUS IX.

VENERABLE BROTHER, Health and Apostolic Benediction—

From your letter of 27th May of this year, addressed to us, we clearly perceive the great attachment and reverence which you, Venerable Brother, cherish for Us and for this Supreme chair of Peter. We cannot find words to express how highly we applaud your pious undertaking in vindication of the rights of this Holy Apostolic See, and of the primacy of the Roman Pontiffs, in the work published by you in the English language. The new edition of this work published this year, and dedicated to Us, in token of your filial attachment and devotedness, which, however, we are unable to read, being unacquainted with English, will, we trust, prove highly useful for the defence of our rights, and of those of the Apostolic See against the impious attacks of our enemies. On which account You yourself, Venerable Brother, can conceive and imagine how great consolation We derive from your undertaking, and especially from the zeal with which you cheerfully devote yourself to the discharge of your pastoral office. Continue, then, to pray earnestly to Almighty God, that He may calm the dreadful storm which rages around us, and grant at length that the church may everywhere enjoy peace in His worship. In the mean time, receive, as a token of our favor and grateful feeling for your good offices, the Apostolic Benediction, which, as a pledge of heavenly happiness, We affectionately impart with our whole heart to yourself, Venerable Brother, to be communicated by you to all the clergy and faithful people over whom you preside.

Given at Rome, at St. Mary Major's, on the 27th July, in the year 1848, in the third year of our Pontificate.

PIUS P. P. IX.

To Our Venerable Brother,
    FRANCIS PATRICK, *Bishop of Philadelphia.*

Preface to the Fifth Edition.

ALTHOUGH but a short space of time has elapsed since the fourth edition of this work was issued, several events have occurred which serve to show the vast importance of the subject of which it treats. The impediments thrown in the way of the exercise of the Pontifical power, by Joseph II., have been voluntarily removed by the present Emperor of Austria, who feels that his first duty and best policy is to acknowledge the Church of God, to respect her rights, and promote the observance of her laws. The Czar of Russia has so far yielded to the sense of the expediency of conciliating his Catholic subjects as to send a minister to Rome empowered to make every suitable concession for the arrangement of the Catholic interests of Poland; and has received, in return, an Extraordinary Envoy of the Holy See, sent to compliment him on occasion of his coronation, which has so recently dazzled the world by its splendor. But the greatest homage rendered to the Papal authority in this age, or perhaps in any other, is the acquiescence of the whole Catholic episcopacy and the Church at large in the definition pronounced two years ago from the Chair of Peter. In the mean time, the want of a tribunal to maintain and guard the revealed doctrines has been seen in the English establishment, by the latitude of opinion allowed by the Queen's Privy Council in regard to Baptismal Regeneration, and by the recent proscription of the doctrine of the Real Presence pronounced in the name of the Archbishop of Canterbury. In our own country, the excitement which prevails on the subject of domestic slavery, and the spread of polygamy in the territory of Utah, evince the advantages of an authority which, independently of local considerations, declares the divine law, and lends moral influence to the support of government and society. May we not hope that the unjust prejudices so deeply rooted and so industriously fostered against this guardian power will at length yield to the evidences which daily multiply of its necessity?

BALTIMORE, November, 1856.

Preface to the Fourth Edition.

THIS work first appeared in the year 1837, in the form of letters to the Protestant Episcopal Bishop of Vermont, John Henry Hopkins, in reply to a work on the Church of Rome, addressed by him to the Roman Catholic Hierarchy. In 1845 it was enlarged, and took the form of a general treatise on the Primacy; and in 1848 it was republished, with an improved arrangement of the matters which it embraced. In 1853 a German translation, made by Rev. Nicholas Steinbacher, S. J., was issued, with some alterations made by me in the last edition. The present edition contains some further corrections, although of little importance. The submission of Mr. Allies to the authority of the Holy See, of which he has become an able defender, rendered it proper to retrench many observations made in refutation of his positions as an apologist of the Church of England. Mr. Manning also, now recognising the centre of unity, no longer deserves the reproach of inconsistency. The many striking avowals made by Dr. J. W. Nevin, late President of Marshall College, Mercersburg, Pennsylvania, are freely quoted in support of the authority of the Catholic Church and of the Holy See, although it may perplex the reader to understand how he should still remain out of our communion. The other alterations in this edition are chiefly verbal. The work now goes before the public in a permanent form, being stereotyped, with the hope that it may serve to dispel those prejudices which withhold so many from union with the See of Peter, of which Augustin has well said that God has established the doctrine of truth in the chair of unity.

BALTIMORE, 1855.

CONTENTS.

PART I.

SPIRITUAL SUPREMACY.

                                                                                  PAGE

CHAPTER I.—Nature of the Primacy... 17
    Organization of the Church by Christ—Necessity of a Central Power—Presumptive Evidence—Motives of Luther—Henry VIII.—Photius—Prejudices against the Papacy—Federal System—Abuses.

CHAPTER II.—Promise of the Primacy.. 24
    Custom of our Lord—Change of Name—Concession of Barrow—Promise—Personal Faith—Admission of the First Converts—Christ the Rock—Difference of Gender—Bloomfield's Admission—Gerard—Thompson—Christ the Foundation—St. Leo the Great—Figure of the Keys—Rebuke to Peter—Rivalry of the Apostles—Prayer for Simon.

CHAPTER III.—The Fathers' Exposition of the Promise............ 34
    Authority of the Fathers—Tertullian—Origen—Mystical Fancies—St. Cyprian—Peter Represents the Church—On him the Church is Built—St. James of Nisibis—St. Cyril of Jerusalem—St. Basil the Great—St. Gregory of Nazianzum—St. Chrysostom—Peter is placed over the entire World—St. Epiphanius—St. Cyril of Alexandria—St. Hilary of Poictiers—Faith of Peter—Arian Heresy—St. Optatus—St. Ambrose—Power of Forgiveness—Equality of Paul to Peter—St. Jerom—Occasion of Schism Removed—On that Rock the Church is Built—St. Augustin—Hesitation—The Church through Peter receives the Keys—St. Leo the Great—Various Interpretations.

CHAPTER IV.—Institution of the Primacy............................. 57
    Manifestation of our Lord—Feed Lambs and Sheep—Union of Jews and Gentiles—One Fold, one Shepherd—Barrow's Avowal—St. Francis de Sales—Perpetuity of the Power—Headship of Peter reconciled with that of Christ—Wisdom of Christ—Bossuet.

CHAPTER V.—Exposition of the Commission........................ 64
    Origen—Cyprian—Unity of the Church—Barrow's Admission—St. Cyril of Jerusalem—St. Chrysostom—St. Ambrose—St. Augustin—St. Leo—St. Gregory the Great—St. Bernard.

CHAPTER VI.—Exercise of the Primacy............................... 70
    Call of Matthias—Remark of Chrysostom—Council of Jerusalem—Result of Peter's Address—Tertullian—St. Jerom—Theodoret—Chrysostom—Model of Councils—Bossuet—Potter—To send sometimes implies superiority—Condescension of Peter—St. Gregory the Great—Cephas at Antioch—Visit of Paul to Peter—The Jews committed to the charge of Peter, the Gentiles to Paul—Address of Peter to his Fellow-Bishops.

CHAPTER VII.—Peter Bishop of Rome................................ 79
    Admission of Cave—Babylon—Clement—Ignatius—Papias—Irenæus—Dionysius of Corinth—Cajus—Origen—Cyprian—Eusebius—Theodoret—Palmer's Admission—Difficulty of arranging Chronology—Both Apostles Founders of the Roman Church—Apostleship compatible with Episcopacy—Silence of St. Paul—Palmer's Admission.

CONTENTS.

CHAPTER VIII.—Roman Church 85

Transmission of the Power of Peter—St. Ignatius M. addresses the Church that Presides—Celebrated Passage of St. Irenæus—Palmer's Admission—Tertullian—St. Cyprian—Root and Matrix—Dr. Hopkins—Authority of Roman Clergy—The Emperor Aurelian's Reference to Roman Bishops—St. Augustin—St. Jerom—Bishops everywhere equal in order—Bishops of Province of Arles—Dignity of Imperial City—Concessions of Emperors—Decree of Valentinian—Concession of Palmer.

CHAPTER IX.—Centre of Unity.

§ 1. *Communion with See of Rome*.. 97

Remark of Hallam—St. Cyprian—To communicate with the Roman Bishop is to communicate with the Catholic Church—Union of Spirit without identity in Faith is chimerical—Episcopate in solidum—St. Ambrose—St. Optatus—Evasion of Palmer—St. Augustin—Roman Catholic.

§ 2. *Interruptions of Communion*.. 103

Meletius—St. Jerom—Liberality of the Holy See—Inconsistency of Palmer—Testimony of John, Bishop of Constantinople—St. Cyprian on Unity.

CHAPTER X.—Ancient Examples of Papal Authority.

§ 1. *Disturbances at Corinth*.. 108

Letter of Clement.

§ 2. *Paschal Controversy*.. 109

Difference of Discipline—Polycarp and Anicetus—Measures of Victor.

§ 3. *Montanism*... 111

Tertullian—Bishop of Bishops—Faber's Admission—Peter's Church.

§ 4. *Controversy Concerning Baptism*... 113

African Decree—Pope Stephen—Asiatic Usage—Vincent of Lerins—Papal Authority—St. Cyprian—St. Jerom—St. Augustin.

§ 5. *Donatism*.. 119

Cecilius of Carthage—Decree of Constantine—Sentence of Melchiades—Council of Arles.

CHAPTER XI.—Guardianship of Faith.

§ 1. *Constancy of the Holy See*... 123

Theophylact—Innocent III.—Early Heresies.

§ 2. *Chief Mysteries*... 124

Divinity of Christ—Dionysius of Alexandria accused—Arianism—Liberius Vindicated—Testimony of Sozomen—Heresy of Apollinaris—Edict of Theodosius—St. Basil—The East as well as the West receives the Decrees of Rome—Nestorius—St. Cyril—Decree of Celestine—Council of Ephesus—Eutyches—Flavian writes to the Pope—Letter of Valentinian—Council of Chalcedon—Acknowledgment of Palmer—Blessed Virgin.

§ 3. *Grace*... 137

African Councils—Innocent I.—Further Examination superfluous—Zosimus—St. Prosper—St. Vincent of Lerins—Paulinus of Milan—Nestorius—St. Leo.

§ 4. *Testimonies of Fathers*.. 143

St. Jerom—St. Leo—Acknowledgment of Casaubon.

§ 5. *Vindication of Honorius*... 145

Anathema—Letters of Honorius—Agatho—St. Bernard—Bishops of Tarragona.

CHAPTER XII.—Governing Power.

§ 1. *Exercise of Authority*... 149

St. Celestine—St. Cyprian—Decree of Siricius—Innocent I.—Zosimus—St. Leo—Just Declaration of Bossuet—Dispensing Power—Boniface I.—Consultations.

CONTENTS. 11

§ 2. *Universal Patriarch*.. 156
    John the Faster—Council of Chalcedon—St. Gregory the Great—Byzantium—Acknowledgment of the Eastern Church—Acts of Gregory—Serenus of Marseilles admonished—Patriarchs address Gregory with reverence—Decree of Phocas.

CHAPTER XIII.—The Hierarchy.

§ 1. *Patriarchal System*.. 161
    Extent of Western Patriarchate—Origin of Patriarchal Jurisdiction—Sixth Canon of Nice—Version of Ruffinus—Suburbicarian Churches—Boniface I.—Council of Chalcedon—St. Leo.

§ 2. *Western Patriarchate*.. 164
    Innocent I.—Pallium—Primates—Guizot—Clinch.

§ 3. *Apostolic Vicars*... 167
    Barrow's Avowal—First Instance of Apostolic Vicar for Illyricum—Pontifical Instructions—St. Leo the Great—Modern Vicars Apostolic—Bishops not mere Delegates.

§ 4. *Papal Relation to Patriarchs*.. 170
    Patriarchal Power—Dependence on the Pontiff—Juvenal of Jerusalem—Bishop of Constantinople—Embassy to Rome—St. Basil.

CHAPTER XIV.—Deposition of Bishops. 175
    Occasional Encroachments—Ancient Reservation to the Holy See—Potter's Testimony—Deposition of Marcian of Arles, solicited by St. Cyprian—Roman Council—Imperial Edict—Mosheim and Maclaine—Zosimus—Celestine—Council of Chalcedon—Ephesus—Bishops of Jerusalem, Antioch, and Constantinople Deposed—Anthimus Deposed by Agapitus—Primate of Byzacium.

CHAPTER XV.—Appeals.

§ 1. *Ancient Examples*.. 183
    Marcion goes to Rome—Basilides—Cyprian's Judgment—Privatus of Lambesita—Cyprian complains of wanton appeals as calculated to defeat justice—Appeal of Athanasius—Letter of Julius—Custom to write first to Rome—Marcellus of Ancyra—Passage of Socrates—Council of Sardica—St. Basil an Illustrious Witness—Appeal of Chrysostom.

§ 2. *African Controversy*.. 195
    Council of Carthage—Appeal of Apiarius—Sardican Canons—Misnomer—Appeals of Bishops—Letter to the Pope—Appeal of Celestius—African Instances of Appeal.

§ 3. *Promiscuous Examples*... 201
    Chelidonius—Flavian—American Editor of Mosheim—Theodoret—John Talaja—Enumeration of Appeals by Barrow—Pope Gelasius.

CHAPTER XVI.—The Church of England.

§ 1. *Britons*... 205
    Introduction of Christianity—British Bishops in Councils of Arles and Sardica—St. Germanus Legate of Celestine to the Britons—Bishops of Cyprus—Autocephalous Character—Forgery of Address of Abbot Dinoth—Fuller's Quaint Acknowledgment—Gregory gives Authority over British Bishops.

§ 2. *Anglo-Saxon Church*.. 209
    Canterbury Founded by Augustin.

§ 3. *Paschal Controversy*... 210
    Britons and Irish follow Old Cycle—King Oswiu decides in favor of the Roman usage.

§ 4. *Anglo-Saxon Hierarchy*.. 211
    Plan Traced by Gregory—Changes made by Vitalian and Agatho—Lichfield raised to Metropolitical Dignity by Adrian—Pallium—Several English Metropolitans go to Rome: some are consecrated by the Pope—Papal Legates.

§ 5. *Acknowledgment of the Primacy*.. 213
    Bede—Alcuin—Anglo-Saxon Pontifical—Councils—Deposition of Bishops—Appeal of Wilfrid.

CONTENTS.

§ 6. *Modern Church of England*.. 217
    Measures of Henry VIII.—Futile Attempts of Palmer—Female Supremacy.

CHAPTER XVII.—Papal Prerogatives.................................... 221
    False Decretals—Presidency of the Universal Church—St. Leo—Right to Judge in Controversies of Faith—Definitions *ex cathedra*—Assembly of 1682—Plenitude of Power—New Organization of French Hierarchy—Hypothetical Argument of Bellarmine—Acknowledgment of Voltaire—Relations of Pope to Councils—Not necessary to define extent of prerogative—Observation of Palmer.

CHAPTER XVIII.—Unbroken Succession of the Bishops of Rome. 232
    Invitation of Augustin—Schism of Novatian—Cornelius Bishop of the Catholic Church—St. Cyprian—Felix Intruded—Schisms—Imperial Interference—Great Schism—Absence from Rome—Simoniacal Elections—Interregnums—Fable of Pope Joan—Elizabeth of England—St. Augustin's Appeal.

CHAPTER XIX.—Papal Election.
    § 1. *Imperial Interposition*.. 241
    Interference of Odoacer, King of Italy—Eastern Emperor—Popes Consecrated without the Imperial Assent—Western Emperors—Oath required by Otho I.—Amount of Deference to Emperors—St. Gregory VII.—*Esclusiva*.
    § 2. *Mode of Election*.. 244
    Office not to be bequeathed—Popular Influence—St. Celestine—Council of Laodicea—Conclave.

CHAPTER XX.—Ceremonies.
    § 1. *Ceremonies after Election*... 246
    Adoration—Kissing of the foot, Ancient Oriental Rite—Chair of State.
    § 2. *Ceremonies of Coronation*....................................... 250
    Burning of Bunch of Flax—Pallium—Gospel in Latin and Greek—Tiara—Cap of Liberty—Address of Council of Baltimore.

PART II.

SECULAR RELATIONS.

CHAPTER I.—Patrimony of St. Peter..................................... 255
    No Earthly Possessions, or Dominion given by Christ—Wealth of the Roman Church—Donation of Constantine—Humane Treatment of Tenants—French Princes—Title of Patrician—Acts of Sovereignty—Heroism of Leo IV.—Relation of Pope and Emperor to the Romans—Gibbon's account of the origin of the Papal Dominion—Anticipations of Dr. Jarvis.

CHAPTER II.—Authority over Princes.
    § 1. *In Matters of Faith and Morals*................................ 270
    Pontiff superior to all members of the Church—Gelasius explains the relations of the two powers—Means employed against Princes.
    § 2. *In Secular Concerns*... 275
    No Civil Power now claimed—Creation of Emperor by Leo III.—British Critic—Remarkable avowal of Voltaire.

CHAPTER III.—Peace Tribunal... 283
    Council of Rheims—Louis the Fat—Princes sought the Pope's Mediation—St. Anselm—Genoese and Pisans reconciled—Pope's Power implored by both parties—Federal Union—Decree of Lateran—War Sometimes Necessary—Truce of God—Improvement in the Laws of War.

CONTENTS.

CHAPTER IV.—Deposing Power.

§ 1. *Origin of the Power*.. 293
Abdication of Wamba—Council of Savonieres—Saxons complain to Alexander II.—Threats of Gregory VII.—Henry IV., seeks his influence to suppress Revolt—Crimes of Henry—Compact—Declaration of Independence—Effects of Excommunication—Views of Gregory.

§ 2. *Subsequent Instances*.. 299
Alexander III. sanctions the Lombard League—Frederick II. deposed in Council of Lyons—Act of the Pope—Impeachment of the President.

§ 3. *Never formally defined*... 302
Bull of Boniface VIII.—Definition—Excellence of Sacred Power—Canon of Lateran—Acknowledgment of Monarchs.

§ 4. *Deposition of Elizabeth*... 304
Object of the Sentence—Armada—Conduct of English Catholics.

§ 5. *Disclaimers*... 306
French Clergy in 1682—Cardinal Antonelli—Bull of Pius VII.

CHAPTER V.—Papal Sanction... 308
Transfer of French Crown—Settlement of Succession—Sanction of Treaties—Invasion of Ireland—Grants to Teutonic Knights—Bull of Alexander VI.—Baluffi, Wheaton, Prescott.

CHAPTER VI.—Papal Polity... 316
Christianity the Supreme Law—Remarks of Arnold—Church and State—Mr. Allies—Ecclesiastical Immunities.—St. Anselm—St. Thomas of Canterbury—Principles of Government—Liberty—Tuscan League—Elective Principle.

CHAPTER VII.—Crusades... 327
Efforts of Sylvester II.—Gregory VI.—State of the Eastern Christians—Peter the Hermit—Councils of Piacenza, Clermont—Discourse of Urban II.—League between Greek Emperor and the Crusaders—Defensive Wars—St. Bernard—Indulgences—Alms—Results of the Crusades.

CHAPTER VIII.—Coercion.

§ 1. *Pagans and Jews*... 342
Liberty of Conscience vindicated by Tertullian—Ethelbert—Council of Toledo—Innocent IV.—Facts regarding the Jews—Rome their Asylum.

§ 2. *Sectaries*... 345
Conduct of Constantine—Right of Property—Imperial Laws—Anti-social Principles—Outrages of Circumcellions—Council of Carthage.

§ 3. *Crusades against Manicheans*.. 348
Canons of Toulouse and Lateran—Excesses of Sectaries—Assassination of Legate—Instructions of Gregory IX.—Testimony of Voltaire.

CHAPTER IX.—Inquisition.

§ 1. *Ancient Tribunal*... 353
Council of Verona—*Quæsitores fidei* sent by Innocent III.—Spirit of Inquisitors—St. Peter de Castelnau—Civil sanction.

§ 2. *Spanish Inquisition*... 356
Ferdinand of Spain—Object—Treasonable designs of Moors—Royal tribunal—Opposition of Popes to its establishment in Naples and Milan.

§ 3. *Mode of Proceeding*.. 358
Secrecy—Requisites for arrest—Mode of trial—Torture seldom used: long abandoned—Searching process—Exaggerations of Llorente.

§ 4. *Roman Inquisition*... 362
Congregation of Cardinals—Temporal attributions—Archives seized by the French—Heresy regarded as a crime against society.

PART III.

LITERARY AND MORAL INFLUENCE.

CHAPTER I.—Personal attainments.. 367
    Gregory the Great misrepresented—Testimony of Agatho—Rome the source of letters to the West—Nicholas Breakspere.

CHAPTER II.—Measures to promote learning.
    § 1. *Libraries*... 372
    Popes collectors of books—Vatican library—Nicholas V.

    § 2. *Schools*... 373
    Schools in England—Literary accomplishments of ladies—Decrees of Roman Councils—Universities.

CHAPTER III.—Mediæval Studies... 376
    Divinity—St. Thomas Aquinas—Aristotle—Modern Spirit—Canon law—Oriental languages.

CHAPTER IV.—Revival of Letters.. 381
    Dante—Petrarch crowned in the Roman capitol—Poets—Historians—Eloquence—Belles Lettres—Tuscan genius—Testimony of Voltaire—Reformation prejudicial to literature—Greek studies—Ippolita Sforza.

CHAPTER V.—Science.
    § 1. *Medicine*... 388
    Salerno—Montpelier—Anatomy—State Physicians—Professorship of Medicine—Natural History—Minerals—Botany.

    § 2. *Astronomy*.. 390
    Virgil, the Irish missionary—Antipodes—Correction of the calendar by Gregory XIII.—Meridians—Earth's motion around the sun—Copernicus—Galileo—Decree of Roman Inquisition—Cassini—Benedict XIV.

CHAPTER VI.—The Arts... 395
    Rome renders the arts tributary to religion—Temples and statues—Paintings—St. Peter's—Landscapes—Miniatures—Engraving on diamonds.

CHAPTER VII.—Art of Printing.
    § 1. *Encouragement of Printers*.. 399
    Printers at Rome in 1467—Activity of the Roman Press.

    § 2. *Restrictions on the Press*.. 402
    Decree of Alexander VI.—Leo X.—Committee appointed by Council of Trent—List of prohibited books—Freedom of the Press.

CHAPTER VIII.—Moral Influence.
    § 1. *Civilization*.. 405
    Struggle of the Popes against Feudalism—Civilization of the Heathen—Missionaries of Germany—Monastic Institutions—Devotion to the Virgin.

    § 2. *Personal Virtues*.. 408
    Charity of Roman Bishops—The Martyr Lawrence—Fortitude—Martyrs—Pius VI.—Pius VII.—Humility—Celestine V.

    § 3. *Recognised Sanctity*... 415

CHAPTER IX.—Charges against the Popes.. 417
    Formosus—Stephen—Weight of Luitprand's testimony—Boniface VIII.—Conduct before receiving orders—Leo X. and Innocent X. vindicated—Alexander VI.—Character of Pontiffs as Sovereigns.—Sixtus IV.—Nepotism.

Catalogue of the Popes.. 429

The Primacy.

PART I.

SPIRITUAL SUPREMACY.

THE PRIMACY.

CHAPTER I.

Nature of the Primacy.

THE first question which presents itself to the mind in reference to the important subject of the Church, is, whether Christ our Lord formed the multitude of His followers into a society, and appointed officers to govern them. There are many at the present day, who confidently answer in the negative, contending that He left it entirely optional with believers in His doctrine, to associate under whatsoever form they pleased for the furtherance of the great objects of His divine mission.* It may appear strange, that this can be maintained by any who admit the Scriptures, which testify, so clearly, the appointment by Christ of teachers and rulers, with a perpetual commission: but it is scarcely so surprising as that some should hold that Christ did organize His Church, and yet deny the main principle of her organization, which is unity, by the government of one man, as the Scriptures no less clearly attest. The fact that Christ appeared on earth as Supreme Teacher, invested with all power and authority, should prepare us for a state of Christian society, in which ONE should hold His place, exercising, by delegation, those powers which He inherently possessed. That such a social form is best adapted to the great ends of revelation, reason itself must convince us, since in order to diffuse and preserve the revealed doctrines, it must be of the highest importance to have a chief depositary and supreme guardian, from whose chair of instruction the voice of truth may issue to the farthest extremities of the earth. The union of believers can best be promoted by a central authority divinely established and protected; and the perpetuity of the Church, which without unity is impossible, can thus be secured. In every form of civil government, however limited may be its sphere of action, unity is necessarily sought by means of a supreme magistrate, with such limitations of his power as the genius of the people may require. The existence of such an officer in the Church is the more necessary, inasmuch as she is composed of an endless variety of nations, who could not unite in one society, unless by means of

---

* See "The Church Member's Manual," by William Crowell. Boston, 1852.

a general head.* She has been often styled "a masterpiece of human policy," because she is so constituted as to resist the many assaults made on her from without, and to be uninjured by the conflict of internal elements. Her strength and power must be ascribed to her unity, which conservative and vital principle of her organization she owes to her Divine Founder. In leaving her a visible head to govern in His Name, He left her the pledge of His own perpetual presence, in virtue of which she repels every attack, and remains secure of victory over all her foes. No greater evidence of His divinity is needed to confound the unbeliever, than the fact that He so framed His Church as to ensure her perpetual duration, whilst every human institution, howsoever wisely planned and powerfully sustained, after temporary prosperity, more or less rapidly dissolves. Apart from positive evidence, we may infer the divine institution of the primacy, from the fact that it effectually tends to unite the followers of Christ in an unbroken and invincible phalanx. That which makes the Church one, and renders her superior to all the efforts of her enemies, is surely not a device of human policy, but the institution of Divine Wisdom.

I would not, however, confine the investigation of the primacy to abstract reasoning. It is a matter of fact, and therefore to be established by positive evidence. The New Testament, as far as it is a record of the institutions of Christ, and of their practical development, presents historical proof to all who regard it as a purely human composition, and divine testimony to such as recognise its inspiration. In an inquiry like the present, the obvious meaning of the words, as gathered from the context, and illustrated by parallel passages, may be fairly urged in proof; and where discrepancy of sentiment exists in regard to the interpretation, the unbiassed judgment of the ancient Christian writers may be justly appealed to. The monuments of antiquity, which attest the actual government of the Church in the early ages, should be examined, in order to ascertain what was believed and acknowledged to be the authority left by Christ for that purpose: since the ancient general and constant persuasion of all Christians, on a matter of public polity, and daily practice, must be held sacred, according to the celebrated axiom of Vincent of Lerins, which is consonant with common sense: *Quod semper, quod ubique, quod ab omnibus.*

Whosoever assails the actual government of the Church must be prepared to prove that it is essentially different from the original design, as delineated by its Divine Founder.† The presumption is in favor of that

---

* The reader will find this, and other arguments, ably presented by the Bishop of Louisville, in his admirable "Lectures on the General Evidences of Catholicity." Lecture x.

† For the full development of the presumptive argument, and the complete exposure of the fallacies of Anglican and Episcopalian theories on this point, I beg to refer to "Reasons for Acknowledging the Authority of the Holy Roman See, by Henry Major, late a Clergyman of the Protestant Episcopal Church." Philadelphia, 1846.

which is established, because it is reasonable to suppose that its claims had been thoroughly examined before they were acknowledged. If the opponent himself had previously recognised the authority, he is still more evidently bound to show cause, why he now seeks to discard it, his arguments being unworthy of attention until all suspicion of improper motives is removed. Luther, after loud protestations of unreserved submission, rose in revolt against the Papal power, when his resentment had been provoked by the condemnation of his errors. Henry VIII. shook off the Papal yoke, when it galled him; the Pontiff refusing to minister to his passions, by divorcing his lawful queen, that he might take an adulteress to his bed. Long before the appearance of the apostate monk, or of the licentious despot, Photius, in the ninth century, assailed the Roman primacy; but only after the Pontiff had resisted his usurpation of the patriarchal chair, to the injury of the rightful occupant, Ignatius. The motives of these opponents of Rome were unquestionably suspicious. Hence the arguments, by which they attempted to disprove the divine origin of the primacy, were to be received with caution and distrust. It should be presumed that an authority which existed in the ninth, as well as in the sixteenth century, and which was opposed by men under the influence of passion, was still more ancient, nay, coeval with Christianity itself. If, as we go back to the earliest times, we meet instances of its exercise in every age, the presumption is strong that it existed then, substantially the same as when it was afterward assailed by ambitious, restless, or licentious men. In the scarcity of ancient documents, and in the obscurity in which the persecutions of the early ages necessarily involved the constitution and internal administration of the Church, it is unreasonable to expect the same degree of evidence of the exercise of power by her officers, as in later times, of which fuller records are possessed, and in which her action was less controlled. "So long as the Church," observes Mr. Allies, "was engaged in a fierce and unrelenting conflict with the Paganism and despotism of the empire, she could hardly exhibit to the world her complete outward organization."* It is reasonable to infer that her government was in substance the same previously, as in the fifth and fourth ages, unless there be conclusive evidence to the contrary. Those who deny the primacy to be an original principle of Church organization, in vain object the insufficiency of the proofs of its operation in the early ages. In order to meet the abundant evidence of its powerful activity at a subsequent period, they should show the time in which it was first established, the means used for its introduction, and explain how it happened that it met with no opposition, or that such opposition was unsuccessful.

Some of the Pontifical acts which I shall have occasion to enumerate, might be referred to mere patriarchal jurisdiction; but the attentive reader

---

* "The Church of England Cleared from the Charge of Schism, by Thomas William Allies, Rector of Launton, Oxon.," p. 15.

will perceive, that they all presuppose the divine institution of the primacy, and the authority of the Bishop of Rome as derived from St. Peter. The proofs here furnished cannot then be eluded, merely by saying, that many of them are explicable on the patriarchal theory: for we must examine whether the Pontiffs rested their claims on this ground, or on the divine commission; and whether the bishops submitted to them on principles of ecclesiastical economy, or in obedience to a divine mandate, which they believed to be delivered in the Gospel. To invent a theory, is not sufficient; we must inquire into a fact, whether the power exercised by the Bishop of Rome throughout the Western patriarchate, as well as in the East, was professedly grounded on the commission given to the apostle, whose chair he occupied. If continual reference be made to this commission in all the documents which have come down from those times, it is in vain to say that the same acts might have been performed in virtue of conventional arrangements, since they actually proceeded from a higher source.

The attempt is vainly made to distinguish the primacy from the supremacy, and by the admission of the former to elude the evidences by which the claims of the Roman Pontiff are supported. Primacy of jurisdiction implies supremacy, since it is a real governing power, extending over the whole Church, as appears from the definition of the Council of Florence: "We define that the holy Apostolic See and Roman Pontiff holds the primacy throughout the entire world, and that the said Roman Pontiff is the successor of the blessed Peter, the prince of the apostles, and is the true vicar of Christ, and the head of the whole Church, and father and teacher of all Christians; and that to him, in the person of blessed Peter, full power was given by our Lord Jesus Christ to feed, rule and govern the Universal Church, as is also contained in the acts of œcumenical councils and in the sacred canons."*

Those who live under republican institutions are naturally prejudiced against an authority which resembles a monarchy, inasmuch as one man, as vicegerent of Christ, governs the Universal Church. I will not insist here on the fact that he is an elective ruler, chosen from the body of cardinals, whose office is not hereditary, but the reward of distinguished merit; neither will I dwell on the limitations of pontifical power arising from the nature of the doctrines and laws of Christ, of which His earthly representative cannot change an iota; still less will I plead the practical limitations which may arise from canonical enactments, national usages, and established precedents. A power in things spiritual which affects conscience alone, cannot be arbitrary and despotic, being an emanation from the power of Christ, and dependent for its successful exercise on the voluntary submission of those whom it regards. It is necessary, however, to approach the examination of this subject with a mind prepared

---

* Conc. Flor., collat. xxii., p. 985. V. ix. col. Hard.

to embrace the authority which Christ has established, without regard to our political prejudices, or national predilections. We are not allowed to model His Church according to our views; we must accept her as she was framed by Him, who has done all things well, and whose providence watches over His institutions, that they may be channels of grace and blessing to mankind. I shall not attempt to present any qualified view of pontifical power calculated to win popular favor, or hesitate to admit the rather invidious terms by which it is commonly designated. Let the constitution of the Church be styled monarchical; provided it be well understood that Christ is the sovereign, whose mild authority must be reflected in the government of His earthly representative. Let her aristocratic character be admitted; but with the just observation, that in her, birth or wealth gives no title of nobility, since her princes are chosen indiscriminately from all classes, wherever virtue finds votaries. Even Voltaire remarks, that "the Roman Church has always enjoyed the advantage of rewarding merit with honors which are elsewhere given to birth."* It would be easy to show what elements of democracy are contained within her: but a divine institution needs not be supported by an appeal to popular prejudice. To borrow the words of James Bernard Clinch, a learned member of the Irish bar in the early part of this century: "Whatever be the authority which exists in the Christian system, that authority, in its application, must be as different from the execution of worldly force as it is superior in its origin. To seek for parallels between the genuine idea of Christian polity, and the several species of human organization of force, I consider to be extreme absurdity. To defend the government of the Church as a pure monarchic, or as an aristocratic, or as a republican system, or as resulting from any temperament of these three forms, must necessarily lead into error; and so far, must estrange the mind from the whole of the salutary and everlasting purposes of the Gospel, which, except in the Catholic Church, are not known, or cannot be realized. If it were lawful to circumscribe the Christian state by any general name, it might more aptly be called a federal system, because its essential compact is unity. There is no monarchy in the Christian Church but that of Christ; there is no aristocracy; there is no power of the commons. There are ministries and offices distinct, and there are subjects amenable to these offices. But the highest magistrate of spiritual things can only be the next representative of Christ for Christians; and Christ has declared that He came not to have servitude performed unto Himself, but to perform it, and to lay down His life as a ransom for multitudes."†

---

* "L'Eglise Romaine a toujours eu cet avantage de pouvoir donner au mérite ce qu'ailleurs on donne à la naissance." Voltaire, Essai sur l'Histoire Generale. Histoire de l'Empereur Henri V.

† Letters on Church Government, by J. B. Clinch, Barrister at Law, Dublin, 1815.

By whatsoever appellation we may designate the constitution of the Church, our attachment to our country and its institutions will not be affected by it, since there is an immense difference between things human and divine. As we must not suffer our political predilections to prejudice us against the form of government which Christ our Lord has established in his Church, so we need not seek to assimilate civil to ecclesiastical polity. It has been well observed by Ranke, that "this religious system has no inherent or necessary affinity to one form of government more than to another."* "The Christian religion," says Count de St. Priest, "which has existed for near two thousand years, is not indissolubly attached to any political form. Under the shadow of absolute thrones or of limited monarchies—on the borders of the republican lake of William Tell—in America, which is still more republican, it flourishes as an imperishable plant, nourished by the juices of earth, and refreshed by the waters of heaven. It is not a local, but a universal religion."† So far back as the fifth century, St. Augustin declared the support which the Church lends to every lawful authority: "This heavenly society," he says, "does not hesitate to obey the laws of the temporal powers which regulate the things appertaining to our mortal life. . . . . Whilst sojourning on earth, the Church gathers her citizens from all nations, and forms her pilgrim host of men of every tongue. She cares not for the diversity of laws and usages which are directed to the attainment or maintenance of peace: she annuls or destroys none of them, but, on the contrary, she adopts and observes them; since although they differ in various nations, they are all directed to one and the same end, namely, public order and tranquillity; provided they do not clash with religion, which teaches us to worship the one supreme and true God."‡

The alleged or real abuses of papal power form no just ground of objection to its admission, since every divine institution is liable to be abused by human frailty. The inquirer after truth should not allow his mind to be pre-occupied with frightful images of excesses committed by popes, either in their public administration or in their private conduct: he should first of all examine, whether their authority is from Christ. On calm investigation, he will find that the grossest exaggerations have been indulged in by their traducers, whilst the benefits which they bestowed on the Christian world have been kept out of view. The contributions, which under the name of Peter's pence, or on any other score, were made for the support of the pontifical government, have been designated extortions, without any regard to their justice and necessity; whilst the unbounded charities of the popes, and their immense expenditures for the general interests of Christendom, are forgotten. The civil commotions and wars, which some-

---

* History of the Popes, vol. i. l. vi. ? i. p. 407.
† Histoire de la Royauté par le Cte Alexis de Saint Priest, l. ii. p. 92.
‡ De Civ. Dei, l. xix. c. xvii.

times followed the exercise of papal power, are represented as its necessary results; whilst the enormity of the evils, which the pontiffs sought to remedy, is lost sight of, and the criminality of the immediate actors who provoked this severity is apparently unnoticed. In investigating the fact, whether Christ has left in His stead a ruler of His Church on earth, we should confine ourselves to scriptural testimonies, and to the monuments of Christian antiquity. Let these be consulted, and there can be no doubt that the result will be entire conviction of the divine institution of the primacy. The importance of the investigation is deeply felt at this day by the many estimable individuals, who, with anxious minds, are struggling to disenthral themselves from error and schism. Mr. Allies rightly said: The whole question now "turns upon the papal supremacy, as at present claimed, being of divine right or not. If it be, then have we nothing else to do, on peril of our salvation, but submit ourselves to the authority of Rome."*

---

* The Church of England Cleared from the Charge of Schism. Advertisement.

CHAPTER II.

Promise of the Primacy.

Our Divine Redeemer was wont to prepare men for His chief institutions by a previous declaration of His intentions. Before He made a formal promise to bestow the power of governing His Church, He changed the name of the disciple, who was to exercise it; and He subsequently declared the import of the name, and the authority of the office. When Simon was presented to him by his brother Andrew, He called him Cephas,* a Syrochaldaic term, equivalent to the Greek $\Pi\epsilon\tau\rho\sigma\varsigma$, that is, Peter, which signifies Rock. Andrew " brought him to Jesus, and Jesus looking upon him, said: Thou art Simon the son of Jona: thou shalt be called Cephas: which is interpreted Peter."† It does not appear that our Lord at that time declared the reason why He so called him: which, however, He afterwards most emphatically signified. Although Andrew had the happiness of discovering Christ before him, Peter soon enjoyed a marked precedency, so as to be designated THE FIRST by the evangelist St. Matthew, in the enumeration of the apostles. "Now the names of the twelve apostles are these: THE FIRST Simon, who is called Peter, and Andrew his brother."‡ Then follow the names of the others, with their commission to preach to the lost sheep of the house of Israel. It is not by mere accident that Peter is here placed first, since he occupies the same place in all the lists given by the sacred writers: which is the more remarkable inasmuch as the order of the names of the other apostles varies, with the exception of Judas, who, on account of his perfidy, is always placed last. St. Matthew, moreover, expressly designates him the first: $\acute{o}\ \pi\rho\omega\tau\sigma\varsigma$, which plainly marks him as leader and chief.

We cannot suppose that Peter is put first on account of the excellence of his personal qualities, when we remember his weakness in the hour of temptation. Whilst our Lord was on earth, He alone was head of His Church, and Peter, although he was leader, had not authority over his brethren. At that time his precedency was rather of order, or rank, than of jurisdiction and government; but it was wisely so ordained, that he might be thus prepared for the high office to which he was to be elevated. In this sense the observation of Barrow may be admitted: "Constantly in all the catalogues of the apostles, St. Peter's name is set in the front; and when

---

* It is pronounced in Syriac *Kipha*, or *Kipho:* in Chaldaic כֵּיפָא, in Hebrew כֵּף.
† John i. 42. ‡ Matt. x. 2.

actions are reported in which he was concerned jointly with others, he is usually mentioned first, *which seemeth not done without careful design, or special reason.* Upon such grounds it may be reasonable to allow St. Peter a primacy of order."* I cannot, however, agree with him, that this primacy was "such a one as the ringleader hath in a dance!" Neither can I admit that primatial authority was not afterwards conferred on him; since this is affirmed, not on the mere ground of this order of names, which, however, furnishes no slight presumptive evidence, but on strong and positive testimonies of Scripture.

In the sixteenth chapter of St. Matthew, we learn that "Jesus came into the confines of Cesarea Philippi: and He asked His disciples saying: Who do men say that the Son of Man is? And they said: Some John the Baptist, and others Elias, and others Jeremias, or one of the prophets." Our Lord's interrogation was not an idle inquiry, proceeding from curiosity to ascertain the current opinions of men, for Jesus "knew all men," and "He needed not that any man should give testimony of man: for He knew what was in man."† He asks, in order to afford an opportunity to Simon to state the various human conjectures, that were prevalent concerning His person, and to declare aloud his own faith.

On the question being put as to the belief of the apostles themselves, concerning him, Peter answered without hesitation: "Thou art Christ, the Son of the living God." This explicit declaration of the divinity of Jesus, was followed by a confirmation, on His part, of the name previously given to Simon, and by the exposition of its mysterious meaning, and of the high office with which it was connected: "Jesus answering said to him: Blessed art thou, Simon Bar-jona: because flesh and blood hath not revealed it to thee, but My Father who is in heaven. And I say to thee, that thou art Peter, and upon this rock I will build My Church; and the gates of hell shall not prevail against it. And I will give to thee the keys of the kingdom of heaven, and whatsoever thou shalt bind upon earth, it shall be bound also in heaven: and whatsoever thou shalt loose upon earth, it shall be loosed also in heaven."‡ Never was the language of Christ more clear and emphatic. Simon confessed Him to be the Son of God, not in the general sense of this appellation, as given to every just man, for this would have called forth no extraordinary praise, but as the natural and true Son of His Eternal Father, by a communication to Him of the Divine Nature, by an ineffable generation. Jesus declares Simon blessed for this profession of faith in His divinity, since mortal man could not have suggested it, but God alone. Thus endowed by the Father with divine faith in the incarnate Son of God, Simon becomes a fit instrument in His hands for the building of His Church, a secure foundation whereon it may rest. His name is confirmed: "I say to thee, that thou art Peter." As Jacob was

---

* A Treatise of the Pope's Supremacy, by Isaac Barrow, D. D., Supposition 1, n. 5.
† John ii. 24. ‡ Matt. xvi. 15-20.

called Israel, because in the mysterious conflict he prevailed over the angel of God;—as Abram was called Abraham, because chosen to be the father of a countless multitude;—so Simon is called Cephas, or Peter, because made, by divine grace, a ROCK of faith. Nor is the firmness of his faith a mere personal endowment; he is to become the foundation-stone of the Church of Christ: "Thou art Peter, and upon this rock I will build My Church;" that is: THOU ART A ROCK, AND UPON THIS ROCK I WILL BUILD MY CHURCH.* The strength of this rock—its immovable firmness—is declared by the impregnable character of the Church which is to be built on it: "the gates of hell shall not prevail against it." Because Christ builds on a rock, the powers of darkness cannot overcome His Church. He is the wise man, who chooses a solid foundation for His building. "The rain fell, and the floods came, and the winds blew, and they beat upon that house, and it fell not; for it was founded upon a rock."† The strength of the building is ascribed to the solidity of the foundation. Christ in choosing Simon for the foundation of His Church, gives him strength and firmness, by which the building itself is made secure. Peter becomes the support of the Church, which, like a strong fortress, is in vain assailed by adverse powers. Such is the import of the name given by Christ to Simon; such is the close and necessary relation of Peter to the Church.

Some who seek to elude the obvious force of the language of our Saviour, contend that Peter is called a rock for the firmness of his personal faith, and is spoken of as the foundation of the Church, because he was the first to profess the divinity of Christ, and because all who thenceforward acknowledged the same truth, were added to and built on him as a foundation. This, however, by no means corresponds with the words of our Redeemer. Peter is called a rock, not as a professor of the faith, but to reward its profession. Because he has made this divinely inspired profession, Christ declares that he is a rock, on which He will build His Church. It is fair to give to a figurative expression the force which its use by the same writer, or speaker, authorizes. Our Lord having used the similitude of a house built on a rock, to illustrate the wisdom of the man who builds his hopes of salvation on the practice of the divine lessons, as on a solid foundation, we must regard the rock as the image of the solidity and strength of the foundation, rather than as expressive of a mere commencement. The unfailing support of the building is the idea which the rock suggests.

This observation equally shows the futility of the attempt to explain this figure as employed merely to mark the instrumentality of Peter in admitting Jews and Gentiles to the Church, by proclaiming the resurrec-

---

* In English, the force of the allusion is not perceived, but in French it is preserved: "Tu es Pierre, et sur cette pierre je bâtirai mon église." The Greek, Latin, Italian, and Spanish, imperfectly exhibit it. The German, as well as the English, conceals it.

† Matt. vii. 25.

tion to the assembled multitude on the day of Pentecost, and exhorting them to receive baptism, and by ordering Cornelius and his family to be baptized.* The figure obviously represents strength, immobility, and consequent support afforded to the building. Peter, as a rock of strength, is placed by the Divine Architect in the foundation, in order that the Church may stand for ever, despite of the storms of persecution and temptation, and of all the assaults of the infernal powers.

Many, with a triumphant air, affirm that the rock on which Christ promised to build His Church, is no other than Christ Himself, the rock of ages: but they plainly violate all rules of just interpretation. Since Cephas signifies rock, and Christ says to Simon: "Thou art Cephas, and upon THIS ROCK I will build My Church;" the relative leaves no room for ambiguity. Besides, there would be a confusion of metaphors and ideas, if Christ should, in the same breath, speak of Himself as builder and foundation. Both figures may be applied to Him separately, under different points of view; but it would be incongruous, not to say absurd, to apply both at one and the same time. God is frequently called a rock, on account of his insuperable and everlasting power; Christ is styled the rock of ages, because He is at all times the strength and refuge of all who flee to Him. He is the spiritual rock, from which the waters of salvation issue, and of which the material rock of the desert was a type. Thus St. Paul, speaking of the Israelites, says, that "they all drank of the spiritual rock that followed them, and the rock was Christ;"† but it is absurd to infer hence that the rock spoken of by Christ, when He said, "upon this rock I will build My Church," is Christ Himself!‡

The attempt to explain "*this rock*" of Christ is by no means countenanced by the difference of gender of the words in the text: σὺ εἶ Πέτρος, καὶ ἐπὶ ταύτῃ τῇ πέτρα. Peter is called Πέτρος, because the Greeks never apply a feminine noun to a man, except in derision:§ the rock is called πέτρα, because this term more properly designates a rock, although the

---

* Bishop Pearson says: "It will be necessary to take notice, that our Saviour, speaking of it, (*the Church*,) mentioneth it as that which then was not, but afterwards was to be: as when he spake unto the GREAT APOSTLE: 'Thou art Peter, and upon this rock I will build my Church;' but when he ascended into heaven, and the Holy Ghost came down, when Peter had converted three thousand souls, which were added to the hundred and twenty disciples, then was there a Church, (AND THAT BUILT UPON PETER, ACCORDING TO OUR SAVIOUR'S PROMISE,) for after that we read: 'The Lord added to the Church daily such as should be saved.'"—*Bishop Pearson on the Creed*, Article IX., p. 506.

† 1 Cor. x. 4.

‡ The rule prescribed by the Protestant critic, Gerard, should here be attended to, 456: "Every term should be considered as it stands, in the proposition of which it makes a part, and explained, not by itself, but so as to bring out the real sense of that whole proposition." He shows the violation of this rule by an Antinomian, who should understand the rock on which the wise man builds his house, Matt. vii. 24, to be Christ, the rock of ages. The rule is equally violated, when the rock, of which Christ speaks, Matt. xvi. 18, is understood to be Himself. See Gerard's Institutes, p. 134.

§ Synopsis Critic., in locum.

other term is equivalent. The relative plainly identifies the subject, and excludes all distinction, as the language in which our Saviour spoke has the same word in both places.* Bloomfield, an Anglican commentator, observes that every modern expositor of note has abandoned the distinction between Peter and rock as untenable.† Bishop Marsh, quoted by him, says, that "it would be a desperate undertaking to prove that Christ meant any other person than Peter."‡ John George Rosenmuller, a German interpreter, coincides in this critical judgment: "The rock," says he, " is neither the confession of Peter, nor Christ, pointing out Himself by His finger, or by a shake of the head, (which interpretations the context does not admit,) but Peter himself. The Lord, speaking in Syriac, used no diversity of name, but in both places said Cephas, as the French word *pierre* is said both of a proper and appellative noun. He pointed out Peter, therefore, either by his finger, or nod; for that gesture suited His purpose, to explain the reason of giving him this name. So it is said of Abraham: 'Thy name shall be Abraham, because I have made thee father of many nations;' of Jacob: 'Israel shall be thy name, for thou actest as a prince with angels and men.' So Christ says: 'Thou art called by Me Peter, because thou wilt be as a rock.' And He promises that He will build His Church on Peter. Allusion is made to the custom prevailing in Palestine, of building houses that are exposed to floods and whirlwinds, on a rocky soil, that they may be able to resist the violence of waters and winds. Matt. vii. 24, 25. 'Therefore whosoever thinks of building a durable house, should above all look around for a rock, or firm ground: the rock is the first thing whence the work is to be begun.' "§

In "Gerard's Institutes of Biblical Criticism" is contained the following

---

* The Syriac version of the New Testament is deservedly of high repute, on account of its early date, and of the near affinity between the Syriac language and the Syro-Chaldaic, which our Lord used, and in which, according to the received opinion, St. Matthew wrote his Gospel. In this version, the words "Peter" and "rock" are expressed by the same characters:

Anath Chipha, vehall hada chipha.

A most ancient Chaldee manuscript of St. Matthew's Gospel, in the collection formerly belonging to Cardinal Barberini, written in characters long obsolete, and professing to have been made in Mesopotamia in the year 330, uses but one word to express Peter and the rock, *sciuha*. See the learned treatise of Ecchelensis, a Maronite, *de origine nominis Papæ, &c.* Romæ, MDCLX.

In the Arabic version, given in the London Polyglot, the same term, *Alsachra*, is used in both places. Another Arabic version employs a different term, *Alsapha*, but in both places alike.

The Persian version is rendered by Walton: Thou art the rock (*i. e.* stone) of My religion, and on thee the foundation of My Church shall be laid.

† In locum.

‡ Comparative View. App. p. 217.

§ Scholia in Novum Test., tom. i. p. 336. Norumb. an. 1815.

just observation—Canon 511: "The most obvious and natural sense is to be set aside only when it is absolutely contradictory to something plainly taught in Scripture." He then remarks, that "the opposite way has been taken by all sects;" and quoting the 18th verse of the 16th chapter of St. Matthew, observes: "Building on Peter is explained, by some, as contrary to the faith that Christ is the only foundation, (1 Cor. iii. 2,) and as favoring the succession of Peter and his successors; but the connection shows that PETER IS HERE PLAINLY MEANT." This avowal loses nothing of its importance from the attempt to confine it to Peter to the exclusion of his successors, in conformity with the prejudices and interests of Protestantism.

Mr. Thompson, of Glasgow, in his *Monatessaron*, on this text, gives three interpretations. He thinks the two first unfounded, and thus quotes the third: "The third opinion is, that both the words πετρος and πετρα are here used as appellations of the apostle; and, consequently, Peter was the rock on which Christ said His Church should be built. To this the connection and scope of the passage agree. There seems to be something forced in every other construction, and an inaptitude in the language and figure of the text in every attempt to construct the words otherwise. Protestants have betrayed unnecessary fears, and have, therefore, used all the HARDIHOOD of LAWLESS CRITICISM in their attempts to reason away the Catholic interpretation."* This perversion of Scripture, to suit party purposes, is deeply to be deplored. Those who have made the humiliating acknowledgments which I have placed under the eyes of the reader, have not failed to torture the text after their own fashion, to eschew the consequences of their involuntary concessions.

The apostle, addressing the Corinthians whom he had brought to the knowledge of Christian faith says: "You are God's building. According to the grace of God that is given me, as a wise architect, I have laid the foundation, and another buildeth thereon. But let every man take heed how he buildeth thereupon. For no man can lay another foundation, but that which is laid—which is Christ Jesus."† These words are often alleged to show that Christ Himself is the fundamental rock on which the Church is built: but the meaning of the apostle manifestly is, that Christ —His doctrine and law—His atonement and grace—are the only foundation on which our hopes for salvation can rest; nor is there salvation in any other; for "there is no other name under heaven given to men whereby we must be saved."‡ This does not exclude the relation of Peter to the Church as established by Christ Himself, since he is the rock placed by the hands of the Divine Architect, from Whom his strength is wholly derived. It would indeed be impious to call Peter the foundation, independently of Christ; his office being merely ministerial and instrumental. The faithful are said to be "built upon the foundation of the apostles

---

* Balt. edit. p. 194.   † 1 Cor. iii. 9.   ‡ Acts iv. 12.

and prophets, Jesus Christ Himself being the chief corner-stone."* Thus it is clear, that the apostles and prophets may be represented under the image of the foundation, without any disparagement to the authority of Christ, since the preaching of the apostles and the predictions of the prophets lead men to Him. They are ministers, agents, heralds of the Great King. So may the term be applied to Peter in a special sense, as being His chief minister and representative, without detracting from His sovereignty. Bloomfield avows that the expression as applied to Peter is easily reconcilable with the application of it to Christ, "since the two expressions are employed in two very different senses."† ST. LEO THE GREAT, who filled the chair of St. Peter in the middle of the fifth century, beautifully exhibits the harmony of the sacred texts, whilst he paraphrases the address of Christ to Peter: "As my Father has manifested My divinity to thee, I make known to thee thy excellency: for thou art PETER, that is, as I am the inviolable rock, the corner-stone, who make both one, the foundation other than which no one can lay—nevertheless, thou also art a ROCK, because thou art strengthened by My power, so that those things which belong to Me by nature, are common to thee with Me by participation."‡

The figure of the keys of the kingdom, which our Lord adds, confirms and develops the idea of power and authority contained in the preceding metaphor: "I will give to thee the keys of the kingdom of heaven: and whatsoever thou shalt bind on earth, it shall be bound also in heaven, and whatsoever thou shalt loose on earth, it shall be loosed also in heaven." The keys are the known symbol of authority. Of Eliacim, who was to be substituted to Sobna in official dignity, it is said: "I will lay the key of the house of David upon his shoulder, and he shall open, and none shall shut; and he shall shut, and none shall open."§ By the aid of this usage some explain the prophetic announcement of the empire of Christ, "the government is upon his shoulder."‖ Potter, Protestant archbishop of Canterbury, says: "Our Lord received from God the keys of heaven; and by virtue of this grant, had power to remit sins on earth: the same keys, with the power which accompanied them, were first promised to Peter, as the foreman of the apostolic college."¶ Since our Lord communicated to Peter the keys which He Himself received from the Father, supreme power was clearly delegated by Him, as may be gathered from the same writer. "Our blessed Lord, as the king of this household, who has the supreme power to admit and exclude whomsoever He pleaseth,

---

* Eph. ii. 20. † In Matt. xvi. 18, 19.
‡ Serm. iv. *de assumpt. sua ad Pontificatum.*
§ Isaiah xxii. 22. "As to the expression 'the keys,' it may also refer to the power and authority for the said work; especially as a key was anciently a usual symbol of authority, and presenting with a key was a common form of investing with authority, insomuch that it was afterwards worn as a badge of office."—*Bloomfield, in locum.*
‖ Isaiah ix. 6. ¶ On Church Government, p. 60.

is said to have the keys of David. The supreme power of the keys, that is, the authority of admitting and excluding, belongs to Christ, the King; but the same is exercised by His apostles and their successors, whom He has appointed to govern the Church, as His stewards, or vicegerents."* The force of the symbol is here admitted, although an attempt is vainly made to render common to all the apostles the power which was distinctly given to Peter alone: "I will give TO THEE the keys of the kingdom of heaven." In the New Testament the kingdom of heaven generally denotes the Church of Christ, which is heavenly in its origin, principles and tendency. To give the keys of this kingdom is to communicate supreme power—to make Peter His special vicegerent. To loose and to bind is the exercise of that power, but the keys signify a pre-eminent power of binding and loosing. The remission of sins or their retention may be effected in virtue of it, whilst other acts likewise are included in this broad commission. To resolve the difficulties of the law, and decide religious controversies, to enact laws binding the members of the Church, and to dispense from their observance, to inflict censures on the refractory, and release the penitent from their bonds, may all be signified by these terms. A similar power of binding and loosing was afterwards promised to all the apostles; but, not without special design, it was promised to Peter first, and alone, that his high authority might be manifested.

These sublime promises are not weakened by the rebuke given on the same occasion, to Peter, for opposing the divine counsels. Our Lord charged His disciples to tell no one that He was the Christ; and in order to check their exultation, He disclosed to them His approaching death: but Peter could not bear the thought of the sufferings of his Divine Master: "Lord, (he said,) be it far from Thee: this shall not be unto Thee. But He, turning, said to Peter: Go after me, Satan, thou art a scandal unto me: because thou dost not relish the things that are of God, but the things that are of men."† By this severe reproof, our Lord would teach us, that the humiliating mystery of His sufferings must be adored with the same faith wherewith His glory is believed. Simon was blessed in the divinely inspired faith by which he acknowledged Christ to be the Son of God; but he became *a Satan*, that is, according to the literal force of the term, an adversary, when he opposed the divine counsel for the redemption of mankind, by the sufferings and death of his Lord. The promise made to him was not recalled, although his earthly views were corrected and reproved. The enemies of the primacy have, however, availed themselves of the popular acceptation of the term *Satan*, to obscure the eulogy previously pronounced, and the promise made to Peter. Severe as the reproof undoubtedly is, it does not suppose any sin on the part of the apostle, but a human error of judgment, proceeding from the ardor of his affection, and his lively faith in the divinity of Christ.

---

* On Church Government, p. 300. † Matt. xvi. 22.

In the solemn circumstance of the approaching passion of Christ, the apostles did not cease to indulge the petty rivalry and jealousy, which, during their attendance on Him, they had often manifested. He had had occasion more than once to rebuke them for their disputes about superiority, and yet they were still contending which of them was the greatest. The many marks of His special favor to Peter, the position of leader which this apostle uniformly occupied, and the promise made to him especially, seemed to leave no room for doubting; but the tender love shown to John, and the kindness and affection exhibited to all, led them to question, whether the actual headship of Peter, or the promised office, rendered him absolutely greater than his brethren. Christ had, on a former occasion, brought forward a child to insinuate humility, and stimulate the apostles to its exercise, by the hope of heavenly exaltation;* in this instance He contrasts the spirit which should animate them, with the domineering pride of earthly princes, and offers Himself as the model which they should copy. "The kings of the Gentiles lord it over them, and they that have power over them, are called beneficent. But you not so: but he who is the greatest among you, let him be as the least: and he that is the leader, as he that serveth? For which is greater, he that sitteth at table, or he that serveth? Is not he that sitteth at table? but I am in the midst of you as he that serveth."† He will not have them act in the lordly spirit of the rulers of this world, or content themselves with flattering titles. Plainly recognising the difference of rank among them, He wishes the greatest to sustain his dignity by the humility of his deportment, even as He had condescended to act as their servant. He then proceeds to intimate the high dignity of all, but marks in express terms the special duty and prerogative of Peter: "You are they who have continued with Me in My temptations: And I dispose‡ to you, as My Father hath disposed to Me, a kingdom, that you may eat and drink at My table, and may sit upon thrones, judging the twelve tribes of Israel." Thus, in return for their fidelity and attachment He bestows on them a kingdom, even as His Father that had made Him King. His kingdom is not, indeed, of this world, but of an order far more sublime, according to which the apostles are made priests and kings to their God, partaking of the mysterious banquet, and sitting on thrones of judgment. These honors are common to all: to Peter peculiar privileges are promised. Satan sought to overthrow their thrones and altars, to sift them, even as the wheat is winnowed, and to cast them away as chaff to the wind. In the impenetrable but just counsels of the Deity, he is suffered to accomplish his wishes in some degree: but Christ interposes with His Father to rescue the throne of Peter, and through him to secure all from ruin. "And the Lord said: Simon, Simon,

---

* Luke ix. 48.
† Luke xxii. 25-28. See also Matt. xx. 25.
‡ Assign, or grant.

behold, Satan hath desired to have you,* that he may sift you as wheat: but I HAVE PRAYED FOR THEE† THAT THY FAITH FAIL NOT: AND THOU, BEING ONCE CONVERTED,‡ CONFIRM THY BRETHREN."§ He had just spoken of the kingdom and thrones of the apostles: He now discloses the dark designs of hell against them: and addressing Peter especially, emphatically assures him, that He had prayed for him in particular, that his faith might not fail. Against him the powers of hell shall not prevail, since they cannot prevail against the Church founded on him. The prayer of Christ is specially offered up for him, as the head of his brethren, whom He charges him to confirm in that faith which cannot fail.

The subsequent fall of Peter is often objected as a proof that he was not the head of the Church; which is true of that time, since although the promise of Christ had been made, and His prayer offered up, the office of chief pastor had not yet been instituted. It was only after His resurrection that our Lord, being about to withdraw His visible presence, gave to Peter the charge of His lambs and sheep. The weakness of one chosen for so high an office must teach us, not to regard in the ministers of Christ, especially in His Vicar, their individual qualities, but the divine authority which they exercise, that our trust may be not in man, but in God. Divine mercy pardoned Peter the base denial of his Master: divine goodness raised him to the highest dignity: divine power was employed to endow him, a frail and sinful man, with an immovable firmness in faith, that, like a rock, he might support the everlasting fabric of the Church.

---

* ὑμας. The English reader, accustomed to the use of the plural pronoun for the singular, is apt not to advert to its force here as embracing all the apostles.

† Περὶ σοῦ. Special prayer was offered for Peter.

‡ This appears to be a Hebraism, denoting the repetition of an action. See Ps. lxxxvi. 7. As Christ prayed for Peter that his faith might not fail, He willed likewise that Peter on *his part* should strengthen his brethren by his exhortations, prayers and example. Maldonat, Genebrard, and other Catholic interpreters give this meaning, which is strongly supported by Grotius, who insists that conversion from sin cannot be meant, since Christ had not yet intimated the fall of Peter. Passaglia, and after him Allies, maintain this interpretation; which is also set forth by Cornelius a Lapide and Rosenmüller, although these present at the same time the more common explanation, conformable to the popular acceptation of the phrase. The ancient Syriac version may be rendered: "turn thou in season;" and may be understood of the act of a superior looking towards those under his charge to direct and animate them. The same verb is used in the Syriac for the turning of Magdalen toward Christ in the garden, (John xx. 14,) and the turning of Peter toward John, (Ib. xxi. 20.)

§ Luke xxii. 31, 32.

CHAPTER III.

The Fathers' Exposition of the Promise.

The ancient writers of the Church, who are styled FATHERS, are deservedly regarded with veneration for their piety, learning, and zeal. From an early period of the revolutionary career of Luther, he professed an utter disregard for their opinions; in which he was followed by almost all the sectaries of the sixteenth and succeeding centuries: but "the Church of England" as the English Establishment is styled, professed a high veneration for them, notwithstanding the efforts of Middleton and others to lessen their authority. At the present day they are looked up to with increased reverence, especially by those who participate in the sentiments of Dr. Pusey, whilst they are necessarily depreciated by such Protestants as wish to retain an appearance of consistency. In the Catholic Church, the unanimous testimony of the Fathers, in favor of a doctrine, is conclusive evidence of divine tradition; and their concordant exposition of a text of Scripture is a certain guide to its true meaning: but their individual opinions, however worthy of respectful consideration, impose no restraint on our judgment, unless the Church by adopting them add the seal of her authority. In interpreting the Scripture they frequently turned aside from the literal meaning, especially where this was obvious, and had recourse to moral applications, or allegorical expositions, exercising considerable ingenuity in applying the divine words to matters of daily practice, or endeavoring to discover, under the surface of the letter, some reference or allusion to the great mysteries which are elsewhere explicitly propounded. This however, should give greater weight to their testimony, when they professedly declare the literal meaning of the sacred text, especially in matters which were exemplified in the government and public usage of the Church. Consequently, their interpretation of the promise recorded in Matthew, cannot fail to arrest the earnest attention of the reader.

TERTULLIAN, a priest of the Church of Carthage, at the close of the second century, is classed among the Fathers, although by his fall into the errors of Montanus in the latter part of his career, he forfeited the glory which he had acquired by his celebrated plea with the heathen magistrates for the Christians, and by his immortal work on "Prescriptions against Heretics." Whilst refuting the absurd pretension of the Gnostics, who were not ashamed to boast of knowledge superior to that of the apostles, he indignantly asks: "WAS ANY THING CONCEALED FROM PETER, WHO WAS STYLED THE ROCK ON WHICH THE CHURCH WAS TO BE BUILT, WHO RECEIVED THE KEYS OF THE KINGDOM OF HEAVEN, AND THE POWER OF LOOSING AND BINDING IN HEAVEN AND ON EARTH?"* He justly judged that Peter, being constituted by Christ the fundamental rock and the ruler of the Church, must have been endowed with the most comprehensive knowledge of divine things. His exposition is the more forcible, as it is not urged with any effort; but given as the obvious meaning, which even his adversaries could not question.

After his fall, the African doctor continued to acknowledge Peter to be the rock on which the Church was built; but as the Montanists denied that the Church could pardon the more enormous sins, he endeavored to explain the power of binding and loosing, as signifying a disciplinary exercise of authority in external government, or of a judicial decision,† or in some other way, so as to elude the proof drawn from it, of the authority to impart forgiveness to the most heinous sinners, on due manifestation of repentance. Feeling the insecurity of his position on these points, he boldly maintained that the power—whatever it might be—was promised to Peter personally—and that it did not embrace his successors, or the Church founded by him, much less the Universal Church. It is not necessary to expose the false and frivolous character of these various expositions, which were devised for the support of the severe principles of his sect, especially since they cannot be consistently advocated by those who, with Pearson and Pusey, admit the continuance in the Church of the power of forgiveness; or indeed by any who will not blindly adopt fanciful interpretations. The calm judgment of Tertullian, whilst he remained united with the Church, must not be set aside on account of subsequent aberrations.

Early in the third century, ORIGEN, a man of sublime genius and vast erudition, taught with great success in the famous school of Alexandria; but having given loose reins to his imagination, he hazarded many conjectural expositions of Scripture, which drew on him suspicion and censure. His allegorical interpretations carry with them no weight; but when he explains the letter of the text, or testifies a fact, he is to be listened to with attention, especially if he be found to harmonize with the other fathers. Many of his writings have perished; from one of which Eusebius, who wrote but a century after his time, has preserved a precious extract. The historian being desirous to prove by the testimony of the celebrated catechist, the authenticity of the first epistle of St. Peter, recites his words, which imply a commentary on the promise. "PETER," he says, "ON WHOM THE CHURCH OF CHRIST IS BUILT, against which the gates of hell shall not prevail, left one epistle which is generally admit-

---

* De Præscr. § xxii. † L. de Pudicitia, c. xxi.

ted."* This incidental interpretation is the more forcible, as it must be deemed the unstudied expression of the conviction of the writer.

The liberty which Origen elsewhere takes of applying the promise to every believer in Christ, cannot lessen the force of this exposition, which is manifestly literal, and used to distinguish Peter from all others; but his reasoning to prove that each of the faithful is insuperable whilst he clings to Christ, may be fairly applied to establish the unfailing character of the authority of Peter: "FOR NEITHER AGAINST THE ROCK ON WHICH CHRIST BUILT HIS CHURCH, NOR AGAINST THE CHURCH, SHALL THE GATES OF HELL PREVAIL."† Heretics in every variety of form assail the truth of Christ as taught in the Church, and endeavor to overthrow her, but in vain: "Every author of a perverse sentiment is a builder of a gate of hell; but many and numberless as are the gates of hell, no gate of hell shall prevail against the rock, or the Church which Christ builds upon the rock."‡ Origen, throughout, insists on the immovable nature of the rock, as well as of the Church, so as inseparably to connect them. His application of the text to every just man is evidently by the way of accommodation; since he even denies that it can be applied to each act of episcopal authority, unless the bishop be a Peter, namely, firm in the conscientious exercise of the power with which he is clothed. In its literal acceptation, it must be restricted to Peter himself, on whom the Church was built, and to his successors in office.

ST. CYPRIAN, who filled the see of Carthage in the middle of the third century, is justly classed among the most illustrious of the fathers.§ In his letter to those who had fallen in persecution, he rebukes some of them who had presumed to address him, as if they were the Church, and employs for this purpose, the words of the promise, in order to show that without the bishop there can be no Church. "Our Lord," he says, "whose precepts and admonitions we ought to observe, establishing the honor of the bishop, and the order of His Church, speaks in the Gospel, and says to Peter: 'I say to thee that thou art Peter, and on this rock I will build My Church, and the gates of hell shall not prevail against it; and to thee I will give the keys of the kingdom of Heaven; and whatsoever thou shalt bind upon earth, shall be bound also in Heaven; and whatsoever thou shalt loose upon earth, shall be loosed also in Heaven.' Thence, through the series of times and successions, the order of bishops and the system of the Church flow on; so that the Church is established upon the bishops, and every act of the Church is governed by the same prelates. Since, then, this is the case, I am surprised that some, with audacious temerity, have ventured to write to me in the name of the

---

* L. vi. Hist. Eccl. c. xxi. † In Matt. t. xii. p. 518. ‡ In Matt. t. xii. p. 522.
§ For a full account of this martyr, and a luminous analysis of his writings, I refer to the articles with his name published in the Mercersburg Review in 1852, over the initials of Dr. J. W. Nevin, president of Marshall College.

Church, whilst the Church consists of the bishop, clergy, and of all the hearers."* Cyprian considers Peter in this circumstance as the representative of the Church, through whom she speaks and declares her faith. He was not bishop at the time when our Lord addressed him, but he was destined to be such, as the nature of the episcopal relation was insinuated by the figure of the foundation, as well as by the terms of the promise. In Peter, Bishop of the whole Church, the relation of each bishop to his flock was exemplified. In this sense the remark of Mr. Allies may be admitted. "It is evident," he says, "that if the see of Peter, so often referred to by St. Cyprian, means the local see of Rome, it also means the see of every bishop who holds that office: whereof Peter is the great type, example and source." † Cyprian, taking the sacred text in its obvious meaning, pointed to the principle of unity established in Peter, the representative of the whole episcopate, and so applied it to the local bishop. It is altogether inconsistent with its manifest import to exclude its direct application to Peter. Hence he employs this text to show that the prevaricators, who were separated by their apostasy from himself, could not call themselves the Church, which name belongs only to the bishop, clergy and faithful. This reasoning implies that Peter is as essential to the Church at large, as each local bishop is to his flock; so that it is absurd to apply the term to an acephalous body, from which he is excluded.

Frequent reference to the same text occurs throughout the writings of Cyprian. Addressing Cornelius, Bishop of Rome, he adverts to the reply of Peter, to the question put by our Lord, on occasion of promising to give His flesh to eat: "Will you also leave Me?" and remarks, "PETER, ON WHOM THE CHURCH HAD BEEN BUILT BY THE LORD, speaking one for all, and answering in the name of the Church, says, Lord, to whom shall we go?"‡ In his letter to Florentius, he says: "Peter, ON WHOM THE CHURCH WAS TO BE BUILT, speaks there in the name of the Church."§ Everywhere Cyprian speaks of Peter as the rock on which the Church is built, the representative of episcopal power, the organ of the Church, and the living personification of the principle of unity. In attempting to support his error, that the remission of sins could not be effected by baptism administered by heretics, Cyprian observes, that the power of forgiving sin was only granted to the prelates of the Church; "for to Peter, in the first place, ON WHOM THE LORD FOUNDED THE CHURCH, AND WHENCE HE INSTITUTED AND SHOWED THE ORIGIN OF UNITY, He gave this power, that whatsoever He had loosed on earth, should be loosed also in heaven. And after His resurrection, He speaks likewise to the apostles, saying: 'As the Father hath sent Me,'" &c.|| Although he draws a wrong inference from the premises, in opposition to the decree of the suc-

---

* Ep. de lapsis, xxxiii.   † Church of England, &c. p. 31.   ‡ Ep. lv. ad Cornelium.
§ Ep. lxix. ad Florentium. || Ep. ad Jubajanum, lxxiii. n. 7.

cessor of Peter, this, far from weakening, strengthens considerably his testimony to the power, as promised first to Peter especially, that the unity of the episcopate and Church might be maintained.

Cautioning the faithful against the false indulgence of schismatical priests, who hastily proffered communion to apostates, contrary to the enactments made by the African bishops, he says: "THERE IS ONE GOD AND ONE CHRIST, AND ONE CHURCH, AND ONE CHAIR, FOUNDED BY THE VOICE OF THE LORD UPON PETER. That any other altar be erected, or a new priesthood established, besides that one altar and one priesthood, is impossible. Whosoever gathers elsewhere, scatters. Whatever is devised by human frenzy, in violation of the divine ordinance, is adulterous, impious, sacrilegious."*

The name of ST. JAMES, Bishop of Nisibis in Mesopotamia, is not so well known among us as that of the great bishop of Carthage; but it is illustrious in the annals of the Church of Syria, which venerates him as one of her greatest doctors. He proved the strength of his faith by his fearless confession in the persecution of Maximin, and he was one of the fathers who bore testimony to the divinity of Christ in the great Council of Nice. We have but a small remnant of his works, in which, however, this passage is found: "Simon, who was called the rock on account of his faith, was justly styled rock."†

ST. CYRIL, raised to the see of Jerusalem in the year 340, shed a bright lustre of learning and sanctity around him, which is still reflected in his most precious writings. His discourses delivered to catechumens, and to neophytes, contain numerous passages expressive of the meaning of the texts regarding Peter; which, as we may infer from the incidental character of the exposition, were thus generally understood. Speaking of the confession of the divinity of Christ by Peter, and of the keys bestowed in recompense of it, he plainly recognises the high privileges and station of this apostle: "All of them," he says, "remaining silent, for the doctrine was beyond the reach of man, Peter, THE PRINCE OF THE APOSTLES AND THE SUPREME HERALD OF THE CHURCH, not following his own inventions, nor persuaded by human reasoning, but enlightened in his mind by the Father, says to Him: 'Thou art Christ,' not simply this, but the 'Son of the living God.'"‡ The high prerogatives of Peter are affirmed by Cyril in his comparison of the apostles with the prophets. "Be not ashamed of thy apostles," he says to each Christian; "they are not inferior to Moses, nor second to the prophets, but they are as good as the good, and better than the good: for Elias was taken up into heaven, but Peter has the keys of the kingdom of heaven, since he heard: 'whatsoever thou shalt loose upon earth, shall be loosed in heaven.'"§ He re-

---

* Ad plebem, ep. xliii. † Apud Galland. t. v. p. 3, n. 13.
‡ Cat. xi. § 1. Πέτρος ὁ πρωτοστάτης τῶν ἀποστόλων, καὶ τῆς ἐκκλησίας κορυφαῖος κήρυξ.
§ Cat. xiv.

lates the wonderful overthrow of Simon Magus at Rome by Peter, to render which credible, he dwells on the extraordinary powers with which the apostle was clothed: "Let it not appear wonderful," he cries, "however wonderful it be in itself, for PETER WAS HE WHO CARRIED AROUND THE KEYS OF HEAVEN."* Again he says elsewhere: "In the same power of the Holy Ghost, Peter, also THE PRINCE OF THE APOSTLES, AND THE KEY-BEARER OF THE KINGDOM OF HEAVEN, cured Æneas, a palsied man, in the name of Christ, at Lydda, now called Diospolis."† Explaining the article of the creed: "I believe in the Holy Catholic Church," he says: "She is also styled a Church, or convocation, on account of the calling and assembling of all in her. The Psalmist says: 'I will confess to Thee in the great Church; I will praise Thee in the numerous people.' Before they sang in the Psalms: 'In the churches bless ye the Lord God from the fountains of Israel:' but after the Jews fell from grace, in consequence of the snares laid for the Saviour, He instituted another society, formed of the Gentiles, our holy Christian Church; of which He said to Peter: 'On this rock I will build My Church, and the gates of hell shall not prevail against it.'"‡ These testimonies to the high prerogatives of Peter, and his relation to the Church, show the ancient faith and tradition of the see of Jerusalem on these important points, as well as the received exposition of the sacred text.

ST. BASIL THE GREAT, Archbishop of Cesarea, is another illustrious witness of the faith of the Eastern churches in the fourth century, as handed down from the beginning. He calls Peter THE BLESSED ONE, WHO WAS PREFERRED TO THE OTHER DISCIPLES, who alone received a testimony above all the others, and who was pronounced blessed, rather than all the others, and TO WHOM THE KEYS OF THE HEAVENLY KINGDOM WERE INTRUSTED."§ He says that "on account of the excellence of his faith, he received on himself the building of the Church:"‖ that is, he was made the foundation on which the Church rests secure. These passages clearly show that he acknowledged Peter to be the foundation of the Church, and its ruler, intrusted by Christ with governing authority. Similar is the language of his brother, ST. GREGORY OF NYSSA, who says: "The memory of Peter, who is the head of the apostles, is revered, and together with him the other members of the Church are glorified; but the Church of God is solidly established on him; for according to the prerogative granted him by God, he is the firm and most solid rock, on which the Saviour built His Church."¶

ST. GREGORY OF NAZIANZUM, the friend of Basil, says: "Do you see that among the disciples of Christ, all of whom were sublime and worthy of their election, ONE IS CALLED A ROCK, AND IS INTRUSTED WITH THE

---

* Περιφέρων. Cat. vi.   † Cat. xvii.   ‡ Cat. xviii.   § Prœm. de judicio Dei.
‖ Adv. Eunom., l. 11.   ¶ S. Greg. Nyss. laudatio altera S. Steph., protom.

FOUNDATIONS OF THE CHURCH; another is loved more, and rests on the breast of Jesus; and the others bear patiently the preference?"* He calls him "the support of the Church,"† "the most honored of the disciples."‡

ST. CHRYSOSTOM, who is celebrated for his literal exposition of the Sacred Scriptures, abounds in passages declaratory of the prerogatives of Peter. In reference to the question put by our Saviour to the apostles, whom believed they Him to be, he asks, "How does Peter act, THE MOUTH OF ALL THE APOSTLES, THE SUMMIT OF THE WHOLE COLLEGE? All were interrogated; he alone answers. What then does Christ say: 'Thou art Simon, the son of Jonas, thou shalt be called Cephas; for since thou hast proclaimed My Father, I also mention him who begot thee.' But since he had said, 'Thou art the Son of God,' in order to show that He was the Son of God as he was son of Jona, namely, of the same substance with His Father, He added, 'and I say to thee that thou art Peter, and upon this rock I will build My Church;' that is, upon the faith which thou hast confessed."§ The Church is said to be built on the faith which Peter professed in the divinity of Christ, because this mystery is the foundation of the whole Christian system. As Chrysostom, in the exposition of this text, had specially in view the Arians, whose heresy was so widely spread, he insists particularly on this truth as fundamental and essential. He does not, however, regard this faith as a mere abstraction; but he considers it as professed by Peter, on whom, he repeatedly affirms, that the Church is built; so that when he says, that the Church is built on the faith which Peter confessed, he plainly means, on Peter confessing this faith. Accordingly, he proceeds to explain the prediction of our Lord as pointing to a numberless multitude of believers, who, under the pastoral government of Peter, profess the same mystery. "Here He manifestly foretold that the multitude of believers would be great, and He elevates the thoughts of Peter, and MAKES HIM THE PASTOR. 'And the gates of hell shall not prevail against it.' If they shall not prevail against it,— much less shall they prevail against Me. . . . . Then He adds another prerogative: 'And to thee I will give the keys of the kingdom of heaven.' What means,—'I will give to THEE?' As the Father has given to thee the knowledge of Me, so I will give to thee. And He did not say: I will ask the Father to give thee: but, though the power was great, and the greatness of the gift ineffable, nevertheless, He says, 'I will give thee.' What, I pray, dost Thou give? 'The keys,' He says, 'of the kingdom of heaven, that whatsoever thou shalt bind upon earth, shall be bound also in heaven; and whatsoever thou shalt loose upon earth, shall be loosed also in heaven.' How then is it not belonging to Him who says—'I will give to thee,'—to grant also to sit on the right hand, and on the left?

---

* Or, xxvi., ὁ μὲν πέτρα καλεῖται, καὶ τοὺς θεμελίους τῆς Ἐκκλησίας πιστεύεται.
† Apolog. ad Patrem Orat. vii.   ‡ Orat. ix.   § Τῇ πίστει τῆς ὁμολογίας.

You perceive how He leads Peter to a sublime idea of Himself, and reveals, and shows Himself to be the Son of God by these two promises. For what God alone can grant, namely, the power to remit sins, and that the Church should remain immovable amidst the swelling surges, and that a fisherman should be stronger than any rock, whilst the whole world wars against him, He promises that He will grant. Thus the Father also said to Jeremiah: 'I have made thee a pillar of iron, and a wall of brass.' But the Father set him over one nation: HE PLACED THIS MAN OVER THE ENTIRE WORLD.* Wherefore, I would willingly ask those who say that the dignity of the Son is less than that of the Father, which gifts appear to them greater, those which the Father, or those which the Son granted to Peter? The Father made to him the revelation of His Son; but the Son spread everywhere throughout the world the revelation both of the Father and of the Son; and to a mortal man gave the power of all things in heaven, giving him the keys. He spread the Church throughout the entire world, and showed that it is stronger than the firmament: 'for heaven and earth shall pass away, but My words shall not pass away.' How is He inferior, who granted all these things—who accomplished these things? I do not speak thus, as if I would separate the works of the Father from those of the Son: 'for all things were made by Him, and without Him was made nothing:' but I speak with a view to silence the shameless tongues of those who utter such things. See in all these things, how great is His power. 'I say to thee, thou art Peter; I will build My Church; I will give to thee the keys of the kingdom of heaven.'† Thus Chrysostom proved that Christ is truly God, equal to the Father, because He gave to Peter powers which God alone could grant, and rendered the Church of which he is pastor, impregnable and indefectible.

In answer to an objection against the divinity of Christ, taken from His having prayed for Peter that his faith might not fail, Chrysostom observes, that as His passion was approaching, it was fit that He should manifest His human nature by the humility of prayer; but he points to the promise of the keys as made without any previous prayer, which shows that He had all things at His disposal. "As He is going to suffer, He speaks humbly, to show that He was man, for He, who built the Church on the confession of Peter, and so strengthened her that no danger, nor death itself, can vanquish her,—He who gave to him the keys of the kingdom of heaven, and intrusted him with so great power, without at all needing to pray for this purpose, how much less should He need it in this circumstance? For He did not say, I have prayed, but He spoke with authority: I WILL BUILD MY CHURCH ON THEE, AND GIVE TO THEE THE KEYS OF THE KINGDOM OF HEAVEN."‡

---

* Πανταχοῦ τῆς οἰκουμένης. † S. Chrys. hom. lv. in Matt.
‡ Hom. lxxxii., alias lxxxiii., in Matt.

In his panegyric on the martyr Ignatius, who was Bishop of Antioch, where Peter had resided for a time, Chrysostom dwells on the great honor thus bestowed by God on that city: "for He set over it PETER, THE DOCTOR OF THE WHOLE WORLD, TO WHOM HE GAVE THE KEYS OF HEAVEN, TO WHOSE WILL AND POWER HE INTRUSTED ALL THINGS."* Panegyrizing both the apostles Peter and Paul, he thus carefully distinguishes the high prerogatives of Peter :—" Peter the leader of the apostles, Peter the commencement of the orthodox faith,—the great and illustrious priest of the Church,—the necessary counsellor of Christians, the depositary of supernal powers,—the apostle honored by the Lord. What shall we say of Peter? the delightful spectacle of the Church; the splendor of the entire world, the most chaste dove, the teacher of the apostles, the ardent apostle, fervent in spirit, angel and man, full of grace, the firm rock of faith, the mature wisdom of the Church, who, on account of his purity, from the mouth of the Lord heard himself styled blessed, and son of the dove: who received from the Lord Himself the keys of the kingdom of heaven. REJOICE, O PETER, ROCK OF FAITH !"† This is, indeed, the language of panegyric: but it would have been utterly unwarrantable, if Peter were not in fact the necessary counsellor of Christians, the teacher of the apostles, the rock of faith. It is not only when expressly engaged in panegyric, that Chrysostom thus speaks of Peter. They are his favorite expressions, which everywhere occur in his writings: "Peter," says he, " is the foundation of the Church,—the fisherman who cast his net into the sea, and caught in it the whole world.‡ He left his ship, and undertook the government of the Church; he was called the key-bearer of the kingdom of heaven.§ He was the chief who occupied the first place, and to whom the keys of the kingdom of heaven were intrusted."|| He was " the pillar of the Church, the foundation of faith, the head of the apostolic choir."¶ "TO HIM THE LORD GAVE THE PRESIDENCY OF THE CHURCH THROUGHOUT THE WHOLE EARTH."**

ST. EPIPHANIUS, bishop of Salamina, in the island of Cyprus, a contemporary of Chrysostom, calls Peter "the first of the apostles, the solid rock on which the Church was built."††

---

* In S. Ignat. M. Barrow admits "the titles and eulogies given to St. Peter by the fathers; who call him ἔξαρχον, (the prince,) κορυφαῖον, (the ring-leader,) κεφαλὴν, (the head,) πρόεδρον, (the president,) ἀρχηγὸν, (the captain,) προήγορον, (the prolocutor,) πρωτοστάτην, (the foreman,) προστάτην, (the warden,) ἔκκριτον τῶν Ἀποστόλων, (the choice or egregious apostle,) majorem, (the greater or grandee among them,) primum, (the first or prime apostle.)"—*A Treatise of the Pope's Supremacy*, Sup. i. § vi.

† In SS. Petrum et Paulum, tom. v. p. 690. This oration, with another, was first edited, at Rome, by Gerard Vossius, in the year 1580, in the original Greek, with a Latin translation. I quote from the translation published in Paris in 1687.

‡ De Verbis Isaiæ, hom. 4, p. 609, tom. i.

§ In duodecim Apost. tom. v. p. 691.

|| In Ep. ad Corinth, i. c. ix., hom. 21.

¶ Hom. 2, de pœn. in Psalm l.

** Ad. pop. Antioch. hom. 80, de pœnitentia.   †† In Ancorato.

St. Cyril of Alexandria observes of our Lord: "He was pleased to call him Peter, by an apt similitude, as the one on whom He was about to found the Church."*

St. Hilary filled the see of Poictiers in Gaul, in the middle of the fourth century. In his treatise *On the Trinity*, he thus distinguishes the teachers, from whom he derived the knowledge of this mystery: "Matthew, from a publican chosen to be an apostle; John, through the familiarity of the Lord, made worthy of a revelation of heavenly mysteries, and after his confession of the mystery, BLESSED SIMON, LYING BENEATH THE FABRIC OF THE CHURCH,† AND RECEIVING THE KEYS OF THE KINGDOM OF HEAVEN, and all the others preaching by the Holy Spirit."‡ Although wholly intent on establishing the divinity of Christ, Hilary strongly declares the distinguishing attributes of Peter, who supports the Church, as a foundation-stone sustains the building, and who has received the keys of the kingdom, as the symbol of spiritual sovereignty. He elsewhere addresses all the apostles as having received the keys, because all received the power of binding and loosing;§ but when distinguishing Peter from Matthew, John, and Paul, he puts the keys as his peculiar characteristic. All may be said to have received them, as far as they are symbols of apostolic power, but to Peter only they were given expressly by Christ, as the proper token of delegated sovereignty.

When speaking of the confession made by Peter, Hilary shows that it was extolled by our Saviour, as divinely revealed, because it was an acknowledgment that He is the true and eternal Son of God the Father: "For praise," says he, "was given to Peter, not on account of the confession of the honor, but on account of his acknowledgment of the mystery, because he confessed not merely Christ, but Christ the Son of God. The Father saying, 'This is My Son,' revealed to Peter, that he might say, 'Thou art the Son of God.' On this rock of confession,|| therefore, the Church is built. This faith is the foundation of the Church: through this faith the gates of hell are powerless against her. This faith has the keys of the heavenly kingdom. What this faith binds or looses on earth, is bound and loosed in heaven. This faith is the gift of the Father's revelation; not falsely to assert that Christ is a creature, drawn forth from nothing, but to confess Him to be the Son of God, according to His natural property. Oh! impious frenzy of wretched folly, that does not understand the martyr of blessed old age and faith, the martyr Peter, for whom He prayed to the Father, that his faith might not fail in temptation—who, having twice repeated the profession of the love which God demanded of him, sighed, on being a third time interrogated, as if his love were doubtful and uncertain; thereby also meriting to hear thrice from the Lord,

---

* L. ii. in c. xii. Joan. † Ædificationi ecclesiæ subjacens.
‡ L. vi. de Trinitate, n. 20. § Ibidem, p. 166.
|| On this confession, as on a rock.

after being purified of his weaknesses by this threefold trial: 'Feed My sheep:'—who, whilst all the other apostles remained silent, understanding, in a manner beyond human infirmity, from the revelation of the Father, that He was the Son of God, merited pre-eminent glory by the confession of his faith! To what necessity of interpreting his words are we now brought! He confessed Christ to be the Son of God: but you, (*Arian*,) the lying priesthood of a new apostleship, urge me to believe that Christ is a creature brought forth from nothing. What violence you offer to His glorious words! He confessed the Son of God: for this he is blessed. This is the revelation of the Father, this is the foundation of the Church, this is the security for eternity. Hence he has the keys of the kingdom of heaven—hence his judgments on earth are ratified in heaven. He learned by revelation the mystery hidden from ages—he spoke the faith—he declared the nature—he confessed the Son of God. Whoever, on the contrary, affirming Him to be a creature, denies this, should first deny the apostleship of Peter, his faith, blessedness, priesthood, martyrdom; and then let him understand that he is estranged from Christ, because Peter, confessing Him to be the Son, merited these things. . . . Let there be a different faith, if there be different keys of heaven. Let there be a different faith, if there is to be another Church, against which the gates of hell shall not prevail. Let there be another faith, if there is to be another apostleship, binding and loosing in heaven what it binds and looses on earth. Let there be another faith, if Christ shall be proclaimed to be a different Son of God from what He is. But if this faith only that confessed Christ to be the Son of God, merited in Peter the glory of all beatitudes, that which declares Him to be a creature from nothing, must necessarily be not the Church, nor of Christ, since it has not obtained the keys of the kingdom of heaven, and is contrary to the apostolic faith and power."*

From these quotations the reader has a full and correct view of the sentiments of Hilary. His object is to show that the Arian heresy had no part or share in the power of the keys, or the privileges granted to Peter, because it had not the faith which obtained for Peter these privileges. There is not the least effort to establish a distinction between Peter and the confession of faith which he made: but the Arians are confounded, by being told, that, as they deny Christ to be the Son of the living God, they have not the power of the keys, and are not inheritors of the promises made to the Church. Peter, then, confessing the divinity of Christ, is the foundation: his is the apostleship, the acts of which are confirmed in heaven: the Church connected with him is that against which the gates of hell cannot prevail: there can be no other faith, no other power, no other Church. In the circumstances in which St. Hilary and other

---

* De Trin. l. vi. p. 169.

fathers spoke, during the prevalence of Arianism, and at a time when no controversy was agitated concerning the prerogatives of Peter and his successors, it was natural for them to employ the text against the formidable heresy which they were engaged in refuting. As Peter had made a glorious confession of the divinity of Christ, and had received his name and privileges in reward of it, they rightly insisted that on this confession the whole fabric of Christianity rests; so that to deny the eternal generation of Christ is to overthrow all revealed religion, and make void all the counsels of God for the salvation of men. The reasoning of Hilary perfectly harmonizes with the obvious exposition of the text, since the confession was the act of Peter under divine illumination; and to say that the Church was founded on the confession of the divinity of Christ made by Peter, is equivalent to declaring that it was founded on Peter, in consequence of his having confessed Christ to be the Son of the living God. In applying the text to the controversy of the day, the fathers did not, even by the remotest implication, deny its direct force for establishing the prerogatives of Peter; which, on the contrary, on so many occasions, they most unequivocally asserted.

In his commentary on the glorious confession of Peter, Hilary observes: "The confession of Peter obtained a suitable reward, because he discerned the Son of God in the man.* Blessed is he, who was praised for observing and seeing beyond what human eyes could see; not beholding what was of flesh and blood, but discerning the Son of God by the revelation of the heavenly Father; and who was judged worthy to be the first to recognise in Christ His divine nature. O! THOU FOUNDATION OF THE CHURCH, HAPPY IN THE NEW APPELLATION WHICH THOU RECEIVEST! O! ROCK, WORTHY OF THAT BUILDING WHICH IS TO DESTROY THE INFERNAL POWERS, AND THE GATES OF HELL, AND ALL THE BARS OF DEATH! O! HAPPY GATE-KEEPER OF HEAVEN, TO WHOSE DISCRETION THE KEYS OF THE ETERNAL PORCH ARE DELIVERED, AND WHOSE JUDGMENT ON EARTH IS AN AUTHORITATIVE ANTICIPATION OF HEAVENLY JUDGMENT, so that those things which are bound or loosed on earth, obtain in heaven the same order and determination."† Any effort to illustrate this passage would be superfluous.

After this illustrious doctor of the Church of Gaul, the order of time presents to us OPTATUS, bishop of Milevis,‡ in Africa, who was among the most learned, eloquent and saintly prelates in the decline of the fourth century. Of him St. Augustin says, that if the Church depended on the virtue of her ministers, his life might serve as a proof of her authority. He wrote against the Donatists, whom he held to be inexcusable for assuming the name of Church, while they remained separated from that see, which, in the person of Peter, received the keys: "Christ," he re-

---

* He recognised Christ as the eternal Son of God, although veiled in human flesh.
† Com. in Matt. c. xvi.   ‡ Mila, near Tunis, or Constantina.

marks, " in the Canticle of Canticles, intimates that His dove is one, that she is a chosen spouse, an enclosed garden, and a sealed fountain; so that all heretics neither have THE KEYS, WHICH PETER ALONE RECEIVED, nor the ring with which the fountain is sealed: and the garden, in which God plants the shrubs, belongs to none of them. What can you say to these things, you who secretly cherish and shamelessly defend schism, taking to yourselves the name of the Church?"* To how many deluded men in our day might not this reproach be addressed!

Let us hear the eloquent bishop of Milan, whose lucid exposition of Catholic truth dissipated the prejudices and errors of Augustin, and prepared his heart for the triumph of divine grace over pride and passion. In his commentary on the fortieth Psalm, AMBROSE says: " This is that Peter to whom Christ said: 'Thou art Peter, and upon this rock I will build My Church.' THEREFORE WHERE PETER IS, THERE IS THE CHURCH, there death is not, but life eternal: and therefore He added: 'and the gates of hell shall not prevail against it: and I will give unto thee the keys of the kingdom of heaven.' Blessed Peter, against whom the gate of hell did not prevail, and the gate of heaven was not closed! on the contrary, he destroyed the porches of hell, and laid open those of heaven: therefore, while on earth, he opened heaven, and closed hell."† Speaking of the question put by our Redeemer to His disciples as to the opinions prevailing among men concerning Him, he observes the silence of Peter in this circumstance; but calls our attention to his promptitude in answering the interrogation as to their own belief. " This, therefore, is Peter, who answered rather than the other apostles, yea, for the others, and he is therefore styled the foundation, because he not only fulfilled his duty individually, but acted in behalf of all. Him Christ eulogized: to him the Father made a revelation: for he, who speaks of the true generation of the Father, learned it not from flesh, but from the Father.‡ Faith, therefore, is the foundation of the Church: for it was not said of the flesh of Peter, but of his faith, that the gates of hell shall not prevail against it: but the confession overcame hell. And this confession does not exclude one heresy only: for since the Church, like a good ship, is lashed oftentimes by many waves, the foundation of the Church ought to prevail against all heresies. The day would close before I should have enumerated the names of the heretics and different sects: but against all of them that faith is available, that Christ is the Son of God, eternally proceeding from the Father, born in time of the Virgin."§ When Ambrose says, that faith is the foundation of the Church, he evidently speaks of faith in the

---

* Opt. Afric. l. 1. † In Psalm xl. enar. § 30.

‡ Ille est ergo Petrus, qui respondit præ cæteris Apostolis, imo pro cæteris, et ideo fundamentum dicitur, quia novit non solum proprium, sed etiam commune servare. Huic astipulatus est Christus, revelavit Pater.

§ De Incarn. c. 4 and 5.

divinity of Christ as professed by Peter, that is, of Peter professing the faith. He is, therefore, styled the foundation, in reward of his promptitude to confess Christ, before the others, and in their name. The confession which he made was, indeed, the expression of his individual faith, but it was made by him in reply to a question that regarded all; nor did he give it in as peculiar to himself. St. Ambrose insists that the Church was not built on the flesh of Peter, but on his faith; because it was no mere natural quality, but his faith in the divinity of Christ, that gained for him this prerogative; and this faith is ever to prove the bulwark of the Church against the endless varieties of heresy. He insists on this for the same reason as Hilary and Chrysostom, in order the more effectually to combat Arianism. In his work on faith, he observes: "That you may know that what He asks as man, He ordains by His divine power, you have in the Gospel what He said to Peter: 'I have prayed for thee, that thy faith may not fail.' And when Peter said before: 'Thou art Christ, the Son of the living God,' He answered: 'Thou art Peter, and upon this rock I will build My Church, and to thee I will give the keys of the kingdom of heaven.' Could He not, therefore, strengthen the faith of him to whom, of His own authority, He gave a kingdom, and WHOM, IN CALLING A ROCK, HE MADE THE STRENGTH OF THE CHURCH? Consider when it is that He prays—when it is that He commands. He prays when He is about to suffer; He commands when He is believed to be the Son of God."* Peter, then, is the rock of strength on which the Church rests: he has received a kingdom from Christ. St. Augustin testifies that in a hymn composed by St. Ambrose, which was in general use, Peter was styled the rock of the Church.†

It is manifest that St. Ambrose interpreted the texts in question precisely as we interpret them, and recognised in Peter special powers and prerogatives not granted to the other apostles of Christ. He was the rock,—the foundation,—the strength and support of the Church,—sustaining all the parts of the vast fabric, holding them together in unity, and imparting to them strength and durability. He received a kingdom from Christ,—that heavenly kingdom whose keys were intrusted to him. Elsewhere Ambrose says: "Christ is a rock: 'for they drank of that spiritual rock which followed them, and the rock was Christ.' He did not deny the favor of this appellation even to His disciple, that he may also be Peter, because from the rock he derives the solidity of constancy, and the firmness of faith."‡ Thus far he retains the literal meaning of the text, and often and strongly inculcates it. He then takes occasion from it for exhortation, and passes to a mystical interpretation, similar to

---

* De Fide, l. iv. This observation coincides admirably with that of St. Chrysostom, above cited, p. 46.

† Hoc ipso, petra ecclesiæ, canente, culpam diluit. Aug. Retract. l. 1. c. xxi.

‡ L. vi. in Luc. n. 97.

one found in Origen. "Peter," he elsewhere says, "is therefore styled a rock for his devotion, and the Lord is styled a rock for His power, as the apostle says: 'they drank of the spiritual rock that followed them, and the rock was Christ.' He justly deserves the communication of the name, who is made worthy to partake of the work, for Peter in the same house laid the foundation. Peter plants, the Lord gives an increase, the Lord waters."*

The last verse of the thirty-eighth Psalm reads thus, in our Vulgate translation: "Oh forgive me, that I may be refreshed, before I go hence and be no more."† On these words St. Ambrose writes: "Forgive me, that is, forgive me here where I have sinned. Unless Thou forgivest me here, I shall not be able to find there the repose consequent on forgiveness: for what remains bound on earth, shall remain bound in heaven; what is loosed on earth, shall be loosed in heaven. Therefore, the Lord gave to His apostles what previously was reserved to His own judgment, a discretionary power to remit sins,‡ lest what should be speedily loosed remain bound for a long time. Finally, hear what He says: 'I will give to thee the keys of the kingdom of heaven, and whatsoever thou shalt bind on earth, shall be bound also in heaven, and whatsoever thou shalt loose on earth, shall be loosed also in heaven.' To thee, He says, I will give the keys of the kingdom of heaven, that thou mayest loose and bind. Novatian did not hear this, but the Church of God heard it: therefore, he is in his fallen state; we are in the way of forgiveness: he is in a state of impenitence; we, of grace. What is said to Peter, is said to the apostles. We do not usurp the power, but we obey the command, lest, when the Lord shall afterward come, and find those bound who should have been loosed, he be indignant against the dispenser who kept the servants bound, whom the Lord had ordered to be loosed."§ In this beautiful vindication of the power of forgiveness, as exercised by the Catholic Church, there is nothing that militates against the distinction which Christ made in the powers of the apostles. Ambrose quotes the words addressed to Peter, to prove that the Church founded on Peter has the power of forgiving sins: and observes that this power was not confined to Peter, Christ having spoken in like manner to all the apostles. He does not say that He spoke precisely the same words, or gave to each one the same power to be exercised independently; much less does He treat here of the governing power of the Church, as represented by the keys of the heavenly kingdom, which were peculiarly given to Peter, but he speaks of the power of forgiveness, which was common to all. The power of the

---

* L. v. § 33.

† The Vulgate version of the Psalms was made from the Greek version of the Septuagint, which, in some places, presents a reading somewhat different from the actual Hebrew.

‡ Peccata remittendi æquitatem. The Vatican manuscript reads: peccata remittendi æquitate solvenda. § Enar. in Psalm xxxviii.

keys, he elsewhere ascribes to Peter alone: "There went up," he says, "to the mountain, Peter, WHO RECEIVED THE KEYS OF THE KINGDOM OF HEAVEN; John, to whom His mother is intrusted; James, also, who first ascended the episcopal throne."* The keys of the heavenly kingdom were consequently the characteristic badge of Peter, as it was the peculiar privilege of John to receive in his charge the Mother of our Lord, and the province of James to govern with episcopal authority the Church of Jerusalem. "Peter, James, and John, and Barnabas," are styled pillars, but Peter is called "an eternal gate, against which the gates of hell shall not prevail."†

The equality of Paul to Peter is asserted by Ambrose, not as to the power of office, but as to the merit of virtue; and this with a view to prove that the choice of the Holy Spirit was full of wisdom. "Being chosen by the command of the Holy Spirit, which is abundant evidence of the excellence of his merits, he was not unworthy of so great a college. For the same grace shone forth in those whom the same Spirit had chosen. Nor was Paul inferior to Peter, THOUGH THE ONE WAS THE FOUNDATION OF THE CHURCH, and the other a wise architect, knowing how to direct the steps of the nations that believe. Paul, I say, was not unworthy of the college of the apostles, since he also may be compared with THE FIRST, and was second to none: for he who does not acknowledge himself inferior, makes himself equal."‡ The meaning is obvious. Ambrose is careful to mark even here the distinguishing characteristic of Peter as *the foundation of the Church*, and *first* of the apostles, while he supposes Paul to be equal to him in merit, and on that account to compare even with the first.

Some passages of the writings of Ambrose are occasionally abused to obscure his testimony to the primacy of Peter. Any one, however, who considers them in their connection, cannot hesitate as to their meaning. Those places in which he gives interpretations evidently mystical, need not be specially explained, since, as we have already remarked, such expositions cannot have weight in doctrinal inquiries.

ST. JEROM, the contemporary of Ambrose, is justly esteemed, not only for his excellent translation of the Scriptures, but also for his lucid exposition of their meaning. In his work against Jovinian, who assailed virginity, and objected that Peter, a married man, was chosen to be prince of the apostles, Jerom replied that his wife was probably deceased; a conjecture rendered likely by the omission of all mention of her in Scripture, as well as by the circumstance, that his mother-in-law, when relieved from the fever, served at table. He proceeded to show that John, on account of his virginity, enjoyed the special love of Christ, and was ad-

---

* In Lucam, l. vii. n. 9. See also in Psalm cxviii. Serm. 20.
† De fide, l. iv. c. 1, ♂ 25.   ‡ L. de Sp. S. ♂ 158.

mitted to great familiarity. He then objects to himself that Peter was chosen to be the foundation of the Church; and observes, that the other apostles likewise received similar powers, though he admits that, to prevent schism, Peter was chosen to be the head of all. He further inquires, why the virgin apostle, John, did not receive this distinction; and answers that the age of Peter was a reason for preferring him: "But, you say," he remarks, "the Church is founded upon Peter: though the same thing is elsewhere done upon all the apostles, and all receive the keys of the kingdom of heaven, and the strength of the Church is consolidated upon them equally: yet ONE IS CHOSEN AMONG THE TWELVE, THAT A HEAD BEING ESTABLISHED, THE OCCASION OF SCHISM MAY BE REMOVED. But why was not the virgin John chosen? Regard was had to age, because Peter was elder, lest a very young man should be preferred to men of advanced age."* It is clear, that while Jerom advocates so strongly the excellence of virginity and its special prerogatives, he is careful to lay down, in clear and precise terms, the primacy of Peter. All the apostles are, indeed, in a certain degree the foundations of the Church, since of the heavenly Jerusalem, which is the Church in glory, it is said: "the wall of the city had twelve foundations, and in them the names of the twelve apostles of the Lamb;"† but Peter is strictly the foundation, since to him only, and not to the others, Christ said: "Thou art Peter, and on this rock I will build My Church." All of them have received the keys of the kingdom, inasmuch as all have received the power of binding and loosing, which is sometimes expressed by that symbol: but it was not without special and high design that to Peter alone was said: "To thee I will give the keys of the kingdom." Jerom maintains that similar powers were granted to the others, on which account it may be justly said, that upon all of them the strength of the Church is consolidated, since all concur to the great work of the ministry, in union, however, with Peter, who is the head, invested with all the authority necessary for maintaining order and unity: a head, by the appointment of whom all plausible pretext for schism is removed. Were not this his peculiar privilege, there was no need of explaining why John was not chosen to be chief.

In his commentary upon the similitude of the wise man, who built his house upon a rock, Jerom observes: "On this rock the Lord founded the Church: from this rock Peter the apostle derived his name. The foundation which the apostolic architect laid, is our Lord Jesus Christ alone: on this stable and firm foundation, and of itself founded with a strong mass, the Church of Christ is built."‡ This, at first sight, may appear not to harmonize with the general interpretation of the fathers; but, by attention to the occasion in which it was written, it will be found not to

---

* Adv. Jov. l. 1, p. 16, tom. iii.   † Apoc. xxi. 14.
‡ Com. Matt. c. viii. f. 12.

be at variance. In reference to the similitude used by our Saviour in His sermon on the mount, it was most natural to observe, that He was the wise man who built His Church upon a rock, and that from this circumstance Peter was styled a rock: but it would be a strange phrase to say, that He built His Church upon Himself, thus confounding the architect with the foundation. Hear Jerom elsewhere: Having quoted a passage from the writings of St. Peter, he exclaims: "Oh sentence truly worthy of the apostle and of the rock of Christ!"* by which he plainly means him whom Christ made a rock of faith. "As Plato was the prince of philosophers, so was Peter of the apostles: ON HIM THE CHURCH OF THE LORD, AN ENDURING STRUCTURE, WAS BUILT."† In his letter to Marcellus he says of Peter: "UPON WHOM THE LORD BUILT HIS CHURCH."‡

The allusion to the text of St. Paul presents a change of metaphor. In the former Christ was the architect, and Peter the foundation: in this Paul is architect, and Christ the foundation. Metaphors admit of this variety, and it would be unjust to transfer what regards one similitude to another somewhat different.

The commentary of Jerom on the promise of our Saviour to Peter, plainly establishes the relation between them. "What means," he asks, "'I say to thee?' Because thou hast said to Me: 'Thou art Christ, the Son of the living God: I also say to thee;' not in vain discourse, void of effect, but I say to thee, because My word effects what it expresses: 'that thou art Peter, and on this rock I will build My Church.' As He gave light to the apostles, that they might be called the light of the world, and they received other appellations from the Lord: so also He bestowed the name of Peter on Simon, who believed in the rock Christ; and according to the metaphor of a rock, it is properly said to him: 'I will build My Church upon THEE.' 'And the gates of hell shall not prevail against it.' I think that the gates of hell are the vices and the sins of men; or certainly the doctrines of heretics, by which men are allured and led to hell."§ Here the learned interpreter applies to Peter the term rock, and explains the promise, as if it were said: I will build My Church on thee. Against this Church neither the vices and sins of men, nor the doctrines of heretics, can prevail. Scandals must come, and may obscure the lustre of the Church, but they cannot effect her overthrow: heresies may be broached, even by those who were children of the Church, but they can never receive her sanction, because Christ teaches in her "all days even to the consummation of the world."

When commenting on the rebuke of Christ, "Go behind me, Satan," Jerom supposes his reader to inquire, how this is compatible with the sublime address made to Peter, and with the powers conferred on him.

---

* Adv. Jovinian, l. 1, c. iv.   † L. 1, adv. Pelag. c. 4.   ‡ Class. 2, Ep. 4, n. 2.
§ Com. in Matt. tom. ix. f. 24, 25. Ed. Bas. an. 1516.

"If," he answers, "the inquirer reflect, he will perceive that the benediction, and beatitude, and power, and the building of the Church upon him, were promised to Peter for a future time, and were not granted at the present time: I *will* build (he says) on thee My Church, and the gates of hell shall not prevail against it: and to thee I *will* give the keys of the kingdom of heaven;'—all in the future tense. Had he given them immediately, the error of a perverse confession* would never have taken place in him."† This enlightened doctor was firmly persuaded that if Peter had been at once constituted primate, the providence of God would have prevented his fall.

St. Jerom unhesitatingly explained the rock of Peter and his successors in the see of Rome. Addressing Pope Damasus to obtain his instructions in regard to the use of the term *hypostasis*, which in the East was understood by some of the Divine Nature, while others used it of the Divine Persons, as it is now employed, he says: "Let it not appear invidious: let the pomp of Roman majesty withdraw: I speak with the successor of the fisherman, and a disciple of the cross. I, who follow no one as chief‡ except Christ, am united in communion with your Holiness, that is, WITH THE CHAIR OF PETER: ON THAT ROCK I KNOW THAT THE CHURCH IS BUILT. Whoever eats the lamb out of this house is profane. Whoever was not in the ark of Noe, must perish in the deluge."§ Respectfully approaching the heir of Peter's faith, Jerom begs that his boldness may be excused; and reminds Damasus, who was encompassed with a splendor like that of imperial majesty, that his greatest dignity is that of successor of the fisherman. This is his imperishable title, his highest glory: as this authority is the fundamental and immovable principle of the Church. We have in this passage the obvious meaning of the text with its application in the most direct and positive manner.

ST. AUGUSTIN, in several places, gives the common interpretation of the texts regarding the primacy; but in the revision of his works, he observed, that he had likewise explained "the rock" of Christ Himself, and he left the reader to judge which of the two expositions was the more probable.|| He was led to doubt by the change of gender observable in the Greek and Latin: a distinction to which no importance can be attached by any one acquainted with the language in which our Lord spoke, which admits of no variation in the term, as we have already seen. His hesitation cannot outweigh the positive judgment of so many fathers, who concur in recognising Peter as the rock of which Christ spoke; especially as the context, by the acknowledgment of most learned adversaries, admits of no other interpretation. He did not, however, hesitate as to the meaning of the whole passage of Matthew, or of the other texts, which he uniformly expounded as declaring the governing authority wherewith

---

* Peter's denial of Christ. † Com. in Matt. tom. ix. f. 24, 25. Ed. Bas. an. 1516.
‡ Primum. § Ep. xv. Damaso. || L. 1, Retract. c. xxi.

Peter was invested. In his discourses on the Gospel of St. John, he observes that our Lord left almsgiving and prayer as remedies for the slighter sins into which even just men fall, and taught us to pray for forgiveness, as we forgive our debtors. "The Church," he says, "happy in hope, does this," (namely, sues for pardon in the name of her frail children,) "in this wretched life: which Church Peter, the apostle, ON ACCOUNT OF THE PRIMACY OF HIS APOSTLESHIP, represented in a figurative universality," (Peter being addressed as the whole Church, which he represented, as her head.) "For, as to what strictly regards himself, he was by nature an individual man, by grace an individual Christian; but by more abundant grace he was an apostle, and THE FIRST: but when it was said to him: 'To thee I will give the keys of the kingdom of heaven, and whatsoever thou shalt bind on earth, shall be bound also in heaven; and whatsoever thou shalt loose on earth, shall be loosed also in heaven,' he represented the whole Church, which in this world is agitated by various temptations, as by showers, floods, and tempests, and which does not fall, because it is founded on the rock, whence Peter derived his name."* Here Augustin departs from the general interpretation of the term rock, yet considers Peter as the representative of the whole Church, receiving from Christ a power to be exercised for the benefit of all. He was not a mere actor in the scene, but an official representative, "ON ACCOUNT OF THE PRIMACY OF HIS APOSTLESHIP," in which capacity he received the promise, and subsequently the power promised, not for his mere personal advantage, but for the benefit of the Church at large. The holy doctor insists on this point, because the Montanists and Novatians denied to the Church the power of forgiveness. "Therefore," says he, "the Church, which is founded on Christ, received through Peter the keys of the kingdom of heaven, that is, the power of binding and loosing sins. For what the Church is really† in Christ, Peter is the same mystically in the rock: according to which signification Christ is the rock, Peter the Church. This Church, therefore, which Peter represented, as long as she is in the midst of evils, is freed from evils, by loving and following Christ. And she follows Him especially by means of those who contend unto death for the truth. But to the multitude is said, 'follow Me;' for which multitude Christ suffered."‡ In pursuing this allegorical explanation, Augustin evidently presupposes that the keys were given to Peter, and that in him,§ the Church received them, inasmuch as not for himself only—"an individual man, an individual Christian"—but for all the Church, he, who

---

* Tract. cxxiv. in c. xxi. Joan. Ev.

† Quod est enim per proprietatem in Christo Ecclesia, hoc est per significationem Petrus in petra, qua significatione intelligitur Christus petra, Petrus Ecclesia. Ib.

‡ Sed universitati dicitur: sequere me. The command is directed to all the Church.

§ Ecclesia ergo, quæ fundatur in Christo, claves ab eo regni cœlorum accepit in Petro, id est potestatem ligandi solvendique peccata. Tract. cxxiv. in Joan.

was "an apostle and first of the apostles," received this power.* "For the benefit of all the saints," says he, "inseparably belonging to the body of Christ, PETER, THE FIRST OF THE APOSTLES, received the keys of the kingdom, for its government in this most tempestuous life, to bind and loose sins,† and with reference to the same saints, John the Evangelist reclined on the bosom of Christ, to express the most tranquil repose of this most secret life." John is said to represent or signify the Church triumphant, inasmuch as, reposing on the bosom of Jesus, he presents an image of the happiness of the saints. The representative character of Peter is clearly marked as *official*, directed to the government of the Church militant in this stormy life. He is the pilot placed by Christ at the helm;—he is the ruler, who received from Christ the keys of His kingdom.

It is in the same sense that St. Augustin insists that not only Peter, but all the apostles, in his person, since he represented the whole Church, received the keys, because the power of forgiving sins was not limited to him alone, being communicated to all of them for the benefit of the whole Church. "For it is evident," he says, "that Peter in many places of the Scripture represents the Church,‡ chiefly in that place where it is said: 'I give unto thee the keys of the kingdom of heaven. Whatsoever thou shalt bind on earth, shall be bound in heaven; and whatsoever thou shalt loose on earth, shall be loosed in heaven.' What! did Peter receive those keys, and Paul not receive them? Did Peter receive them, and John and James and the rest of the apostles not receive them? Or are not those keys in the Church, where sins are daily remitted? But since in meaning hinted, but not expressed,§ Peter was representing the Church, what was given to him singly, was given to the Church. So then, Peter bore the figure of the Church: the Church is the body of Christ.'|| What Augustin inculcates is plainly that the Church received the power of forgiveness, through Peter, who in his official capacity represented her, on account of the primacy of his apostleship. This does not imply that the keys, as symbols of governing power, were not given to Peter in a more special manner.

ST. LEO THE GREAT is most eloquent and forcible in the exposition of the sacred text. He observes: "Christ having assumed him to a participation in His indivisible unity, was pleased that he should be styled what He Himself was, saying: 'Thou art Peter, and on this rock I will build My Church;' that the building of the eternal temple, by the wonderful gift of the grace of God, should rest on the solidity of the rock, strengthening His Church by this firmness, so that neither human temerity could affect it, nor the gates of hell prevail against it. But whosoever attempts

---

* Abundantiore gratia unus idemque primus apostolorum. Ibidem.
† Ibidem. ‡ Personam gestet ecclesiæ. § In significatione.
|| Serm. cxlix. de verbis Actuum Apost. tom. v. 706 B.

to infringe on his power, indulges excessive and impious presumption, in seeking to violate the most sacred strength of this rock, God, as we have said, being the builder."* This exposition loses nothing of its weight from the fact that St. Leo filled, at the time, the chair of Peter. His learning and sanctity, the high esteem which he enjoyed among his contemporaries, and the veneration with which his name has been transmitted to us, do not suffer us to consider him as influenced by personal interest, or pride of station, in expounding the sacred text.' He spoke the truth in Christ, with no other view than that all should adore the divine wisdom and power manifested in the establishment of the Church.

St. Leo freely admits that the power given to Peter was to be communicated to the other apostles; but insists that it was specially lodged in him for the great ends of Christian unity. "The privilege of this power did, indeed, pass to the other apostles, and the order of this decree reached all the rulers of the Church; but not without purpose what is intended for all, is put into the hands of one."† Elsewhere he says: "The Lord hath willed that the mystery of this gift (of announcing the Gospel) should belong to the office of all the apostles, on the condition of its being chiefly seated in the most blessed Peter, the first of all the apostles, and from him, as it were from the head, it is His pleasure that His gifts should flow into the whole body, that whoever dares recede from the rock of Peter may know that He has no part in the divine mystery."‡

The quotations hitherto submitted to the reader, show clearly that the promise recorded by St. Matthew, was understood by the fathers of the first five centuries, as implying special relations of Peter to the Church, as its foundation and ruler. It is in vain that Mr. Palmer asserts that some interpret it of the apostles generally; for it will easily be seen that these fathers, as Ambrose and Augustin, whose words we have quoted, speak of the apostolic powers as declared in other passages, and that they apply and extend to the apostles the text in question, so far only as these powers are implied, without prejudice to the primacy of Peter, which they expressly affirm. The few who speak of Christ as the rock, for the most part use this figure without direct reference to the text of Matthew, for the purpose of declaring the immovable nature of the Church, of which Christ is the support; and when, like Augustin, they refer to this passage, they otherwise acknowledge in unequivocal terms the high prerogative of the prince of the apostles. All who interpret it of the faith as confessed by Peter, perfectly harmonize with those who expound it of Peter himself, so that these two interpretations, which at first sight appear different, are in reality identical. It is worthy of remark, that before the rise of Arianism, no father explained the rock of the confession of Peter; which interpretation was first suggested by the necessity of employing every available weapon against that impiety. It is also to be observed,

---

* T. ii. op. col. 1315. † In anniv. suæ consecr. ‡ Ep. 10.

that no father who declares faith to be the rock, expressly excludes Peter, while many positively mention him conjointly with the confession. The moral application and allegorical expositions of some can by no means weaken the literal exposition so forcibly delivered by the great body of the fathers. We can, therefore, fairly claim their general support in the maintenance of the primacy as divinely promised to Peter. In the words of Dr. Nevin, we may say: "The promise of our Saviour to Peter, is always taken by the fathers in the sense that he was to be the centre of unity for the Church, and in the language of Chrysostom, to have the presidency of it throughout the world. Ambrose and Augustin both recognise this distinction over and over again in the clearest and strongest terms."*

---

* Art. Early Christianity, in Mercersburg Review, Sept. 1851.

CHAPTER IV.

Institution of the Primacy.

THE promise made by Christ to Peter, that He would make him the fundamental rock of His Church, and give him the keys of the kingdom of heaven, and the solemn charge addressed to him to confirm his brethren, prepare us for the bestowal of extraordinary power. The denial of his Divine Master, might, however, seem to be an insuperable obstacle to his elevation to this dignity: but his tears, which were bitter and abundant, washed away his prevarication. Christ, after His resurrection, appearing to him with Thomas, John and James, and two others, besides Nathaniel, of Cana in Galilee, was pleased to fulfil His promise, after He had first elicited from Peter repeated protestations of special love. He presented Himself to them all as they were fishing, and directed them to cast the net on the right side of the ship, assuring them that they should be successful. The verification of this assurance led John to recognise Him; and Peter, being made sensible of the presence of his Master, girded his coat about him. Then, as the other disciples came in the ship, drawing the net, and reached the shore, "Simon Peter went up, and drew the net to land, full of great fishes, one hundred and fifty-three. And although there were so many, the net was not broken."* It cannot be doubted, that by this miraculous draught was typified the wonderful conversion of nations by the apostles, with Peter at their head, acting under the command of Jesus. The occasion was most opportune for declaring the office of Peter. "When, therefore, they had dined, Jesus said to Simon Peter: Simon, son of John, lovest thou Me more than these?" Some have absurdly explained this question, as if Peter were asked, whether he loved his Lord more than the fish; but this cannot be seriously advanced. The comparison is evidently referred to the persons present. Peter declares his affection: "He saith to Him: yea, Lord, Thou knowest that I love Thee." This declaration was followed by the pastoral commission: "Feed My lambs:"† that is, the tenderest, weakest portion of the flock, the little ones in Christ, the faithful who are as lambs in regard to those who have begotten them, or brought them forth in Christ. The question is renewed: "He saith to him again, Simon, son of John, lovest thou Me? He saith

---

* John xxi. 11. † βόσκε τα ἀρνία μυ.

to Him: yea, Lord, Thou knowest that I love Thee. He saith to him: feed My lambs."* The commission is repeated, in a new form, as appears from the Greek text. The former injunction regarded feeding, the present comprises the whole pastoral care—to tend, to watch over, to restrain, to bring back the stray sheep, to remove the contagious, and to do all that a shepherd should do for his flock. " He saith to him the third time : Simon, son of John, lovest thou Me? Peter was grieved, because He saith to him the third time, lovest thou Me? And he said to Him : Lord, Thou knowest all things : Thou knowest that I love Thee. He said to him: feed My sheep."† Thus, on the manifestation of his tender love and enlightened faith, Peter receives the commission to feed the sheep of Christ, namely, those who are to the faithful as sheep to lambs, their parents in Christ. In the presence of the beloved disciple, and of James, Thomas and others, Peter receives a commission, the highest that could be given, by which he becomes, under Christ, the shepherd of the flock. The declaration of special love, which was demanded of him, shows that special power was to be imparted : the repetition of the injunction in various forms, manifests the intention of our Lord to communicate all necessary power for feeding, tending and governing all His flock.

Our Lord had foretold the union of Gentiles and Jews in His Church. " Other sheep I have," said He, " that are not of this fold: them also I must bring; and they shall hear My voice : and there shall be made one fold and one shepherd."‡ This was not to be accomplished by Himself personally, since He was not sent by His Father unless to the sheep that had strayed away of the house of Israel; but by the ministry of His apostles. All His sheep were to be united in one fold, under the charge of Peter.

Apart from all tradition, and on the strictest principles of critical exegesis, the superior authority of Peter is proved from the Scripture. We cannot suppose the keys of the kingdom, the confirming of the brethren, the feeding of the lambs and sheep, to denote no special authority. We cannot capriciously extend to the other apostles a promise, charge, and commission, addressed especially to Peter alone. Christ is the Good Shepherd : He charges Peter to act in His stead. Thus, in withdrawing His sensible presence, He leaves Peter clothed with His authority, and indicates its kind and tender character by an image the most affecting.

In very many circumstances our Lord by His actions signified the special power of Peter. From HIS bark He teaches the multitude : to HIM He gives the command to let down the net, and rewards his obedience

---

* Ποίμαινε τα πρόβατα μου. The Vulgate interpreter read ἀρνία. The Greek term is taken for governing, as kings were called shepherds of the people: ποιμένες λαῶν. See Homer, passim. The same verb is constantly used in the Septuagint to express the government of God, and of Christ. Ps. ii. 9; xxii. 2. Ezek. xxiv. 33. Isa. xi. 9. Mich. v. 2.

† βόσκε τα πρόβατα μου.   ‡ John x. 16.

by a miraculous draught of fishes: to HIM HE promises that he shall henceforth catch men. He commands HIM to walk to Him on the waters, and stretches forth His hand to support HIM, when the weakness of the apostle's faith causes HIM to sink. He pays tribute for HIM, as well as for Himself. All these facts have forced themselves on the attention of the declared enemies of the primacy. Barrow supposes the excellent qualities of Peter for leadership to have disposed our Lord to grant him the precedency. "They," he observes, "probably might move our Lord Himself to settle, or at least to insinuate this order; assigning the first place to him, whom He knew most willing to serve Him, and most able to lead on the rest in His service. It is indeed observable, that upon all occasions our Lord signified a particular respect to him, before the rest of his colleagues; for to him more frequently than to any of them He directed His discourse; unto him, by a kind of anticipation, He granted or promised those gifts and privileges, which He meant to confer on them all: him He did assume as spectator and witness of His glorious transfiguration; him he picked out as companion and attendant on Him in His grievous agony; his feet He first washed; to him He did first discover Himself after His resurrection, (as St. Paul implieth,) and with him then He did entertain most discourse; in especial manner recommending to him the pastoral care of the Church; by which manner of proceeding our Lord may seem to have constituted St. Peter the first in order among the apostles, or sufficiently to have hinted His mind for their direction, admonishing them by His example to render unto him a special deference."* After such admissions, the reader must be surprised to find Barrow denying all authoritative primacy in the apostle.

St. Francis de Sales, with his ordinary simplicity and force, exhibits the privileges of the prince of the apostles, as insinuated under various images in the divine writings: "Is the Church likened unto a house? It is placed on the foundation of a rock, which is Peter. Will you represent it under the figure of a family? You behold our Redeemer paying the tribute as its Master, and after Him comes Peter as His representative. Is the Church a bark? Peter is its pilot; and it is our Redeemer who instructs him. Is the doctrine by which we are drawn from the gulf of sin represented by a fisher's net? It is Peter who casts it; it is Peter who draws it; the other disciples lend their aid; but it is Peter that presents the fishes to our Redeemer. Is the Church represented by an embassy? St. Peter is at its head. Do you prefer the figure of a kingdom? St. Peter carries its keys. In fine, you will have it shadowed under the symbol of a flock and a fold? St. Peter is the shepherd and universal pastor under Jesus Christ."†

The occasion of promising this power was the confession which Peter made of the divinity of Christ, and the declaration of greater love than

---

* Barrow on the Supremacy. † Controverses de S. Franc. de Sales, disc. 42.

that of the other apostles was required, before its collation; yet the office was not merely personal. The reward was the greater, because it was to be perpetuated in his successors. The power promised was directed to the advantage of the Church, which was to last throughout ages: the charge given regarded all the sheep of Christ, who were to be gathered into His fold at any period of time. The image of a foundation presents the idea of permanent support, since no fabric can subsist if the foundation be removed: the kingdom of Christ must always have a ruler, bearing the keys, and exercising sovereign power under Christ; the brethren must always be confirmed in faith: the lambs and sheep of Christ at all times need the care, guidance, and protection of a shepherd, to keep them all in one sheepfold. Since the powers of hell cannot prevail against the Church, the fundamental authority of Peter can never cease: since the visible kingdom of Christ shall endure to the end of time, there must be always a viceroy governing in His name: since the prayer of Christ is always heard for His reverence, the faith of Peter can never fail: there shall be always one fold, and there shall be likewise one shepherd. If any thing be clear in Scripture, it is the promise of the primacy and its institution. "To THEE," says Christ, "I will give the keys of the kingdom of heaven." "I have prayed for THEE that thy faith fail not: and thou being once converted, confirm thy brethren." Feed My lambs, feed My sheep." He distinguishes this apostle from the rest: "Blessed art THOU, Simon Bar-jona." He addresses him repeatedly and emphatically: "SIMON, SIMON." He calls on him for special and reiterated declarations of attachment: "Dost thou love Me more than these?" As the powers given to the apostles generally are continued in their successors—as the authority to teach, baptize, and otherwise concur to the salvation of men by ministerial functions, is perpetual; so must the peculiar privileges of Peter be recognised in the occupants of his See. If among the apostles it was proper that one should preside, for the sake of order and unity, a leader is still more necessary for a body so numerous as their successors. A ruler is indispensable for a kingdom so extensive as the Church actually diffused throughout all nations, lest being divided, it be brought to desolation: a pastor for the whole flock is essential at all times, that the unity of the sheepfold may be maintained. Thus, by the very same line of argument by which we infer the perpetuity of the apostolic ministry, we are led to acknowledge the headship, or primacy, as a permanent institution of Christ.

What, then, is the character of this primacy? Limiting myself for the present to the sacred text, I answer, that it is a fundamental principle of church organization, having the same relation to the universal Church, as the foundation has to the building: it is a central authority uniting all the parts of the sacred edifice, which rest on it necessarily and inseparably. Peter was constituted the vicegerent of Christ, having received from Him the keys of the kingdom, and consequently a plenitude of authority, delegated, however, and subordinate, which his successor inherits. The primate of the Church is bound to confirm his brethren in the faith, which he must maintain as originally delivered, opposing, by all the weight of his authority, every error adverse to its integrity. He is powerful for the truth: powerless against the truth. He must feed the lambs and sheep of Christ with salutary pastures: he must use pastoral vigilance, lest they stray away, and employ due care to reconduct to the fold those that have actually strayed. Since Christ represents Himself under the image of a good shepherd, in giving to Peter the command to feed His lambs and sheep, He imparts the highest authority under the most tender image.

It is not difficult to reconcile the headship of Peter with that of Christ. The apostle tells us that Christ instituted the ministry, "that performing the truth in charity, we may in all things grow up in Him who is the head, Christ; from whom the whole body, compacted and fitly joined together, by whatever joint supplieth, according to the operation in the measure of every part, maketh increase of the body, unto the edifying of itself in charity."* Christ is clearly styled the head in this place, in a way in which Peter cannot be so designated. Every grace by which the mind is enlightened, the will moved, and the Church built up in faith and charity, is derived from Christ; not from Peter, whose office is ministerial and external, and totally dependant on the supreme invisible head. "Christ is the head of the Church. He is the Saviour of His body."† Who has ever thought of ascribing to Peter headship of this nature? Who has ever regarded him as the Saviour of the Church? God the Father hath made Christ "head over all the Church, which is His body, and the fulness of Him, who is filled all in all."‡ No one recognises Peter as head in this sense. Christ is "above all principality, and power, and virtue, and dominion, and every name that is named, not only in this world, but also in that which is to come."§ The like cannot be said of Peter, who, under Christ, was only the visible head of the Church on earth, governing it according to the principles which He taught, and in virtue of the authority which He vouchsafed to delegate. Whoever deems such authority derogatory to the headship of Christ, must consider the viceroy of a monarch an antagonist of his sovereign.

The wisdom of Christ in appointing a ruler and pastor under Himself, to confirm and unite the brethren, is clearly apparent. Order can be maintained in a body of men only by some authority exercised by one, whatever be its origin, or its limits: which authority should be proportioned to the importance of the objects to be attained, and the number of persons to be directed or governed. A certain precedency of rank may suffice in a body, where objects dependent on the will of the members are at stake: but where high interests, independent of the fluctuating views of men, are involved, a binding authority, divinely constituted and

---

* Eph. iv. 15.   † Ibid. v. 23.   ‡ Eph. i. 22.   § Eph. i. 21.

guarded, is necessary. Even among the apostles a certain precedency was enjoyed by Peter, while our Lord was present. When He had withdrawn from the earth, and the apostolic band was augmented by a large number of bishops, and the Church was spread throughout many nations, every appearance of unity would soon have vanished, had there not been a central authority, around which all might gather. This became still more necessary, when the apostles closed their career, and their successors were multiplied, and scattered to the utmost bounds of civilization, and beyond them. Confusion of tongues must have ensued, had there not been a divinely constituted leader. The professed subjection of all to Christ could not have restrained the vagaries of human opinion, or preserved the harmony of believers. Without an infinitude of miracles, in proportion to the number of professors, and the diffusion of religion, there would have been no order, no unity, no faith; and the evidence which our Lord referred to, for convincing the world that He was sent by the Father, namely, the union of His disciples in the profession of revealed truth,[*] would have been utterly wanting. While Christ was visibly present, the disciples gathered around Him, and were one family, He being the Head; when He was about to withdraw His visible presence, He left Peter at the head of his brethren, pastor of the fold, and ruler of the kingdom, and consecrating in his person the principle of unity, He rendered his office perpetual in his successors. To this divine arrangement we owe the preservation of the revealed truths, and the unity of the Church.

To all the apostles Christ promised the power of binding and loosing, which He conferred on all, by authorizing them to remit or retain sins. He gave to all a mission like that which He had received from His Father. He sent all of them to preach His Gospel to every creature, and ordered them to teach all nations all things whatsoever He had delivered; promising them His effectual assistance even to the end of time. The apostolic power of each one was, like that of Peter, coextensive with the world: but Peter was pastor, ruler and superior. They were all equal in the episcopal character, and even in apostolic authority, with this difference, that their power was subordinate to his, and to be exercised necessarily in connection and harmony with his, that even in their persons unity might be exhibited. His universal jurisdiction was a permanent attribute of his office, as pastor and ruler, to descend and continue for ever in his successors; while theirs was a personal prerogative, of which the bishops would partake, without enjoying severally its plenitude. This distinction is gathered from the marked manner in which Christ addressed Peter individually, while He promised and gave authority to the others in common, Peter being necessarily included. As Bossuet beautifully observes: "The power divided among many imports its restriction: conferred on one alone, over all and without exception, it bears the evidence of

---

[*] John xvii. 21.

INSTITUTION OF THE PRIMACY.

its plenitude. All receive the same power, but not in the same degree, nor to the same extent. Jesus Christ commences by the chief, and in the person of the chief develops all His power—in order that we should learn that the ecclesiastical authority, being originally centred in one individual, has been diffused only on the condition that it should always be reflected back on the principle of its unity, and that all they who share in it should be inseparably connected with that See, which is the common centre of all churches."*

---

* Discours sur l'unité de l'Eglise, 1 par.

CHAPTER V.

Exposition of the Commission.

THE charge given by our Lord to Peter, to feed His lambs and sheep, was understood by the early fathers to imply the communication of the highest authority under Christ Himself. ORIGEN, speaking of the excellence of charity, remarks, that our Lord required the profession of it from Peter, as a condition for receiving supreme authority in the Church: "WHEN THE SUPREME POWER TO FEED THE SHEEP WAS GIVEN TO PETER, AND THE CHURCH WAS FOUNDED ON HIM, AS ON A ROCK,* the declaration of no other virtue than charity was required."†

In his admirable treatise on the unity of the Church, CYPRIAN insists, with great earnestness, on the provision made against heresy and schism by the promise made, and the pastoral power subsequently given to Peter. Deploring the havoc of souls made by the enemy of man, who transforms himself into an angel of light, and puts forward his ministers as ministers of justice, he says: "This comes to pass, beloved brethren, because recourse is not had to the source of truth, and the head is not sought after, and the doctrine of the Heavenly Teacher is not regarded. If any one consider and examine these things, there is no need of a lengthy treatise and of arguments. The proof of faith is easy and compendious, because true. The Lord speaks to Peter: 'I say to thee, that thou art Peter, and on this rock I will build My Church, and the gates of hell shall not prevail against it. And to thee I will give the keys of the kingdom of heaven: and whatsoever thou shalt bind on earth, shall be bound also in heaven: and whatsoever thou shalt loose on earth, shall be loosed also in heaven.' And again, after His resurrection, He says to him: 'Feed My sheep.' *Upon that one individual He builds His Church, and to him He commits His sheep to be fed.* And although, after His resurrection, He gives to all the apostles equal power, and says: 'As the Father hath sent Me, I also send you. Receive ye the Holy Ghost: whose sins you shall forgive, they shall be forgiven them; whose sins you shall retain, they shall be retained;' yet, in order to manifest unity, He establishes, by His authority, the origin of the same unity, which begins from one. Even the other apostles were certainly what Peter was, being endowed with

---

* Some manuscripts have: super terram—on the earth.
† In Ep. ad Rom. i. v. n. 10.

equal participation of honor and power; but the beginning proceeds from unity, *and the primacy is given to Peter*, that the Church of Christ may be shown to be one, and *the chair one*. All are pastors, and the flock is shown to be one, which is fed by the apostles with one accord, that the Church of God may be shown to be one. This one Church the Holy Ghost also designates, speaking in the person of our Lord in the Canticle of Canticles, 'My dove is one, My perfect one, she is the only one of her mother, the chosen one of her who bore her.' Does he who does not hold the unity of the Church, imagine that he holds the faith? Does he who opposes and resists the Church,—*who deserts the chair of Peter, on whom the Church was founded*, presume that he is in the Church, while the blessed apostle Paul teaches this same thing, and shows the sacrament of unity, saying: 'One body and one Spirit, one hope of your vocation, one Lord, one faith, one baptism, one God?'"*

The words which I have put in italics were omitted by Erasmus in his edition of the works of St. Cyprian, published in 1521: but restored by Paul Manutius in an edition made from manuscripts of great value, in 1563. They are quoted as far back as the year 582, by Pelagius II. in his second epistle to the Bishops of Istria, which forms a strong presumption in their favor, and they accord with the scope of the writer, and with his language on several other occasions. "Neander remarks, no less than Möhler," as Dr. Nevin reminds us, that "the clauses contain nothing that is not elsewhere affirmed by Cyprian, even more distinctly than here."†

The object of the whole work is to prove the inviolable unity of the Church; and in the passage just quoted, St. Cyprian shows how the efforts of Satan to estrange men from the Church, by corrupting their faith, or engaging them in schism, may be promptly and effectually defeated. He refers to the texts in which our Lord addresses Peter, and makes him special promises. He admits that, in other circumstances, similar promises and equal power were given to all the apostles: "yet to manifest unity He established, by His authority, the origin of the same unity, which begins from one." This cannot mean that Christ merely insinuated and recommended unity by thus beginning with Peter; since Cyprian insists throughout that unity is enjoined, and is essential to the Church: it must mean that Christ established in Peter the principle and means of unity. "The other apostles were certainly what Peter was, being endowed with an equal participation of honor and power:" the apostolic office, dignity, and jurisdiction were the same in all, but there was subordination for the maintenance of unity. The scope and the whole context show, that Cyprian recognised in Peter a central and connecting power, whereby truth should be preserved and order maintained.

Barrow himself admits that the African fathers generally considered St. Peter to have received from Christ a primacy of order, which he styles a

---

* L. de Unit. Eccl.   † Art. Cyprian, M. R. July, 1852.

womanish privilege, as in truth it might be styled, were mere precedence in rank given him; but this is to blaspheme Christ, who cannot, without impiety, be supposed to have bestowed an idle distinction. It is strange how this learned opponent of the supremacy, through a desire to weaken the authorities which support it, should have allowed himself to speak disrespectfully of the luminaries of the African Church. "St. Cyprian," he says, "hath a reason for it somewhat more subtile and mystical, supposing our Lord did confer on him a preference of this kind to his brethren (who otherwise in power and authority were equal to him) that he might intimate and recommend unity to us; and the other African doctors (Optatus and St. Austin) do commonly harp on the same notion!"* He adds, that the fathers generally seem to countenance this primacy! Thus does he virtually abandon the cause which he labors to defend.

The same explanation of the texts in question constantly recurs throughout the works of this eloquent prelate. In his book on the virginal state, he observes: " PETER, TO WHOM THE LORD RECOMMENDS THE FEEDING AND PROTECTION OF HIS SHEEP, ON WHOM HE PLACED AND FOUNDED THE CHURCH, denies that he has silver or gold, but says that he is rich in the grace of Christ."†

ST. CYRIL OF JERUSALEM, speaking of the witnesses of the resurrection, thus distinguishes Peter from the rest: " Peter testifies it, who before indeed denied Him, but who, after having confessed Him thrice, was ordered to feed His spiritual sheep."‡ It is clear that Cyril considered this command to have been given specially to Peter.

In his golden work on the priesthood, by which term he designates the episcopal office, CHRYSOSTOM argues from the charge given by Christ to Peter, to feed His sheep, that this is to be the practical evidence of the love which we bear to our Redeemer. " Speaking with the prince of the apostles, He says: 'Peter, lovest thou Me?' and Peter answering affirmatively, He adds: 'If thou lovest Me, feed My sheep.' He designed to teach both Peter, and us all, His great benevolence and love for His Church: that by this means we also might cheerfully assume the care and charge of it. For why did He shed His blood? Certainly that He might purchase the sheep, the care of which He committed to Peter, and to his successors.§ Justly, therefore, Christ thus spoke: 'Who then is the faithful and prudent servant whom the Lord placed over His family?'"‖ The inference which Chrysostom draws from the text does not imply any thing inconsistent with its special application to Peter, whom he recognises as " endowed by Christ with special authority far surpassing the other apostles: for He says: 'Peter, dost thou love Me more than all these?'"¶ Again, in his commentary on the Gospel of St. John, when expressly engaged in the exposition of the text, he asks: " Why does He

---

* A Treatise of the Pope's Supremacy, Suppos. 1.   † L. de habitu virginum, § x.
‡ Cat. xiv.   § Τοις μετ' ἐκεινον.   ‖ L. ii. de sacerdotio.   ¶ Ibidem.

address Peter concerning the sheep, passing by the others? HE WAS THE CHIEF OF THE APOSTLES, AND MOUTH OF THE DISCIPLES, AND HEAD OF THAT BODY: ON WHICH ACCOUNT PAUL ALSO WENT UP TO SEE HIM, IN PREFERENCE TO THE OTHERS. Showing him at the same time, that he must have confidence hereafter, He cancels the guilt of his denial, and GIVES HIM THE PRESIDENCY OVER THE BRETHREN. . . . And He says: 'because thou lovest Me, preside over the brethren.'"*

The pastoral and governing authority of Peter is clearly set forth by ST. AMBROSE in many places, in which he treats of the commission given to him by Christ, to feed His sheep. In his forty-sixth sermon he observes, "When he was thrice questioned by the Lord: 'Simon, dost thou love Me?' he answered thrice, 'Lord, Thou knowest that I love Thee.' The Lord says: 'Feed My sheep.' This was said thrice; the triple repetition serving to compensate for his former fault: for he who had denied the Lord thrice, confesses Him thrice, and as often as he had contracted guilt by his delinquency, he gains favor by his love. See, therefore, how profitable to Peter was his weeping. Before he wept, he fell; after he wept, he was chosen, and he who had been a prevaricator before, was made a pastor after his tears, and he received the government of others, who before had not governed himself." In his exposition of the 118th Psalm, he says: "On this account Christ enjoined on Peter to feed His flock, and do the will of his Lord, because He knew his love."† In his commentary on Luke, Ambrose says of Peter: "He is afflicted because he is questioned the third time, Dost thou love Me? But the Lord does not doubt: He interrogates him, not to ascertain the fact, but to teach him, whom, when He was about to be elevated to heaven, HE LEFT TO US AS THE VICAR OF HIS LOVE. For thus you have: 'Simon, son of John, dost thou love Me?' 'Thou knowest, Lord, that I love Thee.' Jesus said to him, 'Feed My lambs.' And because he alone of all professes his love, HE IS PREFERRED TO ALL."‡ Peter, then, was made pastor and governor, and vicar of JESUS CHRIST, to perform toward men the kind offices which divine love inspired, and was preferred to all.

The disciple of Ambrose does not differ from his master in the interpretation of the sacred text. AUGUSTIN writes: "For Peter himself, to whom He intrusted His sheep, as to another self, He willed to make one with Himself, that so He might intrust His sheep to him; that He might be the head, the other bear the figure of the body, that is, the Church; and that, as man and wife, they might be two in one flesh."§ This gives us the highest idea of the relation of Peter to Christ and to the flock. In intrusting him with the charge of the sheep, Christ made him as another

---

* In c. xxi. Joan. hom. lxxxvii. t. iii. 'Οτι εἰ φιλεῖς με προΐστασο τῶν ἀδελφῶν. Mr. Palmer translates: 'If thou lovest Me, protect the brethren.' Treatise on the Church, part vii. ch. 1. vol. ii. p. 461. It signifies to preside over προϊςωτες, qui imperium habent.
† Enar. xiii. ‡ In Luc. l. x. n. 175.
§ Serm. xlvi. de past. in Ezek. 34. tom. v. 240 F.

self, putting him in His own place. Peter is said to represent the Church; but evidently in his official character, as pastor of the whole flock, and in this respect he becomes, as it were, one with Christ, as the Church is one with her Divine spouse, by the mysterious union of faith and love. Elsewhere, Augustin teaches that the other apostles were also commissioned to feed the flock, because all were sent to teach and administer the sacraments, but he is careful to mark the prerogative of Peter: "For deservedly, after His resurrection, the Lord delivered His sheep to Peter himself to feed; for he was not the only one among the disciples who was thought worthy to feed the Lord's sheep. But when Christ speaks to one, unity is commended; and to Peter above all, because Peter is the first among the apostles."* St. Augustin justly infers the authority which all bishops have received, to feed the sheep of Christ, since the power granted to him was communicable to others: "Therefore hath the Lord commended His sheep to us, because He commended them to Peter."†

That Peter received charge of the sheep of Christ, in a special manner, is declared by Augustin, when enumerating the motives which retained him in the Church: "I am retained," said he, "by the succession of priests from the very See of the apostle Peter, to whom our Lord, after His resurrection, intrusted the feeding of His sheep, down to the actual bishop."‡

ST. LEO beautifully expounds the pastoral commission in connection with the charge to confirm the brethren, and the prayer of Christ for its fulfilment: "Since, therefore, beloved, we see such a protection divinely granted to us, reasonably and justly do we rejoice in the merits and dignity of our chief, rendering thanks to the Eternal King, our Redeemer, the Lord Jesus Christ, for having given so great a power to him whom He made chief of the whole Church, that if any thing, even in our time, be rightly done and rightly ordered by us, it is to be ascribed to his working, to his guidance, unto whom it was said: 'And thou, being once converted, confirm thy brethren:' and to whom the Lord, after His resurrection, in answer to the triple profession of perpetual love, thrice said with mystical intent, 'Feed My sheep.' And this, beyond a doubt, the pious shepherd doth even now, and fulfils the charge of his Lord; strengthening us with his exhortations, and not ceasing to pray for us, that we may be overcome by no temptation."§ The great power granted to Peter especially, and to his successors, is strongly declared by the holy pontiff, who justly ascribes the constancy in faith which distinguishes the occupants of the See to the prayer of Christ, that the faith of Peter might not fail.

St. Eucherius, who occupied the See of Lyons toward the middle of the

---

* Serm. ccxcvi. in nat. Apost. tom. v. 1195 F.
† Ibidem. Tom. v. 1199 D, 1202 F.
‡ L. contra epist. Manichæi, quam vocant fundamenti.
§ In Anniv. Consecr.

fifth century, in his discourse on the feast of the apostles, Peter and Paul, observes that "our Lord intrusted to Peter, first the lambs, and then the sheep, because He constituted him not only a shepherd, but the shepherd of shepherds. Peter therefore feeds the lambs: he feeds the sheep likewise; he feeds the young, and feeds the mothers: he rules both subjects and prelates. He is then shepherd over all, because besides lambs and sheep there is nothing in the Church."

ST. GREGORY THE GREAT writes: "To all who know the Gospel, it is manifest that THE CHARGE OF THE WHOLE CHURCH was intrusted by the voice of the Lord to the holy apostle Peter, chief of all the apostles. For to him is said: Peter, lovest thou Me? Feed My sheep."* This commission, therefore, implied the charge of the whole Church.

Although I have generally confined my quotations to the fathers of the six first ages, I cannot refrain from giving the reader the benefit of the reasoning of ST. BERNARD, "the last of the fathers in age, but equal to the first in glory," as Mr. Allies describes him. Addressing Pope Eugenius, he says: "You are he to whom the keys were given; to whom the sheep were intrusted. There are, indeed, likewise, other gate-keepers of heaven, and shepherds of the flocks; but you have inherited both titles in a sense far different and more sublime. They have, each of them, their respective flocks severally assigned to them: all have been intrusted to you, as one flock to one man. Nor are you shepherd of the sheep alone, but of the shepherds also; the one shepherd of all. Do you ask me how I prove this? From the word of the Lord. For to which I do not say of the bishops, but of the apostles themselves, were the sheep committed so absolutely and unreservedly? 'If thou lovest Me, Peter, feed My sheep.' What sheep? The people of this or that district, city, or kingdom? 'My sheep,' He says. Who does not manifestly see that He did not particularize any, but assigned them all to him? None are excepted, where no distinction is made. The other disciples were perchance present, when intrusting all to one, He recommended unity to all, in one flock and one shepherd: according to that passage: 'My dove is one, My beautiful one, My perfect one.'"† This exposition, which is strictly literal, is fully sustained by the testimonies of the early fathers, which I have already quoted, as well as by the acts of pastoral authority exercised by Peter, and recorded in the divine writings.

---

* Lib. v. ep. xx.   † L. ii. de Consider. c. viii.

CHAPTER VI.

Exercise of the Primacy by St. Peter.

It is impossible not to be struck with the prominent part which Peter acted in the establishment of the Church. While the disciples were awaiting the fulfilment of the promise of Christ, and preparing by prayer for the coming of the Paraclete, Peter arose, and proposed to fill the vacancy which the fall of Judas had occasioned. Under divine illumination he unfolds the meaning of the sacred oracles, which predicted the treachery of this apostle, and directed that another should take his bishopric: he determines the qualifications of the successor: and if he does not himself choose the individual, it is from no want of power, but to give a laudable example of its moderate exercise. This condescension is justly admired by the eloquent Bishop of Constantinople: "Being fervent and intrusted by Christ with the care of the flock, and being the leader of the band, he is always the first to speak. Why did he not himself alone beseech Christ to give him some one in the place of Judas? Why do not the brethren of themselves undertake the election? See how he does all things with the general consent, nothing arbitrarily, nothing imperiously. Brethren, he says. Since the Lord called his disciples brethren, still more should he style them such. Wherefore he addressed them, all being present. Behold the dignity of the Church, and its angelic state. Why does he confer with them on this matter? Lest it become a subject of dispute, and they fall into dissensions. He leaves the choice to the judgment of the multitude, thus securing their regard for the objects of their choice, and freeing himself from jealousy. COULD NOT PETER HIMSELF HAVE CHOSEN THE INDIVIDUAL? BY ALL MEANS: but he abstains from doing it, lest he should appear to indulge partiality. He is the first to proceed in this affair, because ALL HAVE BEEN DELIVERED OVER INTO HIS HANDS: for to him Christ said: Thou being once converted, confirm thy brethren."* It is gratifying to be able to show in what light this act was viewed by so bright an ornament of the Greek Church—one of the most illustrious men of antiquity—the occupant of the chair of the imperial city, the new Rome. In the conduct of Peter on this occasion, Chrysostom recognises a splendid instance of the moderate use of supreme power.

A still more manifest exercise of the high office of Peter, as guardian

---

* Chrysost. hom. iii. in 1 cap. Act.

of the faith, occurs in the history of the first Council of Jerusalem. Great excitement was caused at Antioch by certain Judaizing Christians, who insisted that the converts from the Gentiles should be subjected to circumcision and the legal observances. "Paul and Barnabas had no small contest with them,"* without being able to induce all to acquiesce in their judgment; wherefore it was determined that they "and certain others of the other side, should go up to the apostles and priests to Jerusalem about this question." "Accordingly the apostles and ancients came together to consider of this matter, and when there was much disputing, Peter rising up said to them: Brethren, you know that in former days God made choice among us, that the Gentiles by my mouth should hear the word of the Gospel, and believe. And God, who knoweth the hearts, gave them testimony, giving to them the Holy Ghost, as well as to us: and made no difference between us and them, purifying their hearts by faith. Now, therefore, why tempt you God to put a yoke upon the necks of the disciples, which neither our fathers nor we were able to bear? But by the grace of the Lord Jesus Christ we believe to be saved, even as they." The result of this address is worthy of attention: "All the multitude held their peace."† There was great contention previously at Antioch, notwithstanding the reverence due to the apostolic character in Paul and Barnabas; it is renewed in the Council; when Peter, rising up, reminds them that he had been chosen to announce the Gospel to the Gentiles, and that God had given evidence of His favor toward them; he reproaches them for seeking to burden them unnecessarily with the multifarious observances of the ceremonial law, and declares the great principle of faith in Jesus Christ, as the only foundation of hope, for Jew or Gentile. No sooner has he spoken than all acquiesce: no murmur, no dissenting voice is heard: all opposition ceases: and whoever rises to speak, only confirms, like Paul and Barnabas, by the narrative of miraculous facts, what Peter had declared, of the favor shown by God to the Gentiles; or, like James, refers to the prophecies, adding the suggestion‡ of measures to be decreed, that the principle might be carried into successful execution. I do not see how any man can read the simple history of this controversy, by the inspired writer, without perceiving the great weight of Peter's authority in its termination. The letter of the Council drawn up in the name of the apostles and ancients, which expresses the principle laid down by Peter, and the practical measure suggested by James, is declared to emanate from the Holy Ghost: "it hath seemed good to the Holy Ghost and to us."§ The writers of antiquity speak of it as the sentence or decree of Peter. TERTULLIAN describes it as the exercise of his power of binding and loosing:

---

* Acts xv. 2. † Ibid. xv. 2.
‡ Κρινω, "I judge," is the simple expression of sentiment, whether authoritative, or void of authority. See Thucydid. iv. 60. It corresponds to the Latin *censeo*.
§ Acts xv. 28.

"the decree of Peter loosed such things of the law as were set aside, and bound fast such as were retained."* St. Jerom calls Peter the author of this decree;† and the celebrated Theodoret, Bishop of Cyr, speaks of the controversy as a matter referred by Paul to Peter, that by his authority it might be definitely settled. Writing to Pope Leo, he says : "If Paul, who was the herald of truth, the organ of the Holy Spirit, had recourse to the great Peter, in order to obtain a decision from him concerning the observances of the law, for those who disputed at Antioch on this subject; with much greater reason we, who are abject and weak, have recourse to your Apostolic See, that we may receive from you remedies for the wounds of the churches, for it is fit that in all things you should be first, since your throne is adorned with many prerogatives."‡ Cave, the learned Anglican critic, explains the words of Paul, that "he went to Jerusalem to see Peter," of his going up on this occasion, "Peter being the leading character in the Council."§

St. Chrysostom calls our attention to the wisdom with which Peter permitted the discussion, before he interposed his authority: "See," says he, "he allows the inquiry and dispute to go on, and then he himself speaks."‖ As an evidence of the harmony and condescension which prevailed in the Council, he remarks that Paul was allowed to speak after Peter had pronounced judgment: "See, Paul speaks after Peter, and no one closes his mouth."¶ Even Barrow cannot dissemble the prominent part which St. Peter bore in this Council and in apostolic assemblies generally: "At the consultation," he observes, "about supplying the place of Judas, he rose up, proposed, and pressed the matter. At the convention of the apostles and elders, about resolving the debate concerning observance of Mosaical institutions, he first rose up, and declared his sense. In the promulgation of the Gospel, and defence thereof, before the Jewish rulers, he did assume the conduct, and constantly took upon him to be the speaker; the rest standing by him, implying assent, and ready to avow his word."**

It has pleased the Holy Spirit to leave on record only a few of the circumstances connected with this model of Councils : which, however, sufficiently show that Peter either called the Council, or assented to its convocation ; that he spoke with authority and effect, silencing all disputation by his discourse; and that the decree was in strict conformity with his judgment. The forms are of little importance where the authority is fully

---

* L. de pudicitia.

† Principem hujus fuisse decreti. S. Hieron. Aug. Ep. 45, alias xi. inter August. T. 8, col. 172, tom. ii. ‡ Ad Leonem. Ep. cxiii.

§ Petrum ibi convenit, occasione, ut videtur concilii apostolici—cujus Petrus pars magna fuit. Sæc. Ap. p. 6.

‖ S. Chrys. hom. xxii. in c. xv. Act. Ap. p. 259, tom. iii. Edit. Paris, 1687.

¶ Hom. xxxiii. p. 260. ** A Treatise of the Pope's Supremacy. Supposition 1.

respected and admitted. To be Prince and Primate in the Church of God, it was not necessary that he should stand alone, separated from his colleagues in the apostleship and episcopacy, and resting solely on the prerogative of his station. It is delightful to see him in the Council of his brethren, causing the ardor of disputation to subside by authoritative instruction, and enlightening the minds of his colleagues, and of the faithful, by unfolding to them the oracles of God. The decree which expresses his judgment, and that of his colleagues, as well as the faith of the whole Church, is no way derogatory to his high prerogative.

The eloquent Bishop of Meaux presents, at one view, the various circumstances in which Peter appears foremost: "Peter," says he, "appears the first on all occasions: the first to confess the faith; the first to express his obligation of love; the first of all the apostles who saw Christ after His resurrection, as he was the first to bear testimony to this fact before all the people. We find him first, when there was question of filling up the number of the apostles; the first who confirmed the faith by a miracle, the first to convert the Jews, the first to receive the Gentiles; in short, every thing covers to establish his supremacy."* Potter remarks: "Our Lord appeared to Peter after His resurrection, before the rest of the apostles; and, before this, He sent the message of His resurrection to him in particular." Having specified the various acts of Peter after the ascension of our Lord, he concludes thus: "From these and other examples which occur in the Scriptures, IT IS EVIDENT THAT ST. PETER ACTED AS CHIEF OF THE COLLEGE OF APOSTLES, and so he is constantly described by the primitive writers of the Church, who call him the Head, the President, the Prolocutor, the Chief, the Foreman of the apostles, with several other titles of distinction."† Even Calvin, in endeavoring to meet the argument in favor of the primacy, drawn from the general visitation of the churches‡ by Peter, admits the fact: "Granting that Peter was the chief apostle, as the Scripture often shows, does it follow," he asks, "that he was the head of the world?"§

Against facts which so strongly mark the superior authority of Peter, a term of equivocal import used by the sacred historian is sometimes objected. "When the apostles who were in Jerusalem had heard that Samaria had received the word of God, they *sent* to them Peter and John."‖ To *send* ordinarily supposes the superiority of him who sends; but the term is often used, where solicitation, counsel, and the expression of desire are only meant. When the tribes of Ruben and Gad, and half the tribe of Manasses, had erected an altar near the Jordan, the children

---

* Discours sur l'unité de l'Eglise.
† On Church Government, p. 72, 74.   ‡ Acts ix. 32.
§ In locum. This qualified concession is very different from that admission which De Maistre most unaccountably ascribes to him, by applying to the Bishop of Rome what Calvin says of the Jewish High-Priest. Du Pape, ch. ix. Calv. Inst. vi. ¿ 11.
‖ Acts viii. 14.

of Israel "sent to them into the land of Galaad, Phinees, the son of Eleazar the priest, and ten princes with him, one of every tribe."* This mission derogated in no degree from the high dignity of the priesthood, since it was doubtless a proposal made and accepted, rather than a command given with authority. When the dispute concerning the ceremonial law arose at Antioch, "they *determined* that Paul and Barnabas, and certain others of the other side, *should go up* to the apostles and priests to Jerusalem, about this question."† This language is certainly as strong, at least, as if it were said: "They sent Paul and Barnabas;" and yet no one thence infers that these apostles were inferior to the faithful, at whose solicitation they undertook this journey. The apostles at Jerusalem sent Peter and John to Samaria, by urging the expediency of the visit, not by a positive injunction: for no one pretends that these apostles were inferior in authority to the rest, as they certainly would have been, if they had acted under a positive command.

The condescension of St. Peter, in explaining the motives of his conduct to the disciples who murmured against him, on account of his having admitted Cornelius and his family into the Church, is perfectly consistent with his official supremacy. Superiors cannot prevent the murmurs of their subjects, or silence them effectually, by an appeal to their own authority. Persuasion must often be employed to convince them that the exercise of power is not capricious, or ill-advised. But if the faithful knew Peter to be supreme ruler of the Church on earth, it is said they would not have dared question the wisdom of his acts. It did not, indeed, become them to question it: yet since the Israelites of old murmured against Moses, whose mission was proved by stupendous prodigies, need we wonder that some of the first believers ventured to dispute the propriety of the course pursued by Peter? The prejudices of nations do not always yield instantaneously to religious influences, and the distinction of castes is not easily forgotten. The Jews regarded the heathens with an aversion bordering on abhorrence, so that with the evidence before them of the communication of the gifts of the Holy Ghost to Cornelius and his family, they were filled with amazement. ST. GREGORY THE GREAT derives from the conduct of Peter, on this occasion, a lesson of humility: "When Peter was blamed by the faithful, had he regarded the authority which he had received in the Holy Church, he might have answered, that the sheep should not dare reprove the shepherd, to whom they had been intrusted. But if, on the complaint of the faithful, he had made mention of his own power, he would not truly have been the teacher of meekness. He appeased them, therefore, in an humble manner, and in the case for which they blamed him, he even brought forward witnesses: 'These six brethren came also with me.' Since then the pastor of the Church, the prince of the apostles, he who performed in an extraordinary manner signs

---

* Josue xxii. 13, 14. † Acts xv. 2.

and miracles, did not disdain humbly to give an explanation of the conduct for which he was blamed, how much more should we who are sinners, when we are blamed for any thing, be ready to appease our censors by humble explanations?"*

The strongest objection adduced against the superior authority of Peter is the resistance made to him by Paul, and the rebuke given him on account of his declining familiar intercourse with the converted Gentiles, through fear of offending the Jews who had recently arrived at Antioch. I have elsewhere stated the doubts entertained by some learned men as to the identity of Cephas with the apostle :† but waiving this critical point, I see nothing in bold remonstrance, such as Paul used, inconsistent with the supremacy of him to whom it was addressed. The matter in question was one of mere prudence and expediency, where offence was sure to be given, whichever course might be pursued; and Cephas having adopted a line of conduct offensive to the Gentiles, and prejudicial to the liberty which we have in Christ, Paul, prompted by zeal for the Gentile converts, remonstrated in strong language, and in a public manner: " When Cephas was come to Antioch, I withstood him to the face, because he was blameable—when I saw that they walked not uprightly unto the truth of the Gospel, I said to Cephas, before them all: If thou, being a Jew, livest after the manner of the Gentiles, and not of the Jews, how dost thou compel the Gentiles to follow the way of the Jews?"‡ What the apostle here calls *walking not uprightly unto the truth of the Gospel*, he terms likewise *dissimulation*, meaning plainly a course inconsistent with the ingenuous and independent avowal of the great principle of Gospel liberty: not a betrayal of divine truth, by teaching erroneous doctrine. No one pretends that either apostle deviated from the faith, or that Paul reproved Peter, as a superior checks an inferior. " Paul reproved Peter," says TERTULLIAN, " for no other reason, however, than the change of his mode of living, which he varied according to the class of persons with whom he associated; not for any corruption of divine truth."§ AUGUSTIN, speaking of this fact, admires the intrepidity of Paul and the humility of Peter: " A just liberty," he says, " is to be admired in Paul, and holy humility in Peter."‖ GREGORY THE GREAT cries out: " Behold, he is reproved by his inferior, and he does not disdain to receive the reproof: he does not remind him, that he has received the keys of the kingdom of heaven."¶

The respect of Paul for Peter is evident from this same epistle; for, although, in order to convince the Galatians of the divine origin of the doctrine which he delivered, he states that those who appeared to be pillars in the Church, contributed nothing to his instruction, and that on his con-

---

* L. xi. ep. xiv.
† Letters on the Primacy, p. 51, and Theologia Dogmatica, vol. i. p. 157. See also Dissertazione 32 su Cefa ripreso da S. Paolo, nella raccolta del Padre F. A. Zaccaria.
‡ Gal ii. 11, 14.   § L. v. contra Marcion, c. iii.
‖ Ep. lxxxii. alias xxii.   ¶ L. ii. in Ezech. hom. xviii.

version he had not gone to Jerusalem to the apostles, who preceded him in the profession of the faith, he adds: "Three years after I came to Jerusalem to see Peter, and stayed with him fifteen days."* This visit is justly considered by ST. CHRYSOSTOM to be an evidence of the high regard of Paul for the official character of Peter. "Peter," he observes, "was the organ and prince of the apostles: on which account Paul went up to see him, in preference to the rest."† Paul, indeed, did not go with a view to obtain instruction, for having been favored with a divine revelation, he entertained no doubt whatever of the correctness of his doctrine: he was equal in the apostolic dignity to Peter: and he may have been greater in personal qualifications and merit; yet he went to him as to a superior, honoring the office which he held by divine appointment. "After so many illustrious actions, although he stood in no need of Peter, or of his instruction, being equal in dignity to him,‡ (for I shall say no more,)§ he goes up to him as to a superior and elder, and he had no other motive for the visit, but merely to see Peter. Remark how he pays them (the apostles) due honor, and regards himself not only as no better, but not even as equal to them. This is evident from his journey; for as many of our brethren now travel to visit holy men, so Paul likewise in a similar disposition, went up to Peter. This was even much more humble on his part: for men now travel for their own improvement; but this blessed apostle went to learn nothing, and to be set right on no point, but for this only motive, to see him, and honor him by his presence. He uses the term ἱστορῆσαι, to become acquainted with Peter; not ἰδεῖν, merely to see Peter. He went in order to become fully acquainted with him, as visitors seek to know thoroughly great and splendid cities."||

St. Paul states, that to himself was committed the Gospel of the uncircumcision, as to Peter was that of the circumcision;¶ whence occasion has been taken to deny the general authority of Peter over Gentiles and Jews; or, in other words, over all the members of the Church. The text, however, cannot be understood of exclusive jurisdiction over either class as belonging to either apostle, since Paul, as occasion presented itself, instructed Jews as well as Gentiles; and Peter received the Gentiles, Cornelius and his family, into the Church. The apostle speaks manifestly of the chief objects of his zeal, since he was emphatically the teacher of the Gentiles, while Peter labored chiefly among the Jews. "St. Peter," says Bloomfield, "was chiefly, but not entirely, occupied by the Jews, and St. Paul chiefly, but not wholly, with the Gentiles."** The universality of the mission of all the apostles is unquestionable—it was not confined to certain classes of men, or bounded by territorial limits—they were sent

---

* Gal. i. 18.   † Hom. lxxxvii. in Joan.
‡ Ἰσότιμος, equally honorable.
§ He insinuates that Paul may have been greater than Peter in merit, talent, virtue, or other personal qualifications. || Chrysostom, in c. i. ep. ad. Gal.
¶ Gal. ii. 7.   ** In locum.

into the whole world, to preach the Gospel to every creature. St. Paul, being called in an extraordinary manner to the apostleship, participated in the plenitude of the original commission, which is not at all inconsistent with the supervision, presidency, and chief government of the whole Church, with which Peter was invested.

Although the language of Peter himself, addressing his colleagues in the sacred ministry, is objected as excluding all idea of superior control, it is, nevertheless, in perfect harmony with his high prerogatives : " The ancients, therefore, that are among you, I beseech, who am myself also an ancient and a witness of Christ."* The term πρεσβυτέρους, *presbyters*, here rendered *ancients*, was then applied to bishops, whom St. Peter addressed, declaring himself their fellow-bishop, συμπρεσβύτερος. Perfect equality cannot be meant by this expression, since, as an apostle, he was certainly superior to a local bishop. The character of bishop is undoubtedly the same as that of an apostle; but the jurisdiction of an apostle, being universal, far exceeds that of him who is charged with a special flock. The very fact of the general address of Peter to the bishops, whom he exhorts, and entreats to perform their pastoral duties in an humble, exemplary and disinterested manner, affords no slight presumption of his general superintendence and control. His language is certainly such as the chief pastor might appropriately employ : " Feed the flock of God which is among you: taking care not by constraint, but willingly according to God : neither for the sake of filthy lucre, but voluntarily : neither as domineering over the clergy, but being made a pattern of the flock from the heart. And when the Prince of Pastors shall appear, you shall receive a never-fading crown of glory."† Grotius has well remarked, that this epistle has an energy of language characteristic of the prince of the apostles.‡

Paul instructed Timothy and Titus, his disciples, whom, with his own hands, he had consecrated bishops: at Miletus he addressed the bishops whom he had called from Ephesus, and who were in like manner his special disciples. Either apostle might direct his admonitions to any bishop: but it seems not without a special design of the Holy Ghost, to mark the universality of his official charge, that Peter, writing to the strangers—proselytes to Judaism first, and then to Christianity, dispersed through Pontus, Galatia, Cappadocia, Asia and Bithynia—gave solemn injunctions to all the bishops of those countries, on their sacred duties.

The exercise of the most important functions of the primacy is, as we have seen, plainly proved from the sacred Scriptures. To provide pastors for the churches is the right and duty of the pastor of the whole flock, a right, however, which is to be exercised with a sacred regard for the interests of the universal Church. This was done by Peter, in supplying

---

. * 1 Pet. v. 1. † Ibidem. 2–4.

‡ Habet hæc epistola τὸ σφόδρον vehemens dicendi genus conveniens ingenio principis apostolorum.

the place of Judas. To see that the pastors perform their duties to their respective flocks, appertains to the same office. To decide, or take a prominent part in deciding doctrinal controversies, is a duty of the chief pastor, which was manifestly performed by Peter, in the Council of Jerusalem. He truly exercised a primatial authority, which shows that the commission given to him imparted power to maintain unity and faith.

It is not necessary to show that Peter actually exercised all and every one of the attributes of spiritual sovereignty, especially since we have no detailed history of the apostolic age; the Acts of the Apostles being confined to a few facts connected with the commencement of the Church, and an account of the conversion and chief labors of St. Paul. Since the promise of Christ, His charge to Peter at the last supper, and His commission after His resurrection, convey the idea of a viceroy, superintendent and pastor; and the prominent part taken by Peter corresponds with this idea: we are warranted in believing him to have possessed and exercised a true supremacy. I am not now anxious to demonstrate what are his essential rights: I ask only that his primacy, which is so clearly established, be admitted. I produce his commission with the seal of the Great King, and demand that it be respected.

CHAPTER VII.

Peter, Bishop of Rome.

HAVING proved from the sacred Scripture, on strict principles of *exegesis*, and according to the general interpretation of the fathers of the first five centuries, that Peter received from Christ an authoritative primacy, which must always continue in the Church, to be exercised by his successors, it becomes necessary to show who succeeds to his privileges. The task is an easy one, as the voice of all antiquity proclaims the Bishop of Rome to be the successor of Peter. Some bold men have, indeed, pushed skepticism so far as to deny that St. Peter ever was at Rome, as some unbelievers have questioned whether Jesus Christ ever existed; but even Calvin, with every disposition to deny the fact, blushed to oppose the testimony of all the ancients;* while Cave strongly and fearlessly affirms it: "We intrepidly affirm with all antiquity, that Peter was at Rome, and for some time resided there." He adds: "All, both ancient and modern, will, I think, agree with me that Peter may be called Bishop of Rome, in a less strict sense,† inasmuch as he laid the foundations of this Church, and rendered it illustrious by his martyrdom."‡ Professor Schaff avows, that "it is the unanimous testimony of tradition that Peter suffered martyrdom in Rome under Nero." Babylon, from which the first letter of St. Peter was written, is understood by learned interpreters generally, Protestant as well as Catholic, to mean Rome; the Christians being accustomed to designate it in this way, on account of its vices, which resembled the corruption of the ancient queen of the East. St. John portrayed the crimes and calamities of pagan Rome under the same name, in the mysterious descriptions of the Apocalypse. Those who assert that Peter visited Babylon on the Euphrates, which was then in ruins, are unsupported by history or tradition: and the critical reasons which they offer for interpreting the name literally, are far outweighed by the arguments in favor of its figurative acceptation. After a review of them, Professor Schaff says: "These difficulties constrain us to return to the earliest and, in ancient times, only prevalent interpretation of Babylon, by which it is taken to mean Rome."§

---

* Inst. lib. iv. c. vi. ? 15.
† This qualification is wholly unnecessary.
‡ Sæc. Apostol. S. Petrus.
§ See Extract from Schaff's Church History, in Mercersburg Review, July, 1851: also Perrone Tract. de locis Theol. p. 1. ? ii. c. ii. n. 560.

For a matter of fact human testimony is entirely sufficient, whenever it is clothed with those qualities which remove all just fear of deception. If it were otherwise, Christianity itself would vanish from our grasp; for its certain transmission to us implies a number of facts independent of any testimony of Scripture; and even the authenticity and integrity of the sacred books are dependent on human testimony, at least, for all who deny the authority of the Christian Church.

CLEMENT, Bishop of Rome, a contemporary of the apostles, who is mentioned with honor by St. Paul, and who was ordained by Peter, according to the testimony of Tertullian, in a letter to the Corinthians, mentions Peter and Paul as having suffered martyrdom at Rome under his eyes.* IGNATIUS, Bishop of Antioch, when led to martyrdom, about the year 107, wrote to the Romans, begging of them to place no obstacle by their prayers to the fulfilment of his ardent desire to die for Christ: "I do not command you," he says, "as Peter and Paul: they were apostles: I am a condemned man."† This shows that the Romans had been instructed by both apostles, and received their commands. PAPIAS, Bishop of Hierapolis, a disciple of John the apostle, or of another John, a contemporary of the Apostle, states that Mark related in his Gospel what he heard from Peter at Rome, and that Peter wrote his first epistle from Rome, calling it Babylon.‡ IRENÆUS declares that Peter and Paul preached the Gospel at Rome, and established the Church, which he calls "greatest and most ancient, known to all, founded and established by the most glorious apostles, Peter and Paul;" and adds the list of bishops from the apostles down to his own time.§ DIONYSIUS of Corinth states, that both apostles, Peter and Paul, instructed the Corinthians, and afterward having passed into Italy, planted the faith among the Romans, and consummated their course by martyrdom in their city.‖ CAJUS, a Roman priest, who lived at the close of the second and beginning of the third century, says: "I can show you the trophies of the apostles; for whether we go to the Vatican, or to the Ostian way, we shall meet with the trophies of the founders of this Church."¶ ORIGEN also testifies that Peter suffered martyrdom at Rome.** ST. CYPRIAN says that Cornelius was chosen bishop "when the place of Fabian, that is, THE PLACE OF PETER, and the rank of the priestly chair was vacant."†† .

That Paul was not the original founder of the Church at Rome, is evident from his epistle to the Romans, in which he states his earnest desire to see them, which up to that time was out of his power, and praises their faith as celebrated throughout the whole world. We must, then, conclude that Peter had already preached the faith there, since all antiquity recog-

---

* Cor. n. 5, 6.
† Ep ad Rom.
‡ Apud Euseb. l. ii. c. xv. Hist. Eccl.
§ L. iii. hær. c. iii.
‖ Apud Euseb. l. ii. c. xxv.
¶ L. adv. Proculum apud Euseb. Hist. Eccl. l. ii. c. xv.
** Ib. l. iii. c. 1.
†† Ep. lii. Antoniano.

nises no other founders of the Roman Church but these two apostles: the conjecture of Dr. Jarvis, that proselytes who were at Jerusalem on the day of Pentecost, introduced and established the faith at Rome, being wholly unsupported. EUSEBIUS, who compiled his ecclesiastical history from the most authentic documents of the early ages, states that Simon Magus, after he had been publicly rebuked by Peter, went to Rome, and that to counteract his efforts, "the all-bountiful and kind Providence which watches over all things, conducted thither the most courageous and the greatest of the apostles, Peter, who, on account of his virtue, was leader of all."* Theodoret, commenting on the passage of St. Paul, in which he expresses his desire to confirm the Romans in the faith, observes: "Because the great Peter was the first to instruct them in the evangelical doctrine, he necessarily said 'to confirm you;' for he says: I do not mean to propose to you a new doctrine, but to confirm that which has been already delivered, and to water the trees that have been planted."† In a word: "The universal tradition of the Church," by the acknowledgment of Mr. Palmer, "ascribes the foundation or first government of the Roman Church to the apostles Peter and Paul, who were the greatest of the apostles."‡

It is, nevertheless, no easy matter to fix with certainty the precise date of the visit of the apostle to the capital of the empire, since ancient writers assign different periods, some probably referring to his second visit, while others speak of the former. With the few lights afforded us by Scripture, in regard to his movements and actions, and with the scanty historical materials remaining, it would be unfair to require of us to adjust the chronological order of events, so as to exclude all question. Learned antiquarians have exercised their skill in arranging them, and we are at liberty to adopt the results of their inquiries, or to remain in suspense as to the particular order of the facts, provided we admit that which is established by most unquestionable evidence, that the apostle Peter preached the faith at Rome before St. Paul addressed his letter to the faithful of that city.§ The letter to the Romans is generally assigned to the year of our Lord 58, the fourth year of the reign of Nero. Orosius, a writer of the fifth century, states that St. Peter came to Rome in the commencement of the reign of Claudius, who was the predecessor of Nero; and St. Jerom, as well as Eusebius, ascribes his visit to the second year of that reign, about the forty-fourth year of our Lord, so that we may consider this fact as attested by three judicious writers, who relied, no doubt, on ancient historical documents. It probably occurred soon after the miraculous deliverance of the apostle from prison, when, rescued by the angel from the power of Herod, he went from Jerusalem "to another place." The See of Antioch had been previously founded by him, as the ancients assure us; but his stay

---

* L. ii. Hist. Eccl. c. xiv.   † Com. in c. 1, ad Rom.
‡ Treatise on the Church, vol. ii. ch. vii. p. 472.
§ De Romano D. Petri itinere et episcopatu, P. F. Foggini.

there was short, although he may have retained the special charge of it for seven years, as many aver: its administration, however, being confided to Evodius, who is the first on the list of its bishops after the apostle. Twenty-five years are generally assigned to the Roman episcopate of St. Peter, which period intervened between the second year of Claudius, who reigned fourteen years, and the close of the reign of Nero, which is also believed to have lasted fourteen years.* The apostle nevertheless was not stationary during that whole period, since he must have returned to Judea, where he was present in the Council of Jerusalem, held in the nineteenth year after the resurrection of our Lord, about the fifty-first of the common era. His return may have been spontaneous, or it may have been occasioned by the edict published in the ninth year of Claudius,† by which all Jews were commanded to quit the imperial city;‡ since the natives of Judea, whether practising Jewish rites, or professing Christianity, were included under this general denomination. While Nero occupied the throne, Peter visited Rome, as Lactantius testifies;§ which must be understood of a second visit, since the authority of Jerom, Eusebius, and Orosius is conclusive as to the visit under Claudius. St. Leo alludes to both, extolling the fortitude of the apostle, who dreaded neither the power of Claudius, nor the cruelty of Nero.‖

The concurrence of both apostles in the foundation of the Church of Rome does not at all interfere with the special prerogative of Peter. Both apostles labored successfully in establishing it; both consecrated it by their martyrdom; both are even styled its bishops by Epiphanius; but, in the stricter sense, Peter was peculiarly its founder and its bishop. The Bishops of Rome are wont to unite the invocation of these glorious apostles, and to act as by their joint authority, because the apostolic power was possessed by each, and the pre-eminence of Peter was not affected by the joint labors and martyrdom of Paul: yet Peter was specially the Bishop of Rome.

Cajus, already quoted, speaks of Victor, Bishop of Rome, as the thirteenth in succession from Peter:¶ and a contemporary writer says that Peter appointed Linus to succeed him in the chair of this great city, "in which he himself had sat." "The Church of Rome," he adds, "organized by Peter, flourished in piety."** Hyginus is mentioned as the ninth occupant of the chair of Peter. Eusebius terms Peter the first Pontiff of the Christians:†† and speaks of Linus as "first Bishop of the Church of the Romans, after the leader Peter."§§ Optatus mentions the establish-

---

* Acts xii. 17.
† Oros. Hist. l. vii. c. vi.
‡ Acts xviii. 2.
§ L. de mortibus pers. c. ii.
‖ Serm. i. in natali ap. Petri et Pauli.
¶ Hist. Eccl. l. v. c. xxviii.
** Contra Marcion carm. inter opera Tertull.
†† Palmer, quoting Chronicle, an. 44. Treatise on the Church, vol. ii. part vii. ch. 1, p. 463.
§§ In Chronico: Primus, post coryphæum Petrum, Romanorum ecclesiæ episcopus.

ment of the episcopal chair at Rome by Peter, as an unquestionable fact; and states that Peter, the prince of the apostles, was the first to occupy it.* St. Chrysostom observes, that Linus was accounted the second Bishop of the Roman Church after Peter."† St. Jerom says: "Clement was fourth Bishop of Rome after Peter."‡ Augustin begins the list from Peter, whom Linus succeeded, and continues it down to his own time.§ That Peter was strictly Bishop of Rome, is clearly established by these most ancient and respectable witnesses. That Paul was not united with him in the episcopal office, although he labored with him in his apostolic character, is plain from the marked distinction observed by all the ancients, who never give Paul alone the appellation of Roman Bishop, which they frequently give to Peter, and from the general and ancient tradition, that there cannot be two bishops of one Church; which was so strongly impressed on the minds of the Roman people, that when Constantius proposed that Liberius and Felix should jointly govern the Church, the faithful protested against the novelty, and cried out: ONE GOD, ONE CHRIST, ONE BISHOP.

ST. LEO, addressing the Romans, on the anniversary of his own consecration, observes: "For the celebration of our solemnity, not only the apostolic, but likewise the episcopal dignity of the most blessed Peter concurs, who does not cease to preside over his own See, and obtains its unfailing union with the Eternal Priest. For that solidity, which he himself being made a rock, received from Christ, he transmitted to his heirs likewise."‖

The alleged incompatibility of the apostleship with the episcopal office arises from a confusion of terms. If Peter were said to be Bishop of Rome in such a way as to confine his authority and vigilance to this local church, it would interfere with his apostolic office and primacy, since he was charged with the care of all the churches, and could not divest himself of this general government: but no one considers him bishop in this sense. He retained the special charge of the Church of Rome, which he founded, without foregoing his general solicitude for the universal Church; and while he cherished the favored flock with peculiar care, he watched incessantly over all the sheep of Christ, wherever they were found, and urged the local pastors to the fulfilment of their duties, as appears from his admirable epistle. Most writers have identified James, Bishop of Jerusalem, with the apostle of that name, which shows that they did not deem the episcopal charge incompatible with his apostolic character, although he would thereby appear exclusively devoted to a single flock; while the Roman bishopric of Peter does not imply any restriction of power or authority. Barrow virtually admits that James the apostle was

---

* L. ii. c. iii.
† Hom. x. in ii. ad Titum.
‡ Cat. Script. Eccl. de Clemente.
§ Ep. ad Generos.
‖ Serm. V. in anniversario assumpt.

the same as the bishop,* and offers reasons why it was proper to give to him this special jurisdiction over the faithful of Jerusalem; which, however, can have no weight, if the apostleship and episcopate cannot be united in the same person.

The silence of St. Paul concerning St. Peter in his letter to the Romans is no argument against the episcopacy of Peter, much less against the fact of his having been at Rome. The letter was written most probably at a time when Peter was not in the city, to silence by his authority the disputants whom Paul labors to enlighten. Besides, a mere negative argument cannot be admitted against positive testimony of contemporary witnesses, sustained by public facts and general tradition.

Mr. Palmer says: "Hence we may see the reason for which the Bishops of Rome were styled successors of ST. PETER by some of the fathers. They were bishops of the particular church which St. Peter had assisted in founding, and over which he had presided; and they were also, as bishops of the principal church, the most eminent among the successors of the apostles; even as St. Peter had possessed the pre-eminence among the apostles themselves."† To express the whole truth unequivocally, he should have stated that, as bishops of that local church, and successors of St. Peter, their pre-eminence was one of jurisdiction and authority extending throughout the whole world.

---

* Treatise on the Supremacy. Suppos. iv. n. 11, 2.
† A Treatise on the Church, vol. ii. part vii. ch. iii. ? 1, p. 473.

CHAPTER VIII.

Roman Church.

FROM the fact that St. Peter was Bishop of Rome at the time of his martyrdom, it follows that his successors in this See are heirs of his apostolic authority. The powers given to the apostles collectively are perpetual, but the bishops do not severally inherit their plenitude, since each receives charge of a special flock, as is intimated in the epistle of St. Peter,* with authority subordinate to that of the general ruler of the Church. Although all bishops are, in a qualified sense, successors of the apostles, no apostle but Peter has a successor in the strictest and fullest acceptation of the term, because he alone was invested with the office of supreme governor, which is essential to the order and existence of the Church in all ages. The primacy being of divine institution, as the words of our Lord plainly prove, it is by divine right vested in Peter, and in his successors: and the fact of his occupancy of the Roman See has determined the succession to the Bishop of Rome. Hence we find all the ancient writers speaking of the Roman Church as the Apostolic See, the head of all the churches.

ST. IGNATIUS, who, in the year 68, succeeded Evodius in the See of Antioch, on his way to martyrdom in 107, addressed a letter to the CHURCH WHICH PRESIDES in the country of the Romans: " Ignatius, also called Theophorus, to the Church that has obtained mercy through the magnificence of the most high Father, and of Jesus Christ, His only begotten Son; the Church, beloved and enlightened through His will, who wills all things that are according to the charity of Jesus Christ our God; which PRESIDES in the place of the Roman region, being worthy of God, most comely, deservedly blessed, most celebrated, properly organized, most chaste, and PRESIDING in charity, having the law of Christ, bearing the name of the Father." This language clearly indicates the pre-eminence of the ROMAN CHURCH.

ST. IRENÆUS, who passed from the East to Gaul, about the middle of the second century, and became Bishop of Lyons in 177, refuting the Gnostics, who boasted of some secret tradition more perfect than the public teaching of the Church, appeals against it to the public tradition of all churches throughout the world, and offers the Roman Church as a compe-

---

* 1 Pet. v. 2, τὸ ἐν ὑμῖν ποίμνιον.

tent and authoritative witness of this general tradition. "All," he says, "who wish to see the truth, may see in the entire Church the tradition of the apostles, manifested throughout the whole world: and we can enumerate the bishops who have been ordained by the apostles, and their successors down to our time, who taught or knew no such doctrine as they madly dream of. But since it would be very tedious to enumerate in this work the succession of all the churches, by pointing to the tradition of the greatest and most ancient church, known to all, founded and established at Rome by the two most glorious apostles Peter and Paul, and to her faith announced to men, which comes down to us by the succession of bishops, we confound all those who in any improper manner gather together,* either through self-complacency, or vain-glory, or through blindness, or perverse disposition. For with this church, on account of her more powerful principality, it is necessary that every church, that is, the faithful, who are on all sides,† should agree,‡ in which the apostolic tradition has been always preserved by those who are on all sides."§ A better or more powerful‖ principality is ascribed to this church, since heavenly empire surpasses earthly dominion; and its influence in maintaining the integrity of Christian tradition, is shown by the necessity of harmony between all the local churches and this ruling church. The attempt to explain away this splendid testimony, by supposing the civil principality to be meant, is utterly futile: since this could be no reason why the churches and faithful should agree with the Roman Church. Hence it is pretended that agreement in doctrine is not meant, although it is manifest that the professed object of the writer is to prove the general tradition of the churches, of which he takes the tradition of the Roman Church as evidence, the succession of its bishops being well known, and its relations to the other churches implying the harmony of their faith. To suppose that

---

* The Greek term συλλεγουσι, "colligunt," is understood, of assembling.

† Undique, as it were κυκλω πανταχη. The central character of Rome, and the convergency of the local churches, as rays to a centre, or focus, is beautifully insinuated.

‡ Ad hanc enim ecclesiam propter potentiorem principalitatem necesse est omnem convenire ecclesiam. The learned Calvinist, Saumaise, admits that this is the force of the phrase, which is Hellenistic. He remarks: *Ad hanc convenire ecclesiam* is a Græcism for *cum hac convenire ecclesia*. "Necesse esse dicit omnem ecclesiam convenire ad Romanam, id est, ut Græce loquutus fuerat Irenæus, συμβαινειν προς την των ρωμαιων εκκλησιαν, quod significat convenire et concordare in rebus fidei et doctrinæ cum romana ecclesia." De primatu Papæ, c. v. *Convenire* as signifying motion, cannot be applied to a church. It could not be said even of the faithful, that it was necessary for them to go to Rome.

§ Maximæ et antiquissimæ et omnibus cognitæ, a gloriosissimis duobus apostolis Petro et Paulo Romæ fundatæ et constitutæ ecclesiæ eam quam habet ab apostolis traditionem, et annuntiatam hominibus fidem per successiones episcoporum pervenientem usque ad nos indicantes, confundimus omnes eos qui quoque modo, vel per sibi placentia, vel vanam gloriam, vel per cæcitatem et malam sententiam, præterquam oportet colligunt. Ad hanc enim ecclesiam, propter potentiorem principalitatem necesse est omnem convenire ecclesiam, hoc est eos qui sunt undique fideles: in qua semper ab his qui sunt undique, conservata est ea quæ est ab apostolis traditio. S. Iren. l. iii. adv. hær. c. iii.

‖ The reading varies, probably because *potiorem* was put by contraction for *potentiorem*.

the fortuitous visits to Rome of believers from various parts are referred to as affording evidence of general tradition, is manifestly inconsistent with the principles laid down by Irenæus, and indicated in the very passage itself; since it is of tradition descending through the succession of bishops that he speaks, and to their testimony and preaching, as divinely guaranteed by the gift, χαρίσμα, inherent in their office, he invariably ascribes all certain knowledge of revealed truth.. Besides, the frequency of the visits of believers to the capital of the empire is a gratuitous supposition, void of probability, when we consider the humble condition of most of the faithful, and their great distance from Rome. Irenæus plainly speaks, not of travellers who happen to visit the city, but of churches which harmonize with this most glorious and apostolic church, on account of her more powerful principality. By the acknowledgment of Palmer: "Irenæus says, 'the necessity of resorting to the Roman Church arose from the principality or pre-eminence of that church.'"*

Dr. Nevin is more explicit: "It is not to be disguised," he says, "that the episcopate is viewed by him (Irenæus) as a general corporation, having its centre of unity in the Church of Rome. Against the novelty of heretics, he appeals to the clear succession of the Catholic sees generally, from the time of the apostles; but then sums up all, by singling out the Roman Church, founded by the most glorious apostles Peter and Paul, and having a certain principality for the Church at large, as furnishing in its line of bishops a sure tradition of the faith held by the universal body from the beginning."†

We have already heard Tertullian contesting the power of forgiveness, which the Bishop of Rome exercised; but acknowledging that he was apostolic, and that the Roman Church was the church of Peter, and that Peter was the rock on which the Christian Church is built. We shall now hear him speak reverentially of the authority of the Roman Church, acknowledging her to be the depositary and guardian of the apostolic doctrine, and its incorrupt professor, in harmony with the African churches, as well as with the other churches throughout the world. The fact of the establishment of this church by Peter and Paul, and the consequent authority of her teaching, are fully testified by him; nor is his testimony weakened by his subsequent pleas in support of Montanism, since evidence given before a public tribunal would not be affected by partisan efforts of the witness against those who were benefited by it.

In the admirable work *on Prescriptions*, in which TERTULLIAN shows that the ancient doctrine alone can be true, because it comes down from the apostles, he thus invites the inquirer to pursue the investigation of truth, by listening to the teaching of the churches founded by the apostles. "Come, then," says he, "you who wish to exercise your curiosity

---

* A Treatise on the Church, vol. ii. part vii. ch. v. p. 502.
† Art. Early Christianity. Mercersburg Review, November, 1851.

to more advantage in the affair of salvation, go through the apostolic churches, in which the very chairs of the apostles continue aloft in their places, in which their very original letters are recited, sounding forth the voice, and representing the countenance of each one. Is Achaia near you? you have Corinth? If you are not far from Macedon, you have Philippi, you have Thessalonica. If you can go to Asia, you have Ephesus. If you are near Italy, you have Rome, whence we also derive our origin.* How happy is this church to which the apostles poured forth their whole doctrine with their blood! where Peter by his martyrdom is made like to the Lord: where Paul is crowned with a death like that of John: where John the apostle, after he had been dipped in boiling oil without suffering injury, is banished to the island: let us see what she learned, what she taught, what she professed in her symbol in common with the African churches."† He passes rapidly over the other churches founded by the apostles, and which even to his day preserved the chairs on which they sat in the performance of their solemn functions, and their original letters. When he has reached the Roman Church, he pauses, exclaiming in rapture, how happy is she in possessing the abundant treasure of apostolic doctrine! He appeals to her tradition, to her teaching, to her solemn profession of faith, in which she was the guide of the African churches. Could we say more in her praise? Need we claim for her higher prerogatives? She is the church whose symbol is the great watchword of faith, and with which the churches throughout the world harmonize.

In urging the character of antiquity as a mark of true doctrine, Tertullian says: "Since it is evident, that what is true is first, that what is first is from the beginning, that what is from the beginning is from the apostles, it also must be equally manifest, that what is held sacred in the apostolic churches must have been delivered by the apostles. Let us see with what milk the Corinthians were fed by Paul; according to what standard the Galatians were reformed; and what instructions were given to the Philippians, Thessalonians, and Ephesians; what also the Romans proclaim in our ears, they to whom Peter and Paul left the Gospel sealed with their blood."‡ The appeal to the other churches chiefly regards the apostolic letters directed to them, while the faith of Rome, as loudly proclaimed within hearing, as it were, of Africa, is specially referred to; for

---

* *Unde nobis quoque auctoritas præsto est.* Christianus Lupus shows that such is the force of *auctoritas*, as used by Tertullian. See Scholia. Also Diss. ii. de Afr. Eccl. Prov. c. 1.

† Si autem Italiæ adjaces, habes Romam, unde nobis quoque authoritas præsto est. Ista quam felix ecclesia, cui totam doctrinam apostoli cum sanguine suo profuderunt: ubi Petrus passioni Dominicæ adæquatur: ubi Paulus Joannis exitu coronatur: ubi apostolus Joannes posteaquam in oleum igneum demersus, nihil passus est, in insulam relegatur: videamus quid didicerit, quid docuerit, cum Africanis quoque ecclesiis contesserarit. De Præscr. Hær. c. xxxvi.

‡ Tertullian, l. iv. adv. Marcionem, p. 505. Quid etiam Romani de proximo sonent, quibus evangelium et Petrus et Paulus sanguine quoque suo signatum reliquerunt.

by its tradition coming down unchanged, through the succession of bishops, from its glorious founders, all heretics and sectaries are confounded. Tertullian boldly challenged them to exhibit any thing bearing a like weight of authority: "Let them then give us the origin of their churches: let them unfold the series of their bishops, coming down from the beginning in succession, so that the first bishop was appointed and preceded by any one of the apostles, or of apostolic men, provided he persevered in communion with the apostles. For in this way the apostolic churches exhibit their origin, as the Church of Smyrna relates that Polycarp was placed there by John; as the Church of Rome likewise relates that Clement was ordained by Peter; and in like manner the other churches show those who were constituted bishops by the apostles, and made grafts of the apostolic seed. Let heretics feign any thing like this."*

St. Cyprian, who, in so many passages, recognises Peter as the rock on which the Church is built, and the one apostle in whom unity was established, is loud in his eulogies of the Roman Church, which he styles THE PLACE OF PETER, THE PRINCIPAL CHURCH—THE ROOT AND MATRIX OF THE CATHOLIC CHURCH. In a letter to Cornelius, Bishop of Rome, he details the irregular proceedings of the schismatics, who had ordained Fortunatus bishop, and subsequently despatched Felicissimus to Rome, to deceive the Pope by false statements concerning his ordination: "A false bishop having been ordained for them by heretics, they venture to set sail, and carry letters from schismatical and profane men TO THE CHAIR OF PETER, AND TO THE PRINCIPAL CHURCH,† WHENCE SACERDOTAL UNITY AROSE; nor do they reflect that they are Romans, whose faith is extolled by the apostle, to whom perfidy can have no access."‡ The strong language of this passage forced from Dr. Hopkins, the Protestant Episcopal Bishop of Vermont, this avowal: "Now here we have, certainly, a beginning of the doctrine of the Church of Rome, showing to us what we anticipated, when examining the evidence of Irenæus, namely, how early the Bishops of Rome endeavored to secure dominion and supremacy. The influence of their efforts, too, we find first showing itself in the neighborhood of Rome, for Carthage, where Cyprian was bishop, lay within a moderate distance from the imperial city. Let·it be granted, then, that in the year 250, about a century and a half later than Polycarp, a century later than Irenæus, and fifty years later than Tertullian, the doctrine was partially admitted that Peter had been Bishop of Rome, and that the unity

---

.* Tert. *de præscr. hær.* Edant ergo originem ecclesiarum suarum : evolvant ordinem episcoporum suorum, ita per successiones ab initio decurrentem, ut primus ille episcopus aliquem ex apostolis—habuerit auctorem et antecessorem.—Sicut Romanorum (*ecclesia*) Clementem a Petro ordinatum.—Confingant tale aliquid hæretici!

† *Cathedram principalem.* The English term *principal* does not fully express the force of the Latin. The edicts of the emperors are often styled *jussiones principales.*

‡ Ep. ad Cornel. lix.

of the Church took its rise in the See or diocese of Peter."* An unbiassed mind would have perceived in the words of Cyprian the echo of those of Irenæus, and recognised the powerful principality of the chair of Peter as the principle of unity and the safeguard of faith.

Writing to Antonian, an African bishop, to remove some doubts concerning the legitimacy of the election of Cornelius, St. Cyprian praises his magnanimity in accepting the pontifical office, which was attended with the manifest danger of martyrdom, since Decius the heathen emperor dreaded more the presidency of the Roman Bishop over the Christian people, than the approach of a powerful enemy: " How great was his virtue in the discharge of the episcopal office! how great his courage! how strong his faith! To sit fearlessly at Rome in the priestly chair, at a time when the priests of God were threatened with dire torments by a hostile tyrant, who would hear with less pain of a rival prince rising up against him, than of a priest of God being established at Rome."† The dignity of the Roman Bishop must have been notorious, as well as eminent, to create such jealousy.

It is objected, nevertheless, that Cyprian always treats Cornelius as a brother and colleague, and that Cornelius reciprocates, so as to appear on terms of perfect equality. This is easily accounted for by the fact, that all bishops are equal in their sacred character, the difference between them being merely of jurisdiction. Thus a Roman Council, in 378, says of Pope Damasus, that "he is equal in office to the other bishops, and surpasses them by the prerogative of the Apostolic See."‡ Even at this day the Pope is wont to address all bishops as "venerable brethren," although at that early period Damasus called them his "most honorable children."

We cannot satisfactorily account for the extraordinary authority recognised in the Roman clergy, during the vacancy of the See, except inasmuch as they were regarded as the depositaries *ad interim* of the power ordinarily exercised by the Roman Bishop over the whole Church. St. Cyprian communicated to them the rules which he deemed it advisable to adopt in regard to those who had fallen in persecution, with a view to obtain their approval: which they gave in terms complimentary to him, and sufficiently expressive of their own authority. Their letter in reply was despatched, as St. Cyprian assures us, not only to himself, but " throughout the whole world, and brought to the knowledge of all the churches and of all the brethren:"§ which shows that the authority of the Roman Church, which they provisionally exercised, extended to all portions of the universal Church.

The eminent dignity of the Roman Bishop, which, as we have seen from

---

* Lectures on the Reformation, by John Henry Hopkins, &c. p. 127. There are some mistakes in the chronological computation. † Ep. Antonian, lv.
‡ Ep. v. apud Constant, t. 1, col. 528. § Ep. xxx. Cleri Romani ad Cyprian.

the testimony of Cyprian, was viewed with jealousy by Decius, was implicitly acknowledged soon afterward by Aurelian. Paul, Bishop of Samosata, had been deposed for heresy by the Council of Antioch, in the year 268, but under the protection of Zenobia, queen of Palmyra, he continued to occupy the episcopal mansion. The Roman army, under the command of the emperor, having defeated the troops of the queen, the conqueror was implored to dispossess the heretical incumbent. Aurelian, feeling himself incompetent to decide a question which involved a point of Christian doctrine, decreed that "the right to the dwelling should be adjudged to him who should receive letters of communion from the Italian bishops of the Christian religion and from the Bishop of Rome."* This reference of a doctrinal dispute between Eastern bishops to the bishops of Italy, and especially to the Roman Bishop, proves that the emperor knew that he was acknowledged by Christians of the East, as well as of the West, to be the chief judge of doctrine. The mention of the other Italian bishops may have been made, because the matter seemed sufficiently important to be examined, and decided in a meeting, and to take the form of a solemn judgment. Ammian Marcellinus, a pagan writer of the following century, is also witness that "the bishops of the eternal city enjoy superior authority;"† which Barrow vainly attempts to explain of mere influence and reputation.

AUGUSTIN, speaking of Cecilian, the successor of Cyprian in the See of Carthage, pays a sublime tribute to the Roman Church, as possessing at all times, the apostolic power in all its fulness. Of the Bishop of Carthage, he remarks, that "he might well disregard the combined multitude of his enemies, while he saw himself united, by letters of communion, with THE ROMAN CHURCH, IN WHICH THE PRINCEDOM OF THE APOSTOLIC CHAIR ALWAYS FLOURISHED, and with other countries, from which the Gospel came to Africa, where he was ready also to plead his cause, if his adversaries should endeavor to estrange these churches from him."‡ There is no possibility of mistaking the force of this testimony. The dignity of the Roman Church is ascribed to its apostolic origin. To its authority and unquestionable integrity Augustin appeals, even in the supposition that the allegations of the Donatists against the African bishops and other bishops in communion with them were true: "If all throughout the world were such as you most wantonly assert, what has been done to you by the CHAIR OF THE ROMAN CHURCH, IN WHICH PETER SAT, and in which Anastasius sits at this day?"§

St. Jerom, who in his own cutting style so often lashed the vices of Rome, and treated with no indulgence the defects of the clergy, speaks with profound reverence of the Roman Church as the venerable See of the apostles, heiress of their faith, as well as of their relics. In his letter to

---

* Euseb. Hist. Eccl. l. vii. c. xxx.   † L. xv.
‡ Ep. xliii. olim clxii. ad Glorium et Eleusium.   § R. contra ii. lit. Petiliani, c. 1.

Marcella, he says: "There indeed is a holy church: there are the trophies of the apostles and martyrs: there is the true confession of Christ: there is that faith which was praised by the apostle: and Christianity is there making new advances daily over prostrate heathenism."* Yet when certain Roman usages were in question, such as the distinctions which deacons assumed, to the prejudice of the respect due to the priesthood and episcopacy, Jerom refused to defer to these local customs, and strongly vindicated the honor of the higher orders. The pretensions of the deacons show the eminence of the Church, whose officers they were, since otherwise there would have been no pretext for their assumption, while his caustic strictures prove his independent character, which must give increased weight to the homage, which he elsewhere renders to the apostolic See. "The Church," he says, "of the Roman city is not to be thought something different from the Church of the whole world. Gaul, and Britain, and Africa, and Persia, and the East, and India, and all the barbarous nations adore one Christ—observe one rule of truth. If authority is sought for, the world is greater than one city. Wherever a bishop is, whether at Rome, or at Eugubium,† or at Constantinople, or Rhegium, or Alexandria, or Tanæ, he has the same dignity, the same priesthood. Neither the power of wealth nor the lowliness of poverty makes a bishop more or less exalted :‡ but all are successors of the apostles. But you say, how is it that at Rome the priest is ordained on the testimony of the deacon? Why do you offer as an objection the custom of one city? Why do you allege, as laws of the Church, the insignificant number, from which haughtiness has sprung? Every thing that is rare is sought after. Their small number makes deacons respected; the multitude of priests brings them into contempt. However, even in the Church of Rome, priests sit while the deacons remain standing."§ Jerom asserted the equality of the episcopacy, evidently with a view to embrace even the priests, in defence of whose privileges he was writing. Will any one, in the face of all the monuments of antiquity, maintain, that the Bishops of Rome and Eugubium, of Alexandria and of Tanæ, were distinguished by no difference of jurisdiction? The episcopal character is, indeed, alike in all; the Bishop of Eugubium is, in this respect, equal to the Bishop of Rome; but the governing power, or jurisdiction, widely differs, for to the one the care of a small portion of the flock of Christ—to the other the charge of all the sheep and lambs is committed.

Jerom cannot be supposed to depreciate the authority of the Roman Church, merely because he condemns the practice of a few deacons, who took occasion from the eminence of that Church in which they enjoyed special distinction, to treat with less reverence their superiors in the sacred

---

* Ep. ad Marcell.
† Gubbio, a small town in the Roman States.
‡ The negation is wanting in some copies.
§ Hieronym. Evagrio.

ministry. Such customs as are peculiar to the local Church of Rome, need not be adopted by the other churches in her communion: and the abuses of individuals among the clergy of that Church, may be condemned, even by those, who, like Jerom, cry aloud that they cling to the chair of Peter—who receive her faith and tradition with reverence, and who cherish her communion, because they "know that it is the rock on which the Church was built."

All the bishops of the province of Arles concurred in a letter to St. Leo, in which, imploring the exercise of his authority in support of the privileges of the See of Arles, they distinctly recognised its apostolic source: "The Holy Roman Church," say they, "through the most blessed Peter, prince of the apostles, has the principality over all the churches of the world."* LEO himself, addressing the clergy and faithful of Rome, dwelt on the favor bestowed on them by the apostles: "They have raised you to such a pitch of glory, that, being made a holy nation, a chosen people, a priestly and royal city, the head of the world, through the sacred See of blessed Peter, you preside over a vaster region by the influence of divine religion, than before by earthly dominion."†

Barrow asserts, that the imperial dignity of the city was "the sole ground upon which the greatest of all ancient synods, that of Chalcedon, did affirm the papal eminency to be founded; for 'to the throne,' say they, 'of ancient Rome, because that was the royal city, the fathers reasonably deferred the privileges.'"‡ This assertion, however, is refuted by the very words of the council addressed to Leo, in regard to Dioscorus, patriarch of Alexandria: "He has extended his frenzy even against your apostolic Holiness, to whom the care of the vineyard was intrusted by the Saviour."§ When the Council speaks of prerogatives as bestowed by the fathers in consideration of the majesty of the city, they cannot be understood of the primacy itself, since this is no other than the care of the Lord's vineyard, which they expressly acknowledge to have been committed by our Saviour Himself to Leo, in the person of Peter. The attempt of Palmer to explain away this solemn recognition of the divine origin of the primacy, as if it meant "by His providence in permitting that bishop to occupy so eminent a position in the Church,"‖ is a perversion so uncandid as not to merit refutation. The privileges bestowed on the Roman See were only in recognition of its rights, by enactments tending to facilitate their exercise, especially by the canons of Sardica, which acknowledged the right of the Roman Bishop to receive appeals, and the propriety of reporting to him from all parts the state of religion, as to one divinely charged with the solicitude of all the churches: "This seems excellent and most suitable, that the priests of the Lord, from the respective pro-

---

* Ep. lxv. inter Leonis ep.   † Serm. lxxxii. in Natali Apost.
‡ Supp. v. ... ix.   § T. ii. p. 655, coll. Hard.
‖ Treatise on the Church, vol. ii. p. vii. ch. iii. p. 476.

vinces, report to the head, that is, to the See of the apostle Peter."* The imperial majesty of Rome was, indeed, the occasion of its being chosen by the apostle himself for the seat of his authority: if we may not suppose him to have been specially directed by Christ our Lord in a point so important. The chief city of a heathen empire, co-extensive with the civilized world, was peculiarly adapted to become the centre of a religion, which was to spread throughout all nations, making captives to Christ the lords of the earth, as well as their subjects, and extending its mild influence beyond the utmost bounds of civilization. The divinity of Christ was manifested in a manner the most striking, when the fisherman of Galilee planted the cross in the city of the Cæsars, and established his chair near the imperial throne, in the confidence that his empire would far surpass theirs in extent, and that it would endure and flourish for ages after theirs had been broken into fragments by the barbarian. Most probably the traveller would now seek in vain for the ruins of Rome, as for those of the eastern Babylon,† had it not been thus selected for the seat of a peaceful empire, far more glorious than that, which it once acquired by the irresistible valor of its legions. We may safely add, that it is destined to continue the fountain of civilization, art, science, and religion:

"Rome dont le destin dans la paix, dans la guerre,
Est d'etre en tous les tems maitresse de la terre."‡

Rome, Heaven awards the world for thy domain;
As once in war, in peace is now thy reign.

Some are willing to ascribe the origin of pontifical supremacy to the concessions of Christian emperors, who were pleased that the Bishop of ancient Rome should preside over his colleagues: but it is manifest, that it is to be traced to no such source. The seat of empire having been removed by Constantine to the city which bears his name, the imperial influence was naturally enlisted in favor of its bishop, who, from being a suffragan of the See of Heraclea, in Thrace, soon sought to become the second dignitary of the Church, to the prejudice of the rights of the Bishops of Alexandria and Antioch, and of other prelates. In 421, Theodosius the younger, overstepping the limits of the civil power, issued an edict, giving him cognizance of ecclesiastical causes throughout all the provinces of Illyricum, which belonged to the Western patriarchate. Honorius, Emperor of the West, remonstrated with his Eastern colleague on this innovation, as prejudicial to the rights of the "Holy Apostolic See." "Doubtless," he says, "we ought specially to venerate the Church of that city, from which we have received the Roman empire, and the priesthood derives its origin." He begs him to "command the ancient order to be

---

* Ep. Rom. Pont. Constant. t. 1, p. 395.
† Mr. Layard has been partially successful. See "Discoveries in the Ruins of Niniveh and Babylon; by Austin H. Layard." ‡ Voltaire, La Henriade, ch. iv.

observed, lest the Roman Church, under the empire of Christian princes, lose what it retained under other emperors."* Theodosius, yielding to this remonstrance, revoked his former decree.

The occupants of the See of Constantinople continued, nevertheless, to aspire after titles and power, with the marked favor of the Eastern emperors, until at length Pope Boniface III., about the year 606, obtained from Phocas the legal recognition of his title, which some moderns mistake for an imperial concession. Long before this period, namely, in 455, the Emperor Valentinian issued a decree, in which he acknowledged the primacy of the Roman Bishop to flow from the princely eminence of St. Peter: "The merit of blessed PETER, WHO IS THE PRINCE OF THE PRIESTLY ORDER, and the dignity of the Roman city, the authority also of the holy synod, strengthened the primacy of the Apostolic See."† The mention of the dignity of the city cannot detract from the force of the first reason, which of itself is sufficient. The principality of Peter is the real and only source of the dignity of the Roman Church; but the remembrance of the former civil importance of the city might be a motive in the mind of a Christian emperor, for viewing with complacency the apostolic prerogatives, with which it was enriched. The authority of the holy synod of Sardica strengthened them, inasmuch as the recognition of them was calculated to increase the reverence of the faithful for this guardian power, established by Christ Himself, who constituted Peter "prince of the priestly order."

Even Palmer says: "It would be a mistake to contend, that the pre-eminence of the Roman Church was derived altogether from the decrees of emperors, or from the canons of Councils, though it was much increased by such causes. It was founded on the possession of attributes, which collectively belonged to no other Church whatever."‡ He might have simply said, that it was founded on the fact, that it was the See of Peter, which, a little before, he himself had acknowledged: "The Roman Church was particularly honored as having been presided over by Peter, the first of the apostles, and was, therefore, by many of the fathers, called the See of Peter."§

With more ingenuousness, Mr. Allies, while still an Anglican, avowed that "the precedency or prerogative of Rome, to whatever extent it reached, was certainly not either claimed or granted merely because Rome was the imperial city. It was explicitly claimed by the Bishop of Rome, and as freely conceded by others to him, as, in a special sense, successor to St. Peter. From the very first, the Roman Pontiff seems possessed himself, as from a living tradition, which had thoroughly penetrated the local Roman Church, with a consciousness of some peculiar influence he was to

---

* Ep. ix. x. xi. apud Coustant. t. 1, col. 1029, 1030.
† Nov. xxiv. in fine eod. Theod. Vide Hallam, Middle Ages, c. vii. p. 270.
‡ A Treatise on the Church of Christ, vol. ii. part vii. ch. iii. p. 473.
§ Ibidem, p. 472.

exercise over the whole Church. This consciousness does not show itself here and there in the line of Roman Pontiffs, but one and all seem to have imbibed it from the atmosphere, which they breathed. That they were the successors of St. Peter, who himself sat and ruled, and spoke in their person, was as strongly felt, and as consistently declared, by those Pontiffs, who preceded the time of Constantine, as by those who followed. The feeling of their brother bishops, concerning them, may have been less definite, as was natural; but even those, who most opposed any arbitrary stretch of authority on their part, as St. Cyprian, fully admitted that they sat in the See of St. Peter, and ordinarily treated them with the greatest deference. This is written so very legibly upon the records of antiquity, that I am persuaded any one, who is even very slightly acquainted with them, cannot with sincerity dispute it."*

---

* The Church of England Cleared, &c.

CHAPTER IX.

Centre of Unity.

1.—COMMUNION WITH THE SEE OF ROME.

THE Bishop of Rome, being successor of St. Peter in the pastoral office, all the sheep of Christ are under his charge. All the bishops, with their respective flocks, constitute the one flock of Christ, under the one pastor, who is consequently the centre of general unity. All must communicate with him, since the members must be connected with the head: through whom they communicate with all their colleagues, even should they have no direct personal intercourse. The Church of Christ is essentially one— one body, one sheepfold—a well-constructed house—a united kingdom. It is plain, from all ancient documents, that the Bishop of Rome was regarded by all antiquity as a necessary bond of the universal Church, and that all bishops who valued Catholic unity, sought it in his communion. It is easy to perceive in Irenæus the necessity of this union and harmony with the Roman Church.* The members must harmonize and be united with the head; the provinces of this spiritual empire must be subject to the ruling power; the local churches and faithful must agree with the principal and ruling church. Thus had apostolic tradition been preserved in its integrity in the Church of Rome down to the time of Irenæus. The succession of bishops from Peter and Paul, her founders, had transmitted their teaching; and the whole body of believers, throughout the world, bore witness to it by the assent, which they gave to the doctrine of the Roman Church, whose communion they cherished as an essential principle of church organization.

ST. CYPRIAN is an illustrious witness to the necessity of communion with the See of St. Peter, which is so strongly asserted by him, that Hallam deems his language more definite than that of Irenæus: "Irenæus," he remarks, "rather vaguely, and Cyprian more positively admit, or rather assert the primacy of the Church of Rome, which the latter seems to have regarded as a kind of centre of Catholic unity."†

Mosheim avows, that the principles laid down by these fathers lead naturally to the admission of a central authority, such as is ascribed to the Bishop of Rome, and alleges that they were too simple and short-sighted

---

* See p. 85. † Middle Ages, c. vii. p. 270, Americ. ed.

to understand the consequences! "Cyprian and the rest cannot have known the corollaries which follow from their precepts about the Church. For no one is so dull as not to see that between a certain unity of the universal Church, terminating in the Roman Pontiff, and such a community as we have described out of Irenæus and Cyprian, there is scarcely so much room as between hall and chamber, or between hand and fingers."*

The letter of St. Cyprian to Antonian, whom the representations of Novatian had caused to hesitate in recognising Cornelius as Bishop of Rome, begins thus: "I received your first letter, most beloved brother, which firmly maintains the harmony of the priestly college, and the communion of the Catholic Church, inasmuch as you intimate, that you hold no communion with Novatian, but that, following our counsel, you are in harmony with Cornelius, our fellow-bishop. You also wrote, that I should forward a copy of the same letter to Cornelius, our colleague, that he might lay aside all anxiety, knowing that YOU COMMUNICATE WITH HIM, THAT IS, WITH THE CATHOLIC CHURCH."† This will enable us to understand the full force of some other passages in the sequel. The Bishop of Rome, at that early day, was the centre and bond of Catholic communion: through him the bishops of every part of Christendom communicated with each other, and thereby formed that episcopal college, of which Cyprian so often speaks—as one in its character, tendency, and spirit.

Antonian had requested to be informed what heresy Novatian had introduced. Cyprian replied, it was a matter of no consequence, as long as he was separated from the Church by his opposition to her lawful bishop: "As to what regards Novatian, concerning whom you have requested me to inform you what heresy he has introduced, know, in the first place, that we should not be curious to know what he teaches, since he teaches WITHOUT. WHOEVER HE IS, AND WHATEVER QUALIFICATIONS HE POSSESSES, HE IS NOT A CHRISTIAN WHO IS NOT IN THE CHURCH OF CHRIST." No one can insist on the necessity of communion with the Apostolic See, in terms stronger than these. Immediately after the words just quoted, Cyprian continues: "Though he boast of his philosophy, or proclaim his eloquence in haughty words, he who does not maintain either fraternal charity, or ecclesiastical unity, has lost what he had been before. Unless, indeed, you regard as a bishop, an adulterer and stranger, who ambitiously endeavors to be made bishop by deserters, after a bishop has been ordained in the Church by sixteen bishops; and, while there is one Church divided by Christ into many members, throughout the whole world, and one episcopacy spread abroad in the concordant multitude of bishops, in violation of the unity of the Catholic Church, which is connected and joined together everywhere, he endeavors to make a human church, and sends his apostles through many cities, to lay the foundations of his new institution; and while, long since, throughout all the provinces, and in every city,

---

* Dissertatio de Gallorum appell. § 13.   † Ep. ad Antonian.

bishops have been ordained—advanced in age, sound in faith, tried in times of oppression, proscribed in persecution, he dares create mock bishops in their stead." It would be absurd to argue that there is no superior authority in the Bishop of Rome above his colleagues, because the episcopate is one; for surely the context shows, that it is not directed to establish the equality of all bishops, but their union for one great purpose—the government of the Church; whence Cyprian concludes, that the refractory intruder, Novatian, by his opposition to Cornelius, was cut off from the communion of all bishops, and of the Church. The very efforts of Novatian to secure the support and gain the communion of the African bishops, and to lay the foundations of his new institution, by means of his emissaries, indicate that the station, which he claimed, was that of a bishop having general authority throughout the Church, on which account he was considered by Cyprian as laboring to establish a new institution, "a human Church," in opposition to the Divine institution of Christ.

The language of this illustrious prelate is stronger than the mere usurpation of an ordinary bishopric, contrary to the rights of the legitimate pastor, would warrant. Such an act, however unjustifiable and criminal, is not in itself an attempt to make a new Church. When Fortunatus had been created bishop, by some schismatics, in opposition to Cyprian himself, this prelate, while strongly reprobating the act, did not look upon it as one involving serious consequences to the universal Church, so that he neglected to inform Cornelius of it, until, on the application of the schismatics for recognition, the Pope wrote to inquire into the facts, and the causes of his silence.* He complains, that the communications from Polycarp, Bishop of the colony of Adrumetum,† which had been, in the first instance, addressed to him by name, had subsequently been directed to the priests and deacons of the Roman Church, which change he traced to a visit which Cyprian and Liberalis had made to the colony. This shows the frequency of the communications with the Roman Church from distant parts, and the right which the Bishop of Rome claimed, that they should be addressed to himself personally. Cyprian, whose mind from the beginning had been made up in favor of Cornelius, explains in his reply, the motives of the change, which was the result of a resolution taken by several bishops, in an assembly held on the subject, to avoid direct communication with either of the claimants, until the return of the ambassadors, whom they had despatched to ascertain the facts. In the mean time they had been careful to cling to the Roman Church: "for," says he, "giving an account (*of this reserve*) we know that we exhorted all who sailed (*hence*) to acknowledge and hold fast to THE ROOT AND MATRIX OF THE CATHOLIC CHURCH." On the return of the ambassadors, all doubt about

---

* Ep. lix. Cyprianus Cornelio.
† Afterward called Heraclea, and recently Herkla, on the eastern coast of Tunis.

the legitimacy of the election of Cornelius being removed, it was determined, as Cyprian assures him, that letters should be written and ambassadors sent to him by all the bishops: "that all our colleagues should strongly approve of you, and hold fast your communion, that is, both the unity and charity of the Catholic Church."* The dignity of the Roman Church as the See of Peter, and the necessity of communion with her, could not be more touchingly expressed.

In his admirable treatise on the unity of the Church, St. Cyprian maintains that martyrdom avails nothing to him who is not in unity. Yet unity is a phantom, unless the central and connecting authority of the Bishop of Rome be admitted. The union of local churches in sentiment and faith cannot be left to the result of mere chance. There may be, at least, as many creeds as there are bishops, if there be not a chief bishop in whom his colleagues recognise their leader and organ, to declare with authority, in the name of all, the common faith. By this means the general tradition can be collected, preserved, and transmitted. The bishops gathering around him may attest the faith of their respective churches, compare it with the unfailing tradition of Peter, and uniting with him in judgment, concur to proscribe all the novel inventions of human pride. Union of charity between churches discordant in faith, is a fond imagination of those, who would cover the shame of disunion, by affecting to cherish, what, at best, is but sympathy for the errors of their fellow-men. The Church is the pillar and the ground of the truth, which must be admitted by her members in all its fulness. She cannot be one without a common principle of government. There can be no permanent order without a controlling power. As in each diocese, the bishop is the ruler, in whom the clergy and faithful unite to form a local church, so all the churches must have a universal bishop, presiding over all, and directing and governing all. As there is one God, one Christ, one Church, one faith, so, according to Cyprian, there is one chair founded by the voice of the Lord on Peter. From him unity began: in his chair the principle of unity is lodged: and the same necessity which obliges us to recognise one Church, leads us to acknowledge one Pastor, one Priest, one Judge in the place of Christ. The plenitude and independence of authority in the several bishops are totally inconsistent with unity. "Would there not have been," asks Mr. Allies, "not only imminent danger, but almost certainty, that a power, unlimited in its nature, committed to so large a body of men, who might become indefinitely more numerous, yet were each independent centres of authority, instead of tending to unity, would produce diversity?"†

St. Cyprian holds the episcopate to be one, as the Church is one: "Does he who opposes and resists the Church—*who forsakes the chair of Peter,*

---

* Ep. xlviii.   † The Church of England Cleared, etc. p. 17.

on whom the Church was founded*—flatter himself that he is in the Church; while the blessed Paul, the apostle, teaches this, and shows the mystery of unity, saying: 'One body, and one spirit, one hope of your calling, one Lord, one faith, one baptism, one God?' This unity ought to be firmly held and maintained, especially by us bishops, who preside in the Church, that we may show that the episcopate itself is one, and indivisible. Let no one deceive the brotherhood by falsehood—let no one corrupt the truth of faith by perfidious prevarication. The episcopate is one, the parts of which hold severally from the whole; the Church is one, which is extended more widely by the increase of her fecundity."† The scope of Cyprian is not to prove that one bishop is equal to another, or that each bishop possesses the entire episcopal power in its plenitude; but that the Church is one, and the episcopate one likewise, each bishop exercising his authority for the same general interest, and in inviolable connection with his brethren. The phrase: *cujus pars a singulis in solidum tenetur*,‡ marks the end and manner of the exercise of episcopal power—the unity and connection in which alone it can be enjoyed, since all bishops, according to Cyprian, are a *collegium*,§ or corporate body, the powers of which are communicated to the individual members with dependence on the general body, especially on the head. Dr. Nevin remarks, "it is enough for us to know that the unity of the Church was taken to stand in the solidarity of the episcopate, and that the proper *radix* and *matrix* of the whole system, as Cyprian has it, was felt to be the *cathedra Petri*, kept up by regular succession in the Church of Rome."‖ The book on the unity of the Church, which was addressed to those confessors of the faith, who had tarnished their glory by supporting the schism of Novatian, was directed to prove, that those, who adhered to a rival of the lawful Bishop of Rome, forfeited all the privileges of the Church, which are only enjoyed in unity, all bishops being necessarily united in communion. As there can be only one bishop in each Church, whoever sets up or supports a rival prelate, by this schismatical act deprives himself of the communion of the whole Church, which can only be enjoyed through the lawful bishop. This was especially true of the Bishop of Rome, the head of all bishops, although the principle may be applied to any diocesan in communion with the chief bishop and the universal Church.

The great Archbishop of Milan, St. Ambrose, relates in praise of his brother Satirus, that on reaching shore after shipwreck, he was careful to

---

* The words in italics are omitted in the edition of Erasmus. I believe them to be genuine, for the reasons elsewhere given; but I have no need of laying stress on them.

† De unit. Eccl.

‡ I have borrowed the translation of Dr. Nevin. For a full exposition of this text, and of the relations of the Pope to the college of bishops, I refer to a work of great value: "The Unity of the Episcopate Considered, by Edward Healy Thompson, M.A.". The author is one of many English converts.

§ Ep. lii. ‖ A Word of Explanation, M. R. March, 1852.

inquire, whether the bishop of the place "agreed in faith with the Catholic bishops, that is, with the Roman Church."* Thus communion with Rome was regarded as an evidence of orthodoxy and Catholicity.

St. Optatus, arguing against Parmenian the Donatist, insists on the notoriety of the fact, that Peter established the episcopal chair at Rome, whence he infers the necessity of communion with the Bishop of that See. "You cannot affect ignorance of the fact, that the episcopal chair was first established by Peter in the city of Rome, in which Peter sat, the head of all the apostles, for which reason he was called Cephas :† in which one chair unity should be maintained by all; that the apostles should not each set up a chair for himself, but that he should be at once a schismatic and a sinner, who should erect any other against that one chair." He gives the succession of pontiffs from St. Peter to Siricius, "who," says he, "is at this day our colleague, with whom the whole world as well as ourselves, agrees in one society and communion by the intercourse of the usual letters."‡ The chair of Peter is thus plainly recognised as the necessary bond of Catholic communion.

Mr. Palmer feebly attempts to elude the force of this remarkable passage, by a qualified concession : "It is not denied that St. Optatus, in arguing against the Donatists as to the 'cathedra,' which they admitted to be one of the gifts of the Church, refers to the chair of Peter at Rome, as constituting the centre of unity in the Catholic Church. It was so in fact, at that time, and had very long been so."§ Truly, very long, even from the time that Peter founded that See : and so necessary was this centre of unity in the mind of Optatus, that whoever erects a rival see is a schismatic and prevaricator.

St. Augustin fully harmonizes with Optatus, in acknowledging the necessity of communion with the Roman See; and calls on the Donatists to embrace it, if they wish to be ingrafted in the vine.‖ St. Jerom identifies the Roman with the Catholic faith, demanding : "What faith does Rufinus call his own ? Is it that which is held by the Roman Church, or that which is found in the writings of Origen ? If he replies : It is the Roman: then we are Catholics."¶ In the conflicting claims to the see of Antioch, of three prelates, of which we will speak more fully hereafter, he manifested the greatest anxiety to discover which of them enjoyed the communion of the Pontiff, that with him only he might communicate.

When the intention of St. Fulgentius to visit the monasteries of Egypt, with a view to attain to the perfection of monastic discipline, became known to Eulalius, Bishop of Syracuse, he effectually dissuaded him from putting

---

* De obitu fratris.

† *Rock*. Some pretend that Optatus confounded the Syriac term with the Greek term κἰφαλη, which signifies *head :* but this is by no means certain, since he might well say that the apostle was called a rock, because he was head of all the apostles.

‡ De Schismat. Donat. l. ii.

§ A Treatise on the Church, part vii. ch. v. p. 503.

‖ Ps. contra partem Donati.   ¶ L. i. in Rufin. n. 4.

it in execution, by remarking that they were separated from the communion of Peter, and consequently out of the way of salvation, whatever austerities they might practise: "You are right," said the bishop, "in aspiring to perfection; but you know that without faith it is impossible to please God. The countries which you desire to visit are separated by dire schism from the communion of Blessed Peter."*

All the ancient symbols and fathers speak of unity as an essential attribute of the Church, as Mr. Manning has fully shown.† This unity was not realized unless by means of communion with the Roman See, as Dr. Nevin candidly avows: "To be joined in communion with the See of Rome was in the view of this period to be in the bosom of the true church; to be out of that communion was to be in schism. It was not enough to be in union with any other bishop or body of bishops; the sacrament of unity was held to be of force only, as having regard to the church in its universal character; and this involved necessarily the idea of an universal centre, which by general consent was to be found in Rome only, and no where else."‡

The sophism of some moderns, who, from the popular use of the terms "Roman Catholic," infer that our claims involve contradiction, is easily refuted. The term "Roman" was applied to the Catholic faith by Pelagius the heretic, who designated in this way the faith of St. Ambrose,§ and by Theodosius the younger,‖ as also by St. Jerom. The union of both appellations is popular, rather than ecclesiastical, for which reason it was objected to in the Congress of Vienna, by Cardinal Consalvi, who preferred that the Church should be styled Roman and Catholic. The popular usage, however, admits of an easy explanation, since the mention of the seat of power does not necessarily limit the extent of empire; and the centre can be pointed to without prejudice to the vastness of the circumference. The Church is Roman, because her visible head is Bishop of Rome: she is Catholic, because her spiritual dominion extends throughout all nations, even to the extremities of the world.¶

§ 2.—INTERRUPTIONS OF COMMUNION.

Although special facts should never be allowed to militate against principles which are certain, it may be useful to consider the particular cases in which prelates or churches are alleged to have been out of the communion of the Roman See, without loss of church-membership or privileges.

---

* B. Fulgentii vita c. xiii.
† The Unity of the Church, by Henry Edward Manning, M. A., Archdeacon of Chichester, ch. i. ii.
‡ Early Christianity. Mercersburg Review, September, 1851.
§ Apud Aug. l. de Gratia Christi, c. xlvi.
‖ In Conc. Eph.
¶ Anglo-Catholic is a modern phrase, involving a real contradiction, since it unites an insular title, implying independent and separate existence, with a claim to universality.

St. Meletius, Patriarch of Antioch, is given as an instance: but it can never be shown that he was deprived of ecclesiastical communion, although for a time he did not enjoy official intercourse with the Pontiff. The Arians had concurred in his election, which threw doubt on his orthodoxy, and determined Damasus to recognise Paulinus, who was subsequently ordained by Eusebius, Bishop of Vercelli, at the solicitation of some Catholics. The suspicions entertained to his prejudice were known to be unjust by St. Basil and other Eastern prelates, who supported him in consequence of the priority of his ordination. Damasus abstained, in his regard, from any positive act of exclusion, or of communion; and Meletius persisted in maintaining his claims, with avowed reverence for the authority of the Pontiff. According to the established discipline of those ages, the patriarch, when duly elected and consecrated, received jurisdiction, under the obligation of communicating his election to the Pope, whose letters of communion confirmed him in the possession of his see: but the withholding of official intercourse, when not followed by positive excommunication, did not strip him of his authority, much less did it place him beyond the pale of the Church. Meletius continued to profess adhesion to the Pontiff, so that when Sapores, the commander of the forces, came to Antioch, by order of the emperor Gratian, to deliver the churches to the bishop in communion with Damasus, Meletius satisfied him that he enjoyed it, and accordingly got possession. Vitalis had been consecrated bishop of the same see, by Apollinaris, and professed the same reverence for the pontifical authority. In fact, the three claimants were loud in their declarations of attachment to Rome. St. Jerom, who was then in Syria, being perplexed by their conflicting pretensions, tells the Pope that, to avoid mistake, he held communion with the Egyptian confessor, that is, with Peter, Patriarch of Alexandria, then an exile in Syria, who had assisted at the Roman Council: "I follow here your colleagues, the confessors of Egypt, and amid the merchant vessels, I lie hid in a little boat. I know nothing of Vitalis—I reject Meletius—I care not for Paulinus. Whoever does not gather with you, scatters; that is, whoever is not of Christ is of Antichrist."* He looked on Meletius with the suspicion with which he was generally viewed in the West, and therefore declined his communion. To relieve himself from perplexity, he addressed a second letter to Damasus: "The Church here being split into three parties, each is eager to draw me to itself. The venerable authority of the monks who dwell around, assails me. In the mean time I cry aloud: WHOEVER IS UNITED WITH THE CHAIR OF PETER, IS MINE. Meletius, Vitalis, and Paulinus affirm that they are united with you: if one only made the assertion, I could believe him: but in the present case either two or all of them deceive me. Therefore, I beseech you, blessed father—by the cross of the Lord, by the becoming zeal for the faith,† by the passion of Christ—as you

---

* Ep. xv.

† Necessary regard for the integrity of faith, which is the glory of the Church.

succeed the apostles in dignity, so may you rival them in merit—so may you sit on the throne of judgment with the twelve—so may another gird you like Peter in your old age*—so may you gain the franchise of the heavenly city with Paul—declare to me by your letter, with whom should I hold communion in Syria. Do not disregard a soul for which Christ died."† This is the language of a man, who feels that it is the duty of a disciple of Christ, in whatever part of the world he may be, to communicate with the Bishop of Rome, through the local prelate enjoying his communion.

A compromise between Paulinus and Meletius was subsequently effected, as Sozomen and Socrates testify, and both prelates were recognised by the Council of Aquileja, held in 381. Meletius presided in a Council of Antioch, held in 379, which solemnly embraced the decree of Damasus and the Roman synod against the errors of Apollinaris, adding anathema to the gainsayers. The acts of this council were accepted at Rome, and placed in the archives of that See, bound up with those of the Roman synod, as appears from ancient manuscripts. The fathers of the Council of Constantinople, held in 382, in which Meletius was present, in their letter to the Pope, bore testimony to the integrity of his faith, of which the acts of the Council of Antioch, which they mentioned with praise, were a splendid evidence. His acceptance of the doctrinal definition of Damasus, and the Pontiff's approval of the proceedings of the Council of Antioch, were solemn acts of direct communion, which show that Meletius did not die separated from unity, from which, in reality, he was never excluded.

It was worthy of the truly liberal spirit of the Holy See to render homage after death to a bishop, whom, for a considerable period, it treated with distrust, under false impressions, which time has removed. The integrity of the faith of Meletius, the legitimacy of his ordination, and the eminence of his virtues, were generally recognised after his death, when rival pretensions and interests could no longer cast a cloud over them. The successors of Damasus united with the East in the celebration of his virtues, and his name was inscribed on the records of illustrious prelates of the Church, who, in difficult times, preserved the faith, and cultivated piety. His example may serve to show, that a man can attain to sanctity and salvation, although, from misconception and misrepresentation, he be not favored by the chief bishop with special marks of communion; but it offers no security to such as persevere in sects separated from the Church, contrary to the divine law, which enjoins submission to our lawful pastors, and contrary to the divine constitution of the Church, of which unity is the distinctive principle. Meletius was neither leader nor member of a sect. He held the truth as it is in Christ; he received with docility the teaching of the chief bishop; he professed adhesion to his authority, and it was his misfortune, not his fault, that he could not for a time succeed in dissipating the suspicions that deprived him of official intercourse.

---

* He wishes him the crown of martyrdom. † Ep. xvi. Damaso.

The great solicitude of the Bishops of Antioch to enjoy the communion of the Apostolic See, appears from the efforts made in their behalf by St. John Chrysostom, on his elevation to the See of Constantinople. Having been priest of that Church, he charged the ambassadors whom he sent to Rome to announce his own election, to use their influence to procure a formal recognition of the actual bishop of Antioch. Ambassadors also came from Flavian himself, as Innocent I. testifies: "The Church of Antioch, which the blessed apostle Peter, before he came to the city of Rome, illustrated by his presence, as a sister of the Roman Church, did not suffer herself to be long estranged from her, for, having sent ambassadors, she sought and obtained peace."* The misunderstanding had lasted seventeen years; but it implied no difference of belief, or breach of unity. It arose from the difficulty of putting facts in their true light, and dissipating prejudices honestly entertained against individuals. ·It is freely admitted, that, in such circumstances, the want of direct communion with the Apostolic See may not be fatal to the claims of membership of the Catholic Church: but the nature of unity and catholicity manifestly forbids us to consider as members of the Church, those who positively reject her communion.

Mr. Palmer, after having assigned unity as a mark of the Church, labors with great industry to prove that it is possible that she may be divided in respect of external communion: thus throwing down with one hand what he builds up with the other. He particularly endeavors to show, that at various times the communion between the Church of Rome and the oriental churches was actually interrupted, as after the death of St. Chrysostom, when the Roman Church, followed by all the West, refused to communicate with the oriental bishops, especially with Theophilus of Alexandria, as long as they declined to re-establish the memory of the holy Bishop of Constantinople. This, however, was not an absolute excommunication, excluding them from the pale of the Church, but a denial of the usual marks of brotherhood, in order to compel them to do justice to the memory of a persecuted prelate. When Acacius, bishop of the same see, was excommunicated by the Pope, he could no longer be a member of the Church, since Christ binds in heaven those whom His vicar binds on earth. The oriental bishops who still adhered to Acacius, violated their duty, and such of them as professed the heresy for which he was condemned, forfeited thereby the communion of the Church: but those who only indulged partisan attachment, without rejecting the faith and communion of the Pontiff, and who were not expressly separated from the Church by his act, might remain included among her members. The period of thirty-five years which elapsed before this dissension was healed, was not one of absolute interruption. The communion between the East and the West was partially suspended, rather than broken off; the Pope refusing to give tokens of his communion to the oriental prelates, as long

---

* Ep. **xxiii**. Bonifacio, col. 852, t. l. Coustant.

as the name of Acacius remained on the sacred tablets. The condition on which a reconciliation took place, was a solemn engagement on the part of John, Bishop of Constantinople, not to allow to be inscribed on the tablets of the Church, the names of any who did not in all things harmonize with the Apostolic See : "We promise," said he, writing to Pope Hormisdas, in the year 515, that "hereafter the names of such as are separated from the communion of the Catholic Church, that is, such as do not in all things harmonize with the Apostolic See, shall not be recited in the celebration of the sacred mysteries."* Thus harmony with the Holy See was declared to be identical with communion with the Catholic Church.

In the great schism between the rival claimants of the papal chair, in the fourteenth century, on which Mr. Palmer lays great stress, there was no rejection of the pontifical authority, which on the contrary all solemnly recognised, although the doubt which existed as to the fact—who was lawful Pontiff—prevented their mutual intercourse. No instance can be produced from the history of the Church to prove, that any one who openly denies the primacy of the Apostolic See, or who is solemnly excommunicated by the lawful occupant of the papal chair, can be regarded as a member of the Church : much less can it be shown that any local church, or any collection of churches, absolutely separated by their own act, or by the act of the Pontiff, from his communion, can be considered as portions of the universal Church. The unanimous teaching of the fathers demonstrates that the unity of the Church is indivisible, and that she is one, not only in each place by her local government, but throughout the world, by the compact connection of all her parts; on which account she is compared by St. Cyprian to a tree, whose branches spread all around, to a spring whose waters flow through numberless channels, and to the sun whose rays shed light abroad throughout the entire earth : "The Church is one, which, by the growth of its fruitfulness, is spread widely into a multitude : as there are many rays of the sun, but one light, and many branches of a tree, but one trunk planted in the clinging root : and though from one source many rivers flow, so that there seem to be many several streams, by reason of the fulness of the abundant flood, yet is the oneness maintained in the original spring. Take off a ray from the body of the sun, the unity of light admits no division; cut off a stream from the source—that which is cut off dries up; so the Church, filled throughout with the light of the Lord, spreads its rays through the whole world; yet is it only one light which is everywhere diffused; nor is the unity of the body severed : by reason of its abundant fulness it stretches its rays into all the earth, it pours widely its flowing streams, yet there is one head, and one beginning, and one mother, teeming with continual fruitfulness."†

---

* Conc. t. ii. col. 1077. † Cyprian de Unit. Eccl.

CHAPTER X.

Ancient Examples of Papal Authority.

§ 1.—DISTURBANCES AT CORINTH.

It is declared by St. Paul that heresies are attended with advantage, inasmuch as they serve to try men, and to distinguish the faithful and stable from the unsteady and perverse: "there must be also heresies, that they also who are approved, may be made manifest among you."* They serve, at the same time, to mark more clearly the faith of the Church, and to render it more illustrious. In like manner schisms, controversies, and scandals, in the designs of Providence, become instrumental for good, afford us a salutary warning to shun strife and crime, and lead us to respect authority.

Toward the end of the first century, before the death of St. John the apostle, violent commotions broke out at Corinth, in which the clergy suffered by the opposition of rash and misguided men. The persecutions which, about the same time, raged at Rome, prevented immediate action in the case on the part of the Church of this city; but as soon as an interval of peace was granted, an effort to restore harmony was made in the name of the Roman Church, and a letter of expostulation and advice was sent, which was so esteemed and venerated, that long afterward it was wont to be read publicly in the Church of Corinth,† and is justly valued among the most precious monuments of Christian antiquity. Messengers were despatched, charged to use every exertion to re-establish order. The terms of the letter may not satisfy a fastidious critic that superior authority was claimed by the writer, because persuasion only is used; but the judicious reader will easily understand, that where passions are excited, they can scarcely be subdued by urging abstract views of power. The interposition of a distant prelate in the internal affairs of the Corinthian Church, cannot be accounted for satisfactorily unless by reference to his universal charge, especially as the apostle John, then residing at Ephesus, was much nearer to the scene of strife, and could hope to exercise greater personal influence, besides the authority of his office.‡ Had not Clement felt it to be his

---

* 1 Cor. xi. 19.   † Dionys. cor. apud Euseb. *Hist. Eccl.* l. iv. c. xxiii.

‡ This forms a difficulty in the mind of Dr. Schaff, that an apostle should be in any way subordinate to Clement, the Roman Bishop; but it is nowise incompatible with his privileges as an apostle to respect the order established by Christ for the benefit of the whole Church.

duty, he scarcely would have ventured, in such circumstances, to address the revolters. That he wrote the letter, although it bears the name of "the Church of God which is at Rome," is attested by Irenæus, a writer of the next age;* and the title is sufficiently accounted for, by the ancient custom of assembling the clergy on occasions of great importance, and acting with their advice and concurrence. The bishop and the church were identified in such acts, since, as ST. CYPRIAN remarks, "the church is the people united with the priest and the flock following its pastor; whence you should know that the bishop is in the church, and the church is in the bishop."†

§ 2.—PASCHAL CONTROVERSY.

The second century affords us more decisive proofs of the official interference of the Bishop of Rome in the affairs of the Eastern churches. A difference of discipline in regard to the time of celebrating Easter existed, from the commencement, between the churches of Asia Minor and the Western churches. The former alleged the authority of St. John the evangelist for celebrating it on the same day as the Jews; thus changing the object of the festival, and commemorating the resurrection of our Lord, while the Jews ate of the paschal lamb. The Western churches, especially the Church of Rome, and also the Church of Alexandria, celebrated it on the Sunday following the Jewish feast; not wishing to appear to retain any thing of the abrogated ceremonial. The matter in itself was indifferent, and the various usages may have been originally sanctioned by the respective apostles, who founded the churches, since variety in discipline may be expedient, according to local circumstances. In places where the converts from Judaism formed the main body of Christians, their transition to Christianity was rendered less difficult by retaining the day of their solemnity; and thus the usages of the Asiatic churches may have had the sanction of St. John. At Rome, and wherever the churches were chiefly composed of converts from heathenism, the same delicate regard to Jewish feelings not being required, it seemed expedient to leave no occasion for supposing that any legal observance was still in force among Christians. Anicetus, who held the chair of St. Peter about the middle of the second century, endeavored to persuade Polycarp, Bishop of Smyrna, on occasion of his visit to Rome, to conform to the more general usage; but the venerable prelate pleaded so strongly in favor of the custom of the Asiatic churches, that Anicetus abstained from any positive prohibition, and treated his illustrious guest with the honor which his virtues and station deserved.

Near the close of the same century, Victor, Bishop of Rome, resolved to procure uniformity, even by having recourse to severe measures, if necessary.

---

* L. iii. adv. hær. c. iii.   † Ep. lxix. ad Pupianum.

The Western bishops were unanimous in desiring it, and among others, Irenæus, Bishop of Lyons, at the head of a synod in Gaul, wrote to the Asiatic churches, strongly recommending it.* A letter to the same effect was issued in the name of Victor, by a Roman synod over which he presided, exhorting the bishops of Asia to hold synods, in order to bring about the change.† At Cæsarea of Palestine a numerous Council was held, which enacted that the Paschal festival should thenceforward be celebrated on Sunday: but Polycrates, Bishop of Ephesus, with a synod in which he presided, persisted in defending the ancient usage. Victor resolved on cutting off the refractory from his communion, which so alarmed Irenæus, that he wrote to him an earnest letter of remonstrance, deprecating the loss of so many churches to Catholic unity, for an observance which had been so long tolerated, and reminding him of the wise indulgence of Anicetus, who treated Polycarp with marked distinction, notwithstanding the tenacity with which he clung to the Asiatic practice.‡ All these facts, which are detailed by Eusebius, are not called in question by any of the learned. It is, however, doubted whether Victor actually pronounced excommunication.

Of the justice and wisdom of the course pursued by Victor, different sentiments may be entertained: but it cannot fairly be questioned that he claimed authority over the Asiatic churches, and, at least, threatened to employ it, in the severest manner, to compel them to conform to the more general usage. The pertinacious adherence of Polycrates and other bishops to the custom of the East, may be used to show that the ancient rites of local churches should not be hastily proscribed, even by the Bishop of Rome: but it does not prove that his authority was called in question. In the letter of the synod, which maintained the usage, precedents are insisted on as justifying it; while the obvious reply is omitted, which would have been at once conclusive, had Victor no right to control the churches of the East. The holding of various local Councils by his orders, the compliance of some of them with his injunction, the plea of ancient precedent strongly urged by others, the remonstrance of Irenæus against precipitate severity, all concur to prove that the authority of Victor was universally admitted, although the justice or expediency of its exercise was questioned by some. This is all that is implied in the words of Polycrates: "I am not at all moved by the threats held out to me: for greater than I have said: 'It behoveth us to obey God, rather than men.'"§ It is plain that he considered Victor as commanding, and menacing; but under the false impression that the festival day prescribed by God to the Jews was still obligatory, he refused obedience to what he deemed an un-

---

* See letter of Irenæus, *inter Ep. Rom. Pont.* Constant. col. 105. t. i.

† See letter of Polycrates to Victor, ibidem, col. 100. He states that he had summoned the bishops at his request.

‡ L. v. Hist. Eccl. c. xxiii. xxiv.

§ Vide inter Rom. Pontif. epist. studio Petri Coustant, t. i. col. 99.

just precept, and an abuse of authority. Had he recognised in the Roman Bishop no power to command, he would surely at once have repelled the attempt to dictate to him, and boldly denied his right of interference.

Whether Victor actually issued an excommunication, or merely threatened to issue it, his claim to superior power is manifest. Potter speaks of his act as unjust, but adds: "however, it is a good evidence that excommunication was used at this time in the Church."* He might have said with equal truth, that it is good evidence that the Bishop of Rome at that early period, claimed power over the bishops of Asia, ordered them to hold synods with a view to put his decree in execution, and threatened them with excommunication, in case of resistance; and that those who resisted his orders, did not call in question his authority. From the narrative of Eusebius, it is clear that his threat was not looked on as an insolent assumption of power, or an idle waste of words, but that every effort was made by argument, remonstrance, and entreaty, to avert its execution. The judgment of the entire episcopal body in the Council of Nice, vindicated the wisdom and foresight of the Pontiff, by classing among heretics the Quartodecimans, who, under the false persuasion, that the Mosaic law was still obligatory as far as the day of the paschal solemnity was concerned, persisted in celebrating the Christian festival on the same day on which the Jews offered the paschal victim. This is not the only instance in which the Popes have proved their deep discrimination, and enlightened zeal to reform usages pregnant with danger to the integrity of Christian faith, and have received the highest homage that could be rendered to their wisdom, by the final adhesion of the episcopal body and of the whole Church to their judgment. Like watchful pilots, they were the first to discern the distant speck, which gradually grew into a thunder-cloud, and burst in fury on the vessel of the Church, whose helm, with steady hand, they directed.

§ 3.—MONTANISM.

The heresy broached by Montanus, of Mysia, in the decline of the second century, prevailed in various parts of Asia Minor and Phrygia. The heresiarch denied the lawfulness of second marriages, and the power of forgiving heinous sins, such as adultery, murder, and apostasy. Every effort was made by his followers to procure from the Bishop of Rome at least an indirect sanction for their errors, by the admission of their abettors to communion: and if the testimony of Tertullian, who embraced the sect, can be relied on, they actually succeeded in disposing him† to write to the Asiatic churches to this effect. However, the timely arrival of Praxeas, who himself had been of their number, defeated their artifices.‡

---

* On Church Government, p. 335. † Tertullian does not give his name.
‡ Tertull. Lib. ad Praxeam.

The martyrs of Lyons addressed Eleutherius, urging him to oppose the progress of the heresy, by the authority of his office, which he accordingly employed for that purpose.* Of this mission, St. Jerom says: "Irenæus, a priest of Pothinus, the bishop who then ruled the Church of Lyons, in Gaul, was sent as legate by the martyrs of that place to Rome, concerning certain ecclesiastical questions."†

The decree of the Bishop of Rome, by which adulterers, as well as other sinners, were declared admissible to communion, after suitable penance, is mentioned by Tertullian in terms that prove him to be a reluctant witness to the pontifical supremacy: "I hear that an edict has been published, and, indeed, a peremptory one: namely, THE BISHOP OF BISHOPS, which is equivalent to the sovereign Pontiff, proclaims: I pardon the sins of adultery and fornication to such as have performed penance. This is read in the Church, and is proclaimed in the Church."‡ The authority from which this decree emanated, was manifestly supreme, since it was thus publicly acknowledged by the solemn promulgation of this "peremptory" edict. The Bishop of Rome, of whom Tertullian confessedly speaks, is styled by him "BISHOP OF BISHOPS,"§ because he acted as having power over other bishops. It is not at all probable, that he employed the language which the Montanist puts in his mouth, since the Popes have always abstained from the use of pompous and offensive titles: but his acts bespoke him to be the chief bishop, which was tantamount, in the mind of Tertullian, to 'sovereign Pontiff,' a title at that time justly detested, on account of the idolatrous functions which belonged to the office, although after the extirpation of idolatry, it was applied, in an innocuous sense, to the High Priest of Christianity. George Stanley Faber admits that the primacy was already claimed: "In the time of Tertullian, whose life extended into the third century, a considerable advance had plainly been made by the See of Rome, in the claim of the primacy, inasmuch as he calls the Bishop of that Church the supreme Pontiff, and distinguished him with the title of Bishop of bishops."‖

In combating this decree, Tertullian maintained that the power given to Peter did not regard the remission of sins, and that, whatever it was, it was conferred on him personally, not communicated to the Church at large, or even to the local Church, of which he was founder. While recognising the Roman Bishop as "Apostolic," that is, successor of the apostle, and the Roman Church as Peter's Church, he insists that the duties of the bishop "are merely disciplinary, to preside, not imperiously, but ministerially," and denies his right to exercise the power of forgiveness: "I now

---

* Euseb. l. v. Hist. Eccl. c. iii. † Cat. Script. Eccl. t. iv. 113.
‡ L. de pudicitia, c. 1.
§ Pontifex scilicet Maximus, quod est episcopus episcoporum. There is an inversion in the sentence, which is quite familiar to Tertullian.
‖ Difficulties of Romanism, by George Stanley Faber. Note, p. 261. Phil. edit.

ask your own sentiment, whence do you claim this power for the Church? "If, because the Lord said to Peter, 'on this rock I will build My Church,' 'to thee I have given the keys of the kingdom of heaven,' or, 'whatsoever thou shalt bind or loose upon earth, shall be bound or loosed in heaven,' you presume, on that account, that the power of loosing and binding has come down to you, that is, to the whole Church allied to Peter;* who are you, to overturn and change the manifest intention of the Lord, who conferred this on Peter personally? 'On thee,' he says, 'I will build My Church, AND TO THEE, (not to the Church,) I will give the keys, and whatsoever THOU shalt bind or loose, not what they shall bind or loose!"† This partisan effort to limit the promise to Peter personally, should meet with little sympathy from those who strive to extend it to all the apostles, and to all bishops: yet Faber triumphs in the sophistry of the Montanist, and remarks with complacency: "He flatly denies that it can be construed as belonging to what then began to be esteemed as PETER'S CHURCH."‡ It is unfair to speak of this as a nascent opinion, since Tertullian uses positive language, and elsewhere refers confidently to the succession of the Roman bishops from Peter, and the authority of their teaching. He is an unexceptionable witness of the claims of the Bishop of Rome in his time, and of the authority which he effectually exercised, and which was courted even by opponents, with a view to betray him into some measure favorable to their errors. It was felt in Phrygia, where the sect numbered a multitude of votaries; and in Africa, where it was assailed by the powerful logician whose subtilties we have exposed. At the same time it was venerated in Gaul, by the martyrs, who from their dungeons implored its exercise, to preserve the faith in its integrity.

§ 4.—CONTROVERSY CONCERNING BAPTISM.

The dispute concerning baptism administered by heretics rose to a high pitch of excitement in the middle of the third century. The various sects that denied the mystery of the Trinity, naturally introduced changes into the form of words used in baptizing, by which it was entirely vitiated; and, of course, no account was had of the act, when converts from them sought to be admitted to the Catholic Church. The custom of baptizing such persons was extended in some parts of Africa to converts from all the sects, even to such as had been baptized with the due form of words; which usage had received the sanction of Agrippinus, Bishop of Carthage, in a Council held early in this century. St. Cyprian, through horror for heresy, and love for Catholic unity, added his approval in several Councils, "reprobating the baptism of heretics, and sent the acts of an African synod held on this subject, to Stephen, who was at that time Bishop of the city of Rome."§ His ambassadors, however, were not received to com-

---

* Ad omnem ecclesiam Petri propinquam. † L. de pudicitia, c. xxi.
‡ Difficulties of Romanism, Note, p. 261. § St. Jerom, Dial. adv. Lucifer.

munion by the Pontiff, who was highly displeased at this attempt to establish a usage different from the general custom of the Church, founded on ancient tradition. In reply, he sent to Cyprian a command in these terms: "Let no change be made, contrary to what has been handed down." This decree was received with murmurs by the bishops of Africa. Cyprian at their head, in a subsequent Council, continued to adhere to the usage which he had previously sanctioned, professing, however, that he did not mean to force others to conform to his practice, since each was responsible to God for the administration of his diocese. "No one of us," he says, "constitutes himself a bishop of bishops, or, by tyrannical terror, compels his colleagues to the necessity of obedience, since every bishop enjoys his own judgment according to the liberty of his power, and can no more be judged by another, than he can judge another. Let us all await the judgment of our Lord Jesus Christ, who alone has the power both to place us in the government of His Church, and to judge of our conduct."* Were these words taken as they sound, they would suppose each bishop absolute and independent; whereas all antiquity attests that the action of individual bishops may be directed and controlled by synodical enactments—not to speak at present of the authority of the Holy See—and that delinquents may be removed for mal-administration, or misconduct. St. Cyprian, then, cannot be understood in this sense. He himself, as we shall hereafter see, had solicited the Pontiff to remove Marcian from Arles, and approved of the deposition of Basilides, which had been made in a Spanish Council. The liberty which he claimed was in matters not decided by the supreme authority of the Church, as St. Augustin testifies.† He stated, with complacency, that neither he himself, nor any of his African colleagues, acted as "bishop of bishops," because all were willing to allow a difference of sentiment and practice in the matter of baptism; which not conceiving to interest faith, they referred to the judgment of God; and he attached the more importance to their harmony in sentiment, as being totally unconstrained and uninfluenced. If he be supposed to use these terms sarcastically, with reference to Stephen, it must be allowed that this Pontiff claimed and exercised the authority of a superior. Such is the tenor of the extant documents, which are considered by most writers as genuine, although their authenticity was questioned by some so far back as the days of St. Augustin.‡

The practice of baptizing anew converts from heresy had also crept into some provinces of Asia, and "Stephen had written concerning Helenus, and Firmilian, and all the priests throughout Cilicia, Cappadocia, and all the neighboring provinces, that he would not communicate with them, for this same reason, that they rebaptized heretics."§ Dionysius, Bishop of

---

* Sententiæ episcoporum, lxxxvii. *de hær. bapt.*
† De Bapt. contra Donatistas, l. iii. c. iii.
‡ Ep. xciii. ad Vincentium Rogat. ¿ 38.
¿ Dionys. Alex. *apud Euseb. l. v. Hist. Eccl.*

Alexandria. who states the fact, wrote to Stephen, deprecating this severity.

This serious dispute shows the authority which the Bishop of Rome then exercised, and which, even when resisted, on account of its supposed abuse, was, in fact, acknowledged. The transmission of the proceedings of the African synod to Rome, was a marked testimony of the pre-eminence of the Roman Bishop; whose immediate action in the case proves that he conceived himself authorized to judge of the correctness of the canons, and to rescind them, when found in opposition to the general and ancient usages of the Church. It was viewed in this light by St. Vincent of Lerins, a profound writer of the fifth century, who points to it as an instance in which novelty was successfully opposed by the successors of Peter. "When, therefore, all cried out from all quarters against the novelty, and all priests, in every place, struggled against it, each according to his zeal, Pope Stephen, of blessed memory, who at that time was prelate of the Apostolic See, resisted, in conjunction, indeed, with his colleagues, but yet more than his colleagues, THINKING IT FIT, as I suppose, THAT HE SHOULD SURPASS ALL OTHERS IN THE DEVOTEDNESS OF HIS FAITH, AS MUCH AS HE EXCELLED THEM BY THE AUTHORITY OF HIS STATION. Finally, in the epistle which was then sent to Africa, he decreed in these words: that 'NO INNOVATION SHOULD BE ADMITTED, BUT THAT WHAT WAS HANDED DOWN, SHOULD BE RETAINED.' What force had the African Council or decree? None, through the mercy of God."*

The history of this controversy plainly proves, that on both sides it was maintained that Stephen held the place of Peter. We are asked how could Cyprian have dared resist, if he had regarded Stephen as his ecclesiastical superior? The answer is obvious: He believed that Stephen rashly employed his authority, to proscribe a practice intimately connected with the unity and sanctity of the Church. Respectful remonstrance is permitted, whenever authority is injudiciously exercised. Cyprian felt that to acknowledge the baptism of heretics was virtually to sanction heresy, by communicating to an adulteress the unalienable privileges of the pure Spouse of Christ; and resting on her acknowledged unity, he rejected the pretensions of every sect. Stephen, relying on ancient usage and tradition, condemned the novel practice, and the decree made in its support; yet he did not issue a formal definition of faith. St. Augustin confidently says, that Cyprian would have readily acquiesced, had the matter been placed in a clear light by the examination and decision of a general Council, which does not imply that he would have submitted to no other authority, but that by this means the general practice of the Church and her ancient tradition would have been clearly proved. In the facts of the case we have evidence of a most unequivocal exercise of superior power on the part of the Pontiff. On the other hand, we behold the advocates of

---

* Commonit. c. viii.

the novel usage deriving an argument against his conduct from his station as successor of St. Peter, and official guardian of Catholic unity. On this point Firmilian of Cappadocia especially relied, in his irreverent invective against the pontifical decree. "I am," said he, "justly indignant at this open and manifest folly of Stephen, who, while he boasts of the rank of his bishopric, and contends that he holds the succession of Peter, UPON WHOM THE FOUNDATIONS OF THE CHURCH WERE PLACED, brings in, nevertheless, many other rocks, and builds the new edifices of many churches, defending their baptism by his authority. The greatness of the error, and the strange blindness of him who says, that the remission of sins can be given in the synagogues of heretics, and does not abide on the foundation of the ONE CHURCH, WHICH WAS ORIGINALLY BUILT BY CHRIST ON THE ROCK, may be understood from this, that TO PETER ALONE CHRIST SAID: 'Whatsoever thou shalt bind on earth, shall be bound in heaven; and whatsoever thou shalt loose on earth, shall be loosed also in heaven.'"[*] Had the claims of Stephen to the place and power of Peter been questionable, Firmilian doubtless would have denied them, in order to show that the decree forbidding innovation was void of all authority; whereas he contents himself with drawing thence an argument for his error, and accuses Stephen of dishonoring the memory of the apostles Peter and Paul, whose place he occupied, by referring to them the usage of admitting the baptism of heretics. The language which he uses toward Stephen is an evidence of the warmth of feeling with which he defended his favorite practice, in opposition to the high authority which condemned it. Had it been in his power to deny the authority itself, he would surely have done it in no measured terms.

Writing to Jubaian, against baptism administered by heretics, ST. CYPRIAN maintained that the remission of sins cannot be imparted by it, because heretics have no share in the powers of forgiveness granted to Peter, the foundation of the Church, and the source of unity, which power was communicated to the other apostles likewise: "It is manifest where and through whom the remission of sins, namely, that which is given in baptism, can be given. FOR THE LORD GAVE THIS POWER IN THE FIRST PLACE TO PETER, ON WHOM HE BUILT HIS CHURCH, AND WHENCE HE ESTABLISHED AND SHOWED THE ORIGIN OF UNITY; that what he would loose on earth, should be loosed also in heaven. And after the resurrection, He speaks to the apostles likewise, saying: 'As the Father hath sent Me, I also send you.'"[†] "The Lord cries out: Let him that thirsteth, come and drink of the streams of living water that flow from Him. Whither shall he who thirsts come? Is it to heretics, where there is no fountain or river of living water, or to the Church, which is one, and WAS FOUNDED BY THE VOICE OF THE LORD UPON ONE, WHO ALSO RECEIVED ITS KEYS?"[‡] Although St. Cyprian, under the erroneous persuasion that

---

[*] Ep. Firmiliani inter Cyprian.   [†] Ep. lxxiii. § 7. Jubajano.   [‡] Ibidem, § 11.

baptism administered by heretics is not valid, uses these texts to establish this false position, his acknowledgment of the primacy is in no degree weakened by this circumstance. His admission that Peter was the rock on which Christ built His Church, and that he is the source of unity, is the more important, inasmuch as it was his interest to call it in question, while he resisted a mandate of the bishop, who, he acknowledged, held the place of Peter. "Custom," he says elsewhere, "must not be allowed to prescribe, but reason must prevail. For Peter, WHOM THE LORD CHOSE TO BE FIRST, AND ON WHOM HE BUILT HIS CHURCH, when Paul afterward disputed with him in regard to circumcision, neither insolently claimed, nor arrogantly assumed any thing, saying that he held the primacy, and should be obeyed by those who were recent in the faith and posterior to him in the order of time.* Nor did he despise Paul, because he had been a persecutor of the Church; but he admitted the counsel of truth, and readily agreed to the just reason which Paul alleged; giving us an example of concord and patience, that we should not obstinately cherish our own sentiments, but rather adopt as our own those which are sometimes usefully and wisely suggested by our brethren and colleagues."† This observation is evidently directed to show that Stephen should not rest on his superior authority; but rather imitate the condescension of Peter, who, waiving the consideration of his own primacy, yielded to the remonstrance of Paul.

Mr. Allies, with his accustomed candor, avowed that St. Cyprian acknowledged the primacy, notwithstanding his resistance to the decree of Stephen: "I most fully believe, be it observed, that Cyprian acknowledged the Roman primacy, that he admitted certain high prerogatives to be lodged in the Roman Pontiff, as St. Peter's successor, which did not belong to any other bishop."‡ If any thing occur in his writings apparently derogatory to the pontifical authority, we may decline replying to it in the words of Augustin: "I will not review what he uttered against Stephen in the heat of dispute."§

It is not certain that St. Cyprian finally conformed to the decree of St. Stephen. ST. JEROM says: that "his effort (*to change the ancient custom*) proved vain; and finally those very bishops, who with him had determined that heretics should be rebaptized, turning back to the ancient custom, issued a new decree."‖ St. Vincent of Lerins does not name him as the defender of the African usage. Eusebius does not state any act done by him in support of it, subsequently to the pontifical prohibition.¶ ST. AUGUSTIN supposes him to have retracted, if he at all entertained the er-

---

* Called after him to the apostolate.
† Cypr. ad Quint. Ep. lxxi. p. 297. Ed. Wirceb.
‡ Church of England Cleared, &c. p. 32.
§ L. v. Contra Donat. c. 25.
‖ Dial. adv. Lucifer.
¶ L. vii. c. iii. Hist. Eccl.

roneous views imputed to him, of which he insinuates a doubt, while he strongly insists that he persevered in unity, and atoned for his involuntary error, by the abundance of his charity, and the glory of his martyrdom. In reply to the Donatists, he says: "Cyprian either did not at all think, as you represent him to have thought, or he afterwards corrected the error by the rule of truth; or he covered this blemish of his fair breast with the abundance of his charity, while he defended most eloquently the unity of the Church spread throughout the whole world, and held most steadfastly the bond of peace."* "If this glorious branch," (*of the mystical vine,*) he elsewhere says, "had in this respect any need of any purification, it was cleansed by the pruning-knife of martyrdom, not because he was slain for the name of Christ, but because he was slain in the bosom of unity for the name of Christ; for he himself wrote, and most confidently asserted, that they who are out of unity, though they should die for that name, may be slain, but cannot be crowned."† "You are, indeed, accustomed to object to us the letters of Cyprian, the opinion of Cyprian, the Council of Cyprian: why do you take the authority of Cyprian for your schism, and reject his example for the peace of the Church?"‡

We shall take leave to add the reflections of Dr. Nevin on this controversy. "As it is, the whole case tells strongly in favor of the supremacy of the Roman See, and not against it as is sometimes pretended. How came Stephen to assert such authority, in opposition to whole provinces of the Church east and west, if it were not on the ground of previously acknowledged prerogative and right? Or how could the pretension do more than call forth derision, if no such ground existed for it in fact in the general mind of the Church? It is easy to talk of his presumption and pride, and of a regular system of usurpation kept up with success on the part of the Roman pontiffs generally. But that is simply to beg the whole question in dispute. The hypothesis is too violent. It destroys itself. Stephen was neither fool nor knave; and yet he must have been both on a grand scale, to play the part he did here out of mere wanton ambition, usurping powers to which he himself well knew, as all the world knew besides, he had no lawful claim whatever. Both Cyprian and Firmilian are themselves witnesses, in fact, that a true central authority did belong to the Bishop of Rome. What they complain of is its supposed abuse. They feel the force of it very plainly in spite of themselves. This is just what makes them so restive under its exercise. Had it been mere false pretension, they could have afforded to let it pass by them as the idle wind. They knew it however to be more than that. Then again, it turned out in the end that Stephen was in truth right. His judgment proved to be, with proper distinctions afterwards, the real voice of the Catholic Church, and has remained in full force down to the present time."§

---

* Ep. Vincent. † Ep. cviii. ad Macr.
‡ L. ii. de bapt. contra Donat. c. iii. p. 98. § "Cyprian," M. R. November, 1852.

§ 5.—DONATISM.

The Donatists were originally engaged in a mere personal contest, in which the disappointed ambition of Majorinus was chiefly interested. They sought to induce the Emperor Constantine to second their efforts against Cecilian, the Catholic Bishop of Carthage, who had been ordained by Felix of Aptugna, a bishop whom they accused of having delivered the sacred books to the heathens in time of persecution. "Constantine," says St. Augustin, "not daring to judge a bishop, committed to bishops the trial and decision of the case: which took place in the city of Rome, Melchiades, Bishop of that Church, presiding, amid many of his colleagues."* The emperor ordered the parties to sail to Rome, and present themselves before the Bishop of that See, with three bishops of Gaul, as was conformable to the Divine law.† This law required that a bishop should be judged, not by a secular tribunal, but by bishops, in a case where the very title to his office depended on the issue of the trial. The same law constituted the Bishop of Rome chief or supreme judge, whence the sentence is ascribed to him by St. Augustin and St. Optatus. The dignity of the See of Carthage, to which the primacy of all the African churches was attached, rendered it fit that the charges against its prelate should, in the first instance, be laid before the highest tribunal.

That Melchiades sat in judgment of his own right as the highest ecclesiastical judge, appears from the freedom with which he acted, in selecting a number of Italian bishops to aid him in the trial. The Donatists had sought to induce Constantine to submit the case for examination to the bishops of Gaul, where persecution had not raged under Constantius Chlorus; from which circumstance they affected to hope for a more impartial investigation of the alleged guilt of the African bishops. The emperor so far yielded to their importunities as to associate with Melchiades three bishops of that nation; but the Pontiff feeling that their presence was intended to satisfy the Donatists of the impartiality of the trial, without interfering with the rights of his see, summoned fifteen Italian bishops to unite with them in hearing the cause: a liberty which he could not have taken, had he been a mere delegate. He thus plainly showed, that the imperial commission was not designed to add to, or take from his official authority, although it was calculated to give civil force to his sentence, and secure its execution.

The moderation and indulgence of Melchiades in the case of the Donatists are justly admired by St. Augustin. A secular judge rigorously decides according to the letter of the law, and the merits of the case, having generally no power to qualify or mitigate the sentence. The ecclesiastical judge has truth and justice always in view; but he is empowered to tem-

---

* Epist. cv. olim. xvi.   † Vide ep. Constantini Miltiadi.

per the exercise of justice, so as to procure the salvation of the guilty, and dispose them for submission, not only by remitting the penalty, but even by extending favor. Thus it was that Melchiades, after he had pronounced Cecilian innocent, undertook to conciliate his prosecutors. "How admirable," exclaims AUGUSTIN, "was the final sentence of Melchiades! how faultless! how upright! how provident and peaceful! By it he did not venture to remove from the college of bishops his colleagues, against whom nothing had been proved; but, having passed special censure on Donatus alone, whom he had found to be the author of the whole disorder, he gave to the others the opportunity of regaining a sound state, being ready to give letters of communion even to such as were known to have been ordained by Majorinus; so that wherever there were two bishops, in consequence of the dissension, he ordered him who had been first ordained to be confirmed in the see, and another flock to be committed to the government of the other. O! excellent man! O! child of Christian peace, and father of the Christian people!"* The power and authority of Melchiades are manifest from this decision. He regulates the claims of the contending parties, and requires from some such sacrifice of rights as is necessary to promote harmony. For the general interests of Christian unity, he removes bishops to other sees, according to the accidental circumstance of priority of ordination. In a word, he arranges the affairs of the distant churches of Africa with entire freedom, but with a strict regard to charity and peace.

The complaints of the Donatists to Constantine of the injustice of the Roman sentence appear to some to have assumed the form of an appeal; which, however, was not strictly the case, since it is not usual for judges, from whose sentence the appeal is lodged, to sit in the higher court, and revise the cause with their colleagues.† It is certain that Constantine granted a new trial, which may be more properly called a *revision* of the proceedings, to take place in a numerous assembly at Arles, in which the Roman judges were present, and Melchiades was represented by his legates. This was a measure which the emperor declared to be altogether unnecessary; but he wished to confound the boldness of the Donatists, by the number of their judges, who, he felt confident, would renew the sentence already passed on them. The matter as yet was personal, rather than doctrinal: the trial of a bishop was acknowledged to be of ecclesiastical cognizance: Constantine could well have closed their mouths for ever, by insisting on the execution of the Roman sentence; but he suffered himself to be importuned, until he granted that which was irregular. The weakness of the prince, who was not yet a Christian, only served to show forth more splendidly the eminent dignity of the Pontiff; who, consenting

---

* Ep. xliii. olim. clxii. n. 16.
† This however, takes place in the Supreme Court of the United States.

to the revision of the cause, despatched his legates to preside in his place, being unwilling to leave any thing untried which could place the facts in clearer light, and lead the misguided to the peace and unity of the Church. It is true that St. Augustin does not, in stating these facts, expressly censure the conduct of the emperor in granting a new trial, but no doubt can be entertained that he deemed it irregular, since, when the Pelagians, after their condemnation by Pope Innocent, clamored for a new examination of their doctrines, he cried out: "Why do you still seek an investigation, which has already taken place before the Apostolic See?"[*]

In the Council which was held at Arles in 314, bishops were assembled from Sicily, Campania, Apulia, Dalmatia, Italy, Gaul, Britain, Spain, Mauritania, Sardinia, Africa, and Numidia, who, at the conclusion of their proceedings, addressed "the most beloved, most glorious Pope, Sylvester," in terms of deserved reverence, denoting his apostolic authority: "Would to God, most beloved brother, you had been present at this great spectacle! we feel convinced that a severer sentence would have been passed on them, (*the Donatists;*) and you sitting in judgment with us, our assembly would have experienced greater exultation. But you could not leave those parts WHERE THE APOSTLES SIT, (*in judgment,*) and their blood[†] incessantly attests the Divine glory."[‡] The fathers made known to the Pontiff their decrees on various points, that through him, who had the great dioceses[§] under his charge, they might be communicated to all the churches. The greater power of the Roman Bishop appears from the severity of the sentence which was expected from him; and his office, as successor of the apostles, is clearly marked as the source of his authority.

The Donatists appealed, as in a secular and profane cause, to the final judgment of the emperor, who, yielding again to their solicitations, took cognizance of it, but confirmed the decision.

I am not obliged to prove, that Melchiades, of his own right, could have tried and judged the African bishops, without the aid of any Council, or the liberty of appeal. It is enough for my present purpose, that the eminent authority of the Roman Bishop was manifest in the proceedings, and that he exercised a power which the emperor could not delegate, by his enactment in regard to the Donatist bishops returning to unity.

Thus it is clear, that in the chief controversies of the second, third, and fourth centuries, the authority of the Roman Bishop was exercised and

---

[*] Oper. imperf. contra Julianum, l. ii. c. ciii.
[†] The memory of their martyrdom.
[‡] Ep. ii. Syn. Arelat.
[§] "Qui majores diœceses tenes." From the ancient plot of the empire, (*Vetus Notitia Imperii*) it appears that the six provinces of the West were so styled, namely, Africa, Illyricum, Italy, Spain, Gaul, and Britain.

admitted. To imagine that he interfered in Asia and in Africa, and menaced the bishops with excommunication, without having any authority superior to theirs, is to indulge in the speculations of fancy against the evidence of facts. To ascribe his authority to ecclesiastical arrangement, is to mistake its character altogether, since it was exercised before any General Council had been convened, and was always referred, not only by its claimants, but even by those who, in particular cases, opposed it, to a divine origin, namely, the privileges bestowed by Christ on Peter.

CHAPTER XI.

Guardianship of Faith.

§ 1.—CONSTANCY OF THE HOLY SEE.

As the confession of the divinity of Christ gave occasion to the sublime promise of the primacy, and the prayer of Christ was offered for Peter that his faith might not fail, it is the chief duty of his successors to guard with jealous care the integrity of divine revelation. St. Chrysostom says that "Christ ordained Peter teacher of the world."* Theophylact, a Greek writer of the eleventh century, thus paraphrases the address of our Lord to Peter at the last supper: "Since I regard thee as prince of the disciples, after thou shalt have wept for denying Me, confirm thy brethren, for it behoves thee to do so, since thou, after Me, art the rock and foundation of the Church."† This duty has been strictly discharged by the Bishops of Rome, whose primacy has been signally exercised in proclaiming the divine truths without reserve, and proscribing every error opposed to them. In the confidence that the prayer of Christ was effectual, each Pontiff exercised his high prerogative, giving to Him the glory: "What He asked He obtained," says INNOCENT III., speaking of the prayer of Christ, "since He was always heard for His reverence: on which account the faith of the Apostolic See has never failed in any difficulty, but has always remained entire and undefiled, that the privilege of Peter might continue inviolate."‡

From a very early period, heretics sought to corrupt the doctrine of the Roman Church, whose faith, even before St. Paul visited it, was celebrated throughout the whole world; but in nothing has the providence of God been more manifest, than in its preservation, and in the energy with which the Roman Bishops have maintained it. They can affirm with propriety that their weapons "are powerful through God to the destruction of fortifications, subverting of counsels, and every height that exalteth itself against the knowledge of God, and bringing into captivity every understanding to the obedience of Christ, and having in readiness to revenge every disobedience."§ In condemning error, the Pope is guided by the tradition of the Roman Church, derived from her founders, as St. Irenæus

---

* Τῆς οἰκουμένης ἐχειροτόνησε διδάσκαλον. Hom. lxxxviii. in Joan. t. viii. p. 527, edit. Montf.
† In Luc. xxii.   ‡ Serm. ii. in consecr. Pont. Max.   § 2 Cor. x. 4.

states, and by the tradition of all the churches, which, being in close communion with him, concur in their testimony. The faith of which he is the guardian, is not his mere private sentiment, much less his conjecture; but that which the Father revealed, and which having been once delivered to the Saints, can never be lost, or adulterated, while the promises of Christ retain their force. It is not any prevailing opinion among the clergy of Rome which he proposes to be believed; but that doctrine which is contained in the symbols of faith, and in other authoritative documents, which, together with his colleagues throughout the world, he has received from his predecessors. When Leo sent to Flavian, Bishop of Constantinople, the exposition of the mystery of the Incarnation, he only undertook to state "what the Catholic Church universally believes and teaches," as he declared in his letter to the emperor Theodosius.* The Pope receives and venerates the doctrinal definitions made in General Councils, even as he venerates the four Gospels;† and he claims no power to take from the original deposit of revelation, or to add to it, or to remove the limits which the fathers have placed. It is his duty to watch over the entire kingdom of Christ, from the high tower on which he is placed as sentinel, and to sound the alarm when the enemy approaches. Heresy, in every shape and form, instinctively hates him, since, as Bossuet remarks, he always strikes the first or final blow at every innovation. Before the middle of the second century, Valentine, Cerdon, and Marcion came from the East to Rome, and endeavored to spread there, in public and in private, their heresies, which were levelled at the very foundations of Christianity. The integrity of the Roman faith suffered nothing from their attempts; so that Cerdon, despairing of success, dissembled his errors, professed repentance, and underwent public humiliation in the Church, in order to obtain her communion: but his hypocrisy being laid open, he was again forced to flee from the assembly of the faithful.‡ The heresies of Marcion, and his flagitious conduct, prevented his being restored to communion. Montanism also, as we have seen, was effectually opposed by the Bishop of Rome. Sectaries knew him to be the authorized and supreme teacher of the Church, and the faithful revered him as the guardian of revelation against every assailant.

§ 2.—CHIEF MYSTERIES.

The divinity of Christ was triumphantly maintained in all ages, by the successors of Peter, against the subtle errors by which it was from time to time impugned. At the close of the second century, Theodotus, a currier of Byzantium, during the rage of persecution, had the weakness to deny Christ; and subsequently, as if to extenuate his crime, he added heresy

---

* Ep. xxix.   † St. Gregory M. Ep. xxv. alias xxiv. ad Joan. Cp.
‡ Irenæus, l. iii. c. iv.

to apostasy, alleging that Christ was but man. The zeal of Pope Victor led him to cut off the heresiarch from the communion of the church.* Zephyrinus, who succeeded him, and who was an equally strenuous defender of the faith, admitted to communion Artemon, a bishop of the sect, after a public abjuration of the profane error. "Clothed with sackcloth, with ashes sprinkled on his head, and with tears in his eyes, he cast himself at the feet of Bishop Zephyrinus—and with difficulty was received to communion."†

Dionysius, Bishop of Alexandria, fell under suspicion of entertaining erroneous opinions in regard to the same mystery, so that, as St. Athanasius informs us, some of his brethren went to Rome, and accused him before his namesake, the bishop of that city.‡ The accused prelate, far from denying the competency of the tribunal, sent a satisfactory exposition of his faith. Such was the acknowledged authority of the Roman Bishop in the middle of the third century. In a Roman synod held on this occasion, the orthodox faith was solemnly defined.

During the violent and long struggle with Arianism in all its forms, the Holy See was the constant defender of the Nicene faith. To this symbol, as final and essential, reference was always made by the Pontiffs and their legates; by which means the artifices of the Arians and Semiarians were effectually defeated. They spoke of the 318 fathers of the Council of Nice, as of the host of faithful Abraham, by whom the enemies of the divinity of Christ were routed; and they adhered to their definition as made under the guidance of the Holy Ghost. While many bishops proved recreant to their trust, and either openly abandoned the ancient faith, or exposed it to corruption by the profane novelty of words, the successor of Peter, constantly rejecting every suggestion of expediency, whereby the divine truth might be endangered, held to the form of sound words delivered by the Nicene fathers, and acknowledged Jesus Christ to be GOD OF GOD, LIGHT OF LIGHT, TRUE GOD OF TRUE GOD, CONSUBSTANTIAL WITH THE FATHER. Amid the perplexity which distressed pious minds on seeing Arians intruded by imperial power into many episcopal sees, it was consolatory to hear the successor of Peter proclaiming, without hesitation and without disguise, the divine truth which the apostle learned from the Father. Ursacius and Valens obtained communion from Julius, on renouncing the Arian heresy, embracing the communion of Athanasius, and promising not to be present without permission of the Pope, at any

---

* Irenæus, l. iii. c. iv. n. 3. Euseb. l. iv. c. xxviii. Theodor. l. ii. hær. fab.

† Ex antiqui scriptoris libro adversus Artemonis hær. apud Constant. Epist. Rom. Pontif. vol. i. col. 110.

‡ "Romam ascenderunt, ibique eum apud Dionysium ejusdem nominis Romanum præsulem accusaverunt." De Sent. Dionys. Alex. p. 345. Also de Syn Nic. p. 371. Bishop Bull makes mention of "the Roman synod held under their Bishop Dionysius, in the cause of Dionysius of Alexandria, who was accused by some of the Church of Pentapolis of denying the consubstantiality of the Son of God." Discourse iv. p. 189, vol. ii. Oxford Edit. 1816.

Eastern synod, even if called to it by their former partisans to account for their return to Catholic unity. They declare to him that they were encouraged by his clemency to renounce the sect; "because your Holiness, according to your innate goodness, has vouchsafed to pardon our error;"* and they submit to him a profession of faith, to satisfy him of their orthodoxy. Afterward they were again cut off from the church by Damasus, on their relapse into heresy.† In these acts we have the clearest evidence that the Roman Bishop, as the highest judge and guardian of faith, exercised unequivocal authority over other bishops.

It was alleged, and for a long time admitted without contradiction, that LIBERIUS, whom Constantius drove into exile for his attachment to the true faith, purchased his liberty and regained his see by the sacrifice of his principles and conscience. His defence of orthodoxy before, as well as after his banishment, is unquestionable, and he is known to have rescinded, by the authority of the blessed Peter, the acts of the Council of Rimini. The want of his sanction is relied on by Damasus, in his letter to the Bishops of Illyricum, as proof of the invalidity of the decrees, since "the Roman Bishop, whose sentiment above all should be regarded, did not consent to them."‡ I am not interested in denying his fall; for the weakness of a prisoner, however culpable, cannot destroy the prerogatives of the successor of Peter, when acting with the freedom of authority; but the account given by Theodoret, a Greek historian almost contemporary, leaves no doubt on my mind that it was a fiction of the Arians, which was believed on mere popular rumor, and received without examination by subsequent ages. St. Athanasius informs us, that the zeal of Liberius against Arianism excited the abettors of this heresy to make efforts to corrupt him, knowing the influence of his station and example: "If we succeed," said they, "in gaining Liberius to our opinion, we shall soon overcome all."§ Constantius commissioned the eunuch Eusebius to treat with him, in order to induce him to condemn Athanasius; but he proved inflexible: "Such is not," he replied, "the tradition which we have from the fathers, and which they received from the blessed and great apostle Peter."‖ Insisting on the reception of the Nicene faith, before he would admit any to communion, he preferred exile to the occupancy of his see, if the betrayal of his duty were the condition on which it depended. His replies to the emperor, at the audience at Milan, which display the greatest intrepidity, are recorded with praise by Theodoret.¶ When Constantius promised that he should return to his see, provided he made peace with the Oriental bishops, the enemies of Athanasius, Liberius answered: "I have already bidden farewell to the brethren at Rome, for the laws of the church are dearer to me than my residence at Rome."

---

* Ep. v. apud Constant. t. i. col. 405.   † Ep. ad Afros.
‡ Ep. iii. t. i. Constant. col. 486.   § Ad vitam solit. agentes.
‖ Athanas. hist. Arian. ad monach. n. 37.   ¶ L. ii. Hist. Eccl. c. xv. xvi.

That Liberius never swerved from this determination is perceived from Theodoret, who says: "The glorious champion of truth went therefore into Thrace, as was ordered." His return is ascribed by the historian to the entreaties of the Roman matrons, who presented themselves in a body to Constantius, on his visit to Rome, in 357. The emperor wished, indeed, that Felix, whom he had intruded into the see, should share with Liberius the administration; but the people cried out: "ONE GOD, ONE CHRIST, ONE BISHOP." "After these pious and just acclamations of the most Christian people, the admirable Liberius returned."* It is utterly improbable, that Constantius should have promised to the people to restore Liberius, and yet made the execution of his promise depend on the fulfilment of a condition repugnant to the faith and principles of the people, as well as of the Pontiff! It is unlikely that Theodoret should have known nothing of such terms, or knowing them, should have passed them over in silence, and heaped praise on Liberius! Sulpicius Severus, a cotemporary writer,† and Socrates,‡ ascribe his return to seditions of the Romans; which is easily reconcilable with the statement of Theodoret, since the fear of tumult may have concurred to dispose the emperor to lend an ear to the supplications of the matrons. Sozomen says that "the Roman people ardently loved Liberius, a man in all respects illustrious, who bravely resisted the emperor in the cause of religion."§ ST. ATHANASIUS says of Liberius and Osius: "They preferred to suffer every calamity, rather than betray the truth, or our cause."‖ St. Jerom testifies that the Roman people, who were utterly opposed to the Arians, went forth to meet him on his return, and that he entered the city in triumph.¶ Nevertheless, if his writings be not interpolated, Jerom believed the reports spread by the Arians, of the criminal condescension by which Liberius obtained his liberty; but his opinion can scarcely counterbalance the inference which the triumphant reception of the returning Pontiff warrants, or the positive testimonies of Theodoret, Socrates, and Sulpitius. The passages in Athanasius which affirm the fall of Liberius, appear to be interpolations, since they do not at all harmonize with his assertion concerning the continued sufferings of the Pontiff for his cause. The fragments of Hilary, which pronounce anathema to Liberius, are evidently supposititious, and unworthy of the great writer to whom they have been ascribed.**

Liberius, although himself free from reproach, showed lenity to the bishops who, in the Council of Rimini, had been beguiled by the artful professions of the Arians, and coerced into acquiescence. Writing to the bishops of Italy, he declares that the authors of the deception should be treated with severity; but that those who had been the victims of fraud

---

* L. ii. c. xvii. † L. ii. Hist. Sacr. ‡ L. ij. Hist. c. xxxvii.
§ L. iv. Hist. c. xv. ‖ Apol. ii. ¶ In Chronico.
** See Dissertazione di Giosafatte Massari sopra la favolosa caduta di Liberio xi. nella Raccolta di Zaccaria, t. iii.

and violence, should be allowed to retain their sees, on making anew the profession of the Catholic and Apostolic faith, as declared at Nice.*

Sozomen tells us that Eustathius of Sebaste, Silvanus of Tarsus, and Theophilus of Castabala, were sent as ambassadors from Lampsacus, Smyrna, Pamphylia, Isauria, and Lycia, where Councils had been held, to Liberius and the bishops of the West, to beseech them to concert measures, and correct whatever was amiss in the Eastern churches, "since they (the Western bishops) retained the true and lasting faith delivered by the apostles, and ought, above all others, to interest themselves in the concerns of religion."† Liberius, in the beginning, repelled them, as the known enemies of the Nicene faith; but on their declaring that they had abandoned Arianism, and subscribed the Nicene creed, he admitted them to communion. In their address they style him: "Lord brother and fellow-priest." In the reply written by him, in his own name, and in the name of the Western bishops, he proclaims the faith of Nice, and condemns with anathema the blasphemies of Rimini.‡

The faith and sanctity of Liberius are testified by St. Ambrose, who speaks of him as a man of great holiness and blessed memory: § without any intimation that he had ever betrayed the cause of truth. There is, then, the strongest reason for regarding him as the constant and faithful defender of the Nicene creed, which his predecessors had gloriously maintained.

The influence and authority of the Bishop of Rome in controversies of faith were fully recognised in the East at this period. Soon afterward the heresy of Macedonius, Bishop of Constantinople, who denied the divinity of the Holy Ghost, called for the exercise of the apostolic authority. "When this question was agitated," says Sozomen, "and the excitement daily increased, the Bishop of the city of Rome, being informed of it, wrote to the churches of the East, that, together with the Western bishops, they should confess the consubstantial Trinity, equal in honor and glory. All acquiesced in this; the controversy being terminated by the judgment of the Roman Church, and the question appeared to be at an end."‖

Apollinaris, Bishop of Laodicea in Syria, in the decline of the fourth century, denied that the Divine Word had assumed a human soul. Damasus, Bishop of Rome, was the first to condemn the error, as Sozomen testifies. Peter, the patriarch of Alexandria, driven from his see, fled to Rome for redress, and was present at the Council in which this heresy was condemned.¶ The heretic and his disciple Timothy were both deposed by the judgment of the Apostolic See.** The decree of faith was received and subscribed by Meletius, Bishop of Antioch, and by more than one hundred and fifty Oriental bishops, in a synod held at Antioch, in the

---

* Ep. xiii. inter ep. Rom. Pont. Constant. t. i. col. 450.   † Sozomen l. vi. c. xi.
‡ Ep. xv. Constant. t. i. col. 458.   § De Virginibus, l. iii. c. i.
‖ L. vi. c. xxii.   ¶ Ibidem, vi. c. xxv.
** Ep. Damasi, xiv. ad Orientales.

year 379, in terms most expressive of unqualified adhesion to the doctrine. At the end of the decree it is said: "This is the end of the epistle, or exposition, of the Roman synod held under Pope Damasus, and transmitted to the East, with which the whole Eastern Church, having held a synod at Antioch, agrees, believing the same faith; all of whom consenting to the faith so explained, severally confirm it by their subscription." The first subscription, which is that of the patriarch himself, is in these terms: "I, Meletius, Bishop of Antioch, agree to all that is written, believing and thinking in like manner; and if any one think otherwise, let him be anathema."*

Even the civil authority looked up to the Roman See as a sure guide in all that appertained to faith. The Emperor Theodosius, about the year 380, issued a decree to this effect: "We wish all the nations governed by our clemency to profess the religion which was delivered to the Romans by the apostle Peter, as the religion handed down by him to the present time declares: and which is manifestly followed by Pope Damasus, and by Peter, Bishop of Alexandria, a man of apostolic holiness;† namely, that according to the apostolic institution, and evangelical doctrine, we should believe the one Deity of the Father, and Son, and Holy Ghost, with equal majesty and venerable Trinity."‡ The reason why the name of the Bishop of Alexandria was united with that of the Pope, was not only the dignity of his see, but likewise his well-known orthodoxy, since he had been present at the Roman Council, in which the doctrine had been defined. The high authority of the Pontiff suffers nothing from the concurrence and support of his colleagues.

While the Roman Bishop was thus regarded as the legitimate expounder of the faith, he scrupulously adhered to the symbol of Nice, and required its unqualified subscription from all who desired his communion. ST. BASIL, speaking of Eustathius, and his adherents, reproaches him with deviating from the Nicene faith, which he had subscribed at Rome, a copy of which he had brought back with him to the East: "I am surprised," he says, "that they do not reflect that the confession of the faith of Nice, which they subscribed, is preserved at Rome, and that with their own hands they presented to the synod of Tyana the book from Rome, which we still have, containing the same faith. They have forgotten their own harangue on that occasion, when, advancing to the middle of the assembly, they mourned over the mistake, into which they had been betrayed, in subscribing the document prepared by the faction of Eudoxius; wherefore, they thought on this plea for their error, that GOING TO ROME, THEY MIGHT THERE RECEIVE THE FAITH OF THE FATHERS, so as by introducing

---

* Ep. iv. apud Coustant. t. l. col. 500. Vide supra, p. 105.
† Dr. Jarvis strangely mistakes him for another Peter, who had suffered martyrdom eighty years before! Reply to Dr. Milner, p. 189.
‡ L. i. Cod. de Fide Catholica. Vide et Sozomen, l. vii. Hist. Eccl. c. iv.

a better formulary, to repair the evil which they had caused to the churches by their previous assent to error."* Rome, then, was acknowledged to be the incorrupt guardian of the faith of the fathers, so that those who drank of her pure fountain, were qualified for spreading revealed truth in its integrity, throughout those regions in which error had before prevailed. The Roman Bishop, acting as the superior of the Eastern bishops, who applied to him for the privileges of communion, insisted that they should give unequivocal evidence of orthodoxy, by subscribing the Nicene creed; and he caused the document to be recorded, that it might serve to confound them, in case they should ever relapse into the errors which they had abjured.

The authority of the Apostolic See was constantly invoked in all the controversies which, in the fourth and fifth centuries, agitated the East, about the great mysteries of the Trinity and Incarnation. It was manifested in the case of Vitalis, a priest of Antioch, who, having fallen under suspicion, repaired to Rome, and by using Catholic language, succeeded in gaining the approbation of Damasus, by whom, however, he was remanded with letters referring his case to the discretion of his bishop. Subsequently, toward the close of the year 378, in consequence of doubts raised concerning his sincerity, a Roman synod was held, from which a decree of faith issued, which Damasus sent to Paulinus, Bishop of Antioch, requiring Vitalis and his adherents to subscribe it, if they wished to enjoy Catholic communion.†

These are most solemn evidences that the Bishop of Rome was considered throughout the Eastern churches as well as in the West, as the chief guardian and expounder of the faith. From all parts recourse was had to him: every novel error was denounced to him: priest and prelate were alike subject to his judgment. He propounded the mysteries of faith in all their plenitude, declaring anathema to the gainsayers, and requiring assent to his doctrinal definitions as a necessary condition for enjoying ecclesiastical communion. The Eastern patriarch, with his whole synod of bishops, received the pontifical decree with reverence, subscribed it without reserve, and gloried in harmonizing in faith with the successor of Peter.

The mystery of the Incarnation of the Divine Word, which infinitely transcends the sublimest conceptions of the human mind, was from the beginning an occasion of scandal to such as did not absolutely and unreservedly adhere to the simplicity of revelation. The apostle St. John declares, that "the Word was made flesh, and dwelt among us; ‡ and St. Paul says, that "being in the form of God, he thought it no robbery Himself to be equal to God; but debased Himself, taking the form of a servant, being made to the likeness of men, and in shape found as a man."§

---

* Ep. ccxliv. Patrophilo.   † Ep. v. Constant. col. 507.
‡ John i. 14.   § Phil. ii. 6.

The Church has always believed that the Divine Person of the Word assumed human nature in the womb of the Virgin, so that the same Person is at once true God and true man. Nestorius ventured to sound the depth of this mystery, and listening to the whisperings of reason, fancied that the human nature of Christ had a distinct subsistence, or personality, and was only morally united with the Divine Nature and Person, which, he said, dwelt in it, as in a temple. His pride revolted at the thought of attributing to God, even in an assumed nature, birth, sufferings, and death, such as Catholics were wont to ascribe to the Divine Word in human flesh. This error, which impugned the Incarnation itself, and destroyed the infinite value of the atonement, in Constantinople, where it was first broached, met with vehement opposition on the part of the laity, as well as of the clergy; and the report of the scandal having reached Alexandria, St. Cyril, its illustrious patriarch, wrote with learning and zeal against the profane novelty. Feeling entire confidence that he was maintaining the truth originally delivered, he did not hesitate to hurl anathema against the various forms of this recent error; yet knowing his own place in the Church of God, and the respect which he owed to superior authority, he sent his writings on this subject to Celestine, observing that he had not openly withdrawn from the communion of Nestorius, awaiting the instructions of the Pontiff, which he begged might be communicated to all the Eastern bishops: "We do not withdraw from his communion openly, until we communicate the facts to your Holiness. Wherefore vouchsafe to declare to us your judgment, and whether we should at all hold communion with him, or openly forbid any one to communicate with him, while he holds and teaches such sentiments. It behoveth the judgment of your Holiness to be manifested by letter to the bishops most reverend and most beloved of God, throughout Macedonia, and to all the bishops of the East."* In the Roman Council, held in the year 430, St. Celestine quoted Ambrose, Hilary, and Damasus, as harmonizing with Cyril in their expositions of the mystery, and showed that the error of Nestorius had been condemned by anticipation, by his predecessor Damasus, in the decree which he had sent to Paulinus of Antioch.† In his letter to Cyril, he declares that the putrid member must be cut off, and that Nestorius must not hope to enjoy his communion, if he persevere in his opposition to the apostolic doctrine.‡

To Nestorius himself, CELESTINE addressed a solemn letter, threatening him with excommunication, unless he speedily retracted his error: "Know then," he wrote, "that this is our decree, that unless you preach concerning Christ our God what the Church of Rome, and of Alexandria, and the whole Catholic Church holds, and what the holy Church of the great city

---

* Ep. Cyril. viii. ad Cœlest. t. i. col. 1094, Constant.
† Arnobius, l. ii. de conflictu cum Serap.
‡ Ep. xi. t. i. col. 1106, Constant.

of Constantinople has steadfastly maintained until your time; and unless, by an explicit confession in writing, you condemn this perfidious novelty, which attempts to separate what the holy Scripture unites, you are cast forth from the communion of the entire Catholic Church." At the same time he wrote to Cyril, directing him to act as his vicar, and use the authority of the Apostolic See, together with his own, and charged him most strictly to execute the sentence of excommunication, if Nestorius should not retract within the time specified. He also informed John of Antioch, Juvenal of Jerusalem, Rufus of Thessalonica, and Flavian of Philippi, of the measures adopted against the new heresy. "We have separated from our communion the Bishop Nestorius, and all who follow him in his preaching, until he shall condemn, by a written profession of faith, the perverse error which he has broached, and shall declare that he holds the faith which, conformably to the apostolic doctrine, the Roman and Alexandrian and Catholic universal* Church holds, and venerates, and preaches, concerning the birth from the Virgin, that is, concerning the salvation of the human race." "Know that this sentence has been passed by us—rather by Christ our God—concerning the said Nestorius, that, within ten days from the day on which he shall be notified hereof, he must condemn in writing his sacrilegious preaching concerning the nativity of Christ, and profess that he follows the faith of the Roman and Alexandrian and Universal Church, or, being removed from the college of bishops, understand that his own pernicious error has caused his ruin."†

Whoever wishes to comprehend fully what degree of authority in matters of faith the Roman Church claimed and exercised in the early part of the fifth century, needs only peruse these documents, and consider the action of the Council of Ephesus. When the letter of Celestine was read in that venerable assembly of two hundred bishops from various parts, exclamations burst forth on all sides: "This is a just judgment—to Celestine, the guardian of the faith—to Celestine, who harmonizes with the synod—to Celestine, the whole synod returns thanks. There is one Celestine—one Cyril—the faith of the synod is one—the faith of the world is one." No greater tribute could be paid to the Apostolic See. The fathers were eager to induce Nestorius to abjure his error, embrace the pontifical definition, and thus escape censure: but the heresiarch, relying on the support of John of Antioch, and other Eastern bishops, who were personally attached to him, refused to obey the summons for trial. They accordingly proceeded, although with reluctance, to the fearful duty enjoined on them to cut him off from communion, "constrained so to do," say they, "by the canons and by the letter of our most holy father and fellow-minister, Celestine, Bishop of the Church of Rome."‡ All this took place before

---

* The latter term is used as explanatory of the former.
† Ep. xii. apud Coustant. t. i. col. 1111.
‡ Hard. col. conc. t. i. p. 1462.

the arrival of the legates, whom the Pope had despatched to preside in the Council with Cyril, his legate extraordinary. When they appeared, Juvenal, Bishop of Jerusalem, inquired of them whether they had read over the act of deposition. Philip, the priest, one of the legates, replied that they had, and that they felt satisfied that all had been done in strict accordance with the canons; yet he requested that the acts should be read anew in the Council, that, in compliance with the orders received from Celestine, they might confirm what had been decreed!* The request was granted without difficulty: and the decrees having been read, the legate thus began the confirmatory sentence: "It is not doubted by any one, but rather it was well known in all ages, that the holy and most blessed Peter, the prince† and head of the apostles, the pillar of faith, and the foundation of the Catholic Church, received from our Lord Jesus Christ, the Saviour and Redeemer of mankind, the keys of the kingdom: and power to bind and loose sins was given to him, who, down to the present time and for ever, LIVES AND JUDGES in his successors. His successor, then, in regular order, the occupant of his place, our holy and most blessed Pope, the Bishop Celestine, has sent us to this holy synod to supply his presence." The legate proceeds to state the obstinacy of Nestorius, who suffered the time prescribed by the Apostolic See to elapse, without retracting his error; and then, ratifying the act of the Council, he declares that the sentence passed against him, by the consent of the bishops of the East and of the West, IS FIRM, and that he is cut off from the communion of the Catholic Church. The other two legates spoke to the same effect, after whom Cyril, the patriarch of Alexandria, proposed that the proceedings of both sessions should be presented to the legates for subscription. Arcadius, one of them, observed that the proceedings of the holy synod were such that they could not but confirm them. The synod replied, that as the legates had spoken in a manner becoming them, it now remained for them to fulfil their promise, and subscribe the acts, which they accordingly did. Thus in all things was seen, as Philip the legate observed, the union of the holy members with their holy head, "for you," he said, addressing the fathers, "are not ignorant that the BLESSED APOSTLE PETER IS THE HEAD OF ALL FAITH, OR EVEN OF THE APOSTLES."‡

No more solemn and splendid testimony could be given of the general belief at that period of the divine institution of the primacy. The bishops who composed this venerable assembly, with the exception of the Roman legates, were oriental or African: yet they heard, without a murmur, the strong assertions of the legates concerning the prerogatives of Peter and his successors; they submitted their acts to them for confirmation—and

---

* Ὅπως ἡμεῖς ἀκολυθήσαντες τῷ τύπῳ του ἁγιωτάτου Πάπα Κελεςίνου—δυνηθῶμεν τα κεκριμένα βεβαιῶσαι.

† Ἔξαρχος.—Actione 3, Conc. Eph. p. 1476 and 1477. Tom. i. Hard. Col.

‡ Ἡ κεφαλὴ ὅλης τῆς πίστεως ἢ καὶ τῶν ἀποςόλων.—Act. 2, col. 1472, tom. ii. Edit. ii. Head of all who profess the faith, and guide in all matters of faith.

they declared themselves constrained to execute the sentence of Celestine against Nestorius.

Xystus III., successor of Celestine, says that what his predecessor had written on faith was sufficient, but that the Apostolic See is not remiss in urging it, since the solicitude of all the churches presses on it.* On the submission of John of Antioch, who, from personal attachment and jealousy, had for a time sustained Nestorius, Xystus wrote to him: "You have experienced by the issue of the present affair what it is to be of one mind with us. The blessed apostle Peter delivers in his successors what he learned. Who will choose to separate himself from his doctrine, whom the Master Himself taught first among the apostles?"†

It was the mental malady of those early ages, to endeavor to scan the unfathomable mystery of the Incarnation. Scarcely had the destructive heresy of Nestorius been exploded, when the monk Eutyches, in shunning it, plunged into another gulf not less dangerous. Nestorius had divided Christ from the Word, by ascribing a human personality to the human nature: Eutyches confounded the divinity with the humanity, by affirming that there was but one nature, as well as person, after the union. It is not easy to determine the precise character of his error; whether he supposed the Divine nature to be merged in the nature of man, which is so plainly repugnant to the glorious and unchangeable attributes of Deity as to be scarcely imaginable: or whether he thought that the human nature was swallowed up in the Divine, and transformed, and deified: or whether he fancied a composition of both natures, from which a distinct nature resulted. The error was most probably conceived in a confused and inconsistent manner; but Flavian, Bishop of Constantinople, perceiving clearly that revealed truth was assailed, did not hesitate to cut off from the communion of the Church the author of the pernicious novelty. Eutyches had no just ground of appeal from the sentence. However, he determined on interesting the Roman Bishop in his behalf, and addressed Leo, as if he had lodged an appeal in form, beseeching him to grant him relief from the injustice of his immediate ecclesiastical superior. He likewise solicited the support of St. Peter Chrysologus, Bishop of Ravenna, from whom he received this significant reply: "We exhort you, most honored brother, to attend obediently in all things to whatever shall be written to you by the most blessed Pope of the city of Rome, since blessed Peter, who lives and presides in his own chair, imparts the truth of faith to those who seek it: for we, through zeal for peace and faith, cannot take cognizance of a cause which regards faith, without the consent of the Bishop of Rome."‡ Flavian, addressing the Pope, styles him: "Most Holy Father," and assures him that Eutyches had lodged no appeal, although with a view to defeat justice, he declared he had done so. He solicits his approbation of

---

* Ep. 1. t. 1. col. 1235.   † Ep. vi. ib. col. 1260.
‡ Ep. xxv. Petri Chrysologi inter S. Leo. ep.

the canonical deposition of Eutyches, and states that his sentence will crush the heresy, and supersede the necessity of a general Council, which could not be convened without great commotion in the Christian world.* Leo finally sent to Flavian a sublime exposition of the Catholic faith, in which he confirmed the condemnation already pronounced against Eutyches, and despatched, at the same time, as his legates, a bishop, priest, and deacon, with a notary, to execute the sentence,† and hold his place in the Council convened by Theodosius the younger, emperor of the East,‡ who had solicited the authority of the Apostolic See to give effect to his pious desires for the peace of the Church.§

The proceedings of the second Council convened at Ephesus being irregular, through the violence of Dioscorus of Alexandria, the legates of the Pope "constantly protested in the synod that the Apostolic See would by no means receive the decision;"‖ and declared that "they would not on any account deviate from the clear and explicit statement of the faith which they had brought with them to the synod, from the throne of the most blessed apostle Peter."¶ The Pope, with all the Western Council of Bishops, reprobated the acts of this conventicle,** and exhorted the emperor to withdraw his favor from the heretical faction, for which purpose he also implored the empress Pulcheria to use her influence, and to regard herself as if delegated by St. Peter himself. To the clergy and people of Constantinople he addressed strenuous exhortations to cling to the orthodox faith, and consoled Flavian in his sufferings. To the priests and monastic superiors, he gave instructions to avoid the heresy of Eutyches, and hold the communion of Flavian. Valentinian, the emperor of the West, on coming to Rome, and visiting the basilic of St. Peter, being witness of the deep affliction caused by the proceedings at Ephesus, addressed a letter to Theodosius, at the request of Leo, and a synod of bishops, exhorting him to preserve the ancient faith unchanged, and to show the becoming veneration for the Apostolic See: "We ought," he says, "with becoming devotion to defend the faith handed down by our ancestors, and preserve undiminished in our days the measure of proper veneration for the blessed apostle Peter, so that the most blessed Bishop of the city of the Romans, to whom antiquity gave a priesthood above all, may have scope and opportunity to judge about faith and priests."†† This was said to induce Theodosius to summon a Council to be held in Italy, where Leo, with the bishops, might pronounce judgment according to the truth of faith, as Valentinian proceeds to state. Galla Placidia, the mother of Theodosius, at the earnest request of the Pontiff, wrote to her son, imploring him to "preserve the faith of the Catholic religion in its

---

* Ep. xxvi. inter Leonis ep.
† Ep. xxviii.
‡ Ep. xxix.
§ Ep. xxxiii. ad Eph. Syn. secundam.
‖ Ep. xliv. ad Theodosium.
¶ Ep. xlv.
** Ep. Hilarii diaconi ad Pulcheriam, inter S. Leo. ep.
†† Ep. lv. inter Leonis ep.

integrity, that, according to the form and definition of the Apostolic See, which we likewise venerate as presiding, Flavian continuing in his priestly station, might be sent over for trial in the synod of the Apostolic See, in which that chief, who was made worthy to receive the keys of heaven, has manifestly established the sovereign pontificate."* She wrote also to Pulcheria to urge her interposition, that the proceedings at Ephesus might be set aside, and the matter referred to the Apostolic See, "in which the most blessed apostle Peter, who received the keys of heaven, established the high priesthood."† A Council was convened at Chalcedon, by Marcian, successor of Theodosius, at the earnest solicitation of Leo; and the letter of the Pontiff, in which the mystery was propounded, was received with acclamation, as the genuine declaration of the ancient faith. On the reading of it, all cried out: "This is the faith of the fathers—this is the faith of the apostles. All of us have this belief—the orthodox believe this. Anathema to him who does not believe this. PETER HAS SPOKEN BY LEO."‡ In their letter to the Pope, they declare that "he is appointed for all, the interpreter of the voice of Peter the apostle."

Thus did the successors of Peter maintain the faith which he professed under divine inspiration, when he said: "Thou art Christ, the Son of the living God." The consubstantiality of the Son, which is implied in these words, and which was defended by the Nicene fathers against the subtleties of Arius, and his followers, was proclaimed by Sylvester, Julius, Liberius, and the other occupants of that see, conformably to the faith originally delivered. The identity of the Person, who was at once the man Christ, and the Son of God, was declared by Celestine, against the impiety of Nestorius. To Leo belongs the glory of exploding the contrary error of Eutyches, who, confounding the natures, derogated from the unchangeable majesty of the Deity; while faith recognises the reality and distinction of the divine and human natures, and acknowledges in each its special properties. To the Holy Spirit in the adorable unity of the Godhead, with the Father and the Son, Damasus and his synod, and with them the Council of Constantinople, and the whole episcopal college, rendered supreme homage. The mysteries, then, of the Trinity, Incarnation, and Redemption, which the vast majority even of the sects hold to be fundamental, were propounded and maintained chiefly by the agency and authority of the Roman Pontiffs, as even Mr. Palmer acknowledges.

"We find," he says, "that the Roman Church was zealous to maintain the true faith from the earliest period, condemning and expelling the Gnostics, Artemonites, &c.; and, during the Arian mania, it was the bulwark of the Catholic faith."§

In connection with these mysteries, the honor of the Mother of our Lord

---

* Ep. lvi. τὴν ἐπίσκοπὴν τῆς ἀρχιεροσύνης.
† Ep. lviii.
‡ Act. ii. t. ii. coll. Hard. col. 505.
§ Treatise on the Church, vol. ii. part vi. ch. iii. p. 472.

was vindicated. Jovinian, the enemy of holy virginity and of the Virgin Mother, was condemned, as St. Jerom testifies, by the authority of the Roman Church;* and St. Augustin says that "the holy church which is there, (*at Rome*,) most faithfully and strenuously opposed this monster," (*the heresy*.)† The apostolic decree, by which the heresiarch and his abettors were "by the divine sentence, and by the judgment of the Roman synod," excluded from the church, was sent to the bishops, in the confidence that they would receive it with reverence. St. Ambrose and his colleagues addressed Damasus in reply, and alleged among other things, the authority of the symbol of the apostles in support of the doctrines defined, proving from it that Mary brought forth her Divine Son without detriment to her virginity: "Let them," he cried, "believe the symbol of the apostles, which the Roman Church always guards and preserves inviolate."‡ The prelates assure Siricius that they also condemn the heretics, conformably to his judgment.

The perpetual virginity of the Blessed Mother was defended by the same illustrious Pontiff; and the contrary error was rejected with horror, in his letter to Anysius, his Vicar in Illyricum, and to the bishops of that province.§ Her high dignity as Mother of God was vindicated with immense applause in the Council of Ephesus, when the error of Nestorius was condemned by the authority of Celestine. "This term," says Dr. Nevin, "for the ancient church, was the very touchstone of orthodoxy over against Nestorianism, just as much as the term *consubstantial* was so also, when applied to the doctrine of 'the Saviour's true and proper divinity, over against the heresy of Arius. No man whose tongue falters in pronouncing Mary *Mother of God*, can be orthodox at heart on the article of Christ's Person."‖

§ 3.—GRACE.

The highest authority was always ascribed to doctrinal decisions of the Pope by the bishops in every part of the world, who either besought him to declare the faith, or submitted for his confirmation the definitions which they themselves had framed against heresies infesting their provinces.

The bishops of Africa had recourse to the Holy See to obtain the confirmation of their decrees against the subtle heresy of Pelagius and Celestius. A numerous Council was held at Carthage in the year 416, the proceedings of which were communicated by a synodical letter, addressed to "the most blessed and most honorable lord, the holy brother Pope Innocent." "Lord brother," say the fathers, "we have thought it necessary

---

* Lib. contra Vigilantium initio.
† L. ii. Retract. c. xii.
‡ Ep. viii. Ambrosii, apud Constant, t. i. col. 671.
§ Ep. ix. col. 681, t. i. Constant.
‖ Dr. Berg's Last Words. M. R. May, 1852.

to communicate this measure to your Holiness, that the authority of the Apostolic See may be added to our humble decrees, in order to preserve many in the way of salvation, and lead back some from perverse error. The error and impiety, which have many abettors scattered abroad everywhere, should be anathematized even by the authority of the Apostolic See. For let your Holiness, compassionating us with pastoral tenderness, consider how pestiferous and destructive to the sheep of Christ is the consequence of their sacrilegious disputations, namely, that we should not pray that we may not enter into temptation, which the Lord both admonished His disciples to do, and specified in the prayer which He taught us: or that our faith may not fail, as He Himself testified that He prayed for Peter the apostle." . . . "We entertain no doubt that your Holiness, on examining the synodical proceedings, which are said to have taken place in the East, in the same cause, will pass such judgment, as to give us all cause for rejoicing in the mercy of the Lord. Pray for us, most blessed lord Pope."*

Another Council held at Milevis in the same year, in which St. Augustin bore a conspicuous part, addressed Innocent to the same effect: "We think that, through the mercy of the Lord our God, who vouchsafes both to direct your counsels and hear your prayers, those who entertain such perverse and pernicious opinions, WILL READILY ASSENT TO THE AUTHORITY OF YOUR HOLINESS, DERIVED FROM THE AUTHORITY OF THE DIVINE SCRIPTURES, so that we may have occasion rather of joy at their correction, than of sorrow at their ruin."† Five of the African bishops, among whom was Augustin, wrote a special letter to Innocent, to urge the adoption of measures calculated to defeat the wiles of the Pelagians. "Pelagius," they say, "should be called by your Holiness to Rome, and closely questioned as to the nature of the grace which he acknowledges, if, indeed, he acknowledge that men are aided to avoid sin, and live justly: or this is to be treated of with him by letter."‡ The Pontiff recognised in the reference made to his authority, nothing more than faithful adherence to the examples of antiquity, and due respect for the rights of the chair of Peter. His decree, directed to the prelates of Carthage, begins in these words: "In investigating those things, which it is meet should be treated of with all care by priests, and especially by a true, and just, and Catholic Council, following the examples of ancient tradition, and mindful of ecclesiastical discipline, you have properly maintained the vigor of our religion, not less now in consulting us, than before when you pronounced judgment; since you determined that your judgment should be referred to us, as you know what is due to the Apostolic See, because all of us placed in this station desire to follow the apostle himself, FROM WHOM THE EPISCOPACY AND THE WHOLE AUTHORITY OF THIS ORDER

---

* Apud Coustant, t. i. col. 867. † Ep. 176, olim. 92, p. 620.
‡ Ep. xxviii. Coustant, col. 878.

PROCEEDED: following whom, we know how to condemn what is evil, and to approve what is praiseworthy. Observing, with priestly fidelity, the institutions of the fathers,* you do not allow them to be trodden under foot; for they decreed, not by human impulse, but by divine direction, that whatsoever was done in provinces, however distant and remote, should not be deemed terminated until it had come to the knowledge of this see; that the judgment, which might be found just, might be confirmed with its whole authority, and the other churches (as waters issuing from the fountain, and flowing through the different parts of the whole world, pure streams from an unpolluted source) might thence derive what they might prescribe."† His letter to the prelates of Milevis is also couched in the language of one having authority: "Among the various cares of the Roman Church and occupations of the Apostolic See, in managing with faithful and healing care the affairs of different persons, on which it is consulted, Julius, our brother and fellow-bishop, unexpectedly delivered to me your letters, which, through earnest zeal for the faith, you sent from the Council of Milevis." After some other remarks he proceeds: "Ye do, therefore, diligently and becomingly consult the secrets of the apostolic honor, (that honor, I mean, on which, besides those things that are without, the care of all the churches awaits,) as to what judgment is to be passed on doubtful matters, following, in sooth, the direction of the ancient rule, which you know, as well as I, has ever been observed in the whole world. But this I pass by, for I am sure your prudence is aware of it: for how could you by your actions have confirmed this, save as knowing that throughout all provinces answers are ever emanating to inquirers as from the apostolic fountain? Especially, so often as matter of faith is under inquiry, I conceive that all our brethren and fellow-bishops ought not to refer, save to Peter, that is, the source of their own name and honor, just as your affection hath now referred, for what may benefit all churches in common, throughout the whole world."‡ These documents were not considered to betray any undue assumption, by Augustin or his colleagues; who, on the contrary, rejoiced that "the pestilence had been condemned by the most manifest judgment of the Apostolic See:"§ and maintained that further examination was unnecessary. A few months after the confirmation of the African Councils had reached Africa, addressing his flock, he observed: "Already have the decrees of two Councils on this matter been sent to the Apostolic See: the rescripts from thence have reached us: the cause is decided: would to heaven the error were abandoned!"|| Elsewhere he writes: "The authority of Catholic Councils and of the Apostolic See has most justly condemned the recent

---

* Of Sardica. † Ep. 181.
‡ Inter opera Aug. tom. ii. 639 B. § Ep. 191, olim. 104, p. 709, tom ii.
|| Serm. 131, de verbis Apost. c. 10, col. 645, tom. v. "Causa finita est, utinam aliquando finiatur error!"

Pelagian heretics."* "All doubt," he says, "was removed by the rescript of Innocent."†

Zosimus having received with favor the declaration of Celestius, and written to the African bishops in his behalf, was thought by them to have implicitly believed the statements of this subtle heresiarch: on learning which, he wrote to assure them that he had not at all receded from the decrees of his predecessor. "The tradition of the fathers," says he, "has ascribed so great authority to the Apostolic See, that no one dares call its judgment in question, and it has been so maintained by the canons and rules; and ecclesiastical discipline, which is still regulated by its laws, pays the due reverence to the name of Peter, from whom itself likewise is derived; for canonical antiquity, by common consent, ascribed to this apostle such power, in virtue of the very promise of Christ our God, that he should loose bonds and bind what was loose; and equal power was recognised in those who had, by his favor, inherited his see; for he himself has charge of all the churches, but especially of this one in which he sat: nor does he suffer any privilege to fail, or any decree to vacillate by any breath of air, having established in his name a firm foundation, which cannot be shaken by any effort, and which no man rashly assails without danger to himself. Wherefore, as Peter is head of so great authority, and as he has confirmed the subsequent acts of all our predecessors, so that all laws and regulations, both human and divine, support the Roman Church, whose place we hold, as you are not ignorant, but rather know well, as priests ought to know, yet, although we have so great authority that no one can rescind our decree, we adopted no measure which we did not at the same time communicate to you by letter."‡

In the year 418, Zosimus published, against the Pelagian errors, a decree called *Tractoria*, directed "to all bishops universally."§ It was sent to the churches of Africa, in which the errors had been condemned, to the Eastern churches, to the diocese of Egypt, to Constantinople, Thessalonica, and Jerusalem. ST. AUGUSTIN, quoting a passage from it concerning sin, observes: "In these words of the Apostolic See the Catholic faith, so ancient and well founded, is so certain and clear, that a Christian cannot entertain a doubt of it without impiety."‖

ST. PROSPER says: "A council of two hundred and fourteen bishops being held at Carthage, the synodical decrees were sent to Pope Zosimus, which being approved of, the Pelagian heresy was condemned throughout the whole world."¶ Elsewhere he says, that "the judgments of the Eastern bishops, and the authority of the Apostolic See, and the vigilance

---

* L. ii. de anima et ejus origine, c. xii. n. 17.
† L. ii. ad Bonifac. contra 2 ep. Pelag. c. iii.
‡ Ep. xii. col. 974, Coustant, t. i.
§ Vide Aug. ad Optat. ep. cxc. n. 22.
‖ Ep. cxc. n. 23.   ¶ In Chronico.

of the African Councils, detected the artifices of the Pelagians."* Speaking of those who asserted that St. Augustin had not correctly defended the Catholic doctrine, he dwells "on the greatness of the injury, which, in the person of this one doctor, they inflict on all, and especially on the Pontiffs of the Apostolic See."† He repels the assertion as absurd: "According to your censure, the blessed Pope Innocent erred, a man most worthy of the See of Peter. The two hundred and fourteen bishops erred, who, in the letter which they prefixed to their decrees, thus addressed blessed Zosimus, the prelate of the Apostolic See: 'We have determined that the sentence passed against Pelagius and Celestius by the venerable bishop, Innocent, from the See of the most blessed apostle Peter, shall continue in force, until they most unreservedly confess that we are aided in each act by the grace of God, through Jesus Christ our Lord, not only to know but to perform justice, so that without it we can have, think, say, or do nothing of true and sincere piety.' The holy See of Peter erred, which by the mouth of blessed Zosimus thus speaks to all the world: 'We, nevertheless, through the inspiration of God—for all good is to be referred to its author and origin—have reported all to our brethren and fellow-bishops.'"‡ He shows that these errors, having been once proscribed by Apostolic authority, should not be discussed: 'We are not again to enter into a new conflict with them, (*the Pelagians*,) nor are special contests to be begun as against unknown enemies: their engines were broken in pieces, and they were prostrated, in the companions and princes of their pride, when Innocent, of blessed memory, struck the heads of the impious error with the Apostolic sword .... when Pope Zosimus, of blessed memory, added the seal of his sentence to the decrees of the African Council."§ "See," he says in another place, "the rebels every where laid prostrate by the thunderbolt of the Apostolic decision."‖ He calls Rome "the throne of Peter,"¶ "the throne of Apostolic power,"** the "head of the world, governing with religious empire nations which its arms had not subdued."††

St. Vincent of Lerins, in his celebrated 'Commonitorium,' illustrates his great principle of ancient tradition, "by an instance taken from the Apostolic See, that all might see in meridian light—with what energy,

---

* Ad Ruf. p. 164, App. ad Aug. Ed. Ven. tom. x.
† L. contra Collatorem, p. 171.
‡ Ibidem, p. 176.
§ L. contra Collatorem, p. 195.
‖ ——————— stratosque rebelles
    Oris Apostolici fulmine ubique vide.—Prosp. in Obtrect. Aug.
¶ Ergo Petri solium Romam, et Carthaginis altæ
    Concilium repetant.—Carm. de Ingratis.
** Juris Apostolici solio.—Ib.
†† Sedes Roma Petri, quæ pastoralis honoris,
    Facta caput mundi, quidquid non possidet armis,
    Religione tenet.—Ib.

with what zeal, with what determination the blessed successors of the blessed apostles always maintained the integrity of the religion originally handed down." He then, in the strong language already quoted, mentions the resistance of Pope Stephen to the practice of rebaptizing.* In the penultimate chapter, speaking of the letters of Julius, Bishop of Rome, which were read in the General Council of Ephesus, he observes: "That not only THE HEAD OF THE WORLD, but also its sides, might give testimony for that judgment, the most blessed Cyprian, Bishop of Carthage and martyr, was brought forward from the south; St. Ambrose, Bishop of Milan, from the north." In the last chapter he adduces "two authoritative declarations of the Apostolic See: one, namely, of the holy Pope Sixtus, which venerable man," he says, "now adorns the Roman Church; the other of his predecessor of blessed memory, Pope Celestine. Whoever opposes these Apostolic and Catholic decrees, must first insult the memory of holy Celestine, who decreed that novelty should cease to assail antiquity, and must mock the decrees of holy Sixtus, who judged that novelty should have no indulgence, because nothing should be added to antiquity."†

In terms which beautifully exhibit the unity of the Catholic faith, and the efficiency of the Apostolic See in preserving it, Paulinus, deacon of Milan, author of the Life of St. Ambrose, congratulated Zosimus on the measures adopted against the heresy of Celestius: "The true faith is never disturbed, especially in the Apostolic Church, in which perverse teachers are easily discovered, and properly punished, that their evil conceptions and worse productions may die in them, if they will be corrected, and the true faith may be imparted to them, which the apostles taught, and the Roman Church holds, in union with all the teachers of the Catholic faith."‡

NESTORIUS, Bishop of Constantinople, previously to the condemnation of his own error, consulted Pope Celestine, concerning Julian and others, accused of the Pelagian heresy, inquiring whether he should treat them as heretics: "We wish to be informed what opinion we should entertain of them, for we put them off day after day, awaiting the answer of your Holiness."§ Thus the authority of the Apostolic See in determining matters of faith, was distinctly recognised by the Bishop of the new Rome, at the moment when it was about to be employed to proscribe the heresy into which pride betrayed himself.

ST. PROSPER relates that Pope Xystus was guarded against the wiles of Julian, by the advice of Leo, who was then deacon; and that the disappointment of the artful heretic, who hoped to impose on the unsuspecting Pontiff, filled all Catholics with joy, as if then, for the first time, the Apostolic sword had cut off the head of the proud heresy.‖

---

* Supra, p. 115. † Comm. p. 26, Ed. Aug. Vindelic.
‡ Ep. viii. Coustant, t. i. col. 963. § Ep. vii. Coustant, t. i. col. 1089.
‖ L. contra collat. c. xxi.

St. Leo, understanding that the Pelagians and Celestians were in some places admitted to the communion of the Catholic Church, without a solemn abjuration of their errors, wrote to the Bishop of Aquileja, commanding him to convene a synod, and require of them a formal retraction : "Let them condemn openly and explicitly the authors of the proud error, and detest whatever the universal Church has found worthy of abhorrence in their doctrine, and declare fully, openly, and in written documents subscribed by them, that they embrace, and unreservedly approve of all synodical decrees directed to the extirpation of this heresy, which have been confirmed by the authority of the Apostolic See."* Thus the pernicious errors against divine grace, which pride invented and fostered, to the prejudice of the redemption which we have through Christ, were opposed and extirpated, with untiring zeal, by the successors of Peter

§ 4.—TESTIMONIES OF FATHERS.

The most learned fathers humbly addressed the Bishops of Rome, with childlike dependence on their teaching. St. Jerom, in affecting language, implored the direction of Damasus in the controversies which agitated the East: "Since the East tears into pieces the Lord's coat, and foxes lay waste the vineyard of Christ, so that among broken cisterns which hold no water, it is difficult to understand where is the sealed fountain and the enclosed garden : therefore the chair of Peter and that faith which is praised by the Apostle's mouth is appealed to by me, who now seek food for my soul where formerly I received the robe of Christ."† Writing to Demetriades, a Roman lady, to guard her against the wiles of heretics, he exhorts her to adhere to the doctrine of the actual occupant of the Apostolic chair; at the same time bearing witness to the zeal with which a deceased Pope had exercised his authority for the maintenance of sound doctrine : "When you were a child," he says, "and the Bishop Anastasius, of holy and blessed memory, governed the Roman Church, a dread storm of heretics from the Eastern parts, attempted to adulterate and destroy the simplicity of the faith, which was praised by the voice of the apostle. But a man, very rich in his poverty, and full of apostolic zeal, struck at once the direful head, and broke the hissing mouth of the hydra. Since I fear, and even have heard a report, that these poisonous plants are still in the ground, and bud forth anew, I think it proper charitably to warn you, to hold the faith of the holy Innocent, who is the successor and child of the Apostolic chair, and of the holy man just mentioned, and not to receive any strange doctrine, however prudent and wise you may appear to yourself."‡ Writing to Theophilus, Patriarch of Alexandria, he says : "Be it known to you, that we hold nothing more sacred than to maintain the

---

* Ep. i. ad Aquil. ep.   † Damaso ep. He alludes to his baptism.
‡ Ep. viii. ad Demetriadem.

rights of Christ, and not to move the boundaries which the fathers have placed, but always to bear in mind that the Roman faith was praised by the mouth of the apostle, of which faith the Church of Alexandria glories that she partakes."* Theophilus himself exhorted certain monks to anathematize Origen and other heretics, after his own example, and that of "Anastasius, Bishop of the holy Roman Church, whom the entire synod of the Western bishops follows."† Thus Alexandria and Antioch, as well as the Western patriarchate, followed the authority of the Pontiff, and gloried in his communion. Heretics themselves knowing the Bishop of Rome to be the highest judge in causes of faith, used every stratagem to deceive him. We have seen already the efforts of the Montanists, Pelagians, and many others, to gain his confidence. Sulpicius tells us that Instantius, Salvian, and Priscillian, having been condemned for heresy in a Council of Saragossa, "set out for Rome to justify themselves before Damasus, who was then Bishop of that city;" but that they were not admitted into his presence.‡

With St. Leo we must ascribe the constancy in faith of the Roman Bishops, not to chance or personal merit, but to the aid of Christ: "From whose supreme and eternal protection we also," says he, "have received the strength of apostolic aid, which certainly is not withdrawn from His own work; and the firmness of the foundation on which the high fabric of the whole Church is built, suffers nothing from the mass of the temple which rests on it. For the solidity of the faith, which was praised in the prince of the apostles, is perpetual; and as that which Peter believed of Christ continues always, so that which Christ instituted in Peter always remains." The eloquent Pontiff proves this from the passage of St. Matthew, and then proceeds: "The ordinance of truth therefore continues, and blessed Peter, persevering in the strength of the rock imparted to him, does not abandon the helm of the Church at which he was placed. For he was thus ordained in preference to the others, that while he is styled a rock, while he is declared a foundation, while he is made gatekeeper of the kingdom of heaven, while he is constituted judge of what is to be bound or loosed, with a promise that his decision shall be ratified in heaven, we should understand, by the mysterious appellations themselves, the special relation which he bears to Christ."§

The agency of the successors of Peter in maintaining the integrity of revelation, through a long lapse of ages, was acknowledged by the learned Protestant, Cassaubon: "No one," he remarks, "who is the least versed in ecclesiastical history, can doubt that God made use of the Holy See, during many ages, to preserve the doctrines of faith."|| The same is true of all ages, so that we may at this day repeat the words of Eusebius: "It

---

* Ep. lxiii. clas. 3, an. 397. † Serm. ad quosdam monachos.
‡ L. ii.   § Serm. iii. in anniversario ad Pontif.
|| Exercit xv. ad annal. Baronii.

is certain that our Saviour foretold that His doctrine should be preached throughout the world in testimony to all nations, and that the Church which was afterward to be established by His power, should be invincible and impregnable, and never overcome by death, but should be firm and immovable, as established and founded on a rock. He has, in fact, done what He foretold; for already the fame of His Gospel has filled the world from east to west, and reached all nations, and its preaching spreads daily. The Church, also, receiving her appellation from Him, has taken root; and, being extolled to the skies by the discourses of holy men, shines with the light and splendor of orthodox faith; nor does she flee before her enemies, nor yield to the very powers of death, in consequence of the few words which He uttered: 'On this rock I will build My Church, and the gates of hell shall not prevail against it.'"*

"There are, it is true," writes Dr. Nevin, "predictions enough of trials, heresies, apostacies, and corruptions; but the idea is never for a moment allowed that these should prevail in any such universal way as the (*Puritan*) theory before us pretends. On the contrary, the strongest assurances are given that this should not be the case. These stand forth most conspicuously and solemnly, in those wonderful passages from the mouth of the blessed Saviour Himself, which form, as it were, the charter of the Church, and its heavenly commission to the end of time."†

§ 5.—VINDICATION OF HONORIUS.

A dark cloud long lowered over the Holy See, on account of the condemnation of Pope Honorius by the sixth General Council, held in 680. The fathers of this assembly on reading, among other documents, the answer of Honorius to Sergius, Bishop of Constantinople, rejected it with execration, together with the letter of Sergius, to which it was a reply, and another letter directed to Cyrus, then Bishop of Phasis; and added to their anathemas against various heretics by name, this very solemn condemnation: "We have resolved also to anathematize Honorius, who was Pope of ancient Rome, since we find, from the letter addressed by him to Sergius, that conforming to his views in all things, he confirmed the impious dogmas."‡ They cried out: "To Honorius, the heretic, anathema." In defending the dogma of the primacy, I do not deem it necessary to prove, that no one of the Roman Bishops at any time taught heresy, or was personally heretical; as I insist only on the duty of his office to guard the faith, and on the notorious fact that it has been generally fulfilled: but I owe it to truth and justice, and to the memory of a Pontiff illustrious for zeal, to express my conviction that the charge of heterodoxy advanced against him is without solid foundation.

De præp. Ev., l. i., c. iii.   † "Early Christianity," M. R., November, 1851.
‡ Act xiii.

The letters of Honorius, which are still extant,* express the doctrine of the One Divine Operator, or Agent, in the two natures, which is, in substance, the Catholic doctrine of two operations, each nature having its own operation. "We should confess," says he, "both natures in Christ, united in natural unity, operating in communion with each other; the divine nature doing what belongs to God, and the human nature executing the things of the flesh, not separately, nor confusedly; not teaching that the nature of God was changed into the man, or the human nature into that of God, but confessing the difference of natures to be entire." At the artful suggestion of Sergius, Honorius ordered silence to be observed as to the terms of one or two operations, being content with requiring that Christ should be held to be one Divine Operator in the two natures. This injunction was serviceable to the cause of heresy, which in the mean time spread like a cancer. The abuse made of the good faith of the Pontiff drew down censure on his memory, as if he were the abettor and approver of an error which he did not strongly and instantly condemn: but I may be permitted to observe, that men are often judged by the results of their actions, and that the forbearance of Honorius, and his anxiety to terminate the wordy contest and preserve peace, might have gained the praise of consummate prudence and enlightened zeal, had not the perverse ingenuity of the Monothelites turned the prohibition to the advantage of their cause. The orthodoxy of Honorius never wanted strenuous defenders. John IV., in his letter to the Emperor Constantine Pogonatus, complained that Pyrrhus, Bishop of Constantinople, was abusing and perverting the words of his predecessor. John the Abbot, the secretary employed by Honorius, testified that the implied disclaimer of two wills in Christ, was intended to exclude only the corrupt will of fallen man; and the martyr Maximus, the declared enemy of Monothelism, vindicated the faith of the Pontiff.† A more solemn, though less direct vindication, is contained in the letter of Pope Agatho to Constantine Pogonatus, read with acclamation in the sixth General Council, in which he asserts that his predecessors had never failed in the performance of the high duties of their office: "This is the rule of true faith, which the apostolic Church of Christ, this spiritual mother of your most tranquil empire, warmly held and defended both in prosperity and adversity; which Church, through the grace of Almighty God, is shown to have strayed at no time from the path of apostolic tradition, and to have never succumbed to the perverse novelties of heretics; but what, from the commencement of Christian faith, she learned from her founders, the princes of the apostles of Christ, she incorruptibly retains to the end, according to the promise of our Lord

---

* John Baptist Bartholi, Bishop of Feltri, in an Apology for Honorius, maintains that the first letter to Sergius has been adulterated, and that the second is a forgery, of which nothing was known at Rome.

† In Ep. ad Marin. presbyt.

and Saviour Himself, which He declared to the prince of His apostles, in the Gospel, saying: 'Peter, Peter, lo! Satan hath sought to sift you as one sifteth wheat, but I have prayed for thee, that thy faith may not fail: and thou, being once converted, confirm thy brethren.' Let, then, your serene clemency consider, that the Lord and Saviour of all, whose gift faith is, and who promised that the faith of Peter should not fail, charged him to confirm his brethren; as it is notorious to all that the apostolic Pontiffs, my predecessors, have always fearlessly done."* All this seems expressly directed to repel any charge likely to be made against Honorius; and the applause which followed the reading of the letter, "PETER HAS SPOKEN THROUGH AGATHO," implies the assent of the Council to the statement: yet the records of the proceedings contain censures on the memory of Honorius, which force us to believe that the fathers there assembled considered him to have been guilty, if not of culpable connivance, at least of an untimely dissimulation. Without disrespect to their authority, they may be supposed to have been mistaken in a matter of fact, merely personal, namely, the spirit and intention with which the letters were written.

It is not necessary to insist more particularly on this vindication of an individual Pontiff. I have not undertaken to prove, what, indeed, no Catholic divine asserts, that the Pope may not, by the artifices of heretics, be betrayed into measures prejudicial to the faith; neither have I deemed it necessary to maintain, what I am deeply convinced of, from the special prayer of Christ, that God will never suffer him to propound error in a solemn doctrinal definition directed to the universal Church. My object has been to show that the Popes, as primates of the Church by divine right, exercised high judicial authority in determining and maintaining the doctrines of faith. It is not merely in the eleventh century that language occurs like that which was addressed by St. Bernard to Innocent II.: "It is right that all dangers and scandals which arise in the kingdom of God, especially such as regard faith, should be reported to your apostleship: for I think it proper that the wounds inflicted on faith should be there healed, where faith cannot fail. That is the prerogative of the See."† In the fifth century, Pope Hilarius was addressed by the Bishops of the province of Tarragona, in language almost equally emphatic. The occasion of their writing was a personal or disciplinary affair, of which they availed themselves to express their desire to profit by the instruction of the Holy See: "Even were there," say they, "no necessity of ecclesiastical discipline, we should seek to benefit by the privilege of your See, since the extraordinary preaching of the most blessed Peter, who, after the resurrection of the Saviour, received the keys of the kingdom, shone forth for the illumination of all: the principality of whose Vicar, as it is eminent, is to be feared and loved by all. Wherefore, profoundly adoring

---

* Conc. Constant. iii. act. iii., col. 1081, Coll. Hard. t. iii.
† Ep. ad Innoc. ii.

in you God, whom you serve without reproach, we have recourse to the faith which was praised by the mouth of the apostle; and we seek a reply from that source, where nothing is ordained erroneously, nothing presumptuously, but all with pontifical deliberation."*

We may be allowed to recapitulate in the words of Dr. Nevin: "Examples of the actual exercise of supreme power on the part of the Popes, in the fourth and fifth centuries, are so frequent and numerous, that nothing short of the most wilful obstinacy can pretend to treat them as of no account. In every great question of the time, whether rising in the East or in the West, all eyes show themselves ever ready to turn toward the *cathedra Petri*, as the last resort for counsel and adjudication; all controversies, either in the way of appeal, or complaint, or for the ratification of decisions given in other quarters, are made to come directly or indirectly, in the end, before this tribunal, and reach their final and conclusive settlement only through its intervention. The Popes, in these cases, take it for granted themselves, that the power which they exercise belongs to them of right, in virtue of the prerogative of their See; there is no appearance whatever of effort or of usurpation, in the part they allow themselves to act; it seems to fall to them as naturally as the functions of a magistrate or judge in any case are felt to go along with the office to which they belong. And the whole world apparently regards the primacy in the same way, as a thing of course, a matter fully settled and established in the constitution of the Christian church. We hear of no objection to it, no protest against it, as a new and daring presumption, or as a departure from the earlier order of Christianity. The whole nature of the case implies, as strongly as any historical conditions and relations well could, that this precisely, and no other order, had been handed down from a time, beyond which no memory of man to the contrary then reached."†

---

* Ep. Tarrac. ep. t. ii. conc. Hard. col. 787.
† "Early Christianity," Mercersburg Review, Sept., 1851.

CHAPTER XII.

Governing Power.

§ 1.—EXERCISE OF AUTHORITY.

WE have seen abundant evidence of the most decided exercise of the primacy in the maintenance of faith. The same documents prove that the Bishop of Rome was regarded as the governor of the universal Church, regulating its administration by laws, enforcing their observance, and occasionally mitigating their rigor by opportune indulgence.* But few of the many rescripts which emanated from the Holy See in the early ages, have escaped the flames kindled by the heathen persecutors, or the ravages of time; yet they are amply sufficient to establish the fact, that a governing power was at all times claimed by the Roman Bishop, as successor of St. Peter, by divine right, and that the claim was admitted, and its exercise oftentimes implored, by the bishops throughout the world. The administration of the Church was, nevertheless, conducted on settled principles, because the power was given by the Lord, not for destruction, but for edification; and the canons, or rules, made by the Popes, or by Councils, were sacredly respected, unless when the high interests of religion required a departure from them. "Let the rules govern us," cried out St. Celestine; "let us not set aside the rules; let us be subject to the canons, whilst we observe what the canons command."†

The divine origin of episcopal power is loudly proclaimed by St. Cyprian, whose language is strictly applicable to the Roman Pontiff, the representative and depositary of the plenitude of episcopal authority. In order to show the crime of insubordination, he adduces the well-known passage of Deuteronomy, wherein the decree of the High Priest is enforced with the strongest penal sanction; from which, as well as from other testimonies, he thus concludes: "Since these and many other weighty examples are upon record, by which the priestly authority and power, through divine condescension, are established, what think you of those who, being enemies of the priests, and rebels against the Catholic Church, are not awed, either by the threat of the Lord who forewarns, or

---

* The admirable adaptation of the pontifical enactments to the variety of circumstances, is acknowledged by Voltaire. Of Rome, he says: "Elle a sû toujours tempérer les loix selon les tems et selon les besoins." Sur la Police des Spectacles, vol. v.

† Ep. ad ep. Illyric. t. i. Coustant, col. 1064.

by the avenging judgment that awaits them? For from no other source have heresies arisen, or schisms sprung up, than from not obeying the priest of God, and not reflecting that THERE IS ONE PRIEST, FOR THE TIME, IN THE CHURCH, AND ONE JUDGE, FOR THE TIME, IN THE PLACE OF CHRIST, to whom if all the brotherhood yielded obedience, according to the divine instructions, no one would attempt any thing against the college of priests; no one, after the divine judgment, after the suffrage of the people, after the consent of his fellow bishops, would make himself judge, not of the bishop, but of God; no one would rend the Church of Christ by the breach of unity; no one, through vanity and pride, would form a new heresy apart and without."* It may be contended, not without plausibility, that this is said of a local bishop, namely, of Cyprian himself: but it is difficult to apply language so strong to each individual bishop, since it is certain that on the principle of unqualified obedience to the diocesan, the whole body of the clergy and people of Constantinople would have been perverted, when Macedonius, or Nestorius held that See. The mere episcopal character did not afford a guarantee of orthodoxy— the mere fact of succession did not ensure the truth of the doctrine professed. As Dr Nevin well observes, "It must be the office in unity with itself under a catholic form; the office as representing the undivided and indivisible Apostolical Commission, on which, as a rock centring in Peter, the church was to be built to the end of time."† It is only in the person of the chief bishop, whom Divine Providence wonderfully guards and directs, that the observations of Cyprian are fully verified. His own resistance to Stephen may seem to show that he did not inculcate obedience to the mandates of the Roman Bishop; yet as it arose from a supposed abuse of power, it is reconcilable with the advocacy of the general principle, that obedience should be rendered to the one priest and one judge. Besides, the text is painfully illustrated by the history of that opposition, in connection with the rise of Donatism. Had Cyprian in that instance obeyed the priest of God, and reflected that THERE IS ONE PRIEST, FOR THE TIME, IN THE CHURCH, AND ONE JUDGE, FOR THE TIME, IN THE PLACE OF CHRIST, the scandal of dissension would have been avoided, and the Donatists would have had no pretext for using his venerable name in support of their error and schism.

We have seen that Victor and Stephen acted as persons having authority over the Asiatic and African prelates. The evidences of a similar exercise of governing power multiply during the fourth and fifth ages, when, in consequence of the liberty which the Church enjoyed, there was a development of her power, as occasions presented themselves for its exercise. Pope SIRICIUS, in the year 385, replying to the consultation of Himerius, Bishop of Tarragona, in Spain, says: "We bear the burdens of all who are heavily laden, or rather the blessed apostle Peter bears

---

* Ep. lix., alias liv. lv. † Art. Cyprian, M. R. July, 1852.

them in us, and, as we trust, in all things protects and defends us, the heirs of his authority." The language of this document implies a governing power of the most marked character, by which offences against the divine law are punished with the highest ecclesiastical penalty, and positive enactments are enforced by a similar sanction. Those who re-baptize persons baptized by heretics, are subjected to excommunication. Having pointed to the authorities which condemn this practice, the Pontiff observes: "You must not hereafter depart from this rule, if you do not wish to be separated from our body by a synodical decree." The immediate administration of baptism to infants and persons in danger of death, is enjoined under a similar penalty: "Let this rule be henceforth observed," he says, "by all priests who do not wish to be separated from the solidity of the apostolic rock, on which Christ built the Universal Church." It needs no commentary to show that this is the language of a superior. Incontinent clergymen, who presume to defend their excesses by appealing to the Mosaic code, are threatened with final degradation: "Let them know that they are cast down from all ecclesiastical honor, which they have abused, and that they can never again touch the sacred mysteries." The connivance of the Spanish bishops at abuses, in the promotion of unqualified men to sacred orders, is strongly reprobated, and a rule is laid down which they must follow: "By a general enactment, we decree what hereafter must be followed, and what must be shunned by all churches." This very remarkable document closes with a commendation of the bishop to whom it was addressed, for having reported and proposed the various points to the Roman Church, as to the head; and with an injunction to communicate the decree itself to all the bishops, not only of the diocese of Tarragona, but also of Carthage, Bætica, Lusitania, Gallecia, and other neighboring provinces, that none may plead ignorance, in order to escape the penalties of transgression: "None of the priests of the Lord are at liberty to plead ignorance of the decrees of the Apostolic See, or the venerable definitions of the canons."* Although Spain was in the Western patriarchate, and the decree was not beyond the limits of patriarchal power, the terms show that Siricius relied on his apostolic authority derived from Peter.

Similar language is observable in all the ancient pontifical decrees. Vitricius, Bishop of Rouen, sought to be guided by "the rule and authority of the Roman Church;" and with this view addressed Innocent I., who held the chair of Peter in the commencement of the fifth century. This venerable Pontiff undertook to reply, invoking "the assistance of the holy apostle Peter, through whom the commencement of the apostolic office and of the episcopate was made by Christ." He directs ecclesiastical suits to be terminated in the respective provinces in which they originate, and forbids recourse to foreign tribunals, "without prejudice, how-

---

* Apud Coustant, t. i. col. 623, et seq.

ever, to the Roman Church, to which reverence is due in all cases." The greater causes are to be submitted to the judgment and final decision of the Holy See, conformably to synodical decrees and established usage: " Let them be referred to the Apostolic See, after the episcopal judgment, as the synod decreed* and laudable custom requires."† Writing to the bishops of Macedonia, he resented, as derogatory to the authority of the Holy See, that what it had decreed " as the head of the churches, should be considered as admitting of question."‡

ZOSIMUS, the successor of Innocent, spoke with the same voice of authority, and sent his orders to Gaul, Spain, Africa, and wherever the necessities of the Church demanded his interposition. Addressing Hesychius, Bishop of Salona, who had asked for a command of the Apostolic See, to authorize him to resist those who rashly sought to advance to the priesthood without the necessary preparation, he states that he had already written to this effect to Spain and Gaul, and that even Africa had not been a stranger to his warnings; and he encourages this prelate to oppose such hasty proceedings. "You demand," he says, "a precept of the Apostolic See in harmony with the decrees of the fathers."—" Resist such ordinations: resist the pride and arrogance which ambitiously aspire to advance. You have in your favor the precepts of the fathers: you have also the authority of the Apostolic See." He charges Hesychius to make known the decrees to all the bishops of the neighboring provinces. "Whosoever," he adds, " disregarding the authority of the fathers and of the Apostolic See, shall neglect this, must know that it shall be strictly enforced, so that he may rest assured he shall not retain his dignity, if he imagine that what has been forbidden so repeatedly, can be attempted with impunity."§ This is clearly the strongest language of authority. St. Augustin avows, in reference to ecclesiastical matters, that he and his colleagues were under the necessity of obeying the commands of the Pontiff. Writing to Optatus, he says: "Your letter, which you sent to Mauritania-Cæsariensis, arrived when I was at Cæsarea, whither ecclesiastical duty, enjoined on us by the venerable Pope Zosimus, Bishop of the Apostolic See, had led us."‖ Possidius says that " the letters of the Apostolic See had compelled Augustin, with others of his fellow-bishops, to repair thither, in order to terminate other difficulties of the Church."¶

St. Leo wrote to Turribius, Bishop of Asturia, in Spain, to direct that a Council should be called, and required that if any bishops were found tainted with the errors of Manes or Priscillian they should be at once cut off

---

* According to another reading, custom only is mentioned. The Council of Sardica may be meant by the Synod.
† Ibidem, col. 746.
‡ Ep. xvii. col. 830.
§ Ep. ix. col. 968.
‖ Ep. cxc. alias clvi. n. 1, necessitas ecclesiastica.
¶ C. xiv.

from the communion of the Church. He had given a similar order to the Bishops of Tarragona, Carthage, Lusitania, and Gallecia.* To the Bishops of Mauritiania-Cæsariensis, he wrote, "in consequence of THE SOLICITUDE WHICH," he says, "BY DIVINE INSTITUTION WE HAVE FOR THE WHOLE CHURCH."† He elsewhere expresses the admirable economy of Divine Wisdom in the constitution and government of the Church: "Out of the whole world Peter alone is chosen, and placed over those who are called from all nations, and over all the apostles, and all the fathers of the Church: so that, although there are many priests and many pastors of the people of God, Peter, nevertheless, properly‡ governs them all, who are also chiefly governed by Christ.§ Great and wonderful, dearly beloved, is the communication of His own power, which the divine goodness vouchsafed to him; so that whatever Christ was pleased to communicate to the other princes—whatever he did not withhold from the others—He granted only through him."||

It is manifest that a power was claimed by the Popes over all the churches, in virtue of which laws were enacted, which all were called on to obey, under penalty of ecclesiastical censures. Besides that these claims were made to rest on divine right, there is nothing to warrant us in regarding them as groundless, since in many instances the power was exercised at the solicitation of the parties immediately concerned, and in most cases there was entire acquiescence in the authority claimed. It would be strange, that usurpation could have assumed such consistency, at so early a period, and have commanded the respect of distant prelates, naturally jealous of their own rights and independence. Bossuet deservedly rejects as rash and perverse, the exception taken by some to the evidence derived from papal documents, and loudly declares that "he puts entire confidence in the doctrine and tradition of the Roman Pontiffs concerning the majesty of the Apostolic See.¶

A dispensing power, by which the rigor of the canons was mitigated, for just causes, was also exercised by the Popes from the earliest ages. We have seen the regulation by which Melchiades relaxed the severity of the ecclesiastical law, in order to provide for the Donatist bishops on their return to Catholic unity. Anastasius, in the commencement of the fifth century, was besought by the African bishops to show the like indulgence. They "resolved to write to their brethren and fellow-bishops, and especially to the Apostolic See," to obtain a relaxation of the rigor of the canons of a Council beyond the seas, so that the Donatist bishops, on

---

* Ep. xv. ad Turribium.
† Ep. xii., ad ep. Afric. prov. Maurit. Cæsar.
‡ Proprie. Mr. Allies translates it, "by special commission."
§ "By sovereign power."—Allies.
|| S. Leo, Serm. iv. In anniversario die ejusdem assumpt.
¶ Defens. decl. l. x., alias xv. c. 6.

coming to the Church, might be received with all their honors.* Thus the power of the Pontiff to dispense in the general laws was solemnly recognised.

The Popes, although solicitous for the observance of the canons, were always ready to dispense in them, when the return of the deluded children of error could be promoted by indulgence; in which exercise of clemency they wisely disregarded the censures of the over-zealous, who clamored for the severity of discipline. Some Spanish bishops complained that heretics, on abjuring their errors, were allowed to retain possession of their sees: to whom Innocent I. replied: "If any are pained or grieved at this, let them read how Peter, the apostle, after his tears, was restored to his original station: let them consider that Thomas, after his doubts, retained his former dignity: finally, that the great prophet David, after his open confession, was not deprived of the gift of prophecy."† Yet he acknowledged the wisdom of the general rule, and traced the exceptions to necessity. When some persons ordained by the heretic Bonosus had been received to the Catholic communion, and allowed to officiate in their respective orders, Innocent ascribed this indulgence to necessity, and admitted that it was not conformable to "the ancient rules which the Roman Church received from the apostles, or apostolic men, and which she observes, and commands to be observed by such as are wont to obey her."‡ The same indulgence continued to be shown by his successors, when circumstances demanded it: on which account Leo allowed Donatus, the Novatian Bishop of Salicina, (or Saja,) in Africa, to retain his See, on abjuring Novatianism and sending a satisfactory profession of Catholic faith to Rome; his former adherents passing with him to the Catholic communion.§ Maximus, who had been advanced by the Donatists from the condition of a layman to the bishopric, was allowed to retain his see, on abjuring his errors.‖

In Greece, the Pope exercised the same authority, dispensing in the canons in extraordinary cases, where personal merit and the interests of the Church so required. Boniface I. appointed Perigenes Bishop of Corinth, who had been previously ordained for the See of Patras. Some bishops having resisted this exercise of authority, probably on the ground that the translation of bishops was forbidden by the canons, the Pope insisted that the act of the Holy See could not be called in question. In his letters to the Bishops of Macedonia, Achaia, Thessalia, Epirus, old and new, Prevalis and Dacia, he says: "THE SOLICITUDE OF THE UNIVERSAL CHURCH, which he undertook, RESTS ON THE BLESSED APOSTLE PETER,

---

* Codex can. eccl. Afric. c. lxviii.
† Ep. iii. ad Tolet. Syn. t. i., Coustant, col. 766
‡ Ep. xvi., ibid. col 835.
§ Ep. xii. ad episc. Afric. prov. Maurit. Cæsar.
‖ Ep. xii. ad episc. Afric. prov. Maurit. Cæsar.

BY THE DECREE OF THE LORD, since, according to the testimony of the Evangelist, he knows that it was founded on him : nor can his honor be free from solicitude, as it is certain that all depends on his deliberation. These things expand my mind to the provinces of the East; which our solicitude makes present to us." He proceeds to observe : " The Apostolic See, after mature examination of all the facts, appointed Perigenes Bishop of Corinth ;" and he dwells on the grievousness of the sin of resisting the authority of blessed Peter, " in whom," he says, " our Christ established the high priesthood. Whosoever rises contumeliously against him, cannot become an inhabitant of the kingdom of heaven. 'To thee,' He says, 'I will give the keys of the kingdom of heaven :" into which no one can enter without the favor of the gate-keeper. 'Thou art,' He says, 'Peter, and on this rock I will build My Church.' Whosoever, therefore, desires to be considered a priest in the sight of our God, since we come to God through Peter, on whom, as we before mentioned, it is certain that the Universal Church is founded, should be meek and humble of heart." Boniface, understanding that a synod was to be held at Corinth, to take into consideration the appointment of Perigenes, strongly denied the right to canvass the act of the Apostolic See : " No one has ever dared resist the Apostolical supremacy,* whose judgment cannot be reviewed."† This shows not only his own sense of the Apostolic prerogative, but also his confidence that all the precedents of antiquity were in harmony with his views.

Besides the many positive acts of authority which I have enumerated, the answers given to the consultations of the bishops from every part of Christendom, prove that the Roman bishop was a Superior, to whom all looked up for guidance. St. Jerom testifies that when at Rome, during the pontificate of Damasus, he was constantly engaged, by his order, in answering the synodical consultations that poured in from the East and the West.‡ The papal documents which I have quoted, were generally drawn up in reply to such consultations. Hallam admits that "consultations or references to the Bishop of Rome, in difficult cases of faith or discipline, had been common in early ages, and were even made by provincial and national councils."§

Dr. Nevin observes : " If any thing in the world can be said to be historically clear, it is the fact that with the close of the fourth century and the coming in of the fifth, the Primacy of the Roman See was admitted and acknowledged in all parts of the Christian world. This is granted by Barrow himself, in his great work on the Supremacy : though he tries to set aside the force of the fact, by resolving it into motives and reasons to suit his own cause."

---

* Culmini.
† Ep. xv. Constant, t. i. col. 1042.
‡ Ep. xci. alias xi.
§ Middle Ages, ch. vii. note.

§ 2.—UNIVERSAL PATRIARCH.

It has been asserted that St. Gregory the Great disclaimed the title and authority of Œcumenical or *Universal* Bishop, because he opposed the use of this title by John the Faster, Bishop of Constantinople. The term had been most justly applied to the Pope in various documents of the Council of Chalcedon : but it had not been used by Leo, or any of the predecessors of Gregory, because it appeared ostentatious, and they chose to be, as it were, on a level with their colleagues, by the exercise of humility, whenever there was no need of putting forward the authority of their office. Eulogius, Patriarch of Alexandria, having given this appellation to Gregory, the humble Pontiff wrote to him : "If your holiness calls me Universal Pope, you deny that you yourself are at all what you admit me to be entirely. But God forbid! Away with words which inflate vanity and wound charity."*

In writing to the Patriarchs of Alexandria and Antioch, Gregory designates the title a profane one : "You know," he says, "that this title was offered by the holy Council of Chalcedon to the Pontiff of the Apostolic See, which, by the appointment of God, I occupy : but none of my predecessors ever consented to use so profane a word, since if one is styled universal patriarch, the name of patriarch is denied to the others. But, far, far away be this from a Christian mind, to attempt to usurp a title, by which the honor of his brethren may be in the slightest degree diminished!"† The term, because ambiguous and capable of perverse interpretation, and in fact perversely used by the Bishop of Constantinople, is styled profane; but as employed in documents of the Council of Chalcedon, it was just and proper, although the Popes prudently abstained from its use.

It is not probable that the title was assumed by the Bishop of Constantinople in its worst sense, since he does not appear to have had any idea of discarding the superior authority of the Roman Bishop, or of denying the episcopal character of his colleagues. After the demise of John the Faster, Cyriacus, his successor, sent, as was usual, special messengers to report his ordination, and submit the acts of his synod to the Holy See. Gregory acknowledged that the language of the synod was Catholic ; but he complained that the dangerous title had not been abandoned. It was used, indeed, to signify amplitude, rather than universality of jurisdiction ; for which reason even the Patriarch of Antioch seemed willing to dissemble,‡ lest the peace of the Christian world should be disturbed on account of a term capable of a mild explanation : but Gregory perceived in it the germ of great evils, and justly reproached the ambitious prelate, as preparing the way for future encroachments : "What will you say at the last judgment to Christ, the Head of the Universal Church, whilst

---

* L. iv. ep. xxxvi. † L. v. ep. xliii. ‡ L. vii. ep. xxvii.

you are now striving, under cloak of this appellation, to subject all His members to yourself? Who, I pray, is held up as a model for imitation in this perverse term, if not he, who, despising the legions of angels, to whose ranks he belonged, attempted to rise to extraordinary distinction, that he might appear to be subject to none, and set over all—who even said : ' I will ascend into heaven, I will lift up my throne above the stars of heaven ?' What are all your brethren, the bishops of the Universal Church, but stars of heaven, over whom you wish to set yourself by a haughty term, and whose title, compared with yours, you wish to trample under foot ?"* He shows that even the apostles were but members of the Church under Christ: " Surely Peter, the apostle, is the first member of the holy Universal Church : Paul, Andrew, John, what else are they but the heads of particular nations ?† and yet all are members of the Church under one head."‡ This presents the true relations of the apostles to the Church. Even Peter was but a member of it, under Christ, but the chief member, as being the first of the apostles, and " to him the care of the whole Church was committed." In this sense, only, is he styled head.

The ambition of the Bishop of Constantinople manifested itself at an early period. Although Byzantium was but a suffragan see of Heraclea, up to the middle of the fourth century, the imperial dignity of the new Rome, as the city of Constantine was called, soon emboldened the Bishop to claim titles and privileges similar to those of ancient Rome. The fathers of Chalcedon, dazzled by the splendor of the imperial throne, consented to his wishes ; but Leo the Great annulled their decree, as derogatory to the rights of the Patriarchs of Alexandria and Antioch, which had been recognised by the Council of Nice, and, by the authority of blessed Peter, he declared it of no effect.§ This severe check did not deter John the Faster from aspiring to a title which the same Council had given only to the Roman Bishop, to whom he avowed his subjection, as Gregory testifies. Speaking of certain Sicilian bishops, who murmured at the supposed adoption at Rome of some Oriental usages, at a time when the ambition of the Bishop of Constantinople should be checked rather than fostered, he remarks : " As to what they say concerning the Church of Constantinople, who doubts that it is subject to the Apostolic See ? This is constantly avowed by the most pious emperor, and by our brother, the Bishop of that city."‖ "The Eastern Church," says Mr. Allies, " as its own rituals declare, always acknowledged St. Peter's primacy, and that his primacy was inherited by the Bishop of Rome."¶ The assumption of the offensive title had commenced in the pontificate of Pelagius, the predeces-

---

* L. iv. ep. xxxviii.
† Singularium plebium. He refers to the nations to which those apostles respectively preached the Gospel.
‡ L. iv. ep. xxxviii.
§ Ep. lv. ad Pulcher.
‖ L. ix. ep. xii.
¶ Church of England, p. 111.

sor of Gregory, who, on learning that John had used it, in a synod celebrated by him at Constantinople, in the year 588, "sent letters in which, by the authority of St. Peter the apostle, he annulled the acts of that synod."* In the same determined spirit of opposition to dangerous ambition, when Gregory understood that a synod had been called to meet at Constantinople, he addressed the bishops who were to convene there, and cautioned them against lending themselves to the designs of the Bishop of that city: "For," said he, "if one, as he thinks, is universal, it follows that you are not bishops." He reminds them that, "without the authority and consent of the Apostolic See, their proceedings could have no effect."†

It cannot be thought for a moment, that in rejecting the title Gregory disclaimed any superior authority in himself, as successor of Peter, since he affirmed the contrary, in the most positive terms, and exercised, in the most marked manner, the power of a ruler of the whole Church. "Assuredly," says Mr. Allies, "if there was any Pontiff who, like St. Leo, held the most strong and deeply-rooted convictions as to the prerogatives of the Roman See, it was St. Gregory."‡ His letters abound with admonitions, injunctions, decrees and threats, directed to bishops in every portion of the Church, all of whom he treated as brethren whilst they were blameless; but admonished them as a father, if they erred, and punished them as a judge, when they proved delinquent. When Serenus, Bishop of Marseilles, indignant at the marks of veneration given to a sacred image, broke it in pieces, as an occasion of superstition, and thereby shocked the feelings of the faithful, Gregory sent a special messenger, and wrote to admonish him that the excess, or abuse, should be corrected, without taking sacred images from the Church, in which they served as books for the unlearned.§ On complaint being lodged of excessive lenity, amounting almost to connivance, used toward a licentious priest by the same prelate, he was subjected to such punishment as the Bishop of Arles, Vicar of the Holy See, should inflict: "*nostra hoc sic vice corrigere.*"‖ The proofs of a similar exercise of power throughout Gaul, Italy, Sicily, and Corsica, are abundant. His vigilance extended to Illyricum, where he commissioned the Bishops of Justiniana Prima¶ and of Scutari, to inquire into the alleged invasion of the see by the deposed Bishop Paul, and, in case of his conviction, to confine him to a monastery, and deprive him of the holy communion until death.** It was likewise felt in Africa.

---

* L. v. ep. xliii. † L. ix. ep. lxviii.
‡ Church of England Cleared, &c. p. 156. § L. ix. ep. cv. l. xi. ep. xiii.
‖ L. xi. ep. lv.
¶ A city in Bulgaria, the birthplace of the elder Justinian, was so called. A city in Moesia superior was called Justiniana Secunda: and the ancient city of Chalcedon was styled Justiniana Tertia.
** L. xii. ep. xxx. xxxi.

GOVERNING POWER.

Gregory enjoined on the Council of Byzacium* to investigate the charges made against their primate, and proceed as justice might require.† He directed the Bishop of Numidia, in conjunction with Victor, the primate, and other bishops, to examine the complaints of the clergy against Paulinus, Bishop of Tegessis, and proceed according to justice; and he authorized Hilary, his notary, to be present at the trial.‡ The provinces immediately subject to the patriarchs were not beyond the reach of his authority, although he used it with the moderation which was inspired by respect for his colleagues. Hearing that simoniacal abuses existed in the Church of Alexandria, he addressed the Bishop of that city, exhorting him to abolish them without delay.§ He communicated to the Bishop of Jerusalem the report made to him of simoniacal practices and of strifes which prevailed in that Church, urging him to remedy these evils.‖

The highest dignitaries addressed Gregory in terms expressive at once of his exalted station and personal merit. Anastasius, Patriarch of Antioch, styled him "the mouth of the Lord."¶ He, in return, wrote to them affectionately; and, whilst stating his faith, and explaining his sentiments as to the duties of the pastoral office, gave to all the patriarchs sublime instructions for their own conduct.** To Eulogius, Patriarch of Alexandria, who had extolled the dignity of the chair of Peter, Gregory replied, that Alexandria and Antioch participated in this honor: " Your holiness,†† in your letters, has said many flattering things concerning the chair of St. Peter, prince of the apostles, who, you observe, still occupies it through his successors.—Who does not know that the holy Church is strengthened by the solidity of the prince of the apostles, whose name denotes the firmness of his mind, he being called Peter from the rock? To him Truth itself said: 'I will give to thee the keys of the kingdom of heaven.' And again: 'Thou being once converted, confirm thy brethren.' And again: 'Simon, son of John, lovest thou Me? Feed My sheep.' "‡‡

The contest concerning the use of the title "œcumenical" continued until Phocas, the emperor, in 607, forbade the Bishop of Constantinople to usurp it, and commanded the Apostolic See of Blessed Peter, " which is the head of all the churches," to be maintained in the enjoyment of her legitimate honors.§§ The evil broke out anew in the ninth century, when Photius, the intruder into the patriarchate, found it his interest to disregard altogether

---

* Now part of Tunis. † Ib. ep. xxviii.
‡ L. xiii. ep. xxxii. § L. xiii. ep. xii.
‖ L. xi. ep. xlvi. ¶ L. i. ep. vii.
** L. i. ep. xxv. †† This title was not as yet confined to the Pope.
‡‡ L. vii. ep. xl.
§§ This is attested by Anastasius in *Vita Bonifacii III.*, and by Paulus Diaconus, l. iv. c. xi. de gestis Longobard. Hallam ably shows the absurdity of dating the papal supremacy from this epoch: "The popes," he avows, "had unquestionably exercised a species of supremacy for more than two centuries before this time, which had lately reached a high point of authority under Gregory I."—Middle Ages, ch. vii. note.

the superior authority of the Roman Bishop. No one was better qualified to exemplify in his own person the results of the false principle, which measured the dignity of the bishop by his proximity to the throne, than the courtier who passed to the patriarchal chair through imperial favor His revolt against the paternal rule of the successor of Peter, who maintained the rights of Ignatius, the deposed patriarch, showed that pride and ambition are opposed to the order, which Divine Wisdom has established in the Church. The scandal of this schism was subsequently repaired, and the governing power of the Roman Pontiff fully admitted by the Greeks; but the elements of discord still remained, to burst forth anew with increased fury, in the eleventh century. From that time palliatives were in vain applied; and, after several ineffectual attempts at reunion, the evil became desperate in the fifteenth century, when the sword of the Mussulman was employed by divine justice to punish the obstinacy which no condescension could cure. Thus the vanity of a title and the love of power, gradually brought on calamities which the weak men who first assumed it did not at all anticipate. But wisdom is justified in her children—the event having shown how vain it is to lean on the arm of the flesh, when the divine favor is withdrawn. The throne of the imperial favorite has been overturned, whilst the chair of Peter remains where his hand placed it.

CHAPTER XIII.

The Hierarchy.

§ 1.—PATRIARCHAL SYSTEM.

NOTHING is clearer in the history of the Church, than the distinction of rank among her prelates. In each province one bishop presided, whose see was generally in the chief city, whence he was called metropolitan and archbishop. In some nations, one was designated primate, whose rank was superior to that of the other metropolitans. There were also exarchs, or privileged bishops, who were exempt from dependence on immediate superiors in the hierarchy, although they did not exercise metropolitical authority. The name of patriarchs was given in the fifth century to the Bishops of Rome, Alexandria, and Antioch, each of whom from the commencement extended his jurisdiction over large provinces, or dioceses, as they were anciently called. The Roman Bishop exercised the power of metropolitan over the provinces styled Suburbicarian, which, within Italy, extended from Liguria to the Ionian Sea, and included Sicily; and he enjoyed patriarchal jurisdiction over the dioceses of the West, namely, besides all Italy, Illyricum, Spain, Gaul, Britain, and Africa proper. The Bishop of Alexandria was second in rank, governing Egypt, Lybia, and Pentapolis; and the Bishop of Antioch exercised similar authority throughout the East. That the Roman Bishop was first in rank is not seriously questioned by any one who is conversant with ancient documents. "The Bishop of Rome," says Mr. Allies, "as successor of St. Peter, has a decided pre-eminence. It is very apparent, and is acknowledged in the East, as well as in the West."* "No student of antiquity can doubt the primacy of the Roman See."† Describing the unquestioned constitution of the Catholic Church, at the time of the Council of Nicea, he states that "the three great Sees of Rome, Alexandria, and Antioch, exercised a powerful, but entirely paternal influence on their colleagues, that of Rome having the undoubted primacy, not derived from the gift of Councils, or the rank of the imperial city, but from immemorial tradition as the See of Peter."‡

---

* Church of England, &c. p. 18.
† Church of England Cleared, &c. p. 27.
‡ Ibidem, p. 47.

Although the terms patriarch and archbishop were occasionally applied to the Pope, they were not used as marking a restriction of power within local limits; on the contrary, the epithet œcumenical* was sometimes added, to denote his universal authority; and, although the Popes did, in fact, exercise throughout the provinces of the West immediate jurisdiction and superintendence, such as the Patriarchs of Alexandria and Antioch had in their respective provinces, yet it was not exercised as merely patriarchal, but as a portion of that apostolical authority which was lodged in Peter, and which embraced in its plenitude the whole flock of Christ. All antiquity shows that the Bishop of Rome, at all times, and everywhere, acted as successor of Peter, and pastor of the Universal Church. The patriarchal jurisdiction enjoyed by the Bishops of the other two Sees, was, in truth, originally derived from the will of the apostle, who, as Innocent I. testifies, delegated to his disciple Mark, and to Evodius, a portion of his general solicitude, that they might have a more immediate supervision over their districts;† whilst he reserved to himself the immediate government of the West, besides his general superintendence over the whole Church. The Council of Nice confirmed the rights and privileges of the two Sees of Alexandria and Antioch.

The celebrated sixth canon of Nice is couched in these words: " Let the ancient customs be kept, which are in Egypt, Lybia, and Pentapolis, that the Bishop of Alexandria may have full power over all these places, as this is customary also with the Bishop of Rome. In like manner, also, in Antioch and in the other provinces, let the privileges, dignities, and authority of the churches be preserved."‡ The clause regarding the Roman Bishop, which is used as confirmatory of the Alexandrian usage, marks the similitude of the patriarchal authority as exercised by each, but does not declare that they are in all respects alike. The occasion which gave rise to this enactment shows the object which the fathers had in view. Meletius, a bishop of Egypt, having been deposed by St. Peter of Alexandria, formed a schism, and throwing off all dependence on that See, presumed to establish new bishoprics in that province.§ "This canon was enacted," as Potter avows, "upon a complaint of Alexander, the Bishop of Alexandria, that the metropolitical rights of his See had been invaded by Meletius, the schismatical Bishop of Lycopolis in Thebais, who had taken upon him to ordain bishops without Alexander's consent."|| The fathers confirmed the usage of the Church of Alexandria by reference to the usage of Rome. The learned Clinch observes, that "from the Greek, it appears first, that no confirmation was given at

---

* See various documents read in the Council of Chalcedon.
† Ep. xxiv. ad Alex. Antioch., to Agapitus, apud Fleury, l. xxxii. an. 536
‡ Coll. Hard. p. 432.
§ Apol. ii. Athanas.
|| Church Government, p. 188. See also Theodoret Hist. l. i. c. ix.

Nicea to the usage of the Church of Rome: that on the contrary, the usage of Alexandria was confirmed, because it had the authority of Roman usage. Secondly, it is equally plain, that no boundaries are either marked, or alluded to, within which the Roman Bishop exercised that general authority which the fathers had in view."*

The liberty taken by Ruffinus in his version of this canon, seems wholly unwarrantable, so that the investigation of its meaning should not be embarrassed by his interpolation. It becomes necessary, however, to notice it, as it has acquired importance by the pains which the learned have taken to reconcile it with well-known facts. He interprets the canon as meaning, "that the ancient custom be observed in Alexandria and in the city of Rome, so that the former bishop should have charge of Egypt, and the latter of the suburbicarian churches."† Great disputes have been raised as to the territory designated by the term "suburbicarian," which some have explained of the district of the "præfectus urbis," extending only to the distance of a hundred miles around Rome; whilst Sirmond has proved that it embraced the ten southern provinces of Italy, together with Sicily, Sardinia, Corsica, and other adjacent islands, all of which were subject to the officer styled *Vicarius urbis*. Mr. Palmer asserts that this was the original and legitimate extent of the Roman patriarchate, from which he excludes even the northern provinces of Italy, as well as Gaul, Spain, Britain, and other nations.‡ The learned, however, generally admit that the whole West, including Africa proper, was subject to the patriarchal jurisdiction of the Bishop of Rome, since, in fact, he exercised from the earliest period, a special superintendence over all the Western nations. It is not, indeed, our interest to dispute the position of the Anglican divine; for if the patriarchal power was confined within such narrow limits, the numerous instances in which the Roman Bishop interposed in the ecclesiastical affairs of the more distant countries, can only be accounted for by his authority as primate of the entire Church.

Boniface I., in the early part of the fifth century, in a letter to the bishops of Thessalia, did not hesitate to affirm, that the Nicene fathers had made no decree in reference to the prerogatives of the Holy See, because they were conscious that these flowed from a higher source than ecclesiastical legislation, namely, the will and act of Christ Himself. "The general institution of the rising Church began," he says, "with the honor of the blessed Peter, in whom its government and highest authority centre; for from this fountain ecclesiastical discipline has flowed through all the churches, as religion increased. This is obvious from the laws of the Nicene synod, which did not attempt to enact any thing in regard to him, knowing that nothing could be conferred above his merit, and that

---

* Letters on Church Government, p. 271.   † Hist. Eccl. l. i. c. vi.
‡ Treatise on the Church, vol. ii. part vii. p. 507.

all things were granted to him by the voice of the Lord."* The same Pontiff describes the privileges of the Sees of Alexandria and Antioch as guarded by ecclesiastical enactments, for the purposes of unity, and with necessary dependence on the apostolic chair.

In the great Council of Chalcedon the primacy of the Roman See was solemnly acknowledged and most effectually exercised. "We consider," said the fathers, "that the primacy of all and the chief honor, according to the canons, should be preserved to the most beloved of God, the Archbishop of ancient Rome."† The details of the proceedings show most plainly the power which the Pontiff exercised through his legates, so that Mr. Allies, speaking of this Council, says: "that (the patriarch) of Rome has the unquestioned primacy, and is seen at the centre, sustaining and animating the whole."‡ Leo, of whom he speaks, thus explains the whole economy of the Church: "Though priests have a like dignity, yet they have not an equal jurisdiction, since even amongst the most blessed apostles, as there was a likeness of honor, so was there a certain distinction of power, and the election of all being equal, pre-eminence over the rest was given to one, from which type the distinction between bishops also has arisen, and it was provided by an important arrangement, that all should not claim to themselves power over all, but that in every province there should be one, whose sentence should be considered the first among his brethren; and others again, seated in the greater cities, should undertake a larger care, through whom the direction of the Universal Church should converge to the one See of Peter, and nothing anywhere disagree with its head."§

§ 2.—WESTERN PATRIARCHATE.

The claims of the Bishop of Rome on the obedience of the Western churches, were not dependent on the mere principle of authority, since he begot them in Christ, by means of apostolic men, whom he sent to evangelize them: as INNOCENT I. affirmed, without fear of contradiction: "It is manifest that no one founded churches throughout all Italy, Gaul, Spain, Africa, and Sicily, and the adjacent islands, except those whom the venerable Peter, or his successors, ordained priests."‖

The exercise of papal power over the churches of Western Europe is proved by the very ancient practice of sending the *pallium*, a badge of authority, to bishops of distinguished rank, especially to metropolitans. As early as the year 336, it was used by the Bishop of Ostia, as a mark of his privilege as consecrator of the Bishop of Rome.¶ "It was, about A.D. 500, given by Pope Symmachus to his vicar, or legate, Cesarius of

---

* Ep. xiv.
† Act xvi. col. 637.
‡ The Church of England Cleared, &c. p. 53.
§ Ep. xiv. cap. i. xi.
‖ Ep. xxv. ad Decentium Eugub.
¶ Anastas. in Marci vita.

Arles. The same Pontiff granted it to Theodore of Laureacum,* in conformity with the usage of his predecessors.† It is spoken of as an immemorial usage by Gregory the Great, in whose letters passages abound recording its concession to various prelates. He granted it to Constantius, Bishop of Milan, a metropolitical see; to Maximus, metropolitan of Dalmatia; to Leander of Seville, metropolitan of the province of Bœtica, in Spain; to John of Corinth, metropolitan in the Morea; to Andrew of Nicopolis, metropolitan in Epirus; to John of the First Justiniana, or Ocrida, metropolitan of Dardania; and to the metropolitans of Aquileja, Cagliari, Dyrrachium, Crete, Philippopolis, and Salonica. He also granted it to Virgil of Arles. He directed the pallium to be given to the Bishop of Autun, in a synod, which he ordered to be held, requiring, however, a promise on his part to remove simoniacal abuses.‡ At the same time he assigned to this bishop the next place after the Bishop of Lyons, by his own indulgence and authority.§ Notwithstanding these facts, Palmer says, that "with two exceptions, none of the Western bishops, except the Vicars of the Apostolic See, received the pallium till the time of Pope Zacharias, about 743."|| When Desiderius, a bishop of some place in Gaul, sought to obtain this badge of authority, Gregory answered, that after diligent search in the Roman archives, he could find no document of such a grant to the predecessors of the petitioner.¶ Sending it to the Bishop of Palermo, he observed: "We admonish you that the reverence due to the Apostolic See should be disturbed by the presumption of no one; for the state of the members is sound, when the head of faith suffers no injury, and the authority of the canons continues always safe and inviolate."**

The primacy of the Apostolic See was particularly displayed in the special privileges granted to some bishops, which were modified and changed, according as the interests of religion, in the altered circumstances of various countries, required. The See of Arles from ancient times was invested with extraordinary authority, recognised and confirmed by Pope Zosimus: "We ordain that the Bishop of the city of Arles shall have, as he always has had, chief authority in ordaining priests. Let him recall to his jurisdiction the provinces of Narbonne the first, and Narbonne the second. Be it known that whosoever hereafter, in opposition to the decrees of the Apostolic See, and to the commands of our predecessors, shall presume to ordain any one in the above provinces, without the authority of the metropolitan bishop, or whoever shall suffer himself to be unlawfully ordained, is deprived of the priesthood."†† Not only

---

* The town Enns, in Austria, at the conflux of the river Enns and the Danube, is near the site of Laureacum.
† Conc. edit. Mansi, t. viii. col. 228.   ‡ Ep. cvii.   § Ep. cviii.
|| Treatise on the Church, vol. ii. part vii. ch. viii. p. 521.
¶ Ep. cxii.   ** L. xiii. ep. xxxvii.   †† Ep. i. Coustant, t. i. col. 936.

are the ancient privileges of the See of Arles confirmed, but a most severe penalty is attached to their violation. Bishops who usurp the power of ordaining, in places subject to its jurisdiction, are suspended altogether from the exercise of episcopal functions. This authority, nevertheless, was restricted by St. Leo, who transferred a portion of the province to the See of Vienne,* but it was again enlarged by other Popes, who constituted the Bishop of Arles Apostolic Legate. Guizot attempts to account for these changes, and for the jurisdiction subsequently granted to the Sees of Lyons and Sens, by the jealousy of the Roman Bishop, lest a Gaulish prelate, with extensive authority permanently attached to his see, should become a rival in the Western patriarchate :† but facts and documents plainly show that the papal action was in all cases solicited, and that it was grounded on the representations of those concerned, and the change of local relations. The learned Clinch, with more discernment and justice, has observed : "The synod of Turin adjudged a primatial right to Vienne, as being a civil metropolis. The diocese of Arles appealed from this decision to Rome, and by Rome it was annulled. Leo I. took away from St. Hilary a portion of his diocese, and transferred it to Vienne. The See of Arles obtained from after-Popes a compensation for this loss by an apostolical delegation. The Bishop of Lyons next set up for the primacy, as being successor to Irenæus. In the mean time the ancient civil boundaries are shifted by the introduction of foreign princes; and the metropolitan power, which originally had meant primacy, being divided against itself, and undermined by time, required helps from that authority which alone remained confessedly the first."‡

The terms in which the Bishops of the province of Arles besought Leo to restore the privileges of this see, contain what Mr. Allies designates "this undoubted testimony to the primacy of the Roman Church." "By the priest of this church, (*Arles*) it is certain that our predecessors, as well as ourselves, have been consecrated to the high priesthood by the gift of the Lord; in which, following antiquity, the predecessors of your Holiness confirmed by their published letters this which old custom had handed down, concerning the privileges of the Church of Arles, (as the records of the Apostolical See doubtless prove;) believing it to be full of reason and justice, that as through the most blessed Peter, prince of the apostles, the holy Roman Church holds the primacy over all the churches of the world, so also within the Gauls the Church of Arles, which had been thought worthy to receive for its priest St. Trophimus, sent by the apostles, should claim the right of ordaining to the high priesthood."§

---

* Ep. lxvi.
† Cours d'histoire moderne, t. ii. p. 24.
‡ Letters on Church Government, p. 245.
§ Inter opera Leonis, ep. xlv.

§ 3.—APOSTOLIC VICARS.

The delegation of authority to bishops as Vicars of the Apostolic See, is among the most splendid evidences of the primacy. Barrow acknowledges that in the fourth century the Popes bestowed the title of Vicars on various bishops: "The Popes, indeed, in the fourth century, began to confer on certain bishops, as occasion served, or for continuance, the title of their Vicar, or Lieutenant, thereby pretending to impart authority to them; whereby they were enabled for performance of divers things, which otherwise, by their own episcopal or metropolitical power, they could not perform. Thus did Pope Celestine constitute Cyril in his room. Pope Leo appointed Anatolius of Constantinople. Pope Felix, Acacius of Constantinople. Pope Hormisdas, Epiphanius of Constantinople. Pope Simplicius to Zeno, Bishop of Seville : 'We thought it convenient that you should be held up by the vicariate authority of our see.' So did Siricius and his successors constitute the bishops of Thessalonica to be their vicars in the diocese of Illyricum. So did Pope Zosimus bestow a like vicarious power upon the Bishop of Arles. So to the Bishop of Justiniana prima in Bulgaria, (or Dardania Europæ,) the like privilege was granted (by procurement of the Emperor Justinian, native of that place.) Afterwards temporary or occasional vicars were appointed (such as Austin, in England, Boniface in Germany."*)

When Maximus, a philosopher, had been ordained bishop by some Egyptian prelates, for the See of Constantinople, Damasus addressed a letter to Acholius, Bishop of Thessalonica, and other bishops, reprobating the irregularity of his ordination, and directing them to proceed to the election of a bishop, blameless, orthodox, and peaceful, in a synod to be held in the imperial city. He urged the observance of the ancient canons, which forbade a bishop to be transferred from one see to another, lest ambition should be fostered.† By a special letter he instructed Acholius, as his Vicar, to see, that hereafter a Catholic bishop should be chosen, with whom peace could be permanently had.‡ This is the first instance of the appointment of an Apostolic Vicar throughout Illyricum, the reason of which is conjectured by Tillemont to be, that these provinces having been added by Gratian, in the year 379, to the Eastern empire, the Pope could no longer conveniently exercise a direct inspection over them, as he was wont to do over the remainder of the provinces of the West. Siricius addressing Anisius, Bishop of the same See, directed that " no one should presume to ordain bishops in Illyricum without his consent."§

---

* Treatise on the Supremacy, Supp. vi. p. 733.
† Ep. viii. Damasi ad Acholium et alios, Coustant, t. i. col. 535.
‡ Ep. ix. St. Innocent speaks of Acholius as having been Vicar Apostolic.
§ Ep. iv. Syricii, apud Coustant, t. i. col. 642.

INNOCENT I. constituted Rufus, Bishop of Thessalonica, Vicar, to determine "all cases that might arise throughout the churches of Achaia, Thessalia, Epirus old and new, Crete, Dacia, both *mediterranea* and *ripensis*,* Mœsia, Dardania, and Prævalis;"† alleging the examples of his apostolic predecessors, who had given like power to Acholius and Anysius. BONIFACE, having appointed Rufus, Bishop of Thessalonica, Vicar Apostolic, addressed him as charged with the care of all the churches of Illyricum: "The blessed apostle Peter has entrusted to the Church of Thessalonica all things, in his own stead."—"You have for your defence the blessed apostle Peter, who can oppose your enemies, according to that strength which is peculiarly his own. The fisherman does not suffer the privilege of his See to be lost, whilst you are laboring."‡ Again he says: "THE BLESSED APOSTLE PETER, TO WHOM THE CITADEL OF THE PRIESTHOOD WAS GRANTED BY THE VOICE OF THE LORD, rejoices exceedingly, when he sees that the children of inviolable peace are careful of the honor granted him by the Lord."§ Some of the bishops having resisted the authority of 'Rufus, as Vicar Apostolic, Boniface reproaches and threatens them: "The apostle says: 'What will you? Shall I come to you with a rod, or in charity and in the spirit of meekness?' You know that blessed Peter can do both,—treat the mild with meekness—punish the proud with the rod. Therefore give due honor to the head. Certainly if in any respect the reproof (*given by the Vicar to the bishops*) appeared excessive, since the Apostolic See holds its principality in order that it may freely receive the complaints of all, we should have been addressed on this point, and an embassy sent to us, whom you see charged with the ultimate settlement of all things. Let there be an end to this novel presumption. Let no one dare hope for what is unlawful. Let no one strive to set aside the regulations of our fathers, which have been so long in force. Whoever considers himself a bishop, let him obey our ordinance."‖

Xystus sustained Anastasius, Bishop of Thessalonica, in his privileges as Vicar Apostolic, and reminded Perigeues, Bishop of Corinth, to respect his authority, as he owed his own place to the favor of the Holy See.¶ Addressing the synod of Thessalonica, he insisted on the maintenance of the authority of the Vicar.**

ST. LEO THE GREAT, acting in accordance with the example of his predecessors, committed to Anastasius, Bishop of Thessalonica, the authority of Vicar over all the churches of Illyricum, assigning as the reason of this delegation his anxiety to discharge his duty as general pastor.

---

* That part of Dacia which bordered on the Danube was called *ripensis;* that part which was remote from this river was called *mediterranea*, or inland.
† Ep. xiii. n. 2.   ‡ Constant, t. i. col. 1035.
§ Ep. iv. col. 1019, t. i. Hard.   ‖ Ep. xiv. Constant.
¶ Ep. vii. Constant, t. i. col. 1262.   ** Ep. ix. col. 1263.

"Since," he says, "our solicitude extends to all the churches, as the Lord requires of us, who entrusted to the most blessed apostle Peter the primacy of the apostolic dignity, as a reward of his faith, establishing the Universal Church in the solidity of the foundation itself, we communicate this necessary solicitude to those who are united with us by the affection of brotherhood. Following, therefore, the example of those whose memory we venerate, we have constituted our brother and fellow-bishop Anastasius our Vicar, and enjoined on him to see, from his watch-tower, that nothing unlawful be attempted by any one; and we admonish you, beloved, to obey him in all that regards ecclesiastical discipline: for your obedience will not be rendered to him, but to us, who are known to have entrusted him with this office in those provinces, in consequence of our solicitude."* In this letter Leo decreed that the disputes of bishops should be terminated by his Vicar; to whom likewise he reserved the consecration of all metropolitans throughout the province: directing, at the same time, that no bishop should be consecrated by any metropolitan without his knowledge and authority. All these documents plainly prove that the power delegated was founded on the divine commission to Peter, for the government of the whole Church. In his letter to the Vicar, he expressly says that he appoints him to fulfil the duty "which, in virtue of our headship," BY DIVINE INSTITUTION, we owe to all churches.†

The term "Vicar Apostolic," in modern usage denotes a bishop whose title is not derived from the see or territory committed to his charge, which he governs rather as the delegate of the Holy See, during the good pleasure of the Pontiff. Some fancy the episcopal tenure to be universally of this precarious character, so that all bishops are but as tenants at will; or officers of the Pope, to be dismissed when he judges proper. This, however, is not the sentiment of the Pontiff himself, who treats all titular bishops as his colleagues, and claims no right to remove them but for canonical causes, unless in extraordinary emergencies in which the highest interests of religion are at stake. The most ardent supporters of the papal privileges give us no other views. "The power of the Pope," says Ballerini, "although supreme, is not the only authority left by Christ in His Church, since bishops are called to share in his solicitude; and although in the fulness of his power he can regulate and limit the exercise and use of their faculties, as he may deem it expedient for the good of the Church, nevertheless he cannot monopolize and assume to himself all their faculties, or make them as his mere vicars, or regard all the dioceses as his own: whence it follows that not the Pope alone throughout the whole Church, but the bishops likewise in their respective dioceses have ordinary jurisdiction, by divine right."‡ Bolgeni also denies that bishops

---

* Ep. v. ad episcopos metrop. per Illyricum. † Ep. x.
‡ Vindiciæ auct. pontif. contra Just. Febron. c. iii. n. 12.

are mere vicars of the Pope.* Their dependence on the Apostolic See is without detriment to their rank in the Church, as is evident from the reservation made in the oath of consecration: SALVO MEO ORDINE. They can address the actual Pontiff in the words which St. Augustin addressed to Boniface: "To sit on our watch-towers and guard the flock belongs in common to all of us who have episcopal functions, although the hill on which you stand is more conspicuous than the rest."† In truth their submission to the chief bishop is the great guarantee of their true independence, which they sacrifice to regal or popular caprice, when they attempt to set themselves free from the authority which Christ has placed over pastors and people. "In better times," as Mr. Allies ingenuously avows, "doubtless every bishop felt his hand strengthened in his particular diocese, and had an additional security against the infraction of his rights by his brethren, when he was able to throw himself back on the unbiassed and impartial authority of the Bishop of Rome.‡

4.—PAPAL RELATIONS TO PATRIARCHS.

As the exercise of pontifical power throughout the Western patriarchate, although constantly referred by the Popes themselves to the commission given to Peter, may not appear to all conclusive evidence of supremacy, it is important to consider the relations of the Bishops of Rome to the Patriarchs of Alexandria and Antioch. These governed their respective provinces with full power, ἐξουσία: without recourse to the Pope for the appointment of bishops, or other acts of ordinary jurisdiction; whom, however, they notified of their own consecration, to obtain recognition by letters of communion. St. Leo, writing to Timothy Salophaciolus, who had recently succeeded Timothy Ælurus in the see of Alexandria, observes that his messengers, with the testimonials of his ordination, had come to the Apostolic See, "as was necessary and customary."§ This system having been established from the earliest period, and having been ratified by many acts of the Popes, was altogether sufficient to convey jurisdiction, from whatsoever source it originally flowed. When their own authority was violently assailed, or when faith was endangered, the patriarchs had recourse to the Pontiff. Athanasius fled to Rome, to obtain pontifical aid against his persecutors, and on his return he was recommended to the confidence of his flock by letters of Pope Julius, in which he congratulated them on the success of their

---

* L'Episcopato, vol. i. art. iii. See also Perrone, vol. viii. Tract. de locis theolog. p. 1, s. ii. c. iii.

† Tom. x. 412 B., apud Allies, p. 76.

‡ Church of England Cleared, &c. p. 101.

§ Sicut necessario et ex more fecistis ut per filios nostros Danielem presbyterum, et Timotheum diaconum ordinationis tuæ ad nos scripta dirigeres.—Ep. ci. ad Tim. Alex.

prayers for the restoration of their bishop. Peter found aid in the same paternal authority, and returned to Alexandria in 378, "bringing with him a letter of the Bishop Damasus, in which he testified his faith in the consubstantiality of the Son, and approved of his ordination."* John Talaja, in the following century, sought the papal confirmation to occupy the same see, as Simplicius affirms in his letter to Acacius, "that the succession of a Catholic bishop to the ministry of the deceased, might derive strength from the assent of the apostolic authority."†

The dependence of the patriarchates on the Roman Bishop is further evinced from the pontifical interposition in some extraordinary cases. LEO, writing to Dioscorus, Bishop of Alexandria, to correct some usages which were not in harmony with the traditions of the Roman Church, observed, that the disciple of St. Peter had not certainly departed from the teaching of his master : "for," says he, "since the most blessed Peter received the apostolic principality from the Lord, and the Roman Church perseveres in his traditions, we cannot believe that his holy disciple Mark, who first governed the Church of Alexandria, framed differently the decrees which have come down from him by tradition."‡

The energy with which this holy Pontiff exercised his office throughout the whole Church, is avowed by Mr. Allies: "In truth we behold St. Leo set on a watch-tower, and directing his gaze over the whole Church : over his own West more especially, but over the East too, if need be. He can judge Alexandria, Antioch, and Constantinople, as well as Eugubium, and is as ready too. Wherever canons are broken, ancient custom disregarded, encroachments attempted, where bishops are neglectful, or metropolitans tyrannical, where heresy is imputed to patriarchs, in short, wherever a stone in the whole sacred building is being loosened, or threatens to fall, there he is at hand to repair and restore, to warn, to protect, or to punish."§

The Church of Antioch was avowedly dependent on the See of Peter, as is clear from the testimony of JUVENAL, Bishop of Jerusalem, in the Council of Antioch : "It is customary, conformably with apostolic order and tradition, that the See of Antioch should be directed by the See of the great Rome, and should be judged by it."‖

When the Bishop of Constantinople acquired importance, and claimed patriarchal authority, it was usual to communicate his ordination to the Holy See by a formal embassy. Nectarius being chosen Bishop of Constantinople, ambassadors were despatched by the Emperor Theodosius to the Roman bishop, with a view to obtain his assent and confirmation, as BONIFACE testifies: "Theodosius, a prince whose clemency is in sweet remembrance, considering that the ordination of Nectarius was not

---

* Socrat. l. iv. Hist. c. xxxvii. † Ep. vii.
‡ Ep. ix. ad Dioscorum ep. Alex. § Church of England Cleared, &c. p. 101.
‖ Conc. Antioch. act. iv. t. iv. Conc. Edit. Mansi, col. 1311..

assured, because it was not known to us, sending courtiers from his side with bishops, asked, in due form, a letter of communion to be addressed to him by this Holy See, to confirm his priesthood."* This custom was considered obligatory; so that Pope Hormisdas required Epiphanius, Bishop of that See, to comply with it, not being content with a mere letter of information.† A splendid embassy was sent to Rome, in the year 398, with Acacius of Berœa at its head, to notify the election of St. John Chrysostom.‡ Innocent I. refused to acknowledge Atticus, Bishop of Constantinople, until he should send ambassadors to communicate his election, and prove that he had fulfilled the prescribed conditions of peace.§ St. Leo would not hold communion with Anatolius, until he was satisfied of his orthodoxy, and always spoke of his occupancy of that see as a favor which he owed to Pontifical indulgence.‖ Cyriacus, Bishop of that city, sent ambassadors to Gregory the Great, with the proceedings of the synod, after his ordination.

The authority of the Pope became particularly manifest, when the patriarchates, in consequence of the incursion of heretics, required his interposition. BONIFACE states, "that the greatest Oriental churches, in important affairs which needed maturer discussion, always consulted the Roman See, and when the case required it, sought its aid."¶ ST. BASIL, who was metropolitan of Cæsarea, writing to Meletius, Patriarch of Antioch, communicated to him the design which he had formed of sending to Rome, in order to obtain a visit from some of the Italian prelates, to settle the disturbances of the East. The bearer of this letter was a deacon named Dorothee: "This resolution has been formed," he says, "that this same brother of ours, Dorothee, should go to Rome, and press some to visit us from Italy."** He wrote in like manner to St. Athanasius, Bishop of Alexandria: "It has appeared to us advisable to send to the Bishop of Rome, that he may look to our affairs; and to suggest to him, that if it be difficult to despatch some persons thence by a general and synodical decree, he himself, by his authority, may act in the case, and choose persons able to bear the journey, and endowed with such meekness and firmness of character as would be likely to recall the perverse to correct sentiments."†† Addressing Damasus, Bishop of Rome, he styles him, "Most honored Father!" and states that the hope that harmony and truth would prevail, having hitherto proved deceptive, he

---

* Vide Bonifacii I. ep. xiv. t. i. Constant.
† Hormisdæ, ep. lxviii. alias cxi.
‡ Pallad. de vita Chrysost, c. iv.
§ Ep. xxii. apud Constant, t. i. col. 848.
‖ "Quod nostro beneficio noscitur consecutus."—Ep. liv. ad Martianum Augustum. "Mei favoris assensu Constantinopolitanæ ecclesiæ sacerdotium fuerit consecutus."—Ep. lv. ad Pulcheriam Augustam.
¶ Ep. xvi. apud Constant, t. i. col. 1043.   ** Ep. lxviii.   †† Ep. lxix.

has recourse to him, that he may succor the churches of the East, as Dionysius, Bishop of Rome, had formerly done: "Being disappointed in our expectations, and unable to bear our evils any longer, we have resolved to write, and urge you to come to our relief, and to send to us some men harmonizing in sentiment, who may reconcile those who are at variance, or restore the churches of God to harmony, or, at least, make more manifest to you the authors of disturbance, that you may hereafter plainly know with whom it is proper for you to hold communion. We ask nothing new, but what has been usual of old with other blessed men beloved of God, especially among yourselves; for we know by tradition, being instructed by our fathers whom we have questioned, and by documents which are still preserved amongst us, that Dionysius, the most blessed bishop, who was illustrious among you for the integrity of his faith and his other virtues, visited, by letter, our Church of Cæsarea, and sent persons to ransom the brethren from captivity. Our affairs are at present in a more difficult and gloomy situation, and need greater care: for we now grieve over, not the razing of our earthly dwellings, but the destruction of our churches—we witness not corporal servitude, but the bondage of our souls, which is daily effected by the abettors of heresy, who have the sway. Wherefore, unless you hasten to our relief, in a little while you will scarcely find any to whom you may reach the hand, since all will be brought under the power of heresy."* The language of this address is that of affectionate appeal to superior authority. Damasus was addressed not merely as a brother, sound in faith, and possessing wide influence, but as one clothed with power, whose messengers might gain to truth and peace the rebellious children of error. Were personal influence alone regarded, Basil might be expected to accomplish much more than the envoys of the Roman Bishop; whose high authority, however, would be respected by those who would not yield to the persuasive eloquence of the metropolitan of Cæsarea, or to the commands of the Patriarch of Antioch.

Thus we have seen that the power of the Bishop of Rome was implored by the patriarchs themselves, and was effectually exercised in their behalf, whenever any emergency required his interposition. Mr. Allies asks: "When the ship of the Church was in distress, whom should we expect to see at the rudder but St. Peter?"† That he did not ordinarily interfere in the affairs of their patriarchates, arose from a love of order, which prompted him to leave to his colleagues the care of that which was entrusted to their respective charge, and to confine himself to a general superintendence. The occasions of his interference were, however, sufficiently numerous to mark clearly his right, and the grounds on which he always relied were such as to leave no question as to the divine

---

* Ep. lxx. † Church of England Clenred, &c. p. 25.

source of his authority. He was first among the patriarchs, their superior and judge, not by courtesy, or conventional arrangement, but in virtue of the command of Christ to Peter: "Feed My lambs:" "Feed My sheep:" "Confirm thy brethren."

Mr. Allies with great candor said: "I am fully prepared to admit that the primacy of the Roman See, even among the patriarchs, was a real thing, not a mere title of honor. The power of the first see was really exerted, in difficult conjunctures, to keep the whole body together. I am quite aware that the Bishop of Rome could do what the Bishop of Alexandria, or of Antioch, or of Constantinople, or of Jerusalem, could not do. Even merely as standing at the head of the whole West, he counterbalanced all the four."*

---

* Church of England Cleared, &c. p. 120.

CHAPTER XIV.

Deposition of Bishops.

THE office of bishop is perpetual, a sacred character, which can never be effaced, being impressed in ordination: yet the exercise of the power may for just causes be inhibited; nay, the governing authority, or jurisdiction may be entirely taken away. The eminence of the dignity, which is no less than that of successor of the apostles, does not secure him who is adorned with it from danger of error, should he listen to the whisperings of pride, rather than guard that which is committed to his trust, or of vice, if he be neglectful of the approaches of temptation. For this reason the apostle addressed strong exhortations to Timothy and Titus, to fulfil the duties of their sacred office, and instructed them in what circumstances they should receive accusations against the bishops* subject to their authority. The power of suspending bishops from the exercise of their functions, or of removing them altogether from the ministry, is among the most awful and sublime functions of the higher ecclesiastical dignitaries. In the early ages it was exercised by metropolitans, or other superiors, especially in Councils, where the assembled bishops judged and deposed the delinquents. Territorial limits were not always accurately observed, especially where one of the patriarchs intervened, whose high rank gave a coloring of authority even to acts performed beyond the province in which he presided.† Thus Flacillus, Bishop of Antioch, presided at a Council in which Athanasius of Alexandria was condemned; and Theophilus of Alexandria undertook to try and depose Chrysostom of Constantinople, who, however, protested against his competency. The power was at all times exercised by the Bishop of Rome, in a manner to leave no room for doubt, that he claimed authority to judge and punish, by censure, all bishops, even patriarchs themselves, and that he grounded his claims on his office as successor of Peter. These claims were put forward with entire confidence, as admitting of no question; and the exercise of the power was implored by bishops occupying the highest sees, and submitted to by those against whom it was exercised, or resisted

---

* The Greek term, πρεσβύτερος, was then applied to bishops.

† Cyril acknowledged, that were he himself, or an Egyptian Synod, to pronounce sentence on Nestorius, he might be charged with going beyond the limits of his authority.

ineffectually. St. Leo, in his instructions to his Vicar in Illyricum, directed that cases of difficulty and importance should be reserved to his own judgment;* whence Bianchi maintains† that the deposition of bishops was from that time reserved to the Holy See. The reservation was well established in the ninth century, since the Council of Troyes implored Nicholas I. to provide for the dignity of the episcopal office, by restraining metropolitans, who sometimes attempted to depose bishops without the apostolic judgment, contrary to the decrees of his predecessors.‡ The deposition of Rothade, Bishop of Soissons, by Hincmar, Archbishop of Rheims, gave occasion to this complaint; and Nicholas rescinded the act as unjust, and irregular, it having been done without his knowledge.

Potter records an early instance of the deposition of bishops by the Roman Pontiff: "Three bishops, who ordained Novatian, the schismatic bishop, were deposed, and others ordained to succeed them, by Cornelius, Bishop of Rome; whose proceedings in this matter were generally approved all over the world."§ Cornelius acted as of his own authority, in proceeding to this measure, which met with universal approbation; the crime of the schismatical ordination being deemed by all most enormous, as tending to destroy, or render doubtful, the essential authority of the Church.

Not long afterward another occasion arose for a similar exercise of power, no longer in the neighborhood of Rome, but over a bishop of an illustrious see in Gaul. Marcian, metropolitan of Arles, had openly espoused the cause of Novatian, in consequence of which, the neighboring metropolitan of Lyons, with his suffragans, implored the Roman Pontiff to depose him from the episcopate. This measure having been delayed, they wrote repeatedly to Cyprian, praying him to use his influence for the speedy correction of the scandal: who accordingly addressed a letter to Pope Stephen, urging him to prompt and decisive action: "Faustinus, our colleague at Lyons, has repeatedly written to us, dearest brother, stating what I know has been reported to you also, both by him and by our other fellow-bishops in the same province, that Marcian of Arles has joined Novatian, and has departed from the unity of the Catholic Church, and the harmony of our body, and of the priests.—Wherefore it behooves you to write an explicit letter|| to our fellow-bishops in Gaul, that they may no longer suffer Marcian, an obstinate and proud man, and an enemy to Divine Mercy and to the salvation of the brethren, to insult our body, since being an abettor of Novatian, and imitating his obstinacy, he has withdrawn from our communion, whilst Novatian himself, whom he

---

* Ep. vi. ad Anastasium Thessalonic.   † Dell'esterior politia, t. v. p. 1, p. 478.
‡ Ep. synod. Trienssin. ad Nicolaum I.   § On Church Government, p. 392.
|| Plenissimas litteras.

follows, was formerly excommunicated and judged to be an enemy of the Church; and when he had sent ambassadors to us in Africa, wishing to be admitted to our communion, he received for answer from a numerous Council of bishops, who were assembled, that HE WAS WITHOUT, and that none of us could communicate with him, since, whilst Cornelius was ordained bishop in the Catholic Church, by the judgment of God, and choice of the clergy and people, he was endeavoring to raise a profane altar, and to erect an adulterous see, and to offer sacrilegious sacrifices in opposition to the true priest.—Let your letters be directed throughout the province, and to the people of Arles, in order that Marcian be removed,* and another substituted in his place, and the flock of Christ gathered together, which, hitherto being scattered and wounded by him, is despised."† It has in vain been attempted to explain this call for the interposition of Stephen, by reference to the fact that Novatianism had sprung up at Rome, on occasion of the opposition to the election of his predecessor. This was no reason why the bishops of Gaul should not, of themselves, proceed to the deposition of the heretical metropolitan, if Stephen were not his lawful and proper judge. They were not wanting in zeal against the heresy, since they had already addressed Stephen and Cyprian, urging the former to come to their aid, and begging the influence of the latter for the speedy success of their application. Of Stephen it was plainly expected, that he should remove the perverse teacher; and to him Cyprian looked for official information of the appointment of his successor.

Palmer, taking Du Pin for his guide, says that Cyprian only requested Stephen to write to the people of Arles, and the Gallican bishops to appoint another bishop in his stead:‡ but it is manifest that the authority of the Bishop of Rome was solicited for the deposition of Marcian, *abstento Marciano*. Were personal influence and persuasion only sought, there would have been no need that the Bishops of the neighboring province of Lyons should have written so pressingly to Carthage and to Rome, merely to obtain a letter of advice from the Bishop of Rome to the Bishops and faithful of the province of Arles.

The power of deposing bishops was recognised in the Pope by a Roman Council, held in the year 378, and by the Emperors Gratian and Valentinian. In addressing the emperors, the fathers state that "numberless bishops from various parts of Italy had assembled at the sublime sanctuary of the Apostolic See." They compliment the emperors as "observing the precept of the holy apostles," inasmuch as, having

---

* *Abstento Marciano.* The Latin term was used of the deposition of an emperor, after he had been adjudged to be an enemy of the empire. Cyprian uses it in this letter of Novatian, who was removed from communion of the Church, and condemned as her enemy.

† Ep. lxvii. alias lxviii.   ‡ Treatise on the Church, vol. ii. part vii. p. 489.

12

banished Ursinus, the leader of the schism, and separated his partisans from his society, they had decreed "that the Roman Bishop should try the other priests of the various churches, so that the Pontiff of religion with his colleagues, should judge of religion; and the priesthood should not suffer in its honor, by subjecting the priest to the judgment of a secular judge, as might otherwise happen." They complain that some bishops, his partisans, still endeavor to persuade others "not to submit to the judgment of the Roman priest;" and mentioning several instances of deposed bishops who retain possession of their sees, they ask the aid of the civil authority to give effect to the ecclesiastical sentence. They pray that a bishop, who declines to appear for trial, may be compelled by the governor, or his Vicar, to repair to Rome; or, if he be far distant, to appear before the metropolitan; and if the metropolitan himself be accused, that he be compelled to come to Rome without delay, or to appear before judges appointed by the Roman Bishop. In cases in which the metropolitan, or other judge, is open to suspicion, they wish an appeal to lie to the Bishop of Rome, or to a council of fifteen neighboring bishops.* The emperors granted their petition, giving civil force to the sentence of the Roman Bishop, passed with the advice of five or seven bishops.† These documents clearly prove the eminence of the Bishop of Rome, as occupant of the Apostolic See, and his right to judge other bishops, whether he sat alone, or surrounded by his colleagues. The reason of the qualifications prescribed in the imperial edict was, that the sentence should be passed solemnly, maturely, and advisedly: and although it had ecclesiastical force independently of these circumstances, the emperors thought fit to limit the civil sanction to sentences thus pronounced. Mosheim, and Maclaine, his translator, refer to these measures as imprudent concessions of the emperors and bishops, which prepared the way for Roman supremacy:‡ but it is easy to see, on inspection of the documents themselves, that the belief that Rome was "the sublime sanctuary of the Apostolic See," preceded, and gave rise to them. Those who, in the investigation of ecclesiastical history, set out with the persuasion, that the papacy is an invention of later ages, engrafted on the original system, can only discover in the many documents of an early date, "steps by which the Roman Bishops mounted afterwards to the summit of ecclesiastical power;" whereas they obviously show the exercise of high authority, derived from a divine source, and recognised alike by bishops and by emperors.

So fully acknowledged was the power of the Pope to depose bishops, when false to the faith, or recreant to their duty, that the Eastern prelates solicited DAMASUS to depose Timothy, a bishop infected with the

---

* Ep. vi. apud Coustant, t. i. col. 528.   Ep. vii. ibidem, col. 532.
‡ Fourth Century, part ii. ch. ii. p. 108

heresy of Apollinaris, and received for reply that the sentence of deposition had already been passed by the Apostolic See against the master and the disciple, in a solemn Council at Rome, at which the Bishop of Alexandria was present: "Why do you ask of me anew," said he, "to depose Timothy, who, together with Apollinaris, was already condemned here, by the judgment of the Apostolic See, in presence even of Peter, Bishop of the city of Alexandria?"* The same zealous Pontiff, in a Roman Synod, deposed Ursacius and Valens; for which act he received the thanks of St. Athanasius, who urged him to proceed to the deposition of Auxentius, the Arian occupant of the See of Milan. Tuentius and Ursus having received episcopal consecration unlawfully, Zosimus addressed a letter to the Bishops of Africa, Gaul, and Spain, in which he says: "Dearest brethren, we have sent letters to your holiness, and throughout the whole world, wheresoever and in whatsoever part of the earth the fountain of the Catholic religion flows, that you may not think that Tuentius and Ursus are to be received in any ecclesiastical rank, in the communion of the Church, from which they are wholly cut off by anathema."† Thus did he most effectually depose them from the episcopate.

Celestine directed all bishops holding the errors of Nestorius to be separated from the episcopal body, and ordered John of Antioch to be notified, "that unless he hold our sentiments and condemn in writing the new blasphemy, the Church would take such measures in his regard as the interests of faith might demand."‡

The papal legates in the Council of Chalcedon deposed Dioscorus, Patriarch of Alexandria, in the name of Leo: "The most holy and blessed Leo, Archbishop of great and elder Rome, by us, and by the present holy synod, together with the most blessed apostle Peter, who is the rock and ground of the Church, and the foundation of the right faith, has stript him of the dignity of the episcopate."§ "The Apostolic See," as Gelasius testifies, "by its own authority condemned Dioscorus, the prelate of the second see."

Ephesus was an *autocephalous*‖ see, which Bassian, by the favor of Proclus, of Constantinople, occupied, to the prejudice of that independence which it derived from the apostles Paul and John, its founders. The clergy and people seeing that the intruder cared only to secure his own honor, by compromising the privileges of the Church, accused him to Pope Leo, and having exposed the unworthy means by which he had usurped the see, obtained a sentence of deposition, which was acknowledged and recorded in the great Council of Chalcedon: "The most holy

---

* Ep. xiv. t. i. col. 514, Coustant. † Ep. iv.
‡ Ep. xxii. ad Syn. Ephes. apud Coustant, t. i. col. 1202. § Act iii.
‖ *Independent* Sees, which were not subject to a metropolitan; or metropolitan sees exempt from patriarchal authority were so styled. No see was absolutely independent, since all are necessarily subject to the chief Bishop.

Roman Archbishop Leo deposed him, because he was made bishop contrary to the canons." Sixtus III. deposed Polychronius, Bishop of Jerusalem. Peter Mongus, Bishop of Alexandria, was excommunicated by Simplicius. Peter Cnapheus, Bishop of Antioch, having fallen into various heresies, especially that of Eutyches, was admonished by Felix III., and finally stricken with anathema, and deposed in this solemn form: "Having written two letters to you, I now proceed to pass sentence against you: yea, rather, he (sentences you) who is the head of all pastoral sees, the glorious Peter, truly the greatest of the apostles."[*] Acacius, Bishop of Constantinople, who was charged with the execution of this sentence, and of several others, afterwards himself fell under suspicion, and was summoned to answer in the assembly of bishops to St. Peter, to whom, in the person of Felix, the accusation was made.[†] He was finally cut off utterly from the Catholic Church. "Being separated from the honor of the priesthood, and from Catholic communion, and likewise from the number of the faithful, know that the name and office of the priestly ministry are taken from you, being condemned by the judgment of the Holy Ghost and by apostolic authority."[‡] Mosheim relates the deposition of Acacius in these terms: "The Roman Pontiff, Felix II.,[§] having assembled an Italian Council, composed of sixty-seven bishops, condemned and deposed Acacius, and excluded him from the communion of the Church, as a perfidious enemy to the truth." The opposition of the Greeks to the execution of this sentence the historian takes as a denial of the right of the Roman See to pronounce censure on the Bishop of the imperial city; but he admits that Rome finally succeeded in exacting its acceptance. "Hence," he says, "arose a new schism and a new contest, which were carried on with great violence, until the following century, when the obstinacy and perseverance of the Latins triumphed over the opposition of the Oriental Christians, and brought about an agreement, in consequence of which, the names of Acacius and Fullo were erased from the diptychs, and sacred registers, and then branded with perpetual infamy."[||] This is no equivocal proof that the right of the Roman Bishops to depose even the Bishop of the imperial city, although he was protected and supported by the emperor, was incontrovertible. It is not true that the Orientals generally resisted the sentence. Acacius, indeed, remained obstinate, but died in a few years. Flavita, his successor, sought the communion of the Holy See, which was denied him, unless he removed the suspicions which fell on his faith, and cancelled from the sacred tablets the name of Acacius. Euphemius, who soon succeeded him, a man of sound faith, pleaded in vain that the memory of Acacius might be spared; alleging, among other things, that he should not have been condemned by a single bishop.

---

[*] Hard. t. ii. col. 826.   [†] Ib. col. 829.   [‡] Ib. col. 832.
[§] Others style him Felix III.   [||] Mosheim, Church History, p. 2, ch. v. §xxi.

Gelasius, who then occupied the chair of St. Peter, answered, that Acacius had been condemned in virtue of the Council of Chalcedon, since he professed heresies which it had proscribed; but independently of this fact, the Pontiff relied on the supreme authority of the Holy See, whose judgments are final. He showed that Acacius, previously to his own condemnation, had accepted and executed a commission of the Holy See for the deposition of several bishops: "Timothy of Alexandria, and Peter of Antioch, Peter, Paul, and John, and others, not one only, but several bearing the priestly title, were cast down by the sole authority of the Apostolic See. Of this fact Acacius himself is witness, since he was charged with the execution of the sentence. In this manner, then, falling into company with those who have been condemned, Acacius is condemned."* By embracing their errors, he provoked the like condemnation.

A most splendid instance of the exercise of the papal power occurred on occasion of the visit of Pope Agapetus to Constantinople, at the solicitation of Theodatus, King of the Goths, with a view to persuade the Emperor Justinian to abandon his intended invasion of Italy. His failure in the direct object of his visit made the acts of spiritual authority which he exercised the more remarkable. Anthimus, Bishop of Trebizond, through the favor of the empress, had recently occupied the See of Constantinople, left vacant by the death of Epiphanius. His hostility to the Council of Chalcedon, although artfully dissembled, was known to Agapetus, who could not be prevailed on by the emperor or empress, by threats or promises, to admit the heretical usurper to his presence. He offered, indeed, to allow him to return to his original see, on his unequivocal acceptance of the Council; but in no case would he suffer him to occupy the see of the imperial city. After some delay, in order to give him time for submission and repentance, the Pope convened a Council of bishops at Constantinople, summoned him to appear for trial, pronounced sentence of deposition against him, absent by default, and consecrated with his own hands Mennas in his stead.†

The Emperor of Constantinople solicited Gregory the Great to proceed in the case of the primate of Byzacium;‡ but he hesitated to come to a final decision, not feeling assured of the sincerity of the accused in his professions of submission: "As to his saying," observes the Pope, speaking of the Primate, "that he is subject to the Apostolic See, I know not what bishop is not subject to it, when any fault is found in bishops. But when delinquency does not require it, all of us are equal, on the principle of humility."§

---

* Ep. xlii.   † See Fleury, Hist. l. xxxii. a. 536.
‡ In Africa. Adrumetum, now Mahumeta, was the chief city. It is in the kingdom of Tunis.
§ Ep. lix.

It is unnecessary to give further examples, since those already adduced plainly show that the Roman Bishop, as the superior of all other bishops, judged and deposed them, either in solemn council, or, with less solemnity, by his own act. No prelate, however elevated, was exempt from his judgment. Alexandria, Antioch, Jerusalem, Constantinople, enjoyed privileges; but remained subject to the supervision, correction, and censure of Rome. The imperial favor availed nothing against apostolic prerogative. The successor of Peter did not, however, always appear in a menacing attitude. He could heal, as well as strike; and he was often appealed to, that the wounds inflicted by others might be remedied by his indulgence and authority.

CHAPTER XV.

Appeals.

§ 1.—ANCIENT EXAMPLES.

In all governments there is a tribunal of appeal, whose judgment is final. By it the sentences of the inferior judges are confirmed, when found conformable to justice and law; or, if otherwise, reversed and corrected. The existence of such a tribunal is an evidence of its supremacy: the judge must be the sovereign, or his representative, or the depositary of supreme juridical power, which he, in fact, exercises. The usage of appealing to the Bishop of Rome from the judgment and censures of bishops and Councils, in every part of the Church, which is most ancient, shows that he was believed to possess a power superior to all other bishops.

St. Epiphanius relates of Marcion, that having been excommunicated for a grievous sin against chastity, by his father, the Bishop of Sinope,* he fled to Rome, about the year 141, and sought to be restored to communion; but that the chief clergy, (the see being vacant,) declared, that they could not grant him relief, without the consent of his father, with whom they were united in faith and friendship.† The journey and the application show that he recognised the superior power of Rome; and the refusal which he met with, is an evidence, not of want of authority in the Roman Church, but of discretion and moderation in its exercise. The case may not be strictly styled an *appeal*, since it does not appear that the injustice of the sentence was complained of; but it implies that even a just penalty inflicted by an Asiatic prelate, could be mitigated by the ruler of that Church.

It is evident from the testimony of St. Cyprian, that in his time the Bishop of Rome took upon himself to restore bishops deposed by the Council of their province. Basilides, Bishop of Asturia, in Spain, who

---

* In the early ages, men who had been married but once, ("the husband of one wife,") were often assumed to the ministry; it being difficult, especially on the first preaching of the Gospel, to find persons of mature age who had not been married. The actual discipline of the Church still allows such persons to be ordained after the death of their wives, or on a mutual and voluntary profession of continency.

† Hær. xiii. n. ii.

had been deposed on the charge of idolatry, and other crimes, having repaired to Rome to plead his cause, succeeded in inducing Pope Stephen to restore him. In the interval, another bishop, Sabinus, had been consecrated and placed in the see. St. Cyprian, being consulted by the Spanish prelates, held that Sabinus should not be dispossessed, since the decree for the reinstatement of Basilides had been surreptitiously obtained. "His ordination," he remarks, "which has been regularly performed, cannot be rescinded, merely because Basilides, after the discovery of his crimes, and his own public confession of guilt, going to Rome, deceived Stephen our colleague, far distant from the scene of action, and unacquainted with the proceedings and with the facts which were suppressed, in order to be reinstated in the episcopate, from which he had been justly deposed. This only shows that the crimes of Basilides are not cancelled, but aggravated by the additional guilt of fraud and circumvention, together with his former sins. Nor is he who has been imposed on unadvisedly, so blamable, as he who fraudulently practised on his credulity, is deserving of execration. If Basilides has succeeded in deceiving men, he cannot deceive God, since it is written: 'God is not mocked.'"* St. Cyprian opposed the execution of the sentence, not on the ground of a want of authority, which would have been the obvious method, if the power of Stephen admitted of any question; but because he had proceeded on false information. The right to reverse the sentence, if the merits of the case admitted it, not being denied, must be taken as acknowledged. In maintaining the incapacity of Basilides, and also of Martialis, another deposed bishop, to hold the bishopric, St. Cyprian relies on the law regarding persons guilty of idolatry, made by Cornelius, the predecessor of Stephen: "In vain," says he, "such men attempt to usurp the bishopric, whilst it is manifest that they should neither preside over the Church of Christ, nor offer sacrifice to God, especially since long ago, in union with us and with all bishops, without exception, throughout the whole world, even CORNELIUS OUR COLLEAGUE, a pacific and just priest, and through the special favor of God, honored with martyrdom, DECREED that such men might indeed be admitted to do penance, but are precluded from clerical ordination and priestly honor."† This reference to the decree of Cornelius, to which the whole episcopal body had assented, shows the eminence of his authority.

In a letter to Cornelius, St. Cyprian makes mention of Privatus, a heretic, in the province of Lambesita,‡ who, many years previously, had been condemned by a Council of ninety bishops. He had in vain attempted to have his cause reopened in a Council of Carthage. Disappointed in this effort, he had recourse to Rome, and during the vacancy of the see, he urged the Roman clergy to reverse the sentence. The

---

* Ep. lxviii.   † Ep. lxviii.   ‡ Algiers.

letter of Cyprian put them on their guard; but independently of it, they judged unfavorably of the case. In reply, they commend the conduct of Cyprian in giving them, as was customary, full information, that they might better discharge the duty incumbent on them in behalf of all the churches: "As to what concerns Privatus of Lambesita," they observe, "you have, as usual, been careful to call our attention to the case, as one of moment: for it behooves us all to keep guard for the body of the entire Church, whose members are spread throughout the various provinces. But even before the receipt of your letter, the frauds of the crafty man did not escape our notice. For, when one of his impious band, Futurus, an ardent partisan of Privatus, had come, endeavoring to procure letters from us, his true character was not unperceived by us, on which account he did not receive the letter which he desired."* Thus it is clear that Privatus appealed to the Roman Church, whose authority was exercised by the clergy, during the vacancy of the see, who refused redress, because they knew him to be undeserving. St. Cyprian, nevertheless, complained of the appeals of the minor clergy, as derogatory to the judgment of their bishops and of the Councils by which they had been condemned, and as tending to relax discipline and defeat justice. He also stated in strong terms the artifices of heretics, whereby they sought to abuse the good faith of the Bishop of Rome. Fortunatus had been ordained Bishop in Carthage, in opposition to Cyprian, and had despatched to Rome an abettor of his schism, the priest Felicissimus, to preoccupy the ears of the Pope. Cyprian expresses his surprise at the audacity of the schismatics. "What cause," he asks, "had they to go (to Rome) and announce the false bishop who was created in opposition to the other bishops? For either they are satisfied with what they have done, and persevere in their wickedness, or, if they are sorry, and abandon it, they know whither they may return. For since it has been determined by us all, it is equally just and proper that the cause of every one should be tried where the crime was committed, and since to each of the pastors a portion of the flock is given, which each one may rule and govern, being to render an account of his conduct to the Lord, it is certainly meet, that those over whom we preside should not run about, nor, with crafty and deceitful temerity, destroy the unity and harmony of the bishops, but should plead their cause where the accusers and witnesses of their crime may be present; unless, perchance, a few desperate and abandoned men regard as insufficient the authority of the African bishops, who have already pronounced judgment on them, and have recently by their weighty sentence condemned them as guilty of many crimes, of which they themselves are fully conscious. Their cause has been already tried, sentence has been already passed on them; and it is not consistent with the gravity

---

* Ep. xxx.

of sacerdotal judgment, that it should be rescinded easily and lightly, since the Lord teaches us, saying: 'Let your speech be: yea, yea; no, no.'"* Cyprian was delighted to find that Cornelius had repelled them. He plainly disapproved such appeals, as calculated to encourage insubordination, and screen the guilty from punishment: yet he does not deny in the abstract the right to make or receive them.

The fourth century offers us an illustrious instance of an appeal made by the great champion of the divinity of Christ, the persecuted Bishop of Alexandria. In the year 335, whilst Constantine was still alive, Athanasius had been condemned and deposed by a Council held at Tyre, in which Flacillus, Patriarch of Antioch, presided. Constantine, under the influence of the Eusebians, banished him; but, towards his death, relented: and after his decease his sons, in compliance with his wishes, permitted him to return to his see.—The Eusebians, mortified at his restoration, and resolved on his ruin, sent legates to Constance and Constans, and wrote against him to Pope Julius. Without awaiting any act of the emperors or Pontiff, they held a Council at Antioch in 341, and regarding his restoration as irregular, chose Gregory of Cappadocia, an Arian, to be Bishop of Alexandria, and sent him with the prefect Philagrius, and a military escort, to take possession of the see. They had previously sent Martirius and Hesychius, two deacons, as deputies to Rome; who meeting there the deputies of Athanasius, and failing to sustain the charges which they had advanced against him, found themselves under the necessity of calling for a trial,† that they might not appear utterly to abandon their cause. Julius accordingly called a Council, in order to have a full investigation. In the mean time Athanasius arrived at Rome, having fled from the violence of the intruder Gregory, and his partisans. The Pontiff sent legates to summon the accusers; and determined likewise to institute inquiry into the crimes which they themselves, or their partisans, had committed, and to punish them accordingly.‡ Under various pretexts, they detained the messengers, and in the end, wrote an offensive letter, in which they complained of the intended reopening of the cause of Athanasius, whilst they admitted "the preeminence of the Roman Church, as avowed by all, as having been FROM THE COMMENCEMENT THE SCHOOL OF THE APOSTLES, AND THE ME-

---

* Ep. lix. alias liv. lv.

† "Concilium indici postularunt, literasque et ad Eusebianos, et Athanasium Alexandriam, quibus convocarentur, mitti, ut coram omnibus justo judicio de causa cognosci posset: tum enim se de Athanasio probaturos esse, quod jam nequirent."—Epist. Julii, p. 391.

‡ "Certe fratres nostri Romæ anno superiori infensi prioribus eorum factis, quum nondum scelera ista accesserant, pro ultione sumenda concilium indici, celebrarique voluerunt."—S. Athanas. ad Orthodox, p. 338.

TROPOLIS OF PIETY."* Notwithstanding their opposition, Julius proceeded to examine the cause, in a Council consisting of fifty prelates. The acts of the Synod of Tyre, and of the committee of bishops who were appointed to inquire into the facts at Mareotis,† where they were said to have occurred, being submitted to examination, were found to be irregular and unjust; and Athanasius was acquitted by the unanimous judgment of the fathers. Julius communicated the result of their investigation, in the admirable letter preserved by Athanasius, which unites mild persuasion with authoritative judgment.

The complaint made by the Eusebians, of the re-opening of the cause, shows that they had not seriously asked for a trial, and that the demand made by their deputies was a last subterfuge, when they had failed to substantiate their charges in the less solemn discussion with the deputies of Athanasius.‡ It is for this reason that they expressed their willingness to abide by the judgment of Julius, if he would undertake the investigation. They hoped that he would decline; and when, contrary to their expectations, he consented, those who had sent them shrunk from the trial, and sought by every frivolous pretence to excuse their default. They had applied for a confirmation of their sentence by the only authority which could render it final and conclusive; but as Athanasius sought to be released from their unjust censure, the actual proceedings were in the nature of an appeal. The decision, although made in a synod, and with the assent of all, was emphatically and justly styled the judgment of Julius, even by the Council subsequently held at Sardica. It has all the qualities that constitute a real exercise of judicial authority. Complaints had been lodged against Athanasius with Julius, as with a judge and superior; afterwards, the cause proceeded entirely against the will of the party in whose name the investigation had been demanded. This was manifestly the exercise of a supreme and independent judicial power, not derived from the voluntary act of those concerned. In his letter Julius distinctly claims the right of summoning all the parties to his tribunal. At the head of the accusers was Flacillus, Patriarch of Antioch;—the accused, Athanasius, was Patriarch of Alexandria, the highest dignitary after the Roman Bishop, within whose jurisdiction both were embraced. As a proof of the innocence of Athanasius, Julius alleges that he freely presented himself in Rome, and awaited during a year and a half the arrival of his accusers. He adds that "by his presence, he put them all to shame, for he would not have presented himself for trial, had he not been confident of his innocence; nor would he have

---

* Φερειν μεν γαρ πασι φιλοτιμίαν την ρωμαίων ἐκκλησίαν ἐν τοις γράμμασιν ὡμολόγουν, ὡς ἀποστόλων φροντιστήριον, καὶ εὐσεβείας μητρόπολιν ἐξ ἀρχῆς γεγεννημένην.—Sozomen., l. 3, Hist. Eccl., c. viii.

† A town of Africa, in Tunis.

‡ "Id enim eorum legati, quum se vinci animadverterent, postularunt."—Athanas., ad vitam sol. agentes, p. 440.

appeared spontaneously, but waited to be called to trial by our letters, as we summoned you in writing."* After this, no doubt can be entertained that the judgment emanated from a recognised tribunal. The details of the proceedings, as given in that letter, are such as constitute a trial. The accusations against Athanasius had been communicated in letters written by Eusebius and his adherents; the crimes were stated for which he had been condemned at Tyre, on the report made by a committee of bishops which sat at Mareotis; the records of that trial were presented by Martyrius and Hesychius on the part of the accusers, the chief of whom were absent by default; Athanasius was heard in his defence; a number of witnesses were examined, and a favorable sentence was pronounced, reinstating him in his episcopal dignity. At Mareotis the liberty of defence had been denied him, his witnesses having been excluded, whilst his accuser alone was heard: "This we know," says the Pontiff, "not merely from his statement, but from the records of the acts brought by Martyrius and Hesychius; for, on reading them, we found that Ischyras, his accuser, was present, but that Macarius and Athanasius were not present, and that the priests of Athanasius were not admitted, though they earnestly demanded it. Dearly beloved, if indeed that trial were carried on fairly, it was necessary that not only the accuser, but the accused should be present."† Julius evidently had a just idea of the regular forms of trial. He felt, likewise, that in virtue of his office he could annul this irregular sentence, and that, if Athanasius were guilty, he could condemn him. The merits of the case had been canvassed, no less than the mode of proceeding. It was proved from the very records of the former trial, that the chief accuser, Ischyras, was convicted of perjury by his own witnesses. "Since, then," says Julius, "these things were brought forward, and so many witnesses appeared in behalf of Athanasius, and he made so just a defence—what did it become us to do?—Was it not our duty to proceed according to the ecclesiastical canon? Should we not, therefore, abstain from condemning the man, and rather admit and regard him as a bishop, as in truth he is?"‡ He complains severely of the proceedings of the Orientals while the cause was pending before his tribunal; the Eusebians having violently intruded Gregory into the See of Alexandria, without awaiting the decision: "For in the first place," he continues, "to speak candidly, it was not right that, when we had issued letters for the celebration of a synod, any one should antici-

---

* "Suaque præsentia pudefecit omnes: non enim judicio stetisset, nisi sui fiduciam habuisset, neque sponte, sed litteris nostris ad judicium vocatus comparuisset, quemadmodum vos per litteras citavimus."—Julii. Ep. apud Athanas., Ap. 2, p. 396.

† "Oportebat autem, dilectissimi, siquidem sinceriter illud judicium agebatur, non solum accusatorem, sed et reum præsentem sisti."—P. 394.

‡ "An non quod ecclesiastici canonis est? hominemque proinde non condemnaremus, sed potius reciperemus?"—P. 395.

pate the judgment of the synod." He also intimates that the Eusebians themselves would have been put on trial, had they appeared, accusations having been formally presented against them; and he accuses them of contumacy, and implied confession of guilt, in neglecting to appear to stand their trial.*

This letter must satisfy impartial and discerning readers, that, at that period, the Bishop of Rome exercised real jurisdiction in the most important causes, in whatever part of the world the parties resided, or whatever rank they occupied in the hierarchy. The exercise of his high authority is marked in almost every line. As guardian of the canons, he complains that the ecclesiastical law was violated. To him, as the divinely-constituted ruler of the whole Church, not only Athanasius and Marcellus, "but also many other bishops from Thrace, Cœlosyria, Phenicia, and Palestine," came, complaining of the wrongs which they had endured, and which had been inflicted on their respective churches. The plea which the Eusebians offered for filling the sees of Athanasius and Marcellus, could not be put forward to palliate the violence by which others were driven away from their bishoprics and country. "Suppose," said Julius, "that Athanasius and Marcellus, as you write, were removed from their sees, what can you say of the others, who, as I have said, have come hither from various places, both priests and bishops?—for they also affirm that they have been driven away, and that they have suffered similar outrages. O! beloved! ecclesiastical trials are no longer conducted in conformity with the Gospel, but with a view to banishment or death. If, as you say, they were absolutely guilty, the trial should have been carried on according to the canon, and not in that way. You should have first written to us all, so that what is just might be decreed by all. For they who suffered these things were bishops, and not of an ordinary Church, but of one which the apostles themselves had, by their labor, instructed in the faith. Why, then, have you neglected to write to us any thing, especially concerning the city of Alexandria? DO YOU NOT KNOW THAT IT IS THE CUSTOM TO WRITE FIRST TO US, THAT WHAT IS JUST MAY BE DETERMINED? Wherefore, if suspicions of that kind had fallen on the bishop there, it should have been reported to our Church. Now, after having done as they pleased, without informing us at all, they wish us to approve of their sentence of condemnation, in which we had no share. Such are not the ordinances of Paul—such is not the teaching of the fathers—but this is arrogance and innovation. I beseech you, bear me willingly: I write for the general advantage. I intimate to you what we have learned from the blessed apostle Peter: nor would I write things

---

* "Alacrius a vobis et sine recusatione occurrendum fuit, ne qui hactenus infamia istorum scelerum laborant, contumacia non comparendi in judicio, libellos contra se datos videantur refellere non potuisse."—Ibid.

which I am persuaded you know already, had not the transactions filled us with affliction." Accordingly, Julius recognised Athanasius in his episcopal rank, leaving the formal reversal of the sentence to take place after a re-hearing in presence of both parties, when a Council could be assembled.

MARCELLUS, Bishop of Ancyra, was of the number of those prelates, who successfully appealed to the superior authority of the Roman Bishop, for relief from the unjust judgment of an Eastern Council. Having repaired to Rome, and for a long time awaited in vain the arrival of his accusers, he submitted to Julius a written exposition of his faith. His letter commences with these words: "Since some of those who were formerly condemned for heterodoxy, whom I exposed in the Council of Nice, have dared write against me to your Holiness, as if I did not entertain correct sentiments, conformable to the teaching of the Church, endeavoring to transfer to me their own fault, on this account I thought it necessary to repair to Rome, and suggest to you to send for those who wrote against me, that, on their appearing, I might confound them in both respects, by showing that what they have written against me is false, and that they themselves still continue in their original error, and are guilty of criminal machinations against the churches of God, and against us who preside over them; but since they have declined to come, although you sent messengers after them, and I have waited a year and three entire months at Rome, I have thought it necessary, before my departure, to deliver you the profession of faith, which I have written, in all sincerity, with my own hand, which I have learned, and in which I have been instructed by the Divine Scriptures."* He concludes by requesting Julius to transmit a copy of this profession to the other bishops, that his orthodoxy might thus be manifest. The Council of Sardica, in conformity with the judgment of Julius, acknowledged Marcellus and Athanasius as bishops in the communion of the Church.

Socrates, a Greek historian of the fifth century, relates in the most emphatic terms, the recourse of various bishops to the authority of the Pope: "At the same time (*when Athanasius arrived*) Paul also, the Bishop of Constantinople, Asclepas of Gaza, Marcellus of Ancyra, a city in Lesser Galatia, and Lucius of Hadrianople, each accused of a different offence, driven from their churches, reach the imperial city. When they had stated their case to Julius, Bishop of the Roman city, he, according to the prerogative of the Roman Church, sent them back into the East, bearing with them strong letters, and restored them to their sees, severely rebuking those who had rashly deposed them. They, accordingly, setting out from Rome, supported by the letters of the Bishop Julius, took possession of their churches, and sent the letters to those to whom they

---

* Vide ep. Marcelli inter ep. Rom. Pont., Coustant, p. 390.

were directed."* Sozomen, speaking of the same bishops, says: "The Roman Bishop having taken cognizance of their various cases, and finding them all to harmonize in the Nicene faith, admitted them to his communion. And since, ON ACCOUNT OF THE DIGNITY OF HIS SEE, THE CARE OF ALL BELONGED TO HIM, HE RESTORED EACH ONE TO HIS CHURCH."† With these facts before us, we cannot wonder at the avowal of Hallam: "The opinion of the Roman See's supremacy seems to have prevailed very much in the fourth century. Fleury brings remarkable proofs of this from the writings of Socrates, Sozomen, Ammianus Marcellinus, and Optatus."‡

The restoration of so many Catholic bishops to their sees by the pontifical authority, was viewed with pain by the abettors of Arianism, who, in a conventicle held at Philippopolis in Thrace, combined to prevent it, and gave loose reins to their frenzy against Pope Julius:§ but the Council of Sardica, which was assembled at the same time, came to the support of his prerogative, and enacted canons to regulate the proceedings thenceforward in all cases of appeal. The holding of this Council was necessary for the formal reversal of the sentence of deposition, and to induce the Emperor Constantius to dispossess the Arian Gregory of the See of Alexandria, into which he had been intruded, and restore Athanasius. Accordingly, at the instance of Julius himself,‖ Constans, the Catholic emperor, urged his Arian brother to summon a Council, that the facts might be placed in their proper light, by a full rehearing of the case, in the presence of both parties.

The fathers of this Council observe, that the accusers of Athanasius, though present at Sardica, "did not dare appear in the Council of the holy bishops; from which circumstance the justice of the judgment of our brother and fellow-bishop Julius most clearly appeared, who passed sentence not rashly, but after mature deliberation." In their letter to the Egyptian and African bishops, they mention the accusations against Athanasius, preferred to Julius, Bishop of the Roman Church,—the letters written to him in defence of the accused by bishops of various places—the summons issued to the Eusebians to appear, and their shrinking from the trial: whence they infer their guilt,—"because, being summoned by our beloved fellow-minister Julius, they did not present themselves for trial."¶ In their first letter to the emperors, they implore them not to suffer the public officers to pass sentence on clergymen, or to molest the brethren, but to leave every one at liberty to follow the

---

* Hist. Eccl., l. ii. c. xv. † L. iii. Hist. Eccl., c. vii.
‡ Hallam, Middle Ages, ch. vii. p. 270.
§ See Diss. de appellationibus, c. xiii., a Christiano Lupo.
‖ Sozomen, l. iii., Hist., c. i. Socrates, l. ii., Hist., c. xx.
¶ "Judicio non steterunt."

Catholic and apostolic faith, without being subject to the violence of persecution.

This Council bore the most splendid testimony to the privileges of the primacy. Osius proposed: "If any bishop be condemned in any cause, and thinks that his cause is good, and that a trial should again take place, if it meet your approbation, let us honor the memory of the holy apostle Peter, and let those who investigated the case, write to the Roman Bishop, and if he judge that a new trial be granted, let it be granted, and let him appoint judges. But if he judge that the cause is such that the proceedings should not be called in question, they shall be confirmed. Is this the will of all? The synod answered: It is our will."* Gaudentius, a bishop, then proposed that should an appeal be lodged to Rome, no bishop should be ordained in place of the deposed prelate: which was agreed to. These canons were adopted by the Council, and report was made of the whole proceedings to Julius, in a synodical letter, in which the title of HEAD is given to THE SEE OF THE APOSTLE PETER.†

Thus in this Council, held a few years after that of Nice, Osius being present at both, Rome is recognised as the See of Peter, and the mode of proceeding in ecclesiastical causes is regulated with a marked deference to its Bishop. He is acknowledged to be the head, and is requested to admonish by his letters all bishops not to communicate with those whom the Council had condemned. It has been sometimes said that the Council of Sardica granted the right of appeal; but this is inconsistent with the well-established fact, that appeals had been previously made and heard. A close inspection of the two canons that regard this matter will show, that recognising the right, they only regulated the mode of proceeding. The first enactment which they made on this subject, was intended to correct an abuse, not to confer a privilege. Before, a condemned bishop sometimes succeeded in obtaining a new trial from the bishops of the neighboring province. To prevent this, it was enacted that no new trial should be granted, unless by the special authority of the Holy See, who should appoint the judges. With regard to appeals to the Pope, "from the judgment of those bishops who belonged to the neighboring parts," the Council, at the suggestion of Gaudentius, decreed, that if a bishop "should proclaim that his cause should be heard in the city of Rome, another bishop, pending the appeal, should not by any means be ordained in the place of him who appears to be deposed, unless the cause be determined by the judgment of the Roman Bishop." This enactment supposes the right of appeal, and restrains the provincial bishops from proceeding to the ordination of a new bishop whilst it is pending. It de-

---

* Sardic. Conc., can. iv. tom. i., Conc. Hard., col. 640.
† Ep. Synod. Sardic., apud Hard. Col. Conc., tom. i. col. 653.

termines it to have the effect of *suspending* all provincial acts. The object is manifest from the case of Athanasius, into whose see, whilst his cause was pending at Rome, Gregory had been intruded. Had the right of appeal been conferred by that Council, it would still be worthy of remark, that it was with a view to honor the chair of Peter; and consequently it should be taken as an evidence of the primacy, the exercise of whose prerogatives it was designed to regulate, in a manner conformable to the interests of piety and peace, in the confidence that it would meet with the cordial approbation of the Pontiff. The influence of the Roman Bishop, had it at all originated in the greatness of the imperial city, must have been on the wane, ever since Constantine raised the new seat of empire at Byzantium. The prejudices of Constantius must have made him view with peculiar jealousy every new privilege of a bishop, the avowed and implacable enemy of Arianism, who had so lately sustained Athanasius against the Arian faction. The fathers of Sardica had been called together by the letters of this Arian emperor. Every thing, then, concurred to persuade them to diminish, rather than augment the prerogatives of Rome; and nothing could have induced them to recognise its superiority, or admit its rights, but the deep-rooted conviction that they were the rich inheritance bequeathed by the prince of the apostles to his successors.

The exercise of the power of receiving appeals before the holding of this Council, proves that it was not derived from its enactments. It is a right which clearly flows from the office of Chief Bishop, and which must consequently be deemed of Divine institution. In giving to Peter the keys of His kingdom, Christ made him highest in authority, with a governing power over all; and authorized him to bind all by his decrees; or loose them, by reversing the sentences of his colleagues. This is not to be done capriciously, but justly, in conformity with the Divine law, and with a strict regard to the interests of the Church at large The exercise of the power may vary, and may be regulated by the canons, with the assent of the Pontiff, with a view to order and harmony; but the power itself cannot be taken away or restricted by positive enactments, since it flows from a higher source—the will of Jesus Christ, who constituted Peter, under Himself, chief ruler and chief pastor.

St. Basil is an illustrious witness of the exercise of the privileges of the primacy in absolving, on appeal, a bishop deposed in an Eastern synod. Eustathius of Sebaste, in Armenia, had, in various circumstances, professed Arianism, in consequence of which he was deposed from his see. In a letter to the Western bishops, Basil thus relates the artifice which he employed to recover his dignity: " Being cast out of his bishopric, from which he had been already deposed in Melitina, he thought on this plan of recovering his place, to undertake a journey to you. What things were proposed to him by the most blessed Liberius, and what he consented to, we know not: but he brought back with him a letter reinstating him, which being presented to the synod of Tyana,* he was restored to his place."† No stronger evidence could be given of the papal authority. Liberius reversed the decree of an Oriental Synod, and restored the deposed bishop; in which exercise of authority another Synod acquiesced, even when there was strong reason to believe that the Pontiff had acted on false representations.

St. Chrysostom sent to Innocent I. an embassy, consisting of four bishops and two deacons, to state plainly and clearly all the wrongs which he had suffered from the violence of Theophilus of Alexandria, and his abettors, and to obtain redress without delay. He shows that the Egyptian could have no authority in Thrace; and implores the Pontiff to display becoming fortitude and zeal for the remedy of these disorders: "Lest," he says, "so great confusion should become general, I beseech you to write to the effect that these irregular proceedings, which were carried on in our absence, and from *ex parte* information, whilst we did not decline trial, are of no effect; as they are in fact null of themselves; and that the authors of these illegal measures shall be subjected to the penalty prescribed by the ecclesiastical laws. Grant, likewise, to us, who have not been convicted, reproved, or denounced as guilty of crime, the favor of your letters immediately, and your affection and that of all others as hitherto."‡

In some manuscripts it is stated, that Chrysostom wrote in like terms to Venerius, Bishop of Milan, and Chromatius of Aquileja; but there is reason to believe, that this is an unauthorized observation of some one who supposed that the two letters addressed to these prelates, which are still extant, were written at this time, although their contents be different. If, however, it be admitted that Chrysostom addressed to them letters of the same tenor, it must have been as to the chief bishops of Italy, whose influence with the Pope was presumed to be great.

Innocent, addressing the clergy of Constantinople, who had written to him on the same subject, pronounced the deposition of their bishop irregular, unjust, and void.§ This sentence was intended to replace Chrysostom in his station; it determined his right of possession,‖ without deciding the merits of the case;¶ for which maturer examination and more solemn judgment were desirable. The adverse parties were Theophilus, Patriarch of Alexandria, and the Empress Eudoxia, supported by the emperor in her hostility to the stern reprover of her luxury and injustice. For this reason it was proper that the case should be fully examined in a Synod, in which the Pope, by his legates, should preside,

---

* In Natolia.
† Ep. cclxiii., alias lxxiv.
‡ Ep. iv. apud Coustant, col. 785.
§ Palladius in vita Chrysostomi: ἀδετησας.
‖ In possessorio.
¶ In petitorio et devolutivo.

that the solemnity of the proceedings might conciliate respect for the final sentence. Innocent accordingly directed a Synod to be held at Thessalonica, saying that there was no other method of allaying the storm.* There was no want of authority on his part; but the acts of the Council which had condemned Chrysostom, could not be rescinded with propriety, unless after a rehearing of the case, which it was desirable should be attended with equal solemnity. The aggrieved prelate, who, by providential interposition, was in the mean time restored to his See, felt grateful for the kind solicitude of the Pontiff, whose protection he still implored. "You continue," he says, "to imitate excellent pilots, who are most attentive when they see the waves raised up, the sea swelling, the waters rushing, and thick darkness in the midst of day."† He represents Innocent as manifesting more than parental benevolence and affection in his efforts to relieve him. Thus did the bishop of the imperial city acknowledge and implore the superior power of the successor of Peter. The Alexandrian Patriarch likewise recognised it, by sending ambassadors to support his sentence before the pontifical tribunal.‡

§ 2.—AFRICAN CONTROVERSY.

In the early part of the fifth century, the most splendid testimonies were rendered by the Bishops of Africa to the authority of the Holy See, which they acknowledged to be derived from the Divine Scriptures; yet, at that very time, a controversy arose between them and Pope Zosimus, on the subject of appeals, which is now brought forward to prove that they did not admit his supremacy. We have already heard the complaints of St. Cyprian concerning clergymen, who, by having recourse to a distant tribunal, sought to escape from the just sentence of their bishops. The like dissatisfaction was felt by Aurelius, who occupied the See of the Martyr at the time of which we now speak, and by the African Bishops generally; so that in a numerous Council held at Carthage, in the year 418, canons were enacted with a view to remedy what was felt to be an abuse. It was decreed that clerical causes, with the consent of the diocesan, might undergo a rehearing before neighboring bishops; or, by way of appeal, might come under the cognizance of a provincial Council, or of the primate of the province. In order effectually to preclude any appeal of clergymen to a tribunal beyond the seas—that is, to the Bishop of Rome—the prelates agreed that any such appellant should not be received to communion by any of their number. The appeal of Apiarius, a priest excommunicated by Urban, Bishop of Sicca, brought matters to a crisis. Zosimus immediately despatched Faustinus, an

---

* T. i., ep. Rom. Pontif., col. 799.   † Ep. xi. col. 810.
‡ T. i., ep. R. P., 804.

Italian bishop, with two priests, as papal legates, commissioned to reinstate the appellant, to excommunicate the bishop, in case he persisted in disregarding the appeal, or to send him to Rome for trial, and to regulate all future appeals after the manner prescribed by the Council of Nice: the Pontiff thus designating the canons of Sardica, because they were added to those of Nice in the manuscript of the Roman Church.*
In May, 419, a Council of two hundred and seventeen bishops, assembled at Carthage, received the legates, who delivered to them in writing the Apostolic mandates. The canons referred to were wholly unknown to the prelates, who, however, pledged themselves to observe them, until such time as their authenticity could be ascertained, by consulting the archives of the great Churches of Alexandria, Antioch, and Constantinople. Faustinus urged that, to avoid all appearance of strife, the prelates should rather address the Holy See directly, and seek from it the desired information; which they readily agreed to, without, however, abandoning their intention of sending commissioners to the other churches. The case of Apiarius was settled by his removal to another diocese, and the apparent contumacy of Urban was satisfactorily accounted for, so that, after some warm debate, harmony succeeded. We know, however, from St. Augustin, that Urban himself visited Rome,† most probably with a view to explain his conduct to the Pontiff. The appeal of a priest was the immediate occasion of the Pontifical interposition; but it prompted Zosimus to put the whole matter of appeals on a proper basis. The canons which he cited, left clergymen at liberty to appeal from the sentence of their diocesan to neighboring bishops, without making mention of the Bishop of Rome; and a similar enactment is ascribed to the Council of Carthage, held in the preceding year. Hence surprise is expressed that Zosimus should rely on the canon as sanctioning the appeals of clergymen to the Apostolic See; and that the African fathers should admit it only provisionally. The Pope, indeed, did not labor to prove from it his right to receive the appeals of clergymen, concerning which the plenitude of his authority suffered him to entertain no question; but he meant to show the right of appeal to neighboring bishops, which was recognised by the Sardican canons. The right of appeal was restricted by the African prelates to provincial Councils, or at least to the primates of the province, since the consent of the diocesan was requisite for the rehearing of the case before neighboring bishops, whilst the canon of Sardica recognised the right without any such restriction. The grievance of which Apiarius had complained, was, that the sentence of Urban could not be reversed by a neighboring prelate without the consent of the diocesan. Zosimus wished to throw open a door by which an injured priest could obtain

---

* Cod. Iustelli, apud Ballerin., t. iii., oper. S. Leon, p. 59. Also, apud Bened., in not. ad ep. Zos., xv.

† Aug. ep. cclxiii.

redress, without awaiting the celebration of a provincial Council, or depending on the judgment and good pleasure of the Primate alone. By introducing the Sardican canon, the necessity of appealing to the Holy See in ordinary cases would have been removed, and a fruitful occasion of murmurs avoided; but the African fathers were apprehensive that so great facility of appeal would unsettle discipline, loose the bonds of authority, and lead to relaxation and disorder.

The appeals of bishops, although not at all controverted when this discussion first arose, came under consideration in consequence of the wish of the Pope to have the canons put into full operation. It had always been customary for African bishops to appeal to Rome, as is gathered from St. Cyprian and St. Augustin; but the mode prescribed at Sardica, of trying the appeal by delegated judges, appears to have been new to the Africans, who complained that the bearing of the legate Faustinus savored of imperiousness. For this reason they gave the same qualified and provisional adhesion to the canon regarding episcopal appeals; and when the inquiry, apparently, resulted unfavorably to the authenticity of the decrees, the bishops* who addressed Celestine, in the year 425, extended their remonstrances to episcopal appeals, and earnestly besought him not to receive them easily, nor to send legates into Africa, whose demeanor might exhibit in the Church the pride of secular domination.

I have thus endeavored to unravel† this somewhat intricate controversy, and to gather from the documents, which are apparently discordant, a narrative that may be consistent in itself, and reconcilable with their testimony. The appeal of Apiarius, a priest, being the immediate occasion of dispute, and the African canon expressly regarding the appeals of priests, or inferior clergymen, we are bound to consider the main controversy as confined to such appeals; and the mode and form of episcopal appeals connected with it only incidentally.

The misnomer of the canons by Zosimus greatly embarrassed the discussion, and emboldened the prelates, in their letter to Celestine, to assume a tone which they were not wont to use in addressing the successor of Peter. We may not now easily conceive how canons which were passed at Sardica in 347, should, after seventy years, be ascribed, especially by the highest dignitary of the Church, to a Council which was held in 325: but as many of the Nicene prelates, and especially Hosius, their leader, were present at Sardica, it is not strange that their decrees should have been added to the roll of the proceedings at Nice, and preserved with them in the Roman archives, and thus, in process of time, have become identified and

---

* The names of Augustin, and several others of the former Council, do not appear among them: so that the stress which Mr. Palmer and others lay on his authority, is without foundation in fact. He partook, but in a most conciliatory spirit, of the earlier proceedings.

† See Diss. ii., de Africanæ Eccl. Rom. appell., c. xxviii., a Christiano Lupo.

confounded with them. Very ancient manuscripts show this to have been the fact; and Innocent I., who preceded Zosimus, refers, in several passages,* to the Sardican canons under the title of Nicene, loudly professing that the Catholic Church follows no other canons than those adopted at Nice.† In the scarcity of manuscripts, it was no easy matter to trace the mistake to its origin, and to distinguish the sources of decrees, which came down recommended by the same authority. The Council of the Arians, held at Philippopolis, which had assumed the name of Sardican,‡ had rendered this title invidious, and thus served to involve the proceedings of the Catholic prelates in obscurity. The report of the African commissioners, that the alleged canons were not found in the great churches, left the Pope in the embarrassing situation of one who had failed to substantiate his authorities; of which circumstance the African bishops did not neglect to avail themselves: yet their tone was evidently moderated by the feeling that he whom they addressed, might still do, independently of all positive legislation, that which he had sought to do with the support of the canons of a General Council. Greeting him reverentially as "Lord brother," they say: "We earnestly entreat you not easily to give ear hereafter to such as come hence, nor any more to receive to communion persons excommunicated by us."

It is sometimes imagined that in this controversy Zosimus brought forward the canons as the ground of his claim; but this is wholly incorrect. He did not address any document on this subject to the African fathers, but he sent his legates with instructions how to act, ordering them to reinstate Apiarius, and to procure such enactments by the Council as would harmonize with the canons, and with established usage. In referring to these, he was not pointing to the source of his own authority: he was simply marking out a general plan of proceeding in ecclesiastical causes, approved of by the wisdom of a venerable assembly. No one could assert the supreme authority of his see in terms stronger than those which in the preceding year he had employed, when addressing the African fathers in relation to the appeal of Celestius from the sentence of a former Council. Although the appeals of priests, in personal causes, were generally discountenanced, no objection was made, even by the African Bishops, to an appeal from a doctrinal decision; matters of faith being always considered as *inter causas majores*, belonging of right to the cognizance of the Holy See: but as the appeal of Celestius lay dormant for some years, in consequence of his neglect to follow it up, and the doctrinal points had been defined by Innocent, the prelates complained that Zosimus had permitted the case to be re-opened. On being informed that he had determined on absolving the heresiarch, if within two months his accusers did not establish his heterodoxy, they assembled in Council, in order to com-

---

* Ep. ad Victricium Rothom. † Ep. xxv., ad Constant. clerum et pop.
‡ Aug. l. iii., contra Cresconium, c. xxxiv.

municate to him, in the most solemn manner, their views of the wiles of Celestius. His answer commences with the most ample declaration of pontifical supremacy, of which, among other things, he says: "For canonical antiquity, and the very promise of Christ our God, have given to this apostle (Peter) such power over the sentences of all, that he can loose what is bound, and bind what is loose; and equal power has been given to those who, through his favor, have been made worthy to inherit his see."*

It is an error to suppose that the African Bishops made their submission depend on the result of the inquiry as to the authenticity of the canons. Through respect for the pontifical authority, they submitted at once in the particular case in question, and suffered Apiarius to re-enter on the exercise of sacred functions, although they were convinced that he had deceived Zosimus. The same feeling prompted them to pledge themselves to the observance of the rules proposed, during the interval to be employed in the inquiry. The cause why they reserved to themselves the liberty to act otherwise in the contingency that the canons could not be verified, was because the Pontiff, not urging his own authority in the abstract, professed only a desire to enforce their observance; and he was justly presumed not to wish to interfere with national usages and laws, beyond what zeal for canonical discipline required.

The relapse of Apiarius into crime presented, after a few years, an occasion for renewing the controversy about appeals, the unfortunate delinquent having again sought shelter under the authority of Rome. The legate, believing him to be persecuted, and conceiving it to be a duty to vindicate the Apostolic privileges assailed in his person, acted with the zeal of an advocate, rather than with the impartiality of a judge, on his trial in the Council convened for that purpose. When the minds of the fathers were considerably excited, and the charities which should be mutually cherished by them and the representative of the Holy See, were endangered, remorse seized on the wretched man, who, in the presence of all, acknowledged his guilt, and implored mercy. Thus his case was, at length, brought to an issue; which, however, emboldened the bishops to persevere in their opposition to the appeals, seeing that these served to screen the guilty from punishment. This involved no question as to the supreme authority of the Holy See, which, in each particular case, was respected and obeyed, even when its exercise was deemed a grievance. Hence they confined themselves to remonstrance, and laid before the Pontiff the inconveniences and disorders attendant on the practice, without denying the abstract right, which, on the contrary, they pre-supposed, by expostulating against its undue exercise.

Bishops in Africa, as well as in other parts of the Church, had always

---

* See p. 140.

exercised the right of appeal, as we learn from a letter of St. Augustin to Celestine, written about the year 423, after the controversy about appeals had long been agitated. Anthony, Bishop of Fussala, a diocese formed out of that of Hippo, had been removed from its government by St. Augustin, without being deposed from the episcopate. Having appealed to Boniface, and gained the support of the primate of the province, who gave him commendatory letters, he succeeded in obtaining a favorable rescript, qualified, however, with the proviso, if the facts were such as he had represented. To verify them would have required a formal examination in an ecclesiastical assembly. Without this preliminary proceeding he undertook, with the aid of the civil power, to recover possession of his see, and thus scandalized the faithful. In the letter addressed to Celestine, the successor of Boniface, Augustin does not at all controvert the right of appeal; but he seeks to take away the ground on which Anthony relied, namely, that removal from the charge of a diocese could not take place without degradation from the episcopal office; and points to three recent instances in which the Apostolic See had pronounced similar sentences, or had confirmed sentences which had emanated from inferior tribunals. "There are," he says, "examples of some who, for certain faults, were neither stripped of the episcopal dignity, nor left altogether unpunished, the Apostolic See itself having pronounced sentence, or confirmed the sentences of others. Not to go back to very ancient instances, I shall mention some that are recent."* The confirmation of a sentence supposes that the case had been brought by appeal to the higher tribunal. There is no foundation for the assertion that these instances took place during the interval of inquiry, when the bishops had pledged themselves to observe the canons proposed by Zosimus: there is no probability in the supposition that the ancient examples were to be sought out of Africa: there is no reason for tracing them to the Sardican enactments, which were unknown in those churches. Augustin, speaking of a still remoter period, observed, that Cecilian could well disregard the proceedings of the conventicle of Tigisis against him, and await the examination of his case by the church beyond the sea, where, if his adversaries refused to appear, they would, by their own act, cut themselves off from the communion of the world.† This supposes that it was customary to have trials by the Pontiff, on appeal, long before the Council of Sardica was held.

From the whole proceedings and documents, it is clear, that the power of the Pope to receive appeals was not at all called in question; much less was his primacy disputed, which, on the contrary, was eminently displayed in the doctrinal decisions of Innocent and Zosimus, hailed with acclamation by the African Councils, and by the whole Christian world. The complaints of the fathers, which originally regarded the appeals of

---

* Ep. ccix., alias cclx. Aug. Cælest.   † Ep. clxii.

clergymen, in cases of a mere personal character, afterwards embraced the form of proceeding in episcopal appeals, and finally the appeals themselves; but notwithstanding the disorders which arose from the abuse of the privilege, the right and power were never controverted. Subsequent usage continued to correspond with the earlier examples, and accordingly we find Leo despatching Potentius to Africa, that he might on the spot examine the case of the Bishop Lupicinus, who had invoked the pontifical authority.* St. Gregory the Great directed the Bishop of Numidia to investigate the case of Donadeus, deposed by Victor, and to treat the prelate with canonical severity, if he should be found to have acted unjustly.†

3.—MISCELLANEOUS EXAMPLES.

In the year 443, St. Leo had occasion to exercise the right of receiving appeals in the case of Chelidonius, deposed in a Council at which St. Hilary of Arles presided. Writing to the bishops of the province of Vienne, he confidently referred to immemorial custom as authorizing him to decide at Rome, on appeal, causes originating in Gaul, and to reverse the sentence of the Gallic prelates, contrary to the pretensions of Hilary, who contended that the Pope should appoint judges to review the cause in the province where it was first tried : "You, brethren," said Leo, "will acknowledge with us that the Apostolic See, in virtue of the reverence due to it, has been consulted by the priests of your province likewise, in innumerable instances; and that in various cases of appeals, conformably to ancient custom, the decisions were either rescinded or confirmed."‡ Accordingly, he overruled the objections of Hilary, restored Chelidonius to his see, and obtained a rescript of Valentinian III., that his decree might have civil force, and be put in execution.

The right of hearing appeals was fully acknowledged in the time of St. Gregory the Great. Sending a "defender" into Spain, he directed him to examine the case of Januarius, who had been deposed, and if he found him innocent, to reinstate him in his bishopric, to hand over to his authority the intruder, that he might be confined, or sent to the Pontiff, and to subject the bishops who had pronounced the unjust sentence, to penance in a monastery, and deprive them of holy communion for six months.§ On this case, in conjunction with another, Guizot remarks : "The power of the Papacy in Spain was so real, that in 603 two Spanish bishops, Januarius of Malaga and Stephen, having been irregularly deposed, Gregory the Great sent a commissary, named John, with orders to investigate the matter; and without assembling any Council, without looking

---

* Ep. xii., ad ep. Afric.
‡ Ep. x., ad ep. per prov. Vien.
† L. xii., ep. viii.
§ L. xiii., ep. xlv.

for the assent of the Spanish clergy, John declared the deposition irregular, annulled it, and reinstated the two bishops, thus exercising the acts of the most extensive supremacy."*

We have elsewhere seen that Eutyches, when condemned by Flavian, in the Synod of Constantinople, had recourse to Leo, falsely alleging that he had lodged an appeal, which shows that the right of appeal existed. Flavian himself, being unjustly condemned by Dioscorus, in the tumultuous assembly of Ephesus, put into the hands of the apostolic legates an appeal against the iniquitous sentence.† The Pope annulled the acts, recognised Flavian as of his communion, and cautioned the people of Constantinople against receiving any other bishop in his lifetime.‡ Gelasius, speaking of the appeal of Flavian and Chrysostom, says: "The Apostolic See, by not consenting to the sentence, absolved them."§ The American editor of Mosheim's Church History observes, that "Flavian before his death appealed to Leo; and this appeal, pursued by the Pontiff, occasioned the Council in which Eutyches was condemned, and the sanguinary Dioscorus deposed."‖

Theodoret, Bishop of Cyrus, was condemned in the false Council of Ephesus, but, like Flavian, he appealed to the just judgment and high authority of the Apostolic See. Writing to Leo, he says: "I await the sentence of the Apostolic See, and I implore and entreat your Holiness to succor me, who appeal to your righteous and just tribunal." He adds, that "this most Holy See has, on many accounts, the principality over all the churches throughout the universe."¶ He asks a command to present himself at Rome, that he may there render an account of his faith. Leo recognised his orthodoxy, annulled the sentence pronounced against him, and restored him to his see. "Blessed be our God," says he in a letter addressed to Theodoret, "whose invincible truth, according to the judgment of the Apostolic See, has shown you to be clear of all taint of heresy."** When the bishop presented himself at the Council of Chalcedon, he was hailed by the fathers: "Let the most reverend Bishop Theodoret enter in, to partake in the proceedings of the Synod, since the most holy Archbishop Leo has restored him to the bishopric."†† In the course of the proceedings, the formal action of the Council was asked, that he might be put into actual possession of his see, conformably to the pontifical decree, or, as the acts express it, "that he might receive his church, as the most holy Archbishop Leo has judged."‡‡ The bishops

---

* Cours d' Histoire Moderne, t. iii. p. 66.
† Leo., ep. xliv., Ball. edit. col. 915, Liberatus, cap. xii.
‡ Ep. xliv. et xlv. § Ep. xiii.
‖ Church History, p. 2, c. v. p. 152. Note.
¶ Ep. cxiii. ad Leon. Also ep. cxvi., inter lit. Theodoret.
** Ep. cxx., Ball. edit. col. 1226. †† Act I. ‡‡ Act viii.

with acclamation assented: "Theodoret is worthy of his see." "Leo has judged conformably to the Divine judgment."*

John Talaja was raised to the chair of Alexandria, in the decline of the fifth century. Acacius, the heretical Bishop of Constantinople, contrived to draw down on him the anger of the Emperor Zeno, who banished him from his see, and substituted Peter Mongus in his place. Calendion, Bishop of Antioch, to which city he fled, advised him to seek redress from Simplicius, Bishop of Rome, to whom he gave him letters of recommendation. Liberatus, a writer of the sixth century, relates that "having got letters of intercession from Calendion, Patriarch of Antioch, he appealed to the Roman Pontiff, as the blessed Athanasius had done."† The Pope, recognising the justice of his cause, endeavored to have him restored, since the pontifical decree for that purpose could not be executed without the imperial concurrence; and his successor, Felix III., finding the obstacles insuperable, gave him the administration of Nola, a bishopric in Italy, without taking from him his title of patriarch. A priest named Solomon, degraded by Acacius, Bishop of Constantinople, appealed to the same Pontiff, who wrote to the clergy of that city, instructing them to treat him as a brother.

Barrow admits numerous cases of appeal: "Thus did Marcion go to Rome, and sue for communion there. So Fortunatus and Felicissimus, in St. Cyprian, being condemned in Africk, did fly to Rome for shelter, of which absurdity St. Cyprian doth so complain. So likewise Martianus and Basilides, in St. Cyprian, being ousted of their sees, for having lapsed from the Christian profession, did fly to Stephen for succor to be restored. So Maximus (the Cynic) went to Rome to get a confirmation of his election at Constantinople. So Marcellus, being rejected for heterodoxy, went thither to get attestation to his orthodoxy, (of which St. Basil complaineth.) So Apiarius, being condemned in Africk for his crimes, did appeal to Rome. And on the other side, Athanasius being with great partiality condemned by the Synod of Tyre; Paulus and other bishops being extruded from their sees for orthodoxy; St. Chrysostom being condemned and expelled by Theophilus and his accomplices; Flavianus being deposed by Dioscorus, and the Ephesine Synod; Theodoret being condemned by the same,—did cry out for help from Rome. Chelidonius, Bishop of Besancon, being deposed by Hilarius of Arles, (for crimes,) did fly to Pope Leo. Ignatius, Patriarch of Constantinople, being extruded from his see by Photius, did complain to the Pope."‡

The authority of the Holy See to receive appeals, from any quarter of the Church, was strongly asserted by Pope Gelasius. Answering the objection of Euphemius, Bishop of Constantinople, who alleged that

---

* Ibidem.
† Breviarium controversiarum Nestorianæ et Eutychianæ, c. xviii.
‡ Suppos. v. n. 12.

Acacius was uncanonically condemned, because no Council had been summoned to investigate his case, as its importance seemed to demand, he says: "They object to us the canons, which they violate, whilst they refuse to obey the first see, that asks nothing of them but what is just and right. The canons direct that appeals of the whole Church should be made to this see, and no appeal should lie from it, so that it should judge the whole Church, and itself be judged by none, and no one should revise its judgments."* It is not probable that language so strong would have been used by the Pontiff to the Bishop of the imperial city, if it admitted of contradiction. To the Bishops of Dardania he wrote: "The whole Church, throughout the world, knows that the See of blessed Peter the apostle has the right to loose what has been bound by the sentences of any bishops, since it has power to judge every church."†

---

* Apud Fleury, l. xxx. § xxviii.
† Ep. vii., ad episcopos Dardaniæ, anno 495, t. ii., coll. Hard. coll. 909.

CHAPTER XVI.

The Church of England.

§ 1.—BRITONS.

THE special interest attached at present to the "Church of England," may justify a distinct review of the relations of the ancient Britons and of the Anglo-Saxons to the Holy See. The existence of Christianity in Britain in the decline of the second century, is known from the testimonies of Tertullian,* Origen,† and Arnobius.‡ Bede, doubtless on the authority of ancient documents or tradition, states that in the time of the Emperor Aurelius, Lucius, a British king, sent to Eleutherius, Bishop of Rome, to ask for instructors in the Christian law.§ That there is a great weight of authority for this statement, is admitted by an unfriendly reviewer of Dr. Milner's History of Winchester. "The truth is," says Dr. M., "all our original writers, British, as well as Saxon and Norman,‖ together with the records of our ancient abbeys, the martyrologies and histories of foreign countries, and existing manuscripts of the most ancient date, (to say nothing of coins,) prove that the first Christian king reigned in our island, as the first Christian emperor was afterwards born in it."¶ The attempt of Dr. Burgess to ascribe the origin of the British churches to St. Paul, is wholly unsupported by proof, and purely visionary.** In the absence of evidence, we cannot say positively how the succession of bishops was provided for, from the first arrival of those whom Eleutherius despatched to Lucius; but it was no doubt according to some plan originally adopted with pontifical sanction. It is not improbable that the British churches may have been immediately dependent for ordination on the See of Arles, whose

---

* Adv. Judæos, p. 189. † Hom. vi., in Luc. c. i.
‡ In Ps. cxlvii. § L. i., Hist. Eccl. Angl.
‖ Gildas, Nennius, Bede, Asserius, Malmesbury.
¶ Postscript to History of Winchester.
** See its complete refutation in the History and Antiquities of the Anglo-Saxon Church, by John Lingard, D.D., vol. i. app., a. London, 1845. I avail myself freely of this valuable work.

bishop, from very ancient times, was clothed with the powers of Vicar Apostolic; which is the more likely as the civil prefect of Gaul embraced Britain in the sphere of his jurisdiction. Augustin received episcopal consecration from that prelate. The Bishops of London, York, and Lincoln, were present at the Council of Arles in 314, in which a splendid testimony was rendered to the primacy, and other British prelates at the Council of Sardica, so justly celebrated for its decrees regarding appeals to the Pontiff. Three were also at Rimini, whose poverty obliged them to avail themselves of the provision made by the emperor for their support whilst in attendance.* The communion of the British bishops with the Holy See is evident from their presence in the two former Councils. In the last they shared the misfortune of the others, who were beguiled by the artifices of the Arians.

The exercise of the pontifical authority in Britain for the extirpation of the Pelagian heresy, is attested by an unexceptionable witness, St. Prosper, a native of Gaul, contemporary with St. Germanus, and secretary of Pope Celestine: "At the instance of the deacon Palladius, Pope Celestine sends Germanus, Bishop of Auxerre, IN HIS OWN STEAD, in order that he might drive out the heretics, and guide the Britons to the Catholic faith."† Elsewhere he says: "With no less solicitude he freed Britain from this disease, when he banished from that remote island certain enemies of grace, natives of the country, and having ordained a bishop for the Scots (Irish,) whilst he labors to preserve a Roman island in the Catholic faith, he made even a barbarous island Christian."‡ Britain is here called Roman, because subjected by the Roman arms; whilst Ireland is styled barbarian, as being beyond the limits of the empire. The enthusiasm with which Germanus and Lupus of Troyes, his companion, were received by the Britons, and the success of their mission, prove that the authority of the Roman Bishop, in whose name they appeared, was fully recognised. Constantius, a priest of Lyons, who wrote the Life of St. Germanus, about fifty or sixty years after this event, relates their mission in detail; as also Venerable Bede, guided by the tradition and monuments of the British churches. The discipline of the Britons became subsequently relaxed, and their ecclesiastical position was scarcely discernible after the separation of their island from the empire: but a glimpse of it is afforded us by Gildas, a British author, who wrote about the middle of the sixth century, in his complaints of the ambition of some clergymen, who traversed lands and seas for its gratification, and on their return made parade of their authority. This plainly has reference to Rome, as the source of ecclesiastical dignity.§ The succession of bishops was maintained down to the time of Augustin, the

---

* Sulp. Sev., Hist., p. 401.   † In chronico ad an. 429.
‡ Contra Cassian, c. xli.   § Hist. Gild., p. 76.

missionary despatched to England by St. Gregory the Great. Those who assert the original independence of the British churches, and their *autocephalous* character, forget their Roman origin, the presence of their prelates in Councils in which the prerogatives of the Holy See were distinctly recognised, and the interposition of Pope Celestine to extirpate the heresy of Pelagius, through his envoy Germanus. Our ignorance of the arrangement by which the succession of bishops was provided for, does not warrant any inference adverse to the primacy, since any mode originally sanctioned by the Pontiff was a sufficient exercise of his right; and the fact that the Britons continued in his communion proves that their ordination had received his approval. In the Council of Ephesus the Bishops of the island of Cyprus contested the claims of the Patriarch of Antioch to control their ordinations, asserting that their predecessors had performed them from the beginning without his interference: which fact being controverted, the fathers of the Council confined themselves to a general decree, that the ancient usages and privileges of the various churches should be respected. This case, although frequently alleged in support of British independence, is not of any advantage to those who urge it, as long as the fact of the Britons having exercised a free power of ordination, without recourse to Rome, is not established. Were it, however, conceded that the British ordinations were performed without any reference to the Pope, or his Vicar, it would only show that the freedom of the Britons on this point should have been respected, unless most weighty reasons required a change of system. If relaxation and immorality ensued from this "domestic ordination" and partial independence, the great interests of religion, which far outweigh ecclesiastical privileges, would authorize the chief pastor, who is charged with the care of all the churches, to interpose, and reserve to himself the choice or approbation of those who thenceforward should be raised to the responsible office of bishops. Whatever may have been the usage in this respect, it is wrong to infer from it the entire independence of the Britons, since the enjoyment of special privilege does not necessarily imply exemption from all authority. Well does Mr. Allies say: "There can be no independence, strictly so called, in the Church and body of Christ."*

A document was first produced by Spelman, in the year 1639, purporting to be an address of the Abbot Dinoth, on behalf of the British bishops, to Augustin, the missionary of Gregory the Great, who urged them to submit to his authority, he being vested by the Pope with the powers of archbishop. It is unnecessary to expose in detail the reasons for regarding it as a forgery, especially as Fuller, the Protestant historian,

---

* Church of England Cleared, &c. p. 120.
† Spelman, Conc., t. i. p. 108.

abandons its defence: "Let it shift as it can for its authenticalness."* After a feeble effort to account for a glaring anachronism, he is compelled by its modern phraseology to make this avowal: "A late Papist much impugneth the credit of this manuscript (as made since the dayes of King Henry the Eighth,) and cavilleth at the Welsh thereof, as modern, and full of false spelling. He need not have used so much violence to wrest it out of our hands, who can part with it without considerable loss to ourselves, or gain to our adversaries; for it is but a breviate, or abstract of those passages which in Bede, and other authours, appear most true, of the British refusing subjection to the See of Rome. Whilest, therefore, the chapter is canonicall, it matters not if the contents be *apocrypha* (as the additions of some wel-meaning scribe.) And though THIS WELSH BE FAR LATER THAN THE DAYS OF ABBOT DINOTH, and the English later than the Welsh; yet the Latin, as ancienter than both,† containeth nothing contrary to the sense of all authours, which write this intercourse between Augustine and the Welsh nation." The forgery of this document was detected by Tuberville, and is now generally admitted, as Dr. Lingard testifies.‡

It is untrue that the document in question harmonizes with the statements of Bede, "the only real authority which we possess." He does not say a word of any pretensions of the Britons to independence of Rome; but he merely states that they refused to acknowledge Augustin for their archbishop, because he did not rise to receive them as they approached, which neglect a hermit had disposed them to look on as a token of an imperious and domineering temper.§ The apprehension of the severity of his government is the only cause assigned for their declining to recognise him. This refusal is easily reconcilable with the abstract admission of the power of the Pontiff, in whose name he appeared, since men are slow to admit a painful exercise of authority. Gregory, however, had not made the consent of the Britons a necessary condition for the exercise of metropolitical rights by his envoy, but in the consciousness of the power with which he was clothed by divine appointment, he bade him use them freely for the interests of piety: "We commit the care of all the British bishops to you, brother, that the unlearned may be instructed, the weak strengthened by advice, and the perverse corrected with authority."‖

---

* The Church History of Britain Endeavored, by Thomas Fuller. London, 1656. P. 61.

† Spelman says that he added it for the use of foreigners; it was not in the manuscript.

‡ Anglo-Saxon Church, vol. i. p. 71. Note.

§ Bede, l. ii., Hist. c. ii. ‖ Ep. lxiv.

§ 2.—ANGLO-SAXON CHURCH.

We need not discuss more fully the question of the independence of the British churches, since the Church of the Anglo-Saxons was a purely papal creation, having been founded, organized, and fostered by the Popes. Augustin, the envoy of Gregory, acted in all things by his direction, and with entire dependence on him. When he failed to conciliate the Britons, abandoning them to the punishments which their disorders called down from heaven, he foretold that the sword of the enemy would execute the divine judgments on them, as took place after his death. In the mean time he pursued his apostolic mission among the Anglo-Saxons, and succeeded in laying the foundations of that splendid edifice, which afterwards rose in fair proportions, with the admiration of the Catholic world. He fixed his See in Canterbury. Gregory, in sending him the pallium, the emblem of metropolitical power, admonished him that he must not consider himself as authorized to encroach on the jurisdiction of the bishops of Gaul, his power being limited to the British prelates. "We give you no authority over the Bishops of Gaul, because from the ancient times of my predecessors, the Bishop of Arles received the pallium, whom we must not deprive of the authority with which he is invested."* "You, brother," says the Apostolic mandate, "will, moreover, have subject to you not only the bishops whom you or the Bishop of York may ordain, but all the bishops of Britain, by authority of our God, and Lord Jesus Christ, that they may learn from your instruction to believe correctly, and from your example to live religiously."†

The establishment of this new hierarchy throughout the island generally superseded that of the British prelates, and took away all pretext for relying on their privileges, which were certainly not communicated to their rivals. For above a century, nevertheless, the ancient order of bishops was continued, but with entire separation from the new line derived from Augustin, so that even as late as the days of Bede, the Britons had as lieve communicate with pagans as with the Anglo-Saxon Christians.‡ At length they utterly disappeared, and the successors of Augustin and his colleagues were everywhere found; so that, as Dr. Lingard confidently affirms, in contradiction to Mr. Soames, "not a single county, from London to Edinburgh, can point to the ancient Church of Britain as its nursing mother in the faith of Christ."§

St. Aidan, an Irish monk, was the apostle of Northumbria, and other

---

* Ep. lxiv. † Bed., l. i. c. xxix.
‡ Bede, Eccl. Hist., l. ii. c. xx.
§ History and Antiquities of the Anglo-Saxon Church, ch. i. p. 43. Note. Second English edition.

of his countrymen preached the Gospel with success in various parts of England: but the Roman origin of the Anglo-Saxon church and hierarchy was in no degree affected by the co-operation of these missionaries, since Ireland itself traces her Christian privileges to Patrick, the companion of Palladius, who was ordained by Pope Celestine for the *Scoti*, according to the testimony of Prosper. Besides, the Irish missionaries recognised the existing hierarchy, and incorporated their converts into the church.

§ 3.—PASCHAL CONTROVERSY.

The Britons, as well as the Irish, differed from Rome in the calculation of the paschal time, through ignorance of the correct mode of determining it, which was adopted after the first quarter of the fifth century. They were not, however, *Quartodecimans*, as those were styled who celebrated Easter on the same day as the Jews. The tenacity with which they adhered to the method prescribed to them by the early missionaries, was an occasion of some controversy, which, nevertheless, had no serious results. It is in vain alleged as evidence, that both islands had originally received the faith from Oriental missionaries, since the mode of calculation adopted in Britain and Ireland was different even from that which was used in the East, and they invariably celebrated the feast on Sunday, contrary to the practice of those who imitated the Jewish solemnity. The day of their festival was calculated according to the cycle used by the Roman Church before the Council of Nice.* The dissension of the Roman and Irish missionaries on this point, led Oswiu, King of Northumbria, to summon them to his presence, in order to ascertain the grounds on which each relied. Wilfrid, the chaplain of Prince Alchfrid, seeing that Colman, the Bishop of Lindisfarne, placed the strength of the Irish cause on the authority of St. Columba, insisted that the usage sanctioned by the apostle Peter, on whom the Lord founded His Church, and to whom He gave the keys of His kingdom, should prevail. The king, having questioned Colman as to the high prerogative of the apostle, obtained a willing acknowledgment of it, and put an end to the discussion by declaring his desire to enjoy the favor of the gate-keeper of heaven. The narrative of this interesting debate, which is given by Venerable Bede,† shows that the authority of the prince of the apostles was fully recognised by both parties. The adherence of the Irish missionaries to the custom of their ancestors in a matter of discipline, is no evidence of opposition to the teaching of the Roman Church, or of estrangement from her communion, since, whilst condemning the Quartodecimans, who retained the Jewish festival-day, she tolerated those who merely differed

---

* This is certified of the Scots by Goodall, *ad Hist. Scot.*, introd. p. 66.
† L. iii., Hist. c. xxv. xxvi.

in the mode of calculation. St. Columban, who with great vehemence defended the Irish usage, without becoming deference to the Pontiff whom he addressed, rendered, in the same letter, unequivocal homage to the authority of the Holy See. Those of the South of Ireland yielded to the admonition of Pope Honorius,* and the Northerns not long afterwards conformed to the Roman usage. The Britons persisted in their ancient practice the more pertinaciously, because the Anglo-Saxons, whom they held in detestation, observed the festival on a different day. The controversy was rather chronological than theological, as Dr. Lingard well observes.

§ 4.—ANGLO-SAXON HIERARCHY.

The plan of the Anglo-Saxon hierarchy was traced out by the hand of Gregory. He authorized Augustin to consecrate twelve bishops, one of whom, the Bishop of London, should have the pallium, and should be consecrated by his own Synod, that is, be chosen by his suffragans, and consecrated by one of them, with the assistance of two others, which, however, was dispensed with when impracticable. The Bishop of York had power to consecrate twelve bishops, over whom he had the authority of metropolitan, although he was subject to Canterbury, and, according to seniority, preceded or followed the Bishop of London.† The changes which took place in the civil governments, prevented the execution of this plan, which was modified by the Popes Vitalian and Agatho. The latter, by the authority of the blessed Peter, prince of the apostles,‡ determined and decreed that there should be only twelve bishops in the whole island, under the government of the Archbishop of Canterbury, "decorated for the time by the Holy See with the honor of the pallium." Egbert, Bishop of York, succeeded in recovering the ancient dignity of his see from Gregory III., who sent him the badge of metropolitan."§ The See of Lichfield was erected into an archbishopric in 787, by the authority of Pope Adrian, who sent the pallium to its prelate, at the urgent solicitation of Offa, King of Mercia. Cenulf, who subsequently occupied the throne, in seeking the revocation of this measure, protested unqualified submission to the decrees of the Pontiff, "which no Christian dares gainsay;" but at the same time declared that the statements of Offa were not founded in truth and justice. Accordingly, Leo III. rescinded the act of his predecessor, and restored to Canterbury its ancient rights over all the other bishops. Æthelheard, the archbishop, who had pleaded his cause

---

* L. ii., Hist. c. xix. l. iii. c. iii.   † Ep. lxv.

‡ " Ex auctoritate beati Petri apostolorum principis—definimus et statuimus, ut unumquodque regnum in Britannia insula institutum habeat secundum moderationis mensuram episcopos ita statutos," &c.—Labbe, tom. vii. 601. Spelman, Conc. 159.

§ Chron. Sax., an. 735. Malm. de Pont., l. iii. p. 153.

successfully at the Roman court, on his return, published the apostolical decision in the Council of Cloveshoe, and made enactments in accordance with it, with the consent and permission of the Pontiff. Thus the supremacy of the Holy See was exercised in the most unequivocal manner, in the original organization of the Anglo-Saxon Church, and in its subsequent modification. Guizot might well say to his pupils: "As to the Anglo-Saxon Church, you know that having been founded by the Popes themselves, it was placed from the commencement under their most direct influence."*

The successors of Augustin in the See of Canterbury, like him, received from the Pontiff the pallium, as the necessary token of his sanction for the exercise of metropolitical authority. Justinus obtained it from St. Boniface V., and Honorius from his namesake, who then occupied the Holy See. Paulinus, of York, received it from the latter Pontiff. So essential was it deemed, that Eanbald, who had been consecrated bishop, as coadjutor to Archbishop Ælbert, with right of succession, did not omit, on the death of Ælbert, in 780, to despatch Alcuin to Rome to obtain it, after which he was solemnly inaugurated. His successor, of the same name, awaited a year for its reception, on which he was confirmed archbishop. Ælfsy, of Winchester, archbishop elect, died on his journey to Rome, which he had undertaken to procure for himself the pallium. In the ninth century, the indulgence of the Holy See, which previously spared the archbishop elect the necessity of travelling to Rome to obtain it, was withdrawn, so that each had to seek it in person, to testify more solemnly his dependence on the chair of St. Peter.

Aldred, Bishop of Worcester, aspiring to the See of York, in the year 1059, repaired to Rome, in company of Gison, Bishop elect of Wells, and Walter, elect of Hereford. These latter two prelates, being unexceptionable, received consecration from the hands of the Pontiff, who declined to promote Aldred, against whom a charge of simony had been advanced. The disappointed prelate had scarcely left the city, when, falling into the hands of brigands, he was despoiled and forced to return. His misfortune accomplished what his merit had failed to procure, and the Pontiff consented that he should pass to the See of York, on relinquishing the other diocese. Two cardinals went to England, probably to see that this should be faithfully executed, and having approved of the election of Wulstan to fill the vacant bishopric, assisted at his consecration.

Lanfranc, Archbishop elect of Canterbury, going to Rome, in the year 1071, for the pallium, readily obtained it, with extraordinary marks of honor and affection, from Alexander II., who had been his pupil. The Pontiff gave him that which he himself was wont to use in the cele-

---

* Cours d'Histoire Moderne, t. iii. p. 67.

bration of mass, besides another, such as was granted to every metropolitan.

Several of the occupants of the See of Canterbury were consecrated by the Popes themselves. On the death of Wighard, archbishop elect, who had come to Rome for consecration, Pope Vitalian, in 668, chose Theodore, a Greek monk, to fill his place, and having consecrated him with his own hands, despatched him to govern the Anglo-Saxon Church.* Five centuries afterwards, Alexander II. consecrated for the same see, Richard, Prior of Dover, at the solicitation of Henry II., who had implored the Pontiff not to regard the pretensions of his revolted son, who sought to fill the churches with his creatures and supporters.

The Metropolitan of Canterbury was accustomed to receive the powers of Apostolic Vicar, which constituted him Legate of the Pope. Gregory II., writing to the bishops of England respecting Tatwine, the second in succession from Theodore, says: "We have authorized him to act in our stead in all things in that country." Formosus speaks in like manner of Plegmond, who filled the same See.† Pope John addressed St. Dunstan to the same effect, in conformity with the usages of his predecessors. In 1117, Henry I. solicited Paschal II. to relieve his kingdom from the necessity of receiving papal legates, alleging that, by the concession of Gregory the Great, the Archbishop of Canterbury was invested with legatine powers. The Pontiff called for documentary proof of the concession. Celestine III., in 1194, constituted Hubert of Canterbury his legate. In the contest about privileges between the Sees of York and Canterbury, the whole question turned on the pontifical grants, which were preserved with great care in the archives of each church, as its most valid titles. Lanfranc, in his report to Alexander II. of the proceedings in this case, observes: "For the final strength and support of the whole case, the privileges and writings of your predecessors, Gregory, Boniface, Honorius, Vitalian, Sergius, also of another Gregory, and of the last Leo were produced, which had been given or transmitted at various times to the prelates of the Church of Canterbury, and to the English kings."‡

§ 3.—ACKNOWLEDGMENT OF THE PRIMACY.

The terms in which Bede, and all the Anglo-Saxon writers, speak of St. Peter, and of the Bishops of Rome, are such as leave no room to

---

* Of this Hallam says: "The consecration of Theodore by Pope Vitalian, in 668, is a stronger fact," (*than the appeal of Wilfred,*) "and cannot be got over by those injudicious Protestants, who take the bull by the horns."—Middle Ages, ch. vii. Note.

† Dr. Lingard, on the authority of Eadmer, defends the authenticity of this letter. Vol. i. p. 89.

‡ Apud Baron, an. 1072, p. 409.

question their faith in the divine institution of the primacy, and its perpetual duration for the government of the entire Church. The venerable historian says that Gregory "was invested with the first" (that is, supreme) "pontificate in the whole world, and was set over the churches converted to the true faith."* The celebrated scholar Alcuin, avows that "the Lord Jesus Christ had constituted Peter shepherd of His chosen flock;"† and acknowledges Adrian I., the actual Pontiff, as "Vicar of Peter, occupying his chair, and inheriting his wonderful authority."‡ Huelbert, Abbot of Wearmouth, addressed Gregory the Great as "divinely intrusted with the government of the whole Church."§ The Bishops of Rome were even designated presidents of the world.|| In the Anglo-Saxon Pontifical a prayer is prescribed for the consecration of the sovereign Pontiff, which expresses in the strongest terms the eminence and authority of his station. It styles him " this Thy servant, whom Thou hast made prelate of the Apostolic See, and primate of all priests in the world, and teacher of Thy universal Church, and whom Thou hast chosen for the ministry of the high priesthood."¶

By order of Pope Agatho, a Council was held at Hatfield, by Theodore, Archbishop of Canterbury, and his suffragans, in presence of John, Abbot of St. Martin's, deputy of the Holy See, to declare the faith of the Anglo-Saxons, and subscribe the doctrinal definition of Martin I. against Monothelism: which desire of the Pontiff was religiously complied with.

In a Council held at Cloveshoe, in the middle of the eighth century, at which Cuthbert, Archbishop of Canterbury, opened the assembly by the lecture of two writings, received "from the apostolic lord, the Pontiff held in reverence by the whole world, the Pope Zachary, which, as he by his apostolical authority had commanded, were first read openly in Latin, and then in an English translation. In these he admonished the Anglo-Saxon inhabitants of this island of Britain, expostulated with them, and conjured them; and then threatened to cut off from the communion of the Church all who should despise his warning, and obstinately persist in their wickedness."** Their first canon, directed to the reformation of their own order, was avowedly made to prevent the execution of this threat. Yet there have been some writers so ingenious as to discover evidence of the independence of the Anglo-Saxon Church in the decrees of this Council!

The legates of Adrian visited England during the administration of Jaenbyret, Archbishop of Canterbury, bringing with them from the Holy

---

* Bede, Hist., ii. c. i.
† Alc. Oper., l, 65, 134.
‡ Ad Adrian Oper., l. 25.
§ Apud Bed., op. Min. 150, 329.
|| Eddius, Vit. Wilf., c. v. p. 45.
¶ Pont. Egb., p. 32. Pont. Gemet., p. 41.
** Wilkins, conc. 94. Spelman, conc., 245.

See canons for the reformation of morals: which, in an amended form, were read and adopted in two Councils, with solemn promise of obedience on the part of the prelates.

The authority of the Holy See was also manifested in the deposition of Anglo-Saxon bishops. The legates of Alexander II. deposed the Bishop of Litchfield, who retired to a monastery.* Celestine III., on complaints made against Godfrey, Archbishop of York, brother of King Richard, commissioned the Bishop of Lincoln, with others, to take cognizance of the case, authorizing them to suspend him from the government of his diocese, if he were found guilty. The Pontiff himself, subsequently, pronounced the suspension.†

The Holy See was recognised in England as a high court of appeal, to which bishops, oppressed by unjust judgments of their colleagues, might have recourse, with confidence of obtaining redress. In 664, Wilfrid was chosen Bishop of Northumbria: but thirteen years afterwards, Theodore, Archbishop of Canterbury, without his knowledge, consecrated three bishops for his territory, which he thought proper to divide into separate dioceses. The injured prelate, by the advice of his colleagues, appealed to the Pontiff, from the judgment and act of the metropolitan, and repaired to Rome to prosecute his appeal in person. Cœnwald, a monk, appeared there in behalf of Theodore, and the parties urged their reasons before a Council summoned by Pope Agatho for the trial of the cause. The Pontiff decreed that Wilfrid should be reinstated in his bishopric, under penalty of excommunication to be incurred by the archbishop and by King Egfrid, at whose instance he had acted. The division of the diocese was, however, insisted on, but the choice of the new prelates was left to Wilfrid. The violence and intrigues of the monarch prevented, during several years, his return to his diocese, although the archbishop himself urged the necessity of obeying the pontifical decree. Aldfrid, who succeeded Egfrid, in 685, restored to him the See of York and the monastery of Ripon, but afterwards, under threats of vengeance, sought to force him to make the latter the see of a new bishop. The affrighted prelate fled into the dominions of the King of Mercia, and during nine years remained an exile from his see, until Brithwald, the successor of Theodore, invited him to attend a Council. In this assembly he was urged to resign, but he appealed again to the just tribunal of the Roman Pontiff. After hearing the agent of the metropolitan, and the bishop, in a tedious trial, John VI. pronounced judgment in favor of Wilfrid. The king, however, for a time resisted the execution of the sentence, alleging that he had been previously condemned by the metropolitan, by the envoy of the Apostolic See, and by almost all the bishops of Britain: but in a few weeks being overtaken by death, he declared his

---

* Baron., an. 1095.   † Ibidem, an. 1159.

wish to be reconciled with the injured prelate. After his death the dissension was amicably terminated to the satisfaction of all parties. "It has been often said," remarks Dr. Lingard, "that the great object of Wilfrid was to establish in Northumbria the authority of Rome: but it must be evident to every reader, that he found the authority of Rome already established, and had recourse to it only to protect himself from oppression. The result proved the utility of this supreme jurisdiction claimed by the Pontiff: for we read no more, from the time of Wilfrid till the reign of Edward the Confessor, of any arbitrary deposition of bishops at the will either of the king or of the metropolitan."*

It may gratify the reader to peruse the quaint statement of this case by a Protestant historian. Speaking of the solicitations to resign, made to Wilfrid by the Council, Fuller says: "In a Council convened for the purpose, the bishops endeavored in vain to induce him to resign. Wilfride persisted loyall to his own innocence, affirming such a cession might be interpreted a confession of his guiltinesse, and appealed from that Council to his Holinesse, and this tough old man, being seventy years of age, took a journey to Rome, there to tugg it out with his adversaries. . . . The sentence of Pope John the Seventh† passed on his side, and his opposers were sent home with blame and shame, whilst Wilfride returned with honour, managing his successe with much moderation; equally commendable, that his innocence kept him from drooping in affliction, and his humility from insulting in prosperity. Bertuald, Archbishop of Canterbury, humbly entertained the Pope's letters in behalf of Wilfride, and welcomed his person at his return; but Alfride, King of Northumberland, refused to re-seat him in his bishoprick, stoutly maintaining, that 'twas against reason to communicate with a man twice condemned by the Council of England, notwithstanding all apostolick commands in favor of him. But soon after he fell dangerously sick, a consequent of, and therefore caused by his former stubbornnesse; as those that construe all events to the advantage of the Roman See, interpret this a punishment on his obstinacy. Suppled with sicknesse, he confessed his fault; and so Wilfride was restored to his place."‡ Thus the king finally yielded to the authority of Rome, and put her judgment in execution. The right of the Pope to receive appeals, and grant relief, was acknowledged in England, as in every other part of Christendom.

---

* History and Antiquities, &c. ch. iii. The reader will find there, and in the appendix, the full statement of the facts, and the refutation of modern misrepresentations.

† Dr. Lingard ascribes the sentence to his immediate predecessor, of the same name.

‡ The Church History of Britain Endeavored, by Thomas Fuller. London, 1656. Century viii., book ii. p. 93.

6.—MODERN CHURCH OF ENGLAND.

It is vain to plead the apology of the Church of England on the ground of the patriarchal system, which presupposes the primacy. Even by this system the Church of England stands condemned, since she refuses obedience to the Roman Patriarch, whose jurisdiction she had acknowledged up to the moment that a licentious prince forced her to abjure it: "Henry the Eighth fixing his supremacy on a reluctant church by the axe, the gibbet, the stake, and laws of premunire and forfeiture."* The refusal to admit that the Pope is universal bishop is not the head and front of her offence, as has been sometimes alleged; for she is not called on to approve a title which the Pontiffs have never assumed, or to adopt any theory about the extent of pontifical prerogative, but simply to accept the primacy, as defined by the Council of Florence, and to place herself in that position which she occupied from the time when Augustin founded and organized her. Mr. Allies, whilst defending the Church of England, unconsciously gave up the cause: "If the charge were that we refuse to stand in the same relation to the Pope that St. Augustin of Canterbury stood in to this very St. Gregory, that we refuse to regard and honor the successor of St. Gregory with the same honor with which our archbishops, as soon as they were seated in the government of their church, and were no longer mere missionaries, but primates, regarded the occupants of St. Peter's See, I think both the separation three hundred years ago, and the present continuance of it on our part, would, so far as this question of schism is concerned, be utterly indefensible."†

Mr. Palmer observes, that the clergy qualified the admission of the royal supremacy‡ by the very important clause: "as far as it was consistent with the law of Christ:" but he forgets that this was in 1531, at the commencement of the changes, and that soon afterwards they pledged themselves, "on the word of a priest," to obey the king in spiritual matters.§ The papal power was transferred to the king, which Mr. Palmer says was merely suppressed: for by the 25 Henry VIII., c. 19, the right of appeal from the sentence of metropolitans, which previously lay to the Pontiff, was granted "to the king's majesty, in the king's Court of Chancery;" to be heard "by such persons as shall be named by the king's highness." "This statute," Mr. Lewis remarks, "is the origin of the court of delegates, which has lately made way for the judicial committee of the privy council, in which resides, now, the

---

* Church of England Cleared, p. 172.
† Ibidem, p. 194.
‡ Treatise on the Church, vol. i. p. ii. ch. iii.
§ See Act of Submission in Wilkins, iii. 754, 755.

supreme jurisdiction of the Anglican Church."* Mr. Palmer strangely confounds this recourse to the king, as supreme head on earth, with the usage, or rather abuse, which exists in some countries, of invoking the protection of the State against alleged encroachments of the ecclesiastical authority. *L'appel d'abus*,† is in itself an enormous abuse, from which no sanction can be derived for the still more unjustifiable practice of appeal to the royal tribunal as supreme in all causes, ecclesiastical as well as civil. The papal power in regard to the appointment of bishops, was abrogated by the same act, c. 20, and declared to belong to the king, who, by his *congé d'elire*,‡ determined the choice of the electors, under severe penalties, and by the grant of the pallium conferred metropolitical authority. Dispensations hitherto obtained from Rome were, by c. 21, to be sought from the archbishop, and in extraordinary cases the king's license became necessary. The spiritual prelates were authorized by this statute "to use, minister, execute, and do all sacraments, sacramentals, and divine service." By the statute 26 Henry VIII., c. 1, the king, as "only supreme head in earth of the Church of England," was declared to have all pre-eminences, jurisdictions, privileges, authorities to the said dignity belonging, and especially full power to repress, correct, and amend all heresies and abuses which by any manner spiritual authority or jurisdiction, ought to be repressed, corrected, or amended." Mr. Palmer explains this of " temporal means and penalties in concurrence with the judgment of the Church of England," but he betrays his want of confidence in this interpretation by observing: "The bishops understood it in *some such sense*, for they not only offered no opposition to the passing of this bill, but immediately after swore to the king's supremacy." This only shows that they meanly crouched at the feet of the tyrant. The appointment of Thomas Cromwell, a layman, to be Vicar General of the king, "sounded ill," according to the apologist. There was full evidence that it was intended in a heterodox sense, since he was empowered to correct archbishops and bishops, to summon Synods, and preside in them, to excommunicate, and to use his authority in all causes touching the ecclesiastical jurisdiction. The servility of Cranmer in seeking from the boy Edward a renewal of his jurisdiction, and the acknowledgment of the other bishops that all jurisdiction, both ecclesiastical and civil, flows from the royal power,§ leaves no room for the subtleties of Mr. Palmer. "Authority of jurisdiction, spiritual and temporal," says the statute of 1 Edward VIII., c. 2., "is derived and deducted from the king's majesty, as supreme head of these churches

---

* Notes on the Nature and Extent of the Royal Supremacy in the Anglican Church, by David Lewis, M.A.—of which valuable essay I shall avail myself freely.

† "Appeal against an abuse."

‡ A writ of leave to elect a prelate.

§ Wilkins iii. 797, 798.

and realms of England and Ireland." Although Elizabeth disavowed her right to administer the sacraments, she persisted in claiming the powers exercised by her father and brother, as is evident from the following enactment: "Such jurisdictions, privileges, superiorities and pre-eminences, spiritual and ecclesiastical, as by any spiritual or ecclesiastical power or authority hath heretofore been, or may lawfully be, exercised or used for the visitation of the ecclesiastical state and persons, and for reformation, order, and correction of the same, and all manner of errors, heresies, schisms, abuses, offences, contempts and enormities, shall forever, by authority of this present parliament, be united and annexed to the imperial crown of this realm."*

The acts of Elizabeth prove that her royal supremacy was not an empty name. She issued her commission June 24th, 1559, to certain laymen, with one doctor in divinity, to visit several dioceses "both in the head and the members," giving them power to deprive the bishops. She undertook to place Matthew Parker in the See of Canterbury, "supplying, by her supreme authority," any defects or impediments to his ordination, and then, by the agency of her obsequious parliament, declaring it valid.† In him she laid the foundation of a new fabric, which she herself modelled, "the Church by law established," which subsists to this day. Mr. Lewis observes: "The civil power abolished the papal jurisdiction, and established the royal supremacy in its place; the Anglican Church adopted the work of the State, binding itself by oath at the most solemn time, in the reigns of Henry VIII. and Edward VI. Twice it approved deliberately of the acts of Elizabeth, and at this day, in the 36th Article of her religion, acknowledges the legislation of Henry and Edward not to be superstitious and ungodly."‡ "The King, or Queen, as the case may be, is with most terrible reality, and not simply by fiction of law, Head of the Established Church."§ Truly has the rejection of the shepherd whom Christ appointed, resulted in weakness and in shame.‖ A "human Church" has been erected on the ruins of the magnificent fabric which Gregory planned, Augustin founded, and his successors constructed. Bishops of royal creation have knelt in homage to the power from which *their* jurisdiction flowed: and a boy or a girl, a bold woman or a brutal man, has controlled functions which are connected with the immortal destinies of mankind. The

---

* 1 Eliz. c. i.

† For a full view of this question I refer to the work entitled, "The Validity of Anglican Ordinations examined," by Peter Richard Kenrick, Archbishop of St. Louis. Philadelphia, 1848.

‡ Notes on the Royal Supremacy, p. 95.

§ Dr. Nevin, Art. Cyprian, M. R., July, 1852.

‖ See "The Anglican Church, the Creature and Slave of the State," by Rev. Peter Cooper. London, 1844.

words of the prophet have been fulfilled: "Dabo pueros principes corum, mulieres dominabuntur eis."*

Has not the time arrived when a nation, so enlightened and illustrious, will look back to the source from which she originally derived the knowledge of Christianity, and fulfil, as far as regards herself, the almost prophetic words of her erratic poet?

> Parent of our religion! whom the wide
> Nations have knelt to for the keys of heaven!
> Europe, repentant of her parricide,
> Shall yet ————————
> ———— sue to be forgiven.†

---

* Isaias iii. 4, 12.   † Byron, Childe Harold, canto iv.

CHAPTER XVII.

Papal Prerogatives.

THE chief prerogatives of the Pontiff may be gathered from the facts and documents which have been submitted to the reader: belonging to the first six ages of the Church, and consequently not open to the objection of those who complain, that by means of the false decretals of Isidore, which first appeared in the ninth century, the papal power was immeasurably enlarged. I have purposely avoided all reference to this compilation, in order to furnish no pretext for questioning the authorities on which I rely, or the extent of prerogative which I vindicate. Although the materials out of which the decretals were constructed are of far greater antiquity, being for the most part taken from ancient decrees of the Popes, or of Councils, or from the Cæsarean laws, or the writings of the fathers, I willingly forego all advantage to be derived from them, and confine myself to documents unquestionably authentic. Some have rashly charged the Popes with originating this imposture, with a view to the enlargement of their prerogatives: but the learned trace its origin to Mentz in Germany, and allow that the extension of papal power was not the primary object of the compiler. "It was not in fact," says Guizot, "compiled for the exclusive interest of the Popedom. It appears rather, on the whole, according to the primitive intention, more especially destined to serve the bishops against the metropolitans and temporal sovereigns."* The imposture consisted in giving the decrees an undue antiquity, and false inscriptions, by ascribing them to the Popes of the first three ages. The success of the fraud is accounted for by the fact, that the actual discipline was the basis of the arrangement, so that scarcely any innovation was introduced abhorrent to general usage. Had they been brought forward to sanction novel and exorbitant pretensions, their authenticity would scarcely have escaped question, even in a less enlightened age. It is absurd to trace the prerogatives of the Holy See to these false decretals, whilst unquestionable documents of far higher antiquity plainly establish them.†

---

* Cours d'Histoire Moderne, t. iii. p. 84.

† Hallam, after Schmidt, remarks that St. Boniface in his synod held at Frankfort, in 742, anticipated the system of Isidore.—Middle Ages, ch. vii.

The primacy extends to the entire world, since the commission given to the apostles is to teach all nations, and preach the Gospel to every creature : but none are subject to it who have not by baptism entered within the pale of the Church. It is called by St. Chrysostom "the presidency of the universal Church,"* which, he observes, Christ committed to Peter, after his fall. In virtue of his office, the Pontiff teaches with authority, and directs his teaching to all the children of the Church, wherever they may be found, pastors and people : he pronounces judgment on all, whose faith is suspected, to whatever rank they belong; he condemns heresy, wherever it may have originated, or by whomsoever it may be supported : he calls on his colleagues, the bishops, to concur in the condemnation : he assembles them in Council, to investigate and judge with him the controversies that are raised, or to concur by their harmonious judgment and action in rooting out condemned errors : he confirms and promulgates their definitions of faith, and incessantly guards the sacred deposit of divine doctrine. All these acts have been performed in all ages of the Church by the Bishop of Rome, as successor of St. Peter : and have been universally acknowledged to be the prerogatives and duties of his office. St. Leo, after expatiating on the divine strength imparted to Peter and his successors for the discharge of these functions, observes that it "is assailed with impious presumption by whosoever attempts to infringe on his power, following passion, and abandoning the tradition of the ancients."†

It is the undoubted right of the Pope to pronounce judgment on controversies of faith. All doctrinal definitions already made by General Councils, or by former Pontiffs, are landmarks which no man can remove; but as the human mind may assail revelation in endless varieties of form, there must be always in the Church an authority by which error, under every new aspect, may be effectually condemned. Nothing can be added to the faith originally delivered to the saints; but points contained in the deposit of revelation, may be expressly declared and defined, when the obscurity which may have existed as to the fact of their revelation has been dissipated. The assembling of a General Council is always attended with immense difficulty, and is oftentimes utterly impracticable. The chief Bishop is "the natural organ of the Church,"‡ as Peter is styled by St. Chrysostom "the mouth of the apostles." In pronouncing judgment, he does not give expression to a private opinion, or follow his own conjectures; but he takes for his rule the public and general faith, and tradition of the Church, as gathered from Scripture, the fathers, the liturgies, and other documents; imploring the guidance of the Divine

---

* Τὴν ἐπιστασίαν τῆς οἰκουμενικῆς ἐκκλησίας ἐνεχείρισε. Ad. pop. Antioch. hom. v., de pœnit.

† Ep. x., ad episc. per prov. Vien.

‡ Thoughts and Sights in Foreign Churches, by Frederick W. Faber. This estimable writer has since passed to the Catholic communion.

Spirit, and using all human means for ascertaining the fact of revelation. It has been warmly disputed whether a solemn judgment thus pronounced, wherein a doctrine is proposed to the Church generally as necessary to be believed, under pain of anathema, or an error is proscribed as opposed to faith, with the same sanction, may possibly be erroneous. The *personal* fallibility of the Pope in his private capacity, writing or speaking, is freely conceded by the most ardent advocates of papal prerogatives. His official infallibility, *ex cathedra*, in the circumstances just specified, is strongly affirmed by St. Alphonsus de Liguori, and a host of divines, in accordance, as I believe, with ancient tradition, although the assembly of the French clergy in 1682 contended that his judgment may admit of amendment,* as long as it is not sustained by the assent and adhesion of the great body of bishops. Practically, there is no room for difficulty, since all solemn judgments hitherto pronounced by the Pontiff have received the assent of his colleagues. The Pontiff never has been isolated from his brethren: the harmony of faith being always exhibited in the teaching of the episcopal body, united with their head. The authority of the Pope in matters of faith appeared most conspicuously in the fourth and fifth centuries. The decrees of Damasus, and Innocent, and the doctrinal letters of Celestine and Leo, were hailed by the bishops, severally, and in solemn Councils, as the correct expositions of the mysteries of the Trinity and Incarnation. For the maintenance of this faith the Pontiffs sent legates to the Eastern emperors and Councils, urging it above all other things. Their indefatigable industry, their untiring solicitude, their disregard of every selfish consideration, when the integrity of faith was in question, are marked on every page of history. Faith evidently is the vital principle of papal authority.

The plenitude of pontifical power in all that appertains to the government of the universal Church, is affirmed in the Florentine decree. It is certain that this power must be used for edification, not for destruction: for the interests of faith and piety; for the maintenance of order and unity; in a word, for the good of the Church. It is a government of justice, order, and law, to be conducted, not arbitrarily and capriciously, but according to established *canons*, or rules. It admits, however, of exceptions and dispensations, since the rigorous enforcement of uniformity, in a government embracing so many different nations, would render it intolerable. Whilst, then, the papal authority should be exercised in conformity with the canons or laws of general Councils and preceding Pontiffs, unless the altered condition of things require a change of legis-

---

* Bouvier denies that the declaration was meant to affirm that the judgment of the Pope was fallible, since to avoid this assertion, Bossuet insisted on the use of the term "*irreformabile.*"—*Tract. de Vera Eccl.*, p. 111, § ii. sect. iv. *punct.* ii. n. 4. It is probable that he took the assent of the bishops as the test to distinguish a solemn judgment *ex cathedra* from a less formal decision.

lation, a dispensing power must exist, and be exercised by the Supreme Executive. Individuals, for a just reason, may be freed from the observance of a general law, at the discretion of the Pontiff. The ancient usages of local churches are to be respected, and their established order is to be maintained; but if the higher interests of the universal Church require the suppression of a local usage, or if the existence of the local Church be in jeopardy, unless the order be changed, there is room for the exercise of pontifical supremacy. The French hierarchy had flourished from the days of St. Remigius down to the execution of the sixteenth Louis, when the fury of the revolutionists immolated several of the venerable prelates, and drove the remainder into banishment. The temples of religion were profaned, and the Christian worship proscribed. Amidst the anarchy there arose a daring soldier, who, in the name of liberty, grasped an iron sceptre, and offered to become the protector of religion, on condition that the exiled prelates should renounce their rights, and the Church of France should be re-organized conformably to the new civil divisions of territory. Pius VII. called on the bishops to make the sacrifice of their undoubted rights and just attachments, and using the plenitude of his authority, stripped those who hesitated of all claims to their sees, and gave to France a new ecclesiastical organization.* The extreme necessity of the case justified, in the eyes of the Church at large, this unprecedented act of pontifical supremacy.

It is difficult to assign precise limits to a power which must be adapted to the exigencies of the Church in an endless variety of circumstances. It cannot, however, command any thing immoral. The hackneyed misrepresentation of the hypothetical argument of Bellarmine deserves to be noticed only to guard the unsuspecting against gross deception. This eminent controvertist, maintaining the official infallibility of the Pope, extends it to decrees regarding morals, since an error in moral principle would imply an error in faith itself, and expose the Church at large, in obeying her head, to a practical absurdity and defilement. It is agreed by moralists, that in matters which are doubtful, the presumption is in favor of the superior, and obedience is consequently due, when what is ordered is not manifestly wrong. Taking this moral principle as the basis of his reasoning, Bellarmine constructs on it an hypothetical argument in favor of pontifical infallibility in moral matters; imitating mathematicians, who, from the absurdity of a consequence, infer the falsehood of an hypothesis, and thereby establish the truth of the opposite principle. "I prove," says he, "that the Pope cannot err in morals intrinsically good or evil, for the Church could not, in that case, be truly called holy; —and besides, she would then necessarily err in faith: for Catholic faith teaches that all virtue is good, all vice is evil: but if the Pope should err

---

* See Bulls *Ecclesia Christi*, 15 Aug., 1801, and *Qui Christi Domini*, 29 Nov., 1801.

in commanding vice, or forbidding virtue, the Church would be bound to believe vice to be good, virtue to be evil, unless she chose to sin against conscience: for in doubtful matters the Church is bound to acquiesce in the judgment of the sovereign Pontiff, and to do what he orders, and to avoid what he forbids; and in order not to act against conscience, she is bound to believe that to be good which he orders, that to be evil which he forbids."* All may not acquiesce in the correctness of this reasoning; but no one can seriously pretend that Bellarmine makes the belief of the Church as to what is virtue or vice dependent on the caprice of the Pontiff. It is remarkable that no decree ever issued from the papal chair sanctioning any immoral principle: whilst on the contrary, the rash propositions in moral matters which were hazarded by some divines, were sifted by the Popes with nice discrimination, and condemned, whether they favored relaxation of morals, or affected a severity not compatible with the mild maxims of the Gospel. It was not the learning or the wisdom of the individual Pontiffs that enabled them to steer the vessel of the Church through rocks and shoals, on which the wisest and most learned men had made shipwreck: it was the overruling providence of God which directed their judgment. Even Voltaire acknowledges, in reference to their anathemas against duellists, that their decrees were always wise, and always advantageous to the Christian world, wherever their personal interests were not in question; which are certainly not connected with decisions on abstract principles of morality.† The Pope may enjoin, in matters ecclesiastical, what he judges to be expedient for the maintenance of order, the extirpation of vice, and the promotion of piety. His power is chiefly employed in maintaining the general laws already established, regulating the mutual relations of the clergy, and mitigating the strictness of disciplinary observance, whensoever local or individual causes demand it. He only addresses conscience: his laws and censures are only powerful inasmuch as they are acknowledged to be passed under a divine sanction. No armies, or civil officers, are em-

---

* "Quod autem non possit pontifex errare in moribus per se bonis vel malis, probatur.. Nam tunc ecclesia non posset vere dici sancta. .... Secundo, quia tunc necessario erraret etiam circa fidem. Nam fides Catholica docet omnem virtutem esse bonam, omne vitium esse malum: si autem papa erraret præcipiendo vitia, vel prohibendo virtutes; teneretur ecclesia credere vitia esse bona et virtutes malas, nisi vellet contra conscientam peccare. Tenetur enim in rebus dubiis ecclesia acquiescere judicio summi pontificis, et facere quod ille præcipit, non facere quod ille prohibet: ac ne forte contra conscientiam agat, tenetur credere bonum esse quod ille præcipit: malum quod ille prohibet."—De Romano Pontifice, l. iv. c. v.

† "Les decrets des papes, toujours sages, et de plus toujours utiles à la chretienté, dans ce qui ne concernait pas leurs interets personnels, anathématisaient ces combats."—Essai sur l'Histoire Générale, t. iii. ch. cxvii.

ployed to give them effect.* The fears which are sometimes expressed that he may abuse his power to the detriment of national or individual rights, are wholly groundless. It is employed to sustain right and justice, not to violate them. "For ourselves," Dr. Nevin observes, "we say it plainly, we believe the acknowledgment of the Pope's spiritual primacy is just as little at war with a true American spirit, and carries in it just as little peril for our American liberties, as the acknowledgment of any like primacy in either of the Presbyterian General Assemblies, or in the American Episcopate, or in the private judgment simply of any true-blooded Puritan Independent, who holds himself at liberty, if need be, to brave on the plea of conscience all human authority besides."† It is well observed by De Maistre, that whatever may be said in the abstract of the plenitude of pontifical power, any attempt to exercise it wantonly, would provoke general and successful resistance. "What," he asks, "can restrain the Pope? Every thing—canons, laws, national usages, sovereigns, tribunals, national assemblies, prescription, representations, negociations, duty, fear, prudence, and especially public opinion, the queen of the world."‡

The providing of pastors necessarily appertains to him to whom the charge of the whole flock has been entrusted by Christ our Lord: yet the exercise of this power admits of much variety, according to the circumstances of time and place, as is evident from ecclesiastical history. Whatever arrangement may be made for the election or appointment of bishops, with the concurrence and approbation of the Holy See, may be deemed just and proper. In the United States they are now appointed by the Pope, on the recommendation of the bishops of each ecclesiastical province, and of all the metropolitans. They are not, as I have already observed, mere deputies or vicars, much less vassals of the Pope; but successors of the apostles, exercising under him and with him the powers of binding and loosing, and respecting his high rank, without detriment to their own. Their order is perpetual, and their jurisdiction should not

---

* Of Rome, Voltaire has written:

"L'univers fléchissait sous son aigle terrible:
Elle exerce en nos jours un pouvoir plus paisible
Elle a sû sous son joug asservir ses vainqueurs,
Gouverner les esprits, et commander aux cœurs;
Ses avis sont ses lois, ses decrets sont ses armes."
La Henriade, ch. iv.

Once her proud eagle hovered o'er the world,
But now her peaceful banner is unfurled!
The wild barbarians that o'erspread her lands
Yield to her voice—obey her meek commands.
Their minds she governs, whilst their hearts she charms:
Her laws her counsels, her decrees her arms.

† "The Anglican Crisis," M. R., July, 1851.
‡ Du Pape, ch. xviii.

be capriciously withdrawn; but if they abuse their power, they are amenable to his high tribunal.

The relations of the Pope to a General Council have been the subject of much discussion. The right of summoning them to meet in solemn consultation for the general interests of the Church manifestly belongs to him, as he is the only one whose authority extends to all; but his free acquiescence in the act of another who may have called them together, or in a spontaneous convention, is equivalent to his personal summons. The great Council of Nice was convened by Constantine; yet according to the sixth general Council, Sylvester concurred in the convocation.* The Emperor Theodosius, in like manner, at the request of Damasus, assembled the Oriental bishops at Constantinople.† Marcian, at the solicitation of Leo, summoned the Council of Chalcedon. The obvious reason of the interference of the Emperors was because, according to the laws, no public assembly could then be held without the imperial mandate, which was accompanied with the privilege of the free use of the public vehicles. Since the Christian religion has extended far beyond the limits of the empire, and the bishops live under various governments, there is no civil ruler whose mandate could ensure universal attendance; but the voice of the Chief Pastor reaches to the most distant regions, and is respectfully heard by all his colleagues.

The right of the Pontiff to preside in the assembly of his brethren, which results from the eminence of his station, is universally admitted. In the Eastern Councils it was always exercised by legates, who, to whatever rank they belonged, even if only deacons, obtained precedency of the highest prelates, as representatives of the Chief Bishop. In the Nicene Council, Vitus and Vincentius, priests of the Roman Church, legates of Sylvester,‡ took precedency of the Patriarchs of Alexandria and Antioch; and Osius, Bishop of Corduba, an obscure diocese in Spain, was honored in like manner, doubtless in his representative capacity, which, although not declared in the acts now extant, is attested by Gelasius of Cyzicum, a Greek writer of the fifth century, and is fairly inferred from the fact, for which no other plausible reason can be assigned.§

At Ephesus, Cyril of Alexandria presided, by special delegation of Celestine,‖ whose legates, sent directly from his side, came with instructions not to mingle in the discussions, but to pronounce judgment. At Chalcedon, Paschasinus and Lucentius, most reverend bishops, and Boniface, a most religious priest, presided, "holding the place of the most holy and most beloved of God, Leo, Archbishop of ancient Rome."¶ In the synodical letter of the fathers to Leo, they say, that he presided

---

* Act. xviii. † Theod., l. v. Hist., c. viii.
‡ Theod., l. i. c. viii. § See Fleury, l. xi. sect. v., Hist. Eccl.
‖ Letter of Celestine to Cyril, c. xiii., Act. conc. Eph., col. 3123, Hard., t. i.
¶ T. ii., Hard., p. ii., p. 64.

over them by his legates, "as the head over the members." The fathers of the fifth Council earnestly besought Vigilius to preside over them* at their deliberations "on the three chapters," and having failed to induce him to be present, they read his letter, permitting the examination, as their authority for proceeding in his absence. Two priests and a deacon are mentioned in the sixth Council, at the head of all the bishops, as "holding the place of the most blessed and holy Archbishop of ancient Rome." The like is observable in the acts of the seventh and eighth Councils, in which the legates qualified their assent, by reserving to the Pontiff final judgment on the decrees.

It was customary also to seek from the Roman Bishop the solemn confirmation of the decrees of the Council. As the Nicene acts are imperfect, and the first Council of Constantinople was not œcumenical in its original character, and the doctrinal letter of Celestine which preceded the Council of Ephesus was its guide in the proceedings, I shall at once refer to the synodical letter of the fathers of Chalcedon, in which they beseech the Pope to confirm their decree in favor of the Bishop of Constantinople: "We pray you to honor our judgment by your decrees; and as we have added the harmony of our assent to our head in what is good, so may your Holiness vouchsafe to supply what is wanting in your children." The Pope, nevertheless, felt it to be his duty to annul this decree, as contrary to the ancient usages and rights of the patriarchs recognised at Nice. It is needless to exhibit in detail the proofs of the exercise of those prerogatives in the Western Councils, in several of which the Pope presided in person, and subsequently ratified their decrees by his solemn confirmation. The fathers of Trent acted in conformity with the examples of antiquity, when they gave to the pontifical legates the presidency of their assembly, and at the close of their proceedings sought from the Pope the confirmation of their acts, whereby they might be recommended to the veneration and observance of all the churches. So far back as the fourth century it was an established usage, having the force of law, that no canonical enactment could be made without the sanction of the Roman Bishop.†

I deem it unnecessary to pursue the inquiry into papal prerogatives in further detail, or to speculate on possible contingencies. In the convulsions of the Church at the period of the Council of Constance, when three pretenders claimed the keys, the assembled fathers deemed that they could do all things which might be necessary to restore unity and order. Nearly three centuries have elapsed since the last General Council, during which time the Church has been governed with wisdom and moderation by a series of holy and enlightened Pontiffs. The heresy of

---

* Collat. i. p. 62, col. Hard., t. iii.
† Sozomen, Hist., l. iii. c. viii. x. Socrates, Hist. ii., ch. xvii.

Jansenius, and numberless kindred errors, have been condemned: the purity of Christian morals has been vindicated against relaxed casuists, and the sweetness of the yoke of Christ has been maintained, despite of the repulsive austerity of innovators: discipline has been enforced, or mitigated, as circumstances rendered expedient: and all things appertaining to the government of the Universal Church have been regulated by the foresight, discretion, and zeal of the Roman Bishop. He has had the services and aid of enlightened counsellors, composing the various standing committees or congregations of cardinals, to whose examination he commits the different matters on which he is to pronounce judgment; he has also been seconded and sustained by his colleagues throughout the world: but the Providence of God, as if to cut short the disputes of the schools, has suffered this long period to elapse without a General Council, as was also the case in the first three centuries of the Church. The great Leibnitz strongly states the necessity of a permanent authority in the Church, such as is exercised by the Bishop of Rome: "As from the impossibility of the bishops frequently leaving the people over whom they are placed, it is not possible to hold a council continuously, or even frequently, while at the same time *the person of the Church* must always live and subsist, in order that its will may be ascertained, it was a necessary consequence, by the divine law itself, insinuated in Christ's most memorable words to Peter, (when He committed to him specially the keys of the kingdom of heaven, as well as when He thrice emphatically commanded him to feed His sheep,) and uniformly believed in the Church, that one among the apostles, and the successor of this one among the bishops, was invested with pre-eminent power; in order that by him, as the visible centre of unity, the body of the Church might be bound together; the common necessities be provided for: a council, if necessary, be convoked, and when convoked, directed; and that in the interval between councils, provision might be made lest the commonwealth of the faithful sustain any injury. And as the ancients unanimously attest that the apostle Peter governed the Church, suffered martyrdom, and appointed his successor in the city of Rome, the capital of the world; and as no other bishop has ever been recognised under this relation, we justly acknowledge the Bishops of Rome to be chief of all the rest."* It seems to me superfluous to discuss what power a Council may exercise in certain extraordinary circumstances, since the actual government of the Church is plainly in the hands of the Pontiff. If the object be to point out the limits of pontifical power, and the remedy for its abuse, I must avow that there is but a faint ground of hope in an assembly, the holding of which is generally of extreme difficulty, if not utterly impracticable. Our true security lies in the nature of the pontifical authority, which, being derived

---

* "Systema Theologicum," translated by Dr. Russell.

from Christ, is essentially just and paternal. Our hope is in the ever-watchful Providence which guards the Church, that the passions of men may not defeat the divine counsels. If in calamitous circumstances an extraordinary remedy be necessary, the same Providence will apply it: but the discussion of the powers of an assembly convened at such a crisis, is, in my opinion, safely left to its members.

It is not within my scope to explain in detail the power which the Pope exercises, in pronouncing judgment on the sanctity of deceased servants of God, or in granting indulgences, or in many like ways, as it has not been my intention to write a treatise with the precision of a canonist or scholastic divine. My object has been to give a just idea of the main exercise of pontifical authority.

It is unnecessary to define the extent of papal prerogative, in order to determine the necessity of admitting the primacy. If Christ has established a general governor of the Church in the person of Peter, his authority must be acknowledged such, as it is exercised and admitted by the Church herself. Divine Providence will not suffer its practical exhibition at any period to differ essentially from its original institution, so that if it be exercised with more or less amplitude in different ages, this must be ascribed to the change of circumstances, rather than to any substantial alteration in its character. The overthrow of the patriarchal thrones by the Mussulman rendered the intervention of the Bishop of Rome in the affairs of the East more direct and frequent than while they subsisted. The encroachments of the civil power in various countries made the Pontiffs more jealous of their prerogatives, and the abuses of privileges once enjoyed by the clergy and people, in the election of the prelates, caused their withdrawal. God has always come to the aid of the Popes in their struggles for truth, and the liberty of the Church, and made their worst enemies instruments for the manifestation of the authority divinely entrusted to them. By loosening the ties which connected the Church with the State, under the ancient dynasty, her freedom in France has been greatly advanced, and sound views with regard to the papal power have been effectually diffused. Even the overthrow of the ancient French hierarchy, so venerable and illustrious, the closing of the celebrated universities, and other calamitous events of the revolution, which threatened the extinction of Christianity, resulted in an exercise of pontifical authority, which, by a single act, decided a thousand vain disputes, and created a new order of things, in which the Chief Bishop and the French prelates are united by more intimate ties. Setting aside all minor considerations, the reader should fix his whole attention on the main controversy, since, as Mr. Palmer remarks: "The doctrine of the primacy of the Bishop of Rome over the Universal Church, is the point on which all other controversies between the Roman and other churches turn: for if our Lord Jesus Christ instituted any official supremacy of one bishop in the Catholic Church to endure always: and if this supremacy be inherited by the Bishop of Rome, it will readily follow that the Catholic Church is limited to those of the Roman obedience, so that the Councils, doctrines, and traditions of those churches are invested with the authority of the whole Christian world."*

---

* A Treatise on the Church of Christ, by Rev. William Palmer, M. A., part vii. vol. ii. p. 451. Americ. edit.

CHAPTER XVIII.

Unbroken Succession of the Bishops of Rome.

It is important to establish, beyond all contradiction, the fact that the present Bishop of Rome, by uninterrupted succession, holds the place of Peter. We are aided in this undertaking by the labors of the venerable ancients, several of whom gave lists of the Roman Bishops from the apostle down to their own time. St. Irenæus enumerated them as far as Eleutherius, who was still living when he wrote.* The historian Eusebius, availing himself of authentic documents, continued the series far on in the fourth century.† St. Optatus closed his list with the name of Siricius, who, in his day, occupied the apostolic chair.‡ St. Augustin gave a similar catalogue, and challenged the Donatists to examine closely the order of succession: "Come to us, brethren, if you wish to be engrafted on the vine. We are afflicted in beholding you lying cut off from it. Count over the bishops from the very See of Peter, and mark in that list of fathers how one succeeded the other. THIS IS THE ROCK AGAINST WHICH THE PROUD GATES OF HELL DO NOT PREVAIL."§

The schism of Novatian, who, after the death of Pope Fabian, in the year 253, set himself up in opposition to Cornelius, his lawful successor, served to mark more clearly the series of Pontiffs, and the authority with which they presided in the Church. In vain did the usurper, sending his partisans to Africa, and to the churches generally, "seek to draw into schism the members of Christ, and to divide and rend asunder the one body of the Catholic Church." They were told by St. Cyprian and his colleagues, that "it was impious to forsake their mother," and that "if they professed themselves followers of the Gospel, and of Christ, they should return to the Church."‖ The letter of Cornelius, announcing his ordination, according to ancient custom, was publicly read in the Church of Carthage, and letters were despatched by Cyprian, as primate of Africa, to the bishops of his province, in which they were admonished to write in reply, and send ambassadors to the Pontiff, as Cyprian himself

---

* L. iii., adv. hær.   † Hist. Eccl., l. iii. c. iv
‡ De Schism, Donat., l. ii.   § Ps. contra partem Donat.
‖ Cyprianus Cornelio, ep. i., inter Rom. Pont., ep. i., Coustant, t. i. col. 126.

had done.* The adherents of Novatian are represented by the African primate as "refusing the bosom and embrace of her, who is root and *matrix*," by which terms he designates, not only in this passage, but frequently elsewhere, the local Church of Rome, from which, as from a root, the African churches had grown, and in which, as in the maternal womb, they had been conceived: figurative expressions which he applies to it also in reference to the whole Catholic Church. The creation of a rival bishop, in the person of Novatian, is declared to be "contrary to the mystery originally delivered of the divine organization of the Church,† and of Catholic unity."‡ Although this might be said, in a qualified sense, of any schismatical ordination, it manifestly implies, in the mind of Cyprian, a special divine ordinance in regard to the Bishop of Rome, as centre of Catholic unity.

The letter which the zeal of St. Cyprian led him to address to the schismatics, exhorting them "to return to their mother, that is, the Catholic Church," resulted in the conversion of several of them, who, in the most explicit terms, solemnly recognised the lawful Pontiff. "We know," said they, on occasion of their public reconciliation, "that Cornelius was chosen by God Almighty and Christ our Lord, Bishop of the most holy Catholic Church. We are not ignorant that there is one God, one Christ the Lord, whom we have confessed,§ one Holy Spirit, and that there should be one bishop in the Catholic Church."|| The obvious force of this language is such as to present to us Cornelius as Bishop of the whole Church, since a local bishop could not be styled, without qualification, Bishop of the Catholic Church. St. Cyprian urges strongly the titles of the lawful Pontiff to veneration, and regards his opponents as cut off from the communion of the Church. "Cornelius," he remarks, "was made bishop in accordance with the judgment of God, and of His Christ, with the testimony of almost all the clergy; and he was selected from the college of aged priests and good men, at a time when no one had been appointed before him; and when the place of Fabian, that is, THE PLACE OF PETER, and the dignity of the priestly chair, was vacant, which place being occupied by him according to the will of God; and he being supported therein by the consent of us all, whosoever now seeks to become bishop, must necessarily be WITHOUT, nor can he who does not hold the unity of the Church have ecclesiastical ordination. Whosoever he be, though he vaunt himself, and put forward great claims, he is a profane man, a stranger, he is WITHOUT. And since after the first there can be no second, whosoever was made bishop after the one who alone should be

---

* Apud Coustant, ep. ii. t. i. col. 128.
† "Divinæ dispositionis."
‡ Ibidem, ep. iii. col. 131.
§ They had confessed Christ as Lord before the heathen tribunals.
|| Quoted in letter of Cornelius to Cyprian.

such, is not the second : he is no bishop."* This may imply a denial of the validity of the ordination, conformably to the opinion of Cyprian, in regard to sacraments administered out of unity : but what now concerns us, is, that Cornelius was believed to hold the place of Peter, and that his opponent was regarded as an alien from the Church. Thus, in the Providence of God, this schism served to make more manifest the relation of the Bishop of Rome to the bishops of the Church throughout the world, and to render more evident his succession to the place of Peter.

The intrusion of Felix, in the middle of the fourth century, into the Apostolic See, during a year and three months, by the power of the Arian Emperor Constantius, who caused Liberius, the lawful Pope, to be dragged into exile, made no breach in the series, since the forced suspension of the pontifical administration did not take away the authority.† Vigilius, in like manner, in the sixth century, through the influence of the Empress Theodora, for two years usurped the place of Sylverius, after whose death he was recognised by the Church at large, having atoned for his unlawful occupancy of the chair by the integrity with which he fulfilled its duties. No doubt as to the succession can be raised in consequence of the schismatic rivalry of the deacon Ursicinus, who, with armed satellites, opposed Damasus; of the archdeacon Eulalius, who set himself up against Boniface; of Cælius Laurentius, who disputed the election of Symmachus; of the priests Theodore and Peter, who resisted the lawful claims of Conon; of Theophylactus, a layman, who by violence held possession of the See for thirteen months, to the prejudice of Paul; or of Zinzinus, the adversary of Eugenius. In all these cases, the lawful Pope prevailed over his opponents, after a short struggle, and his rights were acknowledged by the universal Church. It is not to be wondered that a station so exalted should attract the ambitious, whose elevation was justly resisted by the friends of religion. Hence it should be no matter of surprise, that thirty instances of schism, on occasion of papal elections, are enumerated by Church historians: but thanks are due to the Providence which always guards the Church, that, in most instances, they were of short duration, and that eventually no doubt remained as to the legitimate successor of Peter. The fidelity with which they have been recorded, strengthens the evidence that the succession was maintained.

The relations subsisting between the Popes and the emperors of the West, afforded a pretext for imperial interference, which often resulted in schisms of a more or less disastrous character; while the national jealousy of the Romans, and the want of any permanent form of civil government at home, led sometimes to results equally to be deplored. In the middle of the ninth century, the Emperor Louis II. lent his authority to the priest Anastasius, in his aggressions on Benedict III., who, how-

---

* Ad Antonian. † Some think that Felix acted as Vicar of Liberius.

ever, soon recovered his power. The close of the same century was disgraced by the struggles of Sergius, the deacon, against Pope Formosus, and of the anti-pope, styled Boniface VI., against Stephen VII. The opening of the tenth century witnessed the forced abdication of Leo V. to give place to Christopher, who in his turn was ejected by Sergius. The Emperor Otho I., intruded the anti-pope Leo VIII. to the prejudice of the rights of John XII. and of Benedict V., who, on the death of John, was chosen by the clergy and people of Rome. On the other hand, the imperial authority supported Gregory V., a lawful occupant of the See, whose right was disputed by John of Piacenza, aided by the Roman prefect Crescentius. St. Henry, the emperor, lent his aid to expel Gregory, whom the Romans intruded into the place of Benedict VIII. Three pretenders to the power of the keys appeared before the middle of the eleventh century; the right of Benedict IX., who was intruded into the chair by his father, the Count of Tusculum,* being contested by Sylvester III. and John XX. A compromise of their claims, brought about by Gregory VI., terminated this unhappy struggle, and the abdication of Gregory himself, whose pecuniary sacrifices to satisfy the contending parties, left his own election open to the charge of simony, led to a permanent peace. A series of holy Pontiffs, of German origin, elevated to the See of Peter through the influence or with the assent of the emperor, healed the wounds which disorderly intruders had inflicted on the Church; but after the middle of the eleventh century, Mincius, Count of Tusculum, rose against Nicholas II., the lawful Pontiff; and again, Cadolaus Pallavicini disputed the right of Alexander II. St. Gregory VII. had the affliction to witness the creation of an anti-pope without living to see his downfall; yet the Church at large easily distinguished the series of lawful Pontiffs from the usurper, who, during twenty-one years, took the title of Bishop of Rome. Aginulph, styling himself Sylvester III., pressed on the footsteps of the anti-pope Clement III., and Gregory VIII. (as Maurice Burdin styled himself) followed, supported by the Emperor Henry V. The submission of Victor IV., the successor of the anti-pope Anacletus II., terminated a schism which had lasted eight years, during the pontificate of Innocent II. In a similar way, a schism which broke out under Alexander III. was happily extinguished by the submission of Calixtus III., the successor of two anti-popes. Peter de Corbario, whom the Emperor Louis of Bavaria intruded into the Apostolic See, sought and obtained pardon of his usurpation from the lawful Pontiff, John XXII. In the last two schisms which afflicted the Church, the submission of each pretender put an end to all doubt: Clement VIII. having implored pardon of Martin V., and Felix V. having yielded to Eugenius IV. During four hundred years, the Church has been free from this awful calamity. In all the in-

---

* Frascati.

stances, which I have rapidly reviewed, the succession was manifestly uninterrupted, because the schisms generally were of very short duration, and the pretensions of the usurpers were, for the most part, destitute of plausibility, resting chiefly on imperial power, or factious violence, while the true Popes were easily discernible by the regularity of their election, and their unswerving devotedness to the great interests of religion. In cases of doubt, the final submission of the claimants to the authority of the Pontiff, recognised by the Church at large, or the extinction of the schism by the demise of the pretender, made manifest, beyond all contradiction, the true successor of Peter.

The only case of apparent difficulty is the schism which began under Urban VI., towards the close of the fourteenth century, and continued about thirty-seven years. After the death of Gregory XI., at Rome, to which he had returned from Avignon, fear being entertained that the cardinals, who were chiefly natives of France, would elect a Frenchman, who might establish his residence at Avignon, where a series of French Popes had resided, the Romans surrounded the conclave, and with threats insisted that a Roman, or at least an Italian, should be chosen Pope. Under the apprehension of actual violence, the cardinals hastened to bring their proceedings to a close, by electing the Archbishop of Bari, who assumed the name of Urban VI. Whatever objection existed to the election, as not having been made freely, seemed to be removed by the subsequent acquiescence of the cardinals, who, during four months, continued to acknowledge him, in public documents addressed to the bishops throughout the world. However, at the expiration of that time, several of them fled from Rome, and under the pretext that the former election was null, chose Robert, Count of Geneva, who assumed the name of Clement VII., and abode at Avignon. The opinions of men being divided, the nations supported one or other of the claimants; France, Castile, and other countries adhering to Clement, as the free choice of the electors; while Germany and England acknowledged Urban, on account of the priority of his election, and its free ratification by the electors during a considerable time. It soon became difficult for the most conscientious and enlightened men to pronounce with certainty which of the two claimants was entitled to occupy the apostolic chair. The demise of both did not terminate the contest : since a usurper, Benedict XIII., as Peter de Luna, the successor of Clement, was styled, sat at Avignon above twenty years, while Boniface IX., Innocent VII., and Gregory XII., continued the Roman series. To relieve the Church from the scandal of these conflicting pretensions, some cardinals of each *obedience*, or party, resolved on summoning a Council at Pisa, and requiring the two pretenders to submit their claims to the judgment of the assembled fathers; but neither would recognise the authority of this tribunal. The assembly, nothing daunted by this denial of its competency, proceeded to depose both as guilty of contumacy, schism, and heresy, and elected Peter Filargo to the vacant chair, under the title of Alexander V. St. Antonine, and many others, deeming the proceedings utterly void, refused to recognise the new claimant, whose election served only to aggravate the evil. His death, after ten months, gave occasion to the election of Balthassar Cossa, under the name of John XXII.; who, in order to extinguish this dire schism, summoned a General Council to be held at Constance. In this assembly, he himself, being deposed, by his acquiescence in the sentence put an end to all question as to the competency of his judges. Gregory XII. refused to recognise the legitimacy of the Council, regarding it as convened by a usurper of the Apostolic See, but he consented to abdicate, on the observance of some formalities which served to save his pretensions. Neither threats nor persuasion could influence Peter de Luna, whom the Council at length deposed. The general acquiescence of all Christian nations in the election of Martin V., which ensued, left no room to question the legitimacy of the proceedings, although the deposed pretender continued to assert his claims, which, at his death, he charged the few cardinals who still adhered to him, to perpetuate. His successor, after four years, renounced his empty title, to enjoy the communion of the Pontiff, whom the whole Church recognised.

This long schism, however, involves the succession of the Bishops of Rome in no doubt. It may be questioned whether those who sat at Rome, or those who sat at Avignon were the true successors of Peter; although the judgment of the learned generally seems to have decided in favor of the former: but there is no ground for questioning the fact of the succession. One or the other series was certainly legitimate, and both having terminated, in the Council of Constance, in the election of Martin V., he was the undoubted heir of the apostolic authority, through whichsoever channel it flowed.*

The long absence of the Popes from Rome, during their stay at Avignon, which, like the captivity of Babylon, as the Romans sarcastically designate it, extended to about seventy years, affords no reason for questioning the succession, because the authority of a bishop does not depend

---

* I may be allowed, by way of illustration, to refer to a collision of claims between two courts in one of the United States, within my own remembrance. The Legislature of Kentucky, being dissatisfied with the proceedings of the Court of Appeals, the Supreme Judiciary, passed an act for its reorganization, in order, by this summary proceeding, to avoid the tardy and uncertain process of impeaching the judges. Accordingly, a new court was organized, in conformity with this law, and judges were appointed, who proceeded to take cognizance of suits brought before them. The judges of the old court considered that the new law was unconstitutional; and, disregarding it, continued in the exercise of their judicial power. For several years these rival tribunals existed, until, at length, a compromise was effected: yet no one will pretend that the conflicting claims destroyed the judiciary of the State, or the special court in question.

on his residence in his see. Those Pontiffs who resided at Avignon were truly Bishops of Rome, having been elected under this title by the college of cardinals to fill the place of Peter. They governed that See by means of a Cardinal Vicar, whilst they personally applied themselves to the government of the universal Church.

The long vacancies which have sometimes occurred in the Roman See, do not interfere with the succession, since, in the general opinion of mankind, they were not so protracted as to destroy the moral connection between the incumbents. Some interval must necessarily elapse between the demise of one Pontiff and the election of his successor. The longest space which has been assigned to a papal interregnum is three years and eight months, after the death of Marcellinus; which computation, however, is generally denied by the learned. The longest actual vacancy was during two years and nine months, on the demise of Clement IV. Either period was not such an interruption in the long series of Pontiffs as to effect a moral separation in its connecting links. In reality, the interval was much less than it appears, because it was counted up to the day of the consecration of the new Pope, which was often long delayed in order to obtain the assent of the Eastern emperor.

The simplicity of some writers once gave currency to a ridiculous fable, which even the Calvinist Blondell, the skeptical Bayle, and the infidel Gibbon, have shown to be inconsistent with well-ascertained facts of history. In some interpolated copies of Marian Scotus, a writer of the eleventh century, it was stated, that an English female, in male attire, pursued her studies at the schools of Athens, and in process of time succeeded in being elevated to the papal chair, on the death of Leo IV. After two years five months and four days of pontifical administration, her sex is said to have been discovered by her being delivered of a child, in a solemn procession to the church of St. John of Lateran. This ill-concocted tale, which is in itself incredible, concerning Pope Joan, as she is styled, is totally irreconcilable with the statements of contemporary writers, who assure us that on the death of Leo IV., which took place on the 17th July, 855, Benedict III. "immediately" succeeded, and was consecrated on the 1st September of the same year. Gibbon acknowledges that "the contemporary Anastasius indissolubly links the death of Leo and the elevation of Benedict." (*Illico, mox.*)*

A ridiculous precaution is alleged to have been adopted against the recurrence of the imposture: but it is enough for me to explain the real object of the ceremony to which allusion is made. From the year 1191, down to the time of Leo X., on occasion of taking possession of the basilic of St. John of Lateran, it was usual, among other ceremonies, to place the new Pontiff in front of the portico, on a white marble chair,

---

* Decline and Fall, ch. xlix., A.D. 800–1060.

which, from the verse chaunted on the occasion, was popularly styled *stercoraria:* "Raising up the needy from the earth, and lifting up the poor out of the dunghill, that He may place him with princes, with the princes of His people." The object was evidently to inspire the Pontiff with becoming sentiments of humility, and to give praise to God for having raised him to the high dignity of prince and ruler in His Church.*

Although the fable of Pope Joan is now utterly exploded, some still refer to it for mere annoyance; not reflecting that what could not take place in the Catholic Church, unless by an incredible combination of circumstances favorable to imposture, is really exhibited in the Church of England, by a necessary consequence of the principles broached on its separation from the See of Peter. The Sovereign, for the time being, was proclaimed head of the Church throughout his dominions: but, as if to put to shame the abettors of this system, God permitted, on the death of Henry VIII, the boy Edward to succeed him, who was followed by Mary and Elizabeth. The former queen hastened to divest herself of the title and authority which the law ascribed to her in ecclesiastical matters; whilst Elizabeth unblushingly asserted her supremacy, and struck terror into the bishops of her own creation.† When she was informed by her prime minister that the professors at Lambeth had pronounced a theological censure on certain propositions concerning free-will and predestination, she called Whitgift, Archbishop of Canterbury, to her presence, and with bitter irony intimated to him the legal penalties, to which his connivance at this encroachment on her royal prerogative subjected him. "Whitgift," said she, "I hear that you are amassing great wealth for my use." The archbishop replied, that his wealth was not great, but that all he possessed was at her Majesty's service. She resumed: "You fancy that you speak as a dutiful subject; but I maintain that all you have is already mine, by the law of the land, since you have incurred *præmunire.*" The prelate, understanding the drift of her language, pleaded that the Lambeth professors had not meant to pronounce a decision, but had merely expressed a theological opinion; which, however, in order to appease her, he promised to suppress.‡ She suspended Archbishop Grindall from the exercise of episcopal jurisdiction, and threatened to make examples of bishops, in case they neglected

---

* The whole ceremony is described in verse by Cardinal James, in his second book on the Coronation of Boniface VIII., which is found in the Bollandists, t. iv., Maji, p. 471. See also Mabillon, t. i., Musæi Italici, p. 1, p. 59.

† "Vè aqui una cosa admirabile. Al mismo tiempo que los Protestantes se esforzaban à insultarnos con la disparatada especie de una Papisa, elegida en Roma, ellos erigieron otra Papisa en Inglaterra, constituyendo cabeza de la Iglesia Anglicana è su adorada Reyna." Cartas Eruditas por D. Fr. Benito G. Feyjoó, t. v. c. iii. p. 146.

‡ Articulorum Lambethæ exhibitorum historia, juxta exemplar Londini editum, A.D. 1601. P. 6, et seq.

to suppress certain religious exercises. Such was her jealousy of any interference with her rights as head of the Church!

The unbroken succession of the Bishops of Rome is a fact the most unquestionable, established by direct and collateral evidence, and manifest from the continued exercise of the pontifical authority. No difficulties that may be raised in regard to interregnums, rival claimants, or intruders, can create a doubt as to the public exercise of power in every age by the Bishop of Rome as successor of Peter. The continuance of the succession is a moral miracle, which may well be reckoned among the most splendid evidences of Christianity. "The Papacy itself," says Dr. Nevin, "is a wonder of wonders. There is nothing like it in all history besides."* Dynasties have succeeded one to another; powerful empires and kingdoms have passed away; republics have been destroyed by the conflicting elements within them; yet the See of Peter remains, and an heir of his authority is always found, whether taken from low estate, or of noble parentage. The numberless internal causes of dissolution, and violence from without, do not affect its continuance. The city may be trodden down by the barbarian conqueror, and the Pontiff may perish; but there is a vitality in the See that renders its destruction impossible. Those inquirers who now stand at the portals of the Church, perplexed and embarrassed, should say to themselves with Augustin: "Shall we hesitate to take refuge in the bosom of that Church which from the Apostolic See, through the succession of bishops, even by the acknowledgment of mankind generally, has obtained supreme authority, heretics raging around in vain, condemned as they have been, partly by the judgment of the people themselves, partly by the authority of Councils, partly also by the splendor of miracles? To reject her authority is truly either the height of impiety, or desperate presumption."†

---

* Early Christianity, M. R., Nov., 1851. † De util. cred., c. vii.

CHAPTER XIX.

Papal Election.

§ 1.—IMPERIAL INTERPOSITION.

No authority in sacred things was ever acknowledged by the Church to reside in emperor, king, or other potentate, even when he was a Christian, although they were sometimes implored to sustain, by the civil arm, the rights of lawful prelates against ambitious and disorderly men, who endangered or violated public tranquillity. In this sense, as also in regard to the general support which they owe to religion, the Council of Trent declared that "God wills Catholic princes to be the protectors of our holy faith and of the Church."* The Council of Aquileja besought the Emperors Gratian, Valentinian, and Theodosius, to use their authority, and prevent Ursicinus from disturbing Damasus, the legitimate occupant of the See of Peter.† Eulalius, having ambitiously set himself up in opposition to Boniface, the lawful Pope, the Emperor Honorius, on the report of Symmachus, ordered Boniface to be banished from the city; but on receiving from the Roman clergy a correct statement of the facts, and being informed of the return of Eulalius, contrary to his command, he supported the rights of Boniface. To provide for public tranquillity, he decreed that, in case of a contested election, both candidates should be banished from the city.‡ This law is said to have been enacted in consequence of an application made by Boniface himself, for some measure to prevent tumults.

Odoacer, King of the Heruli, having in 476 established himself King of Italy, on the death of Simplicius in 483, alleged an agreement made with him by the deceased Pontiff that the Prefect, in the name of the king, should be present at the election of his successor; but the claim was resisted by the clergy, and the concession disregarded as a nullity. Symmachus, chosen Pope in 498, forbade all laymen, even of royal dignity, to interfere in the election; yet Theodoric, King of Italy, in 526, forced Felix IV. on the Roman clergy and senate, who reluctantly acquiesced, on con-

---

* Sess. xxvi. c. xx., de Ref. † Conc. Aquil. ep., t. i., conc. Hard., col. 837.
‡ Ibid., col. 1237.

dition that the ancient freedom of election should be thenceforward inviolable. The royal assent or confirmation of the election was, however, to be sought, which was to follow as a matter of course, if the proceedings were regular. King Athalaric, successor of Theodoric, required the payment of three thousand crowns of gold on the occasion.

On the extinction of the Gothic power in Italy in 553, the Emperor Justinian exercised the same prerogative of confirming the election, in the person of Pelagius I., chosen in 555. The confirmation was not waited for on the election of Pelagius II. in 578, it being impossible to obtain it, since the city of Rome was actually besieged by the Lombards. It was also neglected in the case of John IV., elected in 640, and of Martin in 649. The tax, which seemed to be the chief object of the imperial court, was remitted by Constantine Pogonatus in 680; who, in 684, completely restored the ancient freedom of election, so as not to require any longer the imperial assent. His successor, Justinian II., renewed the claim in a mitigated form, allowing the exarch of Ravenna to assent in his name, and thus prevent delay. There is no instance of any election having been set aside by the emperor, who regarded the right of confirmation as a mere measure of finance.

The Western emperors soon emulated the prerogatives of those of Constantinople. Louis the Pious, in 818, required the Pope to send him an embassy immediately after his consecration. In 824 he sent his son Lothaire to Rome, to terminate the contest which had arisen on the election of Eugenius II., who was opposed by the anti-pope Zinzinus; whence the young prince took occasion to publish an imperial edict, requiring that the consecration of the Pope should take place in presence of the imperial ambassadors, if the emperor himself were not present. This regulation is stated by Pagi to have originated with Eugenius himself, and to have been confirmed by John IX. in 898, through an anxiety to prevent tumults and irregular promotions. The ambassador of Lothaire came to Rome in 827, to examine the election of Gregory IV., and in 855 the report of the election of Benedict III. was forwarded to the imperial court for examination.

The canonical freedom of election was vindicated from time to time by decrees of the Pontiffs. Constantine, an anti-pope, having obtained possession of the See, by the aid of armed men, Stephen IV., in 769, forbade any layman, of any rank whatever, to interfere in papal elections.* Adrian III., in 884, decreed that the Pontiff elect might be consecrated without the presence of the king or his ambassadors.

It does not appear that the emperors exercised or claimed any right over the election, beyond the mere examination of its regularity, until the middle of the tenth century. After Otho I., in 962, had been

---

* Conc. Rom., act. iii., apud Holstenium, in collect. Rom., par. i. p. 260.

crowned emperor by John XII., he exacted an oath from the clergy and people, that no Pope should thenceforward be consecrated without previously making, in presence of the imperial ambassadors, or of the son of the emperor, or of the public, a promise which is not distinctly specified, but is described as intended "for the satisfaction of all and for their future preservation," such as Leo IV. had spontaneously made. This pledge seems to have been directed to secure the imperial interests in Rome. Otho soon acted as if he could at will create and depose the Pope, having attempted to set aside John, and substitute the anti-pope Leo VIII. In this usurpation he was imitated by two emperors of the same name.

Henry I. restored the freedom of papal elections, which his successors Conrad and the second Henry also respected; although the latter required that the imperial ambassadors should be present at the consecration It must be owned that the disorders of popular elections at Rome, and the violent intrusion of several unworthy men, gave an appearance of expediency to this intervention, which might have been salutary, if it did not prepare the way for unjust influence, amounting to control. Alexander II. directed that the imperial authority should be awaited, unless dangerous circumstances forbade delay.

The imperial influence was exercised beneficially in several instances. At the solicitation of the clergy and people of Rome, Henry II. recommended Suidger, Bishop of Bamberg, for promotion; who, accordingly, under the name of Clement II., adorned the Apostolic throne by his virtues. Bruno, Bishop of Toul, was recommended by the Council of Worms to the emperor, and by him proposed to the Roman clergy; but the holy bishop entered Rome as a private individual, and refused to exercise any authority until the clergy and people freely elected him. He is known to us as St. Leo IX. Gebhard, Bishop of Aichstat, who was reluctantly yielded by the emperor to the urgent prayers of Hildebrand, filled the See as Victor II.

The deference shown to the emperors did not amount to an acknowledgment of any strict right on their part to control the elections, as is evident from the fact that many Popes were consecrated without awaiting the imperial assent. Leo IV., in 847, was consecrated in the absence of the ambassadors; and only five out of nineteen Popes who lived in the ninth century waited for the confirmation of their election. Stephen X. was consecrated within a few days after the death of Victor II., when it was impossible to have received the confirmation. When in the minority of Henry IV. the right was claimed by the Regency, in virtue of an alleged grant of Nicholas II. to the emperor, and complaint was made that Alexander II. had been consecrated without the imperial assent, the representatives of the Holy See strongly denied that even a Pope could give to the emperor a right of peremptory control, since the election of the

Vicar of Christ must necessarily be free. The concession was shown to be a personal privilege granted in critical times, to be exercised without detriment to the liberty of election. St. Gregory VII., by soliciting the emperor to withhold his assent and defeat his election, seemed to acknowledge in him a power of *veto;* but he grounded it on usage, or on the concession of his predecessors: while otherwise he is known to have zealously maintained the freedom of the Church, as of divine right. From his time the imperial pretensions were either altogether abandoned, or defeated by the constancy of the clergy. Gibbon remarks: "The removal of a foreign influence restored and endeared the Shepherd to his flock. Instead of the arbitrary or venal nomination of a German court, the Vicar of Christ was freely chosen by the College of Cardinals, most of whom were either natives or inhabitants of the city. The applause of the magistrates and people confirmed his election: and the ecclesiastical power that was obeyed in Sweden and Britain, had been ultimately derived from the suffrage of the Romans."[*]

From a careful consideration of documents and facts, it results that no right of interference in the election of the Head of the Church exists in emperors, or kings, or earthly rulers of any kind, and that an attempt on their part to control it is a violation of the liberty of the Church. The privileges which they once exercised were granted them by the Church herself, as the guardians of public order, in order to secure regularity in the proceedings, and the support of the civil power for the elect. Whenever they were used in an absolute or arbitrary way, or were assumed independently of the concession or assent of the Pontiffs, they were usurpations, which can neither prove nor give any right whatever.

In modern times it has been customary for the electors to treat with respect the remonstrances of the chief Catholic powers, Austria, France, and Spain, so as not to urge the promotion of an individual objected to by any of them, provided the objection be made before the election is completed by the consent of two-thirds of the electors. Each power can exercise this prerogative only in one instance. No strict right of *veto*, however, is acknowledged by this deference to the *esclusiva*, or *ammonizione pacifica*, as this expression of the wishes of the crowned heads is called. Thus the liberty of the Church remains inviolate, while a just regard is had for the representatives of great national interests.

§ 2.—MODE OF ELECTION.

The plenitude of power with which the Pope is clothed, might appear to authorize him to provide a successor, when old age warns him of the approach of death, especially if he has reason to fear that intrigues, dis-

---

[*] Decline and Fall, ch. lxix., A.D. 1000–1100.

orders, and violence may occur during the vacancy of the See. The language used by Irenæus in regard to Peter, who is said to have committed to Linus the administration of the Church, may be understood of the appointment of a successor; but all antiquity teaches that the bishopric should not be as a legacy, dependent on the mere will of the actual incumbent. The elective principle, which was originally common to all episcopal sees, is still held sacred in regard to the Apostolic See, to which it is utterly forbidden to give the appearance of an inheritance. Hilary, in a Roman Council, declared that no Pope should choose his successor; which important declaration was repeated and confirmed by Pius IV. after the lapse of eleven centuries. Pius added that no Pope could, even with the assent of the cardinals, choose a coadjutor, with the right of succeeding him. Boniface II., in 530, designated Vigilius for his successor, with the view of preventing the intrusion of an unworthy incumbent by the King of the Goths; but on maturer reflection, he committed his decree to the flames, lest his example should give an hereditary appearance to the sacred office. When Gregory XIV. lay at the point of death, he exhorted the cardinals to proceed to the election of his successor; which, however, they respectfully declined. Several Popes, on their death-bed, recommended to the cardinals the person whom they deemed most worthy to succeed, as Clement VII., dying, said, that he would choose Cardinal Farnese, if the office could be bequeathed. His recommendation was adopted, but generally such expressions of desire were neglected. By a decree of Symmachus, in 499, renewed by Paul IV. in 1558, it is forbidden, under pain of excommunication, during the lifetime of the Pope to treat of his successor. It is likewise forbidden, under the same penalty, to make wagers concerning the future Pontiff, when the See is actually vacant, lest any person should use improper measures to obtain a choice favorable to his interests.

It is beyond a doubt that the people, for many ages, had a great share in the election of bishops, although it does not appear that they had at any time a strict right of suffrage. Their favorable testimony had considerable weight, their just wishes were respected, and the clergy willingly aided in the promotion of those who were most likely to secure popular respect and obedience. In those times, however, the chief pastor did not fail to admonish the clergy, that they must not be driven forward by the popular impulse, which they should rather prudently direct and control. "The people," said St. Celestin, in the fifth century, "should be taught, not followed; and we should admonish them, if they be ignorant of what is lawful and what is forbidden, nor should we yield to them."* In the preceding age, the Council of Laodicea had decreed that the "multitude must not be allowed to make the election of those

---

* Ad ep. Apuliæ.

who are to be raised to the priesthood."* The publicity and popular character of the elections continued at Rome down to the twelfth century. Nicholas II., who in 1058 was elected by the clergy, in presence and with the concurrence of the people, decreed that the right of election belonged, in the first place, to the cardinal bishops, who were to fix upon the candidate, and next to the cardinal priests and deacons, whose concurrence was to be sought; and that the clergy and people should express their assent, following the cardinals as guides. The people continued to be present at the elections, and, by their acclamations, signified their assent to the individual chosen by the cardinal bishops, with the consent of the clergy. Innocent II., in 1130, to remedy the disorders attendant on these popular assemblies, attempted to exclude the people from the election; but they rose in arms, and maintained their immemorial privileges, so that Eugene III., in 1145, was elected by the general wish of the clergy and people; and in 1154, the clergy and laity, with acclamation, enthroned Adrian IV. In the third Council of Lateran, held in 1179, under Alexander III., it was decreed, that in case of a division at the election, the person having two-thirds of the votes of the cardinals should be acknowledged as true Pontiff. The people, consequently, thenceforward ceased to have any participation in the choice; and they were effectually excluded from witnessing the election, when it became customary to hold it within an enclosure, called the *conclave*, which was occasionally done, even before it was specially decreed by Gregory X., in 1274.

The exclusion of the laity from the elections was rendered necessary by the tumults and sanguinary scenes that oftentimes attended popular assemblies. It was the wish of Gregory of Nazianzum, so early as the fourth age, that the choice of the prelates of the Church were reserved to a small number of good men.† This is verified in the body of cardinals, who are never more than seventy in number, as seventy elders aided Moses in the government of the people, and who generally are men of great experience and unblemished morals. Six of them are bishops of the neighboring Sees of Ostia, Porto, Albano, Preneste, Sabina, and Frescati. Fifty belong to the order of priests, and fourteen to that of deacons: all of whom have titles taken from the ancient Churches of Rome, over which they preside; and consequently they are the chief clergy of the Roman Church.

The election is conducted in a manner best calculated to result in a happy choice. A solemn mass is celebrated each day to implore the light of the Holy Ghost. A sermon is delivered at the opening of the conclave, in which the electors are exhorted to choose a worthy successor of Peter. All external influence is studiously excluded, no person being

---

* Can. xiii., apud Hard., t. i. col. 784.   † Orat. xix.

allowed to speak in secret, or to communicate by letter with any cardinal, under penalty of excommunication. Any elector, who, by gifts, promises, or entreaties, attempts to influence the votes of others, incurs the same awful penalty. The election is made by ballot, care being taken, by the ingenious folding of the tickets, that no one can know how another has voted, and that no deception be practised in the counting of the votes. At the close of each ballot all the tickets are burnt. When the electors please, they make an open election, or without voting, rush, as it were, by general inspiration, to venerate as Pope the individual who is known to be acceptable to all. Each cardinal, when depositing his vote in the chalice, on the altar, solemnly swears that he gives it according to his conscientious judgment: "I call to witness Christ the Lord, who is to judge me, that I choose the person who, before God, I judge ought to be elected." Two-thirds of the electors must concur to a choice. Each morning and evening the ballot takes place; and in case of no choice being made, a supplementary ballot immediately follows, in order to give the electors an opportunity to supply the number of votes necessary. This is called the *accesso*. The cardinals continue confined within the conclave, like jurors in a jury-room, until the election is made

CHAPTER XX.

Ceremonies.

§ 1.—CEREMONIES AFTER ELECTION.

AFTER the election of the Pope, his consent is demanded, and he is asked by what name he chooses to be thenceforward called. The custom, which was introduced in the tenth century, of assuming a new name, although not originally so designed, corresponds with the example of Simon, who received the name of Peter, on being called by our Lord. The Pope then kneels before the altar in prayer, and retires behind it to lay aside the robes of cardinal and assume those of Pontiff; clothed with which, he seats himself in front of it, on a chair, where he admits the cardinals to kiss his hand and embrace him. Wearing the mantle called the cope, and the episcopal mitre, he is then placed on the altar of the Sixtine chapel, where, as the representative and Vicar of Christ, he receives the homage of the sacred college, in a manner far more solemn and expressive. They kiss his foot, and also his hand covered with the sacred robe, and embrace him, approaching their cheek to his, on each side. The placing of him on the table of the vacant altar, probably arose from considerations of convenience, since the aged cardinals could scarcely perform the obeisance, unless he were in a high position. If, however, we regard it as designed to present him as representative of Him who is our Great High Priest, as well as victim, there is nothing in the rite which should shock our sensibilities or Christian feeling. This ceremony has been popularly styled *adoration*, in the free sense in which this term was generally used, corresponding with respect, veneration, or homage. Novaës justly remarks, that it does not even denote in this place veneration such as is given to the saints, but respect.* The Rubricists term it *obedience*, because used in token of submission to the authority of the Pontiff. The kissing of the foot is an ancient Oriental rite, expressive of honor and affection, and is peculiarly suitable to the apostolic office, since the feet are beautiful of him who proclaims to Sion:

---

* "Con questo nome noi qui intendiamo col Cardinal Bellarmino un atto di rispetto." Introd. alle Vite dei Ss. Pontef., per Giuseppe de Novaës. Roma, 1822. T. i. p. 237.

"Thy God shall reign."* The penitent kissed the feet of our Divine Master; and the devout women, who met Him after His resurrection, held fast His feet, no doubt kissing them affectionately. Cornelius, the centurion, cast himself at the feet of Simon Peter, venerating the messenger of God. From the acts of St. Susanna, a virgin who suffered martyrdom about the year 294, it appears that the custom of paying this mark of respect to the successors of the apostle existed at that early period, since Præpedigna is related to have kissed the feet of Pope Cajus, according to custom. The most powerful princes at various times gave this profound honor to the Popes. The Emperor Justin I., in 525, prostrated himself at the feet of Pope John: Justinian I. honored Agapetus in like manner: Justinian II., with the imperial crown on his head, kissed the feet of Pope Constantine in 710: Luitprand, King of the Lombards, kissed the feet of Gregory II.: Rachis honored Zacharias in the same way: Charlemagne gave the like honor to Adrian I.; and, to pass over many other examples, the Emperor Charles V. honored Clement VII. and Paul III. with the same mark of veneration. No one who knows the war waged by Charles against Clement will ascribe this homage to pusillanimity, or superstition. Since the time of Gregory the Great, as rubricists state, it has been customary with the Popes to wear the cross on their sandals, that the honor might be referred to Christ crucified. If, however, it be given directly to the Pope, as His earthly representative, there is nothing in it which reason may condemn. Besides, the Pope himself every year, on Holy Thursday, kisses the feet of thirteen priests, after having washed them in imitation of our Blessed Redeemer. Can his admission of others to perform in his regard a similar act, be a just cause of scandal?

The splendid chair on which the Pope is borne aloft on the shoulders of twelve men, to the basilic of St. Peter, is used in consideration of his age, which is generally advanced, and in order to render him visible to the faithful, who should, on this solemn occasion, distinctly recognise their chief Pastor. The peacock feathers, which wave on each side of it, are symbolical of his universal inspection, as if he had as many eyes as appear in the plumage of the proud bird.

I deem it superfluous to explain in detail the ceremonies practised in the basilic of St. Peter, where, after adoring the Blessed Sacrament, the Pope receives the same homage as had been given him in the chapel. Three cardinal priests are admitted to kiss his mouth and breast on this occasion: in token of the affection which they bear him, and of the reverence with which they will receive the words which he shall utter in the name of Christ.

---

* Isa. lii. 7.

§ 2.—CEREMONIES OF CORONATION.

The solemn coronation takes place generally a week after the election. In this ceremony, a long plated cane, surmounted with a bunch of flax, is carried by the master of ceremonies, who lights it, bends the knee, as is usually done toward sovereigns, and says: "Holy Father, thus passeth away the glory of this world." This ceremony is repeated three times, that the Pontiff may never suffer his mind to be dazzled by the splendor with which he is surrounded.

On the altar where Mass is to be celebrated, seven candlesticks are lighted, as is usual whenever any bishop celebrates in his own diocese, in conformity with the vision of the Evangelist, to whom our Lord appeared amid seven candlesticks, symbols of the seven churches of Asia Minor.

After the confession in the commencement of Mass, the Pope is placed on the seat on which he was carried to the church; the pallium is blessed by the three first cardinals, and is then hung on his shoulders, by the first cardinal deacon, who says to him: "Receive the holy pallium, the fulness of the pontifical office, for the honor of Almighty God, and of the most glorious Virgin Mary, His Mother, and of the blessed apostles Peter and Paul, and of the Holy Roman Church." The mention of the Blessed Virgin and the apostles, in conjunction with the Deity, is conformable to scriptural precedent, where the agent of divine power is mentioned conjointly with God himself. Thus Moses* and Gideon† are mentioned with God.

The cardinal deacon, accompanied by the judges of the tribunal called *Rota*, and by the consistorial advocates, goes to the tomb of St. Peter, and thrice invokes Christ in behalf of the Pontiff: "Hear us graciously, O Christ," he cries; and those around him answer, praying: "Long life to the Sovereign Pontiff and Universal Pope destined by God." "Saviour of the world," cries the cardinal deacon; they answering: "do Thou help him." The aid of the prayers of the archangels and saints is then asked in a short litany.

The Gospel is sung in Latin and Greek, to represent the union of those two great portions of the Church, whose rite and language are different.

After the Mass, the Pontiff, seated in the great balcony in front of the church of St. John of Lateran, in the presence of the whole people, is crowned with the tiara, by the first cardinal deacon, after the choir has sung the verse of the Psalmist: "A golden crown is on his head!"

It is a curious fact that the tiara, in its original form, is no other than the cap used by the ancient Romans as the symbol of liberty, because

---

* Num. xxi. 5. † Judges vii. 20.

given to liberated slaves. In the ancient images of the Popes, all who preceded the reign of Constantine are represented with the head uncovered; Sylvester, who was contemporary with him, appears with the simple Roman cap. Papebroeck conjectures that the reason of this is that when peace was granted to the Church by Constantine, Sylvester, either of his own accord, or by order of the emperor, took the cap as the symbol of liberty, according to Roman usage.* The Bollandists concur in this view, and explain its signification as relating to the liberation of the Church by Constantine, from heathenish oppression, and the many immunities which he granted to her.† Novaes, a Portuguese, writing at Rome in the beginning of the present century, adopts the same opinion, and expressly says, that the tiara was originally the Roman cap, the symbol of liberty.‡ An ornamental circle, which is called by many a crown, is observable around the lower part, in the ancient pictures of the Popes who succeeded Sylvester; but there is no evidence of any coronation of a Pope before the time of Nicholas I., in the middle of the ninth century, or at least before Leo III., in 795. I, therefore, incline to believe, that this ornament was first added when the Popes had acquired a temporal principality, and was used as a secular ornament, symbolical of their sovereignty over the Roman States. The circumstance of the tiara being blessed and placed on the Pope in the balcony of the church, and the fact of its never being worn at Mass, favor this view. Innocent III. speaks of it as the symbol of temporal power: but his words seem to regard the power which, as Vicar of Christ, he claimed over sovereigns, *ratione peccati*, as far as the morality of their actions was concerned. "The Church," he says, "has given me a crown as a symbol of temporalities: she has conferred on me a mitre in token of spiritual power: a mitre for the priesthood—a crown for the kingdom: making me the vicar of Him who bears written on His garment and thigh: 'The King of kings, and Lord of lords.'"§ Some think that Boniface VIII., who began his reign in 1294, added a second circle, or crown, to the cap, to express more forcibly this same power over sovereigns: but if the testimony of Benzo can be relied on, the two circles were on the cap worn by Nicholas II., who was chosen Pope in 1053.‖ Innocent III., however, makes no allusion to the second circle. The third circle was added, as many think, by Benedict XII., in 1334, but more probably by Urban VI., chosen in 1362.· The ancient images of the Popes preserved at Rome favor this latter opinion. I know of no document which determines the meaning¶ of the three circles. They

---

* In conatu ad S. Silvest., n. 5.   † Acta SS. Maji, l. iv. die 19.
‡ Diss. v., Della solenne Coron. del Ponf., p. 87.   § Serm. in festo S. Silvest.
‖ De Rebus Henrici III., l. vii. c. 2.
¶ "Qual che siane il significato simbolico." Lunadoro.

may have been added for mere ornament, without any special signification.

The tiara was generally worn only in the solemn ceremony of the coronation, until the time of Paul II., chosen Pope in 1464, who used it on many occasions. Some Popes wore it on the chief festivals.

The address made to the Pope when the tiara is placed on his head, which mentions the three crowns, must have been composed or amended since they were adopted. The cardinal deacon says to him: "Receive the tiara adorned with three crowns, and know that thou art the father of princes and kings, the ruler of the world on earth,* the Vicar of our Lord Jesus Christ, to whom is honor and glory throughout all ages." This language might be considered as implying all that was claimed by Gregory, Innocent, or Boniface; but it is also capable of an interpretation consistent with the more moderate pretensions of the Popes, who, since the days of Sixtus V. or Gregory XIV., during two centuries and a half, have filled the chair of the fisherman. The Pontiff is truly "the father of princes and kings," venerated as such by all the children of the Church, who, in their highest elevation, recognise him as the general head of the whole Christian family. He may be styled "ruler on earth of the world," because the Church, in which he holds the primacy, is spread throughout the world, and he is charged to promulgate to every creature the law of God, to which every soul must be subject. He holds the place of Christ, being entrusted by Him with the care of His sheepfold.

---

* "Rectorem orbis in terra." Some put a comma after *orbis*, and refer "*in terra*" to *vicarium:* but the other punctuation seems correct. "Orbis in urbe" is found in Ovid, and signifies a multitude in a city.

The Primacy.

PART II.

SECULAR RELATIONS.

CHAPTER I.

Patrimony of St. Peter.

THE primacy is essentially a spiritual office, which has not, of divine right, any temporal appendage: yet the Pope is actually sovereign of a small principality in Italy, designated *the Patrimony of St. Peter, or the States of the Church.* It is so styled because it has been attached to the pontifical office, through reverence for the prince of the apostles. As it has no necessary connection with the primacy, and as Catholics, not living within the Roman States, are not subject to the civil authority of the Pope, it is not necessary to treat of it: yet it is a matter of no small interest to trace its history, and observe by what a combination of events Providence has annexed it to the Holy See, and most wonderfully maintained it, amid the revolutions of empires and kingdoms.

Christ sent forth His disciples without scrip or staff, giving them no dominion over the least spot of earth. In making Peter the ruler of His kingdom, He did not give him dominion, or wealth, or any of the appendages of royalty. The Master had not whereon to lay His head; and the chief disciple was unprovided with any earthly possession. Gold and silver he had not, but he had powers of a supernatural order, for the government of men in order to salvation.

The generous zeal with which the first disciples devoted themselves to the service of God, led many of them to sell their property, and lay the purchase-money at the feet of St. Peter, to form thence a common fund for the general necessities: yet we have no reason to suppose that it rose to any great amount, since the constantly-flowing streams of beneficence left but little in the common reservoir. When the apostle closed his career, he bequeathed to his successors no inheritance but the labors and dangers of his office. For three centuries they continued exposed to the fury of persecution. Nevertheless, the generosity of the faithful consecrated to the service of religion, under their direction, a considerable portion of their worldly riches; so that a public treasure was formed, by means of which the clergy and a large number of indigent persons were supported. In the middle of the third century, Pope Cornelius, in a letter to Fabius, Bishop of Antioch, stated that there were then at Rome forty-six priests, seven deacons, seven sub-deacons, forty-two acolytes, fifty-two exorcists, lectors, and janitors; that is, clergymen in minor orders; and one thousand five hundred widows, with other afflicted and distressed persons,—to all of whom the grace and bounty of the Lord furnished support.* The heathens believed the wealth of the Church to be great, since the deacon Lawrence, in time of persecution, was called on to deliver it up to the public officer. To avoid doing so, he distributed all to the poor, whom he presented at the appointed time, saying: "Here are the treasures of the Church!"

It is certain that the Emperor Constantine bestowed large possessions on the Bishop of Rome. Although the document which purports to be the instrument of donation is supposititious, yet, as the acute De Maistre observes, nothing is more certain than the donation of Constantine. Voltaire avows, that "he gave in reality to the cathedral church of St. John, not to the Bishop of Rome individually, a thousand marks of gold, and thirty thousand marks of silver, with a revenue of fourteen thousand pence, and lands in Calabria. Each emperor successively increased this patrimony. The Bishops of Rome stood in need of it. The missionaries whom they soon sent to pagan Europe, the exiled bishops to whom they afforded a refuge, the poor whom they fed, put them under the necessity of being very wealthy."† The palace of Lateran was in possession of the Pope in the early part of the fourth century, since Melchiades held there a Council to decide the Donatist controversy, and the church erected beside it still bears the name of the generous emperor. Fleury testifies, that from the ancient monuments of the Roman Church it is apparent that Constantine gave to the baptistery of St. John of Lateran, which is attached to the Constantine basilic, so many houses and farms, not only in Italy, but likewise in Sicily, Africa, and Greece, that the annual revenue amounted to 30,394 marks of gold.‡ Secular influence naturally followed wealth, and the withdrawal of Constantine from the ancient capital of the empire, left the Bishop of Rome in a position almost independent; the pontifical chair being no longer overshadowed by the imperial throne. When Pope Leo the Great was invited to a general Council by the Emperor Marcian, he pleaded, besides the want of precedent on the part of his predecessors, the danger to the public peace should he absent himself from the city. "The very uncertain state of affairs at present does not allow me to withdraw from the population of this city, since the minds which are agitated would be cast into despair, were I to quit the country and the Apostolic See for a cause of an ecclesiastical nature."§ This shows that his presence was connected in the public mind with the peace and safety of the city: on which account he writes to the emperor: "temporal necessity does not

---

* Ad Fabium Antioch, col. 150, Coustant, t. i.   † Essai sur l'Histoire, t. ii.
‡ Hist., l. xi., A. C. 326.   § Ep. xxviii. ad Pulcheriam Aug.

allow me to leave the city."* Necessity forced him to act as protector and father of the Roman people, when his interposition alone could avert the wrath of some fierce barbarian rushing forward to lay the fair city in ruins, and fill her streets with her slaughtered citizens. When Attila, " the scourge of God," at the head of five hundred thousand Huns, advanced to its destruction, the mild eloquence of Leo disarmed him. Two years afterward, the Pontiff discharged the same office of mediator with Genseric, who, at the head of Vandals and Moors, came to wreak vengeance on the queen of nations; but he could only save the lives of the citizens by delivering the city to pillage. Even in times of tranquillity, Leo exercised some acts of civil authority, since he summoned the Manichees to trial, and, on conviction, banished them from the city.† Although the Bishop of Rome was not as yet a temporal sovereign, yet his spiritual power was surrounded with so great secular influence, that he almost ranked as a prince, and felt that wrongs inflicted on his representatives in the imperial court were violations of the rights of sovereignty. In 484, St. Felix complained to the Emperor Zeno, that the laws of nations had been violated by the injurious treatment of his legates.

The moderation and indulgence with which the Popes treated their dependents, made men desirous to enjoy their protection. St. Gregory the Great exhorted Sabinian, Bishop of Callipolis,‡ a city dependent on the Roman Church, to see that the citizens should not be overmuch burdened.§ Pantaleon, the notary of Syracuse, having reported to him that injustice had been practised in the name of the Roman Church on her dependents, he praised him, and directed strict inquiry to be made into the wrongs already committed, that they might be repaired : " for," he says, " like the Teacher of the nations, I have all things, and abound : and I do not seek money, but a heavenly recompense."|| He instructed Peter, his agent in Sicily, to cause restitution to be made, if, as was alleged, the possessions of individuals, or their personal property, or their slaves, had been seized in the name of the Roman Church, within the preceding ten years, and to save the aggrieved the trouble of coming to Rome for redress. Strict impartiality was enjoined by him, as the best evidence which the agent could give of his devotedness to the Apostolic See : " for then," says he, " you will be truly a soldier of St. Peter, if in cases which concern him, you maintain what is right, without regard to his interests."¶ Guizot, after citing some humane regulations of Gregory, observes : " It is easy to understand why people were at that time eager to place themselves under the dominion of the Church : lay pro-

---

* Ep. xxxiv. ad Theodosium Aug.   † Ep. ii. ad ep. per Italiam.
‡ A seaport in Otranto, Naples.   § L. ix. ep. c.
|| L. xiii. ep. xxxiv.   ¶ L. i. ep. xxxvi.

prietors were certainly far from showing like solicitude for the well-being of the occupants of their domains."*

The possessions of the Roman Church† were regarded as a trust for the poor, whose interests St. Gregory felt that he was guarding, while he attended to the collection of the revenues, which he dispensed with liberality and discernment. He directed two thousand bushels of wheat to be given by the deacon Cyprian, his agent in Sicily, to the Bishop Zeno, for the relief of the poor of his city.‡ Sending the priest Candidus into Gaul, to manage the small patrimony of the Roman Church in that kingdom, he ordered the revenues to be employed in buying clothes for the poor, and in purchasing English boys of seventeen or eighteen years of age, that they might be rescued from the bondage of error and sin, and instructed in some monastery, where they might serve God.§ He thanked the prefect of Africa for the protection afforded by him in what regarded the interests of the poor of blessed Peter, prince of the apostles.|| Talitan, another guardian of the patrimony, was exhorted by him to defend it, as being the portion of the poor. Truly did Gibbon say: "In the use of wealth he acted like a faithful steward of the Church and the poor, and liberally applied to their wants the inexhaustible resources of abstinence and order."¶

Property, in those ages, brought with it dominion over the occupants of the soil: whence "the agents of the Church of Rome had acquired a civil and even criminal jurisdiction over their tenants and husbandmen."** Although the feudal system was not as yet developed, yet much that characterized the ages strictly designated feudal, was observable in the relations of landlord and tenant; so that the remarks of Guizot, applied to that period, may help to solve the enigma of the exercise of a power apparently supreme in many respects, and yet confessedly subordinate to the imperial authority. "The landed proprietor, as such, exercised in his possessions some of the rights now reserved to the sovereign. He maintained order, administered justice, or caused it to be administered; led forth, or sent forth to battle the occupants of his lands, not in virtue of a special power styled political, but of his right of property, which included various powers."†† In fact, we find Gregory issuing orders to the defender—that is, agent or officer charged with the care of the patrimony—in an authoritative form:‡‡

---

* Cours d'Histoire Moderne, t. iv. p. 259.

† These are called "*justitiæ S. Petri*," in various documents of the eighth century. The term was probably used for "*jura*," *rights*, and borrowed from the Vulgate, which uses it with great latitude. See *Discorso Storico supra alcuni punti della Storia Longobardica per Manzoni*, ¿ iv.

‡ L. vi. ep. iv.   ¿ L. v. ep. vii.

|| L. x., ep. xxxvii.   ¶ Decline and Fall, &c. ch. xlv.

** Decline and Fall, &c. ch. xlv.   †† Cours d' Histoire Moderne, t. iii. p. 75.

‡‡ *Præcepti nostri pagina.* L. ix., ep. xl., et. l. x., ep. x.

and confirming his acts in the most express manner, to prevent their being called in question.* He directed his attention to the case of an injured woman, whose complaints had reached him, and ordered an inquiry to be made into it, by arbitrators to be chosen by the parties.† He prescribed rules to be followed in trials of the right of property, and directed possession during forty years to be taken as a presumptive proof, barring any adverse claim.‡ He instructed Sergius, the defender at Otranto, to force Fruniscendus to answer a claim made against him, and to pronounce and execute the sentence, without admitting any appeal.§

It may be questioned whether Gregory acted as a landed proprietor, in several instances, in which he took upon himself to direct military movements for the defence of various parts of Italy. Doubtless he had vast interests at stake; but zeal for the common safety may have prompted him to give orders, which all were disposed to receive with gratitude and reverence from one whose social position was already so eminent. We find him appointing Constance, the tribune, to guard the city of Naples, and exhorting the soldiers to obey him.|| Maurentius, another officer in command of the troops at Naples, was directed to relieve Theodosius, abbot of a monastery in Campania, from the necessity of guarding the walls.¶ Apprehending that Ariulph, the Lombard, might attack Ravenna or Rome, he issued orders for defence to the commanders of the troops.** He apprised Januarius, Bishop of Cagliari, and Genadius, who appears to have been a layman in high office, of the danger of the invasion of Sardinia by the Lombards under Agilulph, that they might prepare to repel it, declaring that on his part he would neglect nothing in his power in order to be in readiness.

The negotiations which Gregory carried on with the Lombard king, show that his own position was equivalent to that of an independent prince. He urged Severus, the assessor of the exarch, to advise him to make peace with Agilulph, intimating that should he decline any arrangement, the king had offered to come to an arrangement with himself: this shows that he was in a position nearly equal to that of a sovereign.†† He afterward made peace with the Lombards, on terms nowise prejudicial to the commonwealth.‡‡ He wrote to Agilulph, to thank him for the peace, urged him to see that his officers observe it, and assured him that he received his messengers affectionately, as bearers of good tidings.§§ At the same time he addressed letters of thanks to Theodelinda, the wife of the king, for her kind offices in procuring peace, and begged her to con-

---

* *Per hujus tuitionis paginam confirmamus.* L. ix., ep. lvii.
† Ep. lxxxiii.   ‡ L. i., ep. ii., et. l. vii., ep. xxxix.
§ L. ix., ep. ci. || L. ii., ep. xxxi.
¶ L. ix., ep. lxxiii.   ** L. iii., ep. xxix. xxx.
†† L. v., ep. xxxv.   ‡‡ Ep. xl.
§§ Ep. xlii.

tinue them, that Agilulph "may not reject the society of the Christian republic."* "Disappointed," says Gibbon, "in the hopes of a general and lasting treaty, he presumed to save his country without the consent of the emperor or the exarch. The sword of the enemy was suspended over Rome: it was averted by the mild eloquence and seasonable gifts of the Pontiff, who commanded the respect of heretics and barbarians. The merits of Gregory were treated by the Byzantine court with reproach and insult; but in the attachment of a grateful people, he found the purest reward of a citizen, and the best right of a sovereign."†

That he had civil authority at Rome, appears from the plea of Boniface of Africa, who offered as an excuse for not presenting himself to give an account of his faith, that his friends feared the employment of force against him: "Those," says the Pontiff, "who partake of your doubts, if they will come to me, have no reason to fear that I will employ my authority against them; for in all causes, but especially in those which regard divine things, we are eager to bind men by reason, rather than by force."‡ His great civil influence is apparent from his observation, when he was calumniated as having caused the death of the Bishop Malchus: "On this point it suffices for you to remark to our most serene lords, that if I, their servant, had been willing to cause the death of the Lombards, the Lombard nation would, at this day, have neither king, nor dukes, nor counts, but would be in unutterable confusion."§ He was not, however, free from all dependence on the empire, since we find him promulgating a law enacted by Mauritius, although it did not accord with his own judgment. The terms of his remonstrance indicate the submission of a subject to his sovereign.||

At a subsequent period, the fanatic zeal of Justinian to procure the approval of the Trullan Council, and the persecuting measures of the Iconoclasts, caused the Romans and Italians to rally round the Bishop of Rome. When Zacharias, an imperial officer, attempted to execute the order which he had received for the arrest and transportation to Constantinople of Pope Sergius, who refused to sanction the innovations of the Trullan prelates, the military of Ravenna, of the dukedom of Pentapolis, and of the neighboring districts, rushed to the defence of the Pontiff, and, but for his interposition, would have torn the officer to pieces. The Lombards vied with the Romans in protecting the person of Gregory II. against the satellites of the Iconoclast emperor, Leo the Isaurian. From that time, the military took a conspicuous part in the election of the Pope, being allowed, on more than one occasion, to declare their assent by subscribing the document which certified that he was chosen by the

---

* Ep. xliii.   † Decline and Fall, &c. ch. xlv.
‡ L. iv., ep. xliii.   § Ep. xlvii.
|| "Ego quidem jussioni subjectus—imperatori obedientiam præbui." L. iii. ep. lxv.

clergy, soldiery, and people. Notwithstanding this attempt on his own life, Gregory continued to support the imperial authority, forbidding the Italians to revolt, as they had determined, when Leo the Isaurian decreed the destruction of the sacred images. Prompted by humanity and religion, several Popes adopted measures for the protection of the Romans against the barbarian hordes that overran Italy; and with this view raised walls around the city, and provided it with means of defence. Through the neglect of the Eastern emperors to succor and protect their Italian subjects, the imperial power soon became extinct, and the Popes, unable to cope with the Lombards, were compelled to seek aid from the Franks. " Any effectual assistance," as Hallam avows, "from the Emperor Constantine Copronymus, would have kept Rome still faithful."* When Rome was besieged by Aristulph, Stephen III. called on Pepin to succor the Roman Church, and "his people, the citizens of the republic of the Romans." On his victory over the Lombards, in 755, Pepin restored to the Pope twenty cities, which his valor had recovered. This can scarcely be considered a mere donation, since a great portion, if not all, of the territory had already belonged to the Pope: whence Stephen IV., in the year 769, urged the French princes, Charles and Carloman, as a matter of duty which they owed to St. Peter, to see that his property usurped by the Lombards should be fully restored. "If you neglect or delay to enforce his just claims, a thing which we cannot believe, know that you shall render a strict account of them to the prince of the apostles himself, before the tribunal of Christ."† Language so strong cannot be applicable to a mere gift of their father. "The Popes," says Hallam, "appear to have possessed some measure of temporal power, even while the city was professedly governed by the exarchs of Ravenna, in the name of the Eastern empire. This power became more extensive on her separation from Constantinople."‡ It is not easy to define with accuracy the relations of the Romans to the king and the Pontiff; but the latter may be regarded as limiting his sovereignty to the exercise of a protectorate, while the Romans were virtually a republic; and "the Patrician," as Pepin was styled, was to support the existing order; by his intervention in cases of extraordinary danger from external assaults or domestic dissensions. By his counsels and influence, rather than by the display of power, the Pontiff reigned over his people, who cheerfully obeyed their father and benefactor, unless when excited passion drove them to temporary acts of insubordination and revolt. As it did not become him to use the sword, he called to his aid a temporal prince, to employ that coercion which was necessary to restrain rebellious spirits, reserving to himself the exercise of the milder attributes of sovereignty.§

---

* Middle Ages, ch. i.   † Ep. xlvi. Cod. Carol.   ‡ Middle Ages, p. 1, ch. iii.
§ Something like this is seen in the actual relations to the Papal government of the French and Austrian troops now occupying the States of the Church.

When some desperate men, in attempting to assassinate the holy Pontiff Leo III., mutilated and disfigured him, he became intercessor in their behalf with Charlemagne, as yet only patrician, and obtained their pardon. Yet, on a subsequent occasion, when a similar attempt had been made, and the assassins had been found guilty of a crime punishable with death, according to the laws of the Romans, he suffered the sentence to be executed, lest extreme lenity should embolden the wicked.

> "Mercy is not itself, that oft looks so;
> Pardon is still the nurse of second wo."*

Among the acts of sovereignty which the public danger forced the Pontiffs to exercise, was the repelling of barbarian troops that invaded the Roman territory. In the reign of Leo IV., the Saracens endeavored to effect a landing at Ostia, in order to advance against Rome. The heroic Pope fulfilled the duties of a sovereign, without prejudice to his spiritual character, as Voltaire acknowledges: "Pope Leo IV., taking upon himself at this crisis an authority which the generals of the Emperor Lothaire seemed to abandon, showed himself worthy to be the sovereign of Rome, by his successful defence of it. He had employed the riches of the Church in repairing the walls, raising towers, and extending chains over the Tiber. He armed the troops at his own expense, engaged the inhabitants of Naples and Gaeta to come to the defence of the coasts and port of Ostia, without neglecting the wise precaution of requiring hostages from them, as he well knew that those who are strong enough to aid us, are equally so to do us injury. He himself visited all the posts, and met the Saracens on their approach, not clad in military attire, as Goslin, the Bishop of Paris, had appeared in a still more critical conjuncture, but as a Pontiff exhorting a Christian people, and a sovereign intent on the safety of his subjects. He was a native of Rome. The courage of the first ages of the republic revived in his person, at a period of degeneracy and corruption, like some splendid monument of ancient Rome, now and then discovered among the ruins of the modern city. The attack of the Saracens was bravely met, and half of their vessels having been destroyed by a storm, a portion of the assailants, who escaped shipwreck, were chained, to be employed in public works: the Pope deriving this advantage from his victory, that the very hands which were raised for the destruction of Rome were employed in fortifying and adorning it."†

Similar occasions for the exercise of a protective sovereignty occurred from time to time. In the early part of the tenth century, John X. successfully repulsed the Saracens, who had attempted to invade the Roman

---

* Measure for Measure.—Shakspeare.
† Voltaire, Puissance des Mussulmans, ch. xxiv.

territory. Benedict VIII., in the following age, drove them from the Italian shores, and compelled the Greeks, who inhabited Apulia, to sue for peace. St. Leo IX. accompanied his troops in their expedition against the Normans, who ravaged the south of Italy, to inspire confidence by his presence; but he took no part in the strife, being content, like another Moses, to uplift his hands in prayer. God, whose counsels are mysterious, suffered the barbarians to prevail, and His servant to become their captive: but such was the influence of his sacred character on their minds, that instead of insulting him in misfortune, they knelt to do him homage.

The occasional exercise of supreme power over the Romans by the emperors, has led Guizot to observe, that "the sovereignty was not fully ascribed either to the Pope or to the emperor; uncertain and undivided, it floated between them."* It appears, by numberless facts, that the Pope was sovereign, while an efficient protectorate was acknowledged in the emperor, who came, at his solicitation, to support him, and, in that conjuncture, with his assent, exercised some acts of a temporary sovereignty. "We acknowledge," said Alexander III., "the lord emperor, in virtue of his dignity, advocate and special defender of the Holy Roman Church."† The prefect of the city took the oath of allegiance to him up to the time of Innocent III., who required the senator and barons of the Roman States to pledge their fealty to himself, and nominated the subordinate magistrates. In the oath taken to the emperor Arnulph, a clause saving their fidelity to Pope Formosus was contained. The municipal government of Rome seems to have been always in the hands of popular officers, after the manner of a republic, so that even the power of the Pope was seldom felt in the details of civil administration. He interfered chiefly when the public danger required that the vessel of the State should be guided by a superior mind and firm hand; and he called for the support of the emperor, when physical force was necessary to subdue the rebellion of his own subjects. "The spirits, and even the institutions of the Romans," as Hallam remarks, "were republican. Amid the darkness of the tenth century, which no contemporary historian dissipates, we faintly distinguish the awful names of senate, consuls, and tribunes, the domestic magistracy of Rome."‡ The origin of the pontifical sovereignty is traced by Gibbon to the necessity which the Romans felt of superior direction and support, to which we must add the voluntary submission of various cities, anxious to share the blessings of a mild protectorate. "By the necessity of their situation, the inhabitants of Rome were cast into the rough model of a republican government:

---

* Cours d'Histoire Moderne, t. iii. p. 76.
† Apud Baron., an. 1159, p. 439.
‡ Middle Ages, vol. i. ch. iii. par. i. p. 234.

they were compelled to elect some judges in peace, and some leaders in war: the nobles assembled to deliberate, and their resolves could not be executed without the union and consent of the multitude. The want of laws could only be supplied by the influence of religion, and their foreign and domestic councils were moderated by the authority of the Bishop. His alms, his sermons, his correspondence with the kings and prelates of the West, his recent services, their gratitude and oath, accustomed the Romans to consider him as the first magistrate, or prince, of the city. The Christian humility of the Popes," he adds, in a tone of irony, " was not offended by the name of *Dominus*, or Lord: and their face and inscription are still apparent on the most ancient coins. Their temporal dominion is now confirmed by the reverence of a thousand years, and their noblest title is the free choice of a people whom they had redeemed from slavery."*

Rome long preserved her republican character. Saint-Priest says: " Rome, from the age of Constantine, under the title of republic, which she never lost, had become a kind of free city, which, for illustration sake, I shall compare to the Hanseatic cities of the north of Germany."† The Pope might well be styled the father and protector of the Roman republic. The desolation of the city, sometimes by famine, and often by hostile armies, imposed on him the necessity of succoring it; and his treasury, containing the revenues arising from the possessions of the Roman Church in other places, was exhausted to furnish provisions to the famishing people, and to protect the remains of the imperial city from the incursions of hostile armies. With paternal solicitude, the third and fourth Leo directed their efforts to secure the church of St. Peter by a wall, enclosing the Vatican mount, or, what was styled from their name, the city of Leo: *civitas Leonina*. At the entreaty of the nobles, who complained of the Saracen depredations, Leo IV. determined to execute what his predecessor had designed, and accordingly summoned the citizens to council, arranged his plans, ordering the cities dependant on the republic, and the monasteries themselves, to furnish mechanics, and for four years he spared no personal labor or exposure, until the work was completed. There are traces of republican deliberation in this narrative, and every thing warrants us in regarding the Pontiff as the father, rather than lord of his people.

Of the temporal monarchy of Rome, Hallam observes : " Her ultimate sovereignty was compatible with the practical independence of the free cities, or of the usurpers who had risen up among them. Bologna, Faenza, Rimini, and Ravenna, with many other less considerable, took an oath, indeed, to the Pope, but continued to regulate both their internal

---

* Decline and Fall of the Roman Empire, ch. xlix., A.D. 728.
† Histoire de la Royauté, l. iii. p. 284.

concerns and foreign relations at their own discretion. The first of these cities was far pre-eminent above the rest for population and renown, and, though not without several interruptions, preserved a republican character till the end of the fourteenth century."* The Roman magistrates often went beyond the limits of a municipal power, and reduced the Papal sovereignty to a protectorate void of all efficiency. They frequently assumed to themselves supreme power, as Hallam again testifies: "In the twelfth and thirteenth centuries, the Senate, and the senator who succeeded them, exercised one distinguishing attribute of sovereignty, that of coining gold and silver money. Some of their coins still exist, with legends in a very republican tone."† For a considerable time the Romans freely chose their Senator, by which name they designated a magistrate who exercised supreme control during the period of his government; and they even gave this title to Martin IV., as a personal privilege, expressly stipulating that it should not be considered as inherent in the pontifical office.

Under the influence of the seditious declamations of Arnold of Brescia, the Romans, during a considerable part of the twelfth century, were in revolt. Several Popes were forced to flee from their capital, and erect their chair in Perugia, Viterbo, or some other city of Italy, or to take refuge in France, which gained the glorious title of the asylum of Popes. Sometimes the emperor came to their relief, and replaced them in safety on their throne. On other occasions, Heaven itself seemed to take their cause in hand, and by pestilence brought the disobedient Romans to a sense of duty. In 1230, after a calamitous visitation of this kind, caused by the inundation of the Tiber, they sent an embassy to Gregory IX., who for two years had been an exile in Perugia, beseeching him to return and bless his penitent children. The venerable Pontiff, on his return, lavished gifts on them, and "built a noble palace for the use of the poor," as his biographer assures us.

The character of the pontifical government has been at all times paternal and protective; whence, although popular discontent has often manifested itself, especially through the intrigues of schismatical emperors, many of the surrounding cities sought to enjoy its advantages. In the eighth century, as we learn from Anastasius, "some of those of Spoleto and Rieti came to Rome, entreating to be shaved *'alla maniera de' Romani*,' in token of their subjection to the Pope, rather than to the Lombards," and after the defeat of the Lombard king, Desiderius, the entire dukedom eagerly sought the same privilege. The paternal character of the pontifical government is stated in a letter from the Senate and the Roman people to King Pepin, in the year 763, in the pontificate of Paul I. "They protest that they are firm and faithful

---

* Middle Ages, vol. i. ch. iii. p. 11.   † Ibidem.

servants of the holy Church of God, and of our most blessed father and lord, Pope Paul, because he is our father and excellent pastor, and labors incessantly for our salvation, as his brother Pope Stephen likewise did, governing us as reasonable sheep committed to him by God, and exhibiting clemency always, and imitating St. Peter, whose Vicar he is."* On the elevation of Innocent III., Conrad, Duke of Spoleto and Assisi, seeing the eagerness of his subjects to enjoy pontifical protection, freed them from their oath of allegiance, and surrendered various fortresses into the hands of the Pontiff. Rieti, Spoleto, Assisi, Foligno, and Nuceria, with their whole districts, thus came into his power. Perugia, likewise, Eugubium, Todi, and the city of Acquapendente, Montefiascone, and all Tuscany, acknowledged his authority.

The pontifical principality was greatly embarrassed by the high pretensions of the princes or barons within the States of the Church, until the reign of Alexander VI., when they were crushed by the strong arm of Cesar Borgia.† From that time, the papal sovereignty was more extensively felt in the confederacies of princes: but for a long period the Pontiffs have maintained a complete neutrality.

Although the splendor of a throne may seem to correspond but ill with the lowly beginnings of the Roman Church, when the Syrian fisherman, preaching the folly of the cross, came unnoticed or despised into the city of the Cesars, we cannot doubt that Divine Providence has clothed his successor with this adventitious power, that he might exercise more independently the attributes of his spiritual office. His civil dominion is large enough to inspire respect, while it is not of such extent as to render him formidable. It enables him to foster many ecclesiastical institutions of vast advantage to the Universal Church, as well as to be a munificent patron of learning, art, and science. Were he the subject of a temporal prince, the exercise of his authority would be always liable to the suspicion of constraint, or undue influence, and he might become, like the Bishop of Constantinople, "a domestic slave under the eye of his master, at whose nod he alternately passed from the convent to the throne, and

---

* This letter is the "thirty-sixth of the Caroline letters." I quote from "Rome as it was under Paganism, and as it became under the Popes," &c. Vol. ii. p. 317.

† Roscoe observes: "Alexander might surely think himself justified in suppressing the turbulent barons, who had for ages rent the dominions of the Church with intestine wars, and in subjugating the petty sovereigns of Romagna, over whom he had an acknowledged supremacy, and who had in general acquired their dominions by means as unjustifiable as those which he adopted against them."—Life of Leo X., vol. i. ch. vi. He adds in a note: "Oliverotto da Fermo had obtained the chief authority in the city from which he derived his name, by the treacherous murder of his uncle, and several of the principal inhabitants, whom he had invited to an entertainment. This atrocious deed was perpetrated on the same day, in the preceding year, on which he afterward fell into the snare of Cesar Borgia. The other persons put to death by Borgia, had also supported themselves by rapine, and were the terror of all Italy."

from the throne to the convent."* The great Bossuet has well observed: "God wished this Church, which is the common mother of all kingdoms, not to be dependent on any kingdom in temporalities, that the See, in which all the faithful should preserve unity, might be above the partialities which the different interests and jealousies of States might occasion. The Church, independent in her head of all temporal power, is thereby able to exercise more freely, for the common benefit, and under the protection of Christian kings, this heavenly power of governing souls; and holding in her hands the balance, in the midst of so many empires often at enmity, she maintains unity in all bodies, sometimes by inflexible decrees, and sometimes by wise temperaments."†

In our own Government, we have a striking illustration of the principle on which the patrimony of St. Peter is exempted from any local sovereignty but that of the Pontiff. In order to preserve the independence and free action of the General Government, it was deemed proper by the sages who planned our constitution, that a small district, of not more than ten miles' circumference, should be free from any State or local authority, and immediately dependent on Congress, with a municipal administration. To prevent all intrigue and partisan effort, by which the Government might be put in jeopardy, the citizens of the district are denied the right of suffrage in the election of the chief officers of the United States. Thus the District of Columbia is, in regard to the States, what Rome and the patrimony of St. Peter are in reference to the Church. The independence and purity of the General Government being thus provided for, its moral influence extends everywhere, while its physical power is so restricted as to prevent any just apprehension of any exercise of authority to the prejudice of State sovereignty.‡

It must be acknowledged that there are inconveniences connected with the union of temporal sovereignty and spiritual supremacy in the one person; yet it should be remembered that the powers are altogether distinct, since the former regards only the inhabitants of the Roman States, while the latter reaches to the ends of the earth. The Pope is not as the Roman emperor, who in quality of sovereign Pontiff exercised religious supremacy, controlled by no law but his will, and coextensive with imperial sway. The civil administration is carried on by tribunals and officers distinct from those that are charged with the general affairs of the Church, so that there is no confusion of powers. The mild government of the Popes, and the light taxation to which the Romans were formerly

---

* Decline and Fall, &c. ch. xlix., A. D. 726.

† Discours sur l'Unité de l'Eglise, vol. xv. Op. Bossuet. See also the Bull of excommunication: *Quum memoranda*, published by Pius VII. on 10 June, 1809.

‡ This analogy is ably developed in an essay entitled: "The Papal States analogous to the District of Columbia," by A. P. Thompson. Galveston, 1849.

subjected, provoked the envy of strangers, who regarded them as the happiest people in the world, but for the sanguinary collisions of the nobles,* which have long since ceased. In truth, the lenity of the administration is its chief defect; but it still merits the tribute paid to it by the infidel historian: "If we calmly weigh the merits and defects of the ecclesiastical government, it may be praised in its present state as a mild, decent, and tranquil system, exempt from the dangers of a minority, the sallies of youth, the expenses of luxury, and the calamities of war."†

Under the present illustrious occupant of the pontifical throne, the paternal character of the government appears with increased lustre. With generous solicitude for the happiness of his subjects, he anticipated their desires, by adopting, of his own accord, measures for the amelioration of their condition. The base ingratitude with which his clemency, which threw open the prison-gates, was repaid, and the revolution effected by his seditious subjects, spurred on and supported by the active enemies of Christianity and society, gathered together from various countries, are melancholy facts, which make us blush for our race: but the speedy overthrow of the mock republic, infamous for pillage and assassination, by the arms of republican France, and the triumphant return of the exiled Pontiff to his people and throne, are among the many extraordinary instances of Divine interposition.‡ However, "the better principality" which the Roman Church possessed in the days of Irenæus, is altogether independent of earthly sovereignty; it will survive every change of governors, and modes of government, and will shine forth from a dungeon as well as from a throne. No vicissitudes of the Roman States can affect that spiritual authority, which, going forth from the See of the fisherman, is felt even in the midst of its enemies. The death of Pius VI. in exile, and the captivity of his successor, left little human hope that the States of the Church would be restored, or that the See itself would continue: but God, who casts the mighty from their seats, replaced the persecuted Pius VII. on the throne of Peter, amid the boundless acclamations of a devoted people, while his oppressor was left to perish on a desert island.

It is a stale calumny that Catholics are vassals, or subjects of the Pope: although we everywhere profess, with his full knowledge and entire approbation, unqualified allegiance to the respective civil governments under which we live. The fathers of the fifth Council of Baltimore took occasion to state this distinctly in their address to the late

---

* Decline and Fall, ch. lxx., A. D. 1459. † Ib., A. D. 1500.

‡ The late Samuel Farmar Jarvis must be added to the list of mistaken interpreters of prophecy, since he ventured to mark the year 1847, in which he wrote his tardy reply to Dr. Milner's End of Religious Controversy, as the period of the overthrow of the Papacy.

venerable Pontiff, which was most graciously received.* At the request of the sixth Council, his present Holiness has simplified the oath taken by bishops at their consecration, omitting the terms and phrases which savor of feudal times, although they do not anywhere receive a feudal interpretation. Thus all pretext for questioning our allegiance is removed, although our adversaries still object to us the acts of former Popes, who interfered in the civil concerns of Christian nations, and in the controversies of princes. It will not be uninteresting to review, historically, those facts, in order to reconcile our present professions with past events.

---

* See Acts of V. Council of Baltimore.

CHAPTER II.

Authority over Princes.

§ 1.—IN MATTERS OF FAITH AND MORALS.

THE Roman States form but a small principality, which gives little importance to its ruler, and the Bishop of Rome, of divine right, has no political or civil power; yet, in the things of salvation, he is above all the members of the Church, whatever be their rank—the monarch of vast dominions, as well as the lowliest slave. All men are naturally equal, and all the members of the Church are children of God, subject to His authority, which on earth is exercised especially by the Chief Bishop. The divine sovereignty requires that every soul be subject to God, rendering homage to His truth, and obedience to His commandments. The acts of the Pontiff, in the lawful discharge of his ecclesiastical supremacy, are to be respected by all who acknowledge him to be, under Christ, the ruler of the Church. Hence, when Pope Felix, in 484, had deprived of communion Acacius, the Bishop of Constantinople, he made known the fact to the Emperor Zeno, urging him to give the support of his authority to this decree, and observing, that it was more for his advantage to obey the Church in this matter, than to attempt to control it, by countenancing the heretical prelate. Yet none were more explicit than the Pontiffs in avowing the independence of the civil power within its own sphere, and in giving to sovereigns the honor due to their high station. With a jealous regard to the interests of truth, they united an unfeigned deference for civil rulers. The mutual relations of the ecclesiastical and civil authorities were beautifully expressed by Pope Gelasius, at the close of the fifth century, in a letter of apology written to the Emperor Anastasius, who had complained that the Pontiff had not congratulated him on his accession to the imperial throne. Well-grounded suspicions of heterodoxy had caused this reserve, to which Gelasius alludes: "God forbid that a Roman prince should feel offended at the declaration of the truth! There are two things, august emperor, whereby this world is governed, namely, the sacred authority of the Pontiffs and the royal power, wherein the weight of priestly authority is so much the greater, as in the divine judgment priests must render to the

Lord an account for kings themselves. For you know, most clement son, that although you preside over men, you devoutly bend the neck to the dispensers of the divine mysteries, and ask from them the means of salvation : and in the reception and proper administration of the heavenly sacraments, you know that you should be subject to them according to the religious rule, rather than preside over them. You are aware, then, that as to these things you depend on their judgment, and that they are not to be forced to compliance with your will. For if, as regards public order, the prelates of the Church, knowing that the empire has been confided to you by Divine Providence, obey your laws, lest they should appear to oppose your will in things of this world, with what affection should you obey them, who are appointed to dispense the awful mysteries! Wherefore, as the Pontiffs incur a serious responsibility, if they suppress what they should declare for the honor of the Deity, so the danger is great of others who insolently refuse obedience. And if the hearts of the faithful should be submissive to all priests in general, who treat divine things properly, how much more should assent be yielded to the Prelate of this See, whom the Supreme Lord ordained to preside over all priests, and whom the piety of the Universal Church has always honored! You clearly understand that no one can, by any human device, oppose the prerogative or confession of him, whom the voice of Christ preferred to all others, whom the holy Church has always acknowledged, and whom she now devoutly regards as her Primate."*

This has been deservedly regarded as an admirable exposition of the relations of Catholic princes to the prelacy. The power of the prince is supreme in the civil order : the power of the Pontiff is supreme in things spiritual. The civil and the ecclesiastical powers are from God : the former by His implied sanction of the means for maintaining social order ; the latter by the direct institution of Christ. In both, the sovereignty of God must be honored. The civil power extends to all things necessary for the maintenance and welfare of society; but it cannot command any thing opposed to the divine law. The ecclesiastical authority is engaged in the promulgation of truth and the maintenance of discipline, with a due respect for public order, as regulated by the civil power. These principles were not lost sight of in the Middle Ages, since we find them set forth, in the very words of Gelasius, in a Council held at S. Macra in 881,† and in the Council of Trosley, in 909.‡ Gregory II., in 730, addressing Leo the Isaurian, bade him confine himself to the affairs of the empire, as the bishops applied all their solicitude to religious matters. " The bishops," he said, " being set over the churches, abstain from civil

---

* Gelasii, ep. iv., ad Anastasium, col. 893, t. ii., Hard.

† Conc. col. reg., vol. vi. col. 350. See also the letter of Stephen V. to the Emperor Basil, ib., col. 365.

‡ Ib., col. 307, cap. ii.

affairs; so let the emperors abstain in like manner from church matters, and apply to the things which are intrusted to their charge."

Catholic sovereigns, as members of the Church, are bound by her laws, and subject to the penalties which are attached to their transgression. The prince and the peasant, the master and the slave, share her privileges on the same conditions, and are liable to be deprived of them in punishment of infidelity or disobedience. Her arms are not carnal, but powerful before God—she strikes with the apostolic rod, chastising the children whom she loves with maternal fondness, that they may correct the evil of their ways, and prove themselves worthy of the heavenly inheritance. The Pope, as head on earth of the Church, exercises, by divine right, authority over Catholic princes in the things that are of salvation. When by flagrant crimes they cause the name of God to be blasphemed, he may admonish and reprove them, as Nathan reproved David by the divine command: and, in case of contumacy, he may inflict on them ecclesiastical censures. The exercise of this power peculiarly suits the Chief Bishop, since local prelates could scarcely venture to say to their prince, "Thou art the man!" The majesty of the sovereign is also guarded, by reserving cases in which he is concerned to the mature and unbiassed judgment of the Pontiff.

The means which, in the Middle Ages, were employed for the reformation of princes, after admonition and threats, was the actual infliction of ecclesiastical censures. These were of two kinds, interdict and excommunication. By the former the solemnities of public worship were suspended throughout the whole kingdom, the sacred functions of absolute necessity being, however, permitted at all times, and the mysteries privately celebrated. This interruption of religious worship, casting a gloom over the whole nation, was a significant expression of the horror of the Church for the crime of the sovereign, in which respect it served as a reparation of the scandal. It was hoped, also, that by the general affliction which it occasioned, he would be awakened to a sense of his misconduct, and that he would, by speedy repentance, ward off any personal censure. The clouds which thickened around the throne foreboded the thunderbolt which was soon to fall on the impenitent monarch. When every other measure had failed to produce amendment, excommunication, the highest penalty which the Church can inflict, followed. By it the transgressor was cut off entirely from the communion of the faithful, and cast forth as a heathen and publican. Even as the incestuous Corinthian was delivered over by St. Paul to Satan for the destruction of the flesh, that the spirit might be saved in the day of Christ, the scandalous prince was deprived of all spiritual privileges, separated from the Church of God, and left to perish eternally, unless by repentance he atoned for his transgression. The infliction of this penalty was plainly within the sphere of ecclesiastical power, which can bind as well as loose, with the assurance that Heaven will ratify the just exercise of this spiritual authority. In the commencement of the sixth century, Pope Symmachus excommunicated the heretical Emperor Anastasius, whom his predecessor, Gelasius, had addressed in the solemn language of admonition. The success with which this power was exercised, is attested by Leibnitz: "It is beyond question that the Popes checked many disorders, by their efforts in season and out of season, remonstrating with princes, as their authority enabled them to do, and threatening them with ecclesiastical censures."*

Instances of this exercise of pontifical zeal abound in the history of the Church. CLEMENT IV., on learning the victory obtained by James, King of Aragon, over the Moors, congratulated with him, admonishing him at the same time to subdue his own passions, by putting away from him Berengaria, the object of unlawful attachment. The prince pleaded the infirmity of his wife, Therasia, and asked for a divorce. The reply of the Pontiff began with these words: "How shall the Vicar of God separate those whom God has united?" Subsequently, James, having communicated to Clement his determination to engage in the holy war, was again admonished by him to dismiss his concubine in the first place, since no effort of zeal could otherwise be acceptable to our Lord: "You cannot," he observes, "please our crucified Lord, or avenge His wrongs, if you will not abstain from offending Him. Moreover, we wish you to understand, that unless you obey our admonitions, we shall force you, by ecclesiastical censures, to dismiss her."†

Ladislaus, King of Pannonia,‡ giving himself over to unbridled licentiousness, after several solemn admonitions, was excommunicated by the legate of Martin IV. The nobles, indignant at his excesses, rose up against him, and drove away his concubines.§

In several instances injured queens found succor and protection from the father of the faithful, who, by the threat of ecclesiastical censures, forced their lord to restore to them their rights. Theutberge, the wife of Lothaire I., was divorced from her husband on an allegation of incest, which, although groundless, she was prevailed on to admit, and under this pretext the divorce was approved of in the local Councils of Metz and Aix-la-Chapelle. Even the legates of Nicholas I. were induced to sanction it: but the Pope himself nobly vindicated the cause of the calumniated queen; annulled the decrees of the Councils, and the acts of his legates; ordered the monarch, under penalty of excommunication, to dismiss Waldrade, his concubine, whom he had taken as a lawful wife; refused to give any credit to the forced confession of the queen, and successfully maintained her rights. Guizot remarks, that this exercise of

---

* Dissert. i., de act. publ. usu op. t. iv. p. 299. † Raynald, an. 12&.
‡ Now Sclavonia, and part of Hungary. § Ib., an. 1281.

18

pontifical supremacy was applauded by the nation generally, because it was well known to be founded on justice. It is no slight eulogium of the Holy See that it successfully supported the cause of an injured woman against a licentious and powerful prince. Celestine III., and his successor, Innocent III., with admirable constancy maintained the cause of Ingelburga, the wife of Philip Augustus.* Friendless in a foreign land, the object of aversion to him to whom she had plighted her affections, the unfortunate Danish princess felt that though France was false, her voice could reach her spiritual father, at whose rebuke the proudest monarchs trembled. After sixteen years of banishment from the palace, she was reinstated in her rights.

Philip I. of France, dismissing his lawful wife, gave to his people the enormous scandal of living in open adultery with Bertrade, who had forsaken her husband, Fulco, Count of Angiers. Urban II., first by his legate, and afterward in person, hurled excommunication against him in two successive Councils. The licentious prince soon presented himself as a penitent in the Council of Nemours, and obtained absolution, on putting away the object of his unlawful attachment. Having subsequently relapsed, he was punished with the same censure, from which he was again released by the authority of Paschal II., on appearing in an assembly of bishops, with bare feet, in the attitude of penance, and swearing on the holy gospels that he would shun all criminal intercourse, and all just occasion of suspicion. This was an act of homage to the Christian law—an atonement for its violation. It was well that the prince who had caused the name of Christ to be blasphemed, should sue for pardon, by making public acknowledgment of his sin, and giving satisfactory evidence of amendment. Hallam observes: "The submission of such a prince, not feebly superstitious, like his predecessor Robert, nor vexed with seditions, like the Emperor Henry IV., but brave, firm, and victorious, is perhaps the proudest trophy in the scutcheon of Rome."†

In many instances the Popes inflicted censures on princes who violated the ecclesiastical law, by marrying within the forbidden degrees. The justice of this exercise of authority will strike only those who acknowledge the force of those laws. I would merely remark, that the princes were subject to them equally as the humblest of the faithful, and consequently liable to be punished by ecclesiastical censures for their violation. One end of these laws is to preserve the purity of morals, by taking away the hope of intermarriage from such as are placed in intimate relations in domestic life, by reason of kindred. If their force had not been maintained in regard to princes, as well as their subjects, not only would discipline have suffered, but Christian morals would have been

---

* See Life of Innocent III., by Hurter. While German Reformed Superintendent of Schaffhausen, in Switzerland, Hurter devoted twenty years of diligent research to the compilation of this splendid biography. † Middle Ages, ch. vii.

deeply injured. Robert, King of France, was commanded by Gregory V. in the Roman council, in 998, to separate from Berta, his blood-relation, under penalty of anathema. The prince yielded to the threat. "It is known," says Michaud, "that the excommunication fulminated against Philip I., as well as others subsequently hurled against Louis VII. and Philip Augustus, were in a great measure grounded on the violation of the laws of marriage. It may then be observed that the power of the Popes served to maintain the sanctity of an institution which is the first basis of society. In barbarous ages, what other barrier could be opposed to licentiousness in a contract in which the passions have so great a share?"*

§ 2.—IN SECULAR CONCERNS.

Nothing is more remarkable in the history of the Middle Ages, than the interference of the Popes in the controversies of princes and the internal dissensions of kingdoms and republics. To understand this phenomenon, we must take into consideration the position which they occupied in regard to the temporal powers. The conversion of princes to Christianity disposed them to regard with reverence the teaching of the Church, and to seek counsel and direction in the moral difficulties which occurred in the exercise of the governing power. They felt bound to use it conformably to the laws of God and of His Church, and pledged themselves to do so by the oath of coronation. When they bowed to receive their diadems from the consecrated hands of the Pontiff, they regarded themselves as exercising, with dependence on the King of kings, a delegated sovereignty. The independent action of the Bishop of Rome, freed from the yoke of Eastern emperors, and endowed with a considerable principality, was rendered sacred by his spiritual supremacy. The memory of the glories of ancient Rome was almost obliterated, since barbarian hordes had overrun her territories, and all was confusion and disorder, when Leo III., at the opening of the ninth century, felt himself impelled to call Charlemagne to the imperial throne. At the unexpected salutation given to the prince, amid the solemnities of mass, at the altar of St. Peter's, thousands of Romans and strangers re-echoed with deafening acclamations: "Long live the august emperor of the Romans!" All regarded the act as inspired, and doubted not that order and harmony would arise from chaos, at the bidding of the holy Pontiff. From that time the Bishop of Rome necessarily enjoyed an immense influence over the empire, and the kingdoms which arose under its shadow; and he was regarded by princes and people as their father and

---

* Histoire des Croisades, l. i. n, 102.

judge.* He created the new order of things, assigning to each potentate his place in the political world, and controlling by laws the movements of each, in order to maintain the general harmony. His relations to the empire were most direct, since he determined who should elect the emperor, and enjoyed the right of examining whether the individual chosen was admissible. The power exercised by the Popes in designating the emperor, and giving the royal title to the chiefs of various nations, in a word, regulating the whole political order, cannot fairly be branded as an usurpation, since it was vested in them by the force of circumstances; their spiritual office placing them at the head of the Christian world, and inspiring confidence in the justice and wisdom of their acts. It was not a result of positive concessions made by the respective nations, although it was acquiesced in and confirmed by the free and frequent acts of people and princes. Neither was it a divine prerogative of their office; but it naturally grew out of their ecclesiastical relations to the body of Christians, and was strengthened and sustained by their sacred character. The imperfect civilization of the Northern nations converted to the faith, after their invasion of the Southern provinces of Europe, rendered it necessary for them to be guided and directed, and disposed them to regard with reverence the acts of that authority which their Christian teachers had led them to consider as supreme in the things of salvation. Thus, without effort, the Popes found themselves invested with a kind of temporal supremacy, and enabled to bestow crowns and sceptres, while they themselves possessed only a small principality, which was embarrassed or controlled by a municipal administration, and often wrested from their hands. It so happened that the authority of the Pope was invoked in support of the reigning princes, or to recall them to duty: and his tribunal was regarded as the supreme court of the Christian confederacy. It seemed a common instinct of all Christian nations to appeal to his justice, for the redress of every grievance for which the local authority proved insufficient, and to implore his power for the punishment of those whose station placed them beyond the reach of municipal law. He was, in fact, by common consent, judge, not only in causes strictly ecclesiastical, or in the private concerns of obscure individuals, but in civil matters, where flagrant wrongs were perpetrated by crowned heads. He was called on to interpose his authority: he was blamed if he hesitated: he was feared by delinquents of every class, by the haughty baron and proud emperor, as well as by the humble vassal; and when the thunder of his censure rolled, the prison doors flew open, the hand of avarice let fall the wages of injustice, and the knees of the oppressor beat together.

It is certainly in the power of nations to constitute a supreme tribunal to adjust their controversies; and the fact of its establishment is equally

---

* See Manuel d'Histoire du Moyen Age, par J. Moëller. Vol. i. ch. viii. § ii. p. 118.

proved by their acts, as by any formal compact. If they thereby parted with any portion of their sovereignty and independence, it was with great advantage to their common interests. Voltaire himself has remarked, that "the interest of mankind requires a restraint on sovereigns, and protection for their subjects: this power might be in the hands of the Popes, in virtue of a universal compact. The Pontiffs, interfering in temporal disputes only with a view to settle them, admonishing kings and nations of their duties, reproving their crimes, reserving excommunications for great enormities, would have been always regarded as holding the place of God on earth; but men now prefer to have the laws and usages of their country as their only protection, although the laws are frequently disregarded, and corrupt usages prevail."* "We must," says Saint-Priest, "agree with the Roman school, that the temporal power of the Holy See was far less the result of usurpation, than a consequence of the policy, or rather of the false position of princes. The secular powers themselves, in their rivalries, wars, remorses, and scruples, invoked pontifical intervention, and sought its support sometimes for their inferiority in arms, sometimes for their trepidation and weakness of mind."† We may be allowed to think that the position thus taken was at once natural and advantageous to society, since it was conformable to the relations in which the princes already stood in the spiritual order, and it was calculated to bring about an amicable adjustment of dangerous controversies, and prevent the horrors of war, into which nations are so often plunged by the temerity of their rulers. What diplomacy effects in modern times by management and mutual concession, was accomplished in the Middle Ages by the judgment and persuasion of the father of princes and people. Michaud, the recent historian of the Crusades, says: "Complaints were sometimes made of the injustice of the judgment pronounced by the head of the Church, but his right to judge Christian princes was scarcely called in question, and the nations almost uniformly received his judgments without a murmur."‡

---

* This extraordinary avowal is made in reference to the penance performed by Henry II. for having given occasion to the assassination of St. Thomas Becket. The reader will be pleased to read the original words: "Il devait se repentir d'un assassinat; l'intérêt du genre humain demande un frein qui retienne les souverains, et qui mette à couvert la vie des peuples. Ce frein de la religion aurait pû être par une convention universelle dans la main des Papes, comme nous l'avons déjà remarqué. Ces premiers pontifes en ne se mêlant des querelles temporelles que pour les appaiser, en avertissant les rois et les peuples de leurs devoirs, en reprenant leurs crimes, en réservant les excommunications pour les grands attentats, auraient toujours été regardés comme des images de Dieu sur la terre; mais les hommes sont réduits à n'avoir pour leur défense que les loix et les mœurs de leur pays: loix souvent méprisées, et mœurs souvent corrompues." Essai sur l'Histoire Générale, ch. xliv. t. ii.
† Histoire de la Royauté, vol. ii. lviii. p. 359.
‡ Hist. des Croisades, t. iv. p. 163.

It may be proper to give instances of the eagerness with which princes sought from the Popes the recognition of their royal titles, or to be promoted to the royal dignity, and of the submission which they professed to the pontifical authority. John VIII. reminds Michael, King of the Bulgarians, that, on embracing Christianity, he submitted to the government of Peter the apostle, and of his successors, and promised obedience.* St. Stephen, King of Hungary, acknowledged to have received his crown and title from Sylvester II. Alphonsus, Duke of Portugal, received the royal title from Alexander III., in reward of his exploits against the Arabs. Premislaus was recognised as King of Bohemia by Innocent III., at the solicitation of the Emperor Otho. Calo-Joannes obtained from the same Pontiff the crown and title of King of the Bulgarians. Peter of Aragon was not content with the title which his predecessors had borne, but asked of Innocent to be solemnly crowned, that a religious sanction might be given to his authority. Stephen, on succeeding to the crown of England, swore to preserve the liberty of the Church, and avowed that he had been chosen king with the assent of the clergy and the people, and had been confirmed in the kingdom by Innocent, Pontiff of the Holy Roman See.† Theobald, King of Navarre, asked of Alexander IV. the privilege of being anointed king with the solemn rite prescribed by the Church; which being granted, he afterward sought permission for his successors to use the royal title, when in accordance with the national usage they should be chosen to occupy the throne, being raised on a shield, or on the shoulders of men, before the unction was performed.

The King of Servia, on abandoning schism, sent an embassy to Honorius III. to obtain the pontifical recognition of his royal title. This act was intended to secure to the prince his proper place in the great Christian confederacy. Addressing the Pontiff, he says: "As all Christians love and honor you, and regard you as their father and lord, so we desire to be styled a child of the holy Roman Church, and your child; being anxious that the blessing and confirmation of God, and yours, should always be manifest on our crown and land."‡ Daniel, Duke of Russia, in 1246, obtained the royal crown and title from the legate of Innocent IV. The princes were not insensible of their titles to royal power, as derived from descent, conquest, or popular will; but they felt the advantage of the Pontiff's sanction and recognition, in reference to other sovereigns and to their own people; and they sought for a divine blessing through his ministry. Thus Branimer, a Sclavonian prince, having professed fidelity and obedience to blessed Peter, John VIII., on the feast of our Lord's Ascension, pronounced a solemn blessing on him and on his people, at the altar of St. Peter.§

---

* Ep. lxxv., ad Michaelem regem Bulg. † Baron., an. 1135, p. 341.
‡ Raynald, an. 1220. § Ep. lxxxii. lxxxiii.

Many princes, from a feeling of devotion to the Holy See, freely offered themselves as vassals of St. Peter, which, according to the notions then prevalent, implied no degradation, but rather independence of the imperial power, with a nominal subjection to the Pontiff. The Normans manifested a desire to return to the obedience of the Holy See, as a means of securing their independence of the empire. St. Gregory VII. wrote to Wifred of Milan: "Be it known to you, then, that the Normans are making to us overtures of peace, which they would most willingly have concluded ere this, and have given full satisfaction to Blessed Peter, whom alone, after the Lord, they desire to have for their lord and emperor, had we assented to their petition in certain particulars."* "We suppose that you well know," says he to Grusa, Duke of Hungary, "that the kingdom of Hungary, as also other most noble kingdoms, should enjoy independence, and be subject to the king of no other realm, but only to the holy and universal Church of Rome, our mother, who does not treat her subjects as slaves, but embraces all as children."† The apostolic King of Hungary gloried in this vassalage: the King of Portugal made his dominions tributary: the King of Aragon swore fealty: the King of Dalmatia paid tribute to the Pope as liege lord: and Stephen, and Henry II. of England, before the humiliation of John, acknowledged that England was a fief of the Holy See. It is not just to form to ourselves a false idea of this dependence, and thence to take occasion to despise the princes who acknowledged it, and to censure the Popes who enforced it. It consisted chiefly in the payment of a small annual pension toward the general fund, for the most important wants of the Church, and in the manifestation of greater zeal for the defence of the Holy See, when assailed by powerful enemies. It disposed the prince to listen with docility to the admonitions of the Pontiff, in behalf of religion and of the people, and it procured for him pontifical influence and protection, when the royal authority was assailed by rebels, or by rival princes. When Waldemar, King of Denmark, a vassal of the Holy See, was thrown into prison by Henry, Count of Zeverin, Honorius III., at the instance of the prelates and nobles, interposed his authority to rescue the king, and urged the emperor, Frederick, to come to his relief, beseeching him, however, to spare the life of the rebel count.‡ John, of England, got the support of Innocent against the revolted barons: whose just claims the Pontiff, nevertheless, promised to sustain, if they would consent to lay down their arms. In Sicily, and other original possessions of the Holy See, greater authority was claimed by the Pope, as liege lord; but in kingdoms voluntarily made feudatory, the dependence was almost nominal. Even Hallam avows the favorable influence of this subjection: "Peter, King of Aragon, received at Rome the belt of knighthood, and the royal crown, from the hands of Innocent III.; he

---

* Ep. xv. l. iii.   † Ep. lxiii. l. ii.   ‡ Raynald., an. 1223.

took an oath of perpetual fealty and obedience to him and his successors; he surrendered his kingdom, and accepted it again to be held by an annual tribute, in return for the protection of the Apostolic See. This strange conversion of kingdoms into spiritual fiefs was intended as the price of security from ambitious neighbors, and may be deemed analogous to the change of allodial into feudal, or more strictly to that of lay into ecclesiastical tenure, which was frequent during the turbulence of the darker ages."*

Although the social relations of the Popes to the secular powers gave occasion to their interference in temporal controversies, yet they did not act as temporal superiors, but they availed themselves of their position to apply the maxims of the Christian law to the subjects in dispute, and used their spiritual authority to enforce their judgment by ecclesiastical censures. The principles on which they acted were distinctly stated by Innocent III., when Philip of France resisted his interference, to stop the ravages of war between him and Richard Cœur de Lion. Disclaiming distinctly all right to judge of the title to the fief in dispute,† he insisted that he was authorized to take away the privileges of ecclesiastical communion, from a prince who wantonly shed human blood, while he could obtain his just demands by amicable arbitration: "No one doubts," he says, "that it belongs to our office to judge of the things which appertain to the salvation or damnation of the soul. Is it not deserving of eternal damnation, and of the loss of eternal life, to nourish discord, to attack those who are of the household of the faith, to destroy religious establishments, to give over to pillage the property destined for the wants and advantage of religious men, to oppress virgins consecrated to God?" "Hearken, then, dearly beloved son, not to our word, but rather to the word of the Word, which was in the beginning with God, and which finally was made flesh, and dwelt among us: 'If thy brother sin against thee, go and reprove him between him and thee alone. If he will not hear thee, take with thee two or three, that in the mouth of two or three witnesses every word may stand. But if he will not hear them, tell the Church; and if he will not hear the Church, let him be to thee as the heathen and publican.' Behold! the King of England, your brother, brother not by carnal kindred, but in the unity of faith, complains that you sin against him, and stretch forth your hands to injure him, as you have already done; he has rebuked you already between him and you alone, both by letters and by word of mouth, not once, but frequently, and warned you to desist from injuring him. He has taken with him not merely two or three witnesses, but many nobles, to renew the bonds of peace which were broken, and to use their influence to induce you to

---

* Middle Ages, ch. vii.

† "Non ratione feudi, cujus ad eum spectat judicium, sed occasione peccati, cujus ad nos pertinet sine dubitatione censura." Ep. clxvi., apud Raynald, an. 1203.

desist from wrong. But inasmuch as hitherto he has not succeeded with your highness, he has denounced you to the Church, as sinning against him: and the Church has chosen to address you with maternal affection, rather than to use her judicial power, and therefore she has not authoritatively rebuked you—but mildly admonished you to desist from injuring your brother, and to make with him a lasting peace, or, at least, a truce. What, then, remains, if you refuse to hear the Church, as hitherto you have refused, but, it pains us to say it, to regard you as a heathen and a publican, and to shun you after the first and second rebuke? If we must offend either you or God, we choose rather to appease Him, although we incur your displeasure, than please an earthly king by offending the Divine Ruler.—Shall we hesitate to proceed according to the commandment of the Lord, when we shall have more fully investigated the case, and ascertained the truth? Shall we dissemble the carnage of bodies and ruin of souls, and not declare to the wicked their impiety, and restrain the violent from outrage?"* Honorius III., in 1225, insisted that, as sovereign Pontiff, he had a right to extirpate mortal sin, even when committed by kings.† Even Boniface VIII. rejected, as an absurd calumny, the charge of his having alleged that the King of France held the crown by his concession, or was dependent on him in the civil government, and observed that his studies of jurisprudence during fifty years would not suffer him to entertain so strange a pretension: but he added that the king himself could not deny that, in what regarded sin, he was subject to the high authority of the Pontiff.‡

These views were generally entertained, so that sovereigns themselves put them forward with the greatest earnestness, when they found it necessary to implore pontifical authority against other princes. Richard Cœur de Lion, on his return from Palestine, was treacherously arrested by the Duke of Austria, and thrown into prison. His mother, Queen Eleanor, appealed to Celestine III. to use his spiritual sword, in order to force the duke to relax his grasp. She was confident that her son would be set at liberty, if Celestine menaced to strike with excommunication those who held him a prisoner. Accordingly, Leopold, Duke of Austria, was subjected to this penalty, with which even the emperor and King of France were threatened, being understood to have concurred in the arrest. These measures resulted in the liberation of the captive prince. King Richard himself, when set at liberty, implored the pontifical power for the liberation of his hostages, and induced Celestine to issue an excommunication against the Duke of Austria, and all others who had concurred in his imprisonment, contrary to the security guaranteed to the Crusaders.§ The request was complied with, and the Bishop of Verona was directed by the Pope to issue the sentence, which, however, failed to

---

* Apud Raynald, an. 1203. † Ep. 169, Rai., n. 30.
‡ See Pagi, Brev. Gest. Rom. Pont., vol. iii. p. 540. § Baron., an. 1195, p. 886.

move the duke, until an accident brought him to the verge of eternity, when he humbly submitted to the Papal injunctions.

This may imply authority at all times in secular concerns, as far as they involve moral principle, to be enforced by ecclesiastical censures. The divine law, doubtless, embraces all classes of men, princes and people, and all varieties of human actions, political as well as personal. The chief Pastor of the Church is placed on his high eminence, to proclaim the command of God, and in His name to instruct in justice those that judge the earth. As expounder of the moral law, he speaks to all with power and authority, condemning all that God has forbidden, and inculcating the observance of each divine commandment. He can cast forth from the Church every one, prince or subject, who is notoriously guilty of flagrant immorality, if he will not yield to paternal admonition. But secular concerns are not, of themselves, subject to his cognizance: and the complicated social relations which arise from the free acts of individuals, or from public law, or from the action of the civil authorities, are not the matter of his judgment, unless where they involve a violation of the great principles of Christian morality. In the Middle Ages, kings and nations implored his judgment, and consequently brought within the sphere of his authority those secular transactions and controversies, of which otherwise he might have said, in the words of our Redeemer, to those who called for his interference: "Who hath appointed me judge over you?"* Whencesoever the conviction of his right to take cognizance of them may be supposed to have arisen, it was universally admitted, and it was consequently a part of the public and common law of nations. Guizot testifies that it was generally believed, in the middle of the ninth century, that he was above temporal governments, even in temporal affairs, when connected with religion:† he might have qualified it by adding, in their moral aspect, since he observes that it was by developing the principles of morality ecclesiastics exercised power over governments.

The key to the whole history of the Middle Ages appears to us to be the sentiment then prevailing, that Christian principle should regulate all the departments of government and all the relations of life. We do not think that the authority of the Popes over sovereigns is to be accounted for, merely by reason of the relations in which they actually stood to them, or of the concessions which had been made by former princes. On the contrary, we trace those concessions and relations to the persuasion which was universal, that the head of the Christian Church was the fittest arbiter of the respective obligations of princes and their subjects, and the natural judge of all, in what regarded the application of the Christian maxims to society.

---

* Luke xii. 14. † Cours d'Histoire Moderne, t. iii. p. 81.

CHAPTER III.

Peace Tribunal.

PHILANTHROPISTS often speculate on the propriety of establishing a peace tribunal, to settle, without "the proud control of fierce and bloody war," the various controversies which may arise among nations: yet they seldom reflect that such a tribunal existed in the Middle Ages, in the person of the Roman Pontiff. The warlike spirit of the Northern barbarians, which still survived in their descendants, should be understood, in order fully to appreciate the services which the Popes, in restraining it, rendered to society. Their efforts were not always successful, but their merit was not on that account the less in endeavoring to stem the torrent of human passion; and their success was sufficient to entitle them to the praise of having effectually labored to substitute moral and religious influence for brute force. As ministers of the Prince of peace, they often interposed spontaneously, and with arms powerful before God opposed the crowned marauder, who rushed forward to shed human blood. The fathers of the Council of Rheims, in 1119, under the presidency of Calistus II., were engaged in ecclesiastical deliberations, when the Pontiff communicated to them overtures of peace, which had reached him from Henry V. He informed them that he must repair to the place which the emperor had appointed for an interview, promising to return to close the Council: "Afterward," said he, "I shall wait on the King of England, my god-child and relative, and exhort him and Count Theobald, his nephew, and others who are at variance, to come to a reconciliation, that each, for the love of God, may do justice to the other, and according to the law of God, all of them being pacified, may abandon war, and with their subjects enjoy the security of perfect peace. But such as obey not our admonitions, and continue to disturb the public peace, I will strike with the awful sentence of anathema."[*] The benevolent intentions of the Pontiff were defeated for a time by the wiles and machinations of the fifth Henry, who, however, after many vain struggles against the authority of the Church, at length renounced his pretensions to the right of investing prelates with their sacred office by delivering to them the ring and crosier, the symbols of ecclesiastical

---

[*] Conc. Rhemens. acta, col. 241, t. xxi., coll. Mansi.

authority, and was content with giving them the temporal appanage of their office by stretching toward them the royal sceptre. Thus, in the year 1123, was happily terminated the strife between the Popes and emperors, which had fiercely raged during half a century.

In the same venerable assembly appeared Louis the Fat, King of France, surrounded by his nobles; and having advanced forward to the platform on which the Pope was enthroned, he urged his complaint against the English king: "I come," he said, "with my barons, to this holy assembly to seek counsel, my lord the Pope: and you, reverend prelates, hear me. The King of England has violently invaded Normandy, a province of my kingdom: he has treated in a detestable manner Duke Robert, his own brother and my vassal, whom he has seized, and at this time actually holds prisoner. I have frequently demanded his liberation, through bishops and counts, whom I sent to him for this object, but all without effect. William, the son of the captive duke, stands here before you, despoiled of the inheritance of his father."* This address shows the confidence with which sovereigns themselves appealed to the Pontiff, in the most solemn circumstances, to obtain through his influence what might not be otherwise hoped for, without the shedding of much blood.

Long before this period, the mediatorial offices of the Pope were sought by princes unable to resist the superior force which threatened them. In the year 787, Thassilo, Duke of Bavaria, implored Adrian I. to intercede with Charlemagne, and obtain for him equitable terms. The charity of the Pontiff led him to accept the commission; but when the ambassadors of the duke professed themselves unauthorized to accede to the conditions which were agreed on with the emperor, Adrian judged that he could employ the censures of the Church against him, on account of his bad faith, and declared that the monarch would be guiltless of the blood which might be shed in chastising the perfidious prince. While the imperial troops beseiged the capital of Hungary, the king, Andrew, sought the mediation of St. Leo IX. The Pontiff willingly undertook the journey to Germany, in order to procure peace, which, however, the jealousy of some courtiers or the fickleness of the king prevented.†

Gregory IV., on presenting himself to Louis, against whom Lothaire, his son and colleague in the empire, had revolted, protested that he came only to restore peace, which our Divine Redeemer wished to be maintained by all His disciples. The refusal of the emperor to come to an accommodation, led to the defection of his troops, which forced him to abandon the contest.

The Emperor Henry II. complained to the Council of Tours, over which Victor II. presided, that Ferdinand, King of Spain, took on him-

---

* Ibidem, col. 238.

† Wibert in vita S. Leonis, l. ii. c. 8. Herman Contractus throws the blame on the king.

self the imperial title. The Council menaced to excommunicate the king, and lay the kingdom under interdict, if he did not abandon his pretensions: to which he accordingly consented, declaring his entire submission to the judgment of the Apostolic See. On the death of the emperor, great apprehensions were entertained of disturbances on the part of several princes, to avert which the Pope, to whom the emperor, when dying, had intrusted the charge of his son, a youth, assembled a Council at Cologne, and gained over Baldwin and Godfrey, and effectually prevented civil war. Thus he successfully employed his influence and authority to preserve peace.

It was at the instance of Paschal II. that St. Anselm used his best efforts to bring about an amicable settlement between Henry I. of England, and his brother Robert, who, by right of seniority, claimed the crown. When every overture for peace was rejected, the prelate, on the eve of battle, exhorted the nobles to be true to their allegiance, which they had pledged to Henry, threatening Robert with excommunication if he continued to disturb the public peace. These measures proved effectual, the prince choosing rather to forego his claim than fall under the censures of the Church, by engaging in a bloody contest.

On occasion of war between the republics of Genoa and Pisa, Innocent II. repaired to the latter city, and summoned thither the reprentatives of the Genoese interests, who, together with the Pisans, swore to abide by his commands, and accordingly made peace. Clement III. sent a cardinal legate to Henry II. of England and Louis VI. of France, exhorting them to peace, in order to unite in the effort to liberate the Holy Land. Entreaty, persuasion, and threats were successively employed, until at length the princes consented to abide by the judgment of the legate, and of four archbishops, two on the part of each king. In proceeding to the adjudication of this controversy, the judges threatened to excommunicate any one who should strive to prevent the conclusion of peace.

Innocent III., in the Council of Lateran, enjoined a general peace among all Christians, for four years at least.* He fell sick unto death on a journey which he undertook with a view to induce the Pisans, Genoese, and Lombards, to make peace, and unite in the Crusade. When James, King of Aragon, had made war on Simon, Count of Montfort, Honorius III. despatched ambassadors to enjoin peace, offering to take cognizance of the causes of dispute, if the parties would submit them to the apostolic judgment, and threatening them with anathema in case they persevered in the war. Honorius III. sent a legate to Louis VIII. of France, to induce him to make a truce with Henry, King of England, which, however, he failed to accomplish. He strictly forbade Henry to attack Louis while engaged in the Albigensian war.

---

* Expeditio pro recup. terra sancta.

JOHN XXI. exerted all his influence with Philip, King of France, and Alphonsus, King of Castile, to produce a reconciliation between them, that both princes might unite in succoring the Eastern Christians. To the former he wrote in these terms: "We admonish, ask, and earnestly exhort and beseech your royal highness, by the sprinkling of the blood of Jesus Christ, attentively to reflect that the execution of the affairs connected with the divine glory, in which you are to be the chief actor, is impeded by this misunderstanding, and to turn to meekness what seems disposed to anger, and prepare and change your royal mind to the good of peace, and unity of concord." The Pontiff proffered his kind offices to settle the matters in dispute: "If any dispute shall remain between you and the aforesaid king, the solicitude of the Apostolic See will not be wanting; she offers herself, without sparing labor, to extinguish, to the utmost of her power, all matter of disagreement between you and the aforesaid king, and to procure and maintain unity with great care."* He authorized his legate to restrain by ecclesiastical censures both kings, or whichever should attack the other.

Nicholas III. urged Michael Palæologus, the Greek emperor, Charles, King of Sicily, and the Emperor Philip, to submit their disputes to his decision, rather than engage in war.† By his persuasion Rodulph, King of the Romans,‡ made peace with Charles, King of Sicily, and yielded to him Provence, saving the rights of Margaret, Queen of the French.

Edward of England, and Philip the Fair of France, being engaged in war, Boniface VIII. sent ambassadors, most earnestly exhorting them to peace. He authorized the legates to threaten the infliction of censures, should they persist; declaring it to be unworthy of Christian princes to lead their subjects to mutual slaughter. What to us may appear strange, is, that the Pontiff took upon himself to order a truce to be observed for a year between the contending princes, and prolonged it for two years, under penalty of excommunication.§ The attempt to interfere with the military operations of sovereigns, is an extraordinary instance of ecclesiastical power; but it was then thought that the penalty of exclusion from the Church might be inflicted by her ruler on princes acknowledging her authority, who recklessly sacrificed human life in a contest, which, during the suspension of hostilities, might be amicably adjusted. Both kings, in fact, sent commissioners to Rome to represent their respective rights, and the Pontiff pronounced judgment between them, dis-

---

* Apud Rayn., an. 1276. † Ibidem, an. 1278.

‡ This title was given to the emperor elect, before his coronation. Speaking of the right over Italy acquired by the emperor chosen by the German princes, Hallam says: "It was an equally fundamental rule, that the elected King of Germany could not assume the title of Roman emperor until his consecration by the Pope. The middle appellation of King of the Romans, was invented as a sort of approximation to the imperial dignity." Middle Ages, p. i. ch. iii.

§ Apud Rayn., an. 1296.

pensing, at the same time, in the ecclesiastical laws, that their reconciliation might be insured by intermarriage of the English king and his son with the sister and daughter of the French monarch. With threats of censure, Boniface likewise commanded Adolphus, King of the Romans, to desist from hostilities against Philip, and urged the three princes to submit their disputes to the pontifical decision. He was entirely successful in his efforts to reconcile Charles II., King of Sicily, with James of Aragon. When the Venetians and Genoese threatened each other with war, Boniface enjoined a truce, that their mutual complaints might be heard by him, and adjusted without bloodshed. The Venetians acquiesced in the proposal, in despite of which the Genoese made hostile demonstrations, which the Pontiff left the more docile Venetians free to repel.

Oftentimes both parties simultaneously invoked the pontifical judgment, making the Pope umpire for the termination of their disputes. Thus Honorius III. was called on to judge between Frederick II. and various cities of Lombardy, and he succeeded in effecting a reconciliation. When the war had broken out anew, through the perfidy of the emperor, Gregory IX., who then occupied the papal chair, acted in the capacity of pacific judge, providing with paternal solicitude for the imperial interests, and for the security of the cities.

The Pontiff was sometimes implored by the legitimate claimant of a throne to use his spiritual authority against an unlawful aspirant. At the solicitation of Louis II., the legal heir of the kingdom of his deceased brother, Adrian II. threatened the nobles with censure, should they favor the usurpation of Charles, the uncle of the deceased sovereign.* John VIII., in like manner, came to the aid of Charles the Bald, when his dominions were invaded by his brother Louis, and commanded the bishops, under pain of anathema, to use their influence to prevent further depredations. This interference was in accordance with the general feeling of the age, which regarded the act of the Pontiff as a declaration of right, by which even a weak prince was supported in his struggle against superior force, and a powerful monarch received moral strength in public opinion, which could not be derived from mere success on the field of battle.

When nations were involved in the horrors of civil war, or were threatened with them, the religious influence of the Pontiff was often implored by sovereigns and subjects to restore order, and secure the rights of all. King Louis of France complained to the bishops assembled in Council, in the year 948, at Ingilenheim, under the presidency of the Pope's legate, of the revolt and usurpation of Hugh, Count of Paris: against whom the fathers, in conformity with the fourth Council of Toledo, threatened excommunication, if he persisted in his rebellion.†

---

* Fleury, Hist. Eccl., l. li. an. 869.   † Conc. col. reg., vol. vi. col. 605.

Pope Agapetus, in a Roman Council, confirmed their sentence. Not long before, Stephen IX. had used his influence and authority successfully to induce the French nobles to return to the obedience of Louis VI., against whom they had revolted. In this he followed the maxims of the apostles, who taught men to obey their rulers, even if personally unworthy; and his remonstrances were listened to the more patiently and respectfully, because he addressed them as the common father of all, not as a royal partisan, and employed his influence in their behalf, to obtain for them justice and pardon from the sovereign.

Henry II., on the rebellion of his son, sought the interposition of Alexander III., avowing himself a vassal of the Holy See: "Since God has raised you to the eminence of the pastoral office, that you might give the knowledge of salvation to His people, although I be absent in body, yet present in spirit, I prostrate myself at your knees, demanding salutary counsel. The kingdom of England is of your jurisdiction, and to you alone I am responsible, and am bound as to what regards the obligation of feudatory right. Let England see the power of the Roman Pontiff; and since he does not employ material arms, let him defend the patrimony of blessed Peter with the spiritual sword."* The Pope accordingly issued an excommunication against all who should disturb the king's peace. Clement IV. succeeded in bringing to an amicable issue a strife of long continuance between Bela, King of Hungary, and his son Stephen, and united them in lasting peace.

It is plain that the pontifical interference, when thus invoked by princes or their subjects, was calculated to remedy grievances in a manner most consistent with the general interests. The monarch, however powerful, could not hope to crush by force his subjects, when sustained by the moral influence of the Pontiff; and a feeble prince was protected by the shield of religion, against the violence of a rampant nobility or a restless people. Between sovereigns accustomed to decide their disputes on the battle-field, his interposition, as the common father of princes, was calculated to prevent a recourse to arms. His judgment being regarded as the expression of right, gave a moral support to the just cause: it served

> "To give us warrant from the hand of Heaven,
> And on our actions set the name of right
> With holy breath."†

Leibnitz regarded this mediatorial office of the Pope as one among the most beautiful evidences of Christian influence on society, and expressed the desire, which, however, he did not hope to see realized, that a peace tribunal were established anew at Rome, with the Pontiff as its president, that the controversies of princes and the internal dissensions of nations

---

* Baron., an. 1173, p. 60. † King John.—Shakspeare.

might, under the mild influence of religion, be decided without bloodshed. "Since we are allowed to indulge fancy, why," says he, "should we not cherish an idea that would renew among us the golden age?"*

In order to judge rightly of these acts, it should be remembered, that the Christian nations of Europe, in consequence of their common faith, became almost insensibly a great confederacy, bound together by stronger ties than any conventional compact. "The nations belonging to the Roman communion appeared to be one great republic."† The integrity of Christian faith was its fundamental law, the violation of which was punished with expulsion from the confederacy. The Pope was charged to watch over its observance, and in case of the apostasy of any inferior lord, to declare the forfeiture which he had incurred, and to proclaim that his territory might be seized by any Catholic potentate. The action of the Pontiff, in such case, was not an exercise of his primatial authority, farther than his sentence determined the guilt of heresy: it proceeded from a power attached to his office by general consent for the interests of the Christian commonwealth. The penalty was specially enacted in reference to the Manichean heresy, which subverted public morals, as well as faith.

The fourth Council of Lateran, held in the year 1215, under Innocent III., decreed, that if a secular lord, after request made of him, and admonition given him by the Church, should neglect to clear his territory of *this heretical filth,* he should be excommunicated by the bishops of the province; and in case he continued contumacious under excommunication during an entire year, the Pope should be informed of it, that he might declare the vassals thenceforward free from their allegiance, and leave the territory open to be occupied by Catholics, who might drive away the heretics, and hold it by an unquestionable title, without prejudice to the rights of the liege lord. The same was to be observed in regard to such as had no principal lords,‡ that is, lords paramount. It is clear that the body of the enactment regards inferior and dependent lords. The tenure of their fiefs was thus limited, with the general consent of the secular powers present in the Council, which contained the representatives of the Emperor of Constantinople, and of the Kings of France, England, Hungary, Jerusalem, Aragon, and of many other sovereigns. The ravages of the Manichees, which are described by the fathers, appeared to require the concerted efforts of all the civil powers to suppress them, so that neglect to do so was deemed treason against the Christian confederacy. On this account it was punished with the forfeiture of feudal rights: and accordingly, in the Council itself, Innocent deprived the Count of Toulouse of his principality, and transferred it to Simon de Montfort, the

---

* Lettre II., à M. Grimaret, op. t. v. p. 65.
† Voltaire, Essai sur l'Histoire Générale, t. ii. ch. xlviii.
‡ Can. iii., apud Labbe, conc., t. xi. par. i. p. 147.

leader of the crusade against the Albigensians. Honorius III. justified himself by this enactment with Henry, King of England, for having called on Louis, King of France, to occupy the territory of the Count of Toulouse.* The enactment does not regard sovereigns, the clause which is attached to it being only designed to include allodial† proprietors, who were bound to no military service, or other feudal duty. It may be thought that the principle is equally applicable to sovereigns: but where penal laws are in question, it is not allowable to argue from parity of reason, and sovereigns are never understood to be embraced by general enactments, unless they be specially mentioned. The whole enactment is, indeed, founded on the principle that heresy—especially Manicheism—is a crime against Christian society, to be punished and extirpated by the civil authorities, which was undisputed in that age, when the violence and disorders of sectaries gave melancholy evidence of the anti-social character of their tenets.

It is undeniable that the Pontiffs sometimes invited sovereigns to aid in executing their sentences against other sovereigns, whose territories they encouraged them to invade. Postponing to another opportunity to explain the grounds on which this was done, I wish, at present, merely to meet the objection as regards their pacific character. Whenever war is necessary to vindicate the oppressed, and put a stop to outrage, its justice must be the apology of him who lends it his sanction. It is for the interests of peace and of humanity that a powerful monarch should interpose for the protection of the defenceless, and awe, by a formidable display of force, the tyrant who is deaf to paternal remonstrance. Of the Papal authority as exercised by the Gregories and Innocents, a recent writer says: "It bestowed order, civilization, and, as far as was possible in such fierce and warlike times, peace."‡

In connection with the office of the Pontiffs as pacificators, we may mention the restraints which they imposed on military operations. It would have been vain to enjoin on the nobles of those ages to abstain altogether from the use of arms, since mutual injuries provoked resistance and retaliation, and tribunals of justice were not at hand. Each baron exercised the rights of sovereignty, as far as his own interests were at stake, and undertook the redress of wrongs by the sword. The utmost which could be successfully attempted, was to restrain men from violence at certain times, and especially on days consecrated to religious duties: on this account Cardinal Hugo, in a Council held at Gerona in Spain, in the year 1068, by the authority of Alexander II., confirmed "the truce of God," as there observed, and extended it from the octave of Easter Sunday to the octave of Whitsuntide, requiring its observance during that period, as well as during Lent, under penalty of excommunication.

---

* Vide Fleury, Hist. Eccl., l. lxxix. § xxviii. † See Blackstone, l. ii. c. iv.
‡ London Quarterly, for February, 1836.

Urban II., likewise, in the Councils of Melfi and Clermont, confirmed, by his authority, the decrees of some bishops, who had enjoined a suspension of hostilities from Wednesday evening of each week until Monday morning, and during the whole of Advent and Lent. The wisdom of this ordinance is acknowledged by Mills, who observes: "The clergy did much toward accustoming mankind to prefer the authority of law to the power of the sword. At their instigation private wars ceased for certain periods, and on particular days, and the observance of *the Truce of God* was guarded by the terrors of excommunication and anathema. Christianity could not immediately and directly change the face of the world; but she mitigated the horrors of the times by infusing herself into warlike institutions."*

In 1187, during the pontificate of Gregory VIII., which did not last quite two months, the Cardinals, in order to promote the Crusade which was then undertaken, agreed, with the assent of the Pope, to establish a general peace between all Christian princes for seven years, subjecting to excommunication all who should violate it. The assumption of this power was in accordance with the general principles and usages of the Middle Ages, and was certainly favorable to the interests of humanity.

Hallam, although he regards the Papal interference as an usurpation, admits that the project of Gerohus, a writer who lived early in the twelfth century, to refer all disputes among princes to the Pope, was calculated to find favor with benevolent minds, sickened by the cupidity and oppression of princes. "No control but that of religion appeared sufficient to restrain the abuses of society; while its salutary influence had already been displayed both in the Truce of God, which put the first check on the custom of private war, and more recently in the protection afforded to Crusaders against all aggression during the continuance of their engagement. There were certainly some instances where the temporal supremacy of Innocent III., however usurped, may appear to have been exerted beneficially. He directs one of his legates to compel the observance of peace between the Kings of Castile and Portugal, if necessary, by excommunication and interdict."†

It may surprise the reader to learn that an improvement in the laws of war, which John Adams, Benjamin Franklin, and Thomas Jefferson, as American commissioners, proposed to the Prussian minister, in the year 1784, was anticipated, more than six hundred years, by Innocent II., in the Council of Lateran. Using the civil influence with which he found himself invested, he decreed that "priests, monks, strangers, merchants, peasants, going or returning, or employed in labors of husbandry, and the animals with which they plough, and which carry the seeds to the field, should be secured from all molestation."‡ The proposition of the

---

* History of Crusades, ch. i. p. 22. † Middle Ages, ch. vii.
‡ Cap. Innovamus II., de Treuga et Pace.

commissioners was "to improve the laws of war, by a mutual stipulation not to molest non-combatants, as cultivators of the earth, fishermen, merchants, and traders in unarmed ships, and artists and mechanics, inhabiting and working in open towns."* Another instance may be added, in which the humane and enlightened views of the Popes anticipated and surpassed some of the modern improvements on the laws of war. Paschal II., in a Council held at Troyes, in 1107, decreed that in war houses should not be set on fire.† It is now deemed unlawful wantonly to destroy public buildings. Chancellor Kent truly observes, that "the history of Europe, during the early periods of modern history, abounds with interesting and strong cases, to show the authority of the Church over turbulent princes and fierce warriors, and the effect of that authority in meliorating manners, checking violence, and introducing a system of morals which inculcated peace, moderation, and justice."‡

---

* Kent's Comm., vol. i. p. 91. Note. † Chronic. Malleacense.
‡ Commentaries on American Law, by James Kent. Lecture

CHAPTER IV.

Deposing Power.

§ 1.—ORIGIN OF THE POWER.

WHOEVER is at all acquainted with the history of the Middle Ages, cannot be ignorant of the political influence which the bishops exercised, conjointly with the secular nobility. This arose from the religious feeling of the people, which disposed them to respect their judgment, rather than from the temporal possessions attached to the sees.* Besides, as Hallam avows, "the bishops acquired and retained a great part of their ascendency by a very respectable instrument of power, intellectual superiority."† Their concurrence was sought in every change of rulers, whether the sceptre passed by election to the heir of a deceased monarch, or by some revolution, into the hands of a new dynasty. In the decline of the seventh century, on the resignation of King Wamba, the Spanish bishops assembled at the instance of his successor, Ervigius, who sought at their hands the ratification of his title: and on the deposition of Louis by his son Lothaire, a French Council lent its sanction to the measure. In 859, in the Council of Savonières, Charles the Bald avowed his willingness to submit to the judgment of the bishops, and complained that he had been deposed without their sanction. They, in reality, were the chief nobles, who chiefly constituted the public council and national legislature. The Pope especially possessed immense influence in civil affairs. His judgment sealed the deposition of Childeric, and the transfer of the sceptre from the Merovingian to the Carlovingian race. When Eadbert, a clergyman, regardless of his sacred engagements, was chosen by intrigue to occupy the vacant throne of Kent, in 796, Leo III., at the instance of Ethelheard, Archbishop of Canterbury, struck the ambitious aspirant with excommunication, for the violation of his religious obligations, and threatened to exhort all the inhabitants of Britain to unite in punishing his disobedience, should he refuse to return to the clerical profession.‡ People and princes alike appealed to the Pope in their controversies, and sought redress at his hands. The Saxons complained to Alexander II. of Henry IV., King of Germany, whose oppression and licentiousness were intolerable. The

---

* Middle Ages, ch. viii. p. 111.   † Ib. ch. vii.   ‡ Lingard, Hist. England, l. i. ch. iii.

prince was accordingly summoned to answer at the tribunal of the Pontiff, whose death, however, interrupted the proceedings. Two centuries before, Nicholas I. threatened to interdict King Lothaire unless he dismissed Waldrada: which menace was understood by the Bishop of Metz to involve the throne itself in danger.

Although, from these facts, it is plain that St. Gregory VII. was not the first who claimed or exercised authority over princes, he appears to be the first who actually undertook to depose them. In the year 1074, he wrote to the French bishops, complaining of the crimes of Philip I., whom he designated, not a king, but a tyrant, and requiring of them to admonish him, and lay the kingdom under interdict; adding a solemn threat, that if these measures failed, he would leave no means untried to free the nation from its unworthy ruler, as he could no longer suffer so illustrious a kingdom and its vast population to be ruined by the misconduct of one man. This presents to us a principle very popular in our days, that royalty is but a trust for the people, and that when the public interests are trampled under foot by the prince, he is a tyrant, unfit to hold the reins of government, and no longer entitled to the obedience of the people. Similar views had been delivered by Nicholas I. in the ninth century. To propagate this doctrine, leaving to every one to determine for himself when it is that the ruler has forfeited his rights, would be to preach revolution and anarchy. The assumption, however, of the right of judgment between subjects and their sovereign, has been represented as a daring usurpation. But as all the kingdoms of Europe had arisen under the protection of the Holy See, and all by the very profession of Christianity were considered as acknowledging its parental guidance, which by express acts they declared in the most solemn manner, the Pope was expected to interpose in all great controversies, whether domestic or external. His interference was generally sought, even when he seemed to act unsolicited.

In the Roman Council of the year 1075, excommunication was denounced against Philip, in case he should not yield to the admonitions of the apostolic legate despatched for his correction. The zeal of the Pontiff was soon enkindled against a more powerful prince, Henry IV., King of Germany, and emperor elect. In the lifetime of his father, Henry III., he had been chosen, with the assent of the German nobles, to succeed to the imperial throne, on the usual condition that he should govern justly.* The violation of this pledge had, as we have seen above, provoked the complaints of the Saxons, who subsequently revolted; and having, in an assembly at Gersteng, declared him unworthy to reign, on the accession of Gregory they most urgently besought him to come to their relief,† while Henry at the same time implored his authority against

---

* "Si rector justus futurus esset." Herman. contract., ad. an. 1057.

† "Quibus ut, vel per se, vel per nuntium, genti pene perditæ consolator esset, suppliciter oraverunt." Bruno, de bello Saxonico, apud script. rerum Germ., t. i. p. 133.

the rebels. "When the Saxons revolted," Saint-Priest observes, "the Emperor Henry IV., at the foot of the throne of Gregory VII., accused them of sedition and sacrilege. Thus the King of Germany made the Pope judge of his German subjects."* Gregory, accordingly, expostulated with the insurgents, calling on them to desist from violence, and despatched legates to them and to the king, with a view to bring their disputes to a peaceful termination. In the mean time, Henry threatened with death all who had appealed to the tribunal of the Pontiff. It was then that the measure of his iniquities seemed to overflow, so that Gregory took upon himself to forbid him to govern the kingdom of the Germans and of Italy, and absolved all Christians from the oath by which they had bound themselves to obey him as king.

This extraordinary act naturally leads us to inquire by what authority it was attempted. In a letter to the German bishops, nobles, and people, Gregory states that "Henry was guilty of crimes so enormous, as to deserve not only to be excommunicated, but, according to all divine and human laws, to be deprived of the royal dignity." The various historical documents specify those crimes, namely, utter disregard of the public interests, the cruel oppression of his subjects, the dishonor of the wives and daughters of the princes, and the butchery of many innocent persons. In the national Council held by the German princes, in 1076, they complained that Henry had wantonly shed the blood of his subjects, and laid an intolerable yoke on the necks of a free people. He had, likewise, committed great crimes against religion, by the sale of bishoprics, which he bestowed on unworthy men, and above all, by the sacrilegious attempt to depose the sovereign Pontiff. Both classes of crimes, those against society and religion, concurred to provoke his condemnation, because, as king, he had bound himself to protect the Church, and maintain her rights inviolate: but the last act, in that state of society, was justly deemed treason against the head of the Christian commonwealth. Christianity was the basis of society and its supreme law, and the Pontiff was regarded as its guardian and expounder.

It was the firm persuasion of the German princes that Henry, by his violation of the compact which, at his coronation, he had sworn to observe, had forfeited his title to the throne. "Freemen," says a writer almost contemporary, "put over themselves Henry as king, on condition that he should judge his constituents with justice, and govern them with royal care: which compact he has constantly broken and disregarded. Therefore, even without the judgment of the Apostolic See, the princes could justly refuse to acknowledge him any longer as king, since he has not fulfilled the pledge which he gave at his election; the violation of which brings with it the forfeiture of kingly power."† They sought,

---

* Histoire de la Royauté, par Saint-Priest, l. x. vol. ii. p. 549.

† "Liberi homines Henricum eo pacto sibi præposuerunt in regem, ut electores suos juste judicare, et regali providentia gubernare satageret, quod pactum ille postea præ-

nevertheless, the sanction of the Pope, whose influence on the public conscience was at that period unbounded.

The sentence of Gregory was professedly grounded on the power of binding and loosing which Peter received from Christ: but it presupposed the radical annulling of the oath of allegiance, by the failure of Henry in the fulfilment of the correlative obligations; so that, although bearing the form of a sentence, it was in reality an authoritative declaration that the oath had ceased to bind. In no circumstance did he assert, or insinuate, that he could loose the bond at will; but he uniformly relied on the fact that the king had violated his own oath, and thus virtually released the people from their duty to him. Voltaire has happily expressed the relations which then subsisted between the monarch and the people:

> " Before this sacred shrine he swore
> Justly to wield the power he bore;
> And such the tie that binds in one
> The nation's heart and monarch's throne:
> The day that breaks his oath, annuls our own."*

The feudal principles which prevailed in the Middle Ages, led men to regard the relations of subjects to the sovereign as depending on his fidelity in discharging the duties which he had assumed. The barons owed him no unqualified allegiance, and their liege men felt more strictly bound to their immediate lord than to the king or emperor, to whom they stood in no direct relation. Hallam observes: " The relation established between a lord and his vassal, by the feudal tenure, far from containing principles of any servile and implicit obedience, permitted the compact to be dissolved in case of its violation by either party. This extended as much to the sovereign as to inferior lords."†

The judgment of the Pope was awaited, lest the relations of the people to their rulers should be capriciously dissolved. The Saxons had implored it most earnestly, and Gregory, after much hesitation, and many efforts for the correction of Henry, issued at length the awful sentence. He did not proceed in this matter from the impulse of his own feelings, but with the advice and at the earnest solicitation of the Council which he assembled to take it into consideration. The prince himself, when he sought and obtained absolution from the censure, accepted with apparent

---

varicari et contemnere non cessavit, &c. Ergo et absque sedis apostolicæ judicio, principes eum pro rege merito refutare possent, cum pactum adimplere contempserit, quod iis pro electione sua promiserat, quo non adimpleto nec rex esse poterat." Vita Gregorii VII., in Muratori Script. rerum Italic., t. iii., p. 342.

* A cet autel auguste
———————————— il jura d' être juste :
De son peuple et de lui tel etait le lien ;
Il nous rend nos sermens, lorsqu' il trahit le sien.
Voltaire, Brutus, Acte I., Scene 2.

† Middle Ages, ch. viii. p. 111.

readiness the condition of awaiting the issue of a full investigation, to be made in the presence of the German princes, at a time and place to be appointed by the Pontiff, promising, in the mean time, to lay aside the regal robes, and abstain from all interference in the government of the empire. Should he fail in any of these engagements, or shrink from the trial, he consented to be held as guilty, and agreed that the princes should be deemed free from every obligation contracted by their oath of allegiance, so that they might without further delay proceed by election to fill the vacant throne.*

Without pretending that the cases are in all respects parallel, I beg to refer to the Declaration of Independence, in which, after the enumeration of grievances endured by the American colonies from the King of Great Britain, this remarkable sentence occurs: "We, therefore, the representatives of the United States of America, in general Congress assembled, appealing to the Supreme Judge of the world for the rectitude of our intentions, do, in the name and by authority of the good people of these colonies, solemnly publish and declare that these united colonies are, and of right ought to be, free and independent States; THAT THEY ARE ABSOLVED FROM ALL ALLEGIANCE TO THE BRITISH CROWN; and that all political connection between them and the State of Great Britain is, and ought to be, totally dissolved." Although Congress did not assume the power of the keys, or claim any control over conscience, it certainly set aside, as far as in it lay, the oath of allegiance, on the ground that the correlative duty of protection had not been fulfilled by the British crown. So far, this is precisely a case in point to that for which odium has been heaped on the memory of the holy Pontiff. His act, if in the main just, because declaratory of right, does not cease to be such from the circumstance that he brings to its performance all the spiritual authority of his office, invoking the prince of the apostles to ratify what he undertakes, in virtue of that power of binding and loosing, which he received from Christ. He did not rely on this alone: he did not interfere unsolicited: but his authority having been implored by both parties alternately, he issued a sentence, giving it all the force which his social and ecclesiastical position enabled him to impart to it: and yet suspending its final effect for a year, in order to give the tyrant an opportunity of avoiding the penalty by a change of conduct.

In an assembly of the German princes held at Triers, most of them manifested an anxiety to avail themselves of the opportunity which was thus presented of deposing Henry; but, in the end, they sent an embassy to him, proposing to submit their grievances anew to the judgment of the Pope, in an assembly of all the nobles, to be held at Augsburg; to which proposition the affrighted prince assented. "This was," as Voltaire observes, "a recognition of the Pontiff as the natural judge of the

---

* See Lambert. Schnafnaburg, cited by Pagi Brev. Pont. Rom.

emperor and empire. It was the triumph of Gregory VII. and of the Papacy. Henry IV., reduced to these extremities, increased still more his triumph."*

By a law of the empire, as well as by general usage, the loss of civil rights was attached to the sentence of excommunication, in case of contumacy, manifested by neglect to obtain absolution during an entire year. The sentence of Gregory was but the application of this general law to the case of a ruler, and was not designed to take full effect unless after the lapse of that space of time. Accordingly, as the end of the year drew nigh, Henry manifested extreme anxiety to be released from the censure, and for that purpose he crossed the Alps in the depth of winter, to meet the Pontiff, who had stopped at Canosa on his journey to Augsburg. In the garb of a penitent, he presented himself at the gate of the fortress; but obtained admittance only after three days, Gregory being distrustful of the sincerity of his professions. This apparent sternness was fully justified by the prompt relapse of Henry into his usual excesses. When taking the communion, Gregory, holding in his hand the body of our Lord, appealed to Him as witness of his innocence of the crimes which Henry had laid to his charge, and then challenged him to do likewise: "Do, my son, what you have seen me do. The German princes daily stun my ears with charges against you, imputing to you many enormous crimes, for which they think you deserve not only to be deprived of the government, but to be removed from the communion of the Church, and from all civil society to the end of life: they earnestly demand that a day and place be appointed for the examination of the charges which they bring against you." Consciousness of guilt withheld the monarch from making the appeal.

After the relapse of Henry, and the election of Rudolph by the German princes, contrary to the wishes of Gregory, who still cherished the hope of his amendment, he made several ineffectual efforts to terminate the contest, and resisted the importunate solicitations of the ambassadors of Rudolph, and of others, who urged him to strike the prevaricating prince with the apostolic sword. At length, in the year 1080, he drew it from the scabbard, in a Roman Council, "subjected him to excommunication, binding him with the chains of anathema, forbidding him anew, on the part of Almighty God and of the apostles Peter and Paul, to take on himself the kingdom of the Germans and of Italy." By his solemn sentence, the Pontiff took from Henry all power and dignity, forbidding any Christian to obey him, and absolving from their oath all who had sworn allegiance to him. On the same occasion, he recognised as king, Rudolph, whom the Germans had chosen to occupy the throne, and, with the ardor of prophetic zeal, he besought the apostles "to show by the event that they could take away and grant, according to the respective

---

* Essai sur l'Histoire Générale, ch. xlii., Henri IV. et Gregoire VII.

deserts of each one, empires, kingdoms, principalities, and all varieties of earthly dominion." The apostles were invoked, that, by their powerful influence at the eternal throne, they might obtain such a manifest interposition of Providence, as would show to the world that Christ had confirmed the just sentence of His earthly vicegerent.

The immediate issue of the contest did not give to this appeal the character of prophecy, for Rudolph, at the moment of victory, perished on the field of battle. An anti-pope created by the conqueror, in the person of Guibert, Bishop of Ravenna, and enthroned in St. Peter's, usurped the tiara during the reign of three lawful Pontiffs; and Henry, for twenty years after the death of Gregory, wore the insignia and claimed the title of emperor, which at length he abandoned, after his own son had risen in revolt against him. Having closed his career under the ban of the Church, his corpse was denied Christian sepulture. Gregory, to escape the power of his persecutor and of his rival, retired into the Castle of Sant' Angelo, from which he came forth under the protection of Robert Guiscard, the Norman duke, and passing to Salerno, closed his career of suffering, calm and resigned. "I regret not," said he, "my sufferings, being sustained by the consciousness of having loved virtue and hated iniquity." Henry V. imitated his father for a time by his encroachments on ecclesiastical authority, but in the end made a satisfactory arrangement with Pope Calixtus II. "At his death, in 1125, the male line of the Franconian emperors was at an end."* It is thus that God often cuts off the race of sovereigns who abuse their authority to the prejudice of the Church.

§ 2.—SUBSEQUENT INSTANCES.

Notwithstanding the sufferings of St. Gregory in his struggles against the oppressor, his example was followed by his successors. In the year 1168, Alexander III. excommunicated Frederick Barbarossa, and released his subjects from their allegiance. The sacking of Milan, one of the most horrible events recorded in history, provoked, and, even in the judgment of Voltaire, justified this exercise of pontifical authority.† The Italian cities, encouraged by the Papal sentence, succeeded in shaking off the imperial yoke, and, through gratitude to the magnanimous Pontiff, built a city, which they called from his name, ALEXANDRIA. "Milan, which was rebuilt, Pavia, Brescia, and so many other cities, thanked the Pope for having restored to them the precious liberty for which they fought; and the holy father, penetrated with a pure joy, cried out: 'God has been pleased to cause an old priest to triumph, without combating,

---

* Hallam's Middle Ages, ch. v.
† Essai sur l'Histoire Générale, l. ii. ch. xliv.

over a powerful and terrific emperor.'"* Shall we hesitate to applaud the triumph of liberty and natural right over a cruel despot? The sentence of the Pontiff was plainly a declaration of the rights of the Italian cities, for whose relief it was specially issued. Frederick himself bent his proud neck to the Vicar of Christ,† and, to repair his misdeeds, with heroic courage led the army of the cross to the plains of Palestine.

A most solemn sentence of deposition was pronounced in the year 1245, in the Council of Lyons, by Innocent IV. against Frederick II. There were present in that venerable assembly the Patriarchs of Constantinople, Antioch, and Aquileja, with archbishops and bishops to the number of one hundred and forty, and the Emperor of Constantinople, with several representatives of the civil powers. It is unnecessary to enumerate the measures previously adopted against Frederick, and the long-continued career of crime by which he provoked the censures of the Church. His advocate, Thaddeus, in vain attempted to ward off the blow. Innocent, after preliminary proceedings, in the third session thus pronounced judgment: "The aforesaid prince having rendered himself unworthy of the empire and kingdom, and of all honor and dignity, and being cast off by God on account of his iniquities, that he should not reign, or command; and being bound fast by his own sins, and cast away, we show and denounce him as deprived by the Lord of all honor and dignity; and, nevertheless, by our sentence we deprive him, and absolve forever from their oath all who are bound to him by the oath of allegiance."

In this instance, at least, the sentence was effectual, which shows how general was the conviction that it emanated from a competent authority, and rested on just grounds. "After his deposition by the Council of Lyons," says Hallam, "the affairs of Frederick II. went rapidly into decay. With every allowance for the enmity of the Lombards, and the jealousy of Germany, it must be confessed that the proscription of Innocent IV. and Alexander IV. was the main cause of the ruin of his family."‡

Although the solemnity of this sentence does not give it the character of a doctrinal definition, yet it demands our particular consideration. I am not of those who rely on the circumstance that it is said to have been passed in the presence of the Council, without any intimation that the fathers approved of it; for they certainly concurred in the awful ceremonial of excommunication, and not having protested against the

---

* Essai sur l'Histoire Générale, l. ii. ch. xliv.

† The fable of Alexander putting his foot on the neck of the penitent emperor, is exploded. Voltaire disbelieves, likewise, the statement of Hoveden, that Celestino III., at the age of eighty-four, while crowning Henry VI., son of Frederick, kicked the crown off his head: "Ce fait n' est pas vraisemblable." Voltaire, ibid.

‡ Middle Ages, ch. vii.

deposition, they must be considered as assenting to it, especially as the Pontiff declares that it was decreed after diligent deliberation with them. The obvious reason why it is ascribed to Innocent, rather than to the Council, is because it was believed to be his prerogative to judge the emperor, whom he had crowned. On this rite great stress is laid by Nicholas I., who speaks of the imperial dominions as passing by hereditary right, confirmed by the authority of the Holy See, and by the act of the Pontiff, who placed the crown on his head.* I am not disposed to admit that the act of Innocent was an exercise of usurped power, an unwarrantable encroachment of the ecclesiastical on the civil authority; neither do I contend that it proceeded from the divine commission given to Peter. In the state of society which then existed, which, as we have seen, was in the main a Christian confederacy, having the Gospel as its fundamental law, the head of the Church being placed in such intimate relations with the emperor, could declare that he had forfeited his rights to the throne, by violating the compact in virtue of which he reigned. It is true that he does not speak of this compact, or point to any human source of the power which he exercised, but neither does he declare its divine origin: and by enumerating the crimes of the tyrant, he plainly intimates that these deprived him, in the sight of God, of all title to the throne. The right to depose an unworthy sovereign was not seriously questioned in that age, so that its exercise met with the general concurrence of all who were not under his immediate influence, and needed no proof to recommend it. In reference to this sentence, Michaud observes: "We must acknowledge that the pretensions of the Popes in this respect were favored by the contemporary opinions."†

The provision made in the Constitution of the United States for the trial of the president on impeachment, bears some resemblance to the mode of proceeding against the emperor, at that time, when the Christian nations of Europe virtually formed a federal commonwealth. "The Church," as Chancellor Kent remarks, "had its Councils, or convocations of the clergy, which formed the nations professing Christianity into a connection resembling a federal alliance, and those Councils sometimes settled the titles and claims of princes, and regulated the temporal affairs of the Christian powers."‡ In the Middle Ages, the emperor stood in the relation of the highest executive in all that regarded civil and coercive administration. We may justly consider a General Council as the senate of the Christian confederacy, the Pope as its chief-justice. According to the Constitution, the president is to be tried by the senate, under the presidency of the chief-justice. There may appear to be a striking contrast between the two cases in this respect, that two-thirds of the senate must concur to the condemnation of the president, while

---

* Ep. xxvi.   † Histoire des Croisades, l. xiv. p. 163.
‡ Commentaries on American Law, by James Kent, lect. i. p. 9, 10.

the judicial power of the Pontiff is independent and unrestricted; but, in fact, he never proceeded in a case of this importance unless with the advice and assent either of a General Council, as in the present instance, or of a numerous assembly of bishops, like the Roman Synods under Gregory VII. The chief-justice is empowered to remove the president from office, when found guilty, but he cannot affect life or limb by his sentence. The Pontiff, in like manner, in deposing the delinquent emperor, left his person free and inviolate.

§ 3.—NEVER FORMALLY DEFINED.

It is certain that St. Gregory VII. issued no solemn definition of his right to depose sovereigns. In asserting it he relied on the power of binding and loosing, which Peter received from our Lord: but he did not formally define that it was included in this commission. He had specially in view the religious obligation of the oath, by which the natural duty of allegiance to the established authority is sanctioned, and he claimed the power of absolving from it only in circumstances where the ground of the obligation was withdrawn. All lawful engagements are obligatory independently of the authority of the Church, which enforces them with a general sanction, and claims no power to interfere with the rights of others. Obligations originally legitimate may cease by reason of the breach of conditions on which they were based; in which case the injured party may be considered free, without any ecclesiastical intervention: but if they were sanctioned by oath, respect for this religious bond requires the act of a prelate of the Church to loose the tie, in virtue of the power received from Christ. What is true of the relative obligations of individuals, was applied in the Middle Ages to the duties of sovereigns and subjects, both classes professing submission to the same ecclesiastical authority. While, therefore, no power was claimed to interfere with these duties, the Popes felt authorized to loose the religious bond by which they were sanctioned, when, by the violation of the correlative conditions, the obligation had ceased. This was the substance of the action of Gregory.*

Boniface VIII. is considered as having most formally asserted the right to depose sovereigns. Philip the Fair, King of France, was guilty of debasing the public coin, to the great injury of his subjects, and of other acts of injustice, besides the violation of ecclesiastical immunities. The Pope admonished him with the authority of a father, applying to himself the words of the Prophet Jeremias, which Honorius III. had used on a similar occasion: "God has placed us over kings and kingdoms, to root up, pull down, waste, destroy, build up, and plant in His name and by His doctrine. Wherefore, imagine not that you

---

* The Dictatus, which bears the name of Gregory, is proved to be a forgery. See Pagi, ad an. 1077.

have no superior, and that you are not subject to the head of the Church."* As the prophet certainly had no secular power, Boniface cannot be thought to have claimed it, merely because he used the words which God addressed to Jeremias, and which meant only reproof, exhortation, and correction. The Pope removes all ambiguity, by adding this qualification, "in His name and by His doctrine." He expressly disavowed, through the cardinals, all claims to temporal domination :† but he asserted his right to judge of the morality of the acts of the king, which, *ratione peccati*, fell under his cognizance. As these were flagrantly criminal, he laid the kingdom of France under interdict, in the hope of striking terror into the delinquent monarch. The famous Bull, *Unam Sanctam*, published by Boniface, affirms that the temporal power is of its nature subordinate to the ecclesiastical, as earthly are to heavenly things; and defines the necessity which is incumbent on rulers, as well as their subjects, of admitting the authority of the chief bishop: "We declare to every human creature,‡ we affirm, define and pronounce, that it is altogether necessary for salvation, to be subject to the Roman Pontiff." Beyond this the definition does not go, so that no more is taught, as of faith, than what all Catholics hold, namely, that subjection to the Pope in matters of salvation is a necessary duty. The terms in which it is affirmed are not stronger than those employed by St. Jerome, when addressing Damasus. The allegorical reasoning contained in the Bull concerning the two swords—the spiritual sword wielded by the Pontiff, the temporal sword by the prince, but at the bidding of the Pontiff—is taken from St. Bernard,§ who means no more than that princes should use their power justly, and protect the ministers of religion in the exercise of their sacred functions. The power of deposing sovereigns is not at all asserted, much less is it defined.

The superiority of the pontifical or sacerdotal power to that of princes or emperors, which is affirmed in this and various other documents, is to be understood of moral excellence, not of temporal relation. Justice and right are superior to brute force—the divine law is above all human authority; and the Priest or Pontiff, from whose lips the law is sought, is, in this respect, above the highest earthly potentate. As all power emanates from God, its exercise must necessarily be subordinate to His law, which binds rulers as well as their subjects, nations as well as individuals. Arnold, in reviewing the history of the strifes between the Popes and emperors,

---

* *Ausculta, Fili.* The Bull begins with these words.

† Fleury, Hist. de l'Eglise, l. xc. ₴ 16.

‡ Omni humanæ creaturæ. Allusion is made to the commission to preach the gospel to every creature. In some manuscripts it reads: omnem humanam creaturam; which would imply that every one should be subject to the Pontiff,—kings, as well as their subjects. This is strictly true of all members of the Church, in all that regards salvation.

₴ De consideratione, l. iv.

perceived clearly that it was, originally at least, a struggle for principle; and although he was not disposed to favor the Papal claims, he was forced by his convictions to acknowledge the justice of the cause: "The principle in itself was this: whether the Papal or the imperial, in other words, the sacerdotal or the imperial power was to be accounted the greater. Now conceive the Papal power to be the representative of what is moral and spiritual, and the imperial power to represent only what is external and physical; conceive the first to express the ideas of responsibility to God and paternal care and guidance, while the other was the mere imbodying of selfish might, like the old Greek tyrannies, and who can do other than wish success to the Papal cause? Who can help being, with all his heart, a Guelf? But in the early part of the struggle, this was, to a great extent, the state of it: the Pope stood in the place of the Church, the emperor was a merely worldly despot, corrupt and arbitrary."*

The third canon of the fourth Council of Lateran, which we have already examined, has been often alleged as sanctioning the deposition of sovereigns. Even if this were true, it does not bear the character of a doctrinal definition. It is an enactment, which, by the consent of the secular powers represented in the Council, might have embraced even sovereigns; but there is no proof that it actually embraces them. Yet it cannot be doubted that by a general law, practically recognised by all Christian nations at that time, forfeiture of royal power was incurred by apostasy from the faith, this being admitted even by Henry IV., who contended that in no other contingency was he liable to deposition. It was, however, a principle of action, but not a defined dogma. Even Frederick II. acknowledged that if he were guilty of the crimes laid to his charge, especially of heresy, he would deserve deposition; and the advisers of St. Louis agreed, that in case of his guilt and conviction, he should not be supported by the French monarch.† At present, the principle is reversed, since the English crown would be forfeited by the profession of the Catholic faith.

§ 4.—DEPOSITION OF ELIZABETH.

Among the latest attempts to exercise the deposing power, were the excommunication and sentence of deposition fulminated by St. Pius V., and renewed by Sixtus V., against Elizabeth of England. The grounds of this sentence were her illegitimacy, the declaration of which stood unrepealed on the statute-book of England,‡ her profession of heresy,

---

* Introductory Lectures on Modern History, by Thomas Arnold, lect. v. p. 228 American edition.

† See Fleury, diss. v., in Hist. Eccl.

‡ See History of England, by Dr. Lingard, vol. vii. ch. iv.

which, by the ancient fundamental law of England, as in other Christian countries, induced the forfeiture of regal power,[*] her crimes against religion, and especially her persecution of her Catholic subjects. The special object, however, of the Bull of Pius, was to rescue the Queen of Scots from impending death: a circumstance which does honor to his humanity. "The Pontiff," says Dr. Lingard, who is no advocate of the measure, "considered himself bound to seek the deliverance of the captive princess; he represented to the Kings of France and Spain that honor, and interest, and religion, called on them to rescue Mary from imprisonment and death; and the moment that he knew that Elizabeth had committed her cause to the commissioners at York and Westminster, he ordered the auditor Riario to commence proceedings against the English queen in the Papal court."[†] After the Bull had been prepared, the Pontiff delayed affixing to it his signature, until he received the intelligence that eight hundred individuals had perished on the scaffold, in punishment of an unsuccessful insurrection. The news of this wholesale butchery fixed his determination. To all these considerations was added, in the renewal of the sentence by Sixtus, the barbarous murder of the Queen of Scots, under color of legal process. Philip II., of Spain, prepared to give effect to the Papal decree, by a formidable fleet, the *Armada*, which, by a mysterious act of Providence, became the sport of the winds, leaving the bold daughter of Anne Boleyn to pursue securely her career. Yet it is remarkable, that although Henry left three children, each of whom successively occupied the throne, sterility marked them all, and the sceptre passed from the grasp of the haughtiest woman of the Tudor race to the son of Mary Stuart. Sir Henry Spelman remarks: "They all successively sway his sceptre, and all die childless, and his family is extinct; and, like Herostratus, his name not mentioned but with his crimes."[‡]

The Catholics of England were foremost in demonstrations of loyalty to Elizabeth, at the time of the threatened invasion, feeling themselves bound to recognise her as their queen, because she was so acknowledged by the nation at large. In the sentence of deposition, St. Pius followed the precedents of holy and eminent Pontiffs, and relied on grounds which in themselves were not trivial: but the temporal supremacy of Rome had passed away, and the strength of Catholic faith was to be manifested in the patient endurance of persecution, over which it was finally to triumph.

---

[*] Leges Eduardi regis, art. xvii., alias xv., apud Wilkins, Leges Anglo-Saxonicæ, p. 200. Spelman, concilia, &c. Londini, 1639.
[†] History of England, vol. viii. ch. i.   [‡] De non temerandis ecclesiis. Preface.

§ 5.—DISCLAIMERS.

The deposing power continued for a long time to be a subject of bitter controversy, the English government requiring the abjuration of the opinion in terms that condemned it as impious and heretical; and Rome being slow to sanction any formulary that implied censure on the acts of holy Pontiffs, or even to relinquish a power which she had once effectually wielded for the interests of humanity and religion. Louis XIV. induced the French clergy, in the assembly of 1682, to deny it formally, at a time when there was no disposition on the part of the Pope to exercise it. At length the excitement of controversy passed away : the oath abjuring the opinion, without any offensive censure, was generally taken by the Catholics of the British empire, without blame from the Holy See: the opinion was disclaimed by many Catholic universities, and Pius VI., through Cardinal Antonelli, prefect of the Propaganda, answering the Irish bishops, made the following important declaration: "The See of Rome never taught that faith is not to be kept with the heterodox :— that an oath to kings separated from the Catholic communion can be violated :—that it is lawful for the Bishop of Rome to invade their temporal rights and dominions. We, too, consider an attempt or design against the lives of kings and princes, even under the pretext of religion, as a horrid and detestable crime."

When Napoleon despoiled Pius VII. of his temporal principality, the Pontiff hurled against him the thunders of the Church, without putting forth his hand to remove the imperial crown from his head. The haughty emperor boasted that the arms had not fallen from the hands of his soldiers, in consequence of the excommunication, as if it was but a vain attempt to stop him in his victorious career: but lo! soon afterward, in the Russian campaign, the frozen troops let fall their arms, by what Dr. Arnold designates "a direct and manifest interposition of God."* The conqueror, who during so long a time had sported with crowns as with toys, soon fell from his eminence, and became a prisoner and an exile.

The deposing power was essentially grounded on the principle, that the people are the immediate source of civil government, which is established for their benefit, with liability to forfeiture if abused.† Lest anarchy should arise, through the intrigues of demagogues, the delicate point of declaring when forfeiture was incurred, was reserved, in Catholic nations, to the judgment of the Pontiff. Charles Butler, an English jurist, decidedly opposed to the power, justly observes, that " the deposing doctrine of Persons and Mariana bears a nearer affinity to the whiggish doctrine of resistance than is generally supposed. The whigs maintain

---

* Lecture iii. p. 161.
† See Bianchi, Della indiretta dipendenza della potestà temporale, l. i. § 1.

that the people, where there is an extreme abuse of power,—of which abuse the people themselves are to be the judges,—may dethrone the offending monarch. The good fathers assigned the same power to the people, in the same extreme case, but contended that, if there were any doubts of the existence of the extremity, the Pope should be the judge. Of the two systems, when all Christendom was Catholic, was not the last, speaking comparatively, the least objectionable?"* He further observes, that "it was not found to be in practice quite so mischievous as is generally described. It had even this advantage, that, on several occasions, during the boisterous governments of the feudal princes, it often proved a useful restraint, in the absence of every other, both on the king and the great nobility, and protected the lower ranks of society from their violence and oppression."† It was, in fact, as a recent Italian writer observes, "a spiritual tribuneship, which effectually pleaded for the people when sovereigns went beyond the just limits of authority."‡ Our own Brownson, even before he had set his foot on the threshold of the Church, eloquently remarked: "Wrong, wrong have they been, who have complained that kings and emperors were subjected to the spiritual head of Christendom. It was well for man, that there was a power over the brutal tyrants called emperors, kings, and barons, who rode rough-shod over the humble peasant and artisan—well that there was a power, even on earth, that could touch their cold and atheistical hearts, and make them tremble as the veriest slave." . . . "It is to the existence and exercise of that power, that THE PEOPLE owe their existence, and the doctrine of man's equality to man, its progress."§

---

* Historical Memoirs of the English Catholics, v. iii. § 4.
† Ibidem, L. xxv. 7.   ‡ Audisio, Educazione del clero. Turino, 1844.
§ Boston Quarterly Review, January, 1842, p. 13.

CHAPTER V.

Papal Sanction.

SEVERAL acts of the Popes in regard to temporal sovereigns may be fairly regarded as implying no more than a religious sanction of what was in itself just and lawful. The judgment pronounced by Zacharias, at the solicitation of the Frank nobles, may be viewed in this light. Pepin, Mayor of the Palace, governed the Franks in the name of Childeric III., who altogether neglected the duties of a sovereign, which he was naturally disqualified from performing. The nobles having applied to Pope Zacharias to sanction the transfer of the crown and title to the actual governor, obtained his approval, whereby the Merovingian race was set aside, to make room for the Carlovingian dynasty. This decision was, in reality, but an authoritative declaration of the right of a nation, through its leaders, to choose for ruler a man capable of protecting the public interests. That the inert heir of royalty—*magni nominis umbra*—may be displaced, to make room for an active and capable ruler, when the public safety is in jeopardy, no supporter of the received theories of civil polity will question. The nobles invoked the authority of the Pontiff, in order that all might know that justice and the common good were solely had in view, and that no occasion might be furnished for tumult or disorder. It was an easy means of revolution, without shedding human blood. The conscience of the people at large was interested, lest they should appear to resist the divine ordinance, and purchase to themselves damnation. The father and judge of Christians was consulted, who deemed the reasons of the change just and sufficient. Whatever influence in civil matters was thus given him, was the consequence of a free act of those who sought his counsel, or implored his judgment. He decided with authority a case of conscience of the highest importance, with evident advantage to the nation. Hallam justly observes: "The circumstances under which the crown was transferred from the race of Clovis are connected with one of the most important revolutions in the history of Europe." A sanguinary struggle was prevented, and the impartial judgment of one removed from local influences, which might bias the mind, was received with general acquiescence. "An answer," says Gibbon, "so agreeable to their wishes, was accepted by the Franks as the opinion of a casuist, the sentence of a judge, or the oracle of a prophet."* Zacharias decided, not as a mere casuist, emitting an opinion, nor yet as a prophet inspired of God, but as a judge, determining with authority the extent of a moral obligation. Guizot remarks: " Never was a revolution accomplished with less effort and noise: Pepin possessed the power: the fact was changed into right: no resistance was made: no reclamation was deemed sufficiently important to be recorded, although doubtless some was made. All things appeared unaltered: a title alone was changed. It is, nevertheless, beyond all question, that a great event was then accomplished: no doubt this change was the symptom of the end of a certain social state, and of the commencement of a new state,—a crisis, a true epoch in the history of French civilization."† The change effected was plainly this, that royal descent was deemed an insufficient title to the crown, where personal disqualifications existed, and that the general interests of the nation were deemed paramount to the claims of an individual. The relations of the Pontiff to the new dynasty were rendered more intimate by his concurrence in their elevation to the throne, and his influence with the people in civil affairs was confirmed and increased. Nations and princes thenceforward viewed him as the expounder of their duties, and arbiter of their disputes. Five hundred years later, Innocent IV. showed a more delicate regard for the rights of the nominal sovereign. Sanchez, King of Portugal, surnamed the *Cowled*, from his monastic temperament, proving inadequate to the government, the Bishops of Braga and Conimbra, with some of the secular nobility, were commissioned to solicit the Pope, in the Council of Lyons, that he might be deprived of the crown. Innocent declined acceding to the request, but consented that Alphonsus, who was heir-apparent to the throne, being the brother of Sanchez, who was childless, should be charged with the administration, while the title of king and a becoming maintenance should be given to the impotent monarch.

The pontifical sanction was eagerly sought by kings to secure the succession to the throne, that strife and bloodshed might be avoided. The coronation of a young prince by the Pope settled the title more effectually than a modern act of Parliament for the better regulating of the succession. His person was thenceforward considered sacred, since the judgment of the Pontiff and the mysterious ceremony had ratified his claim to the throne. Ethelwulf, King of the Western Saxons, sent to the eternal city his son Alfred, that he might be crowned by the Pope, and thus declared heir to the throne then occupied by his father.‡ The son of Demetrius, King of Russia, went to Rome in the time of Gregory VII.,

---

* Decline and Fall, &c. ch. xlix., A. D. 754.

† Cours d'Histoire Moderne, t. ii. p. 226.

‡ As he had elder brothers, Dr. Lingard thinks that the ceremony was designed to secure his succession, after their death, to the exclusion of their children, as the will of Ethelwulf directs. Hist. England, vol. i. ch. iii.

swore fealty to blessed Peter, and alleging the consent of his father, obtained the recognition of his right to succeed him, through the gift of St. Peter.* Suger, Abbot of St. Denis, considering the delicate state of the health of Louis the Fat, suggested to him to avail himself of the presence of Innocent II., then at Rheims, to have the young prince crowned, in order to prevent strife between aspirants to the throne. The king accordingly came to Rheims, with his queen and son, and the nobles of his court, and had his son Louis VII. crowned as his successor, in the presence of bishops from France, Germany, England, and Spain. Mendog, King of Lithuania, obtained the consent of Innocent IV. that his son should be crowned king.

In cases where the order of succession could not be observed without danger to the public interests, the sanction of the Pope was asked for the necessary departure from the usual course. At the close of the twelfth century, the King of Armenia sought authority of Innocent III. to give effect to the will of Raymond, Prince of Antioch, who excluded his brother, the Count of Tripoli, from the succession, that the principality might pass to his own son and grandson. There were three claimants to the throne of Castile in the year 1218. Ferrand, who was chosen king by the majority of the nobles, was disqualified by his birth, inasmuch as the marriage of his parents was incestuous and invalid. To prevent civil war, Honorius III. legitimated his birth, and ratified the election. Gregory IX. was implored to confirm the title to the throne, which the King elect of Norway, whose birth was illegitimate, derived from the will of his father, to the prejudice of the rights of the legitimate heir. The Christian nations in those ages felt confident that the Pontiff would weigh well the respective claims of the aspirants to royalty, with a sacred regard to the national interests.

Kings and other potentates, in the Middle Ages, eagerly sought the sanction of the Pope for their treaties. "The oldest treaty now extant between any of our kings," says Dr. Lingard, "and a foreign power, is drawn up in the name of the Pope, and confirmed by the oaths and marks of one bishop and two thanes on the part of Ethelred, and of one bishop and two barons on the part of Richard."† It is, in fact, in the form of a decree of John XV., addressed to all the faithful, in which he states the success of the measures taken by his legate to put an end to the quarrel between the English king and the Norman duke.‡ Richard, King of England, on the conclusion of peace with Tancred, of Sicily, addressed Clement III. in these terms: "The actions of princes are crowned with greater success when they are strengthened and favored by the Apostolic See, and directed by consultation with the Holy Roman Church."§ The Venetians and French having formed a treaty for the

---

* S. Gregor. VII., ep. lxxiv.   † History of England. Vol. i. ch. v. Ethelred.
‡ Conc. col., vol. vi. col. 713.   § Apud Baron. Annal., an. 1190.

affairs of the Eastern empire, the Emperor Baldwin, and Dandolo, Doge of Venice, applied to Innocent III. to sanction it, by threatening the transgressors with anathema: which, however, for weighty reasons, he declined.* "Nothing was more common," as Leibnitz remarks, "than for kings in their treaties to submit to the censure and correction of the Pope, as in the treaty of Bretagny, in 1360, and the treaty of Etaples, in 1492.†

Much odium has fallen on the memory of Adrian IV., for having, as is alleged, given Ireland to Henry II. It is, however, a mistake, to understand as a grant of dominion what was merely a sanction of the enterprise. The king had only sought counsel and favor, which the Pontiff gave, without employing any terms that imply a transfer. He asserts, indeed, that Ireland, and all other islands on which the light of Christian faith had shone, are under the authority of blessed Peter: "*ad jus beati Petri pertinere*," which, it appears, had already been avowed by the monarch, in his application for the pontifical sanction. To understand the nature of this claim, we may be permitted to refer to a Bull of Urban II., issued in the year 1092, which says: "Since all islands, by common law, belong to the first occupants, we hold it as certain that the Emperor Constantine gave the ownership of them to St. Peter and his Vicars."‡ Whether this persuasion arose from the supposititious "donation," or from the munificence actually exercised, in other respects, by the emperor, is not apparent; but the Pontiff seems to have claimed the rights of a feudal sovereign over all those countries which were not included within the limits of the empire, and which embraced the faith on the preaching of Roman missionaries. These pretensions were conformable to the prevailing ideas of those ages, in which men conceived all countries either as portions of the empire, having the emperor as lord paramount, or as free from imperial sway, and governed by their own rulers, under the protection of the Pontiff. In virtue of this feudal sovereignty, he felt himself authorized to sanction the enterprise of Henry, which was professedly directed to establish order where anarchy prevailed; and, as head of the Church, he favored the effort to restore discipline, which was said to be in a most relaxed condition. It is far from my intention to advocate the claim to feudal sovereignty, if, indeed, it be contained in the document, which is denied by ardent supporters of the Papal rights:§ but in justice to the poor scholar, whose merits raised him to the pinnacle of ecclesiastical power, I take leave to state my conviction, that he acted

---

* Apud Raynald, an. 1205. See also Fleury, Hist., l. lxxvi. § 16.
† Diss. 1, de act. publ. usu. Op., t. iv. p. 299.
‡ Apud Ughell., t. iii. p. 413.
§ Bianchi, Della potestà e della politia della chiesa, t. ii. l. v. § xiii. p. 353. This author is of opinion that the Pope put forward no claim to temporal dominion; but availed himself of his spiritual supremacy to sanction a measure which appeared fraught with advantages to religion.

in accordance with the prevailing sentiments as to the prerogatives of his station, and from motives worthy of one who was charged with the interests of religion. I do not affirm that the condition of the Irish Church was such as was represented, or that the prince, whose hostility to ecclesiastical liberty led to the assassination of St. Thomas of Canterbury, was influenced by religious zeal in his pledges to reform it; but the general character of Adrian for zeal and piety prevents my subscribing his condemnation.

The grants made by some Popes to Christian kings, and to the Teutonic knights, and others, to possess and govern such territories as they might gain from pagans by force of arms, must necessarily be reduced to sanctions of their military enterprise, as justified on general principles of law. The state of those countries was such, that it appeared lawful to invade them in the common interest of the human species, in order to stop unnatural excesses, and to extend civilization. This could be done most effectually under a religious sanction, which was given by the Pope to those who enrolled themselves under the banner of the Cross, having in view to prepare the way for the diffusion of religion, by an enterprise that was otherwise lawful. It belongs to the followers of Mohammed, not of Christ, to make proselytes by the sword. The expeditions in question were directed to reclaim men from a savage state, while they served to protect the ministers of religion in the exercise of their sacred functions, and to secure to converts freedom to profess and practise religion. Cistercian and Dominican missionaries had preceded the knights in their expeditions, and had gained many to the faith. Innocent III., writing to the faithful of Saxony and Westphalia, observed : " As the discipline of the Church does not allow any one to be forced to embrace the faith, so the Holy See freely offers protection to believers, and exhorts Christians to defend the neophytes, that they may not repent for having come to the faith, and return to their former errors. Wherefore we beseech you, and enjoin on you, for the remission of your sins, that unless the pagans, who live on the confines of Livonia, make and observe peace with the Christians, you take arms for the defence of your brethren."* Innocent IV., in granting to Duke Casimir such lands as he might acquire from the pagans, added the condition that their profession of Christianity should be spontaneous. When the Teutonic knights with military force invaded these territories, the Pope, on complaint of the duke, confirmed his rights as being prior to their invasion, and obliged them to depart. Thus it was evident that the Papal concessions were directed to regulate the title and claims of Christian princes, and to favor the diffusion of religion, without prejudice to the free will of the conquered people.

The barbarous habits of the Prussians, who were wont to destroy all

---

* Apud Fleury, l. lxxvi., § xxx.

female children but one of each mother, and who otherwise committed unnatural excesses, are the most obvious justification of the war made on them, under the sanction of Honorius III., since writers on the laws of nations hold that a civilized people may interfere, even by force of arms, to prevent a continuance of savage outrages.* The Pope, besides, was solicited by a bishop already established in that country, who complained that the Christians were forced to apostatize, or violate their duty, and sought protection from these lawless acts. The advantages accruing to society from this and similar enterprises, are acknowledged by those who condemn them. Michaud says, "while condemning the excesses of the conquerors of Prussia, we must avow the advantages which Europe derived from their exploits and victories. A nation, separated from all others by its manners and usages, was united with the Christian republic. Industry, law, religion, which followed in the footsteps of the conquerors, to mitigate the evils of war, spread their blessings on savage hordes. Many flourishing cities sprang up in the midst of the forests; and the oak of Romové, beneath which human victims used to be immolated, gave place to churches wherein charity and all the evangelical virtues were taught."† " At the sight of the cross in the midst of deserts and forests, there arose cities : Dantzick, Thorn, Elbing, Konigsberg, &c. Finland, Lithuania, Pomerania, Silesia, became flourishing provinces under the standard of Christ; new nations sprang up, new states were formed; and to complete these prodigies, the arms of the crusaders marked the spot where was to be raised a monarchy unknown to the Middle Ages, and which, in the present age, has risen to the rank of the great powers of Europe. At the end of the thirteenth age, the provinces whence the Prussian monarchy derives its name and origin, were separated from Christendom by idolatry and savage habits: the conquest and civilization of these provinces were the result of the Crusades."‡

Christian princes who undertook to explore undiscovered regions, sought the Papal sanction, lest other potentates should interfere with their rights, and deprive them of the fruits of their enterprise. About the year 1438, Eugene the Fourth granted to the King of Portugal an exclusive right to all the countries which might be discovered by his subjects from Cape Non to the continent of India; and Nicholas V., in 1454, recognised his right over Guinea. It is in vain to say that the Pope had no authority to dispose of these countries; for he was only called on to protect the discoverers against the unjust interference of other princes, by recognising the right which, according to the law of nations, accrued from discovery. This he was perfectly competent to do, from the relation which he bore to the Christian powers generally : and

---

* See Notes of Barbeyrac on Puffendorff, *Du Droit de la Guerre*, l. viii. ch. vi. See also Grotius, *de Jure belli et pacis*, l. ii. ch. xx. n. 40.

† Histoire des Croisades, l. xii. p. 514.   ‡ Ibidem, l. xxii. p. 205.

accordingly, as Robertson remarks, "all Christian princes were deterred from intruding into those countries which the Portuguese had discovered, or from interrupting the progress of their navigation and conquest."* On the remonstrance of John II. of Portugal, Edward IV. of England forbade his subjects to open a trade with the coast of Guinea, lest they should violate the Papal prohibition.

The Bull of Alexander VI., fixing limits for the discoveries of the Kings of Spain and Portugal, is frequently represented as the most extravagant instance of Papal pretensions: yet learned men, Protestant as well as Catholic, regard it only as a solemn sanction of rights already acquired according to the laws of nations, and as a measure directed to prevent war between Christian princes. It is certain, as Washington Irving well observes,† that Ferdinand and Isabella conceived, and in their application to the Pontiff stated, that their title to the newly-discovered lands was, in the opinion of many learned men, sufficiently established by the formal possession taken of them by Columbus, in the name of the Spanish crown; but they desired a public recognition of their right, lest others should profit by the discovery, who had not shared in the enterprise. From the position which the Pope long occupied as father of princes, and highest expounder of law and of the principles of justice, his act was the most solemn confirmation of the title, and the greatest safeguard against encroachment. The terms of "giving, granting, and bestowing, of the plenitude of authority," are only designed to express in the fullest and strongest manner the pontifical sanction and confirmation. "The Roman Pontiffs," says Cardinal Baluffi, "as universal fathers, not because they imagined themselves to be lords of the whole earth, but in order to prevent the effusion of Christian blood, found themselves, at the epoch of the discovery of America, in circumstances which rendered it desirable that they should divide the countries, and mark mutual limits to the conquests of the nations that took arms against unknown nations."‡ Wheaton, in his great work on international law, observes: "As between the Christian nations, the sovereign Pontiff was the supreme arbiter of conflicting claims. Hence the famous Bull issued by Pope Alexander the Sixth, in 1493."§ "This bold stretch of Papal authority," says Prescott, "was in a measure justified by the event, since it did, in fact, determine the principles on which the vast extent of unappropriated empire in the Eastern and Western hemispheres was ultimately divided between two petty states of Europe."‖ It should not surprise us that the right to give, as it were, a charter for the discovery of unknown lands to a national corporation in the Christian confederacy, should be

---

* History of America, l. i.
† Life and Writings of Christopher Columbus, l. v. c. viii. p. 186.
‡ L'America un tempo Spagnuola, da Gaetano Baluffi. Ancona, 1844.
§ Elements of International Law, part ii. ch. iv. p. 240.
‖ Ferdinand and Isabella, vol. ii. ch. xviii.

recognised in him whose office imposed on him the duty of spreading the Gospel throughout all nations.* This temporal attribution might easily attach itself, by general consent, to his spiritual supremacy, the exercise of which in the diffusion of religion it facilitated, by the support and protection given in return by the princes whose enterprise was favored. The personal character of the Pontiff did not disqualify him, in their minds, from discharging the high function of arbiter between them; and Divine Providence gave to the world this sublime instance of the salutary influence of the Papacy, in directing an enterprise which has resulted in the discovery of the New World.†

---

* See Barbosa, de officio et pot. episcopi, tit. iii. c. ii. n. 41, et seq.
† See Du Pape, L. ii. c. xiv., par le Comte De Maistre.

CHAPTER VI.

Papal Polity.

To judge fairly of the acts of the Popes, we must consider the general principles by which they were governed, and which, in a greater or less degree, were common to the ages in which they lived. The first great principle, which was the very basis on which all social order reposed, was, that the Christian revelation and law must be the supreme rule for princes and people, for nations singly and collectively. Christianity was, in fact, the supreme law of all Christendom. Hence it is still considered as a part of the common law of England,* and as such it is even received in this country,† although the Constitution of the United States and the several State Constitutions have virtually annulled its legal consequences, by ignoring its doctrines. Arnold contends that the State has a right to adopt Christianity, if it think proper: "A State may as justly declare the New Testament to be its law, as it may choose the Institutes and Code of Justinian. In this manner the law of Christ's Church may be made its law; and all the institutions which this law enjoins, whether in ritual or discipline, may be adopted as national institutions, just as legitimately as any institutions of mere human origin."‡ The nations, in the Middle Ages, did not feel themselves morally free to adopt or reject the Christian law, which, as they acknowledged it to be from God, they held to be binding, independently of their act; so that they felt bound to conform their municipal and international legislation to its prescriptions. The Popes instinctively acted on this principle, and regarded as null and sacrilegious every human enactment which was opposed to the divine commandments. Michaud remarks: "In reading over the annals of the Middle Ages, we cannot but admire one of the most charming spectacles ever presented by human society, namely, Christian Europe acknowledging but one religion, having but one law, forming as it were but one empire, governed by one chief, who spoke in the name of God, and whose

---

* Blackstone, Comm., l. iv. n. 60.

† "In the United States there is no established Church: it has been considered, however, that we received the Christian religion as part of the common law." American editor of Blackstone, in loc.

‡ Introductory Lectures on Modern History, by Thomas Arnold, D.D. Appendix to Inaugural Lecture, p. 69.

mission was to make the Gospel reign on earth. In the eleventh and twelfth centuries, the nations of Europe, subject to the authority of St. Peter, were united, one with the other, by a stronger tie than that of knowledge, and directed by a more powerful impulse than that of liberty: this bond was the Universal Church."*

The great effort of the Church was to make rulers and their subjects alike submissive in all things to the authority of God. She applied the divine laws to all classes, and urged their observance under the severest penalties which she could inflict, the highest of which was ejection from her fold. Feeling that she could not surrender or compromise the privileges and rights which she had received from her Divine Founder, she calmly but perseveringly protested against every attempt on the part of the State to encroach on her rights, or to control her in the legitimate exercise of her authority. She taught her children to render to Cesar the things which are Cesar's; but she enjoined on them most especially to render to God the things which are God's. Giving a religious sanction to the civil authority, in its proper sphere, she claimed an exclusive right to regulate what appertains to the supernatural order, and to govern men in the things of salvation. Hence Ranke has well remarked, that "in this separation of the Church from the State consists, perhaps, the greatest, and most pervading, and most influential peculiarity of all Christian times."† Dr. Nevin says: "The separation of the temporal and spiritual powers, and the independence of the latter with respect to the former, has had much to do, no doubt, with the formation of that spirit of liberty which is characteristic of modern civilization."‡ The great struggle between the Popes and temporal princes, in regard to *investitures*, was an effort on the part of the Popes to drive them back within the limits of their own jurisdiction, and recover the territory of the Church which they had invaded. Under the pretext that, as civil rulers, they bestowed lands and other temporal advantages on the Church, they took on themselves to install bishops, by placing in their hand the pastoral staff, and putting the episcopal ring on their finger. Thus they insensibly came to control their election, and sometimes put on the episcopal chair the companions of their debauch, or the ministers of their vengeance. The enormous scandals which defiled the sanctuary, in the tenth and eleventh ages especially, were mainly to be traced to this usurpation: to resist which, St. Gregory VII., and his successors, exposed themselves to suffering and persecution. Paschal II., treacherously made prisoner by Henry V., yielded to the advice and entreaties of some who implored him to save his own life, and the lives of his adherents, by conceding the privilege: but he soon felt that he had betrayed his duty, and in a solemn Council he deplored, with tears, his momentary weakness. The bonds of

---

* Histoire des Croisades, l. xiii. p. 98. † History of the Popes, vol. i. ch. i. p. 29.
‡ "Modern Civilization." M. R., March, 1851.

the Church were by successive efforts burst asunder, and her liberty was attended with the renovation of her prelacy, who shone forth in the beauty of holiness. Emperors and kings occasionally became her benefactors, and atoned for the wrongs which their predecessors had inflicted. "It is somewhat remarkable," writes Mr. Allies, "that that Church which maintains a standing protest against the interference of the State with spiritual matters, (a protest for which she is worthy of all respect and admiration,) should owe to the support of the State, in different periods of her history, very much more of her power than any other church. It may be that God rewards the fearless maintenance of spiritual rights by the grant of that very temporal power which threatens them with destruction."* I believe that her indebtedness to the State is very small.

The compacts made between the people and the sovereign, which were confirmed by the rite of coronation, embraced the immunities and privileges of the Church, which the prince bound himself to maintain inviolate. Hence, when these were invaded, holy prelates resisted the perjured sovereign, professing their submission to his just authority, but their unwillingness to betray the interests of religion intrusted to their charge. The Pope encouraged them by his approbation, threatening to hurl the censures of the Church against the violator of her rights. We are not now to inquire whether these immunities ought to have been originally conceded. They actually formed part of the compact in virtue of which the monarch reigned, and could not be disregarded without a breach of his sworn engagement. In enforcing them, the Pontiff acted in accordance with the general usages and public law of the age; at the same time offering to sanction such contributions by the clergy to the public burdens as might appear just and necessary.† Boniface VIII., while resisting Philip the Fair, who forced the clergy to raise subsidies according to his pleasure, consented that they should, of their own free and concerted action, contribute to the public wants, and that in case of any general or special necessity of the kingdom, they should be bound to give supplies. The privilege in question was the right of self-taxation, which in this country, and wherever the representative system prevails, is now exercised by the nation at large, through their representatives.

Some of the most illustrious prelates that adorned the English hierarchy are celebrated for their intrepid maintenance of ecclesiastical immunities. St. Anselm, with sacerdotal fortitude, contended for the privileges and freedom of the Church against William Rufus and Henry I., while he most sincerely professed submission to the lawful authority of the sovereign: "In the things of God I shall obey," he said, "the Vicar of St. Peter: in what regards the dignity of my lord the king, I shall give my best counsel and aid to maintain it."‡

---

* Church of England Cleared, &c. p. 114. † Conc. Lat. iv. § xlvi.
‡ Conventus Rochinghamiensis, t. x., Conc. p. 494.

St. Thomas of Canterbury deemed it the duty of his office to maintain the ecclesiastical immunities against the encroachments of his temporal sovereign, and ventured to rebuke him as deviating from the line of duty which became a Catholic prince. Addressing Henry II., he says: "If you are a good and Catholic king, and wish to be such as we believe and desire you to be, if I may say it with your leave, you are a child of the Church, not her ruler; you should learn from the priests, not teach them; you should follow the priests in ecclesiastical matters, not go before them. You have power peculiar to yourself, bestowed on you by God for the administration of the laws, that, being grateful for His favors, you may do nothing contrary to the order divinely established."* "Most beloved king, God wills that the direction of the things of the Church should belong to His priests, not to the powers of the world, which, if they be faithful, He wishes to be submissive to the priests of His Church."†
Innocent III. wrote to Sanchez II. of Portugal in these terms: "We beseech you, most beloved son, through the mercy of Jesus Christ, to be content with the authority which God has given you, and not at all to stretch your hands to matters ecclesiastical, as we do not stretch our hands to matters of royal prerogative."‡ The justice of this distinction, and the favorable influence of the independence which is here vindicated, are too often overlooked by many advocates of civil liberty, who most inconsistently claim for the State an unlimited control, even in matters which strictly belong to the province of the Church. "Strange," says Dr. Nevin, "that the advocates of equilibrium and counterpoise, who make so much of the policy of dividing powers to prevent tyranny, should not have felt the profound wisdom of this old church doctrine, even in a simply political view."§

With reference to the principles of civil government, it may be safely asserted that the Popes were uniformly favorable to popular rights and liberty, although with strict regard to public order and established authority. St. Gregory the Great rebuked an imperial officer for extreme severity in punishing crime, which, he said, reflected disgrace on the power which he exercised, the subjects of the emperor being freemen, not slaves: "This is the difference between the kings of the nations, and the emperors of the Romans,—that the kings of the nations are lords of slaves, the emperor of the Romans is the lord of freemen. Wherefore, in all your acts, you should, in the first place, have a strict regard to justice, and next, you should preserve liberty in all things."‖ Gregory IX. reproached Frederick II. with being at once a "persecutor of the Church and a destroyer of public liberty," by the unjust laws which he threatened to promulgate. In opposing the union of Sicily with the empire, the Popes guarded against the accumulation of power in the hands of one

---

* Apud Baron., an. 1166, p. 535.   † Ibidem, p. 536.
‡ Apud Raynald., an 1211.   § "Modern Civilization." M. R., March, 1851.
‖ L. x., ep. 41.

man; and in the various acts of Papal opposition to imperial encroachment, the liberty of Italy, Germany, and the nations generally, was vindicated. Michaud avows: "But for the Pope, it is probable that Europe would have fallen under the yoke of the emperors of Germany. The policy of the sovereign Pontiffs, by weakening the imperial power, favored in Germany the liberty of the cities, and the increase and duration of the small States. We do not hesitate to add, that the thunders of the Holy See saved the independence of Italy, and perhaps of France."*
"This policy of the Popes resulted in freeing Italy from the yoke of the German emperors, so that this rich country for sixty years did not behold the imperial troops."† "Liberty and the Church" were inspiring watchwords of the Lombard league. Venice, Verona, Padua, Vicenza, combined against Frederick, *pro tuenda libertate*, in defence of liberty.‡ Pope Alexander was their friend and ally; so that when the Lombards listened to overtures made on the part of Frederick, they made an express proviso in behalf of the Roman Church, and of their own liberty; and, on the other hand, when the Pope was solicited to accede to some proposals of the emperor, he declined any final action without the concurrence of the Lombards, who had nobly fought, as he publicly declared, for the welfare of the Church and the liberty of Italy.§ The like sympathies manifested themselves on many occasions. "Tuscany," says Hallam, "had hitherto been ruled by a marquis of the emperor's appointment, though her cities were flourishing, and, within themselves, independent. In imitation of the Lombard confederacy, and impelled by Innocent III., they now (with the exception of Pisa, which was always strongly attached to the empire) founded a similar league for the preservation of their rights. In this league the influence of the Pope was far more strongly manifested than in that of Lombardy."‖

All the cities of Italy enjoyed that independence which Hallam ascribes to those of Tuscany, since even those which acknowledged the empire, had municipal rights on the largest scale, including the election of their own officers and judges, and every thing appertaining to internal government. The evil of those times was the excess of liberty, which, for the want of a general authority, to combine and preserve in harmony the various cities, degenerated into licentiousness, intestine feuds, and mutual warfare. Each city was a republic, whose citizens were most jealous of their rights, so that they limited the powers of the presiding officer to a short period, sometimes of six months only, and guarded by every possible means against the abuse of his authority, or its continuation in the same individual.¶

---

* Histoire des Croisades, l. xlii. p. 97.   † Ibid., l. xvi. p. 454.
‡ Baronius, an. 1164.   § Baronius, an. 1177.
‖ Middle Ages, vol. i. ch. iii. par. i. p. 259.
¶ See Hurter, Tableau des Institutions et des Mœurs du Moyen Age, ch. xl. vol. ii. p. 531.

It was the constant study of the Popes to guard against the perpetuity of the imperial authority in the same family, by mere title of descent, and to maintain the elective principle. In the vacancy of the empire under Innocent III., the majority of votes were for Philip of Swabia, who was deemed by Innocent totally unworthy, and in whose election the necessary conditions had not been attended to. Frederick had in his favor hereditary right, being son of the deceased emperor. The opposition of the Pope to both candidates led some of the princes to murmur, as if he sought to take from them the privilege of electing the emperor, which, in his instructions to his ambassadors, he denied most unequivocally: "In order effectually to close the mouth of such as speak unjustly, and to prevent credit being given to the slanders of those who assert that we mean to take from the princes the liberty of election, you should oftentimes, by word of mouth, and in writing, repeat to all that we have had regard to their liberty in this matter, and have sought to preserve it inviolate: for we have not chosen any one; but we have favored, and we still favor him who was chosen by the majority of the persons entitled to a vote in the choice of the emperor, and who was crowned in the proper place, and by the proper person; since the Apostolic See should crown him emperor who was duly crowned king. We also stand up for the liberty of the princes, while we utterly deny our sanction to him who claims the empire on the score of succession: for it would appear that the empire was not conferred by the election of the princes, but by succession, if, as formerly, the son succeeded the father, so now the brother should succeed the brother, or the son succeed the father, without any intermediate person."* In speaking of Rudolph, Duke of Swabia, whom an assembly of revolted princes raised to the throne in place of Henry, Hallam observes: "We may perceive in the conditions of Rudolph's election, a symptom of the real principle that animated the German aristocracy against Henry IV. It was agreed that the kingdom should no longer be hereditary, nor conferred on the son of a reigning monarch without popular approbation. The Pope strongly encouraged this plan of rendering the empire elective."† He otherwise labored to confine the imperial power within just limits, and to the Papal vigilance it must be ascribed that "before Charles V., the emperors durst not assume despotic power."‡

The several monarchies which under the favor of the Popes arose in the Middle Ages, were virtually republics, with presidents during good behaviour, the sovereigns being considered only a degree above the nobles, and liable to forfeit their power, should they abuse it. Voltaire, speaking of the thirteenth century, observes: "Castile and Aragon were kingdoms at that time; but we must not imagine that their sovereigns were abso-

---

* Ep. liv., apud Raynald., an. 1201. † Middle Ages, vol. i. ch. v. p. 460.
‡ Voltaire, Essai sur l'Histoire Générale, t. iii. cxvii.

lute: *there were none such in Europe.* The nobles in Spain, more than elsewhere, confined the royal authority within strict limits. The people of Aragon still repeat the ancient formulary used in the inauguration of their kings. The chief-justice of the kingdom, in the name of the various classes of citizens, said: 'We, who are as good as you, and more powerful than you, make you our king and lord, on condition that you preserve our privileges, and not otherwise.'"* "The oath made by the kings (of Poland) on their coronation contained an express call on the nation to dethrone them, in case they did not observe the laws which they swore to respect."† "No mistake can be greater," says Dr. Nevin, "than that by which the exaggeration of the authority of rulers, at the cost of popular rights, is held to be the natural and necessary doctrine of Catholicism, as distinguished from the genius of Protestantism. History plainly teaches a different lesson."‡ As long as the Pope was revered as the father and judge of kings, these felt that there were limits which they could not pass without peril: but when it was proclaimed that kings are answerable only to God, a deep wound was inflicted on popular liberty in the attack on pontifical supremacy. Royalty itself paid the penalty of its independence. When the Pontiff let fall from his hand the mace which he had brandished to awe tyrants, the people, seizing it, wielded it with brutal force, and left even just monarchs weltering in their blood. England saw Charles I. perish by the hands of the public executioner; and France doomed the meek Louis XVI. to the same ignominious end. Never was a Papal sentence of deposition exhibited on a scaffold!

While the Popes labored to instruct kings in justice, they cherished with paternal fondness the Italian republics, which grew up under their fostering protection. At the request of the Doge of Venice, Gregory IX. became the special protector of that republic, and gave her the ocean as her dowry. She flourished long in arms and arts, commerce and enterprise of every honorable kind, the ally and friend of Rome, until Sarpi and other false men disturbed that harmony, by disregarding the ancient immunities of the clergy, which, in the zenith of her power, she had respected. The eternal city still stands in her strength, while the queen of the waters has forfeited her portion; and the German soldier guards the palace, where her merchant princes once deliberated whether they would grant the favors which sovereigns did not disdain to ask at their hands. The Pontiffs always favored the republic, unless in circumstances of this unfortunate character, in which usages, which for ages had been deemed laws of the whole Christian confederacy, were wantonly violated. Many interesting examples of Papal interposition to appease the dissensions of republics, one with the other, or within themselves, are recorded. Speaking of the struggles for office between the aristocracy and

---

* Voltaire, Essai sur l'Histoire Générale, t. ii. ch. lx.   † Ibidem, ch. cxv.
‡ Ibidem, ch. cxv.   § Modern Civilization, M. R., March, 1851.

commonalty, Hallam says: "In one or two cities, a temporary compromise was made through the intervention of the Pope, whereby offices of public trust, from the highest to the lowest, were divided in equal proportions, or otherwise, between the nobles and the people. This is no bad expedient, and proved singularly efficacious in appeasing the dissensions of ancient Rome."* It is pleasing to be able to point out such examples of pontifical interposition to regulate the social relations so as to satisfy every class of the community. The general tendency of such interposition was of this character, which is proved by the result, as testified by a distinguished writer. "It is historically certain," writes Dr. Nevin, "that European society, as a whole, in the period before the Reformation, was steadily advancing in the direction of a rational, safe liberty. The problem by which the several interests of the throne, the aristocracy, and the mass of the people were to be rightly guarded and carried forward in the onward movement of civilization, so as by just harmony to serve and not hinder the true welfare of all, was one of vast difficulty; which, however, in the face of manifold disturbing forces, we may see still approximating, at least, more and more toward its own full and proper solution. The simple position of these several elements relatively to each other, at the going out of the Middle Ages, is of itself enough to show how false it is to represent the old Catholicity as the enemy of popular liberty: for we see that European civilization, at this time, after having been for so many centuries under the sole guardianship of that power, presented no one of these interests as exclusively predominant."†

When the Gospel was first preached, slavery prevailed among the most civilized nations, and the apostles, careful not to disturb the actual order of society, inculcated submission to the slave, to the master humanity. The Popes faithfully followed their example, as has been shown by the late lamented Bishop of Charleston, in his learned letters on this subject. Yet, while respecting existing relations, they did much to mitigate the evils of servitude, and to raise the slave to that moral elevation, which might fit him for the enjoyment of civil liberty. Encouragement was given to the manumission of slaves; the natural rights of man, in regard to the freedom of marriage, were held to be inviolable, notwithstanding his social dependency; and religious privileges were communicated to all, without distinction. The salvation of the slave was especially had in view. In the middle of the eighth century, Zachary gave a noble example of zeal and humanity. Some Venetian merchants had purchased at Rome a great number of slaves, with a view to sell them at a higher price, for transportation to Africa. The Pope, shocked at the thought of the danger of salvation to which the poor slaves would be exposed, generously indemnified the merchants for their outlay of money, and set the

---

* Middle Ages, vol. i. ch. iii. par. i. p. 278.
† "Modern Civilization." M. R., March, 1851.

slaves at liberty. In the same spirit, Alexander III., in the year 1167, in the Council of Lateran, forbade Christians to be held as slaves by Jews or Saracens.*

It is impossible to overrate what the Popes have done for the proper organization of society, and the maintenance of order. In the confusion of the Middle Ages, when an appeal to the sword was the first resort of half-civilized nobles and their followers, they raised their voice in behalf of justice. Not only did they regulate the proceedings of the ecclesiastical tribunals, so as to present a model for the civil powers, but, going beyond the precise limits of Church authority, they made several enactments of a civil character, to secure the attainment of right, and prevent fraud and violence. The great Council of Lateran, held in 1215, contains several decrees of this kind. I shall give one remarkable instance, which to the present day is followed in the practice of the courts of the United States, as well as throughout the British Empire. The mode of proceedings in criminal cases prescribed by it, still serves as the rule of criminal jurisprudence, in secular, as well as ecclesiastical courts. Where a public report prevails of the commission of crime, inquiry is to be made by the judge, and information sought. Such is now the practice of the Grand Jury as a Court of Inquest, preparatory to their making a presentment.† The canon, however, requires the individual whom the report regards, to be present at the investigation, unless he absent himself contumaciously. He is to be apprized of the charges made against him, that he may have an opportunity of defending himself. The judge is directed to communicate to him the names of the witnesses, and their depositions, and to receive his objections and defence. The Roman law required that the accusation should be given, in writing, to the judge; which regulation was inserted in the decretals of Isidore: but the entire process above delineated may be fairly ascribed to the eminent Pontiff, Innocent III.‡

The Councils of the Church were deliberative assemblies, which, in the Middle Ages, assumed a mixed character, from the presence of princes and nobles, whose wishes were respected, and whose consent was awaited in matters of a temporal nature. These prepared the way for the *cortes*, *chambres*, parliaments, and other legislative assemblies of later times, in which the general interests of the respective nations are provided for, by enactments made by their representatives. "The system, indeed, of ecclesiastical Councils, considered as organs of the Church, rested upon the

---

* In former editions, the praise of having abolished the slavery of Christians is given to this Pontiff, on the authority of Bancroft and Voltaire, with whom Fuller and De Maistre agree. The canon xxvi. of the Council does not imply so much. Carrière is of opinion that there is no other ground for the assertion.—De Justitia et Jure, t. i. p. i. ᔕ i. c. iii. 50, p. 75. Mœhler, treating on the abolition of slavery, does not make mention of Alexander III. See "Le Christianisme et l'Esclavage," par Thérou.

† Blackstone, Comm., l. iv. n. 301.

‡ C. Qualiter et quando, 24, de accus. extra.

principle of a virtual or an express representation, and had a tendency to render its application to national assemblies more familiar."* The clergy have no longer that influence which once enabled them to direct legislation in a manner subordinate to the higher interests of religion, and the laity, who now almost everywhere exclusively constitute those assemblies, have forgotten that they originated in the enlightened policy of the Popes and bishops.

Although the established usages and the laws of the various nations were necessarily treated with wise toleration and indulgence, the Popes labored incessantly to correct whatever was reprehensible in them, and to promote a general system of legislation. As the Gothic code of laws contained no penalty for sacrilege, John VIII., in a Council held at Troyes, undertook to supply this defect from the Roman law, modified by the milder legislation of Charlemagne.† With the same views, the study of the civil or Cesarean code was also effectually encouraged. Nicholas I. made frequent reference to it in answering the inquiries of the Bulgarians. The common law, which is justly regarded as the basis of society, here as well as in the British Empire, is perhaps not, as Blackstone affirms, the result of the wisdom of Alfred or Edward, whose lost enactments are gathered from judicial decisions from time immemorial,‡ but rather, as Spelman avows, is derived partly from the laws and customs of Germans and Saxons, and especially from the canon and civil law. "Two other principal parts, (as from two pole stars,) take their direction from the canon law, and the law of our brethren, the Longobards, called otherwise the feodal law, generally received throughout all Europe. Another great portion of our common law is derived from the civil law."§

We may then fairly claim for the Pontiffs the merit of having laid the foundations of order, justice, liberty, and all that appertains to modern civilization. Left to themselves, the nations would have sunk deeper and deeper into barbarism, while, by the mild influences of religion, their fierceness was subdued, their vices corrected, and the controlling power of law successfully established. Had they been isolated, they would have been known to one another only by predatory incursions, or other acts of barbarian aggression; but the acknowledgment of a common father bound them together, despite of national antipathies, and made of them one great family. "During the Middle Ages," says Wheaton, "the Christian States of Europe began to unite, and to acknowledge the obligation of an international law, common to all who professed the same religious faith. This law was founded mainly upon the following circumstances: first, the union of the Latin Church under one spiritual head, whose authority was

---

* Hallam's Middle Ages, ch. viii. p. 111. † Conc. col. reg., vol. vi. p. 198.
‡ Comm., l. iv. n. 301.
§ The Original of the Four Terms of the Year, by Sir Henry Spelman, c. viii.

often invoked as supreme arbiter betwen sovereigns and between nations. Second, the revival of the study of the Roman law, and the adoption of this system of jurisprudence by nearly all the nations of Christendom, either as the basis of their municipal codes, or as subsidiary to the local legislation in each country."*

The principles of this universal faith contain the elements of true liberty, independent of the various forms of government, all of which may practically assume the character of despotism. The relations of men to one another, when governed by Christianity, necessarily assume a mild and just form, and are insensibly divested of the asperity which they might otherwise involve. Domestic as well as social ties are hallowed and ennobled by this influence, and the strongest guarantee of right is found in the general conscience.

---

* Elements of International Law. Preface to third edition.

CHAPTER VII.

Crusades.

THE influence and power of the Pope in temporal matters, connected with the interests of religion, appeared in the most extraordinary degree, in the great movements of the European powers for the recovery of the Holy Land. It has long been fashionable to condemn these wars as fanatical, if not wholly unchristian; but we should be slow to censure what met with the universal approbation of the most enlightened and holy men, during several centuries. It is more becoming to inquire into the principles on which they acted, and judge them according to their motives. My object, however, is to explain the part which the Popes took in these wars, and the influence which they exercised.

Jerusalem and all the parts of Palestine consecrated by the footsteps of our Divine Redeemer, were viewed with special veneration by all Christians, from the earliest period. In the seventh century, they fell under the Mohammedan yoke, and were thenceforward, for three centuries, subject to the Caliphs of Bagdad and of Cairo, alternately, until the power of the Egyptian sultan prevailed. In 1076, Jerusalem was wrested from his dominion by Malek Shah, a prince of the Seljuk Turks from Tartary, who, some time previously, had invaded Syria, and other provinces. The struggle of the hostile clans continued for eighteen years, when the Egyptians again regained the ascendancy. In the mean time, the pilgrims, who flocked from Europe to the holy places, experienced the ferocity of the new lords of Palestine, and the Christian inhabitants of that country were most cruelly oppressed. The sufferings of the Eastern Christians had awakened the sympathy of their brethren in Europe, in the tenth century; at the close of which, "Pope Sylvester II., the ornament of his age, entreated the Church universal to succor the Church of Jerusalem, and to redeem a sepulchre which the Prophet Isaiah had said should be a glorious one, and which the sons of the destroyer, Satan, were making inglorious."* The subsequent success of the Turks filled with alarm the Emperor of Constantinople, Michael Ducas, who, in 1073, applied to Gregory VII. to obtain aid against an enemy formidable to all the Christian powers.† The magnanimous Pontiff received the application favor-

---

* History of the Crusades, by Charles Mills, ch. i. p. 20.
† Hallam, Middle Ages, vol. i. ch. i.

ably, especially as hope was held out, that the reunion of the Greeks with the Church would result from the efforts of the Latins in their behalf. When enlisting an army for the defence of his possessions in Campania, against the Normans, he expressed the hope, that the enemy would be deterred from battle by the military preparations, so that the troops raised might be employed for the succor of the oriental Christians. In an encyclical letter he solicited the aid of the faithful generally, that he might send the desired relief. Fifty thousand soldiers were ready to march to the East, but the difficulties in which he himself was involved, prevented the prosecution of the generous design. Victor III., who succeeded him, encouraged the citizens of Pisa, Genoa, and other towns of Italy, to follow up the undertaking, especially as the Saracens infested the Mediterranean, and threatened the Italian coasts. The combined forces of these Christian powers made a successful descent on the coast of Africa, and reduced under their power Al Mahadia and Sibila, in the territory of Carthage, and obliged a king of Mauritania to pay tribute to the Holy See.*

Alexius Comnenus, who occupied the imperial throne, in 1094, implored the succor of the West, through ambassadors, who, in a Council held at Piacenza, at which Urban II. presided, urged the demand. Four thousand clergymen and thirty thousand laymen, congregated in the open air, received the proposals with acclamation. The narrative of Peter the Hermit, a Frenchman, who had just returned from Palestine, contributed not a little to excite the sympathy and inflame the zeal of the Pontiff. He had been an eye-witness of the cruel oppression of the Eastern Christians, and had been charged by the Patriarch to represent their sad condition, and implore aid of their European brethren. From the court of Rome he hastened back to his native country, and everywhere repeated the tale of wo, so as to move to tears all who heard him. In 1095, a Council was called at Clermont; and, as the numbers who assembled could not be contained in any of the churches, an open square was chosen for the deliberations. Urban, who presided, spoke with an eloquence that seemed supernatural; and as he concluded his exhortation to hasten to the relief of their suffering brethren, the immense assemblage, as if by inspiration, cried out: IT IS THE WILL OF GOD.

The enthusiasm with which the address of Urban was received, and the promptitude wherewith the glorious badge of enrolment was assumed, should convince us that the motives for the expedition were plainly just and sacred. It is not to be thought that in any age, or under any circumstances, thousands and tens of thousands would abandon their country and home, and expose life, for an object not evidently just, at the bidding of an individual, however elevated in station. Nobles, with generous enthusiasm, left the court for the distant plains of Palestine, to fight for the liberation of their suffering brethren, and, at a great sacrifice, sold their

---

* Histoire des Croisades, par Michaud, l. i. p. 88.

domains to procure money for the expedition: their vassals felt honored in being allowed to follow them to the field, where the conflict was not with a rival lord, but with the enemies of religion and of man. The monks went forth from their cloisters, to console and succor the crusaders; and the bishops, with large numbers of their flocks, were seen hastening to the sacred standard. The zeal of the Pontiff led him to visit various other cities of France, and to address fervent exhortations to the immense multitudes that everywhere assembled at his call. Although countless numbers perished on the journey by disease, and in conflict with the people of Hungary, Bulgaria, Greece, and other places, who resisted their progress, and refused them provisions, he nowise relented in his grand purpose; but meeting at Lucca a host of crusaders, who accompanied the Count of Vermandois, he placed in his hands the standard of the Church, that he might go forth to fight the battles of the cross.*

The crusaders are sometimes represented as influenced by no other motive than the desire of rescuing the Holy Land from the infidel. This, however, is not the fact. For three centuries Jerusalem had been in the power of the Caliphs, without any effort having been made by the Christians to wrest it from their hands: it was the ferocity of the Turks which filled Europe with alarm and indignation.† The spirit of the crusades abated, when the Syrian Christians ceased to be so grievously oppressed. The ardor with which all Europe engaged in the struggle, was owing to the picture of suffering presented to them by the Hermit and the Pontiff. Doubtless their enthusiasm was increased by the consideration that the scene of those sufferings had been hallowed by the presence, miracles, and sufferings of Christ: but this does not detract from the lawfulness of the war, as undertaken for the relief of their fellow-Christians. "They were armed," as Michaud remarks, "in behalf of the wretched and the oppressed. They went forward to defend a religion which awakened their sympathies for distant sufferers, and caused them to discover brothers in the inhabitants of countries unknown to them."‡

I know not whether it will be denied, that it was lawful for the nations of Europe to make war upon the Turks, in consequence of the outrages committed on European pilgrims, and the constant oppression of the Christians of Palestine. At this day nations resent the affronts and injuries of foreign powers to individual citizens sojourning in distant countries. Governments also connive at the raising of volunteers to aid the oppressed in asserting their rights, and sometimes openly join in the struggle. In many extreme cases, there seems to be no other means of rescuing the people from cruel despotism, than the intervention of a

---

* Michaud, Histoire des Croisades, l. ii. p. 177.
† Robertson's View of the State of Europe, sect. 1.
‡ Histoire des Croisades, l. iv. p. 512.

foreign power, demanding that the citizens be governed on principles of humanity and justice. If it be ever lawful for foreigners to interpose, it was surely so when fierce barbarians trampled under foot every natural right, delivered the daughters of Christians to dishonor, forced their sons to apostatize, and butchered the parents. The meek and suffering spirit which the Christian religion breathes, does not deprive men of the rights of humanity, or take away from nations the power to make just war. Individuals are taught to respect public authority, even when abused for purposes of persecution: but nations can appeal on the battle-field to the God of hosts, to vindicate justice and right. The actual government of Palestine had not prescription in its favor. The Turks were invaders, who, a short time before, had seized on the reins of power; and the Egyptians, when for a time successful, had not recovered pacific and secure possession. There was nothing in the title of the rulers of Syria, to form a bar against the interference of the European powers, who were anxious to rescue their Eastern brethren.

The crusades were undertaken in the name of humanity, as well as of religion; and the destruction of the infidel was vowed, not as an act in itself acceptable, but as a necessary means for vindicating the oppressed. The shedding of human blood is to be abhorred: yet when it becomes necessary to maintain order, or put an end to outrage, God himself has given it His sanction. Hence we must consider the appeal of Urban II. to the Christian people, as an exhortation to a just war, and a wise effort on his part to give a proper direction to the warlike propensity of the age, by pointing to a legitimate object what for the most part manifested itself in acts of lawless violence. "Be ye armed," he cried, "dearly beloved, with the zeal of God; let each gird his sword upon his thigh most powerfully. Be ye ready, and be ye valiant: for it is better for us to die in war, than to see the evils of the people and of the holy places. Go forth, and the Lord will be with you, and turn against the enemies of the faith, and of the Christian name, the arms which you have criminally stained with the blood of one another."* This language may seem unbecoming the representative of the Prince of Peace: but if the relation of the Pope to society at that period be considered, he will be seen to have only spoken as the necessity of the case required. As the actual head of the confederacy of Christian nations, the only one who could effectually rouse them to a general effort, he raised his voice in behalf of justice and humanity. To exhort to just war was more humane than to suffer in silence the continuance of the outrages of which the Syrian Christians were the victims.

Mills admits that, "if Europe had armed itself for the purpose of succoring the Grecian emperor, the rendering of such assistance would have been a moral action; for the Saracenian march of hostility would not have

---

* Apud Baron., an. 1095.

stopped with the subjugation of Constantinople, and it is incumbent on us to prevent a danger as well as to repel one."* This was the case precisely. Michael Ducas and Alexius Comnenus had successively applied for aid to preserve the seat of empire, which was threatened by the Turks. The Pope acted at their solicitation; and his action, thus fully justified by the law of nations, did not cease to be just, because it was at the same time influenced by the prayers of the Patriarch of Jerusalem, and of the Oriental Christians, and by the sublime consideration of the holiness of the place that was to be rescued from the grasp of the unbeliever. Mills himself states, that "in some minds political considerations had weight, and Europe was regarded as the ally of Constantinople."† The advantages derived to the emperor from the first efforts of the crusaders are acknowledged by Hallam, who does not conceive, as Mills, that the danger had passed away before relief was afforded. "In this state of jeopardy," he observes, when describing the advances of the Turks, "the Greek empire looked for aid from the nations of the West, and received it in fuller measure than was expected, or perhaps desired. The deliverance of Constantinople was, indeed, a very secondary object with the crusaders. But it was necessarily included in their scheme of operations, which, though they all tended to the recovery of Jerusalem, must commence with the first enemies that lay on their line of march. The Turks were entirely defeated; their capital of Nice restored to the empire. As the Franks passed onward, the Emperor Alexius Comnenus trod on their footsteps, and secured to himself the fruits for which their enthusiasm disdained to wait. He regained possession of the strong places on the Ægean shores, of the defiles of Bithynia, and of the entire coast of Asia Minor, both on the Euxine and Mediterranean seas, which the Turkish armies, composed of cavalry, and unused to regular warfare, could not recover. So much must undoubtedly be ascribed to the first crusade."‡

Alexius, on the arrival of the crusaders, entered into an express league with them, binding himself to unite his forces with theirs, supply them with provisions, and aid them in the assault on Jerusalem, while, on their part, they promised to deliver into his hands, or receive of him as fiefs the cities of the empire which they might retake from the infidels.§ This confirms the fact that they acted originally as his allies. After the establishment of the kingdom of Jerusalem, it was regarded as a colony, which the Western princes felt bound to protect.|| The king earnestly and repeatedly sought the support of his European brethren; and when the kingdom was overthrown, the Eastern Christians cried out piteously for aid. If at any time they seemed indifferent, or averse to the interference of their European brethren, it was when despair induced them to

---

* History of the Crusades, ch. xviii. p. 243. † Ibid., ch. ii. p. 24.
‡ Middle Ages, vol. i. ch. vi. p. 519. § Histoire des Croisades, l. ii. p. 194.
|| Histoire des Croisades, l. vi. p. 170, Note

bear their chains without a murmur, rather than provoke the tyrant to rivet them anew. Thus, the third crusade, proclaimed by Celestine III., having failed, they seemed unwilling to share in the responsibility of another effort made by the same Pontiff, in the ninetieth year of his age. Notwithstanding this reluctance, the European powers felt that they had a right to protect the colony, since the general interests of Christendom were at stake.

It is impossible not to perceive that the crusades were, from the commencement, and still more in their progress, virtually defensive wars, directed to repel Turkish aggression, and preserve the nations of Europe from the Mohammedan yoke. The Moors from Africa, imbued with Mohammedan superstition, were already masters of Spain; the Saracens had reduced under their power the southern provinces of Italy, and they frequently hovered over its coast, spreading desolation wherever they lighted; the Turks, fresh in the career of conquest, placed no bounds to their ambition : they "became masters of the Asiatic cities and fortified passes; nor did there seem any obstacle to their invasion of Europe."* The struggle between them and the Christian forces, which continued for ages with various success, proves that their power was in the highest degree formidable. It was, then, a master-stroke of policy to carry the war into their own territory, and to dispute with them the possession of their actual dominions, lest, proceeding in their course, they should obtain an easy victory over each European potentate, singly battling for his own safety. The union of all the Christian powers, which was the only means of effectual resistance, was wisely devised by Urban II. His words prove that this plea for the crusades is no ingenious after-thought, no invention of modern apologists : "We admonish you," said he, "and in the Lord we exhort you, and enjoin on you, for the remission of your sins, to sympathize with our afflicted and suffering brethren, the inhabitants of Jerusalem and its vicinity, coheirs with us of the heavenly kingdom, (for we are all members one of another,) and coheirs of Christ, and to restrain by just coercion the insolence of the infidels, who aim at subjecting to their power kingdoms, principalities and powers, and to oppose with all your might their efforts to cancel from the earth the Christian name."† The same argument was advanced by Innocent III., to rouse the Christian powers to the fifth crusade. He represents the Mussulmen as glorying in their success: "What remains for us," say they, "but to drive away those whom you have left in Syria, and to penetrate to the far West, and cancel forever your name and memory from among nations ?"‡ If the crusaders showed but little apprehension of this danger, it only proves the more generous sentiments by which they were influenced : but the danger was not imaginary, or even remote, as the intelligent Pontiffs well perceived.

---

* Hallam, Middle Ages, ch. vi. p. 519. † Apud Baron., an. 1095, p. 663.
‡ Michaud, Histoire des Croisades, l. x. p. 81.

The manifest lawfulness of the crusades may be fairly inferred from the approbation which they received from the most holy men, and from the miracles which were wrought by some who proclaimed them. The eminent sanctity of Bernard, the famous Abbot of Clairvaux, who was an active promoter of the second crusade, is acknowledged, even by many Protestants. In the year 1145, Eugene III. having received the afflicting intelligence that Edessa had fallen into the hands of the Saracen, and that Antioch and Jerusalem were in danger, forgetful of his own perils and necessities, turned all his attention to the succor of the Christian King of Jerusalem. Louis VII. resolved to second his pious desires, with whom Conrad, Emperor of Germany, united his forces. In a numerous Council held at Chartres, Bernard was chosen as leader, who, however, declined this office, as unsuited to his religious state. The holy abbot, nevertheless, justified the crusade, as a necessary measure of defence against the ever-increasing violence of the Mohammedans : " Since they have commenced the attack, it behoves those who, not without cause, bear the sword, to repel force by force. Christian clemency, however, must spare the conquered, as Christian valor should subdue the proud."* He fervently exhorted the faithful to enlist under the sacred banner; the Lord, as his ancient biographer assures us, confirming his preaching by the signs that followed it, which were so numerous that they could not be recorded in detail.† The faithful, fully persuaded that the undertaking was of God, rallied under the standard of the cross, leaving the cities and towns almost deserted, as Bernard himself testifies.‡ The failure of an enterprise thus divinely sanctioned, is among the instances of the mysterious counsels of God. The perfidy of the Greek emperor and the temerity of the crusaders were the immediate causes of defeat; which may also be ascribed to the unworthiness and sins of the princes and people. St. Bernard asks : " How does human temerity dare censure what it cannot comprehend?"§

The idea of encouraging the crusades by indulgences, has afforded abundant matter of reproach. These, however, were intended to reward the generous devotedness with which the crusaders undertook a long and toilsome journey, and exposed their lives in a just war connected with religion. The condition of true penance was always prescribed in order to gain them; and, in fact, multitudes of most abandoned sinners were won to Christ by the assurance of unqualified forgiveness to the penitent crusader. The terms of the concession were not to be mistaken : " Trusting to the mercy of God, and authority of the blessed Apostles Peter and Paul, we remit the heaviest penances for sins to such faithful Christians as shall take arms against them, (the Turks,) and take on themselves the labor of this journey. Whosoever shall depart from life in sentiments of

---

* Ep. cccxxii., Ep. Spir.   † Vita S. Bernardi, l. iii. c. iv.
‡ Ep. ccxlvi.   § De Considerat., l. ii.

true penance, shall doubtless receive the pardon of sins and an eternal reward." "Whosoever, through pure devotion, not for glory or hire, shall undertake the journey to liberate Jesusalem, shall be considered as having fulfilled all his penance."* Contrition of heart, with the humble confession of sin, is invariably required in the Bulls of Eugene III., Gregory VIII., Innocent III., and the other Pontiffs. Guibert tells us, that, up to the time of the crusade, the whole kingdom of the French was convulsed by internal strife; pillaging and assassination were common, and incendiaries abounded: but that, on its publication, there was an extraordinary and general change: dissensions were suddenly healed, and all the public calamities ceased.† Orderic Vitalis states, that "thieves, and marauders, and other like sinners, under the influence of the Holy Ghost, rose from the depth of their iniquity, and engaged in the crusade, with a view to atone for their sins."‡ The preaching of the fifth crusade by Foulques de Neuilly was attended with extraordinary conversions, and abundant fruits of piety, besides the enthusiasm which it enkindled. To his contemporaries he appeared as another Paul, raised up by God for the conversion of sinners, of whom he considered himself the greatest. Of the first five crusades Michaud says, that "during them religion and evangelical morality resumed their ascendancy, and scattered their blessings around; at the voice of the holy orators, Christians embraced penance, and reformed their lives; all political storms were quelled at the mere mention of Jerusalem, and the West continued in profound peace."§ Even Mills acknowledges, that the crusaders religiously prepared themselves for death, when about to set out on their journey: "Throughout the crusades, most persons, considering the difficulty of the journey, and the perils of war, performed those acts which men on the point of death observed; such as settling their family affairs, and making restitution to the Church or private persons."‖ In pointing to the crusade as a means of expiating sin, the Pope considered that the toils of the journey and the exposure of life in just war, offered up to God in a penitential spirit, might, in some measure, atone for past excesses. "Redeem," said Urban, "by this act, well pleasing before God, theft, arson, plunder, homicide, and other crimes, the doers of which shall not possess the kingdom of God, that these works of piety and the intercession of the saints may specially obtain for you the pardon of the sins, by which you have provoked the Lord to anger." There was no pardon for the impenitent; but the contrite of heart could not give a greater proof of their sorrow, than to expose their lives for their brethren in Christ, and willingly to accept all the sufferings and privations incidental to warfare. No penance which

---

* Canon Conc., Clarom. II.   † Guibert Abb., l. I. c. vii.
‡ Hist. Eccles., recueil des Histor. Norm., par Duchesne.
§ Histoire des Croisades, l. xiii. p. 102.
‖ History of the Crusades, ch. iii. p. 37, Note.

could be inflicted, or assumed, could be compared with constant exposure to a scorching sun, or with thirst and hunger, such as they endured. The thirst which they at one time experienced, was intolerable to the strongest soldiers, of whom it carried off five hundred in one day.* During the siege of Antioch, hunger forced them to eat weeds and briars, dogs, reptiles, and every unclean animal.†

Alms given toward defraying the expenses of the crusades were accepted in lieu of actual service, from such as could not enter on the journey; Frederick Barbarossa, in 1189, having obtained the Pope's consent to this commutation.‡ Innocent III. offered indulgences not only to the crusaders, but to all who contributed to equip and maintain them; and directed boxes to be placed in the churches, in which the faithful might deposit their alms.§ It is unfair to represent this mode of proceeding as a sale of indulgences, since these were not given for a stipulated sum of money, to be paid to an individual for his own use, but they were offered to all who would contribute, according to their ability and devotion, to an undertaking connected with the interests of religion and the independence of the Christian nations. If it was laudable to contribute to this object, it was certainly allowable to stimulate the charity of the faithful by offering to them a release from penitential observances. God himself encourages alms-giving, by promises of abundant rewards in this life and in the next. The Church imitated the divine economy, in dispensing her spiritual treasures to such of her children as might freely offer a portion of their worldly substance in support of the Christian enterprise. An instance of a similar concession occurred eighty years previously, when Gelasius II. offered a remission of penance, at the discretion of the bishops, to such as would contribute to the rebuilding of the church of Saragossa, which the Saracens had destroyed, and to the support of the clergy of that city.

The results of the crusades not being as splendid as the vast number of the crusaders and their enthusiasm might lead us to expect, many who judge from the issue of things, loudly decry them; yet their effects were by no means inconsiderable. The crusaders effectually checked the Mohammedan power; they established and maintained, during almost a century, the kingdom of Jerusalem; and, for another century, they retained the dominion of some places in Syria. When the disadvantages under which these wars were undertaken are considered, even their partial success may be a matter of wonder. A crusade was an army of volunteers, directed by no common leader, and commanded by officers accustomed to feudal domination. They fought on a strange territory, with no knowledge of the places, and in the midst of enemies, numerous, thoroughly ac-

---

* Michaud, Histoire des Croisades, l. ii. p. 237.   † Ibidem, p. 281.
‡ Ibidem, l. vii. p. 374.
§ Ep. Innoc. III. Quia major. inter ep. ad conc., Lat. iv. spectantes.

quainted with the places, and of desperate resolution. They were dependent on chance for the necessary provisions, and they often suffered intensely from hunger, thirst, and every natural want. Nevertheless, the first crusade was eminently successful. Nice, Edessa, Antioch, and Jerusalem, successively yielded to the Christian arms. "The first result of this crusade," says Michaud, "was to fill the Mussulman nations with terror, and put it out of their power, for a long time, to make any attack on the West. Through the victories of the crusaders, the Greek Empire extended its borders; and Constantinople, which was for the Saracens the high-road to the West, was safe from their attacks. In this distant expedition, Europe lost the flower of her population; but she was not, like Asia, the theatre of a bloody and disastrous war."* "When we consider that this weak kingdom, (*Jerusalem*,) encompassed by enemies, stood for eighty-eight years, we have less reason to be astonished at its fall, than at its duration for so long a period."† "On all occasions in which bravery alone was wanting, nothing is found comparable with the exploits of the crusaders. When reduced to a small number of fighting men, they were not less successful than when their forces were innumerable. Forty thousand crusaders took possession of Jerusalem, garrisoned by sixty thousand Saracens. Scarcely twenty thousand remained, when they had to engage with all the forces of the East, on the plains of Ascalon."‡

The constancy with which the Popes pursued their favorite object, the recovery of the Holy Land from the infidel, shows the strength of the religious principle by which they were actuated. The disasters of Louis VII. and of the Emperor Conrad, did not deter Frederick Barbarossa, Richard Cœur de Lion, and Philip Augustus of France, from entering on the same career of danger, at the bidding of the Pontiff. "Gregory VIII. not only endeavored to deprecate the wrath of Heaven, by obtaining fasting and prayer throughout Christendom, but issued a Bull for a new crusade, with the usual privileges to the *croisés*. Gregory went to Pisa, and healed the animosities between that city and Genoa, knowing well the importance of the commercial States of Italy to the Christians in the holy wars."§ Celestine III. again sounded the sacred trumpet, to summon volunteers to the relief of Palestine. Innocent III. used all the influence of his station to rouse the princes of Europe to undertake the fifth crusade, which, contrary to his intentions and wishes, resulted in the taking of Constantinople. With the applause of the fourth Council of Lateran, the same great Pontiff set a sixth crusade on foot, and contributed largely from his treasury to its expenses. His plate and golden vessels were melted by his orders, to be employed for this purpose, in place of which, wooden or earthen vessels were used at his table. "As germs of division subsisted between several States of Europe, which

---

* Histoire des Croisades, l. iv. p. 516. † Ibidem, l. vii. p. 351.
‡ Michaud, l. iv. p. 509. § Mills, History of the Crusades, ch. xi. p. 148.

might prevent the success of the holy war, the Pope sent in every direction his legates, as angels of peace, to induce reconciliation. He himself repaired to Tuscany, to terminate the dissensions of the Pisans and Genoese: his exhortations reunited all hearts; at his voice the most implacable enemies promised to consign to oblivion all their disputes, that they might go and fight against the Saracens."*

To the incessant vigilance of the Popes against the progress of the Turkish power, the European nations are deeply indebted for their independence. When, in 1259, Mogul hordes penetrated into Poland and Hungary, and spread terror everywhere, Alexander IV. addressed the princes and prelates of Europe, exhorting them to repel the invaders. At his suggestion, prayers, processions, and fasts were everywhere employed, to avert the wrath of Heaven. On that occasion, the petition, "Lord, deliver us from the invasion of the Tartars!" was added to the Litanies. Urban IV. walked in his footsteps. After Ptolemais had fallen into the hands of the enemy, and the last hopes of the Eastern Christians had vanished, Boniface VIII. raised his voice in their behalf. Clement V. endeavored to resuscitate the extinct spirit of the crusades. John XXII. pleaded in behalf of the suffering Christians of Armenia. Benedict XI., in conjunction with the republic of Venice and the King of Cyprus, sent troops to Smyrna; and Urban V. proclaimed a new crusade, which resulted in the taking of Alexandria. In the day of their distress, the emperors of Constantinople had no surer refuge than the Pontiff, who employed all his influence to obtain succor for the Greeks, notwithstanding the repeated instances of their bad faith. Eugenius IV., in an eloquent strain, appealed to the princes of Europe in behalf of the imperial city, when threatened by the Turks; but the hour was come in which her faithlessness should receive retribution. The prodigies of valor of Hunniades and of Ladislas, at Warna, could not prevent the victorious Ottoman entering Constantinople in triumph. When his hosts advanced to Belgrade, and all Europe trembled at their approach, Calixtus III. sought to rouse all to the rescue, inviting the faithful to implore help for their Hungarian brethren, by the repetition of the angelic salutation, thrice each day, at the sound of the bell. The victory, which appeared miraculous, may well be ascribed to these prayers, no less than to the piety of St. John Capistran, or the valor of Hunniades.

The efforts of Pius II. against the Turks, before and after his elevation to the pontificate, deserve the admiration and gratitude of Christian Europe. At his earnest solicitation, an assembly of the representatives of the various States was held at Mantua, in which he presided, and, in energetic language, described the ravages of the enemy in Bosnia and Greece, and their advances, like a spreading flame, on Italy, Germany, and all Europe. He declared that he would not leave Mantua until he received, from all the princes and States, pledges of their devotedness to the com-

---

* Michaud, Histoire des Croisades, l. xii. p. 403.

mon cause; adding, that if he were forsaken by the Christian powers, he would advance alone to the combat, and die in defending the independence of Europe and the Church. "The language of Pius II.," says Michaud, "was full of religion, and his religion full of patriotism. When Demosthenes and the Greek orators mounted the rostrum, to urge their fellow-citizens to defend the liberty of Greece against the aggressions of Philip, or the invasions of the great king, they doubtless spoke more eloquently; but they were not inspired by higher interests, or more exalted motives."[*] The frontiers of Illyricum were soon laid waste by the enemy; the isles of the Archipelago and Ionian Sea submitted to his power; and the dangers of Italy and all Europe became daily more imminent. Pius, although bending under the weight of years, resolved to go at the head of the Christian army, and, like Moses, to lift his hands in prayer for the people of God, in the hour of conflict. "What war," he cried, "was ever more just and necessary? The Turks attack all that is dear to us, all that Christians hold sacred. As men, can you be without sympathy for your fellow-mortals? As Christians, religion commands you to relieve your brethren. If you are unmoved by the calamities of others, take compassion on yourselves. You imagine that you are safe, because you are far from danger: to-morrow, the sword may be raised over your own heads. If you neglect to succor those who stand before you, exposed to the enemy, those who are in your rear may abandon you in the struggle."[†] The heroic Pontiff, in June, 1464, left his capital for Ancona, on his way to the scene of danger; but a fever, which the fatigues of the journey aggravated, soon brought him to the end of his earthly career. His last words were an earnest exhortation to the cardinals to pursue the work for which he had sacrificed his life. Paul II. endeavored in vain to enkindle the zeal of Christian princes for the enterprise; and gave to the brave Scanderberg a sword, with pecuniary aid. Sixtus IV. displayed like zeal, with somewhat greater success, having sent a small fleet, in company with the Venetian and Neapolitan navy, to the coasts of Ionia and Pamphylia, in order to compel Mohammed II. to retire from Europe, to the defence of his own possessions. When Otranto had fallen beneath the Ottoman arms, the Pontiff assembled around him the ambassadors of all the Christian powers, and concerted with them measures of prompt defence for the other cities of Italy and Europe. Even Alexander VI. earnestly solicited the princes to unite in repelling the common enemies of the Christian faith. A crusade was decreed in the fifth Council of Lateran, which was commenced by Julius II., and terminated under Leo X. Soliman took Belgrade in 1521, the year of Leo's death; and, a short time afterward, the Isle of Rhodes, which was defended in vain with astonishing valor by the Knights of St. John. Buda fell in 1523, after the direful battle of Mohacs.

While Clement VII. was a prisoner in the castle of St. Angelo, and

---

[*] Histoire des Croisades, L xx. p. 373.   [†] Ibidem, p. 378.

the troops of Charles V. occupied his capital, he did not cease to interest himself for the safety of Europe from the attacks of the Turk. "From the prison in which the emperor detained him," Michaud observes, "Clement VII. watched for the defence of Christian Europe: his legates journeyed to Hungary, to exhort the Hungarians to fight for God and their country. . . . It may not be useless to observe, that most of the predecessors of Clement, as well as he, had employed great diligence to discover the plans of the infidels. Thus, the heads of the Church did not limit their efforts to the rousing of Christians to defend themselves on their own territory, but, like vigilant sentinels, they kept their eyes incessantly fixed on the enemies of Christianity, to warn Europe of the dangers by which it was menaced."* "When the emperor had loosed the chains of Clement VII., the holy Pontiff consigned to oblivion the outrages which he had suffered, and occupied himself with the safety of the German empire, which was about to be attacked by the Turks. In the diets of Augsburg and Spire, the legate of the Pope endeavored, in the name of religion, to awake the ardor of the Germans for their own defence."† While Luther paradoxically denounced opposition to the Turks as resistance to the divine will, Clement continued to provide for the safety of the Christian commonwealth. When the army of the Sultan was at the gates of Vienna, seeing no human hope remaining, he appealed, not in vain, to the God of hosts. Famaugusta and Nicosia, in the Isle of Cyprus, subsequently fell into the power of the Turks, and the butchery of their brave defenders followed the capture. Before their fall, Pius V. had succeeded in forming a league with the republic of Venice, and with Philip II. of Spain, to aid the island: but the fleet reached its destination after the triumph of the Turk. To this fleet, however, of which the pontifical navy formed a considerable portion, the glory was reserved of giving a fatal blow to Turkish aggression. In the Gulf of Lepanto, where Augustus and Antony had contended for the empire of Rome, the naval battle was fought between the Christians and the Turks. The flag of St. Peter, which John of Austria, the high admiral of the fleet, had received from the hands of Pius V., floating aloft, was hailed with joyous shouts by the Christian combatants, who cast themselves on their knees to implore the aid of Heaven, ere they raised their arms to engage in battle. Two hundred Turkish vessels, captured, burnt, or sunk, were the result of a naval contest, such as the world had never before witnessed, and which virtually decided the great struggle between the Mohammedan and Christian powers. The efforts of Saint Pius, and perhaps still more his prayers, obtained this victory. This single action, which closed his earthly career, ought, even in the judgment of Voltaire, to render his memory sacred.‡

In the decline of the seventeenth century, Dalmatia and Candia were

---

* Michaud, Histoire des Croisades, l. xx. p. 464. † Ibid.
‡ Essai sur l'Histoire Générale, t. iv. ch. clvi.

attacked, and Hungary, Moravia, and Austria were invaded by the Turks. The voice of Alexander VII. was raised to urge the Christian princes to unite in repelling them. The Emperor Leopold fled from his capital in dismay. The Pope sent soldiers and money to his aid, and shared with the King of France, and other confederates, the glory of a decisive victory, obtained on the plains of St. Gothard. When Candia had fallen under the Turkish yoke, the Pontiff again addressed the Christian States, and especially the heroic King of Poland, John Sobieski, exhorting them to check the insolence of the triumphant foe. Vienna was soon rescued from the three hundred thousand Mussulmen that surrounded it, by a valiant though comparatively small host, on the memorable 13th of September, 1683. The Venetian republic concurred with the Pontiff; and the banners of St. Peter and St. Mark waved in triumph on the ramparts of Coron, Navarino, Patras, Napoli de Romagna, Corinth, Athens, and throughout the Archipelago. Clement XI., in 1716, made great contributions in money, sent troops to aid the Christians in Hungary, who were assailed by Achmet III., and exhorted the Christian States to do in like manner. The victory of Prince Eugene at Peter-Waradin, and the recovery of Belgrade, filled the Pontiff with joy for the success of the Christian arms, to which he himself had so effectually contributed.

I have rapidly reviewed the efforts made by the Popes during six centuries, for the relief of the Eastern Christians, and for the safety of the European nations, that the reader might form a just idea of the motives which actuated them, and of the services which they rendered to Christendom. Their views were evidently more enlarged than those of secular princes, and their sympathy for the suffering Christians of the East was not less admirable, than their vigilance to preserve the independence of Europe. Their policy was of no narrow, selfish kind. With scrupulous fidelity they employed in those just enterprises whatever the charity of the faithful committed to their dispensation, to which they added much from their own resources.* From those wars they sought no augmentation of territory; but cheerfully left to the crusaders the conquered country, with the spoils and honors of war. In order to gain the infidels to the faith, they assured them that no sacrifice of temporal interests was desired. "We seek not your kingdom, but yourselves," said Gregory XI. to the Caliph of Bagdad, and to the sovereigns of Cairo and Damascus; "We do not wish to lessen your honors or power: our most earnest desire is to raise you above this world, and to ensure your happiness here and hereafter."† With these elevated views they continued their endeavors in the cause of humanity and religion, incessantly opposing Turkish aggression. The Papacy in those ages, as has been well observed, "was constantly endeavoring to advance the borders of the Christian world—to reclaim the hea-

---

* See letter of Honorius III., apud Michaud, vol. iii., Pièces justificatives.
† Raynaldi, Annales Eccles., an. 1233.

then barbarism of the north of Europe—or to repel the dangerous aggressions of Mohammedanism."*

Spain owes her liberty to the crusades against the Moors, which sprang from the same principles as the Eastern crusades. "The celebrated victory of Tolosa, obtained over the Moors, was the fruit of a crusade published throughout Europe, and especially in France, by order of the Sovereign Pontiff. The expeditions beyond the seas were useful to the Spaniards, inasmuch as they kept within their own territory the Saracens of Egypt and Syria, who might otherwise have joined those of the African coast. The kingdom of Portugal was conquered and founded by the crusaders. The crusades gave rise to the orders of chivalry, which were formed in Spain, in imitation of those of Palestine, without whose aid the nation could not have conquered the Moors."†

I shall not dwell on the advantages to commerce, civilization, literature, and freedom, which were derived from the crusades, as Robertson fully acknowledges.‡ Although the all-absorbing thought of the Pontiffs was to rescue the suffering Christians and free the Holy Land, they were never inattentive to the social advantages which might flow from these enterprises. During them, navigation greatly advanced, and the commercial republics of Venice, Genoa, and Pisa, rose to great wealth and power. The barriers which separated the European nations, which had hitherto retained much of the estrangement from social intercourse characteristic of barbarous tribes, were broken down; society was formed on a vast scale, on the great principles of a common faith and common interests; and the East and the West were bound together by hallowed ties. The serfs felt themselves made freed-men of the cross; cities sprang up in every direction, with municipal privileges bestowed in consideration of largesses made for the holy war; and their inhabitants, during the long absence of the feudal lords, acquired the habits and sense of freedom. Learned exiles from Greece, and valuable manuscripts transferred from the East to Europe, laid the foundation of a new era in literature, which the enlightened Pope, Nicholas V., laboured to accelerate.§

---

* London Quarterly, for February, 1836.
† Michaud, Histoire des Croisades, l. xxii. p. 222.
‡ Survey of the State of Europe, sect. I.
§ See Michaud, Histoire des Croisades, l. xxii.

CHAPTER VIII.

Coercion.

§ 1.—PAGANS AND JEWS.

It is an axiom universally admitted, that the worship of God must be voluntary, in order to be acceptable. Liberty of conscience was claimed by Tertullian for the Christians, as a right grounded on the very nature of religion. "It is," said he, "a right, and a natural privilege, that each one should worship as he thinks proper: nor can the religion of another injure or profit him. Neither is it a part of religion to compel its adoption, since this should be spontaneous, not forced, as even sacrifices are asked only of the cheerful giver."* The duty of worshipping God conformably to His revealed will being manifest, every interference with its discharge is a violation of the natural right which man possesses to fulfil so solemn an obligation. The use of force to compel compliance with this duty, is likely to result in mere external conformity, which, without the homage of the heart, is of no value whatever. The missionaries of Gregory to England instructed Ethelbert, the Saxon king, to abstain from all compulsion, and limit his zeal to the inducing of his subjects, by persuasion, to follow his example in embracing Christianity; observing, that the service of Christ should be voluntary, not forced.† Nicholas I. forbade Michael, King of the Bulgarians, to use violence for the conversion of idolaters.‡ The fourth Council of Toledo forbade violence to be offered to any one with a view to force the profession of the faith and the reception of baptism.§ Even amid the military expeditions which were undertaken in the Middle Ages to extend civilization and religion over the northern provinces of Europe, Innocent IV. declared that the discipline of the Church does not allow compulsion to be used for the propagation of the faith. We have already offered the reader an explanation of the principles on which the crusades in Prussia, and other countries, were conducted, which, although apparently directed to spread the faith by military terror, were in reality designed to put an end to unnatural enormities, and extend civilization, while they protected the preachers of the Gospel, and

---

* "Tamen humani juris et naturalis potestatis est unicuique quod putaverit colere: nec alii obest, aut prodest alterius religio: sed nec religionis est cogere religionem, quæ sponte suscipi debeat, non vi: cum et hostiæ ab animo libenti expostulentur." Ad Scapulam, c. ii.
† Bede, Hist., l. i. c. xxvi.   ‡ Resp. ad cons. Bulg., c. xvii.   § Can. lvii.

converts, from molestation on the part of unbelievers. The profession of Christianity was at all times to be the free act of those who were convinced of its divine origin. Force was sometimes necessary to preserve the public peace and protect the faithful against those who interfered with their worship. Chief Justice Clayton thus meets the objection of those who are unwilling that Christianity should be supported against assaults by any legal penalties or safeguards : "We would reply, that while Christianity requires no aid from force, the peace and order of civil society do require much aid from it, to repel force and to prevent persecution; that, while Christianity asks not to be guarded by fines and forfeitures, man has been compelled to make courts and prisons to guard him both by fines and forfeitures; that, while Christianity stands secure in the armor of truth and reason, the public peace, which is altogether a different thing, has never stood secure in the armor of mere truth and reason, without the co-operating aid of some public punishment to assist them ; that political and legal enactments are among the best means by which the peace has been preserved in every country; and that while the law, too, seeks mildly and peaceably to establish her precepts in the hearts of the people, yet, if the people will the law to stand, it must be so administered as to compel obedience from such as do not yield it without force."*

Liberty of conscience was especially maintained by the Popes in regard to the Jews, whom they would by no means allow to be coerced to the reception of baptism. Numerous facts place this beyond contradiction. It was so well known to the Jews themselves, that it was not unusual for them to have recourse to the Pope, when they felt aggrieved by the acts of inferior prelates. The Bishop of Terracina was denounced by Joseph, a Jew, to Gregory the Great, for having taken possession of a synagogue, under the pretext of giving to its members another place of worship, which he was now seeking to take from them. The Pontiff directed redress to be given, observing that unbelievers are to be drawn to the faith by meekness, kindness, and persuasion, not to be forced by threats and penalties.† When a converted Jew had erected a crucifix and an image of the Blessed Virgin, in a synagogue at Cagliari, the Pope, on complaint being lodged of the injustice thereby done to its owners, ordered the images to be reverently removed, and the house left to its original purpose. He advised moderation to be observed toward the Jews, that they might freely hearken to the ministers of the Gospel, observing that they must not be forced against their will, since it is written : "I will freely sacrifice to Thee."‡ Some Italian Jews, who frequented the port of Marseilles, having informed him that their brethren were constrained to receive baptism in that city, he wrote to Virgil, Metropolitan of Arles, and to Theodore, Bishop of Marseilles, praising their good intentions, but expressing his fears that the

---

* Chief Justice Clayton; *State* vs. *Chandler*, 2 Harrington, Delaware, p. 573.
† L. i., ep. 3, 4.   ‡ Ps. lliii. 8, apud Greg., l. vii. ep. 5, ind. 2.

results would be injurious; and directing them to instruct and prepare the candidates for baptism, that their conversion might be sincere.* In the middle of the eleventh century, Alexander II. praised the Spanish bishops for having protected the lives of the Jews from the violence of those Christians who were engaged against the Saracens. He justified the war with the latter, on account of the persecution which they carried on against the Christians, whom they expelled by force from their cities and dwellings; while the Jews everywhere submitted to the established authorities.† Innocent III., in 1199, in conformity with the examples of his predecessor, took the Jews under the special protection of the Holy See, forbidding any violence to be offered them to force them to receive baptism, or their property to be taken, or their usages to be interfered with; but he forbade neophytes to be allowed to practise the Jewish rites, which they had of their free will forsaken, on receiving baptism.‡

When, in 1236, the crusaders in France had committed various outrages on their persons and property, the Jews appealed to the humanity and justice of Gregory IX., who immediately wrote to the Archbishop of Bordeaux, and other French prelates, reminding them that the soldiers of the cross should prepare themselves for battle in the fear of God, by the exercise of charity. He added, that no one should be forced to receive baptism, since man, having fallen from innocence by his free will, must co-operate freely with grace, in order to rise again. The Council of Tours, in accordance with these instructions, forbade any one to offer violence to the Jews, observing that the Church desires not the death, but the salvation, of those that err. Soon afterward a similar appeal was made by the German Jews, who had also suffered. Innocent IV. accordingly addressed the bishops, and directed them to obtain for the Jews compensation for the outrages committed against them. John XXII. stood forward as their protector in the year 1320, when sectaries called Shepherds renewed like scenes of violence in Languedoc, and other French provinces; and Clement VI., under penalty of anathema, forbade them to be slain or beaten. This was in accordance with the teaching of the great St. Bernard, who loudly advocated the exercise of humanity toward them. "The Jews," he said, "must not be persecuted, or put to death, or even banished."§

Rome has always been the asylum and home of this oppressed people, as Voltaire himself acknowledges; and Avignon, because it was for a long time the residence of the Popes, shares with the eternal city this honorable distinction.|| The restrictions to which the Jews have been subjected, even in Rome, in being confined to a certain quarter, and otherwise limited in their intercourse with the other inhabitants, have been owing more to

---

* L. i., ep. 45.   † Ep. xxxiv. Conc. col. reg., vol. vi. col. 1100.
‡ Conc. Lat., clxx.   § Ep. cccxxii. Ep. Spirensi.
|| "Il n'y a guères que Rome qui les ait constamment gardés. . . . Ils sont restés constamment à Avignon, par ce que c'était terre papale." Essai sur l'Histoire Générale, t. iii. ch. xcix.

COERCION.

the fear of dangerous collision, than to any unkind feeling on the part of the Popes: and, we rejoice to add, these restraints are now melting away before the benign influence of our present illustrious Pontiff.

§ 2.—SECTARIES.

The Emperor Constantine, in proclaiming liberty of conscience for the professors of the Christian religion, left the Pagans in the enjoyment of equal privileges, and gave protection to the Jews: but by a subsequent edict, he excluded heretics from the benefit of the laws in favor of Christians.* He is even alleged, by the Donatist Parmenian,† to have ordered the execution of some Donatists, convicted of accusing falsely Cecilian, Bishop of Carthage, and of disturbing the public peace.

Occasion was given for the interference of the civil power to determine the right of occupancy of churches and episcopal sees. In case a prelate abjured the faith, or corrupted it by heresy, it was unjust that he should hold the chair of authority and enjoy the revenues appropriated for the maintenance of a true pastor. His removal became necessary to avoid sanguinary collisions between his partisans and the professors of the original faith. We have elsewhere seen that the authority of the pagan emperor, Aurelian, was implored to dispossess Paul of Samosata of the episcopal residence, and that he wisely determined that the right of occupancy should depend on the fact of communion with the bishops of Italy, especially the Bishop of Rome. The decree of St. Felix I. in favor of Domnus, the Catholic bishop, was executed with the imperial sanction.‡ Christian emperors took on them to dispossess heretical incumbents, and in order to prevent tumult, banished them from their sees. In very many instances Catholic prelates suffered from their misguided zeal. The infliction of penalties for the profession of heresy may be justly ascribed to the excesses and outrages of sectaries. The immoral and anti-social principles of the Manicheans provoked the severity of Valentinian; which was imitated by Gratian, his brother and successor. Theodosius followed in their footsteps, and declared that the Donatists were included in the general proscription. The penalty to which they were subjected, was a fine of ten pounds of gold, and incapacity for any legal act; to which, in some cases, banishment was added. St. Augustin states that he knew of no law subjecting them to death.§ The blame of these coercive measures is justly imputed to themselves. "We daily," he says, "suffer incredible outrages, far worse than those of robbers and marauders, from your clergymen and circumcellions;" (a class of Donatists so styled from their destroying the huts of the Catholic peasantry;) "for, armed with every kind of weapons, they rove about, spreading terror everywhere, and disturbing the peace, I

---

* Tit. v., cod. de hæret. et Manich.   † Aug. contra ep. Parmen, l. i. c. viii.
‡ Euseb., Hist. Eccl., l. vii. ch. xxiv.   § Contra litt. Petiliani, l. ii. ch. xx. n. 46.

do not say of the Church, but of the public at large. They attack by night, and pillage the dwellings of the Catholic clergy: they seize on the inmates, beat them with clubs, mangle them with various instruments, and leave them almost lifeless. Moreover, by a new and unprecedented kind of cruelty, they put a mixture of lime and vinegar in their eyes; and, instead of scooping them out at once, they choose to torture them slowly." He proceeds to describe the horrible mutilation of Servus, a Catholic bishop, prefacing it by this remark: "I pass over the enormities previously committed, by which THEY FORCED THE EMPERORS TO ENACT THE LAWS of which they complain, and which are tempered with Christian meekness, rather than marked by the severity which such enormous crimes deserve."*
We may not wonder, then, that the Catholic Bishops in the Council of Carthage, held in 404, implored the imperial protection; and that Augustin himself, who, in the beginning, was averse to all coercive measures, changed his opinion, and wrote an elaborate defence of the imperial laws, by which these banditti were restrained.† It does not appear, however, that he at all advocated the infliction of capital punishment on them: on the contrary, he addressed the most solemn adjurations to the public officers, that no blood should be shed to avenge the outrages committed against religion or her ministers.‡ Lenity was so characteristic of the episcopal office, that when the Emperors Arcadius and Honorius deemed it necessary to decree capital punishment against such as might perpetrate enormous outrages against the clergy, they cautioned the provincial governors not to await any action on the part of the Catholic bishops, lest the law should remain without effect. "If any one," say they, "fall into the crime of sacrilege, rushing into Catholic churches, to offer violence to the priests and ministers, or disturb the worship and profane the place, let the offence be punished by the governor of the province: and let the governor of the province know that the injury done to the priests and ministers of the Catholic Church, and to the place itself, and to the divine worship, is to be punished by capital sentence against convicts or culprits who confess their guilt: nor let him wait for the demand of justice by the bishop who has suffered injury, since the holiness of his office leaves to him the glory of pardoning."§

The imperial laws, so far as they are directed to restrain and punish outrage, are justifiable on the plainest principles of justice and order. The general proscription of sectaries was the result of those acts of violence which usually characterized them. The Manicheans, who denied the lawfulness of marriage, especially fell under this proscription. By the edict of Theodosius, "the Manicheans were to be expelled from the cities, and given up for capital punishment; since no resting-place should be allowed

---

* Contra Crescon. Donat., t. iii. c. xliii. n. 47.   † Ad Vincentium Rogat., ep. xciii.
‡ Ep. c., alias cxxvii., Donato.   Ep. cxxxiii., Marcellino.
§ Cod., L. i. tit. iii. 10, de episcopis et clericis.

anywhere to men who commit outrages against the elements themselves."*
This severity was provoked by the immoral practices of which they were guilty. St. Leo the Great, as we have before stated, held a court of inquiry, composed of laymen as well as ecclesiastics, and, on the fullest evidence, proclaimed to the world the crimes which were usually committed in their nightly meetings. These induced him to speak in terms of approbation of the laws which proscribed them; but he was careful to observe, that the lenity of the Church shrinks from any sanguinary measure. "Our fathers," he says, "in whose time this abominable heresy broke forth, were earnest in their efforts, throughout the whole world, that the impious frenzy should be banished from the entire Church; and justly so, since even the princes of the world detested this sacrilegious madness to such a degree, that, with the sword of the public laws, they cut off its author, with many of his followers. For they perceived that all regard for probity was destroyed, all bonds of marriage were dissolved, and divine and human laws were at once overturned, if men professing such errors were allowed to live anywhere. That severity was for a long time serviceable to the lenity of the Church; which, although content with the sentence of the priesthood, she rejects sanguinary vengeance, is, nevertheless, aided by the severe enactments of Christian princes; since those who fear corporal punishment, sometimes have recourse to the spiritual remedy."†

The first instance of the capital punishment of heretics, under the imperial laws, occurred at Triers, in Germany, in the year 383. Up to that period, the Catholic bishops had suffered most sanguinary persecution from the Arians and Donatists, without invoking the severity of the law against their oppressors. St. Chrysostom had laid it down as a maxim, that "it -is not lawful to slay a heretic, for this would lead to interminable strife;"‡ and St. Augustin besought Donatus, proconsul of Africa, through Jesus Christ our Lord, to be mindful of Christian lenity, and not to punish sectaries as their crimes against society deserved. "We desire them," he says, "to be corrected, not to be slain."§ At length two Spanish bishops, Idacius and Ithacius, impelled by zeal which was not according to knowledge, denounced to the imperial tribunal Priscillian, and five of his abettors, as guilty of violating the laws, by the propagation of Manichean errors, a crime which was aggravated by licentious practices. Two of the most illustrious prelates of the Church, St. Martin of Tours, and St. Ambrose, condemned this proceeding, as unworthy of Christian bishops, and refused to hold communion with their vindictive colleagues. Of the meek spirit of St. Ambrose, a signal instance is recorded. While he was in the act of celebrating mass, hearing that an Arian priest had fallen into the

---

* Cod. Theod., l. i. tit. v. n. 5.
† Ep. xv., alias xcii., ad Turribium, Asturicensem episcopum. See also Ep. ii. ad episcopos per Italiam.
‡ Hom. xlvi., in Mat. § Ep. c., alias cxxvii. Donato.

hands of a Catholic crowd, with tears he besought our Lord in the mystery to protect him from violence; and despatched, without delay, priests and deacons to his relief. Yet it can scarcely be questioned, that the Popes generally adopted the views of St. Leo, and approved of legal coercion, as necessary to preserve public morals, and prevent outrage. At the same time, they strongly insisted that no one should be violently compelled to external compliance with religious duty. Pope Hormisdas, being informed of the violence offered to his legates, who were engaged in restoring the Eastern churches to the communion of the Holy See, and of the murder of a Catholic bishop, wrote to the legates : " Even if these be the facts, we, nevertheless, make no complaint against the people. It is in the power of the respected prince to punish the injury done to his authority, and to a Catholic bishop, as he may think proper; but our duty is, and we charge you to attend to it in our stead, to see that no one embrace unity without knowledge of the truth, or profess the true faith in such a way as to have occasion to complain of being forced to it by the prince, without the necessary instruction."* John I., at the instance of Theodoric, the Arian king of Italy, undertook a journey to Constantinople, to dissuade the Emperor Justin from measures of coercion against the Arians, which the king threatened to retaliate on his Catholic subjects. The Pontiff succeeded in obtaining for them the free use of their churches : but, as he did not ask that the converts from the sect should return to it, he fell under the displeasure of Theodoric, and died in prison for his fidelity to duty.†

On a review of the acts of the Pontiffs up to the twelfth century,‡ I am convinced that they cannot fairly be charged with having made any coercive enactment, or sanctioned any sanguinary measures. We shall now consider the share which they had in the measures adopted after that period against the sectaries that infested the southern provinces of France.

§ 3.—CRUSADES AGAINST MANICHEANS

In a Council held at Toulouse, in the year 1119, at which Callistus II. presided, it was enacted that the Manicheans should be restrained by the secular powers. In order to understand the justice of this enactment, we must take into consideration the conduct of these sectaries, of whom many were the followers of Peter de Bruis, and of Henry, his disciple. When Henry entered a city, in modest garb and with an affected air of sanctity, he was wont to address the people in language which excited them to violence and bloodshed. The clergy were the immediate objects of popu-

---

* Ep. lxii. † See Pagi, Brev. Gest. Rom. Pont.

‡ John VIII., toward the close of the ninth century, is alleged by Llorente (vol. i. ch. i. art. iii.) to have promised a plenary indulgence to such as might fall in war with the infidels. He, however, neglects to state that the war was of a defensive character, for the protection of Rome, besieged by the Saracens. See Fleury, l. lii. § xl.

lar fury; their dwellings were plundered, and often razed to the ground, and they themselves were stoned, or assassinated, unless the nobles came to their relief.* The third Council of Lateran, held in 1179, under Alexander III., speaking of the various sects of that age, says: "They practise such violence against Christians as not to spare churches or monasteries, widows or orphans, aged persons or children, age or sex; but, heathen-like, they destroy and devastate all things."† The venerable Peter, Abbot of Cluni, assures us that the followers of Peter de Bruis "profaned the churches, overturned the altars, burned the crosses, scourged the priests, imprisoned the monks, and forced them to marry, using threats and torments for that purpose."‡ Elsewhere he says: "Where they can, or dare, they plunder, strike, whip, sometimes even (nay, oftentimes) kill, without discrimination of persons, ranks, or dignities." Hence he maintains that the swords of the knights templars might be employed against them with equal justice as against pagan violence: "The Christian who unjustly suffers violence from a Christian, is no less to be defended by your counsels, and even by your swords, than a Christian should be who suffered like violence from a pagan."§ The desolation produced by the marauding troops was such that Stephen, Abbot of St. Genoveffa, as he passed through Toulouse, saw the ruins of churches which had been torn down, the ashes of other sacred edifices which the fire had destroyed, the very foundations being dug up, and the beasts ranging freely where the dwellings of men had lately been.|| Of the Coterelli, who infested the province of Berry, Antonine, quoted by Baronius, relates, that "they devastated the country, pillaging it, and dragging the inhabitants into captivity, violating their wives in their presence, burning the churches, insulting and beating the priests often unto death, trampling under foot the Divine Eucharist, breaking the chalices in pieces, and applying the sacred linens to profane uses."¶ The Count de Foix is related by Peter of Vaux-Cernay to have attacked monasteries and pillaged them, filled religious houses with courtesans, treacherously assassinated many of the faithful, and put to death those who surrendered on a promise of life being spared. He treacherously seized, and after a mock trial, at which Raymond, Count of Toulouse, presided, hung Baldwin, brother of this count, who, with savage cruelty, gave countenance to this atrocious deed.** Bernard Casvacio, Lord of Doma, and his wife, treated the Catholics with the utmost cruelty: one hundred and fifty persons, of both sexes, were found at Sarlat, whose eyes had been scooped out by the tyrant: the wife causing the breasts of the women to be amputated, that they might not give suck, and their thumbs cut off, that they might not procure support by their labor.††

* Fleury, Hist., l. lxix. ₴ xxiv.   † Can. ult.   ‡ Bibl. Clun., p. 1122.
₴ Petr. Clun., l. vi. ep. xxvii. || Steph. Tornac., ep. 75, al. 91, apud Fleury, l. lxxiii. ₴ xxxvi.
¶ Apud Baron., an. 1183, p. 769.
** Histoire des Croisades contre les Albigeois, par Barrau, vol. ii. p. 66.
†† Raynald., an. 1214.

Lawless fury generally characterized all the sectaries of those ages. A sect called Shepherds, under the guidance of a Hungarian apostate from the Cistercian order, assumed to themselves sacred functions, and declaimed against the clergy. Queen Blanche suffered them to pass through Paris without molestation, regarding their exhibitions rather as evidences of folly and delusion, than as crimes threatening the peace of society. Emboldened by this toleration, they went to Orleans, and, in despite of the bishop, harangued the people, who warned the clergy, under pain of anathema, not to be present at their meetings. Among those who, prompted by curiosity, disregarded the prohibition, was a student, who, unable to repress his indignation, contradicted the preacher, charging him with deceiving the simple-minded people. The words had scarcely escaped his lips, when his head was cleft in two with a hatchet in the hands of one of the Shepherds. A general attack was then made on the clergy: their dwellings were broken into and plundered: their books committed to the flames: themselves wounded: several of them killed, or thrown into the Loire; so that twenty-five perished on this occasion. Above one hundred thousand of these Shepherds traversed France, spreading disorder and desolation in their course. Their arrival at Bourges was signalized by murder, arson, and pillage: which provoked the people to rise against them, and engage in a bloody contest, in which the banditti were dispersed.

In order to understand why crusades were proclaimed in those ages against sects committing acts of violence, we must remember that there was as yet no standing army in the various nations of Europe, and that there was scarcely any code of laws, or tribunal of justice. The vassals of each baron followed their lord to the field: but in case of lawless violence, such as that of the sects, which did not directly interest a potentate, there was no means of repressing it, save the summoning of volunteers: there was no rallying power so great as the standard of the cross, and no allurement so attractive as the indulgences of the Church. In a Council held at Poictiers, in the year 1004, it was decreed, that in case of outrages being committed against the Church, regular process should be formed before the prince, or the local judge; but if the aggressors should resist the execution of the sentence, the bishops and nobles were to be summoned to compel submission by laying waste the lands. This was somewhat in the nature of a *posse comitatus*, called forth to aid the public officers in an emergency for which ordinary force was insufficient. Hence the third Council of Lateran, premising the words of Leo the Great, in which he declares that the Church, content with the priestly judgment, shuns sanguinary vengeance, did not hesitate to exhort the faithful to rally to the defence of the sacred virgins, and holy places, when violently assailed. "We enjoin," the fathers say, "on all the faithful, for the remission of their sins, to oppose manfully such havoc, and to defend with arms the Christian people."*

---

* ₰ xxvii. col. 1683.

The immediate occasion of the great crusade against the Albigensians was the assassination of the Pope's legate, which, however, was preceded by many other atrocities. During the contest, awful scenes occurred on both sides, which stamp a character of cruelty on the age. Among other instances, fifteen cities, infested by Albigensians, rose suddenly on the Catholic garrisons, and on the Catholics dwelling among them, and made a general massacre, by way of retaliation for the sack of the city of Toulouse.* Of the spirit, however, which animated the Popes, I find an evidence in the instructions of Gregory IX. to the commander of his forces, in a crusade for the defence of his own territory. "The mighty Lord," he says, "wishes the liberty of His Church to be maintained in such a manner, that neither humility prevent necessary defence, nor the defence go beyond the bounds of humility. Whence it follows, that although the defender of ecclesiastical liberty sometimes, but rarely and unwillingly, uses the material sword against tyrants and persecutors of the Church, without forgetting the ordinary humility, he does not, however, use it in such a way as to thirst for blood, or desire to be enriched to the detriment of others; but he rather seeks to recall those that are in error to the path of truth, and, in all meekness, to preserve them in their liberty when recalled. Who can bear with patience that a man whose life could be preserved, should be slain or mutilated by the army of Jesus Christ,† and that the image of the Creator Himself should be thus disfigured, as, we have been informed, has taken place in these days, which has grieved us to the heart? Brother, it is not expedient for us who invite the faithful, and even the erring children to the breast of our Mother the Church, to provoke them by outrages, and exult in the effusion of blood! God forbid that the Roman Church, which is wont to rescue from the sword of justice criminals worthy of death, should slay or mutilate her children, whom she is bound to gather under her wings."‡ Gregory ordered that the lives of the prisoners taken in war should be spared: "We have thought it necessary to entreat and exhort you, and by our apostolic writings strictly to enjoin on you, to cause such as the right hand of Him who exalts us may have delivered into the hands of the army of Jesus Christ, to be carefully guarded, without any slaying, maiming, or mutilation of limbs, which we utterly abhor; that so, in captivity, they may enjoy more liberty than when, under Egyptian bondage, in the name of liberty, they obeyed Pharaoh and his ministers, the officers of his army."§

Of the humanity of the Popes we have some consoling instances, which relieve the mind afflicted at the horrors of those wars. Voltaire admits that there were instances of Papal interposition that reflect the highest honor on the court of Rome, of which he gives one example. Peter I. of Aragon fell fighting on the side of the Count of Toulouse, against the

---

* Histoire des Croisades, par Barrau, vol. ii. p. 274. † The Crusaders were thus styled.
‡ Apud Fleury, l. cxxix. §liv. § Raynald., an. 1229.

crusaders, who took his son prisoner. "His widow, Mary of Montpelier, who had retired to Rome, pleaded for her son with Innocent III., imploring him to employ his authority for his liberation. There were moments highly honorable for the court of Rome. The Pope ordered Simon de Montfort to restore the youth to the people of Aragon, and Montfort obeyed. Had the Popes always used their authority after this manner, they would have been the legislators of Europe."* Such they were in reality; which affords no slight grounds for believing that the general exercise of their authority was paternal and just.

The wars carried on against the sectaries of the thirteenth century were professedly directed to their *extermination*, not by their indiscriminate slaughter, but by compelling them to disband, or flee from the provinces which they infested. Not only the integrity of religious faith, and the purity of public morals, but order and civilization were at stake. The sects were in revolt against the general Christian confederacy, which was bound together by one faith and one law, of which the Pope was the recognised teacher and interpreter. While the organization of society was advancing on this basis, the sectaries threatened its dissolution, and involved the Christian commonwealth in a struggle for its own existence. What Chief Justice Clayton has said of our English ancestors, and their common law and judicial tribunals, may be said of the Christian nations generally which opposed Manicheism: "He who reviled, subverted, or ridiculed Christianity, did an act which struck at the foundation of civil society, and tended, by its necessary consequences, as they believed, to disturb that common peace of the land of which (as Lord Coke had reported) the common law was the preserver."†

---

* Essai sur l'Histoire Générale, t. ii. ch. lx.
† The *State* vs. *Chandler*, 2 Harrington, p. 557.

CHAPTER IX.

The Inquisition.

§ 1.—ANCIENT TRIBUNAL.

It was with a view to put an end to the horrors of the wars provoked by the sectaries, that a permanent tribunal for their trial and punishment was established, by the concurrent action of the ecclesiastical and civil powers. In a Council held at Verona, in the year 1184, at which the Emperor Frederick I. was present, Pope Lucius, by the advice of the bishops, condemned with anathema all heresies, especially the various forms of Manicheism. The canon proceeds to observe that "inasmuch as the severity of ecclesiastical discipline is sometimes disregarded by such as know not its power," clergymen convicted of heresy should be deposed and degraded, and "delivered over to the secular power, to undergo the punishment which they deserve, unless the culprit, when detected, abjure his heresy before the bishop of the place. Let the same be observed if the culprit be a layman, and let him be punished by the secular judge, unless he abjure; and let such as relapse after abjuration be left to the secular tribunal, and let them not be further heard."* This is certainly a formal recognition of the imperial laws against heresy, and an implicit approbation of them. If the character of the sectaries be borne in mind, it will not be difficult to account for this sanction.

The *quæsitores fidei*, or Inquisitors, were first appointed by Innocent III. At the commencement of the thirteenth century, this strenuous Pontiff despatched two Cistercian monks, Guy and Ranier, to the south of France, to oppose the Manicheans, and charged them to use all diligence for their discovery and conversion, authorizing them to absolve them, when penitent, from all ecclesiastical censures. These commissaries had no civil attributions; but they were directed to urge the employment of coercive measures by the civil authorities, when persuasion and exhortation had proved fruitless. The means employed by them and their associates, were preaching, exercises of piety, and other ordinary appliances of Christian zeal. They were men of holy life, burning with divine love, and thirsting for the salvation of souls. St. Dominick, who was of their number, succeeded in reclaiming thousands to the faith, by examples of

---

* Conc., t. x. p. 1737.

apostolic poverty and charity. Another, St. Peter de Castelnau, a monk of Citeaux, who was, besides, invested with the authority of Papal legate, desired most ardently to shed his blood for the deluded sectaries; and, as if by prophetic instinct, said to his companions: "We shall accomplish nothing for the cause of Jesus Christ, in this country, unless one of us suffer for the faith: God grant that I may be the first to fall beneath the sword of the persecutor!" His prayer was soon fulfilled. An assassin, hired by the faithless Count of Toulouse, plunged a dagger into his side, and the martyr, as he fell, meekly said: "God forgive you, my friend, as I forgive you."

The imperial laws, published in the year 1220, subjected the Manicheans, under their various denominations, to the penalty of death; and an edict published in 1224 gave civil force to the sentence of the inquisitors, inasmuch as the judges and officers were commanded to take into custody convicts by them declared guilty of heresy. This may be considered the origin of the tribunal of the inquisition, which, however, had not for a considerable time a stationary character or fixed form. The first General Inquisitor is believed to be John Cajetan, appointed in the year 1277. The inquisitors preached to the people, inviting them to come forward, avow and abandon their errors. They searched out those who neglected to avail themselves of this indulgence, and on conviction of obstinacy and contumacy, handed them over to the civil power. This was enjoined on those of Italy in 1238, by Gregory IX. The turbulence of the sectaries, which is fully attested by the records of the times, is the only justification which I shall offer for these coercive measures. Many of the early inquisitors were assassinated. One of them, St. Peter of Verona, is honored as a martyr.

The ecclesiastical character of the tribunal is evident from its judges, who were clergymen, from the chief matter of cognizance, which was heresy, and from its original organization, which was planned and directed by the Pontiff. It assumed a secular character by the action of the emperor, and of other potentates, who attached civil effects, especially capital punishment, to its sentence. For this reason, it could nowhere exist without the concurrence of both authorities. Raymond VII., Count of Toulouse, introduced it into his dominions in 1229, in order to prevent a renewal of the civil war which had raged there during twenty years, in the lifetime of his father, the protector of the Albigensians. James, King of Aragon, by the advice of St. Raymond of Pennafort, established it in his kingdom in 1232. St. Louis obtained of Alexander IV. its extension to all France in 1255. Premislaus, King of Bohemia, procured it for his kingdom in 1257. From the sanction which it received from the meek Louis, as well as from other holy men, we may reasonably infer that it was not designed to be a sanguinary tribunal; it was intended as a measure of police, which would intimidate those who, in the name of religion, spread disorder and perpetrated outrage.

The mode of proceeding prescribed in the Council of Beziers, in 1246, by order of Innocent IV., was calculated to prevent the necessity of recourse to coercion. On the arrival of the inquisitor in any city or town, the clergy and people were assembled, and addressed by him; all who were conscious of the guilt of heresy being exhorted to come forward within a specified time, which was called *the time of grace,* and abjure their errors. Such as avowed them, with marks of repentance, were exempt from capital punishment, perpetual imprisonment, banishment, and confiscation of property. Those who were denounced by others, and who did not spontaneously appear within the time, were to be specially summoned, informed of the charges advanced against them, and heard in reply. If their defence was not satisfactory, they were liable to be condemned, according to the nature of the evidence. Those who avowed heretical sentiments were to be privately admonished in the presence of a select number of prudent Catholics, that they might be induced to abjure their errors. Such as were obstinate were required to acknowledge their sentiments publicly, that sentence might be pronounced on them in the presence of the civil magistrate, to whom they were handed over. Relapsed heretics, fugitives from justice, and those who suppressed the truth, were liable to perpetual imprisonment. This punishment, however, could, after some time, be remitted with the advice of the bishop, on security being given for the performance of suitable penance. Such as were not imprisoned were to enlist for a time in the crusades, and to present themselves on Sundays and festivals in the church, in a penitential habit. Those who were condemned to death forfeited their property to the public treasury. By subsequent enactments, the tribunal obtained the benefit of these forfeitures: yet its funds were often so low that it could not pay the very moderate salaries of its officers.

From all the means employed to induce the sectaries to retract their errors, it may fairly be inferred that comparatively few experienced the extreme rigor of the law. Llorente* makes a most extravagant estimate of the sufferers under the operation of the ancient system, although he himself acknowledges that its activity was chiefly confined to the thirteenth century, that it had considerably abated in the fourteenth, and still more so in the fifteenth, when it did not punish with confiscation of property,

---

* This writer was, in 1789, and the two following years, secretary of the Spanish Inquisition; but he was subsequently deprived of his office, and sent to do penance in a convent, for a breach of confidence; it being discovered that he had communicated to some philosophers the secrets which he was sworn to keep. On the invasion of the French, he attached himself to the interests of Joseph Bonaparte, who placed at his service the archives of the inquisition, many of which he burned—a fact which betrays an apprehension that their examination would expose his misstatements. His history of the tribunal, although professedly composed from authentic documents, is a most malignant misrepresentation of its spirit and proceedings. It betrays a deadly hatred against the Catholic Church, the Pope, the religious orders, and the clergy generally, and a deep sympathy with the deistical clubs.

much less with death. Puigblanch says that "in Italy, and in Rome itself, the inquisition soon declined."* Voltaire states that "it languished in Aragon, as well as France, without functions, without order, and almost forgotten."† We may, then, regard it as a tribunal erected in a disorganized state of society, to repress sectaries of a turbulent character, which, after having for a time manifested an awful energy, soon lost its terrific attributions. It gives us an idea of the fierce character of the age, which could have required or admitted so violent a remedy for the disorders committed against religion.

§ 2.—SPANISH INQUISITION.

The modern tribunal of the inquisition may be denominated Spanish, because it has displayed its fearful power chiefly in the dominions of the King of Spain. At the solicitation of Ferdinand, Sixtus IV., in the year 1478, authorized the erection of a tribunal of inquisition, throughout the Spanish dominions. The object which the monarch had in view was, doubtless, the security of his throne, which was endangered by the number of false Christians, professed converts from Judaism, or Mohammedanism, who secretly practised their former superstitions, and kept up treasonable correspondence with the Moors of Barbary. Puigblanch says: "It is, indeed, true, that the Moors of Granada had in agitation, several years before, to deliver up the kingdom to the Barbary powers, or to the Grand Turk."‡ Guizot is right in the opinion that Ferdinand was guided by motives of policy, and that he sought to maintain order by means of this vigilant and strict police.§ Prescott partially admits it, although he maintains that religious zeal was the inspiring motive of Isabella, who desired to provide for the integrity of Catholic faith. It is probable that both considerations influenced the royal counsels; and certainly, regarded in a human point of view, it was a master-stroke of policy, well calculated to defeat the machinations of the secret enemies of the crown.

The Spanish inquisition may be styled a royal tribunal, since the king appointed the supreme inquisitor from among the bishops, with the assent of the Pope, and otherwise exercised an influence equivalent, in many instances, to control. Voltaire,∥ De Maistre,¶ and Ranke,** agree in recognising its royal character. Cardinal Baluffi observes: "It is notorious that the tribunals of Spain and Portugal were royal, and acted independently of Rome, and often in opposition to her wishes."†† For this rea-

---

* Inquisition Unmasked, p. 13. † Essai sur l'Histoire, t. iv. ch. cxxxvi.
‡ Inquisition Unmasked.
§ "Elle fut d'abord plus politique que religieuse, et destinée à maintenir l'ordre plutôt qu' à defendre la foi." Cours d'Histoire Moderne, t. v. lec. ii.
∥ Essai sur l'Histoire Générale, t. iv. ch. xxxvi.
¶ Lettres sur l'Inquisition Espagnole, let. i. p. 12.
** Turkish and Spanish Empires. Spanish Empire, ch. ii.
†† L'America una volta Spagnuola, vol. i. pref., vol. ii. p. 139.

son Paul III. encouraged the Neapolitans in opposing its introduction among them by Charles V.; and Pius IV. countenanced and sanctioned the resistance of the people of Milan, when Philip II. attempted to impose this yoke on them. The Popes oftentimes and loudly complained of the excessive rigor of the Spanish tribunal, and in many instances interposed, by authorizing the secret absolution of numbers of persons, and by absolving those who fled to their clemency from the national judges. They even removed several of the inquisitors for cruelty. Llorente is an unwilling witness to the humanity of the Pontiffs, which he unjustly ascribes to interested motives. "The result," he says, "of the policy was favorable to humanity, since it preserved for those who implored the clemency of the Holy See, their honor and fortune, and those of their children."*

An *auto-da-fé*, or act of faith,† was celebrated at Rome, before St. Peter's Church, under Alexander VI., in a manner not unworthy the earthly representative of Him who came to call sinners to repentance. Two hundred and fifty Spaniards, who fled from the terrors of the national Inquisition to the clemency of the Pontiff, had avowed themselves guilty of relapsing into Jewish superstitions. Dressed in the penitential habit called *san benito*, on bended knees they supplicated to be reconciled with the Church. By the authority of the Pope, who from an elevated situation looked down benignly on his repentant countrymen, they were absolved from ecclesiastical censures. Two by two they then entered the great basilic of the prince of the apostles, and thence proceeded in the same manner to the church of St. Mary *supra Minervam*, where the officers of the Inquisition resided. Having given thanks to God for His boundless mercy, they laid aside the garments of humiliation, and exulted in their restoration to Christian privileges.‡ This surely was a scene at which the angels of heaven might rejoice. Such scenes occurred also in Spain. On 12th February, 1486, 750 culprits underwent public penance in an *auto-da-fé* at Madrid, 900 on the 2d April of same year at Toledo, 750 on 1st May, and 950 on 1st December of same year. Of all these not one was executed.§ What can be more glorious for the Popes than the confidence with which their authority was appealed to, which enabled Sixtus IV. to style the Holy See: "oppressorum ubique tutissimum refugium,"‖ the certain refuge of the oppressed of every clime? This Pontiff did not hesitate to plead with the king for those who might shrink from public exposure, but who would eagerly seek pardon, if their private humiliation

---

* Histoire Critique de l'Inquisition d'Espagne, par D. Jean Antoine Llorente, traduite par Alexis Pellier, vol. i. ch. vii. art. iii. § viii.

† It was so called because the penitents made a public profession of the faith. The punishment of the impenitent took place after the inquisitors had withdrawn; generally on the day following.

‡ Llorente, vol. i. § xxxvi.

§ See Llorente, quoted by Hefele in his late work, "Der Cardinal Ximenes," &c. Tubingen, 1844.

‖ Breve, 29 January, 1481.

were accepted. "Since," he says, "shame of public correction sometimes drives those that are in error to wretched despair, so that they prefer to die in sin than live dishonored, we have judged it necessary to come to their relief, and conformably to the Gospel-teaching, by the clemency of the Apostolic See, to bring back the sheep that had strayed, to the flock of the true Shepherd, our Lord Jesus Christ."* He added, that "clemency alone makes us equal to God, as far as human nature is capable," and he besought the king and queen, by the tender mercies of our Lord Jesus Christ, and exhorted them, in imitation of Him whose property it is to show mercy and to spare, to pardon the penitent, and give them full security in the enjoyment of their property. These are consoling evidences of the disposition of the Popes to procure the exercise of the royal clemency, in an institution that wears a terrific aspect for those who are obstinate in error.

§ 3.—MODE OF PROCEEDING.

A veil of impenetrable secresy formerly shrouded the proceedings of the Inquisition, which gave occasion to surmises and imputations of the most odious kind; but nothing can now be considered secret, since the most confidential instructions by which her officers were guided, have been made public, by the treachery of some of them, and all her archives have been explored by her enemies. Secresy was enjoined especially with a view to protect accusers or witnesses from the vengeance of the culprit, or his friends, and to preserve the character of those whose faith was called in question, until their heterodoxy should have been fully ascertained, as also to keep revolting crimes from public view. Concealment was not designed with a view to injustice, for in no tribunal were greater precautions taken to arrive at a knowledge of the facts, which were recorded in the greatest detail. Many persons were employed in the examination and other proceedings, and powerful safeguards were placed in the dependence of local tribunals on the supreme Council. Before an arrest could take place, if the local officers were not unanimous as to the sufficiency of the grounds for it, the Council *of the Supreme*, as it was styled, was consulted. All the officers were sworn to do justice, and to be strictly impartial, under penalty of ecclesiastical censure, in case they indulged malice. They were required, like jurors, to keep their minds unbiassed, and attend strictly to the evidence. Although the witnesses were not, at least in the early stages of the proceedings, confronted with the accused, or their names communicated to him, yet he was made acquainted with the nature of the charges and evidence, in a manner calculated to enable him to justify himself, if innocent. No aid was afforded him to conceal guilt, or defeat the searching power of the tribunal, but every thing was directed to elicit the truth. He was allowed the aid of counsel, with whom, how-

---

* Breve, 2 Aug., 1483.

ever, he conferred in the presence of an inquisitor, because professional aid was given to direct him in a just defence, but not to enable him to evade the law by subterfuges, or artifices. He was interrogated on oath, as was formerly usual in all criminal tribunals, and thus put under the necessity of criminating himself; but he had an advantage allowed in no other tribunal, that his avowal of guilt, when accompanied by signs of repentance, exempted him from punishment, or secured a great mitigation of its rigor. Twice he could be absolved and set free, on satisfying his judges of his conversion to the truth, on which account mercy as well as justice was incribed on the banner of the Inquisition; but after reiterated relapses they could no longer screen him from the penalties of the law.

The use of the *torture* was common in all tribunals, at the time when the Inquisition was established: hence it should not be made a matter of special reproach, particularly by the admirers of the ancient Romans and Greeks, from whom it passed to the Christian courts. It was very rarely resorted to in this tribunal; and only in cases wherein either positive proof or strong presumptive evidence of guilt existed. In the edict of 2d September, 1561, it was qualified as a dangerous means, to be employed only in extraordinary cases. It could not be used unless the local inquisitors were unanimous in decreeing it. In all cases of disagreement, *the Council of the Supreme* had to be consulted, whose sanction was not given unless after a canonical trial by twelve jurors.* The accused had the right of appeal to the Supreme Council, in case the local inquisitors were unanimous, who, however, might neglect the appeal, if it seemed to them wanton and groundless. Llorente acknowledges that the decisions of the Council were generally characterized by justice and clemency. He also confesses that the torture has long since been entirely abandoned, although the prosecuting attorney continued to demand its application, according to an ancient formulary, and sometimes every preparation was made to apply it, in order to intimidate the culprit into an avowal of the truth.†

The treatment of the prisoners was humane: their cells were lightsome and airy, and with ground attached to them for exercise; not deep, damp dungeons, as novelists are wont to imagine. Chains were never used, unless to restrain some one who appeared bent on self-destruction. All this is testified by Llorente,‡ notwithstanding his desire to represent the institution in the worst possible light. Puigblanch is also compelled to acknowledge the attention which was paid to the comforts of the prisoners, some of whom were attended by their own domestics.§

Although the Inquisition left no means untried to discover the guilt of persons denounced to it as entertaining heretical sentiments, yet it had the strictest regard to truth and justice. It was a formidable tribunal, because it thoroughly sifted every charge and testimony: weighed every

---

* Llorente, Histoire Critique, vol. ii. ch. xiv. art. iii. § xv.
† Ibidem, vol. i. ch. ix. art. vii.   ‡ Ibidem, art. iv.
§ History of the Inquisition, l. ii., ch. xviii.

expression and act, and, without deference to rank, wealth, learning, or other qualifications, extended its searching power to all classes, penetrated the most secret recesses, and struck with its awful penalties all whom it found tainted with heresy. The meek vestals were reponsible for the hasty expressions of confidential communication in their deep solitudes—the learned professors had to answer at its bar for the opinions delivered to their pupils—the fervid preachers, whose zeal won multitudes to the faith, were called on to explain some inaccuracy of language in an extemporaneous burst of eloquence : and even Spain's own primate, Carranza, was its prisoner, and almost its victim. The holiest men could not entirely escape unscathed. St. Ignatius of Loyola, St. John of God, St. Joseph Calasanctius, John D'Avila, and many others most sound in faith, fell under suspicion. Had it only watched with jealousy over the integrity of doctrine, and, with the rod of ecclesiastical censures, driven from the temple the false and faithless, it would have deserved the commendation of all the friends of religion ; but I cannot contemplate without feelings of horror the flames which consumed the impenitent sectary. If humanity shudders at every execution, however necessary for public safety, the punishment inflicted in the name of religion on the most criminal fanatic awakes a still deeper feeling. It is not Voltaire alone that states, that "after the conquest of Granada, the Inquisition throughout all Spain displayed an activity and severity which never characterized the ordinary tribunals. . . . . . The Popes had erected the ordinary tribunals through policy, and the Spanish inquisitors stained them by their barbarity."* Cardinal Baluffi avows that "their proceedings caused grief and shame to the Roman Inquisition, and excited the horror of all nations."†

The number of sufferers cannot be ascertained, since many of the records have been destroyed by Llorente and others, who prefer estimates to statistics, and, without any regard to facts, indulge the most extravagant calculations. If the estimate of two thousand mentioned by Mariana‡ be correct, as the number of those who suffered during the administration of Torquemada, it is indeed awful : but Llorente deceives his readers when he leads them to suppose that these were executed in the city of Seville, in a single year, and makes it the basis of other estimates. Prescott discovers the trick, and yet exculpates its author from any wilful exaggeration, remarking, however, that "one might reasonably distrust Llorente's tables, from the facility with which he receives the most improbable estimates in other matters."§ The multitude of the early sufferers is accounted for by the solicitude of the Spanish sovereigns for maintaining the national independence, of which the Judaizing Christians were the secret enemies.|| Don Melchor de Macanaz, a statesman high in the

---

* Essai sur l'Histoire Générale, t. iv. ch. cxxxvi.
† L'America una volta Spagnuola, prefaz.   ‡ Historia de Espana, l. xxiv.
§ History of Ferdinand and Isabella, vol. iii. ch. xxvi. part ii. n. 155.
|| See Balmes, Protestantism and Catholicity, ch. xxxvi.

court of Philip V., and who himself had suffered from the action of the Inquisition, subsequently defended it, and affirmed, that "with the exception of very few cases intended to stop the progress of Lutheranism in the reign of Philip II., scarcely three persons had been sentenced."* Puigblanch, who quotes him, denies the correctness of his assertion, and refers to the *auto-da-fé* under Charles II. The actual statistics given by Llorente present, indeed, sixteen sufferers on one occasion, in many others a much smaller number; but even three, or one, are too many not to excite our horror. Philip V. did himself honor by refusing to assist at an exhibition of this kind, which, happily, was extremely rare under succeeding sovereigns. It is proper to observe, that sodomites were sometimes the subjects of this punishment, as in 1506, when ten of them were burned at Seville.† Indeed many of those executed were convicted of crimes which by another form of process would have been capitally punished in every civilized state, at least according to the legislation then prevailing. Since the year 1781, or 1783, no one has suffered death under the operation of the Spanish Inquisition. "Most of the sentences passed for the last fifty years," says Llorente, writing in the early part of this century, "were of this character," namely, obliging the culprits to abjure their errors in the hall of the Inquisition, "and we must do justice to the inquisitors of our days, by stating, that with the exception of very rare cases, they have followed a system of moderation which does them honor."‡

The abolition of the Spanish Inquisition was decreed by Napoleon on the 4th December, 1808, the same day on which Madrid capitulated. Ferdinand VII. restored it on 21st July, 1814, but it has since entirely ceased. It is now only a matter of history. In justice to the illustrious nation in which its frightful power was displayed, we must take into consideration the motives which impelled the inquisitors, and reconciled the people to the scenes which were enacted. Jealousy of national independence in the early stages of the tribunal, and at a later period the fear of outbreaks on the part of the abettors of the new doctrines, prompted the inquisitors to take effectual measures for repressing innovation, and punishing apostasy. The civil wars of Germany and France convinced the Spanish sovereigns that for the safety of their dominions they must oppose the progress of the Reformers, on which account they wished the Inquisition to exert all its vigilance to discover the latent elements, which might suddenly explode and spread destruction. The number of those who suffered was doubtless small, if compared with the thousands upon thousands who perished in bloody strife in the other nations, where religious feuds armed the citizens against each other. In the judgment of Paley, "the slave-trade destroys more in a year than the Inquisition does

---

* Critical Defence of the Inquisition, quoted in Inquisition Unmasked, ch. v.

† Llorente, Histoire Critique, vol. i. ch. x. art. iii. § i.

‡ Ibidem, ch. ix. art. xiii. § v.

in a hundred, or perhaps hath done since its foundation."* If recrimination were argument, we could point to the atrocities committed against Catholics, to force them to abandon the faith of their fathers: while the power of the Inquisition was employed only against those who proved recreant to the faith which they had once professed.

§ 4.—ROMAN INQUISITION.

The progress of the new opinions awakened the zeal of Paul III., who, in the year 1543, organized a Council of Cardinals, under the title of the Congregation of the Supreme Inquisition. Six cardinals originally composed it, to whom two more were associated by St. Pius V. They are strictly an ecclesiastical tribunal, charged with the affairs regarding the integrity of faith throughout the world. Hence doctrinal matters are referred to them for examination, and the orthodoxy of clergymen especially, whose sentiments may be called in question, is decided by their judgment. The Pope is Supreme Inquisitor, as the highest guardian of faith. The tribunal has no temporal attributions out of the Roman States, and its action within them is very circumscribed, being little more than the injunction of penitential observances, or, in some cases, imprisonment, for crimes against religion, in connection with the order of society. The providence of God permitted its archives to fall into the hands of Napoleon, who caused them to be transported to Paris; but nothing has ever been brought to light to its prejudice, which, as Cardinal Pacca well observes, shows that its proceedings were found unexceptionable. Viscount de Tournay, who was prefect of Rome under Napoleon, from 1810 to 1815, bears testimony to "the moderation of its decisions, and the gentleness of its proceedings." "The size of the prisons," he adds, "and their healthiness and cleanliness, are a proof of the feelings of humanity of those who preside over them."† "The Inquisition," says Count de Maistre, "is of its nature good, mild, and conservative: such is the universal and indelible character of every ecclesiastical institution: you see it at Rome: you will see it wherever the church has influence. If the civil power, adopting this institution, thinks proper for its own safety to render it more severe, the church is not responsible."‡

The praise of moderation is justly awarded to the Roman tribunal, and the efforts of the Popes have been constantly directed to moderate the action of the Spanish Inquisition. Pontiffs, whose personal character was most humane, and whose piety was tender, such as Nicholas III. and Pius V., before their elevation, exercised the office of Inquisitor, and used their best efforts to check the progress of heresy, by severity, tempered

---

* Evidences of Christianity, vol. ii. p. 2. ch. vii.
† Etudes Statistiques, vol. ii. p. 47.
‡ Lettres sur l'Inquisition Espagnole, let. i.

with mercy: yet, while theoretically intolerant, they were often found in practice more forbearing and indulgent than the loud advocates of universal toleration. Balmes observes: "The Popes, armed with a tribunal of intolerance, have not spilled a drop of blood :* Protestants and philosophers have shed torrents. What advantage is it to the victim to hear his executioners proclaim toleration? It is adding the bitterness of sarcasm to his punishment. The conduct of Rome in the use which she made of the Inquisition is the best apology of Catholicity against those who attempt to stigmatize her as barbarous and sanguinary."† The Reformers most inconsistently advocated and practised intolerance, while they maintained as a Christian *privilege* the right of private judgment. Yet it is undeniable that the whole system is founded on the principle that heresy is a crime against society, punishable by the civil power. This was formerly held to be an axiom. Luther, as Limborch observes, " was, indeed, against putting heretics to death, but for almost all other punishments that the civil magistrate could inflict, and, agreeably to this opinion, he persuaded the electors of Saxony not to tolerate in their dominions the followers of Zuinglius, in the opinion of the sacrament, because he esteemed the real presence an essential or fundamental article of faith. John Calvin was well known to be in principle and practice a persecutor. So entirely was he in the persecuting measures, that he wrote a treatise in defence of them, maintaining the lawfulness of putting heretics to death. And that by heretics he meant such who differed from himself, is evident from his treatment of Castellio and Servetus."‡ His followers, above a century afterwards, embodied the principle in their confession of faith, in which they profess that "the civil magistrate hath authority, and it is his duty, to take order that all blasphemies and heresies be suppressed;"§ in proof of which references are given at the bottom of the page to texts of the old law, which prescribe confiscation of goods, banishment, imprisonment, and death. The National Covenant of the Kirk of Scotland, republished in Philadelphia in the year 1838, approves of the sanguinary laws against Catholics which so long disgraced the English statute-book, and contains an oath of the members of the League, to resist all errors and corruptions according to their vocation, to the uttermost of that power which God had put into their hands! The implied avowal of such principles may well occasion surprise here, where the General and State Constitutions extend protection to all citizens, whatever their religious views may be, as long as they do not violate the peace of society or commit crimes against public morals.

---

* Some few executions certainly took place, as that of Aonius Palearius in 1566, and Giordano Bruni in 1600, but other crimes generally concurred with heresy to provoke the punishment.

† Protestantism and Catholicity compared, ch. xxxvi.

‡ History of the Inquisition, Introd., p. 62.

§ Westminister Confession, ch. xxiii.

Happily for mankind and for religion, the ages of coercion have passed away, and men are now left to worship God according to the dictates of their own conscience. None rejoice more than Catholics in this liberty, and none are less willing to see it abridged. Although we hold it to be necessary to believe all that God has revealed, and to obey all His commandments, we are pleased that the divine truths should be made known only by the preaching of the Gospel, and that obedience should be secured by the promises and threats, which are the sanctions of revelation. No principle of the Catholic Church obliges us to approve of coercion in matters of religion. The legislation of the thirteenth century may have been rendered necessary by the ferocity of sectaries; but now that civilization is general, and order and law prevail, we rejoice that the Church presents herself without any adventitious support, that the homage given her may be not only free, but unsuspected. It seems reserved for our age to behold new triumphs of religion, when men who prize highly their civil rights, and spurn restraint, shall yield to the multiplied evidences by which God has rendered His revelation worthy of belief.

The Primacy.

PART III.

LITERARY AND MORAL INFLUENCE.

CHAPTER I.

Personal Attainments.

REVELATION enlightens the mind by the communication of supernatural knowledge, without extinguishing the lesser light of reason, or preventing the exercise of the natural faculties. It must, then, be useful to inquire how far the chief ministers of religion have contributed to the development of our natural powers by the cultivation of letters, science, and art, and what distinction they themselves have attained to, by their genius and research. The question of the primacy is, of course, entirely independent of these considerations; but a prejudice is raised against the conclusion, as if it necessarily blunted the faculties of the human mind, and prevented their legitimate expansion. Ignorance and mental darkness are alleged to be the results of submission to an authority which undertakes to direct and control the mind, by reducing all men to a common standard of belief. If it shall appear that the Roman Pontiffs were generally men of a high order of intellect, who by their industry and talent acquired distinction, and who in their elevation honored and patronized learning, it will effectually silence those who clamor against them as enemies of mental progress. Nothing, indeed, is clearer in history than that they were generally superior to their contemporaries in those endowments which best became their office, and that they exerted all their efforts to encourage even profane literature, but still more sacred science. Although our Divine Redeemer chose fishermen for His apostles, to manifest more clearly His wisdom and power by the success of their preaching, yet He did not exclude the learned and wise from His ministry. Clement of Rome, one of the earliest successors of St. Peter, has left us indubitable evidence of learning and eloquence, in his powerful epistle to the Corinthians, which, seventy years after it was written, continued to be read publicly in the assemblies of the faithful, with veneration almost approaching that given to the inspired writings. The letters of St. Cornelius to St. Cyprian are composed in a pure style, and with the dignity which became the chief Bishop. Pope Julius wrote with force and propriety, in vindication of St. Athanasius. Damasus was distinguished for his learning and genius, and obtained praise for his poetical essays. The few relics that have been preserved of the writings of the Popes of the first four ages, give us a high opinion of their talents and acquirements, and make us regret the loss of the other many valuable letters which were addressed by them, on various occasions, to their colleagues, and to the faithful generally.

It is unnecessary to state that the pontifical documents of the fifth age continued to be distinguished for perspicuity and dignity, without any affectation of meretricious ornament. Leo the Great, in his sermons, has left us proofs of superior eloquence; the language of ancient Rome falling from his lips with something of the majesty and power with which Tully thundered in the forum. The energy of his diction, as well as the sanctity of his office, contributed to win to mercy the proud Attila, and had its share in the moral miracle, by which the triumphant barbarian was stopped suddenly in his march toward the Eternal city, which he had threatened to lay in ruins. Whoever reads the work of Gregory the Great, "on the Pastoral Office," must admire the simplicity and force of his language, the solidity of his judgment, and his acquaintance with the difficult science of governing men. Although he may not claim praise for profane erudition, or elegance of style, he must be allowed to have possessed the knowledge which best suited his station, and to have expressed his sentiments impressively. He is often represented, on the authority of a writer several centuries posterior, as having banished mathematicians from his palace, and consigned the Palatine library to the flames. This statement, even by the avowal of Gibbon,* deserves no confidence; but, were it certain, it would not prove his hostility to learning, since astrologers formerly passed under the name of mathematicians; and the multitude of superstitious works which, doubtless, filled the Palatine library, might be consumed without much detriment to the republic of letters. It is, however, beyond doubt that he reproved Dedier, Bishop of Vienne, for devoting himself to the teaching of grammar, by which he seems to mean the classics, and declared that the praises of Jupiter should not resound from a mouth consecrated to God;† but this can only imply a disapproval of such studies when pursued to the prejudice of sacred learning, and of the important duties of the episcopate. John the Deacon, his biographer, in language that savors of hyperbole, describes the favor which he showed to learned men: "He was surrounded by the most erudite clergymen and religious monks. . . . Wisdom seemed at that time to have built for herself a temple at Rome, and to have raised the Apostolic See on the arts, as on seven most precious columns. None of the attendants of the Pontiff, even of the humblest class, manifested any thing uncouth in his language or deportment; but the Latin language, with the full Roman ornaments, was dominant in the palace. The various arts were flourishing."‡ Making all due allowance for the bias, or contracted views of the writer, which may have led him to overrate the state of literature at the Roman court, we may safely say that Gregory was no enemy of polite literature.§

---

* Decline and Fall, vol. v. ch. xlvi.   † L. xi., ep. liv., ad Desider. op. Vien.
‡ Joan. diac. vit., l. ii. n. xiii.   § See Tiraboschi stor. let., t. iii. l. ii. c. ii.

In consequence of the inroads of the northern barbarians, learning rapidly declined in Italy and the south of Europe generally, in the following centuries, since letters could not be easily cultivated amid the din of arms. The Popes, however, continued to be respectable for their personal attainments, and to show special esteem for those who applied themselves to literature. Vitalian, being anxious to place a worthy prelate in the See of Canterbury, fixed his eyes on Adrian, who added to great knowledge of the divine Scriptures a familiar acquaintance with the Greek and Latin languages: but this humble monk pleaded bodily infirmity, to escape the burden. At his instance, Theodore, of Tarsus, was substituted in his stead, who was even still more distinguished than Adrian for sacred and profane learning.

Pope Agatho, in the decline of the seventh century, sent bishops, priests, and others of inferior rank, as legates to the East, to assist at the sixth Council, with letters to the emperor, in which he said : " We do not send them as if to display their knowledge; for who can expect a perfect acquaintance with the Scriptures in men that live in the midst of barbarians, and with great distress of mind procure their daily subsistence by manual labour? In simplicity of heart and without hesitation, we hold the doctrines which have been defined by our Apostolic predecessors, and by the five venerable Councils, and the faith handed down from our fathers; and we ask of God, as a special grace, that we may keep the words of their definitions and their meaning unchanged, without adding to them, or taking from them any thing. We have furnished these legates with some texts of the fathers, whom this Apostolic See venerates, and with their books, which, if you wish, they will show you, to explain, not with the ornaments of worldly eloquence, of which they are destitute, but in the sincerity of that religion which we have learned from our infancy, the faith of this Apostolic Church, your spiritual mother."* This beautiful apology for the simple faith of those times should be remembered by those who ascribe the introduction of novelties to the ignorance of the Middle Ages. In the literary obscurity in which the successors of Peter found themselves, they held fast to the tradition of their fathers, being careful to add nothing to it, and suffering nothing to be taken away.

Notwithstanding the decline of secular learning, the Popes continued to be distinguished for the study of the sacred Scriptures, which is mentioned in commendation of Leo II., Benedict II., John VI., and John VII. The superior attainments of Eastern clergymen, when the West was overrun by barbarians, caused several of them successively to be elevated to the Apostolic See; it being the fixed sentiment of all, that the ruler of the Church should be distinguished by the ornaments of literature, as well as by his virtues. Gregory III., a Syrian, and Zachary, a Greek, both of

---

* Conc. Mansi, tom. xi. col. 235. Act. iv., Conc. Constant. iii.

them well acquainted with the Greek and Latin languages, occupied the chair of Peter toward the middle of the eighth century.

In the decline of the same century, Hadrian I., a Roman, governed the Church. His reply to the Caroline books affords evidence of much erudition, and still greater reasoning powers. Leo III. has gained praise as a patron of learning. The visit of Charlemagne to Rome, during his pontificate, led the prince to form a high idea of the importance of letters. "The ruins of Rome," as Voltaire avows, "furnished all things to the West, which was still in an embryo state. Both Alcuin the Englishman, who at that time enjoyed celebrity, and Peter of Pisa, who instructed Charlemagne in the rudiments of grammar, had studied at Rome."*

The genius and piety of Sergius II., when a boy, attracted the notice of Leo, who attended to his education, and thus prepared a worthy occupant for the Papal chair. St. Nicholas I. possessed learning and eloquence far beyond his contemporaries. Stephen VI. left after him a discourse abounding in Scriptural quotations, which were the food with which his soul was nourished, and which he distributed to his spiritual children.

After a dark and dreary interval, in which ignorance and vice contended for the sway, Gerbert, a Frenchman, of great mechanical genius, and of much erudition, occupied the Holy See, at the close of the tenth century, under the name of Sylvester II. Hallam describes him as a man "who, by an uncommon quickness of parts, shone in very different provinces of learning, and was, beyond question, the most accomplished man of the dark ages." He "displays, in his epistles, a thorough acquaintance with the best Latin authors, and a taste for their excellencies. He writes with the feelings of Petrarch, but in a more auspicious period."†

Alexander II., the pupil of the learned Lanfranc, did honor to his station by his learning, and showed his gratitude and esteem for his professor, by rising to embrace him, when, as Metropolitan of Canterbury, he presented himself to do homage. Lest the bystanders should be astonished at this departure from the ordinary rules of court etiquette, the Pope observed that it was a scholar who greeted his master.

The history of Nicholas Breakspere, an English boy, is full of interest. After his father had entered a monastery, the youth was wont to present himself at the convent-gate asking for bread; which led the father to chide him for neglecting to procure it by his industry. Stung by the reproach, he crossed the seas, and tried his fortune at a monastery of Regular Canons, in France, where, by the performance of every humble office, he earned his support, and by his pleasing manners gained favor. Being received among the inmates, he applied himself to sacred studies with great success, and attained to offices of much distinction; until, at length, he was raised to the Apostolic throne, under the title of Adrian IV.

---

* Loix èt usages du temps de Charlemagne, ch. xv.
† Literature of Europe, ch. i. n. 78.

Alexander III. was professor of sacred Scripture in the University of Bologna, before his promotion to the pontifical chair. Of the learning and vigorous intellect of Innocent III., it were superfluous to speak, since his letters and other writings fully attest them. John XX. was styled "a general clerk," because he was familiar with all the branches of learning which were then taught. He attained to special distinction in the science of medicine. Boniface VIII. was the most eminent jurist of his age.

The early career of Benedict XI. was not unlike that of Adrian IV. Being of humble parentage, it was not without difficulty that he procured the facilities of learning; of which he soon availed himself to teach other youths the rudiments of education, that he might gain a subsistence, and have means of further advancement. He subsequently entered into the order of St. Dominic, and passed rapidly forward, until, by his persevering genius, he reached the goal of ecclesiastical preferment.

The surname of *Fournier*, that is, *Baker*, was given to a French boy, whose father followed that trade. The laudable ambition of the son led him to Paris, where, at the University, he bore away from youths of nobler birth the rewards of literary merit. He afterward wore the tiara, under the name of Benedict XII.

In the great schism which convulsed the West at the close of the fourteenth and beginning of the fifteenth century, a man of high reputation for learning and sanctity was chosen in an assembly of cardinals and bishops at Pisa, as the fittest to heal the breach. He assumed the name of Alexander V. His early history is that of a beggar-boy, in whose sparkling eye a Franciscan friar discovered the coruscations of genius. He proved worthy of his discerning patron by the success with which he cultivated sacred studies.

Pius II. ranks high among his Italian countrymen as a scholar and historian. Taste, discernment, and laborious research, gained for him this distinction. Sixtus IV., who is said to have been the son of a fisherman, acquired a familiarity with the Greek language, under the instruction of the celebrated Bessarion. He had filled the chair of professor of philosophy in the most famous universities of Italy, before he wore the triple crown.

It is unnecessary to enumerate the many learned Pontiffs who, during the last three centuries, have adorned the Holy See. They form a bright galaxy, such as illumines no other throne. The literary qualifications of the whole series of Popes are in a high degree respectable, especially when they are considered in reference to the times in which they lived: but their services to literature were not limited to their personal efforts. They were emphatically its patrons.

CHAPTER II.

Measures to Promote Learning.

§ 1.—LIBRARIES.

THE diligence with which the Popes gathered books for the promotion of sacred studies, is truly admirable. From the number of quotations in the letter of Leo the Great to Leo Augustus, we perceive that there must have been a large collection of the writings of the fathers at his command. St. Hilary enriched the Lateran palace with two libraries. Stephen V., toward the close of the ninth century, gave books to the library of St. Paul's. From a letter of Lupus, Abbot of Ferrières, to Benedict III., it is seen that Rome was considered a good place to obtain rare and valuable books. The abbot asks the Pope to send him a portion of the commentary of St. Jerom on the Prophet Jeremiah, which was wanting in the libraries of France; as also the books of Cicero *de Oratore*, the twelve books of the institutes of Quintilian, and the commentary of Donatus on the comedies of Terentius. From this request, it appears that the monks of the ninth century could relish the beauties of the classical authors, and that the Pontiff was thought likely to afford facilities for studying them. Gerbert, who was afterward Pope, at the close of the following age, in a letter to a friend, assures him that the desire of books was great in every city of Italy, and that a large number of persons were employed in transcribing. Victor III., when Abbot of Monte Cassino, occupied his monks in this useful labor, and sought after rare books, to add them to his collection.

The office of librarian of the Roman Church was, from very ancient times, one of great distinction, usually confided to a cardinal. The immense Vatican library is the result of the successive efforts of the Popes, who never abandoned the great work of forming this literary treasure. Nicholas V. so far surpassed all his predecessors in his successful endeavors to collect manuscripts, that he is justly styled its founder. Sixtus IV. increased its treasures, and laid them open to the public. "At present the Vatican library contains 3686 Greek, 18,108 Latin, 726 Hebrew, 787 Arabic, 65 Persian, 64 Turkish, 459 Syriac, 71 Ethiopian, 18 Sclavonic, 22 Indian, 10 Chinese, 80 Coptic, 13 Armenian, and 2 Georgian manuscripts; amounting in all to 24,111, the finest collection in the world; which, with 25,000 duplicates, and 100,000 printed volumes, make a total of 149,494 volumes."*

---

* Rome, Ancient and Modern, by Very Rev. Jeremiah Donavan, D.D., vol. ii. p. 491.

§ 2.—SCHOOLS.

The selection of the learned Theodore for the archiepiscopal See of Canterbury, resulted in great literary advantages to England. As an eloquent writer observes, "the palace of Archbishop Theodore, and the monastery of Abbot Adrian became normal schools for all the kingdoms of the Heptarchy. The fire of emulation which they enkindled, soon illuminated the entire land, extending its humanizing influence from the cloisters to the fortress-castles of the nobility, and to the courts of the royal princes. Even the Anglo-Saxon ladies became inflamed with the general enthusiasm for letters; and their accomplishments and classic taste may well excite the surprise, if not the envy, of their fair descendants of the present age. 'They conversed with their absent friends,' says Dr. Lingard, 'in the language of ancient Rome; and frequently exchanged the labors of the distaff and the needle (in which they excelled) for the more pleasing and more elegant beauties of the Latin poets.' "*

When, in the middle of the eighth century, the lamp of learning burned dimly in Italy, Stephen III. was wont to assemble around him, in the Lateran palace, the clergy of Rome, to hold conferences with them on the Holy Scriptures, which he exhorted them to study, that they might be able to refute the sophisms of unbelievers.

Eugene II., in a Roman Council, held in the year 826, enacted several canons, which show his zeal to dissipate the ignorance which prevailed. Bishops were ordered to suspend from sacred functions, or, if necessary, to depose priests ignorant of their duty; and metropolitans were required to use similar severity toward their suffragans. Schools were to be opened in cathedral and parish churches, and wheresoever else they might be deemed necessary. "We have heard," says the Pontiff, "that in some places neither teachers are found, nor is any regard had to literary pursuits: wherefore, in all episcopal residences, and among the people subject to them, and in other places in which it may be necessary, let care and diligence be used by all means to appoint teachers and instructors who may assiduously teach letters and the liberal arts, and the holy doctrines, since the divine commandments are particularly manifested and declared in these things."† When this enactment had been in a great measure defeated by the general distaste for learning, Leo IV., in 853, contented himself with enjoining the study of the Scriptures and ecclesiastical office: "Although teachers of the liberal arts be usually scarce," he observes in a Roman Council, "let there be at least a professor of the divine

---

* "Rome as it was under Paganism, and as it became under the Popes." Very Rev. Dr. Miley, who is known to be the author, has since written a History of the States of the Church, over his proper signature.

† Mansi, col. conc., t. xiv. col. 1008, can. xxxiv.

Scripture, and instructors in the office of the Church."* There was a school of this kind in the Lateran palace, in which many who sat on St. Peter's chair received their education.

St. Gregory VII., in a Roman synod held in 1078, charged bishops to see that schools be opened in the churches subject to their jurisdiction. The third General Council of Lateran, under Alexander III., in 1179, insists on the necessity of learning for bishops and priests, and orders the poor to be instructed, for which purpose a master must be employed in each cathedral church, to teach them gratuitously; it desires the same to be done in monasteries and other churches. No fee is to be received for license to teach, which must be granted on demand to every person who is duly qualified. In cathedrals, a divine was to be employed in instructing the younger clergy in sacred Scripture. In the fourth Council of Lateran, held in 1215, by Innocent III., it was decreed that each bishop, with the concurrence of the chief clergy, should provide a Latin teacher for the cathedral. The same was to be done in all churches that possessed sufficient income to support the burden. The Scriptures were to be expounded to the clergy and laity by a divine devoted to this task. These various measures, decreed from time to time, and enforced with greater or less success, are unequivocal evidences of the value which the Popes always attached to learning, especially to the study of the Scriptures.

In those ages, throughout all Christian nations, the Pope was considered competent to bestow literary privileges, since civil governments concerned themselves only with matters regarding the public peace and order. Hence all the universities of Spain and France, as well as Italy, relied on some papal document for their prerogatives. One of the chief concessions was, that a student might enjoy the revenues of a Church benefice, without residing at the place where it was situated, when his absence was occasioned by his studies at a University. Another exempted students from the ordinary tribunals, and assigned special judges for their trial, in case they were accused of misconduct. Thousands crowded the halls of the University of Paris, encouraged by the advantages which it offered, through the favor of the Pontiffs. The Universities of Tolosa and Valentia, in Spain, proudly traced their privileges to the same source; and Lisbon acknowledged herself indebted for her university to pontifical munificence. Italy, at that period, wore a literary crown studded with many bright gems. The ancient schools of Pisa, in which theology and canon law were taught in 908, rose to the dignity of a university. Rome, Milan, Pavia, and Florence, each had a similar institution. At Fermo, a university was opened by Boniface VIII.; at Perugia by Clement V.; and at Ferrara by the ninth Boniface. The University of Naples had the honor

---

* Mansi. col. conc., t. xiv. col. 1014.

of the early training of St. Thomas Aquinas, who completed his course at Paris. Padua for a time rivalled Bologna, which, with her celebrated professors, and ten thousand scholars, enjoyed, for the most part, an undisputed precedency in the republic of letters. The multiplication of literary institutions, filled with crowds of eager students, is an incontrovertible proof of a high esteem of learning, which was plainly the result of the reiterated efforts of successive Pontiffs. The light which long glimmered, and seemed almost extinct, was kindled anew by their breath, until it grew into a flame, illumining the nations that long had sat in darkness.

CHAPTER III.

Mediæval Studies.

To some it has appeared that the universities were ill calculated to promote solid learning, and served only for the vain subtleties of scholastic disputation. The fact, however, is, that they rendered immense service to religion, and exercised the reasoning faculties in such a manner as to prepare the human mind for the deeper investigations of after times, when the treasures of antiquity were laid open.

Divinity was not originally studied in most of the universities, Paris for a long time having enjoyed the special privilege of public lectures on that subject. The youth of Italy did not hesitate to cross the Alps to hear the far-famed professors of that city descant on the sentences of Peter Lombard, or, at a later period, explain the summary of the Angelic Doctor. Bologna, however, and other universities, were afterward allowed to teach the same sublime science, which Clement VI. aptly designates, *studium sacræ paginæ*, the study of sacred Scripture. The holy volume was expounded to eager youth by men, who, although not skilled in the original languages, or familiar with classic lore, were, nevertheless, competent to teach accurately the revealed doctrines, and to guard against theological errors. Whoever will take the pains to peruse the works of St. Thomas Aquinas, who flourished in the middle of the thirteenth century, will not consider the scholastic study of divinity a mere exercise of vain dialectics. The whole counsel of God, as manifested and developed in the teaching of the Church, is there declared and sustained, chiefly by the authority of sacred Scripture, although occasionally illustrated by some testimony of ancient Christian writers. Reason herself is introduced as the handmaid of revelation. The difficulties which the pride of man presents to the belief of divine truth, are dissipated by a powerful logic, grounded on divine authority. The searching mind of the Angelic Doctor ventured far beyond the positive doctrine of the Church, and indulged in probable conjectures, which some may brand as idle speculations, but which certainly are not less profitable than many of the disquisitions of men of science in later times. It was his privilege to conceive, almost with the clearness of intuition, the whole revealed doctrine, and to comprehend and combine the sacred oracles, and the teachings of the ancient fathers, but especially to fix his gaze on the Divinity with a steadiness scarcely before granted to an uninspired mortal. In the language of the schools, he was as an angel admitted to view the glory of the Deity, and appointed to unfold to men His counsels. Recent Anglican writers have termed him "the great prophet of the Church," since his mind seems to have grasped in its vision the secrets of futurity, namely, the objections which sectaries in after ages would make to the divine doctrines. The Popes, in commending his works, showed not only their zeal for accurate and precise views of doctrine, but their just appreciation of the admirable method and deep reasoning of this most eminent theologian. "The Summa Theologiæ," says a writer in the British Critic, "is a mighty synthesis, in which Catholic doctrine is bound together in one consistent whole." "It was reserved for St. Thomas Aquinas to survey at one glance the whole of Christian truth as it had been developed in former ages, and to point out the relative bearings of the mighty mysteries to each other."*

I cannot vindicate with the same confidence the homage rendered to Aristotle by the schools of the Middle Ages; yet, although blind deference for the *dicta* of the Stagyrite may have prevented the advancement of science, it cannot be thought that the study of his works, which are learned and profound, was in itself favorable to mental inertness. Urban IV. deserved well of mankind for laboring to revive philosophy, which for ages had been neglected. He enjoined on St. Thomas Aquinas to write commentaries on Aristotle, that the student of his works might not imbibe any error contrary to the doctrine of the sublime Master of Christians. The schools that admitted his authority, corrected his ethics by the maxims of the Gospel, and failed not to adore the Christian mysteries, notwithstanding the abstruseness or erroneousness of his metaphysical views. His sway, however, was that of an absolute monarch, in the realms of natural science. He was heard as an oracle, when he should only have been looked on as a guide; and the student, who should have sought to penetrate further into the recesses of nature, fancied he had reached the goal when he had understood what Aristotle had revealed of her secrets.

It might be a matter of just exultation, that this excessive regard for individual authority has given place to a spirit of inquiry, which assumes nothing, and rests only on demonstration and experience, had not skepticism succeeded faith; the temerity of man extending the philosophic doubt to the very axioms of natural right, and to mysteries divinely revealed. A heathenish system, which abstracts from the fact that God has spoken, and, with the glimmering light of reason, scrutinizes the depths of His nature and works, has taken the place of the old philosophy; and men fancy themselves enlightened and intellectual, in proportion as they are destitute of the certain conviction of revealed truth. The whole structure of religion is placed by many on the sandy foundation of natural reason, unassisted and unenlightened.

---

* Number lxv., p. 110, 111.

Whatever may be thought of the philosophy of the Middle Ages, we should not forget that the great science of legislation, both ecclesiastical and civil, was then effectually cultivated and promoted. The Popes, by their decrees on various cases submitted to their judgment, and the Councils of Bishops, combining their wisdom to remedy prevailing disorders and promote piety, had gradually formed a vast code of laws, of which collections had been made by various persons in the East and West; but it was reserved for Gratian, a Benedictine monk, in the middle of the twelfth century, to classify them, and adapt them to the use of students. This *decree of Gratian*, as the collection of canons has been rather strangely styled, was designed especially for the University of Bologna, to which the Popes likewise were thenceforward accustomed to address the subsequent collections. Those only who are unacquainted with the Canon Law can speak disparagingly of it. The Scripture is its foundation; the fathers of the Church have furnished many of its axioms; and its rules are the fruits of the experience of ages. It combines persuasion with authority, equity with law, and a due regard for forms with an inviolable respect for justice and right. It throws its shield over the humblest individuals, and bears aloft its mace to awe the proud. It tempers the exercise of power by the spirit of charity, sustains dignity without fostering pride; and, in the great variety of orders and offices throughout the Universal Church, presents a compact hierarchy, bound together by mysterious ties in indivisible unity. By encouraging this study, it is manifest that the Popes proved themselves the friends of order and justice, and took from the exercise of ecclesiastical authority all appearance of arbitrary power.

In order to promote true liberty, which needs the salutary restraint of law, the Popes promoted the study of civil jurisprudence. The foundations of social order were laid in various enactments directed to maintain natural rights, and to restrain violence, by the censures of the Church: but it was their earnest desire to see the social fabric rise in just proportions, on the pillars of law; for which end they exerted their utmost influence to introduce everywhere its study. The *civil* law, as we are wont to designate the code used in the Roman empire, had been neglected and forgotten during the tumult and wars consequent on its dissolution, and usages derived from barbarian ancestors were the only rules of conduct acknowledged by the races that were spread over the greater part of southern Europe. It was revived in the Italian universities, especially in Bologna, where professors of great celebrity unravelled its intricacies with untiring ingenuity. Hallam observes: "The love of equal liberty and just laws in the Italian cities, rendered the profession of jurisprudence exceedingly honorable; the doctors of Bologna and other universities were frequently called to the office of podesta, or criminal judge, in those small republics; in Bologna itself they were officially members of the smaller or secret council; and their opinions, which they did not render gratuitously, were sought with the respect that had been shown at Rome to their ancient masters of the age of Severus."*

Innocent IV., although he discountenanced the study of the civil law by clergymen, as likely to occasion the neglect of the more necessary qualifications for the sacred ministry, directed schools of law to be opened at Rome, and founded at Placentia a university, in which it was specially taught. Padua also was for some time the successful rival of Bologna in this science. The Cesarean code is acknowledged to contain the most just arrangement of the family and social relations; and if in any case its provisions were found severe, the mild spirit of the Church tempered its rigor, in the name of *equity*. Thus the confusion necessarily arising from the undefined customs of nations emerging from barbarism was remedied; and, instead of a variety of laws, usages, and tribunals, which threatened society with anarchy, the beauty and order of a comprehensive code were exemplified in all the relations of life.

It was the wish and endeavor of several Popes to introduce into the universities the study of the Greek and Oriental languages. Long before the establishment of these institutions, they had labored to promote the study of Greek, in order more effectually to knit together the two great portions of the Church. Paul I., about the year 766, erected a monastery for monks of the Greek rite. Stephen IV., in 816, founded for them the monastery of St. Praxedes; and Leo IV. introduced them into the monastery of St. Stephen. Mills bears testimony to the efforts of Honorius IV., after the example of his predecessors, to promote the study of the Oriental tongues: "In the year 1285, Pope Honorius IV., in his design to convert the Saracens to Christianity, wished to establish schools at Paris, for the tuition of people in the Arabic and other Oriental languages, agreeably to the intentions of his predecessors. The Council of Vienne, in 1312, recommended the conversion of the infidels, and the re-establishment of schools, as the way to recover the Holy Land. It was accordingly ordered that there should be professors of the Hebrew, Chaldaic, and Arabic tongues in Rome, Paris, Oxford, Bologna, and Salamanca; and that the learned should translate into Latin the best Arabic books."† Mills, indeed, states that these measures were not effectually followed up; but this detracts nothing from the merit of the Popes who devised them, and who, but for the difficulties of the times, would have urged their execution. "The Roman Pontiffs," as Tiraboschi observes, "used every possible means to rescue men from ignorance, and probably would have done much more, had the sad state of the times allowed it; which was the cause of their not deriving that abundant fruit from their efforts which in better times they might have reaped." ‡

---

* Hallam, Literature of Europe, ch. i. n. 63.
† History of the Crusades, ch. xv. p. 211. Note.
‡ Storia della Letteratura Italiana, t. iv. l. i. p. 36.

The partial revival of learning, as well as the great advances toward social order, in the eleventh and succeeding centuries, may be traced to the efforts of the Popes, who sought, in every possible way, to establish law and order, and to promote every study that could improve the mind. This is virtually admitted by Hallam, who ascribes to Italy generally this intellectual and social renovation, which was in reality the work of the Pontiffs. "It may be said with some truth," he remarks, "that Italy supplied the fire, from which other nations in this first, as afterward in the second era of the revival of letters, lighted their own torches. Lanfranc, Anselm, Peter Lombard, the founder of systematic theology, in the twelfth century; Irnerius, the restorer of jurisprudence; Gratian, the author of the first compilation of canon law; the school of Salerno, that guided medical art in all countries: the first great work that makes an epoch in anatomy,—are as truly and exclusively the boast of Italy, as the restoration of Greek literature, and of classical taste in the fifteenth century."*
The same writer justly denies that in the thirteenth century learning declined: "In a general view," he says, "the thirteenth century was an age of activity and ardor, though not in every respect the best directed. The fertility of the modern languages in versification; the creation, we may almost say, of Italian and English in this period; the great concourse of students to the universities; the acute, and sometimes profound, reasoning of the scholastic philosophy, which was now in its most palmy state; the accumulation of knowledge, whether derived from original research or from Arabian sources of information, which we find in the geometers, the physicians, the natural philosophers of Europe; are sufficient to repel the charge of having fallen back, or even remained altogether stationary, in comparison with the preceding century."† Of the period between 1250 and 1494, he says: "It is an age in many respects highly brilliant; the age of poetry and letters, of art, and of continual improvement."‡

"It is a most childish fancy, certainly," observes Dr. Nevin, "to suppose that the revival of learning began properly with the sixteenth century. It dates at least from the eleventh; and there is abundance of evidence that the progress made between that and the age of the Reformation was quite as real and important as any that has taken place since. All sorts of learning were in active exercise before Protestantism came in, to share their credit with the Roman Church. So in the case of criticism, controversy, and the learned languages, Latin, Greek, and Hebrew."§

---

* Literature of Europe, ch. i. n. 81, vol. i.   † Literature of Europe, ch. i. n. 86.
‡ Middle Ages, ch. iii. part ii.   § "Modern Civilization." M. R., March, 1851.

CHAPTER IV.

Revival of Letters.

"DANTE and Petrarch," Hallam observes, "are, as it were, the morning stars of our modern literature." The taste of the Italians for the sublime inspirations of poetry was manifested on the appearance of the *Divina Commedia*, which was soon adopted as a text-book in the Italian universities; men of station and age, as well as the young, crowding the halls where learned professors revealed the deep thoughts of the divine poet. The same ardor was manifested in the following century. Four hundred hearers, most of them of high station and senatorial rank, attended the class of Francis Filelfo at Florence, where he explained Dante, in the time of Eugene IV., who invited him to his court, to reward his learning and genius. The eagerness of the Pontiff to honor the professor proves his liberal encouragement of the study, although Dante had treated some of his predecessors with severity. Nicholas V., on hearing of the arrival of Filelfo at Rome, on his way to Naples, sent for him, and pressed him to accept a present of five hundred ducats for the expenses of his journey. "Petrarch," says Hallam, "formed a school of poetry, which, though no disciple comparable to himself came out of it, gave a character to the taste of his country. He gave purity, elegance, and even stability to the Italian language—and none have denied him the honor of having restored a true feeling of classical antiquity in Italy, and consequently in Europe."* Such was the man on whom the laurel crown was bestowed in the Roman capitol in the year 1341. Clement VI. and Urban V. gave him marks of their favour, and invited him to Avignon. Gregory XI. offered him, in his declining age, whatever could relieve or solace him. This is the more remarkable, as the poet was known to have satirized the papal court. It proves that genius had charms for the Popes, which made them view its aberrations with indulgence.

The favor shown to poets is manifest from many facts. Nicholas V., with his own hands, placed the poet's crown on Benedict of Cesena; and Callistus III., in a Brief, designated Nicholas Perotti "poet laureat," and his secretary. The union of the office of papal secretary with the profession of poet became a matter so usual, that poetry seemed to be a title, or qualification, for this honorable employment. Music gained the ear of the

---

* Literature of Europe, ch. 1. n. 46.

Popes even in an unrefined age; since Guy of Arezzo, in the eleventh century, had scarcely invented the gamut, when John XIX. insisted that he should come to Rome to teach the clergy. Among the endowments of various Popes their knowledge of sacred music is mentioned, which, whatever may be thought of its imperfection, denotes the taste and diligence of those who cultivated it.

History was always deemed an important study. It exercised the diligence of ecclesiastics, even when, from the want of documents and critical light, they were unable to perform the task with success. The chroniclers of the Middle Ages are not without their claims on our gratitude, for having recorded the events of their own times, and preserved much of the history of the past, although sometimes disfigured by fables. As soon as the light of literature beamed anew on the world, the Popes drew around them men of deep research and accurate judgment, who labored to recover the hidden treasures of past ages, and rescue them from the superincumbent mass of fiction. The libraries were thrown open to their researches; coins, medals, vases, inscriptions, statues, and other monuments of antiquity, were dug from the earth, or gathered from remote regions, at the expense of the Pontiffs, and every encouragement was given to the curious and diligent student, in his efforts to retrace the progress of the human race, and to discover the manners and customs, laws and polity of the different nations of antiquity. Eugene IV. gave to Cyriacus of Ancona, in his researches, every facility which the most unbounded munificence could afford. Biondo Flavio, the historian, was secretary of the same Pontiff, and of three of his successors. "His long residence at Rome inspired him with the desire, and gave him the opportunity of describing her imperial ruins. In a work, dedicated to Eugenius IV., who died in 1447, but not printed till 1471, entitled '*Romæ Instauratæ libri tres*,' he describes, examines, and explains, by the testimony of ancient authors, the numerous monuments of Rome. In another, '*Romæ Triumphantis libri decem*,' printed about 1472, he treats of the government; laws, religion, ceremonies, military discipline, and other antiquities of the republic."* Annius of Viterbo, who, although charged with literary imposture, must be acknowledged to have shed much light on the Egyptian, Chaldean, and Tuscan antiquities, was made Master of the sacred Palace, by Alexander VI., who, by this and other acts, proved that he was not incapable of appreciating literary merit. Pius II. led the way in the reform of historical narrative; and in the history of his own times gave proof of great discernment, deep reflection, and elegant taste.

Eloquence and Belles Lettres were cultivated in the fifteenth century, under the patronage of the Popes, who invited to their court the most eminent professors. George of Trebizond was called to Rome by Eugene IV.; and Laurentius Valla received the like honorable invitation from

---

* Hallam, Literature of Europe, 1471–1480, vol. i. ch. iii. n. 48.

Nicholas V. Cardinals and other illustrious strangers thronged the halls of the University of Florence, to hear Charles Marsuppini descant on the art of speaking. Hermolaus Barbaro, John Pico de la Mirandola, with others, bright ornaments of this age, prove that the successful cultivation of *Belles Lettres* was not the peculiar privilege of the sixteenth century. "The Pope nominated Hermolaus to the greatest post in the Venetian Church, the patriarchate of Aquileja."*

The revival of letters was by more than a hundred years anterior to the so-called Reformation, which was highly injurious to literature. The Tuscans, by their innate genius, had succeeded in cultivating learning long before the Greeks sought refuge in Italy. "Florence was already another Athens, and among the orators that came on the part of the various cities of Italy to address Boniface VIII., on his elevation, eighteen were Florentines. We see, then, that the revival of the arts is not owing to the refugees from Constantinople. The Greeks could teach only Greek to the Italians."† "It is probable," says Hallam, "that both the principles of this great founder of the Reformation, (Luther,) and the natural tendency of so intense an application to theological controversy, checked for a time the progress of philological and philosophical literature on this side of the Alps."‡ "Erasmus, after he had become exasperated with the Reformers, repeatedly charges them with ruining literature."§

John Malpaghino, who, toward the end of the fourteenth century, taught Latin at Padua and Florence, and Gasparin of Barziza, his disciple, gave the example of a pure and elegant style. "This," says Hallam, "is the proper era of the revival of letters, and nearly coincides with the beginning of the fifteenth century."‖ "It was from Italy that the light of philological learning spread over Europe."¶ Petrarch, who had loved Malpaghino as a son, had applied himself for a time to Greek, but not quite successfully. Boccaccio had succeeded somewhat better in that study, which in the following century became so general, that scarcely an aspirant to the reputation of learning was unacquainted with this language. Whatever may have been the causes which concurred to produce the enthusiasm with which it was pursued, the Popes deserve praise for having encouraged it, by the honors which they bestowed on learned Greeks, and on others who cultivated the language with success. Chrysoloras, after having discharged the high office of ambassador from the Greek emperor to the Western powers, yielded to the solicitations of many to become professor of Greek at Florence, and afterward in various other Italian universities. He was chosen by John XXII. as his ambassador to the Council of Constance. The elevation of Bessarion to the purple, may be regarded as a reward for his zeal in accomplishing the reunion of the Greeks with the

---

* Hallam, Literature of Europe, 1471–1480, vol. i. ch. iii. n. 116.
† Essai sur l'Histoire t. ii. ch. lxxviii.
‡ Hallam, Literature of Europe, 1471–1480, vol. i. ch. iv. n. 61.   § Ibid. Note.
‖ Ibid., vol. i. ch. i. n. 94.   ¶ Ibid., n. 24.

Latins at Florence; but his solid and elegant learning greatly strengthened his claims to this honorable distinction. His presence at Rome, where, in 1470, he published a work in defence of the Platonic philosophy, became an incentive to Greek studies. Aurispa, a Sicilian, who was eminent in Greek literature, was made secretary of Eugenius IV.; and Manetti, a Florentine, who spoke Greek and Hebrew with almost the same facility as his vernacular tongue, was welcomed to Rome, raised to high honors, and provided with a pension of five hundred golden crowns. Angelo Puliziano, the successful imitator of the Greek and Latin classics, was honored by Innocent VIII. with a letter full of esteem and affection, and rewarded with a gift of two hundred crowns for his translation of Herodian. Domizio Calderino, when only twenty-four years of age, was invited by Paul II. to Rome to profess Greek, in which he had already attained eminence; and was subsequently promoted to the office of secretary by Sixtus IV. It were endless to enumerate instances of papal patronage, by which this study was effectually fostered; but I shall note a fact which shows at once the favor of the Popes, and the success with which the study was pursued. Ippolita Sforza, daughter of the Duke of Milan, and afterward wife of the King of Naples, delivered, in 1456, a Greek oration at Mantua, in the presence of Pius II. This accomplished lady was the representative of a considerable class, who united with the usual graces of the sex a thirst for classic literature, and acquired an astonishing familiarity with the works of the Greek authors. The Pontiff was fully capable of appreciating such literary excellence.

Hallam, after having traced in outline the form of European literature, as it existed in the Middle Ages, and in the first forty years of the fifteenth century, observes: "The result must be to convince us of our great obligations to Italy for her renewal of classical learning. What might have been the intellectual progress of Europe if she never had gone back to the fountains of Greek and Roman genius, it is impossible to determine; certainly nothing in the fourteenth and fifteenth centuries gave prospect of a very abundant harvest. It would be difficult to find any man of high reputation in modern times, who has not reaped benefit, directly or through others, from the revival of ancient learning. We have the greatest reason to doubt whether, without the Italians of these ages, it would ever have occurred."*

It cannot be doubted that the Popes eminently deserve this praise. Hallam himself testifies that Eugenius IV. patronized learning; and he does ample justice to the claims of Nicholas V. on the gratitude of the literary world. "Letters," he says, "had no patron so important as Nicholas V., (Thomas of Sarzana,) who became Pope in 1447; nor has any later occupant of that chair, without excepting Leo X., deserved equal praise as an encourager of learning. Nicholas founded the Vatican library,

---

* Literature of Europe, ch. ii. n. 49.

and left it, at his death, in 1455, enriched with five thousand volumes; a treasure far exceeding that of any other collection in Europe. Every scholar who needed maintenance, which was of course the common case, found it at the court of Rome."* The munificence of the Pontiff amply rewarded the literary labors of the many whom he drew around him. Five hundred golden crowns were bestowed by him on Valla for his translation of Thucydides; fifteen hundred crowns were the recompense of Guarino for his version of the first ten books of the geography of Strabo. Manuscripts were purchased at high prices; and honor and wealth were held forth to all who chose to enrich the republic of letters, by the contribution of rare books, or successful imitations of the ancients.

Alexander VI. deserved well of literature, for establishing, on a large scale, the Roman gymnasium, which Eugene IV. had commenced, and promoting and honoring learned men. Julius II. was an active patron of painting and the fine arts: but the boundless munificence of Leo X. to the lovers of the arts, votaries of the Muses, and cultivators of polite literature, eclipsed all that his predecessors had done, and won for him the admiration of succeeding ages. I leave to others to describe the reunion of men of genius at the celebrated Papal suppers, where the feast of intellect far surpassed the richness of the banquet, and fancy soared aloft to delight the guests by her sublime inspirations. The *academies* of literary men, so frequent in "Leo's golden reign," on the banks of the Tiber, in the *circus maximus*, or in some of the magnificent villas which adorn the eternal city, brought to mind the groves of the Grecian Academus, where Plato descanted on divine and human things, and the Lyceum, where Aristotle perambulated, while delivering his sublime lessons. The illuminated halls, in which the gravest prelates were seen amid the fascinated crowds, listening to the poet of Arezzo, showed the keen sensibility of the Italian mind to the beauties of imagination. Vida, who sang in strains not unlike those of Virgil, and Ariosto, the prince of romantic poets, charmed Leo and the age by the sublime and varied conceptions of their minds. Bembo and Sadolet, his secretaries, in the Papal documents revived the chaste elegance of the Augustan age. The artist who dug from the earth some statue, the work of an ancient master,—the humanist who recovered a manuscript of a classic author,—all the *literati* and *virtuosi* of every class received from the Pontiff rewards proportioned to their merit and worthy of his munificence. But it were wrong to suppose that the patronage of elegant literature was peculiar to Leo; since the praise must be shared with his predecessors, and with those who succeeded him. "Italy," says Hallam, "the genial soil where the literature of antiquity had been first cultivated, still retained her superiority in the fine perception of its beauties, and in the power of retracing them by spirited imitation. It was the land of taste and sensibility; never, surely, more so

---

* Literature of Europe, vol. i. ch. iii. n. 2.

than in the age of Raffaelle as well as Ariosto. If the successors of Leo X. did not attain so splendid a name, they were, perhaps, after the short reign of Adrian VI.—which, if we may believe the Italian writers, seemed to threaten an absolute return of barbarism—not less munificent or sedulous in encouraging polite and useful letters."*

Throughout the sixteenth century, Oriental scholars of considerable reputation were found among the Italian clergy. Even high dignitaries assiduously applied to the study of Hebrew, Arabic, and Chaldaic, among whom I may mention Frederick Borromeo, who was raised to the dignity of cardinal by Sixtus V. Gavanti, the famous rubricist, was familiar with Hebrew, in which language he addressed this cardinal, on occasion of his taking possession of his diocese. Paul V., in 1610, issued a decree requiring the religious orders to have a professor of Greek and Hebrew in all their institutions, and a professor of Arabic in the chief schools. Urban VIII., who himself was familiar with Greek and Hebrew, invited several learned Oriental scholars, among whom was Abraham Ecchellensis, to settle at Rome.

History continued to receive liberal encouragement from the Popes. Charles Sigonio, the great historian of the Western empire, was highly honored by Pius V. Onuphrius Panvinio, an Augustinian friar, published at Rome valuable works, in which he re-examined the *consulares fasti*, already arranged by Sigonio, and otherwise illustrated chronology, as connected with history. Possevino, a Jesuit, who added much to the stores of historic knowledge, was made Papal nuncio, by Gregory XIII., to the court of Sweden, and afterward to Russia. Cardinal Bentivoglio, the historian of the civil wars of Flanders, in the judgment of Hallam, ranks as a writer among the very first of his age. Antiquaries received like patronage. Angeloni, who collected and illustrated ancient medals with great industry, was declared Antiquary of Rome by Clement X. Falconieri, who wrote on the antiquities of Anzio, was raised to the episcopacy by Clement XI. Fabretti, the most celebrated of this honorable class, whose constant researches among caverns and ancient monuments are said to have made his horse instinctively stop when approaching some ruin or cave, was raised to office by Alexander VIII. and Innocent XII. This province, according to the remark of Hallam, is justly claimed by Italy as her own.†

Genius instinctively sought Rome, which inspired the poet with his loftiest strains, and was to him a haven, in which he might rest securely from the storms of life. To it Torquatus Tasso, whose muse rivals that of Homer, twice repaired, and there closed his career, leaving the world astounded at the sublimity of his flights, and the illusions of his disordered imagination. Urban VIII. and Alexander VII. were themselves votaries of the muses.

---

* Literature of Europe, vol. i. ch. v. i.
† Literature of Europe, vol. iv., from 1650 to 1670, ch. i. n. 21.

We need not furnish more recent instances of the claims of the Popes to the gratitude of the learned world for their effectual patronage of belles lettres, and of all those studies which contribute to refinement and intellectual enjoyment. It is a mistake to suppose that Italy is not still the land of genius and of learning. Whatever she possesses, she owes to the benign influence of the Pontiffs. Their smiles have cheered the adventurous youth in his struggle to mount the rugged hill of science, their purse has supplied his wants, and they have been ever ready to bestow the most distinguished honors on the successful aspirant. Hallam truly observes, that genius and erudition have always been honored in Italy; and pays a tribute of praise to the spirit breathed in the works of Italians during the last fifty years, which shows that they are not unworthy of their sires. Byron, in many places, has rendered homage to the ancient glory of Rome, and sometimes avowed her actual literary pre-eminence, notwithstanding the decay of her earthly splendor.

"Italia! too, Italia! looking on thee,
Full flashes on the soul the light of ages;
——— still
The fount at which the panting mind assuages
Her thirst of knowledge, quaffing there her fill,
Flows from the eternal source of Rome's imperial hill."*

* Childe Harold canto iii. cx.

CHAPTER V.

Science.

§ 1.—MEDICINE.

The patronage of the Popes was not confined to the study of languages or of antiquity; it embraced the useful sciences. Even in the Middle Ages these were not wholly neglected in the universities, which must necessarily share with their patrons the praise of whatever was taught within their walls. Medicine, long before it received the necessary attention in most countries, was a favorite study at Salerno, and was subsequently cultivated in the universities generally, among which Montpelier acquired high celebrity. The clergy and monks were among its most diligent students, until it became necessary to confine them to the duties more strictly belonging to their state of life. Hallam bears honorable testimony to the successful cultivation of medical science in the Italian universities. "Nicholas Leonicenus, who became professor at Ferrara, before 1470, was the first restorer of the Hippocratic method of practice. He lived to a very advanced age, and was the first translator of Galen from the Greek."*
"In the science of anatomy, an epoch was made by the treatise of Mundinus, a professor of Bologna, who died in 1326. It is entitled, 'Anatome Omnium Corporis Interiorum Membrorum.' This book had one great advantage over those of Galen, that it was founded on the actual anatomy of the human body."—" His treatise was long the text-book of the Italian universities."† "The first book upon anatomy, since that of Mundinus, was by Zerbi of Verona, who taught in the University of Padua in 1495. The germ of discoveries that have crowned later anatomists with glory, is sometimes perceptible in Zerbi; among others, that of the Fallopian tubes."‡

. In the sixteenth century, medical science received still higher encouragement. Leo X. rewarded with his usual munificence the translation of the medical works of Hippocrates, by Mark Fabius Calvi, of Ravenna; and in noticing the embassy sent to him by the citizens of Padua, he designated with special honor Jerom Accorambuoni, as "an excellent physician." The honor of Roman citizenship was bestowed, in 1563, on Mercuriale, a native of Padua, to reward his eminence in the medical science. Beren-

---

* Hallam, Literature of Europe, ch. ix. n. 9.   † Ibidem, ch. ii. n. 37.
‡ Ibidem, ch. iii. n. 17.

gario de Carpi, the great anatomist, was urged by Clement VII. to fix his residence at Rome. Eustachius was professor in the Sapienza, which Alexander VII. furnished with an anatomical theatre. Many most distinguished physicians and anatomists filled the chair of that university, while others were employed in the immediate service of the Popes. Vesalius, a Belgian, who was professor at Padua, bore away the palm in anatomical science, in the sixteenth century; but Italy, which was the chief theatre of his scientific displays, came well nigh conferring it on her own sons. "Few sciences," says Hallam "were so successfully pursued in this period as that of anatomy. If it was impossible to snatch from Vesalius the pre-eminent glory that belongs to him as almost its creator, it might still be said, that two men now appeared who, had they lived earlier, would probably have gone as far, and who, by coming later, were enabled to go beyond him. These were Fallopius and Eustachius."*—"The best physicians of the century were either Italian or French."†

The seventeenth century presents many instances of the encouragement given by the Popes to these studies. Malpighi was invited to Rome by Innocent XII. to be Papal physician. The services rendered by him to science may best be told in the words of Hallam: "Malpighi was the first who employed good microscopes in anatomy, and thus revealed the secrets, we may say, of an invisible world, which Leuwenhoek afterward, probably using still better instruments, explored with surprising success. To Malpighi anatomists owe their knowledge of the structure of the lungs."‡

The work styled *Medical legal questions*, by Paul Zacchia, physician of Innocent X., is still highly esteemed for the exact specifications in anatomy which it contains. Many other medical works were published under the special patronage of the Popes. Lancisi, a Roman physician, gave his splendid medical library to the hospital of Santo Spirito, on condition that it should be for the general use of the profession. Italy retained her pre-eminence. "The Italians," says Hallam, "were still renowned in medicine."§

In connection with this science, we may be allowed to mention the encouragement given to natural history and botany. The former was cultivated, under Leo X. and Adrian VI., by Mattioli, who published a work of great celebrity on herbs, plants, flowers, and animals. Aldovrandi, professor at Bologna, in a work published in 1574, which has received praise, although qualified, from Buffon, an excellent judge, treated at large of birds, insects, fishes, quadrupeds, and all kinds of animals, as also of metals and of trees. The Vatican Museum, in the time of St. Pius V., contained a vast collection of minerals, and of natural curiosities, which were described by Mercati, the guardian of it, in a work styled "Metallotheca,"

---

* Literature of Europe, vol. ii. ch. viii. n. 39.   † Ibidem, n. 42.
‡ Ibidem, vol. iv. ch. viii. n. 37.   § Ibidem, n. 22.

which was published long afterward, with splendid engravings, at the expense of Clement XI. Botany, especially in its connection with medicine, was a favorite study in Italy. Medical botany was taught in the Roman University under Pius V., and the *Sapienza* was furnished with a botanic garden by Alexander VII.

§ 2.—ASTRONOMY.

It is important that the reader should be made sensible how much the science of astronomy owes to the fostering patronage of the Pontiffs, especially as in some instances they may, at first sight, appear to have opposed its progress. I shall at once offer an explanation of the first fact that gives a coloring to this charge. It occurred before the middle of the eighth century.

St. Gregory II., on being informed that the priest Virgil, an Irishman, taught the existence of another world, and other men under the earth, another sun, and moon, directed Boniface to ascertain the fact, and, if true, to depose him from the priesthood. It is not clear that the opinion of Virgil was the same as that which has since been found to be correct, namely, that *antipodes* exist. The Pope seems to have understood him as asserting the existence of a race of men in another world, altogether distinct from this, not derived from Adam, of whom God made all mankind, and not redeemed by Christ, who is the Saviour of all men. Of the measures actually adopted by Boniface we are not informed, but it is plain that no doctrinal decree was issued on the occasion. If Virgil be the same individual who was afterward created Bishop of Saltzburg, as is more generally believed, he must have satisfied the archbishop and the Pontiff that his sentiment was innoxious. Granting, what is by no means proved, that Gregory wished deposition to take place for the holding of the opinion concerning the existence of antipodes, it does not show any hostility to science, but a jealous care, lest scientific speculations, not yet confirmed by satisfactory proofs, should weaken the belief in the revealed doctrines. This solicitude may, in some instances, be excessive, without implying any disposition to oppose the progress of science, within its legitimate sphere. The Church is not authorized to pronounce on subjects of this nature, unless as far as they manifestly clash with revelation; but she may adopt precautions, lest natural science be abused to cast discredit on revealed truth.

Nicholas V., in 1448, in raising to the dignity of cardinal Nicholas Cusanus, a German, author of a work on statics and a defender of the earth's motion around the sun, gave an unequivocal mark of his regard for science. In Bologna, where astronomy was cultivated with success, this system was probably maintained by Dominic Maria Novara, under whom Copernicus, a native of Thorn on the Vistula, studied at the close of this century. Leonardo da Vinci, a most illustrious astronomer, mathematician, and mechanician, as well as painter, "in a treatise written about the year 1510, speaks of the earth's annual motion as the opinion of many philosophers of his age."* Celio Calcagnini, professor in the University of Ferrara, early in the sixteenth century published a work in support of it; but Copernicus, who, at the commencement of the century, was professor of astronomy at Rome, gave it celebrity, when, after the reflections and observations of thirty-six years, he published his work, under the auspices of Paul III., in 1543. The difficulties in which Galileo was involved in 1616 and 1633, show that his manner of maintaining it, rather than the theory itself, must have provoked the displeasure of the ecclesiastical tribunal, since the system had been advanced without censure, nearly two hundred years before, by a high dignitary of the Church, and had been expressly maintained, with the implied approbation of a most enlightened Pontiff, full ninety years before the sentence pronounced against the Florentine astronomer. Had he confined himself, as he was repeatedly warned, to scientific demonstrations, without meddling with Scripture, and proposed his system as probable, rather than as indubitable, he would have excited no opposition. To urge it absolutely, at a time when it was not supported by observations and calculations, was scarcely reconcilable with the respect due to the sacred text, whose literal meaning should not be easily abandoned. "Mankind," says Hallam, "can in general take these theories of the celestial movements only upon trust from philosophers; and in this instance it required a very general concurrence of competent judges to overcome the repugnance of what called itself common sense, and was in fact a prejudice as natural, as universal, and as irresistible as could influence human belief. With this was united another, derived from the language of Scripture; and though it might have been sufficient to answer, that phrases implying the rest of the earth and motion of the sun are merely popular, and such as those who are best convinced of the opposite doctrine must employ in ordinary language, this was neither satisfactory to the vulgar nor recognised by the Church."†— "It must be confessed that the strongest presumptions in favor of the system of Copernicus were not discovered by himself."‡ It may be added, that even Galileo did not furnish the most convincing proofs of the system, and that his chief reliance was on the flux and reflux of the tides, which no one at this day holds to be a satisfactory demonstration of the motion of the earth. Even long after his time eminent astronomers rejected his system. "In the middle of the seventeenth century, and long afterward," says Hallam, "there were mathematicians of no small reputation, who struggled staunchly for the immobility of the earth." In such circumstances it is not to be wondered that an ecclesiastical tribunal, fear-

---

* History of Literature, vol. i. ch. iii. n. 115.
† Literature of Europe, vol. ii. ch. viii. n. 10.   ‡ Ibidem, vol. iv. ch. viii. n. 32.

ful lest the authority of the sacred Scriptures should suffer in the minds of the multitude, by the bold and unqualified maintenance of a system in apparent opposition to them, enjoined on Galileo, in the year 1616, to observe silence, and when he had violated this order, required him, in 1633, to abjure the theory. It is certain that Urban VIII. did not consider the act of the Inquisition as a definitive decree; and that the theory was publicly taught at the time by two Jesuits in the Roman college. All that has been said concerning the persecution of the astronomer is a tale of fancy. His discoveries gained for him the highest honors from all classes, from the Pontiff to the humblest citizen, in 1615, when he first visited the Eternal city. In 1624 he was again received graciously by the Pope and cardinals; and in 1633, when his contemptuous violation of the injunction provoked their displeasure, his confinement was but nominal, in the apartments of the Fiscal, that is, the prosecuting attorney, of the tribunal. No corporal punishment was inflicted—no dungeon was opened to receive him; but, in consideration of his scientific merits, his pride and contempt were visited with the slightest expression of displeasure.*

The study of astronomy was always encouraged by the Popes, while its abuse, by the superstitions of astrology, was severely prohibited. A splendid evidence of the successful cultivation of astronomical science, under pontifical patronage, was afforded by the correction of the Calendar, by the authority of Gregory XIII. The ancient Calendar, in use since the time of Julius Cesar, and adopted by the Council of Nice, was formed on the supposition that the annual course of the sun is completed in 365 days and 6 hours, which in reality takes place in 365 days, 5 hours, 48 minutes, and 25 seconds: whence, in the lapse of so many ages, a difference of ten days existed in the designation of the vernal equinox; the astronomical being prior to the civil calculation. Even in the eighth century, in the comparatively low condition of the sciences, the error had been pointed out by Venerable Bede, and subsequently by others. In the decline of the fifteenth century it again awakened attention. Sixtus IV. called to Rome Muller, the greatest mathematician of his age, to devise a remedy; but the glory of the sublime task of reconciling the calculations of time with the precise motion of the heavenly bodies, was reserved for Gregory XIII. Luigi Lilio, a man of obscure origin in Calabria, proposed the subtraction of ten days from the month of October, 1582, and to prevent a recurrence of the error, the omission of the leap-year at the close of each century, with the exception of the four hundredth year, which should be bissextile or leap-year. His suggestions, communicated after his death by his brother, were graciously received by the Pontiff, and

---

* The letter of Galileo, published by Tiraboschi, shows that he was treated with extraordinary kindness, the Pope having changed the sentence of imprisonment into an order to remain, for a time, with the Archbishop of Sienna, his personal friend.

submitted to the examination of a body of learned astronomers, among whom was the Jesuit Clavius. Being found just, they were recommended to the whole civilized world by Gregory, who, while acknowledging their source, lost nothing of the glory which the correction imparted. Although the dominion of science belongs not to the Vicar of Christ, it was a sublime spectacle to see him regulating by its aid the calculations of time, and the great festivals of the Church; and when his authority in the things of salvation was proudly rejected by many, fixing a standard to which all nations would, sooner or later, conform. "The new calendar," says Hallam, "was immediately received in all countries acknowledging the Pope's supremacy; not so much on that account, though a discrepancy in the ecclesiastical reckoning would have been very inconvenient, as of its real superiority over the Julian. The Protestant countries came much more slowly into the alteration, truth being no longer truth, when promulgated by the Pope. It is now admitted that the Gregorian Calendar is very nearly perfect, at least as to the computation of the solar year."*

To the learned institutions of Italy this and many other fruits of scientific observation may be fairly referred. I have not space to dwell on the many inventions and discoveries which were made by the professors of the various universities, or by those who had been introduced by them into the halls of science. Ignatius Danti, a Dominican, professor of mathematics in Bologna, left, as Tiraboschi remarks, an imperishable memorial of his astronomical knowledge, in the great meridian drawn by him in the temple of St. Petronius in that city, in the year 1576: which, however, was not as great, or as accurate, as that which the immortal Cassini drew in the following age.

The Pontiffs in the seventeenth century were true to their character as patrons of science. During the reign of Paul V., "a Jesuit, Grassi, in a treatise (*de Tribus Cometis*,) Rome, 1618, had the honor of explaining what had baffled Galileo, and first held them to be planets moving in vast ellipses round the sun." The astronomer Cassini, in 1657, was called to Rome by Alexander VII.; and while there gained new fame by his observations on the two comets, which appeared in 1664 and 1665. His calculations, confirmed by the event, appeared like the predictions of an inspired man. They were followed by other discoveries, which seemed to mark him as one to whom the secrets of the skies were laid open. It was a glorious homage to science when the monarch of a great kingdom sought from Clement IX., as a special favor, that France should be permitted to profit by the extraordinary science of this illustrious astronomer, and the reluctant Pontiff consented to lend him for a time. After a few years, he pressingly called for his return, but Louis XIV. declined parting with a

---

* Hist. of Lit. vol. ii. ch. viii. n. 15. The Gregorian Calendar was finally adopted in Germany in 1777. England introduced the new style in 1752, and Sweden in 1753. Russia only retains the old style, which now differs 12 days from the new.—*Encyclopædia Americana, art. Calendar.*

treasure of so much value; and to bind him to the soil, and identify all his attachments and interests with France, granted him the rights of citizenship. In this, and in many other instances, Italy had the glory of giving to other nations the luminaries of science.

Castelli, a Benedictine monk, disciple and defender of Galileo, was called by Urban to Rome in 1625, to occupy the post of professor of mathematics in the *Sapienza,* when in 1628 he published his celebrated works on the measure of running waters, and its geometrical demonstrations, whereby he has acquired the title of creator of this part of hydraulics. Another disciple of Galileo, Cavalieri, of the order of Jeromites, who is generally reputed the father of the new geometry, was professor of Mathematics, about the same time, in Bologna, where he published in 1632 his treatise on continuous indivisibles.

Benedict XIV. in the last century, followed in the footsteps of his illustrious predecessors, and distinguished himself as the patron of astronomical science. By his orders the obelisk, sixty-seven feet high, mentioned by Pliny,* on which was a dial to mark the sun's shadow, and ascertain the length of the day at various seasons, was dug up from the earth in 1748, and its precious fragments rendered accessible to the learned. Even to this day the Jesuit professors of the Roman College, under the fostering patronage of the Pope, continue to enrich astronomical science by their observations and discoveries. To the lamented De Vico and his illustrious assistant Sestini, who is now in our midst, we are indebted for the discovery of the satellites of Venus, and of the rotatory motion of this planet on her axis; while we owe to Secchi the very recent discovery of a new comet.

---

* Hist. Nat. ch. ix. x. xi.

CHAPTER VI.

The Arts.

THE Popes have, at all times, well understood that art may be fostered without detriment to religion: nay, their enlightened zeal found means to make the arts tributary. "If there be a Church," says Saint Priest, "predestined to a social mission, which, far from throwing obstacles in the way of civilization, has developed and fostered its germs in the focus of ardent faith, the Roman Church must be recognized by these features. We shall see her during the first period of her existence, causing the education of the soul and of the mind to advance with equal pace; cursing in the name of faith the gods of paganism, and protecting their images in the name of art: afterwards, for the interest of both, which she always happily combined, opposing the force of her word to the blind fury of the Iconoclasts. . . . . Her true character was always to unite the maintenance of faith with the exercise of all the human faculties, to regulate them all without proscribing any of them, thus to devote them, in a purified state, to the service of God. Rome attached to the altars of Christ the imagination itself, the rebellious slave of reason."*

The proofs of these enlarged views are found in the acts of the ancient Popes, who, as soon as the danger of idolatry had ceased, availed themselves of the labors of the artist for the decoration of the churches. Paintings, mosaics, and inlaid work of various kinds, were among their ordinary gifts. Paul I. built an oratory of the Blessed Virgin within the precincts of St. Peter's, having a silver statue of a hundred pounds' weight, richly gilded. Leo III. introduced the use of stained glass. Sergius II. raised a vestibule before St. John of Lateran, supported by columns and arches. Silver canopies for the altar, which were then called *ciboria*, were given by various Popes. These are a few instances of their zeal to adorn the house of God, that the facts of sacred history might be read on its walls, and the mysteries of faith constantly kept in view. The elegance of the execution varied according to the general condition of the times; but at all times art presented her best offerings on the altars of religion.

Blind zeal against paganism would have destroyed the temples and statues of the gods, as so many monuments of idolatry: the Popes preserved them with care, wisely judging that the temples might be trans-

---

* Historia de la Royauté, vol. ii. l. v. p. 7.

ferred to the worship of the true God.* No glory could redound to the Deity from the destruction of the statues, wherein the skill of man appears, fashioning the lifeless stone to the imitation of the divine work. Paul II. gathered ancient statues from all parts of the city into his own palace, and rewarded with munificence all who brought them from Greece, Asia, or other countries. What Leo X. did for the recovery of the works of art cannot be told. The monuments rescued by the care of the Popes from the destroying arm of the barbarian, or the fragments gathered up by them from the ruins of the desolate city, came down through ages of tumult as models of perfection, which, in a happier age, were to be rivalled, if not excelled. The Pantheon, the glory of Roman architecture, was to be placed in the clouds by the sublime genius of Michael Angelo; the wondrous dome crowning a temple which far surpasses, in its vast and just dimensions, all the ancient fanes of false deities, and even the august mansion which God Himself chose among His favored people. If the Middle Ages produced nothing worthy of the ancient masters, it was a matter of just glory for the age of Julius and of Leo, that genius revisited the earth, and exhibited on the canvas such animated representations as filled the eye with wonder, and stirred the deep fountains of the heart. The Transfiguration and the General Judgment are miracles of genius, which the world might have never seen but for the munificence and refined taste of the calumniated Pontiffs. "Rome," says Tiraboschi, "was the first theatre in which were collected the most perfect productions of nature and art. Julius II., Leo X., Clement VII., and Paul III., are names of immortal renown in the annals of the fine arts, for the munificence with which they promoted and cherished them during their pontificates. There were seen re-united, almost all at one time, Raphael of Urbino, Julius of Rome, John of Udine, Perino del Vago, Polidore of Caravaggio, Francis Mazzuoli, Baldassar Peruzzi, Anthony of S. Gallo, and James Sansovino, Alphonsus Lombardi, and Baccio Bandinelli,—names so illustrious in painting, architecture, and sculpture; and there, finally, was Michelangelo Buonarotti, painter, sculptor, and architect, uniting in himself all the splendid endowments which were divided among the others. The Vatican basilic would alone be sufficient to render immortal the names of the four Popes above mentioned, to whom its commencement and termination are principally due. In it all the arts seem to vie with one another, which should present the most splendid proofs of the excellence of its professors."† "Sculpture," says Voltaire, "was the art in which the Greeks excelled; and the glory of the Italians is, to have approached the perfec-

---

* St. Gregory wrote to St. Augustin to this effect: "Si fana eadem bene constructa sunt, necesse est, ut a cultu dæmonum ad obsequium veri Dei debeant commodari; ut dum gens ipsa eadem fana sua non videt destrui, de corde errorem deponat, et Deum verum cognoscens ac adorans, ad loca quæ consuevit familiarius concurrat." Greg., ep. ix. 71.

† Storia della Letteratura Italiana, v. vii. p. iii. l. iii. c. vii.

tion of their models. In architecture they far surpassed them; and all nations acknowledge that nothing was ever comparable to the chief temple of modern Rome, the most beautiful, vast, and bold that ever existed in the universe."*

Byron has justly said :—

> "Majesty,
> Power, Glory, Strength, and Beauty, all are aisled
> In this eternal ark of worship undefiled."

The animated portraits of Titian, and his living landscapes, which invite the beholder to walk amid the delightful scenery, found admirers in Leo X. and Paul III.; and the miniatures of Julius Clovio were rewarded by the munificence of Farnese. Sofonisba Anguisciola, of Cremona, employed her pencil with such success in the portrait of the Queen of Spain, that Pius IV., to whom it was forwarded, honored her with a complimentary letter on the excellence of the painting. Thus did the Popes prove themselves patrons of the fine arts, lavishing honors and wealth on those who attained to eminence in their cultivation. They made Rome, as Voltaire acknowledges, the most beautiful city in the world.†

It would be tedious, although not uninteresting, to enumerate instances of encouragement given to all the arts. Engravers, lapidaries, as well as painters and sculptors, are indebted to pontifical munificence for the progress and success of their labors. Martin V. and Paul II. were their special patrons. Clement Birago, a youth of Milan, at the court of Clement VII. first practised the art of engraving on diamonds. "The fine arts continued to flourish in Italy because the contagion of controversy scarcely reached that country; and while blood flowed in Germany, France, and England, for matters that were not understood, (it is Voltaire that speaks,) Italy, at peace since the astonishing sacking of Rome by the army of Charles V., cultivated the arts with increased ardor. The wars of religion spread ruin elsewhere; but at Rome, and in several other Italian cities, prodigies of architecture were witnessed. Ten Popes successively contributed, almost without any interruption, to the completion of the basilic of St. Peter, and encouraged the arts generally. Nothing of the kind was seen throughout the rest of Europe at that period. The glory of genius then belonged to Italy alone, as it had been formerly peculiar to Greece."‡

We cannot easily estimate the improvements in church building and decoration which took place in various countries, under the guidance of Christian missionaries, and the influence of Roman models. To be just, we should estimate these things according to the previous state of the respective countries. Of England, Dr. Miley observes : " St. Wilfrid and St. Bennet Biscop, the great improvers of Saxon architecture, made several pilgrimages to Rome, (the former three or four, the latter no less

---

* Essai sur l'Histoire, t. iii. ch. cxvii.   † Essai sur l'Histoire Générale, t. ii. ch. xlix.
‡ Ibid., t. iii. ch. cxvii.

than five;) and never did they return without a rich importation of manuscripts, chalices, various utensils, vestments, and ornaments for the altar; besides statues and pictures to adorn the temples, which their observation of the Roman and continental structures had enabled them to erect. In these new structures, they exhibited to their admiring countrymen all the wonders of cut-stone walls and towers, lead roofs and glass windows, with sundry other astonishing improvements, 'juxta Romanorum morem.' And it may be well imagined, that not the least attractive of these novelties were the creations of the Italian or Grecian pencil."*

The glory of Rome, as the seat of the arts, remains undiminished. When, in the conclave of 1829, Chateaubriand, the French ambassador, had expressed the necessity of choosing for Pontiff a man of enlightened views, corresponding with the progress of the age, and Cutzow, the Austrian ambassador, had harped on the same subject, Cardinal Castiglioni, in reply, modestly pointed to the Vatican, as an unquestionable evidence of the patronage which the Holy See continues to extend to art and science, and the care with which she fosters mental development. His election to fill the vacant chair was an act of homage to the arts. Byron acknowledged that Italy had still illustrious men in every department: "Italy has great names still—Canova, Monti, Ugo Foscolo, Pindemonte, Visconti, Morelli, Cicognara, Albrizzi, Mezzofanti, Mai, Mustoxidi, Aglietti, and Vacca, will secure to the present generation an honorable place in most of the departments of art, science, and belles lettres; and in some the very highest. Europe—the world—has but one Canova."† We may still address the mother and mistress of churches in the language of this child of genius:—

> "Mother of arts, as once of arms,
> Thy hand was then our guardian, and is still our guide."

---

* Rome under Paganism, &c., vol. ii. p. 243.
† Introd. to canto iv., Childe Harold.

CHAPTER VII.

Art of Printing.

§ 1.—ENCOURAGEMENT OF PRINTERS.

THE zeal of the Popes for the promotion of elegant literature and useful knowledge was displayed, in the most unequivocal manner, on the discovery of, what Berthold, Archbishop of Mentz, did not hesitate to style the divine art of printing. To Germany belongs the glory of this invention; but only a few years had elapsed when Italy rivalled and surpassed her. "The whole number of books," as Hallam testifies, "printed with dates of time and place, in the German Empire, from 1461 to 1470, according to Panzer, was only twenty-four; of which five were Latin, and two German Bibles."—"A more splendid scene was revealed in Italy." Sweynheim and Pennartz, two workmen of Fust, set up a press, doubtless with encouragement and patronage, at the monastery of Subiaco, in the Apennines.—In 1467, after printing Augustin De Civitate Dei, and Cicero de Oratore, the two Germans left Subiaco for Rome, where they sent forth not less than twenty-three editions of ancient Latin authors before the close of 1470.—The whole number of books that had issued from the press in Italy at the close of that year, amounts, according to Panzer, to eighty-two, exclusive of those which have no date, some of which may be referrible to this period."* Another German printer, Udalric Hahn, was patronized at Rome at the same time, and gave to the public the meditations of Cardinal Turrecremata, illustrated with woodcuts. The bishop John Andrew de Bussi, librarian of the Vatican, aided the printers in their literary labors. The example of Rome was eagerly imitated by no less than fifty cities of Italy. Venice soon surpassed her in the number of works issuing from the press; while Milan strove to excel in the magnificence of the execution. All the works of Cicero were printed in splendid style at Milan, in 1498 and 1499; and "an edition of Cicero's epistles appeared also in the town of Fuligno."† "The books printed in Italy during these ten years (from 1470 to 1480) amount, according to Panzer, to 1297; of which 234 are editions of ancient classical authors. Books without date are, of course, not included; and the list

---

* Literature of Europe, vol. i. ch. iii. n. 33. † Ibidem

must not be reckoned complete as to others."* "A translation of the Bible by Malerbi, a Venetian, was published in 1471, and two other editions of that, or a different version, the same year. Eleven editions are enumerated by Panzer in the fifteenth century."† The books printed at Rome down to 1500 are 935, a far greater number than were issued from any other city but Venice, which counted 2835. "Much more than ten thousand editions of books or pamphlets (a late writer says fifteen thousand) were printed from 1470 to 1500. More than half the number appeared in Italy."‡ "The editions of the Vulgate registered in Panzer are ninety-one."§ An edition of the Vulgate, corrected on the Hebrew and Greek texts, was published at Venice in 1484, a copy of which is still preserved in the library of the Baltimore cathedral.‖

The activity of the Roman press was considerably lessened by the wars, of which Italy was the theatre in the early part of the sixteenth century; but was soon restored. "An Æthiopic, that is, Abyssinian grammar, with the Psalms in the same language, was published at Rome by Potken, in 1513."¶ "The Æthiopic version of the New Testament was printed at Rome in 1548."** A splendid edition of the works of Homer issued from the Roman press in 1549, under the superintendence of Anthony Bladus. Paul Manutius, the learned Venetian, on the invitation of Pius IV., established a printing office at Rome in 1561, and gave to the public many works, the expenses of which were defrayed by his munificence. Pius appointed two correctors of the press for the Greek language, and ordered diligent search to be made for manuscripts in the Oriental tongues. When, after an absence for some time, Paul returned to Rome, in the pontificate of Gregory XIII., this enlightened Pope insisted on retaining him there, in his old age, and assigned him a pension, leaving him at liberty to pursue his literary labors as might suit his convenience. "The increasing zeal of Rome," Hallam remarks, "for the propagation of its faith, both among infidels and schismatics, gave a larger sweep to the cultivation of Oriental languages." Sixtus V., in order to place the Apostolic printing office on a permanent basis, spent 40,000 crowns to provide it with Greek, Latin, Hebrew, Arabic and Servian types, and with excellent paper, and all other requisites for elegant execution; and assigned pensions to learned men charged with the supervision of the press. During his pontificate, an elegant edition of the Septuagint was issued from it, which is acknowledged to be the best heretofore anywhere published.†† Thence, also, came forth an edition of the Vulgate corrected chiefly by the collation of manuscripts, and published with his solemn sanction, in which, neverthe-

---

* Literature of Europe, vol. i. ch. iii. n. 44.   † Ibidem, n. 53.
‡ Ibidem, n. 143.   ¶ Ibidem, n. 141.
‖ Fontibus ex Græcis, Hebræorum quoque libris
Emendata satis et decorata simul
§ Literature of Europe, vol. i. ch. v. n. 77.   ** Ibidem, ch. ix. n. 25.
†† See Cyclopædia of Bib. Lit., edited by John Kitto, D.D., F.S.A., v. *Septuagint*.

less, about forty typographical errors were soon discovered, which determined him to issue a corrected edition. His death having prevented the execution of his design, it was delayed until the pontificate of Clement VIII., who allowed the revisors of it to modify and correct many other readings, by reference to the original texts. The discrepancies thus arising between the two editions being very numerous, although for the most part of little moment, the adversaries of the Holy See have taken thence occasion to ring the changes on Papal infallibility, as if this regarded the greater or less accuracy of an edition of the Scriptures. The sanction given by Sixtus was directed to assure the faithful that the edition was substantially correct, and to prevent any changes being made in the readings by private authority. Clement, in publishing the corrected edition, renewed the same sanction with the same views, and gave it as the Sixtine edition revised. This explanation seemed called for by the occasion presented to me of mentioning these editions of the Vulgate, both of which attest the zeal of the Popes for the integrity of the Scriptures.

The munificence of the Popes was employed in encouraging the printing of books to be circulated in the Eastern nations. The first printing office in Europe for the Arabic tongue was established at Fano, by Gregory Giorgio of Venice, at the expense of Julius II., in which language a book issued from it in 1514. Gregory XIII. declared Cardinal Ferdinand de' Medici protector of Ethiopia, and of the patriarchates of Alexandria and Antioch, in order to stimulate his zeal for the conversion of the inhabitants of those countries: in consequence of which the Cardinal gathered manuscripts from all parts; and at an immense expense, cast Hebrew, Syriac, Arabic, Ethiopic, and Armenian types, and employed learned men, especially John Baptist Raimondi, to superintend the press. An Arabic and a Chaldaic grammar issued from it: some works of Avicenna and Euclid were published in Arabic, with three thousand copies of the four Gospels in the same language, for distribution in the East. Raimondi also undertook to publish the whole Bible in ten different tongues. Thus, in the sixteenth century, both before and after the so-called Reformation, the Popes and the cardinals were active patrons of the press, and Bible-distributors! "The Persic grammar was given at Rome by Raimondi in 1614." "We find Ferrari, author of a Syriac lexicon, published at Rome in 1622." In 1627 there were types of fifteen different languages, and, at a later period, of twenty-three, in the printing establishment of Propaganda. There issued from it, in the decline of that age, a work styled "*Bibliotheca magna Rabbinica*," composed by Father Bartolocci, a Cistercian monk, who for thirty-six years had been professor of Hebrew. An Arabic grammar, a Syro-Arabic Latin thesaurus, a Syriac dictionary, a Hebrew dictionary, and other works of a like character, were published there at various times. Three Maronites, namely, Victor Scialac, Abraham Ecchellensis, and Faustus Nairo, were maintained at the expense of the Pope, for the purpose of publishing works in Arabic. In 1621, a great work called "*Hebrew Concordances,*" came from that press, and was so highly esteemed as to be reprinted in London. An Arabic Bible, which was in preparation during forty-six years, was published at Rome in 1671, in three folio volumes. A printing office, furnished with Oriental types, was established in Milan by Cardinal Frederic Borromeo, from which an Arabic dictionary in four volumes issued in 1632. Cardinal Barbarigo established an Oriental printing office at Padua. "A fine edition of the Koran, and still esteemed the best," as Hallam observes, "was due to Marracci, professor of Arabic in the Sapienza, or University of Rome, and published at the expense of Cardinal Barbarigo in 1698."* The munificence of Clement XI., enabled Joseph Simon Assemani, a Maronite of Syria, to publish at Rome, in 1719, his learned work on the Vatican manuscripts in the Oriental languages. The publication of the works of St. Ephrem was also begun by him, and continued by his nephew Stephen Evodius. The Acts of the martyrs of the East and of the West were published in Chaldaic, and translated by the latter; and several other works, composed by others of that family, came from the same press. It is not easy to enumerate all that Rome has done, and is still engaged in doing, to promote Oriental literature. "Who," cries Ranke, "does not know what the Propaganda has done for philological learning?"†

§ 2. RESTRICTIONS ON THE PRESS.

The services of the Popes to letters are forgotten, whilst the restrictions imposed by them on the press are made a matter of reproach. Berthold, Archbishop of Mentz, who esteemed so highly the art of printing, deemed it proper to guard against its abuse, by requiring the examination of books by clergymen appointed for the purpose, previous to their publication. Alexander VI. published a similar decree with special reference to Germany, and Leo X. renewed and confirmed it as a general law. Yet as bad books were multiplied, Paul IV., in 1539, published a list of prohibited books. A committee of divines was appointed by the Council of Trent to form a list of bad or dangerous books; who, having failed to complete the task assigned them before the close of the Council, were allowed to continue their labors, and ordered to submit them to the Pope for approval. The list is daily increasing of books, the reading or retention of which is prohibited under ecclesiastical censures: and although this discipline is overruled by contrary usage in most countries, it serves to give coloring to the charge, that the Popes are hostile to the liberty of the press. In justice to them I must observe, that their sole object has been to re-

---

* Literature of Europe, vol. iv. ch. viii. n. 41.
† Ranke, Hist. Popes, vol. ii. l. vii. p. 59.

strain the press within the limits of the divine law, and that the licentiousness which sends forth impious and corrupt books, to poison the minds of youth, is that which our late venerable Pontiff visited with unmitigated censure. Liberty of the press, considered as a civil right, does not suppose freedom from moral restraint, or impunity from civil penalties for its abuse. Its chief value, in a civil point of view, is to give free expression to public sentiment in regard to the management of public affairs by rulers, and other officers, and thus to prevent oppression, or procure its remedy, by exposing it to general censure. The exercise of such liberty, for the true interests of the country, is nowise opposed to the spirit or discipline of the Church. It is well known that the Popes have permitted the publication at Rome of works on civil polity, which, on account of their liberal and popular principles, were proscribed in several European States;* and that, at all times, they have shown themselves disposed to favor the oppressed, rather than stifle their complaints. Incendiary and seditious works could not, of course, be sanctioned by the rulers of the Church, who are bound to sustain established order, and promote peace; but these are not included in the true notion of liberty of the press; since in France, where this is a constitutional right, they are liable to seizure when discovered; and in this country they expose the authors and publishers to the severity of the law. In all that regards science, literature, and the arts, the utmost freedom of the press may be enjoyed, with no limit but the caution of not advancing on holy ground. The golden age of Spanish literature was precisely that in which the laws of the Index, the tribunal which forms the list of prohibited books, were strictly enforced. How can it be pretended that science is impeded in her legitimate progress, because she is warned not to displace the landmarks of religion? A vast space lies open to research and improvements, without encroaching on the realms of faith. If Locke's Essay on the Human Understanding, and Milton's Paradise Lost, are found on the list of prohibited books, it is because the philosopher artfully undermined the doctrine of the spiritual nature of the soul, and the poet exhibited Christ according to the fancy of the Arians and made of Lucifer a hero. Lest an incautious reader, misled by a great name, should imbibe fatal error, the books were proscribed; but even in countries where the discipline prevails, leave to read them is easily obtained. The Popes have at all times respected the meditations of true philosophy, and honored the inspirations of the Muses, always saving the truth of what God has revealed.

Freedom of the press, as a civil right, in this country, extends to the

---

* The work of Spedalieri, entitled, "I diritti dell' uomo," in which the right of a nation to depose a despot, is supported by the authority of St. Thomas of Aquin, in his letter to the Bishop of Rome, was published at Rome in 1791, dedicated to Cardinal Ruffo, Apostolic Treasurer. Pius VI. who encouraged its publication, rewarded the author by appointing him one of the Canons of the Basilic of St. Peter.

publication of works on doctrinal subjects, without regard to the faith of the Church: so that all the doctrines which we hold to be divine, may be assailed without incurring any civil penalty, which, however, may be inflicted, even here, on an open blasphemer of Christ. To the full enjoyment of this civil right by our fellow-citizens, we make no objection whatever. The Constitutions of the various States, and the principles of the country and age, give it, leaving to each one the responsibility of its enjoyment. For ourselves, believing firmly that God has made a revelation, of which the Church is the guardian, we cannot conscientiously approve of any thing written or spoken in opposition to her teaching. The decrees of the Pope proscribing certain books as containing false doctrines, are for us the warnings of a father against what might pervert the understanding, and corrupt the hearts of his children. Independently of them, we are naturally bound to shun whatever is dangerous to our faith and morals. The youth who, uninstructed in the great evidences of revelation, familiarizes himself with Paine's Age of Reason, exposes himself to the manifest danger of infidelity. The female who, with morbid curiosity, peruses an obscene tale, is liable to lose that purity of heart which is her greatest treasure. In proportion to our information and moral habits, the dangers may be diminished; but it is beyond a doubt, that to the reading of bad books may be traced the infidelity and corruption of innumerable individuals. The restrictions which the Popes imposed would be unjust, if arbitrary; and unreasonable, if those for whom they were intended did not already recognise their pastoral authority: but this being recognised, nothing is more reasonable and just than to turn away the sheep from noxious pastures, by proscribing whatever is contrary to sound doctrine. At all events, the precedent of the proscription of bad books was given by the Apostles, when the vast collection of works of magic belonging to converts from that superstition, were consigned to the flames.* Will the readers of Scripture charge the Apostles with hostility to knowledge? The moral restraints resulting from our discipline serve to avert many of the evils with which the licentiousness of the press deluges the world. The pangs of the broken heart when its shame has been revealed—the desolation of families, whose sorrows have rung on the public ear—the torture of high-minded patriots, writhing under the calumnies of reckless rivals—the fury of a populace maddened to arson and bloodshed by incendiary publications, and the struggles and convulsions of parties, which almost threaten the dissolution of society, are no imaginary evils. Voltaire did not hesitate to declare that the press had become one of the scourges of society.† Even here, abolition publications are regarded with horror, as tending to encourage sedition and endangering the lives of the citizens.

---

* Acts xix. 19.

† "La presse, il le faut avouer, est devenue un des fléaux de la société, et un brigandage intolérable." Voltaire, fragment d'une lettre á un Académicien de Berlin, t. v.

CHAPTER VIII.

Moral Influence.

§ 1. CIVILIZATION.

WHAT we have elsewhere said of the authority exercised over princes for the correction of their morals, must give a high idea of the general influence which the Popes had on morality and order. When the people saw their leaders stricken with the rod of ecclesiastical authority, they were made deeply sensible of the turpitude of crime, which could not escape censure even in the great and powerful. The struggle of the Pontiffs with the fierce passions of the feudal nobility, is graphically described by a writer in the British Critic, who thus represents the position of the Church in the Middle Ages: "Just as she had subdued the intelligence and refinement of the old Roman Empire, it was swept away, and she was left alone with its wild destroyers. Her commission was changed: she had now to tame and rule the barbarians. But upon them the voice which had rebuked the heretic, fell powerless. While they pressed into her fold, they overwhelmed all her efforts to reclaim them, and filled her, from east to west, with violence and stunning disorder. When, therefore, she again roused herself to confront the world, her position and difficulties were shifted. Her enemy was no longer heresy, but vice—wickedness which wrought with a high hand, foul and rampant, like that of Sodom, or the men before the flood. It was not the faith, but the first principles of duty—justice, mercy, and truth, which were directly endangered by the unbridled ambition and licentiousness of the feudal aristocracy, who were then masters of Europe. With this fierce nobility, she had to fight the battle of the poor and weak—to settle the question whether the Christian religion and the offices of the Church were to be any thing more than names, and honors, and endowments, trappings of chivalry and gentle blood; whether there were yet strength left upon earth to maintain and avenge the laws of God, whoever might break them. She had to stand between the oppressor and his prey—to compel respect for what is pure and sacred from the lawless and powerful."* It is impossible not to admire the unflinching resolution with which the Pontiffs contended for moral principle against these potentates. The disorders of those ages

---

* British Critic, vol. 33, p. 7.

shock us by their enormity and frequency: but they would have been unmitigated and unrelieved by any exhibition of Christian virtues, had not the Popes fulminated censure against the prevaricators, and proclaimed to the world maxims of purity and holiness. "These ages of darkness, as they are called," says Dr. Nevin, "were still, to an extent now hard to understand, ages also of faith. The church still had, as in earlier days, her miracles, her martyrdoms, her missionary zeal, her holy bishops and saints, her works of charity and love, her care for sound doctrine, her sense of a heavenly commission, and her more than human power to convert and subdue nations. True, the world was dark, very dark and very wild; and its corruptions were powerfully felt at times in her own bosom; but no one but a simpleton or a knave will pretend to make this barbarism *her* work, or to lay it as a crime to *her* charge. She was the rock that beat back its proud waves. She was the power of order and law, the fountain of a new civilization, in the midst of its tumultuating chaos."†

The Popes did not, however, confine their efforts to those who, by the action of Providence, seemed brought within their reach. With unceasing solicitude they applied themselves to the diffusion of the Gospel, by despatching apostolic men, from time to time, to barbarous and savage nations, to impart to them the knowledge of salvation. In order to estimate their services, it would be necessary to go over the records of missions in various ages, and to consider the condition of the *aborigines*, or early settlers of each country. Children of nature, with no rule but impulse, and no restraint but the fear of vengeance—with no affection but for objects of momentary gratification, and no ambition but to slay an enemy—sunk in sensuality, without even the restraint of shame, they scarcely presented any thing to distinguish them from the brute beast. For the salvation of such degraded beings, the Popes uniformly sighed, and when occasion offered itself, sent forth the heralds of the Gospel to enlighten, humanize, and save them. The naked savage and the painted barbarian stood aghast—the huntsman and the warrior tribe were arrested in their course, at the sight of the missionaries of the cross: the tones of sacred music fell on their delighted ears, and they listened to the tale of wonder which the strangers recounted: finally, they clung to them as fathers, and learned from them to control their unruly passions, and worship the Great Spirit. The condescension of the Popes in yielding to these reclaimed children of the forest whatever the divine law did not forbid, and leading them gradually to the perfection of Christian discipline, shows extraordinary wisdom and true philanthropy.† With zeal tempered by wisdom, they labored incessantly to form them to arts of peace and industry. "The Gregorian school," says Count St. Priest, speaking of St.

---

* "Early Christianity," M. R. Nov. 1851.

† St. Gregory writing to Augustin observes: "Nam duris mentibus simul omnia abscindere impossibile esse non dubium est, quia is, qui locum summum ascendere nititur, gradibus vel passibus, non autem saltibus, elevatur." Greg. ep. ix. 71.

Boniface, the apostle of Germany, sent by Gregory II., "although animated chiefly by the sincerest religious zeal, did not limit their views to the salvation of souls. To clear the land, to change a dry soil and thick forests into fertile plains, to build dwellings which might serve as the commencement of cities, to accustom men to social life, to bind strongly the family tie, and to form bonds of association, and of mutual wants and succors, to unite, to colonize, such were the plans that Winfred revolved in his mind."* What Boniface accomplished in Germany, the apostles of other countries effected in their respective missions. The encouragement given to monastic institutions had this tendency and effect. The tranquility of the cloister had its charms for the warrior, who oftentimes laid aside his armor, to sit at the feet of a holy monk, and learn the science of salvation. The wandering tribes were astonished at the sight of a vast monastery with its gardens and well-cultivated fields, and they learned to imitate the industry which afforded plenty and contentment. Hostile bands trod with reverence on the soil which was sacred to religion and virtue. It is impossible to estimate the effects of these institutions on civilization. Marshes drained, immense wastes reclaimed and fertilized, valleys beautified with varied cultivation, hills crowned with olives, and plains overspread with wheat, are only the immediate fruits of their labors.† The influence of the example of the monks in recommending industry and peace must have been immense.

The conversion and civilization of so many barbarous nations are among the most splendid triumphs and evidences of Christianity, no wise inferior to those which marked the first preaching of the gospel. Hence Dr. Nevin points to them as proofs of its enduring power: "Take the conversion of Saxon England in the time of Gregory the Great, and the long work of moral organization with which it was followed in succeeding centuries. Look at the missionaries that proceeded from this island, apostolical bishops and holy monks, in the seventh and eight centuries, planting churches successfully in the countries of the Rhine. Consider the entire evangelization of the new barbarous Europe. Is it not a work fairly parallel, to say the least, with the conquest of the old Roman Empire in the first ages? Is not the argument of 'miraculous success,' quite as strong here as there?"‡

The veneration of the Blessed Virgin, which the Popes always cherished, was amongst the most powerful means of civilization. Woman was raised from her degradation, and no longer regarded as the slave of a haughty master. She was respected because of HER who was blessed among women. The mild virtues of the Virgin caught the admiration of the fierce sons of Mars, who felt honored in imitating her gentle-

---

* Histoire de la Royauté par Saint Priest, vol. ii. l. viii. p. 223.

† See Tableau des Institutions et des Mœurs de l'Eglise au Moyen Age par Frederic Hurter vol. ii. ch. vii. p. 152. traduit de l'Allemand.

‡ "Early Christianity," M. R. Nov. 1851.

ness and sweetness. Holy purity was loved, because it had been honored in her person. Not only vast numbers of her own sex cherished it with jealous care, but thousands of men vowed to preserve it, and sought the aid of her prayers for that purpose. It is manifest that the devotion to her was developed and exercised in those ages in a remarkable degree; to which we may fairly ascribe all that was bland and meek in manners, all that was pure in morals, all that was tender and affecting in piety. Augustus William Schlegel, although a Protestant, has beautifully observed : "With the virtues of chivalry was associated a new and purer spirit of love, an inspired homage for genuine female worth, which was now revered as the pinnacle of humanity, and enjoined by religion itself under the image of a Virgin mother, infused into all hearts a sentiment of unalloyed goodness."*

Without entering into further details we may confidently say, that to the Popes, as rulers of the Church, we owe the great principles of order and law on which civilization depends. An anonymous writer in the Mercersburg Review avows that to the Church "we are indebted for our modern civilization; for whatever influence besides may have contributed to this end, all must have ever remained impotent, without their mainspring, Christianity. This found its exclusive abode in the body of this church."†

§ 2. PERSONAL VIRTUES.

The personal virtues which distinguished the Popes, necessarily had a most happy influence on the whole Christian world. Placed on the highest eminence, they shone, for the most part, with bright effulgence, and gave occasion to all to glorify God for the good works which they performed. Their charity, which embraced all mankind, was experienced far beyond the limits which their means might have marked for its exercise. In the decline of the second century, Dionysius, Bishop of Corinth, addressed a letter of thanks to the Roman Church, for the relief which Pope Soter had sent to the distressed faithful of the East, conformably to the custom of his predecessors: "From the beginning," he writes, "you were wont to bestow favours on the brethren, and to send means of subsistence to the poor of other churches: here you come to the relief of the indigent faithful, especially of those who are at work in the mines; and as becomes genuine Romans, you maintain the ancient usage of your ancestors. The blessed Bishop Soter was not content with walking in the footsteps of the fathers; besides taking on himself the charge of sending your generous offerings to the faithful, he comforted the brethren who went to him with pious words, uttered with the tenderest affection of a fond father towards

---

* Lectures on Dramatic Literature, translated by John Black, p. 8, American edition.
† Protestantism and Romanism. M. R. March, 1852, S. N. C. Jefferson, Md.

his children."* A century afterwards, St. Dionysius, Bishop of Rome, sent alms to Cesarea in Cappadocia, for the ransom of slaves, with letters of condolence to the afflicted Church.† The treasures of the Roman Church were regarded as the common fund of the poor, so that when the deacon Lawrence was called on by the pagan persecutor to deliver them up, he did not hesitate to distribute them among the poor, whom he presented at the appointed time, saying: "These are the treasures of the Church!"

Charity continued to be the distinguishing characteristic of the Pontiffs. With scarcely an exception, they are all described as fathers of the poor, some of them receiving greater praise for more unbounded munificence. Gelasius, who lived at the close of the fifth century, is said to have been the servant of all men, but especially of the poor of Christ. In the seventh century, John IV. sent a large sum of money to Istria, to be employed in the ransom of prisoners; and John VI. imitated his example, when Gisulph, the Lombard duke of Benevento, had led away many captives from Campania. Paul I., in the following century, paid the debts of prisoners out of his own purse. St. Paschal I. built, at his own expense, a house for the reception and entertainment of English pilgrims, in place of another which had been destroyed by fire. Even in the tenth century this attribute of the pontifical office did not fail. Among the praises of Marinus II., is recorded his generosity to the poor. Benedict VII. is described as a lover of the poor. In the fifteenth century (not to weary the reader with specifications in each age), Eugenius IV., Nicholas V., Callistus III., are all commended for liberality towards the poor of Christ. Clement VIII., a Pontiff of the sixteenth century, always entertained twelve poor men at his table. Innocent X., in the following age, exercised extraordinary generosity to the poor, not confining his alms to the large sum of 100,000 crowns, which his predecessors had been wont to distribute every year, but adding many large donations, especially to families burdened with children. The Romans asked leave of Alexander VII. to erect a statue, in order to perpetuate the memory of his charity, which was manifested in an extraordinary degree when famine and pestilence prevailed. The Pontiff humbly declined the proffered honor, telling them with his usual grace and dignity, that he desired no monument but the kind remembrance which they cherished in their hearts. Innocent XII. called the poor his nephews, and bequeathed to them whatever might result from the sale of the furniture of his palace after his death. On his return from Civitavecchia, he was met by an immense multitude, who insisted on bearing on their shoulders the chair in which he rode. As this triumphal procession advanced to the gates of the eternal city, acclamations rent the air: "Behold! our father comes—the father of the poor!" Clement XII. relieved the distress of four thousand Romans, who by a public conflagration,

---

* Apub Euseb. l. iv. hist. eccl. c. xxiii.   † S. Basil. ep. lxx. alias, cxxx.

were thrown houseless on the world. Benedict XIV. made a visit to the sick at Civitavecchia, waited on them, and gave each of them a small present. The same was done by his successor, Clement XIII., who also left proofs of his munificence with the prisoners whom he visited at Corneto, and devoted ten thousand crowns to the erection of a hospital for women, and a house of education for girls. Clement XIV. called the poor of Christ his family. The charity of Pius VI. was displayed in many instances, especially on occasion of public calamities, as when Bologna and other cities were visited by an earthquake, and the fortress of Civitavecchia was blown up by the accidental explosion of a gunpowder magazine.

Leo XII., in our own age, has merited special praises for his solicitude for the poor; but, in truth, it is the general characteristic of all the Pontiffs, who, in this respect, most certainly have proved themselves worthy representatives of Him who became poor for our sake.

The fortitude with which the Popes have struggled for truth and justice, cannot be considered a mere accidental virtue: it was, no doubt, a divine gift, bestowed on them in the person of Him who, from being a shaking reed, was made a rock of strength. The first three centuries saw a succession of martys fill the papal chair: "During the persecutions," says Ranke, "the Bishops of Rome had exhibited extraordinary firmness and courage: their succession had often been rather to martyrdom and death than to office."* The Donatists endeavored to tarnish the lustre of the Holy See, by a groundless report that Marcellinus, whose pontificate closed the third century, had yielded to the persecutors, and offered incense to idols. The slander was indignantly rejected by St. Augustin, who saw no need of refuting what was supported by no proof. "What need have we," he cried, "to answer the charges brought by Petilian against the bishops of the Roman Church, whom he has attacked with incredible calumnies? Marcellinus and his priests are accused by him of having delivered up the divine books into the hands of the pagans, and offered incense to the idols: but does this prove them to be guilty? is any authentic document produced to show that they were convicted of the crime? He declares them wicked and sacrilegious: I pronounce them innocent."†

It must appear strange that this calumny, embodied by some unknown writer in the forged acts of a Council supposed to have been held at Sinuessa,‡ has crept into the Roman Breviary; but this is accounted for by the want of critical acumen at the time when some of the legends were inserted. It matters not whether the forger of the acts designed evil or good by his clumsy contrivance. The compilers of the Breviary regarding them as genuine, and knowing that the personal prevarication of the Pontiff was possible, recorded it together with his penance and humiliation. The caution which is justly observed by the rulers of the Church, in ad-

---

* History of the Popes, l. i. ch. i. p. 29, American edition.
† L. de unico bapt. contra Petil.
‡ Rocca di Mondragone, a fortress in the kingdom of Naples, is built on its site.

mitting any change in the liturgy and office, has prevented the correction of this and some few other errors, which, although blemishes, detract but little from the general excellence of this beautiful compilation.

Even under Christian emperors, the Popes continued to suffer from time to time for the integrity of faith, which they intrepidly maintained. The fortitude of Liberius, in the imperial audience at Milan, has been already described, and his constancy, whilst an exile and a prisoner, vindicated. Silverius, in the sixth century, finding himself the object of calumny and violence, on account of his known orthodoxy, after prayer to God, put himself in the hands of the general Belisarius, who, in compliance with the wishes of the heretical empress, led him into exile, where he died of famine. In the following century, Martin I. gained the martyr's crown by a similar career of suffering.

To come to recent times, the fortitude of Pius VI. in the maintenance of the cause of religion, which was assailed by the infidel government of the French Revolution, is worthy of all admiration. When Napoleon, in the name of the French Republic, hovered over the Ecclesiastical States like a bird of prey, seeking to glut himself with human victims, the paternal heart of the Pontiff led him to make every concession. "Had we attempted any defence," he observed, "torrents of blood would have flowed to no purpose." The plate of his palace, with all that could be gathered from others, was sacrificed to pay the immense sum which the general, elate with his many victories, demanded; and every humiliating condition was accepted: but when the infidel Directory insisted on his retracting the condemnation of the civil constitution of the clergy, the heroic Pius was inflexible: "The crown of martyrdom," he observed, "is more brilliant than the tiara." After immense sacrifices on his part the French, in violation of the treaty of Tolentino, took possession of his capital, and Cervoni, in mockery, presented him with the French cockade, promising him a pension, but he answered with dignity: "I care for no ornaments but those with which the Church has decorated me. You have full power over my body, but not over my soul, which defies your utmost efforts. I want no pension. A staff and the coarsest garment are enough for me, who, for the maintenance of the faith, am soon to expire on ashes." Cervoni persisting in urging him to resign his temporal principality, and accept a pension, the aged Pontiff replied: "My power comes by free election from God alone, and not from men, and I cannot and ought not to resign it. I am now near the eightieth year of my life, and have nothing to fear. Whatever violence and indignities may be committed against me by those in whose power I am, my soul is still free, and so resolute and courageous, that I am ready to meet death, rather than dishonor myself, or offend God." After separating the Pontiff from all his counsellors and friends, and pillaging his palace, Haller, a Swiss Calvinist, in the name of the French, intimated to him that he must quit Rome. Pius pleaded in vain the weight of his years, his infirmities, which at any moment might terminate in death, and his duty, which required him to remain. The brutal messenger told him he should be forced away, unless he consented. The afflicted Pontiff, after pouring out his complaints at the foot of the crucifix, bowed in homage to the divine will, and as he rose from prayer, exclaimed: "It is the will of God: His holy will be done: let us bow to His just decrees." As he descended the staircase, he was met by a criminal whom he had pardoned, but who, like Semei, exulting in the misfortunes of his sovereign, taunted him: "See, tyrant, your reign is at an end." Pius replied: "Were I a tyrant, you would not be alive." Thus he was hurried away from his capital. On his journey, he received a message of condolence from Ferdinand III., Grand Duke of Tuscany, on which occasion he observed: "My afflictions encourage me to hope that I am not altogether unworthy of being vicar of Jesus Christ, and successor of St. Peter. The situation in which you behold me, recalls to our minds the early ages of the Church, which were the days of her triumphs." When Charles Emmanuel IV., the exiled King of Turin, with his wife, visited him in his retreat at the Cistercian monastery near Florence, Pius exclaimed: "All in this world is vanity. No one can say it more truly than we can. Yes: all is vanity, but to love and serve the Giver of every blessing. Let us raise our eyes to heaven, where thrones are prepared for us, of which men cannot deprive us." After a month, Pius was forced from this peaceful asylum, and, notwithstanding the testimony of medical men, given on oath, that travelling would expose his life to imminent danger, he was inhumanly dragged from place to place, without losing his patience, or sweetness of disposition. When he had reached Turin, and found himself obliged to travel still farther, he exclaimed: "The will of God be done. Let us go cheerfully whithersoever they please." As he was carried up the rugged heights of Mount Cenis, he appeared more happy than when borne on a chair of state in the solemn functions of the Vatican. The calm resignation and noble demeanor of the august prisoner struck with admiration a French Calvinist, who witnessed the eagerness with which the Catholics rushed to venerate him, as he was hurried on through France. A few days before his death at Valence, being presented on the balcony of his residence to gratify the devotion of the faithful, he recalled to their minds the resemblance which he bore to his insulted and suffering Master, and then, for the last time, gave them his blessing. When about to receive the holy Eucharist, as a Viaticum, the officiating prelate having asked him whether he forgave his enemies, the holy Pontiff, raising his eyes to heaven, and then fixing them on a crucifix which he held in his hands, answered: "With all my heart." This was surely a glorious exhibition of fortitude, resignation, and triumphant charity.

Pius VII., although he displayed a tenderness towards Napoleon bordering on indulgence, was, nevertheless, inflexible when faith or principle was in question. No effort could induce him to receive into favour the constitutional bishops, intruded into the episcopal Sees, until, by the retraction of their errors, they had disposed themselves for pardon. No importunities could avail to make him annul the marriage of Jerom, brother of the emperor, with a Protestant lady of Baltimore.

The splendor of the tiara did not dazzle him. He professed himself ready to retire to a convent, or to seek a hiding-place in the catacombs, if the sacrifice of his personal rights could appease his persecutor. The offer of pensions and honors had no influence on his conduct: "We want," he said, "no pension—no honors. The alms of the faithful will suffice for our necessities. Other Popes have been as poor as we are."

In maintaining the rights of his See, he was influenced by a sacred sense of duty. When the ministers of the emperor addressed him in his own palace, with threats of vengeance on their lips, should he resist the imperial will, he replied: "We have done every thing in our power, and we are still ready to do all things for harmony and peace, provided principle be safe. Our conscience is at stake, and we cannot sacrifice it, even were we to be flayed alive. Such is our natural disposition, that we become more inflexible when threats are addressed to us. We fear nothing: we are ready for whatever may befall us."

These heroic sentiments lose something of their grandeur, by the momentary weakness into which Pius, when a prisoner at Fontainebleau, was betrayed by the importunities of his advisers, who urged and almost forced him to subscribe the preliminaries of a treaty with Napoleon, which seriously compromised the rights of his office; but his speedy retraction, and his voluntary humiliation before the cardinals, changed the fault itself into an occasion of new merit. From that time he refused to enter into any terms, until he should be restored to liberty and to his capital. "It may be," he said, "that our sins render us unworthy to see Rome again, but our successors will recover the States which belong to our See. As to the rest, the emperor may be assured that we are not his enemy. Religion forbids it."

God soon cast the mighty emperor from his throne, and raised up the humble Pontiff once more to the pinnacle of power. Napoleon, by a singular disposition of Providence, was compelled to sign his abdication in the very room in which he had treated the venerable prisoner with irreverence. Pius entered Rome in triumph, amidst the enthusiastic acclamations of his devoted people, the brilliant illumination of the eternal city on the night of his return rivalling the meridian blaze. In this miraculous change the devout Pontiff saw no occasion for self-complacency, and indulged no exultation over his fallen oppressor: on the contrary, he interceded with the British government in his behalf, to obtain the mitigation of the rigors of his captivity, and sent a pious priest to console and sustain him by the succors of religion. The eagle which rose with so much pride and daring at Austerlitz, perished on the rock of St. Helena. Pius, notwithstanding his great age and sufferings, outlived Napoleon, and received the intelligence of his death with the feelings which became the fond father of a wayward child.

Humility, likewise, was a favorite virtue of the Popes. This was specially manifested in the reluctance of many of them to accept the office. Leo IV. and Benedict III. were raised to it entirely against their will. Martin IV., with all his might, resisted the cardinals, who wished to enthrone him, so that his mantle was torn in the struggle. Emilio Altieri, at the age of eighty, was declared cardinal by Clement IX. as he lay on his dying couch, who foretold his elevation to the Popedom in the approaching conclave. When elected, he pleaded, with tears, his advanced age, and reluctantly yielded to the wishes of the sacred college. The eleventh Clement, during three days, refused to accept the proffered dignity, and actually fell sick in consequence of the excited state of his feelings. The positive declaration of four eminent divines, that he would sin grievously by continuing to resist the manifest will of God, at length determined his acceptance. Benedict XIII., who had thrice declined the purple, which he finally accepted in obedience to his religious superior, acted under the same orders in yielding to the unanimous vote of the sacred college. Clement XIII. burst into tears when the result of the election was communicated to him. All of these humble Pontiffs seem left in the distance by the hermit Peter of Moroni, who reigned as Celestine V., but finding himself unequal to the government of the Church, descended from the throne, and sought again his loved retreat. Dante, in three words, has immortalized "this great abdication:"

FECE IL GRAN RIFIUTO.

The humility of manner of Innocent XI. was such, that when he called for any of his servants, it was with the reservation, "if it was convenient to them;"* and Clement IX. would have no inscription on his tomb but the acknowledgment that he was dust: CLEMENTIS IX. CINERES.

Purity of life, which is a necessary ornament of the priesthood, and which should be above all suspicion, especially in the representative of the Great High Priest, has ordinarily been the characteristic of the occupant of St. Peter's chair. To speak only at present of the last three centuries, Paul IV. and Pius V., his successor, were distinguished for the most unblemished virtue. Gregory XIV., according to the testimony of Ranke, was "a soul of virgin innocence."† Paul V. died with the reputation of having preserved his virginal integrity, saying as he breathed his soul into the hands of his Creator: "I desire to be dissolved and to be with Christ." A year after his death, on the opening of his tomb, his body was found entire. Of Clement IX., Ranke says: "all those virtues which consist in an absence of vices, such as purity of manners, modesty, temperance, he

---

* Ranke, History of the Popes, l. viii. § xvi. p. 218.
† Ibidem, l. vi. § iv. p. 429.

possessed in an eminent degree."* The same unsuspicious witness testifies of Innocent XI., that he was "of such purity of heart and life, that his confessor declared that he had never discovered in him any thing which could sever the soul from God."† Benedict XIII., heir of the dukedom of Gravina, through love of holy purity, had consecrated himself to God in the order of St. Dominic at the early age of eighteen. "Clement (XIII.) was a man of pure soul and pure intentions: he prayed much and fervently."‡ These are specimens of the general character of the Popes. The good odor of Jesus Christ was spread abroad by most of those who occupied the papal chair.

§ 3. RECOGNISED SANCTITY.

Eminent holiness distinguished most of the incumbents of the Apostolic See, which, on this account, as well as for the purity of its doctrine, may be justly styled *holy*. Besides the martyrs of the first three ages, and some of later times, many others are enrolled in the catalogue of saints. The sanctity of seventy-nine Pontiffs is recognised by the Church, being almost a third of the entire series. They are not confined to the first six ages, although Gibbon has strangely asserted of the apostle of England, that "Gregory is the last of their own order whom they have presumed to inscribe in the calendar of saints."§ The two Gregories, who adorned the eighth century, receive the same honor. The sanctity of the former so impressed Luitprand, the Lombard king, as he stood in a menacing attitude at the gate of Rome, that he abandoned the siege, and entered to worship at the tomb of St. Peter, as the infidel historian himself testifies: "In arms, at the gate of the Vatican, the conqueror listened to the voice of Gregory the Second, withdrew his troops, resigned his conquests, respectfully visited the Church of St. Peter, and, after performing his devotions, offered his sword and dagger, his cuirass and mantle, his silver cross and his crown of gold, on the tomb of the apostle."∥ St. Zachary, the successor of the third Gregory, persuaded Rachis, who occupied the throne of Luitprand, to exchange the battle-field and palace for the cloister. Paschal I. is recognised as a saint. Benedict V., who sat as Pontiff in the decline of the tenth century, and had the gift of prophecy, is mentioned in several martyrologies.

In the eleventh century, St. Leo IX. brought to the papal throne great purity of life, with apostolic zeal. Stephen X., Victor III., and Urban II., are named among the blessed in several martyrologies. St. Alexander II. labored to raise the clergy to that holiness of life, of which he gave the example; but above all the Pontiffs of that age, St. Gregory VII. shines with bright lustre, for the intrepidity and perseverance with which

---

* History of the Popes, vol. ii. p. 158.   † Ibidem, l. viii. § xvii. p. 225.
‡ Ibidem, § xviii. p. 236.   § History of the Decline and Fall, &c., ch. xlv. A. D. 590.
∥ Ibidem, ch. xlix., A. D. 730–752.

he strove to purify the sanctuary, and revive the apostolic spirit in its ministers. St. Celestine V. adorned the thirteenth century. Benedict XI., who reigned in the early part of the following age, is styled Blessed in the Roman martyrology.

The sixteenth century was edified by the austere virtues of St. Pius V. From earliest youth he was devoted to the service of God, and in the highest station he "preserved all his austerity, poverty, and humility."* He is the last of the Popes whose names have been enrolled among the Saints, although since his time, as well as before, many not canonized have been eminent for holiness of life.

---

* Ranke, History of the Popes, l. iii. § viii. p. 217.

CHAPTER IX.

Charges against the Popes.

The charges brought against the Popes are, in many instances, totally destitute of foundation. In the fifth century, a schismatical rival accused Symmachus of many crimes: of which, however, he was declared innocent by a council, to which he voluntarily submitted the cause for examination.

The first serious scandal that occurs in the papal history, took place at the close of the ninth century, when Stephen, who had forcibly taken possession of the See, offered indignities to the corpse of Formosus, the deceased Pontiff, by cutting off the fingers with which he was wont to bless the Roman people. The barbarity of this act, which reflects disgrace on the age in which it was perpetrated, cannot be extenuated by the plea then put forward to justify it, namely, that Formosus had violated the canons, through immoderate ambition, by passing from the See of Porto to that of Rome. His promotion appears to have been the just reward of a long life of virginal purity and Apostolic zeal. The outrage offered to his memory was atoned for by the solemn act of a Roman Council under John IX. It may relieve our feelings somewhat from the horror of this outrage, to know that it was committed by an intruder into the See, not by one who entered by canonical election; and though his name still appears on the list of Popes, Graveson, a judicious historian, disputes the propriety of its insertion. In the scarcity of documents of that period, and in the confusion which was caused by the violent struggles of secular nobles for the mastery of the Church, it is in some cases difficult to distinguish with certainty, whether the intrusion was remedied by the subsequent acquiescence of the canonical electors. These may have yielded to the dire necessity of the times, and borne the shame of tolerating an unworthy incumbent in the apostolic chair, rather than endanger the unity of the Church, by an effort to expel him from a place which he had no right to occupy. We must, in such circumstances, remember, with St. Leo, that the merit of Peter does not totally fail in the unworthy heir of his authority;* and with St. Augustine, that occasion of schism must not be taken from the bad examples of those who are in high station: "of which," he says, "our Heavenly Master so carefully forewarned us, as to give the people an assurance in regard to bad prelates, lest on their account the chair of saving doctrine should be abandoned, in which even bad men

---

* Serm. II. de assumpt. sua ad pontif.

are forced to utter what is good: for what they say is not their own: it is of God, who has placed the doctrine of truth in the chair of unity."*

The moral character of Sergius III. is grievously assailed by Luitprand, a contemporary author, whose testimony, however, is weakened by his known adherence to a schismatical rival of John XII., and his devotedness to the imperial interests. Flodoard, another contemporary writer, represents Sergius as a favorite with the Roman people, and a kind pastor of the flock. It is doubtful whether Lando, whose character is also traduced, should be ranked among the Popes. John X. is charged with licentiousness, and with having been accessary to the death of Benedict VII.: but Baronius, who believed the charges, admits that his administration was better than the means used for his promotion would have led us to expect. Muratori, who with great independence of mind, canvassed facts of history, praises him as a worthy Pontiff.† He also proves‡ that John XI. was son of Albericus, Roman consul, and marquis of Tuscany, although Luitprand brands him as a bastard-son of Sergius. Ratherius of Verona bears testimony to the noble and excellent disposition of John, whom he styles, "gloriosæ indolis." John XII., of the same family, at the age of sixteen or eighteen years, seized on the papal crown, and wore it without shame during seven years, in which he is said to have indulged the worst excesses. The account of his death is marked with the character of fable. The following century witnessed similar scandals in Theophylact, son of Alberic, count of Tusculum, who, whilst yet a youth, was intruded into the chair of St. Peter by bribery and family influence, and thence ejected several times by the Romans, weary of his disorders, till at length he resigned all pretensions to the See, and passed to the monastery of Grotta Ferrata, to expiate his sins by penance. Benedict IX. is his name among the pontiffs.

The struggles for the Papacy in those evil times, were sometimes fierce and sanguinary, the power of the petty potentate, who ruled at Rome as patrician, being often employed in behalf of some member of his family, or some corrupt favorite. The occupant of the chair held it by a very uncertain tenure, and was not unfrequently cast into a dungeon to make room for a successful rival. If such horrors affright us, we should reflect on the general state of Italy at that period, when Saracens and other barbarians spread desolation around, imparting to the oppressed Italians something of their own savage character. The rival princes when unrestrained by the imperial power, which during forty years had been suspended, knew no limits to their ambition, and rushed wildly into excesses which make us shudder. We need not be surprised, that daring and licentious men under such circumstances were sometimes seen to occupy the highest

---

* Ep. cv., alias clxvii., c. v. n. 16. † Annali d'Italia, an. 928.

‡ He quotes: Anonymus Salernitanus, in chron. c. cxliii., et Ostiensis, in chr. casin., l. i. c. lxi.

places in the church: but we must admire the overruling providence of God, which preserved the succession of chief pastors, and gave from time to time bright examples of Christian virtue. The tenth century numbers Theodore, Benedict IV., Anastasius III., and Marin II., among the occupants of St. Peter's See, men worthy of their Apostolical calling; and the eleventh justly boasts of a brighter line of holy pontiffs. The scandals of those ages menaced indeed with destruction the church, which drifted like a shattered vessel, whose pilot had no power or care to direct her course, whilst wave on wave dashed over her, and no light beamed on her but the lightning flash, as bolt after bolt struck her masts: but He who controls the tempest slept within her, and in His own good time, He bade the storm be still, and all was calm and sunshine.

To the causes which produced conflict and disorder we must add national jealousy and love of independence. "The Germans," says Voltaire, "held the Romans in subjection, and the Romans sought every opportunity to break their chains. A Pope chosen by the order of the emperor, or named by him, was an object of execration to the Romans. The idea of restoring the republic was cherished by them: but this noble ambition produced only humiliating and frightful results."*

The charges of ambition, arrogance, and impetuosity, which have been made against Boniface VIII., do not appear to be well founded. If he advised the holy Pontiff Celestine to abdicate an office to whose duties he was inadequate, it need not be ascribed to secret aspirations after the tiara, for which, however, his eminent knowledge and determination of character qualified him. The imprisonment of the unambitious hermit, which has brought censure on Boniface, may have been necessary to guard against the wiles of bad men, who might abuse his simplicity to cause a schism, by persuading him that he could not lawfully part with the power which God had committed to him. In the proceedings against Philip the Fair, Boniface contended for justice and the immunities of the Church, advancing no claim which his predecessors had not put forward, and proceeding with the deliberation and maturity which always distinguish the Holy See. When the emissaries of the monarch prepared to seize on his person, he acted with composure and dignity, declaring, that like his Divine Master, he was betrayed, but that he would die as a Pope; with which view he robed himself in the ornaments of his ministry, and, wrapped in his pontifical mantle, with the tiara on his head, the keys in one hand and the cross in the other, he awaited, with majestic air, the approach of the rebel Colonna, and the daring Nogaret. It is not surprising that the indignities offered to his sacred person should have resulted in his death; but the dis-

---

* It must be acknowledged, that the worst scandals of those times were given by Romans, or other Italians, raised to that high eminence by the prejudices and partiality of their countrymen, or still more by the swords of their kinsfolk: and that the splendor and glory of the pontificate were restored by Popes of German origin, or who rose to office under imperial favor and protection.

covery of his body entire three centuries afterwards, was a splendid refutation of the fable that he had died in the writhings of despair. In the person of this magnanimous Pontiff, God gave us the example of noble demeanor under wrongs, that resemble the insults of the pretorian hall.

> To hide with direr guilt
> Past ills and future, lo! the flower-de-luce
> Enters Alagna, in His vicar, Christ
> Himself a captive, and His mockery
> Acted again. Lo! to His holy lip
> The vinegar and gall once more applied;
> And He twixt living robbers doomed to bleed.—*Cary's Translation.**

The memory of Clement V. comes down to us charged with having ambitiously intrigued for the tiara, by promising to Philip the Fair to rescind the acts of Boniface, and to condescend to his will on some important point, not then disclosed. This compact originally rests on the authority of Villani, a partisan of the schismatical Louis of Bavaria. On the same suspicious testimony, his supposed amours with the countess of Perigord have been too lightly credited, notwithstanding the silence of his early biographers, six in number. But the suppression of the Knights Templars, which resulted in the capital punishment of a large number of them, by the authority of Philip, was a measure of fearful responsibility, the justice of which is an historical problem, perhaps never to be solved. His permission for the opening of the process against the memory of Boniface, which is objected to him as an act of criminal condescension, was probably given in the confidence that it would result, as in fact it did, in his entire acquittal. "All this grand display of Philip the Fair," it is Voltaire who speaks, "resulted in his shame. On the great theatre of the world, you will never see a king of France prevail, in the end, over a Pope."* Villani has attacked the moral character of Clement VI., but I feel dispensed from vindicating it, whilst it is assailed only by the professed enemy of the lawful Pontiffs.

The sudden death of Paul II., who was found dead in his bed, arose from an unwholesome supper on melons; and was not attended with any disgraceful circumstances. Although his life was not austere, there is not any ground for censuring his conduct, unless, perhaps, his failure to observe the conditions to which, in common with the other cardinals in conclave, he had bound himself. This, however, may be accounted for by the necessity of his situation, in which he deemed it injurious to observe

---

* Perchè men paja il mal futuro e'l fatto,
  Veggio in Alagna entrár lo fiordaliso,
  E nel vicario suo Cristo esser catto.
      Veggiolo un altra volta esser deriso;
      Veggio rinnovelár l'aceto e'l fele,
      E tra vivi ladroni éssere anciso.
                    Dante, Purgatorio, c. xx. 85.

* Essai sur l'Histoire Générale, t. ii. ch. lxi.

restrictions unwisely imposed on an authority which Christ willed to be free. Above a century before, Innocent VI. had declared such engagements to be radically null.

Of two Popes, it is certain that previously to their entrance into orders, they had become fathers, either by secret marriages, as some contend, or out of wedlock. John Baptist Cibo, son of a Roman senator, who was made Viceroy of Naples, had two children by a Neapolitan lady, whilst living in his father's court. Chacon affirms that she was his lawful wife. He afterwards entered the ecclesiastical career, in which his conduct won general esteem, and secured his promotion to the episcopacy, and, finally, to the government of the Universal Church. Innocent VIII., as he was thenceforward called, during the first five years of his pontificate, manifested no peculiar tenderness to his children, Franceschetto Cibo and Theodorina: which provoked the remonstrances of Lorenzo de Medicis, then esteemed the wisest man in Italy, but whose judgment may have been warped in this instance by the marriage of his son with Theodorina. The Pontiff-proved himself thenceforward an indulgent parent, and freely bestowed on his offspring the riches of the Church, for which he has deserved censure.

Paul III. owned as his son Pier Luigi Farnese, who was alleged to be the fruit of a secret marriage, before his father entered into orders. His grandson Alexander was promoted to the purple, which he adorned by his virtues. Paul was truly a great Pontiff, whose administration was most advantageous to the Church: but the lustre of his reign was tarnished by family attachments.

Two others are admitted to have fallen into temptation before entering the ecclesiastical state. The ardor of the martial Julius II. betrayed him in youth into excess, of which a daughter was the acknowledged fruit. Her children were promoted to the purple. Since St. Francis de Paula is known to have foretold to him his elevation to the papal throne, we have reason to believe, that after his entrance into orders, his morals were blameless. Ugo Buoncompagno, a jurist of Bologna, who rose into life in the civil service, had a son born out of wedlock. He afterwards entered the sanctuary, in which he acquired esteem for integrity and talent, and, at the age of seventy, he was chosen to fill St. Peter's chair, under the name of Gregory XIII. Ranke acknowledges that "his life and conversation were not only blameless, but edifying."* This being the case, it is extreme rigour to make the frailty of his early life a subject of reproach to him as Pontiff, whilst his subsequent course was so exemplary. No one thinks of disparaging the high character of St. Augustin on account of the disorders of his youth. In estimating the moral influence of the Popes, we should consider especially their public administration, and their

---

* History of the Popes, l. iv. § iii. p. 255.

personal conduct whilst in office, in connection with their whole ecclesiastical career.

The censures which have been passed on Leo X., have no other foundation than the amenity of his manners, his partiality for poets, whose compositions were not always strictly governed by rules of propriety, his fondness for musical entertainments, and other peculiarities, some of which were scarcely consistent with the gravity of a bishop burdened with the solicitude of all the churches. "Leo's gay and graceful court," says Ranke, "was not in itself deserving of censure : yet it were impossible to deny that it was little answerable to the character and position of head of the Church."* Luther and Erasmus both bore testimony to the integrity of his morals. He had his practices of mortification and self-denial, especially the weekly fast of Saturday, and he performed the sacred functions, as Roscoe testifies, with dignity and decorum.

John Baptist Pamfili, at the age of seventy-two, was elevated to the popedom under the title of Innocent X., an honor which St. Felix of Cantalicio had predicted. There is no foundation whatever for any charge against his morals, although he entrusted the management of his palace to his aged sister-in-law, and deferred too much to her caprice. "In his earlier career in the Rota, as nuncio, and as cardinal, he had shown himself industrious, blameless, and upright, and this reputation he still preserved."† Such is the impartial testimony of Ranke, who explains the motives which influenced his conduct in regard to Donna Olimpia. "Pope Innocent was under obligations to his sister-in-law, Donna Olimpia Maldachini, of Viterbo, especially in consequence of the large fortune she had brought into the house of Pamfili. He also regarded it as a high merit on her part, that after the death of his brother, she had never chosen to marry again. This had been productive of advantage to himself, since he had constantly left the economical affairs of the family to her guidance ; it was, therefore, no wonder if she now acquired great influence in the administration of the papacy."‡

There is one Pope, however, who seems to have no advocate to attempt his justification,‡ and but few to offer any thing in mitigation of sentence.

---

* History of the Popes, l. i. ch. ii. p. 61.   † Ibidem, vol. ii. l. viii. ? v. p. 150.

‡ Audin, in his Life of Leo X., has almost ventured. In the lives of the Popes by Platina, a highly favorable account is given of Alexander VI. and his administration. As the historian died in 1481, this sketch, and the preceding, as also that of Pius III., must have been added to his work, in order to continue it down to the reigning Pontiff. The edition before me is of Lyons, 1512. The writer charges Alexander with having changed policy in regard to Charles VIII., and mentions Cesar (under the title of Valentinus) as his son : but praises him for industry, ability, and zeal, as also for his patronage of learned men, and aversion to flatterers. "Felix igitur tanto pontifice Roma . . . quem oscitantem raro comperit quisque, quin aut libris legendis, aut divino cultui, aut rei Christianæ semper attentus esset : temporis jactura nihil perniciosius æstimans." This character is given of him at a time when the memory of his reign was fresh and vivid. He died in 1503. Roscoe says much in extenuation of his vices. (Life of Leo, vol. i. ch. vi.) Guicciardini and Paolo Giovio, almost contemporary writers, but both of them exceptionable,

Roderico Lenzuoli, nephew by his mother to Callistus III., was allowed by his too-indulgent uncle to assume the family name of Borgia, only to attach to it indelible disgrace. The levity of his conduct had provoked reproof from Pius II., but his splendid talents and fascinating manners served to conceal, or partially to redeem his vices. While cardinal, occupying offices of the highest confidence, he became the father of four children, by a Roman lady of noble family; notwithstanding which enormous scandal, he was chosen, at the age of sixty-one, to occupy the Papal chair. His election is alleged to have been accomplished by bribery. Cesar, his favorite son, was promoted to the office of cardinal deacon, but soon released from his obligations, that he might pursue, unrestrained by considerations of decorum, a career better suited to his passions and ambition. His brother, Peter Louis, was assassinated, not without suspicion of the murder being cast on Cesar, although most probably without foundation. The accomplished Lucretia sat for a time in her father's palace, and incurred the foulest censure, as if living in the habitual indulgence of the most unnatural incest: a stain which Roscoe has generously removed.* As Duchess of Ferrara she was esteemed not only for her pure and refined manners, but her literary taste, which was manifested in her patronage of learning, and obtained for her a distinguished place among those who contributed to the revival of letters.† The death of Sizim, brother of Bajazet, the sultan, which occurred shortly after he had been delivered up by Alexander to Charles VIII., was ascribed to slow poison, administered to him by order of the Pontiff: but this most improbable surmise deserves no attention. "Prince Cantemir says that his barber cut his throat. Prince Cantemir and the accusers of Alexander VI. may be mistaken. The hatred entertained for this Pontiff led men to charge him with every crime which he could commit."‡ His apologist is Voltaire, who indignantly rejects the tale of his having drunk by mistake poison prepared by his orders for a cardinal, whose wealth he coveted. The journal of the attending physician certifies that he died of fever, after having received the last sacraments.§ A Spanish critic observes, that the popular hatred no doubt gave rise to most exaggerated reports;|| which Mariana, the great historian, also remarks, hinting, however, that some things were true, while others were calumnies.¶ We must, nevertheless, acknowledge that his elevation was disgraceful, and his government calamitous. In several instances he indeed made wise decrees, and patronized

load him with obloquy. Chacon, who wrote in the decline of the sixteenth century, thinks the charges doubtful: "lapsus fortasse non veros."

* Life and Pontificato of Leo the Tenth, vol. ii. Dissertation on Lucretia Borgia. See also Life of Leo the Tenth, vol. i. ch. vi.
† See Francesco Patrizi, Ded. della mil. rom. Also Roscoe, Diss.
‡ Essai sur l'Histoire Générale, t. iii. ch. cili.
§ Dissert. sur la mort d'Henri IV., also Essai sur l'Hist., ch. cvii.
|| Teatro Critico por D. Fr. B. G. Feijoo, t. iv., disc. viii. p. 212.
¶ Historia de Espana, l. xxvi. c. i.

learning; and the military genius of Cesar contributed to the strength of his civil sovereignty: yet it was an enormous scandal to the Christian world that an immoral man should occupy the Holy See, and cherish, with the blindness of parental love, a licentious and daring soldier.* In such circumstances, the faithful understood the force of the warning of Christ, that we should do what we are taught by those who fill the chair of authority, but should not imitate their perverse actions.

As temporal sovereigns of the Roman States, the Popes have incurred much censure, although they have been truly the fathers of their people. Several of them deserve the praise of great as well as good princes. The clemency of Paul I. toward criminals is marked on the page of history; and his successor, Hadrian, receives commendation for the exercise of the same most comely attribute of sovereignty.

> "No ceremony that to great ones 'longs,
> Not the king's crown, nor the deputed sword,
> The marshal's truncheon, nor the judge's robe,
> Become them with one-half so good a grace
> As mercy does."†

Of Hadrian, Gibbon writes: "He secretly edified the throne of his successors, and displayed in a narrow space the virtues of a great prince."‡ Of those who seized the pontificate in the tenth century, Voltaire remarks: "Those Popes whom posterity has branded as immoral, were far from being incapable princes. John X. was a man of genius and courage, and accomplished what his predecessors had never been able to effect, having driven the Saracens from that part of Italy called Garillan."§ With better reason he praises Martin V., who combined the high qualities of a prince with the virtues of a bishop.‖ Paul II. united justice with clemency, not suffering crime to go unpunished, and yet condemning no one to death. Clement VII. was a sovereign worthy of his name.

Some Popes are accused of extreme severity in the punishment of crime. The mode of the death of some cardinals convicted of conspiracy against Urban VI., is revolting to our sense of humanity; yet Leo X., a Pontiff of acknowledged humanity, condemned to death some others on a

---

* Roscoe says of Cesar Borgia: "Courageous, munificent, eloquent, and accomplished in all the exercises of arts and arms, he raised an admiration of his endowments, which kept pace with and counterbalanced the abhorrence excited by his crimes. That even these crimes have been exaggerated is highly probable. His enemies were numerous, and the certainty of his guilt in some instances gave credibility to every imputation that could be devised to throw his character into deeper shade. That he retained, even after he survived his prosperity, no inconsiderable share of public estimation, is evident from the fidelity and attachment shown him on many occasions."—Life of Leo X., vol. ii. ch. vi. The historian had already stated the attachment of the cities of Romagna to Cesar, whose rule they preferred to that of their former princes, on account of his strict administration of justice, and the repression of banditti.

† Measure for Measure. ‡ Decline and Fall, &c., ch. xlix., A. D. 800.
§ Essai sur l'Histoire Générale, ch. xxxi. ‖ Ibid., ch. lxviii.

similar charge. Treason against the sovereign is everywhere the highest crime against society, and is punished in a manner to strike all with horror. The natural character of Sixtus V. seems to have been humane, since " when his nephew, the husband of Vittoria Accorambuoni, was murdered, he was the first to entreat the Pope to let the investigation drop."* As sovereign of the Roman States, he appeared invested with terrific attributes, because the ravages of the banditti that overspread the country required an extraordinary exercise of justice, and the encroachments of the nobles provoked measures of repression. "After chastising the offending feudatories, he sought rather to conciliate and attach the other barons."†

Sixtus IV. has been charged with participating in the diabolical conspiracy of the Pazzi, a noble family of Florence, which resulted in the assassination of Julian de Medicis, at solemn mass in the Dome of Florence. The presence of the nephew of the Pope, Cardinal Raffaello Riario, on the occasion, and his known partiality for the Pazzi, are the only grounds for suspecting his concurrence in the nefarious plot; which his general character, as well as the sanctity of his station, forbid us to suppose. Blame is ascribed to him for his solicitude to maintain the temporal interests of his See, which, however, as a sovereign, he was bound to guard. In reference to the disputed territory of Rovigno, in Romagna, Ranke observes : " The other powers of Italy were already contending for possession, or for ascendency, in these territories; and, if there were any question of right, the Pope had manifestly a better right than any other."‡ The imputation of bad faith toward his allies seems unfounded. He had solicited the aid of the Venetians to repel the attack of the King of Naples, who afterward, by his unconditional submission, took away all legitimate pretext for continuing hostilities. Sixtus then besought the Venetians to desist from the siege of Ferrara, the duke of that place being son-in-law of the king. When his entreaties proved unavailing, he found himself under the necessity of joining the other Italian princes in a league against his former allies; and, by the advice of a Council held at Cremona, he excommunicated the Venetians for opposing the peace of Italy, which was always dear to his heart.

Julius II. incurred censure for similar causes. In maintaining his temporal rights, he displayed great determination of character, and military courage, not easily reconcilable with his office as representative of the Prince of Peace. Justice, however, was on his side; and his patriotism, which never suffered him to falter in his resolution to drive the barbarians beyond the Alps, has gained the admiration of Voltaire himself.§ His change of policy does not imply a breach of faith. When his French allies seemed disposed to remain as conquerors, where they had appeared

---

* Ranke, History of the Popes, l. iv. § iv. p. 267. † Ibidem, § vi. p. 271.
‡ Ibidem, l. i. ch. ii. p. 47, vol. i.   § Lettre à Mr. Norberg, t. viii.

only to aid him in the recovery of his dominions, it was not inconsistent with his engagements, to join the Venetians, after their submission, in order to force back the French to their own territories, since he never meant to sacrifice the independence of Italy. His princely qualities are witnessed by Ranke: "He endeavored everywhere to appear as a liberator: he treated his new subjects wisely and well, and secured their attachment and fidelity."*

It may be difficult to satisfy all readers of the justice of the measures which the Pontiffs, in their capacity of sovereigns, have from time to time adopted; nor is it necessary that they should meet our approval. "We must distinguish," as Voltaire well observes, "the Pontiff from the sovereign."† As Catholics, we are not concerned with the temporal administration of the Roman States, and need not inquire whether it has been just and paternal, or whether the sovereign has maintained the proper relations to foreign powers. Even the personal character of the Popes no further interests us than as we should naturally desire that the Chief Bishop of the Church should sustain the purity of the Christian law by the influence of his example. Thanks be to Heaven, the general conduct of the successors of Peter has been worthy of their station, and may well be referred to as serving to recommend that authority, which they have exercised for the interests of truth and piety.

Partiality for their relatives, whom they employed in offices of high importance with great revenues, has brought censure on several of the Popes, whose personal conduct was blameless. Nepotism, as this vice is technically styled, has caused, no doubt, great evils to the Church; but it is so natural to favor our own kindred, that it should not be condemned too severely, unless the individuals be unworthy. In fact, we owe to the fond affection of Pius IV. for his nephew, Charles Borromeo, the immense advantages which the Church at large derived from his labors and examples, in the high offices which his uncle lavished on him when but scarcely arrived at manhood. Had the holy Pontiff, Benedict XIII., called to his Council his relatives, who were persons of high probity and exemplary piety, the abuse which an upstart favorite made of his confidence, would have been avoided. Nevertheless, it is but rarely that relatives do not avail themselves of their position for self-aggrandizement; and several Pontiffs might say, at the close of a career otherwise illustrious, with Paul III.: "Had not my relatives ruled, I should have been without stain." The austere virtue of Paul IV. was not proof against the blinding influence of kindred ties; and too late he discovered the iniquities and oppression practised in his name by the Caraffas, whom he at once banished from his court, leaving to his successor, Pius IV., the sad office of condemning two of them to an ignominious death.

Many of the Popes evinced heroic detachment from flesh and blood, not

---

* History of the Popes, L. ii. ch. ii. p. 52.   † Ubi supra.

being willing that the natural ties should contract their hearts, which were made to embrace the entire world. Clement IV. and Martin IV. were distinguished for this virtue. When the brother of Martin repaired to court, the Pope dismissed him, with a small gift to meet the expenses of his journey, observing that he could not employ the riches of the Church as if they were his paternal estate. Leo XI., during a short pontificate of seventeen days, gave evidence of an inflexible determination to indulge no human affection with danger to the interests of religion, since he resisted the pressing solicitations of the cardinals to raise his nephew to their rank. The eleventh Innocent, during thirteen years of pontifical administration, kept himself free from all imputation of inordinate attachment to his relatives. Innocent XII., who called the poor his nephews, made stringent decrees against nepotism. Clement XI., his successor, who during eleven years deferred the promotion of his relatives, although they were men of distinguished merit, on his deathbed could say with truth, that conscience alone had regulated his course in their regard. When the learned and facetious Lambertini was raised to the pontifical throne, under the name of Benedict XIV., he ordered his nephew, who was a senator of Bologna, not to come to Rome until invited, and he took care never to give the invitation. Clement XIV. could not be prevailed on to send special messengers to apprise his three sisters of his elevation, observing that they were not wont to receive ambassadors, and that the poor of Christ were his family. No one could prevail on him to admit any of his relatives to his presence, or to send them any gift. Pius VII. and Leo XII., among the Pontiffs of our own age, have merited the praise of similar detachment. When Pius VIII. was chosen to fill St. Peter's chair, he wrote affectionate letters to his nephews, warning them, however, not to indulge in any pomp or pride, but to pray to God in his behalf. "Let none of you," said he, "leave his dwelling or post. We love you in God."

I shall now relieve the reader from this prolonged investigation, with an appeal to his conscience, whether there ever has existed any series of rulers in the Church or in the State, so illustrious as the succession of Roman Bishops. They have been the defenders of the faith, the fathers of the poor, the friends of order and virtue, and the benefactors of society. While intent on executing the divine commission to teach all nations, they have not considered it inconsistent with their sublime office to cherish genius and reward industry, fostering art, literature, and science, with a partiality that might appear extreme. If a cloud has sometimes passed over that See, which shines in the Church like the sun in the firmament, it soon passed away, and left the world in admiration of its undiminished splendor. Sooner shall the orb of day be extinguished, than the prayer of Christ for Peter fail.

CATALOGUE OF THE POPES.

FIRST CENTURY.

1. ST. PETER from the East, where he founded the See of Antioch, passed to Rome; returned to the East when the Jews were expelled by Claudius; returned to Rome, and died a martyr with St. Paul, on 29th June, 66.*
2. ST. LINUS M.† He died a martyr in 67. Berti says in 76.—Eccl. Hist. Brev.
3. ST. ANACLETUS M.‡
4. ST. CLEMENT M.§

SECOND CENTURY.

5. ST. EVARISTUS M. sat to 108.
6. ST. ALEXANDER M. sat from 2 March, 108, to 3 May, 116.
7. ST. SIXTUS I. M. sat from 116 to 3 July, 126.
8. ST. TELESPHORUS M. died in 137.
9. ST. HYGINUS M. died 10 January, 141.
10. ST. PIUS I. sat ten years, four months, and three days.
11. ST. ANICETUS M. During his pontificate Polycarp came to Rome, in 158. Anicetus died in 161.

---

* According to Foggini and Tillemont. Pagi says, 65. The testimony of the ancient writers is unanimous as to the establishment of the Church of Rome by Peter and Paul, and as to their martyrdom at Rome. It is not easy, however, to determine the precise year of the first visit of Peter to Rome, or of the martyrdom of both apostles.

† Tertullian (l. de præscript.) says that the Roman Church proves the succession of her bishops by pointing to Clement, ordained by Peter; but this does not necessarily imply that he was the immediate successor of the apostle. Irenæus, who was prior to Tertullian, states distinctly that Linus received from Peter the administration of the Church, and immediately succeeded him.

‡ Cletus and Anacletus are found in ancient catalogues, and the learned are not agreed as to their identity. St. Irenæus makes no mention of Cletus, and styles Sixtus the sixth from the apostles, which excludes Cletus. Berti says that Cletus succeeded Linus, and died in 89.

§ Clement is put before Anacletus in the list of St. Augustin (Ep. l. iii. alias clv.,) and in the chronicle of Damasus. Berti says that Anacletus sat during the two years of the exile of Clement. I have followed Irenæus. Pagi says that Clement governed from 67 to 77, and then abdicated. Berti says that he sat from 89 to 98, and after two years spent in banishment underwent martyrdom by drowning. His martyrdom is assigned to 23 November, 10

12. St. Soter M. sat until 170.
13. St. Eleutherius M. sat from 170 until 185.*
14. St. Victor I. M. sat from 12th June, 185, until 28th July, 197.
15. St. Zephyrinus M. sat from 7th August, 197, until 12th July, 217.

THIRD CENTURY.

16. St. Callistus I. M. sat from 217 until 28th September, 222.
17. St. Urban I. M. sat from 222 until 24th May, 230.
18. St. Pontian M. sat from 230 until 14th March, 235.
19. St. Anteros M. sat from 21st November, 235, until 3d January, 236.
20. St. Fabian M. elected 11th January, 236, sat until 20th January, 250.
21. St. Cornelius M. died in banishment on 14th September, 252. St. Cyprian styles him martyr, he having been banished for the faith, although his death was not violent.
22. St. Lucius M. died on 4th March, 253.
23. St. Stephen M. elected on 13th May, 253, sat until 2d August, 257.
24. St. Xystus II. M. died on 6th August, 258.
25. St. Dionysius sat from 22d July, 259, until 26th December, 269.
26. St. Felix I. elected on 28th December, 269, died on 22d December, 274.
27. St. Eutychian elected on 5th January, 275, died on 7th December, 283.
28. St. Cajus elected on 15th December, 283, died on 21st April, 296.
29. St. Marcellinus elected on 30th June, 296, died on 24th October, 304.

FOURTH CENTURY.

30. St. Marcellus I., after an interregnum, sat one year and six months, and died 16th January, 310.
31. St. Eusebius elected 5th February, sat until 21st June.
32. St. Miltiades elected on 2d July, 310, died on 10th January, 314.
33. St. Sylvester I. elected on 30th January, 314, died on 31st December, 335.
34. St. Mark created Pope 18th January, 336, died 7th October, 336.
35. St. Julius I. elected on 26th October, 336, (6th February, 337, according to Pagi,) sat until 12th April, 352.

---

* The list of St. Irenæus closes with Eleutherius. Hegesippus, a convert from Judaism, composed a list at the same time.

CATALOGUE OF THE POPES. 431

36. St. Liberius was elected on 8th May, 352. Felix II. was intruded in 355.* Liberius was restored in 359: he died on 23d September, 366.
37. St. Damasus I. sat from 1st October, 366, until 10th December, 384.
38. St. Siricius sat from 22d December, 384, until 26th November, 398.
39. St. Anastasius I.† sat from 5th December, 398, until 14th December, 401.

FIFTH CENTURY.

40. St. Innocent I. sat from 21st December, 401, until 12th March, 417.
41. St. Zosimus sat from 18th March, 417, until 26th December, 418.
42. St. Boniface I. sat from 29th December, 418, until 4th September, 422.
43. St. Celestine I. sat from 10th September, 422, until 18th July, 432.
44. St. Sixtus III. sat from 24th July, 432, until 11th August, 440.
45.‡ St. Leo the Great sat from 22d September, 440, until 4th November, 461.
46. St. Hilary sat from 12th November, 461, until 21st February, 468.
47. St. Simplicius sat from 25th Februrary, 468, until 2d March, 483.
48. St. Felix III. sat from 6th March, 483, until 24th February, 492.
49. St. Gelasius I. sat from 1st March, 492, until 19th November, 496.
50. St. Anastasius II. sat from 24th November, 496, until 17th November, 498.
51. St. Symmachus sat from 22d November, 498, until 19th July, 514.

SIXTH CENTURY.

52. St. Hormisdas sat from 27th July, 514, until 6th August, 523.
53. St. John I. sat from 13th August, 523, until 18th May, 526.
54. St. Felix IV. sat from 12th July, 526, until 18th September, 529.
55. Boniface II. sat from 21st September, 529, until 16th October, 532.
56. John II. sat from 31st December, 532, until 26th May, 535.
57. St. Agapetus I. sat from 3d June, 535, until 22d April, 536.
58. St. Sylverius M. created 8th June, 536, removed 18th November, 537, died on 20th June, 540.
59. Vigilius intruded, afterward legitimate, sat until January, 555.

---

* Felix is put in the list of Popes by many: St. Augustin omits him.

† The list of St. Augustin ends with Anastasius.

‡ Prosper, a contemporary author, numbers him 47th, as he should be numbered if Anacletus and Felix be counted.

60. PELAGIUS I. sat from 11th April, 555, until 1st March, 560.
61. JOHN III. sat from 18th July, 560, until 13th July, 573.
62. ST. BENEDICT I. sat from 3d June, 574, until 30th July, 578.
63. PELAGIUS II. sat from 30th November, 578, until 8th February, 590.
64. ST. GREGORY THE GREAT sat from 3d September, 590, until 12th March, 604.

SEVENTH CENTURY.

65. SABINIAN sat from 13th September, 604, to 22d February, 606.
66. BONIFACE III. sat from 19th February, 607, to 10th November, 607.
67. ST. BONIFACE IV. sat from 25th August, 608, until 7th May, 615.
68. ST. DEUSDEDIT sat from 19th October, 615, until 8th November, 618.
69. BONIFACE V. sat from 23d December, 619, until 22d October, 625.
70. HONORIUS I. sat from 27th October, 625, until 12th October, 638.
71. SEVERINUS sat from 28th May, 640, until 1st August, 640.
72. JOHN IV. sat from 24th December, 640, until 11th October, 642.
73. THEODORE sat from 24th November, 642, until 13th May, 649.
74. ST. MARTIN I. M. sat from 5th July, 649, until 19th June, 653, when he was carried into banishment. He died on 16th September, 655.
75. ST. EUGENIUS I. was chosen on 8th September, 654, by the clergy, who feared that the emperor would force a heretic into the chair, if they awaited the actual occurrence of a vacancy. The election was approved of by Martin. Eugenius died on 1st June, 657.
76. ST. VITALIAN sat from 30th July, 657, until 27th January, 672.
77. ADEODATUS II. sat from 22d April, 672, until 26th June, 676.
78. DONUS I. sat from 1st November, 676, until 11th April, 678.
79. ST. AGATHO sat from 27th June, 678, until 10th January, 682.
80. ST. LEO II. sat from 17th August, 682, until 3d July, 683.
81. ST. BENEDICT II. sat from 26th June, 684, until 7th May, 685.
82. JOHN V. sat from 23d July, 685, until 1st August, 686.
83. CONON sat from 21st October, 686, until 21st September, 687.
84. ST. SERGIUS I. sat from 15th December, 687, until 7th September, 701.

EIGHTH CENTURY.

85. JOHN VI. sat from 28th October, 701, to 9th January, 705.
86. JOHN VII. sat from 1st March, 705, until 17th October, 707.
87. SISINNIUS sat from 18th January, 708, until 6th February, 708.
88. CONSTANTINE sat from 25th March, 708, until 8th April, 715.
89. ST. GREGORY II. sat from 19th May, 715, until 10th February, 731.

CATALOGUE OF THE POPES. 433

90. St. Gregory III. sat from 18th March, 731, until 27th November, 741.
91. St. Zacharias sat from 30th November, 741, until 14th March, 752.
92. Stephen I.* elected immediately, died in three days.
93. Stephen II. sat from 26th March, 752, until 24th April, 757.
94. St. Paul I. sat from 29th May, 757, until 28th June, 767.
95. Stephen III. sat from 7th August, 768, until 2d February, 772.
96. Hadrian I. sat from 9th February, 772, until 25th December, 795.
97. St. Leo III. sat from 25th December, 795, until 11th June, 816.

NINTH CENTURY.

98. Stephen IV. sat from 22d June, 816, until 24th January, 817.
99. St. Paschal I. sat from 25th January, 817, until 10th February, 824.
100. Eugene II. sat from 14th February, 824, until August, 827.
101. Valentine sat forty days.
102. Gregory IV. sat over sixteen years, until 25th January, 844.
103. Sergius II. sat from 10th February, 844, until 27th January, 847.
104. St. Leo IV. sat from 11th April, 847, until 17th July, 855.
105. Benedict III. elected immediately, consecrated on 29th September, 855, sat until 8th April, 858.
106. St. Nicholas I. sat from 24th April, 858, until 13th November, 867.
107. Hadrian II. sat from 14th December, 867, until 26th November, 872.
108. John VIII. sat from 14th December, 872, until 15th December, 882.
109. Marinus sat from the end of December, 882, until May, 884.
110. Hadrian III. sat from June, 884, until September, 885.
111. Stephen V. elected about the end of September, 885, died in September, 891.
112. Formosus sat from October, 891, until 4th April, 896. Boniface VI. sat only sixteen days. He is not acknowledged by Baronius; but many number him among the lawful Popes. Stephen VI. intruded before 20th August, 896, was strangled in prison in 897.†
113. Romanus sat from September, 897, until February, 898.
114. Theodore II. lived only twenty days after his election.
115. John IX. elected in July, 898, sat until August, 900.

---

* As he was not consecrated, he is passed over in most of the lists, from which circumstance a difference arises in numbering the Popes of that name.

† Stephen is commonly put in the list of Popes, although Graveson holds him to be an intruder.

TENTH CENTURY.

116. BENEDICT IV. elected in August, 900, sat until October, 903.
117. LEO V. elected in October, 903, sat less than two months. Christopher, an intruder, occupied the See during six months.
118. SERGIUS III. was consecrated in June, 904, and sat until August, 911.
119. ANASTASIUS III. sat from the end of August, 911, until October, 913.
120. LANDO sat from October, 913, until 26th April, 914.
121. JOHN X. sat from 30th April, 914, was suffocated in prison on 2d July, 928.
122. LEO VI. sat from July, 928, until February, 929.
123. STEPHEN VII. sat from 3d February, 929, until 15th March, 931.
124. JOHN XI. sat from March, 931, until January, 936.
125. LEO VII. sat from 9th January, 936, until 18th July, 939.
126. STEPHEN VIII. sat from July, 939, until December, 942.
127. MARINUS II. sat from December, 942, until June, 946.
128. AGAPETUS II. sat from June, 946, until August, 956.
129. JOHN XII. Octavian, the first who changed his name, held the pontificate from 20th August, 956, until 14th May, 964. An antipope named Leo VIII. was set up by the Emperor Otto, on 6th December, 963. He died in March, 965.
130. BENEDICT V. elected on 19th May, 964, sat until 4th July, 965.
131. JOHN XIII. sat from 1st October, 965, until 6th September, 972.
132. BENEDICT VI. sat from December, 972, until 974. He was strangled, and Boniface VII. was intruded, who, after a month, was expelled, but again occupied the See during some months, after the death of John XIV.
133. DONUS II. sat until 975.
134. BENEDICT VII. sat from March, 975, until 10th July, 984.
135. JOHN XIV. died in 985, after governing during eight months.
136. JOHN XV.* sat from December, 985, until April, 996.
137. GREGORY V. sat from May, 996, until 18th February, 999. An antipope named John XVI. was set up in May, 997, by Crescentius of Nomentum, who exercised tyrannical sway at Rome.
138. SYLVESTER II. elected on 28th February, consecrated on 2d April, 999, sat until 11th May, 1003.

---

* Another John, son of Robert, died without being consecrated, or was not true Pope, wherefore he is not counted.

ELEVENTH CENTURY.

139. JOHN XVII.,* whose family name was Sicco, sat from 13th June, 1003, until 7th December.
140. JOHN XVIII., named Fasanus, consecrated on 26th December, 1003, died in May, 1009.
141. SERGIUS IV. sat until 18th August, 1012.
142. BENEDICT VIII. succeeded before 23d November, but was expelled by the antipope Gregory, and restored by St. Henry, King of Germany. He died before October, 1024.
143. JOHN XIX. sat nine years and nine days.
144. BENEDICT IX. was elected toward the end of 1033. He was deposed by the Romans in a revolt on 29th June, 1037. In May, 1044, he was driven away a second time, when an antipope, styled Sylvester III., was intruded during three months. Benedict abdicated in favor of Gregory VI., but on the death of Clement II. he returned, and occupied the See during eight months, until 17th July, 1048. He is said to have died penitent at Grotta Ferrata.
145. GREGORY VI. obtained from Benedict the renunciation of his claims in 1044, and sat two years and eight months, but resigned in the Council of Sutri.
146. CLEMENT II. sat from 25th December, 1046, until 9th October, 1047.
147. DAMASUS II. created on 17th July, 1048, sat twenty-three days.
148. ST. LEO IX.† elected on 2d February, 1049, enthroned on 12th, sat until 19th April, 1054.
149. VICTOR II. elected on 13th April, 1055, enthroned on 16th, sat until 28th July, 1057.
150. STEPHEN IX. sat from 2d August, 1057, until 29th March, 1058. On the death of Stephen, an antipope styled Benedict X. was set up by the Romans. He sat nine months and twenty days, and afterward submitted to the lawful Pontiff.
151. NICHOLAS II. sat from 28th December, 1058, until 22d July, 1061.
152. ALEXANDER II. sat from 1st October, 1061, until 21st April, 1073.
153. ST. GREGORY VII. sat from 22d April, 1073, until 25th May, 1085.
154. VICTOR III. elected, after refusing during a year, on 24th May, 1086, fled after four days, was consecrated 21st March, 1087, and died on 16th September, 1087.
155. URBAN II. sat from 12th March, 1088, until 29th July, 1099.

---

* As many documents bore the name of the antipope, John XVI., this Pontiff took the name of John XVII., to prevent his acts being confounded with those of the antipope.

† Leo VIII. was an antipope whom Otho intruded in place of John XII.

TWELFTH CENTURY.

156. PASCAL II. sat from 13th August, 1099, until 21st January, 1118.
157. GELASIUS II. elected 27th January, 1118, consecrated on 10th March, sat until 29th January, 1119.
158. CALLISTUS II. sat from 1st February, 1119, until 13th December, 1124.
159. HONORIUS II. sat from 21st December, 1124, until 14th February, 1130.
160. INNOCENT II. sat from 15th February, 1130, until 24th September, 1143.
161. CELESTINE II. sat from 26th September, 1143, to 9th March, 1144.
162. LUCIUS II. sat from 12th March, 1144, until 25th February, 1145, when he was killed in a sedition by the throw of a stone.
163. EUGENE III. sat from 27th February, 1145, until 7th July, 1153. The Arnaldists forced him to flee from the city in 1146, but he re-entered in 1149.
164. ANASTASIUS IV. elected on 9th July, 1153, sat until 2d December, 1154.
165. HADRIAN IV. elected on 3d, and consecrated on 5th December, 1154, died on 1st September, 1159.
166. ALEXANDER III. elected on 7th, and consecrated on 20th September, 1159, sat until 30th August, 1181.
167. LUCIUS III. sat from 1st September, 1181, until 24th November, 1185.
168. URBAN III. elected 25th November, consecrated 1st December, 1185, sat until 19th October, 1187.
169. GREGORY VIII. elected 20th, consecrated on 25th October, 1187, sat until 17th December, 1187.
170. CLEMENT III. elected on 19th December, 1187, sat until 27th March, 1191.
171. CELESTINE III. elected on 30th March, ordained priest on 13th April, 1191, consecrated bishop on 14th, sat until 8th January, 1198.

THIRTEENTH CENTURY.

172. INNOCENT III. sat from 8th January, 1198, until 16th July, 1216.
173. HONORIUS III. sat from 18th July, 1216, until 18th March, 1227.
174. GREGORY IX. sat from 19th March, 1227, until 21st August, 1241.
175. CELESTINE IV. elected in October, 1241, sat only seventeen days.
176. INNOCENT IV. elected on 25th May, and consecrated on 28th June, 1243, sat until 7th December, 1254.

177. ALEXANDER IV. elected on 12th, crowned on 20th December, 1254, died on 25th May, 1261.
178. URBAN IV. elected 29th August, consecrated on 4th September, 1261, sat until 2d October, 1264.
179. CLEMENT IV. sat from 22d February, 1265, until 29th November, 1268.
180. GREGORY X. elected on 1st September, 1271, crowned on 27th March, 1272, died on 10th January, 1276.
181. INNOCENT V. elected on 21st January, crowned on 22d February, 1276, died on 22d June, 1276.
182. HADRIAN V. sat from 10th July, 1276, only during thirty-nine days.
183. JOHN XXI.* elected on 15th, and crowned on 20th September, 1276, died on 16th May, 1277.
184. NICHOLAS III. elected on 25th November, ordained priest on 18th December, consecrated on the 19th, and crowned on 26th December, 1277, died on 22d August, 1280.
185. MARTIN IV.† elected 22d February, crowned on 23d March, 1281, sat until 29th March, 1285.
186. HONORIUS IV. sat from 2d April, 1285, until 3d April, 1287.
187. NICHOLAS IV. sat from 22d February, 1288, until 4th April, 1292.
188. ST. CELESTINE V. elected on 5th July, 1294, crowned on 29th August, voluntarily abdicated on 13th December, 1294, died on 19th May, 1296.
189. BONIFACE VIII.‡ sat from 24th December, 1294, until 11th October, 1303.

FOURTEENTH CENTURY.

190. B. BENEDICT XI.§ sat from 22d October, 1303, until 6th July, 1304.
191. CLEMENT V. sat from 5th June, 1305, until 20th April, 1314. He was the first Pope who resided at Avignon.
192. JOHN XXII. sat from 7th August, 1316, until 4th December, 1334.
193. B. BENEDICT XII. sat from 20th December, 1334, until 25th April, 1342.
194. CLEMENT VI. sat from 7th May, 1342, until 4th December, 1352.
195. INNOCENT VI. sat from 18th December, 1352, until 12th September, 1362.
196. URBAN V. sat from 28d September, 1362, until 9th December, 1370. He established his residence at Rome in 1367, but returned to Avignon, and died there.

---

* He was styled XXI., probably because an antipope in the time of Gregory V. had been called John XX.

† The Marini have been popularly confounded with those named Martin, and counted with them. He was the second of the name of Martin.

‡ Boniface VII. was an antipope. § An antipope had been called Benedict X.

197. GREGORY XI. sat from 5th January, 1371, until 17th March, 1378. He re-established the Papal residence at Rome.
198. URBAN VI. sat from 8th April, 1378, until 15th October, 1389. Several cardinals created an antipope, Clement VII., who resided at Avignon, and was succeeded by Benedict XII. or XIII.
199. BONIFACE IX.* sat from 2d November, 1389, until 1st October, 1404.

FIFTEENTH CENTURY.

200. INNOCENT VII. sat from 17th October, 1404, until 6th November, 1406.
201. GREGORY XII. was chosen on 30th November, 1406. . He abdicated on the 14th July, 1415, in the Council of Constance. Alexander V. was chosen in the Council of Pisa, on 26th June, 1409, who dying on 4th May, 1410, was succeeded by John XXIII.†
202. MARTIN V. sat from 11th November, 1417, until 20th February, 1431.
203. EUGENE IV. sat from 3d March, 1431, until 23d February, 1447.
204. NICHOLAS V. sat from 5th March, 1447, until 24th March, 1455.
205. CALLISTUS III. sat from 8th April, 1455, until 6th August, 1458.
206. PIUS II. sat from 19th August, 1458, until 14th August, 1464.
207. PAUL II. sat from 30th August, 1464, until 16th July, 1471.
208. SIXTUS IV. sat from 9th August, 1471, until 13th August, 1484.
209. INNOCENT VIII. sat from 29th August, 1484, until 25th July, 1492.
210. ALEXANDER VI. sat from 11th August, 1492, until 18th August, 1503.

SIXTEENTH CENTURY.

211. PIUS III. elected on 22d September, 1503, lived only twenty-six days.
212. JULIUS II. elected on All-hallow-eve, and consecrated on 26th November, 1503, sat until 21st February, 1513.
213. LEO X. elected on 15th March, 1513, died on 1st December, 1521.
214. ADRIAN VI. elected on 9th January, 1522, sat until 14th September, 1523.
215. CLEMENT VII. sat from 19th November, 1523, until 26th September, 1534.
216. PAUL III. sat from 13th October, 1534, until 10th November, 1549.

---

* Two antipopes had borne this name.

† Alexander V. and John XXIII. are found in most of the lists, even in those published at Rome.

CATALOGUE OF THE POPES.

217. JULIUS III. sat from 8th February, 1550, until 23d March, 1555.
218. MARCELLUS II. sat from 9th April, 1555, only twenty-two days.
219. PAUL IV. sat from 23d May, 1555, until 17th August, 1559.
220. PIUS IV. sat from 26th December, 1559, until 10th December, 1565.
221. ST. PIUS V. sat from 7th January, 1566, until 1st May, 1572.
222. GREGORY XIII. sat from 13th May, 1572, until 10th April, 1585.
223. SIXTUS V. sat from 24th April, 1585, until 27th August, 1590.
224. URBAN VII. elected on 15th September, 1590, died on 27th of the same month.
225. GREGORY XIV. sat from 5th December, 1590, until 15th October, 1591.
226. INNOCENT IX. sat from 29th October, 1591, to 30th December.
227. CLEMENT VIII. sat from 30th January, 1592, until 3d March, 1603.

SEVENTEENTH CENTURY.

228. LEO XI. elected on 2d April, 1605, and crowned on the 10th, died on the 27th of same month.
229. PAUL V. sat from 16th May, 1605, until 28th January, 1621.
230. GREGORY XV. sat from 9th February, 1621, until 8th July, 1623.
231. URBAN VIII. sat from 6th August, 1623, until 29th July, 1644.
232. INNOCENT X. sat from 15th September, 1644, until 7th January, 1655.
233. ALEXANDER VII. sat from 6th April, 1655, until 22d May, 1667.
234. CLEMENT IX. sat from 20th June, 1667, until 9th December, 1669.
235. CLEMENT X. sat from 29th April, 1670, until 22d July, 1676.
236. INNOCENT XI. sat from 21st September, 1676, until 31st July, 1689.
237. ALEXANDER VIII. sat from 6th October, 1689, until 1st February, 1691.
238. INNOCENT XII. sat from 13th July, 1691, until 26th September, 1700.

EIGHTEENTH CENTURY.

239. CLEMENT XI. sat from 23d November, 1700, until 19th March, 1721.
240. INNOCENT XIII. sat from 8th May, 1721, until 7th March, 1724.
241. BENEDICT XIII. sat from 29th May, 1724, until 21st February, 1730.
242. CLEMENT XII. sat from 12th July, 1730, until 6th February, 1740.

CATALOGUE OF THE POPES.

243. BENEDICT XIV. sat from 17th August, 1740, until 3d May, 1758.
244. CLEMENT XIII. sat from 6th July, 1758, until 2d February, 1769.
245. CLEMENT XIV. sat from 19th May, 1769, until 22d September, 1774.
246. PIUS VI. sat from 15th February, 1775, until 29th August, 1799.

NINETEENTH CENTURY.

247. PIUS VII. sat from 14th March, 1800, until 23d August, 1823.
248. LEO XII. sat from 28th September, 1823, until 10th February, 1829.
249. PIUS VIII. sat from 31st March, 1829, until 30th November, 1830.
250. GREGORY XVI. sat from 2d February, 1831, until 1st June, 1846.
251.* PIUS IX. elected 17th June, 1846.

---

* The number varies, according as certain individuals are considered intruders, or lawful Popes. This is a matter for critical inquiry, and does not affect the succession.

THE END.

www.ingramcontent.com/pod-product-compliance
Lightning Source LLC
Chambersburg PA
CBHW020536300426